GOVERNMENT AND BUSINESS

A STUDY IN ECONOMIC EVOLUTION

By **HOWARD R. SMITH** *Professor of Economics, The University of Georgia*

THE RONALD PRESS COMPANY • **NEW YORK**

Library of Congress Catalog Card Number: 58–5635

PRINTED IN THE UNITED STATES OF AMERICA

LARRY

RICHARD   *To*   JANET

DAVID

Preface

Several major considerations determined this book's presentation of the interrelationships between government and business. Perhaps the most important was a desire to emphasize the underlying context within which economic policy is formulated, rather than merely particular policies actually set in motion. The reader thereby gains a greater familiarity with the way public policy is made in a democracy and a better understanding both of the policies currently in operation and of the principles behind them.

This emphasis in turn necessitated giving top billing to the sources of public policy, which, speaking broadly, are threefold. There is the institutional framework inherited from the past, for the status quo in any society ministers to values so important to its members that they are typically unwilling to see any but peripheral changes made therein. Second are the difficulties which policy decisions are designed to remedy, for by definition policy changes will not be seriously discussed until the status quo is felt to be inadequate. And lastly, there are the human conflicts which inevitably form around whatever solutions are proposed.

Although, of course, there are other ways of achieving these emphases, it seemed to the author most effective to use a modified historical approach. A variety of advantages derive from this procedure. First, in connection with the order of topics (always so intricately interrelated), this procedure relates policy changes directly to the dynamics of historical evolution. Second, with respect to the relative significance to be attached to particular topics, the technique adopted here gives highest priority to those policy issues which were of greatest importance at every stage in the nation's evolution—each in its proper place. Third, in view of the great complexity of the subject matter, the step-by-step approach makes possible the elimination of many details without detracting from the understanding thus made available.

Another set of advantages deriving from an historical orientation can be seen particularly clearly in the concept highlighted in the book's subtitle—economic evolution. In this way, it is possible to develop a fuller appreciation of the degree to which the current role of government in economic life is a product of the appearance of new problems rather than a change in basic attitudes or, as it is often put, a "softening of the American character." Stated differently, it is not alone either the fact or the extent of the abandonment of laissez faire which requires emphasis; of equal importance are the circumstances under which this change took place. Furthermore, an evolutionary approach makes it possible to modify the onesidedness of so much writing in this field, which concentrates attention upon the impact of government on business, in order to stress also the impact of business on government. Again, this orientation makes easier the necessary distinction between those situations in which recent legislation has broken new ground and those in which it has merely placed reconditioned bricks on old foundations.

Finally, an approach stressing policy formulation as well as actual policies helps keep normative inclinations and moralizing in check. While it is not contended that the present volume has succeeded at this point where others have failed, the focusing of attention upon motivation in the process of decision-making—that is to say, upon the impact of problems on particular interest groups and the concessions required for a satisfactory adjustment of complex conflicts—does serve to minimize author explanations of what should have been done in particular situations or even of what policy decisions should now be made.

Some comments on several less general matters might also be helpful. Part I, it will be observed, deals with democratic decision-making in theoretical terms. Clearly, no understanding of government economic policy in the United States can be fuller than the understanding of democracy which undergirds it. But because space did not permit going into these matters with respect to each important policy development, the next best alternative seemed to be to use these materials as a more general frame of reference; and the reader is urged to grapple seriously at the outset with the relationships developed in these chapters.

Essentially similar considerations suggested the desirability of putting together in Part VII a different kind of summary. Every institutional development can be analyzed at two levels: first, at the level of the basic conflicts out of which it arises; and second, from the standpoint of the still more fundamental changes taking place in the society which give survival value to particular innovations. Although care was taken throughout not to lose sight entirely of the latter of these two levels of analysis, for reasons already mentioned the focus of attention in Parts II–VI was upon the conflict context of public policy decisions. In order, however, to keep this emphasis in proper perspective, a bird's-eye view of the broader process of evolutionary change was also included.

In endeavoring to focus attention upon the forces behind evolving relationships between business and government, it was necessary to make repeated references to the policy position of this or that great interest group. The fact is, however, that because any sizeable body of citizens is to a greater or lesser degree heterogeneous, every such statement is an oversimplification. A choice had to be made, in other words, whether to leave out these observations altogether, or to oversimplify in order to give the reader a core of understanding of forces impinging upon the policy decision under discussion. While there could not have been, in view of the primary purposes behind this presentation, any question of which alternative was to be selected, the greatest of care was nevertheless taken not to mislead the reader by giving majority status to what were in fact minority views.

It should further be observed that, with relatively few exceptions, footnote citations are here used in a somewhat unorthodox way. Thus, they have not been used with a view to "building a case" for a particular line of reasoning, nor have they been used for the purpose of giving weight to a controversial argument. Rather, citations have been given almost exclusively to provide the student with a representative assortment of collateral reading materials on the assumption that the best annotation for a bibliographical item is the text discussion to which it relates most directly.

Inevitably, in connection with a new offering in the government and business field, the question arises whether it is oriented primarily to economics or political science courses. There is, to be sure, no pat answer to this question; tastes and emphasis vary greatly among teachers within each of these disciplines. There are, however, a few observations to be made with respect to this matter which will at least shed light on the author's interpretation of his own work. To begin with, there is at base only one subject matter for a business and government course, and the place of this course in a curriculum does not alter the real world relationships with which it deals. Moreover, an understanding of these relationships requires a comprehension of both political and economic phenomena, and a course on this subject which is not built around both can only shortchange the student. Thus, although the writer of a book in this field will naturally and as often as not unintentionally stress to some extent the topics which interest him most and with which he is most familiar, he must nevertheless work both sides of this street to the best of his ability. Lastly, the formal training of this writer has been primarily in economics.

In short, the intellectual spirit in which this work was undertaken can be conveniently summarized by echoing the following sentiments from the Preface of David McCord Wright's *Democracy and Progress.*[1]

Ten years ago the writer began the study of social problems by concentrating upon detailed analysis of a specific technical question: how to maintain income and employment. He must plead guilty to having thought such inquiries sufficient in themselves. But, over the years of work and discussion, he has found that apparently minor differences ramify deeply. Nearly always a debate over policy has traced back to some more fundamental ethical or social judgment and he is now profoundly convinced *that the man who wishes to avoid nonsense cannot study social policy on a technical level alone.*

H.R.S.

Athens, Georgia
January, 1958

---

[1] (New York: The Macmillan Co., 1949), pp. 13-14; italics added.

Contents

Part I
A POINT OF VIEW

Chapter 1

Meaning of Public Interest

In the field of government-business relationships in the United States, no concept is more widely used than that of "public interest." No doubt one reason for this is the pride Americans take in their democratic institutions; government in a democracy is, ideally, supposed to care for the interests of *all* the people—that is, the public. Another reason, however, and this consideration is perhaps even more important for this discussion, is the fact that so much difference of opinion exists as to the public policies which most nearly conform with the public interest. Indeed, so fundamental are these differences that a conscientious grappling with the issues raised by this question is a prerequisite to a serious study of government and business.

PRELIMINARY DEFINITION

To be sure, little difficulty is created by one form this controversy may take. Where individuals or groups are careless in their arguments, asserting that such and such a policy is preferred by them and is therefore in the public interest, it is at once clear that no genuine concern for the public is involved.

But precisely because this approach is so transparent, it is in practice rarely used. Instead, men almost invariably rationalize their preferences, presenting their arguments for particular policies in the form of abstract principles with which nearly everyone agrees (as long as they are kept sufficiently abstract). The student's problem, therefore, is distinguishing public interest principles which are more or less valid in and of themselves from those which are only a camouflage for individual preferences. And while all too little of a specific nature can be said on this topic with assurance, perhaps a few helpful guide rules can be laid down.

To begin with, it is common to hear it said or implied that a certain policy is in the public interest because it is "right" rather than

3

"wrong"—because it will work out well rather than badly for the community. This approach has a certain superficial plausibility, too; insofar as democracy is thought of as securing for the people what they want, this definition would seem to be a direct application of the democratic ideal.

Unfortunately, however, the problem is not so easily resolved. A judgment as to whether or not a decision is or was democratic must be made in the light of the information available and the attitudes prevailing at the time it was made. On the other hand, a judgment as to whether or not a decision is or was "right" can only be made in the light of experience. In the first case the inquiry must be whether the individuals affected by the decision were in favor of it when it was made, while in the second it must be whether the decision as made was successful.

To illustrate: if a group decided unanimously to declare war on another group and emerged victorious in the fighting, the decision reached would be said to have been democratic and "right." If, however, the aggressor group were defeated and enslaved, the decision reached would be said to have been democratic and "wrong." Clearly these two questions must be kept separate.

An actual instance, one taken from the evolution of business-government relationships in the United States, can make this point still clearer. In the years following his election to a second term as President, Andrew Jackson summarily destroyed the Second Bank of the United States. Was this action "right"? Was it in the best interest of the nation as a whole? It would probably be agreed today by money and banking experts that Jackson's action was not the best policy, that a substantial need existed for the centralization of money and banking mechanisms thus destroyed. At the same time, however, this policy was no doubt approved by a majority of the country's adult citizens. The election of 1832 had been fought out with "The Bank" as the principal issue, and its proponent, Henry Clay, was roundly defeated.

Another frequent approach to the problem of public interest also employs the antithesis "right" versus "wrong," although using these terms in the moral sense. Here the issue turns on whether the outcome is "good" or "bad," contributory to or destructive of particular ethical ideals.

Such an approach resolves quite satisfactorily the problem of time perspective. The question of whether a given war or banking institution is morally defensible can in theory be answered as well before as after the fact. But this is by no means all net gain, for a difficulty now arises which is even more decisive. This conception of the public interest can be demonstrated to be incompatible with belief in democracy.

Democracy is grounded on an insistence upon the value of the individual person. If, however, this fundamental premise is to have practical effect in the ordering of social relationships, both the individual's pattern of values and his judgments regarding courses of action must be respected. Discussion for the purpose of altering values or broadening judgments is, of course, appropriate. But when the discussion is over, and there can be here no element of coercion, the resultant values and judgments must be honored. To whatever extent they are not, democracy has been abandoned.

Furthermore, not only must the question of whether or not a given decision is democratic part company with the question of whether or not it is ethically sound, but the reverse side of this approach to an interpretation of public interest raises an issue still more far-reaching in its implications. Whenever the public interest is envisioned as demanding some concrete policy Absolute, the first step down the road toward totalitarianism has been taken. The acceptance of an Absolute as the standard of "rightness" is the equivalent of asking, not what people do in fact want, but what they ought to want, or what they would want if they were better informed or had "correct" values. Whenever public policy begins to be made with these questions in the foreground, the day of authoritarian government is at hand. Note how soberly and seriously idealist philosophers after Rousseau identified "freedom" with a process of compelling citizens to work for the values they ought to want, and how this road led directly to Hitler and Mussolini.[1]

Lest this interpretation be too hastily dismissed as extreme, it is essential to recognize that the achievement of what people want is a conception of the basic purpose of government to which few would commit themselves without important reservations. Invariably men do erect Absolutes to govern their behavior. Thus most men are to some extent totalitarian at heart; they are simply not willing to give a high priority to what the other fellow wants, even after full discussion and debate.[2] It follows that men are typically willing to jettison democracy when democracy ceases to produce reasonably acceptable results.

This is not, of course, to urge that men "ought" to value democracy more highly than any other item in their hierarchy of values, or to suggest values which "ought" to be more highly prized than de-

[1] W. M. McGovern, *From Luther to Hitler* (Boston: Houghton Mifflin Co., 1941).
[2] J. A. Schumpeter, *Capitalism, Socialism, and Democracy* (New York: Harper & Bros., 1950), pp. 242 ff.

mocracy. The point is rather that the path leading to democracy is difficult and treacherous. Citizens in a democracy want to base their institutions upon moral principles, but are confronted at every turn with the fact that a rigid insistence upon morality as such can easily lead to authoritarianism. Consequently, a definition of public interest stressing the maintenance of democratic institutions must avoid this pitfall.

What more manageable interpretation can be brought into use? What content can be given to the concept of public interest which will relate it constructively to democracy?

One way out of this dilemma immediately presents itself. If democracy is to be insisted upon, the only safe procedure would seem to be to treat democracy and the public interest as synonymous terms. This, therefore, will be the interpretation used in this book. *Whatever is done democratically will be considered to be in the public interest.*

Private Interests Versus the Public Interest

Admittedly this definition creates as many problems as it solves. It is, therefore, necessary to give attention to a clarification of some of the issues thus raised, one of the most important of these being the relationship between private interests and the public interest.

The criticism is often heard that a particular individual or group orients political behavior to selfish preferences rather than to the good of the community as a whole. Now if it be granted that this is often an accurate description of what does in fact take place, how reasonable is this criticism? Is there anything about democracy requiring individuals and groups to work for a public benefit defined in such a way as to bring it into conflict with the individual's or group's private good?

Because it pervades—implicitly if not explicitly—virtually all discussions of democracy, this is a matter which must be dealt with in all candidness. The view to be advanced here stands on the proposition that democracy *cannot* be made to depend upon a conception of public interest conflicting with private interpretations of private interests. A few brief comments will make clear why this is believed to be the correct answer.

First, any other approach could only be based upon a lack of understanding of the human personality. Behavior consists of responses to personality needs, which are in turn intricately interrelated with the meanings particular situations have for the individual.[3] Behind these meanings, and indeed as their only source, stands the entire

[3] Walter Coutou, *Emergent Human Nature* (New York: Alfred A. Knopf, Inc., 1949).

body of the individual's past experiences. It is these meanings that determine what the individual "sees" in a given situation, and what he does not "see." It is also these meanings that determine what he feels to be important or unimportant, right or wrong. In short, they tell him what to do under certain circumstances, and, depending upon how well his personality is integrated, he reacts accordingly.

It follows that no individual can act from the standpoint of the community as a whole, because no individual "knows" the community as a whole. He knows only those parts of society in which he participates or has participated, and therefore understands only the interests of particular groups. These are the interests with which he identifies; these are the sources of the ideals he endeavors to serve.

The significance of this conclusion for present purposes can be seen still more plainly in the form of its corollary. In the final analysis there cannot exist any individual conception of the public interest which is not actually an interpretation from the standpoint of particular private interests. Thus, when an individual or group is accused of acting contrary to the public interest, what is actually involved is that the accuser is identifying his own circle of interests with the public interest. So too, of course, is the accused—and both may be completely sincere.

This can also be made more concrete by means of an example taken from American economic history. The small group of outstanding citizens that assembled in Philadelphia in 1787 to revise the Articles of Confederation came overwhelmingly from the propertied, merchant, and financial classes. They understood that the document they were planning to present for ratification would be opposed by many of their fellow-citizens back home. At the same time, however, it did not seriously occur to these men that a Constitution fulfilling the basic needs of the classes they represented could fail to serve the "public" interest. Similarly, it was taken for granted by the Constitution's opponents that a revision of those clauses in the proposed document prejudicing their interests would be beneficial to the "public." Nor does this mean that the typical American of that day consciously raised the question in his own mind, "What is there in this for me?" Rather, citizens proceeded (exactly as they would to-day) to rationalize their own interests in terms of the general welfare.

In the second place, democracy itself emphasizes the pursuit of private interests. Democratic thinking makes the initial assumption that a government will be operated for the benefit of those who participate actively in it. If it is run by king and nobility, these will be the people who most gain from its operation. If it is run by a landed aristocracy, the aristocrats will reap its fruits. The only assurance that government will not function in the interest of a few is for as many as possible to possess a voice in its functioning. In short, the basic idea behind democracy is the proposition that the motive power of government should be the particular interests of a large number of people rather than of a small number.

This thought can be put differently with profit. The essence of democracy is a government controlled by the governed; the diffusion of power which is democracy's most fundamental characteristic can have no other meaning. But it is only natural for men, given the power with which to control government, to take this responsibility seriously. If, as a result, men use the sovereign power to further their own purposes, it can only be said that it is for this reason that men believe in democracy.

These conclusions, too, are perhaps subject to misinterpretation, and misinterpretation must again be avoided if at all possible. To be sure, an individual does not always and only act to enhance his own personal welfare as narrowly defined. Particular groups may, and often do, stand at the center of an individual's scale of values. Rather, what is suggested is that an individual always and only acts in terms of the values in which he believes—whatever they happen to be. This distinction has been especially well expressed by Bertrand Russell:

> If politics is to become scientific, and if the event is not to be constantly surprising, it is imperative that our political thinking should penetrate more deeply into the springs of human action. All activity is prompted by desire. There is a wholly fallacious theory advanced by earnest moralists to the effect that it is possible to resist desire in the interest of duty and moral principle. I say this is fallacious, not because no man ever acts from a sense of duty, but because duty has no hold on him unless he desires to be dutiful.[4]

Motivation, in short, is always personal. The individual behaves as *he* needs to behave, as *his* groups have taught him to behave; and in consequence behavior is typically oriented toward values much narrower than those held by the total community. Furthermore, in the life experience of most individuals the determining forces tend to be centripetal in their operation rather than centrifugal. That is, the circle of an individual's pattern of values has a tendency to become smaller rather than larger—still another reason why individual values often diverge sharply from the total pattern of community values.

It is quite true, of course, that individuals differ greatly one from another with respect to the comprehensiveness of the values toward which they are oriented. But though this fact is frequently interpreted

---

[4] Bertrand Russell, "The Springs of Human Action," *The Atlantic Monthly*, March, 1952.

as meaning that some individuals work for the public good while others endeavor to further only their own private good, such a conclusion is not warranted. Both groups are in fact oriented only to their own interests from one point of view—and to the good of the public from another. The size of the public differs from case to case, but *it is never the whole public in any event.*

But does this mean that there is no such thing as "public interest groups"? Are there not organizations without "axes to grind" which devote their efforts instead to genuine public interest activities?

Surely the answer must be that there are not. True, there are organizations that lobby for policies more easily defended in idealistic terms than those pursued by the National Association of Manufacturers, the American Farm Bureau Federation, or the AFL-CIO. Some groups are no doubt oriented in their thinking and planning to a broader segment of the values current in the underlying community than others. But once these points are acknowledged and the value of such organizations to democracy properly recognized, it must still be inquired whether the Civil Liberties Union, to take a single obvious example, speaks for the business interests of the country. And against the argument that it does not do this because businessmen are quite capable of taking care of themselves, the fundamental proposition at issue here must be emphatically repeated. Just as no individual can absorb all aspects of the culture of a modern, complex civilization, so can no organization reflect the aspirations and expectations of all segments of the population. In a democracy, since no one is conceded to be competent to say who is to speak for what interests, everyone is implicitly authorized to speak for, but only for, his own interests.

Since this conclusion in turn is so basic to the point of view underlying this book, perhaps one more summary statement will not be amiss. No society can be either built or maintained contrary to interest; no social system which depends upon behavior oriented to causes of which the behaver is not the center can hope to function successfully. As so wise and democratic an observer as Benjamin Franklin said many years ago: "Few men in public affairs act from a mere view of the good of their country, whatever they may pretend; and though their activity may bring real good to their country, they do not act from a spirit of benevolence."

CONSUMER INTEREST AS PUBLIC INTEREST

Another issue raised by the identification of the public interest with the democratic process has to do with a specific common denominator of the general welfare often put forward. Thus, many people insist that because all citizens are consumers, here is a criterion for determining policy which does not make the mistake of postulating behavior contrary to interest, but which at the same time does not wholly surrender to interest conflicts. How well does this criterion conform with the public interest concept used here?

Because the view will be taken that it does not conform at all well, it is only fair that this approach to a solution of the problem be first presented as advantageously as possible. In answer to the question of what guiding rule or standard the government might use in its regulatory activities, V. A. Mund, one of the many who might be cited in this connection, puts it this way:

From an economic standpoint, all citizens have a common interest in a "living." Everyone must secure each day some part of the total national stream of real income—such as food, clothing, housing, medical and dental care, automobiles, radios, and furniture, and so forth. The "consumer interest" is the interest of all citizens in getting more and better goods for consumption at ever lower prices. . . . It follows, therefore, that in so far as government is concerned with promoting the "common interest" in the economic sphere, its decisions should be guided by the "consumer interest."[5]

Within the context of identifying the public interest and democracy, a most urgent question is immediately raised by this emphasis upon consumption as the common denominator of democratic citizenship. Does this approach mean that the individual's consumer interest ought to be advanced regardless of what interest he wishes to stress—that the consumer interest ought to be set up as an Absolute Good, irrespective of what citizens choose to call Good? If so, it differs in no essential way from Rousseau's assertion that the individual who finds himself in the minority actually does not know what he wants and must have what he really wants forced upon him. Can there be any doubt that this is an authoritarian doctrine rather than a democratic one?

But this may, of course, be unfair. Perhaps consumer interest proponents do not really mean this at all. On the other hand, Professor Mund goes on as follows:

Since every producer is also a consumer, it may be asked why consumers are contrasted with producers? What is wrong about promoting the interests of producers as such, since they are also consumers? The contrast between the interests of *consumers* and *producers* is made because an organized group of producers usually stands to gain more from a certain policy (such as legalized price fixing, a curtailment of production, an exclusion of competitors, or a pro-

[5] V. A. Mund, *Government and Business* (2d ed.; New York: Harper & Bros., 1955), p. 75.

tective tariff) than they stand to lose as buyers of the products of others, including their own.

Does this not sound very much like Rousseau's thought processes? Does this not clearly mean that the government is to give priority to the interest of individuals as consumers because, if left to their own devices, they would often choose to give priority to their producer interest instead?

One other interpretation is possible. It can be argued that the several interests confronting the government do not in practice represent "the people" because of defects in our democracy. This is a strong defense, and a legitimate one. At the same time it is one requiring close scrutiny. The proposition that governmental processes in the United States are democratic is hardly to be repudiated by mere assertion. Furthermore, there is particularly good reason for not accepting as evidence supporting such a repudiation the fact that consumer interests are often superseded by producer interests.

This case can most conveniently be made by asking and then endeavoring to answer two closely related questions concerning modern political organization. How realistic is it to expect consumers, as consumers, to organize for political purposes? Under what circumstances can decision-making be considered democratic in the absence of representation of consumers as consumers?

The key to an answer to these questions lies in the nature of today's exchange economy. Real income is typically earned by a roundabout process consisting of (1) the production of a good or service, (2) its sale, and (3) the expenditure of the money received for other goods and services. The real income available to any producer is thus a function of three basic variables: the efficiency of his labor, its price, and the prices of the goods and services he consumes.

Speaking broadly, the producer interest is equivalent to the first two of these terms; the consumer interest may be roughly equated with the third. If a group of citizens decided to organize politically to enhance their income status, in which of these two directions would they ordinarily turn?

Certainly there would normally be little reason to develop a political action group if the emphasis were to be the improvement of efficiency. On the other hand, frequently much can be accomplished politically by way of raising the price of the goods or services being produced. In fact, even where the principal focus of attention is increased output, the complexities of today's industrial economy, camouflaging as they often do the connection between greater effort and greater output, may still dictate political activity for the purpose of securing appropriate recognition for actual output increases. There is, in other words, good reason for devoting political efforts to one's producer interest.

How about the other end of the process? Is the consumer interest a logical basis for political organization?

Two cases must be distinguished. Suppose a question arises involving the price of, say, sugar. As a producer of sugar it is in the interest of a certain individual that the price of sugar be raised. But as a consumer of sugar his best interest will be served by a lower price. Which of these interests will be politically organized? Surely it will be the producer rather than the consumer interest. Most of the real income the individual receives is apt to be tied up with the price of sugar insofar as he is a producer. However, only a tiny fraction of his economic well-being will be related to sugar insofar as he is a consumer. To be sure, he would no doubt rather have a higher price as a producer without paying a higher price as a consumer. But if a choice must be made—and typically it must—the producer interest will be given preference.

This is the most clear-cut case. It demonstrates that in a free-choice situation the producer interest will supersede the consumer interest where the producer's own product is involved. What about the other and more numerous type of situation? Will a threatened increase in the price of sugar mobilize consumers into political action as consumers? There are three reasons for not expecting this result.

First, it is possible that the expenditure of time and money in this direction will do injury to producer interests as such. After all, sugar is only one of the many items entering into the standard of living, and there is no more reason for political activity oriented toward sugar than a dozen other items. If much attention were to be concentrated on such side issues, effectiveness with respect to the more central matter of production could fall sharply.

But suppose, second, many consumers believe that no interference with producer interests is threatened. Will the consumer interest in the case at hand be pressed? Another major hurdle must now be surmounted, the problem of actually putting the required organization together. There would immediately be encountered, of course, many consumers already convinced that the proposed endeavor would interfere with producer interests (and not even the majority of these would be producers of sugar). Moreover, it is difficult to organize a political interest group with large numbers and low geographical concentration. Finally, organization is apt to be more successful as it is more permanent. Thus an organization of sugar consumers today must become an organization of bread consumers tomorrow, with the result that a consumer political group would be constantly shifting in membership and proportionately weak.

Now suppose, third, that both of these problems have been resolved: the activity will not prejudice producer interests, and an effective political instrument can be forged. One more major question remains. How much is to be gained? The fruits of political activity by sugar producers need be shared only with the relative small number of persons included in their own group. Gains accruing from the political activities of sugar consumers, however, must be spread to all consumers of sugar. Assuming the potential gains to be equally great in the two situations, in the one case the per person gains might be significant while in the other they would be scarcely visible.

To summarize, the cost of political activity is high and the resources available must be concentrated where they will bring the greatest returns. And when all things are taken into consideration from this standpoint, it is readily understandable why political action groups are usually producer-centered organizations; this result is virtually decreed by the fact that the modern world is characterized by a highly specialized division of labor. For all practical purposes, therefore, the conception of democracy or public interest around which discussion can realistically be built must take reference from producer interests.

The more fundamental question posed earlier can now also be approximately answered. Under what circumstances can decision-making be considered democratic in the absence of representation of consumers as consumers? Where freedom of association prevails, those groups will form which people believe can best serve their felt needs. If the groups which do form are producer groups, well and good; if they are organizations of consumers, well and good also. The wants and aspirations of the individual, after all, are what democracy is designed to enhance. It is surely not unreasonable to ask democracy to work with the individual life as it grows and develops, and if such is to be its orientation, neither producers nor consumers can be erected into an Absolute. It is easy to agree with Professor Mund and others that organization along producer lines makes life in a democracy more complicated than would otherwise be the case, but there is here no basis for denying the responsibilities imposed by belief in democracy.

Government as "Referee"

Often allied with the idea of a common denominator for the entire community (such as an emphasis upon consumer interests) is another concept which can constructively be commented upon at this point. In a society in which many groups choose to organize on some basis which does not automatically bring them into harmony with other groups, the result is intergroup conflict which can only be resolved by the use of power. This means that every group is compelled to adopt as one of its purposes the securing of such power as is necessary to defend its values against attack by outsiders. However, since the values held by various groups are often mutually exclusive, full emphasis upon the right of groups to satisfy their needs would create a society torn apart by anarchy.

This threat democracy is forced to meet just as it is met in every other form of social organization. A government must be created possessing sufficient power to maintain order—to enforce decisions even though they may benefit some groups at the expense of others. At this point, however, the central problem of democracy is raised in an especially critical way. A government powerful enough to perform this function satisfactorily is apt also to be powerful enough to stifle the individual and group life so vital to democratic living. How can this be prevented?

One explanation of democracy's solution to this problem is to refer to a democratic government as an impartial umpire, as is so important in the play of a competitive game. Questions arising out of the play of the game are referred to a neutral arbiter who makes his decisions from the standpoint of the best interests of all concerned—that is, the "rules of the game" which have evolved out of past play. With the aid of this unfailing criterion of "right" and "wrong," conflicts can be resolved in such a way that the game can go on reasonably harmoniously.

The analogy is, to be sure, not wholly illogical; there are significant parallels between the social process and the playing of, say, a football game. Both activities are dynamic and continuous in the sense that the position achieved at any one moment of the play provides the context within which the next steps must be planned. Both also proceed according to rules which are in general understood and accepted by contestants—rules which are more or less closely enforced as the standard of approved practice by a formally designated referee. And finally, where questions involving application of the rules arise, the decision of the referee is final.

Notwithstanding these similarities, however, this solution of this critically important problem is not convincing. It makes the mistake of dealing with government as though that institution were somehow apart from rather than an integral part of the social process. When government is placed within this context, as it clearly must be, the suggested similarities are more than counterbalanced by three vital dissimilarities.

First, the football referee is by definition an individual who does not care which side wins—or at least is not sufficiently concerned about the outcome for his preferences significantly to affect his judgments. But where basic matters of society are involved, rather than so marginal a matter as an athletic contest, an impartial referee is unavailable. Government officials are a product of the society within which their decisions are to be made. Furthermore, no official will be governed by all the values supported in the larger community—to say nothing of reflecting these values in approximately the same proportions as they prevail in society at large. Rather an official must reflect the conditioning he has received within that part of the culture to which he has been most exposed.

Second, from the start of a football game to its conclusion, the rules under which it is played do not change. After the season is over, to be sure, while no games are being played and when men can deliberate in terms of principles rather than with one eye on teams actually on the field, changes in the rules are made. But while any given game is being played the rules remain fixed.

The "game" played out in society, on the other hand, knows no seasons; there is never a time when rules can be altered except under actual playing conditions—with one eye on the relative positions of teams already competing for supremacy. In other words, changes in rules must be made and put into operation while the game is under way.

A third difference between football and intergroup competition grows out of the procedures by which rule-changes are made. Since such decisions are arrived at in the heat of battle, changes in the rules can only imperfectly be distinguished in practice from the interpretation of existing rules. The consequence is that the umpire not only applies the present rule book but becomes a rule-making official as well. At this point, with a biassed referee having rule-making responsibilities and free to change the rules while the game is in progress, the analogy between government and the referee in a competitive sporting event becomes hopelessly inadequate.

MAJORITY RULE AS THE PUBLIC INTEREST

But if the public interest is not to be thought of in terms of specific policy Absolutes, if individuals are not to be required to repress private wants in favor of the public good, if the consumer interest is not an acceptable criterion of the general welfare, and if the analogy between government and an impartial umpire must be rejected, we are left at this point with very little of what might be called specific content for the concept of public interest suggested above. What can be said, next, to make this concept more precise, to translate the abstract idea of determining policy democratically into a more tangible form?

Ever since the time of John Locke political theory has emphasized the concept "the consent of the governed," and this idea is often thought of as a synonym for democracy. In more modern terminology, consent of the governed is today broadly identified with majority rule. Is there, now, in this arrangement, a set of interrelationships which can meaningfully be interpreted as the public interest?

Here also there is a major issue which must be resolved before the question can be answered affirmatively. As that great student of American democracy, De Tocqueville, said many years ago, majority rule means the "right of the majority to have its way," and many people are critical of democracy because of the "tyranny by the majority" which is thought to result. How valid is this criticism? Under what circumstances does majority rule produce minority coercion? Can a system built on the right of minority coercion be realistically interpreted as consent?

It is of course obvious that a minority can be protected by a majority practicing voluntary restraint. This possibility, however, will be discounted here. No majority can be depended upon to limit itself; because power for all practical purposes is never shared voluntarily, it is now axiomatic with social scientists that power can only be held in check by an opposing power. It follows that ideals can be made effective in the on-going life of a society only if they are built into its power structure. With respect to majority rights and minority protection, how can this be done? How can the ideal of minority rights be incorporated into the power structure of a democratic society? What features in such a society's make-up can force a majority to adopt a moderate program?

Two facts are especially important in this connection. The first is that public policy is not a single thing, but consists rather of an almost infinite variety of facets—each affecting adversely or favorably a different constellation of interests. The second is that public policy is not made once and for all. It is always subject to new interpretations as new situations arise and new alignments are made. Because of the importance of these considerations it is possible for minorities actively to participate in the process of cumulative definition—a participation which provides a solid foundation upon which consent can be said to rest. Put differently, the very fact that a majority is needed to make changes in public policy is a powerful influence operating to limit coercion.

There are several ways in which this force is applied in practice. First, extremists in any direction soon find that they must temper their demands if they wish to be on the winning side. Second, given freedom of association a defeated and hence coerced minority can often secure allies for the purpose of making another try. With new strength the issue on which defeat was suffered may be brought into the political arena again, perhaps with a more favorable outcome. Third, even a minority failing to find satisfaction in this way may be in the majority on the next issue coming up for decision in which its interests are at stake. Fourth, and to complete the circle, the extent of any given defeat is often moderated by the fact that members of a majority are normally compelled to think ahead to the next trial of strength in order to avoid antagonizing members of a minority whose support will later be needed. Thus through what is called "the right to become the majority" a minority can limit the extent to which it is coerced.

But "the right to become the majority" is not always an adequate protection. There are prerequisite conditions which must be met.

A beginning can be made toward describing these conditions by analyzing a hypothetical example. Imagine a legislature of one hundred men in the process of voting on a tariff measure. Suppose further that this body is divided into a majority of fifty-one and a minority of forty-nine. And imagine finally that all members of the majority want a 100 per cent protective tariff, while all members of the minority want a 1 per cent revenue levy. Disregarding the fact that some members of the majority may want to avoid alienating some members of the minority, it is clear that the resulting duty will be 100 per cent. Every member of the majority will get exactly the policy he wants; every member of the minority will be equally and substantially frustrated.

Notice now the difference when this situation is contrasted with the limiting case at the opposite end of the pole—a case much closer to the one most frequently encountered in real life. Suppose here that there is not a clear-cut division of members into a majority and a minority, each of these groups being of one mind on the most desirable tariff policy, but that the views of members are distributed evenly between those of men standing at each extreme. Thus one man wants a duty of 100 per cent, one a duty of 1 per cent, while the other preferences fall at 1 per cent intervals in between. What tariff rate will now be enacted?

Every individual must in this situation seek supporters for his own position, and therefore extensive compromising will be required. Out of the initial confusion it is probable that a high-tariff group and a low-tariff group will be formed—the one endeavoring to pass the highest possible rate, and the other seeking to achieve the lowest possible rate. But when it is discovered that the high-tariff people can command a sufficient majority to defeat a low rate while the low-tariff men can muster sufficient votes to prevent the setting of a high rate, a majority will be created by combining the moderate elements in both groups. The resultant measure will carry a rate of 50 per cent.

The important point to note here is the vital change that has taken place in the incidence of coercion. Whereas in the first case one group of extremists secured exactly the policy it wanted, in this case extremists at both ends of the scale have been similarly frustrated. Put differently, the frustration experienced by low-tariff proponents is no greater and no less than that experienced by those preferring a high tariff, which is in turn only another way of saying that the terms "consent" and "coercion" can be applied equally to either group. And not only is frustration more evenly distributed in the latter situation, but there is substantially less of it—if a quantitative comparison in such a situation is meaningful.

The key to this much more favorable result is that the majority was not homogeneous with respect to the issue at hand. Furthermore, when the situation is broadened to include a succession of issues, another kind of heterogeneity is revealed which contributes to the same end. A majority normally includes people who not only have different ideas about the policy in question, but who also differ from one another with respect to the intensity of their feelings about pending matters. The skillful use of these differences by minority leaders can often shatter majority cohesion and turn a minority into a majority. Called by political scientists "accommodation," this process works as follows.[6]

Imagine a group of interests which appear to constitute a minority. Contemplating their probable minority status, some of these interests will be extremely disappointed while others will feel the anticipated deprivation less keenly. Naturally those who would feel most seriously injured by an adverse decision will give the most attention to the problem of avoiding defeat, and one kind of preventive measure especially will be investigated. By the same token that minority interests differ in the intensity of their preferences, so too do majority interests. If a significant number of those otherwise included in the majority have a low intensity of desire with respect to the issue under

[6] J. A. Corry, *Elements of Democratic Government* (New York: Oxford University Press, 1951).

discussion, perhaps a bargain can be made with them. If they will retreat from their negative position with respect to Policy A, letting the other side win, grateful individuals who would otherwise have been on the small end of that vote will return the favor by retreating from their negative position with respect to Policy B which their colleagues are particularly interested in achieving.

The accommodation process also works in reverse. Minority interests with a low intensity of desire with respect to Policy A may concede defeat and endeavor to bargain with those of their opponents whose intensity of desire is high. In exchange for votes which will assure their own defeat, minority interests will secure support for a Policy B which is of much less importance in the scale of values of their majority allies. Whichever form accommodation takes, however, its essence is the support of policies considered relatively undesirable in exchange for assistance in securing policies considered relatively desirable. In this avoidance of large frustrations by voluntarily accepting smaller ones, a practice which takes place in bewilderingly complex ways in the real world, the distinction between majority and minority tends to disappear. Thus over a period of time and in the course of making a series of policy decisions, defeats and victories have a way of canceling one another out.

Reduced to sociological fundamentals, the key fact in the avoidance of tyranny is diversity.[7] In a richly diversified community such as a democracy strives to be, the very heterogeneity which gives rise to conflict is in the last analysis the principal factor operating to protect minorities from an abuse of majority power. Stated more broadly, because no group is powerful enough to dictate policy on its own terms, every group is compelled to compromise its policy demands. For two reasons, moreover, these compromises will normally be in the direction of greater moderation. On the one hand, those groups standing midway between policy extremes are in the best position to bargain—and are therefore most influential in policy-making. On the other hand, there seems to be in every stable society a normal curve of distribution of policy attitudes, with the largest number of people standing near the center and the smallest number located at the two extremes. Most individuals brought up in a reasonably successful social order identify important values with the *status quo* and will hence not lightly encourage major changes therein.

More specifically, one of the principal characteristics of a complex modern society is what Professor Truman calls overlapping group memberships; individuals frequently belong to more than one

7 R. M. MacIver, *The Web of Government* (New York: The Macmillan Co., 1947).

group.[8] The consequence of this fact is that every group must temper the stand it takes in terms of the values held by those of other groups to which its members also owe allegiance. And while a large number of people is apt to claim membership in at least one liberal organization, the pattern of an individual's memberships is far more frequently conservative, with the result that the real radicals are usually compelled to give up policies they would have preferred to support. Stated differently, the political power of a group is a function of its numbers and cohesion, and these two characteristics are apt to be inversely related to one another. Individuals standing for extreme policies must as a rule either hold to their principles in a group too small to be politically effective, or give up some of those principles in order to participate in a group large enough to wield influence.

Evidently, in short, the most critical problem confronted by majority rule is not insurmountable. On the basis of that assurance, the following summary observations can appropriately be made.

First, *whatever policies are arrived at democratically will in this book be considered to be in the public interest*. Second, arriving at policies democratically means essentially *the promulgation of whatever policies are preferred by the citizen group*. Third, the process of determining what policies are in fact preferred *must rely heavily on some kind of a majority-rule device*. And fourth, stating all of these conclusions more pointedly, *the public interest in a democracy is not wanted because it is the public interest, it is rather the public interest because it is wanted*.

However, in one sense this is only the first step in defining the public interest, for the idea of identifying majority rule with that concept is still by no means obvious. Some there are, indeed, who maintain that majority rule is essentially a contradiction in terms. In order, therefore, to establish the relationship between these two things more securely it will be helpful next to take a closer look at the decision-making process in a democratic society.

QUESTIONS FOR DISCUSSION

1. Why can the public interest not be defined in terms of right and wrong policies?

2. Explain why in a democracy private interests are not to be frowned away on the ground that they are in conflict with something called the public interest?

---

[8] David B. Truman, *The Governmental Process* (New York: Alfred A. Knopf, Inc., 1951).

3. Why is it not realistic to expect consumer interests to be the basis of political organization in a modern industrial economy?

4. What policies can you name that would be greatly changed if consumer interests were a dominant force in policy-making?

5. Why can the government not be properly thought of as a referee? Should the government function in that capacity?

6. What is the principal condition for minority protection in a system of majority rule? How does this operate to protect the minority?

7. In a democracy, must private interests be submerged in the public interest, must the public interest give way before private interests, or does neither of these statements describe the actual situation? Explain.

8. Why is it so important in a democracy that all policies be considered tentative?

Chapter 2

The Decision-Making Process

It is common for the assertion to be made that democracy cannot realistically be defined as "rule by the people." The people, it is said, are too ignorant, impassioned, and cumbersome to do the detailed work essential to the making of concrete policies.[1] It is insisted, furthermore, that when due allowance is made for the fact that in a modern, complex democracy government decisions are made by (or at least through) officials, whether elected or appointed by elected representatives, the people cannot even help frame the broad outlines of policy. All that the people can do is to say "yes" or "no" when asked, and even these broad responses must in the last analysis be limited to a process of passing judgment on whether one individual or another is to hold office.[2] To be sure, judgments about candidates are not wholly divorced from considerations relating to alternative policies, but insofar as this is the basis for votes it is far more often than not past rather than future decisions which are the determining factor.

This picture of democracy is decidedly not a flattering one. So small a role is accorded the citizen as to make one wonder what all the hue and cry over democracy is about anyway. In a study such as this in which the concept of democracy is an integral part of the analytical framework employed, it is necessary to inquire if this view does justice to the democratic process. When the intricacy of the task of governing in today's world is taken into account, is this all that remains of majority rule and the concept of consent?

It will be suggested here that much more is involved—that were the role of the citizen as narrow as the usual view insists, democracy

---

[1] Graham Wallas, *Human Nature and Politics* (London: Constable Co., Ltd., 1938); and Walter Lippmann, *The Phantom Public* (New York: Harcourt, Brace & Co., Inc., 1925).

[2] E. E. Schattschneider, *Party Government* (New York: Rinehart & Co., Inc., 1942).

would indeed be less worth defending. Moreover, it will be urged that this dessicated interpretation arises essentially from a tendency to think of the isolated citizen on the one side standing face to face with an elaborate and impersonal government on the other side. But when thinking about democracy is enriched by the explicit inclusion of the role of groups in social organization, citizen-government relationships take on a more convincing aspect.

DEFINITION OF PRESSURE

The essence of government is decision-making. Struggles to control government and the importance attached to self-government reflect the fact that the decisions government is called upon to make may be favorable or adverse from the standpoint of any particular interest, and whatever control over government is achieved by such interests is utilized toward the end of maximizing favorable decisions and minimizing unfavorable ones. Since decisions are ultimately made by human beings, control over government means the holding of a preferential position in the frame of reference of government officials—that is, placing in office men whose values are as nearly identical with one's own as possible.

Because these relationships are so vital to an understanding of the political, or decision-making process, it is worth while to explore a little further the sociocultural bases of human behavior. Social psychologists tell us that such behavior, including decision-making in government, consists of reactions to a psychological field as perceived by the acting organism,[3] which is perhaps only another way of saying that the individual attributes meanings to the events taking place around him and responds in ways suggested by those meanings. Social psychology further asserts that an individual's behavior can be described as oriented to the task of maintaining and enhancing the self as that self is understood by the individual. What is involved here is a process by which the individual seeks to retain the successes achieved in the past and to go on to greater accomplishments.

But social scientists do not suppose that although the individual is the center of the world in which he lives, he is the only inhabitant. Rather it is emphasized that the groups with which he has been closely associated are also an important part of that world. Before he was mature enough to form independent judgments, these groups

[3] M. Sherif and H. Cantril, *The Psychology of Ego-Involvements* (New York: John Wiley & Sons, Inc., 1947); and Ralph Linton, *The Cultural Background of Personality* (New York: Appleton-Century-Crofts, Inc., 1945).

taught him what meanings to derive from an immense variety of situations. More than this, these groups placed "inside" the individual the values he seeks to attain, and by the same token they judge the extent to which particular values have been achieved and hence the extent to which the individual is to be esteemed because of these accomplishments. In sum, there are in the environment of every individual certain significant persons (other members of the groups to which he belongs) whose approval is basic to that individual's well-being, and behavior is in this sense designed to maintain and increase if possible the flow of approval sentiments.

It should not, of course, be concluded that behavior is conditioned only by interpersonal relationships. Suffice it to say that enough is now known about human motivation to make reasonable the conclusion that this factor is always vital. Nor does it follow that insofar as this is a factor its presence makes itself felt exclusively at the level of conscious awareness. Indeed the most powerful of such influences may operate well below this level. In the case of elected public officials this phenomenon will vary in character all the way from the almost totally subconscious behavior patterns which grow out of past associations, through the sanctions that can be brought to bear by present group intimates, to the leverage exerted by people whose only relationship with the individual in question is the universal franchise. The important point is simply that, because power is fundamentally a set of interpersonal relationships,[4] it is possible to state with a fair degree of precision the largest part of what is involved when a man "makes up his mind" about political issues.

Long and heatedly has the question been discussed whether a representative should vote the way his constituency wants him to or according to the dictates of the principles around which he builds his own life. Within the context here of the way decisions are made it can readily be seen that this question is in large part academic. If voting is done according to constituents' preferences, this means primarily that the representative in question is to a considerable extent governed by the principle that the wielding of power is itself a value of high importance. Where the representative is more willing to risk the loss of votes by taking unpopular stands on significant issues, the meaning here is that power as a value is rated relatively lower in the value hierarchy while other values are ranked relatively higher. (Of course, account must be taken of the fact that it is good politics to insist upon being "a man of principle," whether the principles involved are or are not broader than the winning of the

---

[4] H. D. Lasswell, *Power and Personality* (New York: W. W. Norton & Co., Inc., 1948).

next election, but what in fact happens is not altered by this aspect of the political process in a democracy.) For all practical purposes the politician endeavoring to decide what stand to take on a particular issue is an individual weighing the consequences of alternative decisions for the significant-person approval by which his personality is supported.

The key role played by groups in the life of the individual can meaningfully be summarized as a definition of the term "pressure," which is so important a concept in discussions of politics. Broadly speaking, it can be said that an individual's groups (past as well as present) are always "pressuring" him to behave in one way rather than another; government officials enmeshed in a web of complicated interpersonal relationships and endeavoring to keep their "selves" intact are constantly bombarded with threats of sanctions (withdrawal of approval by significant persons) or promises of rewards (bestowal of approval). Out of this maze of often conflicting pressures comes the behavior which makes up the daily life of every individual—the decisions which are the primary outcome of the governmental process. In short, *pressure is the influence of an individual's groups on his behavior.*

BUILT-IN CONSENSUS

With this definition as a starting point, it is possible to outline a conception of rule by the people which has little in common with the narrow and negative view of this process so often advanced. In the first place, and this is perhaps a more fundamental aspect of the institution of self-government than any other, the people are a silent partner to every decision made by government—as a result of the elaborate socialization process which guides every individual from infancy to maturity.[5] By means of this process, the passing on from one generation to the next of common values and standard ways of feeling and acting, a certain "sense of the community" is built directly into the personality of governing officials. Whenever issues arise which demand governmental action this "built-in" consensus helps make clear what action the people want, and in extreme cases decisions are made on that basis alone.

One such case will illustrate the process. Probably no member of the American Congress in session December 8, 1941, had supposed at the time of his election that he would be called upon to react officially to an attack on the United States by Japan, and therefore

[5] R. A. Dahl and C. E. Lindblom, *Politics, Economics, and Welfare* (New York: Harper & Bros., 1953); and C. A. Hickman and M. Kuhn, *Individuals, Groups, and Economic Behavior* (New York: The Dryden Press, Inc., 1956).

few if any members could have considered themselves "instructed" as to what their response to this situation should be. Furthermore, between the time of the Pearl Harbor attack on December 7 and the time war was declared the next day, there was no opportunity for finding out in any explicit way what the sentiment of the country was. Thus, although without formal guidance from constituents, members were forced to react on their own; by giving expression to their personal feelings representatives expressed the sense of the community no less accurately than if they had had a comprehensive set of instructions. The fact is they did have such instructions—the built-in consensus.

This foundation on which self-government ultimately rests can be generalized as follows. Issues arise which could scarcely have been anticipated at election time; more important, perhaps, even anticipated issues arise in a particular context which was not a part of the understanding on the basis of which votes were cast. The result is that the ordinary citizen is dependent upon the spontaneous decisions of his representatives. Because representatives cannot consult voters directly, they must do the next best thing. They must consult their constituents indirectly through the structure of their own personalities. In other words, to an important extent the community in a democracy is governed by men who can be counted on to do the "right" thing without prompting, who do not need to be watched, rather than by men who must be told what to do on every occasion.

This conclusion can in turn be generalized in another way, and in the process elections in a democracy can be put more nearly in their proper place. Far too much emphasis is customarily placed upon elections as mandates from the people with respect to concrete policies; actually the first and much the most important function performed by elections in a democracy is to provide an opportunity for all elements in the community's consensus to secure their share of the available representation. As emphasized earlier it is an essential characteristic of democracy that the community be heterogeneous, that there exist a wide variety of combinations of interests; some groups will place greatest stress upon certain aspects of the underlying agreement, while other groups will press for different aspects. Every group, however, will endeavor to see to it that the body of government officials includes as many individuals as possible who are rooted in those elements of the consensus in which its members believe most ardently. Democracy demands that the community's representatives taken as a group shall reflect the consensus diversity of the larger society.

ROLE OF LEADERSHIP

This brief glimpse at the function of democratic elections, furthermore, carries with it another implication that is of even greater significance here. It highlights once again the fundamental and unavoidable fact of conflict; every group cannot secure all the policies it desires, and many policies are positively injurious to the values of some groups. This means that decision-making by consensus alone cannot be depended upon; in most instances conflicting interpretations and applications of consensus must be weighed and compromised. If the citizen group at large is to play an important part in day-to-day governing, in short, it must do this also where controversy is a central consideration.

Here, indeed, is the challenge. It is precisely with reference to this problem that much respectable opinion insists that the majority can perform no function. Only leaders can know and understand the relevant facts sufficiently to make intelligent decisions; only the minority can possess the appreciation of reality necessary to policy-making. Is this true? And if it is true (and a most convincing case can be made), what follows? If a minority does enjoy a near-monopoly of facts and the wisdom to master their implications, must it be admitted that the majority cannot in any meaningful sense rule?

No time will be spent here arguing the dubious case that the man-in-the-street possesses his own brand of wisdom, a common sense without which sound decisions cannot be made. Social science has too overwhelmingly taken the other side of this argument for such an enterprise to be attempted with any hope of success. Let it be granted instead that the average individual is basically preoccupied with narrow, personal affairs, and that he is far removed from the reality on the basis of which responsible decisions must be reached. Let it be granted further that those actually making decisions do have the ability and the experience qualifying them to deal with the problems which arise. Is the majority, then, unable to participate in the decision-making process?

The usual view has it that the minority, armed with its superior knowledge and intelligence, makes up its mind what should be done and then "manufactures" a public opinion to support the conclusions thus reached.[6] Certainly there can be no question that this is an important part of what takes place. But at the same time there is reason for doubting that this does justice to the complexities in-

[6] Walter Lippmann, *Public Opinion* (New York: Harcourt, Brace & Co., Inc., 1922); and Gabriel Almond, *The American People and Foreign Policy* (New York: Harcourt, Brace & Co., Inc., 1950).

volved. Specifically, there are two reasons for suggesting that this description exaggerates the policy-making role of the minority relative to that of the majority.

First, in a genuine democracy it is misleading to refer loosely to a minority in contrast with a majority. Where the underlying community is diverse, so too will that community's leadership be diverse. On any issue not decided directly (and hence almost unanimously) by consensus, the heterogeneity of society will guarantee a heterogeneity within the minority of comparable proportions. Instead, therefore, of a clear-cut split between those who are intelligent and informed on one side and those who are less intelligent and less well informed on the other, some of the elite group will be on one side of any given issue and some will be on the other. These two groups will then compete with one another for the allegiance of the majority, and the winner will have the largest share in the framing of policy. Every decision-making official must consciously or unconsciously take account of the attitudes and sentiments of the majority in determining his own stand with respect to any significant issue. Here, thus, is another way in which the people rule in a positive, everyday sense.

Second, not only is the minority in a democracy heterogeneous, but it is also unstable. Particular leaders are always subject to being replaced, and conflicts over group decisions are a typical battleground in the struggle between leaders and their rivals. As these struggles work themselves out against the background of public policy formulation, the majority is given a still more fundamental opportunity to determine the content of decisions.

The point most to be emphasized here is that although the minority is the custodian of "reality," the majority is the custodian of the community's basic values. Democratic theory does not insist that the average citizen has an understanding of the facts essential to the making of difficult decisions, or that he has an especially high intelligence quotient. The only fact about the majority which democracy does insist upon is that here are human purposes all of which have an equal claim to fulfillment. To be sure, ends cannot ordinarily be attained except by the use of intelligent means within the framework of existing institutions. But the danger that the masses will insist on decisions that are in this sense unrealistic is no greater than the danger that the elite will use its superior capacities to interpret the facts from the standpoint of values not shared by other members of society. Thus the critical problem for democracy is the need to bring the realities comprehended by the few into conformity with the values held by the many, and vice versa. How can this difficult task be achieved?

The Process Illustrated

A hypothetical illustration here may be instructive. Suppose the government is called upon to make a decision affecting almost everyone in one way or another. Gradually, as the day of decision approaches, virtually all leaders (both within and outside the government) will be compelled to take a stand, and out of these several stands a policy determination will emerge. What is the process by which the necessary intermixture of reality and values jointly influences the character of such a decision?

Assume, for example, that in the case at hand government officials have the most thorough grasp of the reality involved. This is frequently the actual situation, moreover, because as often as not these are the men who have been most familiar with the evolution which produced the existing state of affairs. For this reason these individuals are likely to be among the first to make up their minds at least tentatively about what ought to be done. However, these men will be surrounded by certain significant people whose approval is essential to their well-being, and therefore they are at once confronted with the problem of convincing these people that the decision tentatively reached is the right one. They must, in short, impart their understanding of reality to those persons on whom their personalities depend most heavily.

It goes without saying that this is more easily said than done. A slave, the victim of an armed bandit, the subject of a totalitarian ruler, are all of course constrained to accept the "official" interpretation of reality without question. Not so in a democracy; within broad limits men do not have to assent unless convinced, and conviction in this kind of situation means at least two things. First, the government official must convey the impression by his manner and his store of information that he has a thorough grasp of the problem at hand. For a man of intelligence who has been reasonably conscientious in the performance of his duties this will be fairly easy. But reality and its interpretation are not Absolutes; the conclusions drawn from facts are a function of the value frame of reference held by the interpreter. It is this frame of reference, the pattern of ideals toward which the official in question is oriented, which determines what facts are important and what irrelevant—and which of the important facts are to be given the most weight. Second, therefore, the government official must convince the significant persons in his environment that his interpretation has been made from the standpoint of a value frame of reference held in common.

For two reasons this task may be difficult. On the one hand, the gap in the understanding of reality is apt not to be large between

officials and their closest nonofficial associates. The latter are normally group leaders in their own right and hence are not without
resources of their own when it comes to mastering the facts of the
situation at issue. Still more important is the fact that although
officials and nonofficials do have some overlapping in their group
loyalties, there will be important differences in the pattern of these
loyalties from individual to individual. Because of the phenomenon
of overlapping memberships, in other words, there will be value-
conflicts between the government official elite group and their nonofficial but also elite associates. And even though there is a difference
in the amount of information possessed by the two groups, a narrow
reality-gap can readily be bridged where the question at issue is the
value frame of reference used in interpretation.

On the other hand, however, there is an even greater difficulty. Because the nonofficial persons involved are group leaders, they are in
turn confronted with the necessity of convincing their following that
a particular decision is the right one. Just as officials must endeavor
not to take a stand they cannot successfully defend, so too must nonofficial group leaders. The reason, moreover, is essentially the same
in both instances. In the case of an official the problem is most immediately that of maintaining prestige and influence among those
whose goodwill he most values, although in some cases his security
in his official position may be directly at stake; in the case of a nonofficial group leader the major problem is to avoid being replaced,
although there are here also considerations having to do with personality supports of a more intimate character. Most groups in a
democracy contain a number of individuals who aspire to top positions, and who are therefore eager to exploit any action by the present leadership which can be used as the basis for an attack. Highly
capable, not greatly inferior to group leaders in their grasp of
reality, these individuals are only too happy to engage in a controversy in which competing interpretations of reality are tested
against the backdrop of the group's scale of values. And here again
the narrow reality-gap between leaders and their rivals is not a
serious handicap where a value position is primarily at issue.

This fundamental social process can also be viewed constructively
from the other end of the political hierarchy. At the grass roots, where
lives the majority with its limited grasp of reality, many citizens are
apt to have exaggerated expectations. As reality interpretations filter
down through the hierarchy above, group members are given the
alternative of rejecting the stand their group is taking and carrying
their expectations elsewhere or accepting this stand and modifying
expectations accordingly. If the latter step is taken, group leaders
are confirmed in the tentative position adopted and major adjust-

ments are not required. But if the interpretation at the top is rejected, significant disturbances may occur in group relationships.

One such disturbance might be the formation of new groups by splinter elements of old groups. This is most likely to happen where potential leaders within old groups are able to hold the loyalty of a minority in opposition to present leadership, but are unable to replace that leadership or force it to alter its stand. Another possibility is the restructuring of power inside existing groups as present leaders are disciplined in one way or another for not effectively caring for group interests as these are interpreted by members. But whichever form the ensuing disturbance takes, the consequence is the strengthening of some groups through an increase in their members or a gain in their cohesion, and a weakening of others through a decrease in their numbers or a loss in their cohesion.

The subtle twistings and turnings of pressures emanating from below are apt to place officials in strained situations. Groups on which they had counted for support are now weaker than had been assumed, while others have emerged in a stronger position from the transformation taking place. Thus at the top the strong will seek to solidify their position by making certain of the availability of essential support and at the same time getting rid of unnecessary support (because the cost of votes not needed is often very great), while the weak will endeavor to improve their position by working out special "deals" or accommodation with interests tentatively committed to the other side. When all of this has been carried as far as is appropriate, a vote is taken to make the resultant lineup official.

Unfortunately, a summary of the decision-making process in hypothetical terms cannot begin to reveal it in all its complexity. For example, it oversimplifies to assume that all government officials agree with one another on the policy to be followed. Normally this is not the case. Rather there will ordinarily be a coalition of official and nonofficial forces on both sides of the question up for decision. Typically, moreover, there will also be conflict between opposing political parties, with the leaders of the opposition party not greatly inferior in their grasp of reality to those presently in power.

And finally, there is the complication introduced by the time dimension of the political process; alterations in group relationships that have become strained under pressure of the necessity of choosing between alternative policies often require a considerable period to work themselves out. Even in a democratic society fluidity is hampered by frictions, and indeed it is in the last analysis these very frictions that give society the underlying stability without which it could not survive. And when the time required to overcome these frictions is considered in terms of the fact that time itself alters the context within which decisions are made, it can be all the more readily understood why policy determinations in a democracy must on the one hand be considered tentative and on the other hand not be confused with the public interest.

Graphically, the democratic process can be visualized as a flow of realities and values up and down the political hierarchy. Interpretations of reality flow down the scale, subject to modification by a flow of values up the scale as the majority informs the minority "where the shoe pinches." In turn the expectations of the majority

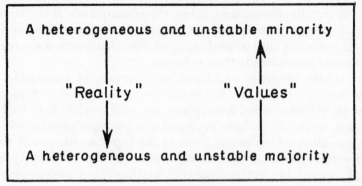

Fig. 1.

are subject to modification in the light of the reality information flowing down to it. Taken together, these two flows are the justification for insisting that in a democracy the people do in fact play an important role in the actual making of government decisions.

Some Implications

There are a number of implications of this analysis which should be frankly faced. The most obvious is its ready acceptance of a situation in which citizens "rule with their hearts rather than their heads"—a condition widely regretted by students of the American scene. Two things need especially to be said about this matter. First, as has already been suggested, discussions of democracy emphasize too much the factor of intelligence in decision-making. On the one hand, the average individual cannot contribute intelligence to the governmental process; and to insist that this is what he must do is to demand the impossible of democracy. On the other hand, the active minority can contribute all of the intelligence needed in government if only that minority continues to be heterogeneous and unstable and if the majority controls this group with its "heart."

Second, it is essential that this emphasis not be misunderstood. Although it does insist that the existence of a gap between the understanding of elite and mass is not a matter of great moment in the development of a workable democracy, it does not follow that it makes no difference how wide this gap becomes. If a situation ever develops in which the reality-gap cannot be bridged in relatively narrow steps as communications move from level to level down the political ladder, the tension between reality and values so essential to a democracy will surely snap. Professor Mannheim's emphasis on the reality-level necessary for successful democracy, the level of understanding of the facts of political life possessed by the average voter, is, in other words, justified.[7]

Another type of question certain to be raised is this: Does not this analysis of democracy place too little emphasis upon the individual citizen's responsibility to inform himself on public policy issues? Does it not make the individual too dependent upon his groups and their leaders rather than reliant upon his own resources? Does it not, in short, reduce the work of the citizen to something that is base and trivial rather than noble and challenging?

It is of course apparent that these queries are only a restatement with a slightly different emphasis of the problem of "heart" versus "head" government, and therefore answers must follow the same general lines. This means that each of these questions must be responded to with a vigorous "no." It is impossible for the individual to separate himself from his groups; this close relationship between individuals and groups is what makes society a society. Because this is impossible, it is unrealistic to define democracy in such a way that it is in fact required.

This conclusion can be stated still more strongly, too. Since political advantage in a democracy goes to those groups having the greatest numbers *and* the highest degree of cohesion, by far the most important political choice a member of the majority can make is to determine which groups he desires to make more powerful. In other words, instead of trying to make up his own mind as to issues and candidates, the average citizen can make his best contribution to democracy by satisfying himself that his chosen groups stand for the same values he does and then voting for the candidates they endorse.

Closely related to this issue is another one. Does not this approach to democracy place too much emphasis upon pressure politics as distinguished from what might be called election politics?

Here again several comments immediately suggest themselves. First, when pressure is realistically defined, there is no useful distinction to be drawn between these two aspects of the political process. Every relationship between ruler and ruled is under pressure; and

[7] Karl Mannheim, *Freedom, Power, and Democratic Planning* (New York: Oxford University Press, 1950), pp. 138 ff.

the major question, therefore, is whether all segments of society have a more or less equal opportunity to exert pressure.

Second, it is important to the cause of democracy that pressure be exerted at the time decisions are being made as well as at the times set aside for elections. From the standpoint of a particular group this suggests that it is more valuable to have the opportunity to support concrete policies when such support can really count than to be limited to the dubious privilege of opposing the election of a candidate who might win. From the standpoint of democracy it means that it is more important for the community to participate in decision-making while issues are still fluid than to have only the opportunity of opposing a decision after it has begun to harden into a tenacious status quo. Through the subconscious operation of consensus, pressure is being exerted constantly on decision-makers rather than episodically; is it not only logical that deliberate pressures be put on the same basis?

Third, if it is argued that this insistence gives a powerful advantage to the active few, other factors can be emphasized. Where freedom of association is a reality everyone has an opportunity to be politically active; if some choose not to take advantage of this opportunity, it is a choice they have every right to make—although in a democracy it may have significant consequences. Furthermore, always at work just beneath the surface are consensus pressures the effectiveness of which do not depend upon formal organization, and hence values which are not supported by overt political activity may yet be protected. It is too often the case, in short, that those who insist that certain interests achieve success only because of lobbying activities carried on at the expense of something referred to as the public interest are guilty of overlooking the elements of consensus reflected in the victorious policy. Let it be remembered that only pressure can offset pressure;[8] government in a democracy is not a neutral agency whose function it is to protect the weak from the strong on the basis of some absolute ethical standard.

Fourth, and perhaps most important of all, this description of the political process makes it possible to suggest in greater detail the purpose of elections in a democracy. Decisions by such a government are unavoidably made, to some extent, in the dark. Men interested in their political futures must necessarily listen most closely to those leaders who speak for the largest numbers of people. But because of overlapping group memberships and differentials in political activity, it is difficult to be sure which leaders are at the head of the largest battalions. This fact creates a situation in which group

[8] Bertrand de Jouvenel, *On Power* (New York: The Viking Press, Inc., 1949).

leaders are given a certain freedom to exaggerate the size of their support, and in which decision-makers in turn are free to indulge in a degree of wishful thinking about the values in which the public believes. As one way of avoiding these potential distortions, the holding of elections at intervals forces the political process into a mold of reality all its own; at intervals a chips-down situation is created in which every individual is given an opportunity to express himself in such a way as to test the basis on which responses to pressures are being made all the way up and down the hierarchy. Just as a carpenter sawing a number of pieces of wood to the same length does not use each succeeding piece as the model for the next one, so do elections provide a true perspective for decision-making which can be referred to often enough to keep erroneous perspectives from becoming policy axioms.

What is true of elections, furthermore, is true of the functioning of legislative bodies. Frequently it is noted that parliamentary discussions often do not center around the issues most fundamental to some decision that is to be made, the obvious converse of this fact being the making of decisions that are not adequately debated. A closely related criticism is that parliamentary debates often take place when the chamber is virtually empty.

Once again misunderstanding arises from an over-intellectualization of democracy. To be sure, information and its uninhibited flow is one of the prerequisites of democracy. But it does not follow that the necessary information consists exclusively of considerations relating to the objective wisdom or unwisdom of some proposed course of action, that the only constructive use of a legislative assembly in a democracy is debate in the most refined sense in which that term is used, or that the most valuable use of time by a representative would include sitting through routine sessions of Congress. For example, it is also of importance that the value reactions of various groups in the larger society become a part of the informational foundation on the basis of which policy decisions are made—and there is no clear reason why these need be trumpeted to the world from the floor of Congress. By the same token, an essential element in the democratic process is the (basically partisan?) appeal from group advantage to public interest. Here flag-waving and all the other techniques of the propagandist take the center of the stage, and because such appeals are often as effective when made for the "record" (for consumption "back home") as when actually heard by legislative colleagues, the size of the immediate audience is not a matter of great significance. And finally, the work of negotiating, compromising, and reconciling, perhaps the most important work done by a legislative assembly, requires the expenditure of countless hours in small groups.

In short, the convening of a legislative group is fundamental to democracy, not so much because representatives can gather under a single roof to be exposed to a full discussion of the pros and cons of various matters, but because they are thereby concentrated in a small geographical area and can communicate with one another more effectively for the purpose of working out the compromises and trades that in the final analysis determine policy. Stated differently, the significance of the representative chamber where all may be within hearing distance of everyone else's voice lies not in the fact that minds are actually made up in such a setting (for that is probably the case only rarely), but in the opportunity thus afforded to test the strength of the promises that have been made and the coalitions that have been formed through a public and a decisive vote.

One final implication may appropriately be noted. Does not this conception of the decision-making process defer too much to the minority which rises to the top in a democracy? Do not these people really range from the mediocre to the inferior in their capacities?

Such questions are often not so well put as they might be, and in this connection it is noteworthy that this charge is most frequently made by individuals who object to particular policy determinations. To be sure, those who possess greatest influence in a democracy are typically not scholars in the library-laboratory sense. But on the other hand surely few would argue that these men as a group are not above average in intelligence. Beyond this, furthermore, it could scarcely be overemphasized that intellectual capacity is by no means the only skill required for the smooth functioning of democratic institutions. Another, and perhaps an even more basic, need is a facility in handling interpersonal relationships[9]—the flexibility of personality which is the foundation of compromise, strategic retreat, and satisfaction with small achievements. Most of the adjustments required in a democracy are made by leaders sensing from their human relationships what stand is to be taken. Democratic decision-making would quickly fall of its own weight if every issue had to be brought to a definitive vote. The men who are skillful at making the necessary interpolations—those whose judgments are most often confirmed when put to the test—are the men who rise the highest in the arena where decisions are made. It is an interesting commentary on the state of thinking about democracy in America that criticisms of politicians are so frequently reducible to the proposition that they are in fact sensitive to pressures emanating from the people.

[9] H. D. Lasswell, *Politics: Who Gets What, When, How* (New York: McGraw-Hill Book Co., Inc., 1936), chap. vi.

POLITICAL IDEALISM VERSUS POLITICAL REALISM

But if, now, the approach to the public interest suggested here is accepted, if the common good is really a by-product of a search for innumerable private goods, is not little place left for the idealism in which discussions of democracy usually abound? Certainly the idea of putting aside personal preferences in favor of the general welfare has a nobility about it which no other approach can match. There is, however, another side to this matter, and perhaps when it has been presented, much of the idealism the approach taken here seems at first glance to repudiate can be reintroduced.

A first point to be noted in this connection is that the general-welfare claims advanced in a public policy debate, claims around which a great deal of the idealism associated with democracy is built, are not real but spurious (because each such claim rests upon some concrete policy alternative expressed as an Absolute), although the presentation of spurious versions of the common good is an indispensable element in democracy. Put differently, the public interest can with some accuracy be identified with the competition for acceptance between two (or more) spurious common goods, but none of the contestant views is to be taken at face value as *the* public interest.

However, does not one of these views become the public interest on being accepted by the majority? No, even this would be an exaggeration. For one thing, the actual decision is apt to be a compromise, embodying elements from all of the views advanced. For another, there is little if anything to be gained and perhaps much to be lost by identifying those stands which are defeated with something thought of as opposed to the public interest. Because in a democracy all policy decisions must be considered tentative, the right of challengers to take their cause into the decision-making arena again and again is one that democracy can never afford to abrogate.

Second, when the issues raised are viewed from this standpoint it can be demonstrated that the public interest as here defined does not advance selfish, divisive interests at the expense of community-wide interests to the extent that may superficially seem to be the case. Actually this conception does not encourage either divisive or cohesive values; it simply reflects democracy's own emphasis upon the values men consider important. To be sure, if men's interests are too divisive for the long-run health of a democratic community, democracy must give way to some other form of organization. But cohesion cannot be secured by exhortation; unless men recognize their mutual dependence upon one another, and the extent to which their society's integrity in a world filled with other societies requires cooperation, democracy is a forlorn hope.

To put this matter in a slightly different context, it is far too easy and far too common to exaggerate the opposition between these two kinds of interests. America's almost unanimous response to the attack on Pearl Harbor was not the result of putting aside private interests; rather vital private interests were seen to be directly threatened by the aggressive power of Japanese imperialism. Private interests were on this occasion rearranged, to be sure, but they were not put aside. Similarly the universality with which theft is condemned in America was not brought about through a sacrifice of personal interests to the general welfare; on the contrary, this policy reflects the high importance of the institution of private property to virtually all citizens. Those who are afraid lest individuals and groups be allowed to press their differences too far either underestimate the cohesive forces which are at work or do not think highly of democracy's ability to resolve differences against a background of fundamental agreement.

Third, despite the fact that it is here assumed that votes are cast from the standpoint of private advantage, there is a sense in which the process when viewed as a whole transcends this factor. Put differently, although there is no way of stopping the game so that decisions can be made apart from considerations relating to teams already in the field, the technique of referring decisions to the entire community still avoids some of the worst consequences of allowing individuals and groups to be judge and jury in their own causes. By means of this device a balance of power is placed in the hands of those less immediately affected, since their representatives too may cast votes on whatever question is up for decision; and a powerful force is thus brought to bear on the decision-making process other than the most direct interests involved. Of course, many individuals and groups making up this balance of power are not wholly neutral parties, but the greater remoteness of some of these interests nonetheless has the effect of generalizing what is done relative to the over-all society to a far greater extent than would otherwise be the case. If it is true that the only idealists with respect to a given issue are those who are not personally concerned with its outcome, the process of referring issues to the entire citizen group is a way of forcing power-seeking into a semi-idealistic framework.

No less an authority than James Madison summed up this feature of democratic living.

The influence of factious leaders may kindle a flame within their particular states, but will be unable to spread a general conflagration through the other states: a religious sect may degenerate into a political faction in a part of the confederacy; but the variety of sects dispersed over the entire face of it, must secure the national councils against any danger from that source: a rage for paper money, for an abolition of debts, for an equal division of property, or for any other improper or wicked project, will be less apt to pervade the whole body of the union, than a particular member of it.[10]

And finally, the very process of making majority-rule decisions is a cohesive force of great significance. In this process the issues which divide men are decided against the background of the ideas and experiences which unite them; men are forced to reaffirm those factors making for cohesion as a condition for the successful stressing of differences. Here, indeed, is democracy's compromise between the individual and the group; a subculture may press its case for uniqueness without challenging the underlying society which in the last analysis sustains it. If, in short, individuals and groups use democracy's processes for their own purposes, it is still more or less true that those individuals and groups reap the greatest rewards who can most effectively appeal to what Calhoun called "the sense of the community." Perhaps it was something like this that Rousseau had in mind when he made his famous (if highly ambiguous) distinction between "the general will" and "the will of all."

The often expressed view that democracy is a paradox is indeed a justifiable one. Few students of this paradox, however, have presented it as clearly as Professors Lasswell and Kaplan in their classic study of power: "The problem of social policy is that of creating conditions under which power can and does act integratively in relation to the major values of society as a whole."[11] In other words, conflict can only be resolved by resort to power, but power must be used in such a way that it contributes to social cohesion even while it is resolving conflicts. These conditions are met as nearly as they can be met when the test of strength is made, as is the case with democracy, the degree of conformity between the particular alternatives proposed and the larger community's hierarchy of values. Surely under these circumstances power is being used "integratively"—as when labor, management, and the general public are all reminded in the course of a bitter contest over labor legislation how fundamental harmony in the economy is to all concerned.

[10] *The Federalist Papers*, Number 10.
[11] H. D. Lasswell and Abraham Kaplan, *Power and Society* (New Haven: Yale University Press, 1950), p. xii.

QUESTIONS FOR DISCUSSION

1. Define "pressure" as the term is used in the text. How adequate do you consider this definition?

2. How do minorities and majorities complement one another in the decision-making process?

3. What is meant by the term "consensus" and how does it contribute to the decision-making process?

4. Distinguish carefully between consent and consensus.

5. Explain the relationships between majority rule and consensus. Between majority rule and consent. Between consent and consensus.

6. In the formulation of economic policy, what is the role performed by successive election campaigns?

7. Why would many people oppose the hiring of "dollar-a-year" men by government? Are these objections valid?

8. Why must the *process* by which decisions are made in a democracy be identified with the public interest rather than the decisions themselves?

9. It is often said that major political parties in the United States are not clearly differentiated from one another in the policies they advocate. Does the analysis in the text suggest any reasons for thinking that this situation might prevail in every democracy?

10. How does the definition of public interest advanced here contribute to the ideals democracy is intended to achieve?

Part II
BEFORE LAISSEZ FAIRE

Chapter 3

Constitutional Beginnings

There is justification, perhaps, for considering the Constitution the first public policy in the government and business field in our country's history. To be sure, the Constitution has its own sources which go far back into the Middle Ages and to the emergence of modern Europe, but there is still reason (since a more or less arbitrary starting point must be taken in any event) for selecting as a point of departure the beginning of the United States as a nation. And not the least part of this reason is the fact that the Constitution is by all odds the most fundamental government-business policy in this country.

But precisely because this document is so fundamental, it is of the utmost importance that it be understood within the context of its own times as accurately as possible. This means that the first task here must be to separate fact from fiction with respect to the Constitution's origins. Thus American folklore has it that the American Revolution and in turn the writing of the Constitution reflected what might be called an "instinct for freedom." According to this interpretation the process of breaking away from the ties and traditions of Europe, coupled with the hardships associated with making a new life in a land as yet barely touched by civilization, created a spirit of individualism which abhorred all government interferences. In two ways which could hardly be more basic, however, this view can be shown to be much exaggerated.

MERCANTILIST ORIGINS

One of the overarching idea-structures that characterized Western civilization as a whole during the colonial period of American history was the pattern of beliefs known as mercantilism. Arising out of the economic anarchy of feudalism, whose petty princes had assumed the power of the state and placed all manner of obstacles in the way

43

of business activity, these beliefs centered on the notion of the state as a political and economic unit.[1] On this foundation a set of practices was built primarily designed to enhance the wealth and power of the nation. Admittedly these practices were often destructive; frequently one nation could be and was strengthened at the expense of another —a possibility frankly accepted as part of the game. But mercantilism did have its constructive side, and this side was historically most significant. Under the influence of this set of ideas the Western world developed the movement known to history as "The Commercial Revolution," and thus gave a tremendous momentum to forces destined to change the course of human civilization.

Speaking broadly, mercantilist thinking took it for granted that a national government might appropriately impose restrictive or promotional regulations or taxes at whatever point in the economic system it deemed desirable, for only by possessing and exercising such powers could the larger community effectively combat the atomism medieval conditions had produced. If the purposes of the state required an import duty on foodstuffs to protect local agriculture, this action was accepted. If the national interest dictated that a colony somewhere be prohibited from engaging in textile manufacturing, such a procedure was assented to. It was, in short, basic to the mercantilist way of thinking that the government might take whatever actions the purposes of a strong and wealthy state required, and this understanding was a part of the intellectual equipment every statesman brought to his tasks.

Nor is it any mystery why this conception of the responsibilities of government was called mercantilism. In practice this regulating, restricting, and promoting more often than not had to do with merchant affairs—trade and commerce. So undeveloped were European economies at this time, so crude and few were the goods produced there, that variety and luxury could typically be added to the standard of living only through foreign trade. In consequence the most absorbing interest of Europe in those days was overseas expansion, and activities which would enhance the wealth and power of the nation were therefore more closely identified with merchant affairs than with any other aspect of the economic order. It was, in other words, a state's relations with other nations which had most carefully to be regulated, and these international economic relations were overwhelmingly in the field of commercial policy.

What was true in Europe, moreover, was also true in the colonies. Though there were vital differences between the conditions under

[1] Witt Bowden, Michael Karpovich, and A. P. Usher, *An Economic History of Europe Since 1750* (New York: American Book Co., 1937), chap. iv.

which life was lived in the New World as compared with the Old, their character was not such as to make America less mercantilist in outlook than Europe. If anything, colonists were propelled even more powerfully in that direction.

In the first place, colonies in America had as great or even greater reason than European nations for giving attention to the problem of attaining wealth and power. To be sure, a Massachusetts, a Virginia, or a New York did not have visions of world domination as did England, France, or Spain. But wealth and power were no less important at the other end of the scale of economic well-being. Thus, in this country a central objective was to maintain status as a going concern amid difficulties constantly threatening to overcome a poor, undeveloped colony far from its mother country. And not only was the arm of England often weak in this part of the world, but during most of the colonial period the colonies were such an insignificant part of the British Empire that it was often not quite certain that England would use the power she possessed to protect the integrity of any given colony.

This factor can be seen especially well in colonial difficulties involving money. For a number of reasons (which can be summarized by saying that money was painfully scarce as a result of the rapid economic development of the Western world and its unfavorable balance of trade with the East) mercantilist regulations in Europe were to a considerable extent preoccupied with the accumulation of money. But if this was a serious problem in Europe where an important consideration was the hoarding of specie in preparation for the next war, it was of even more vital concern in economies which would be compelled to remain in a precarious infancy if a way could not be found to replace commodities as the circulating medium. It is thus no wonder that mother England was almost perpetually plagued with colonial attempts to improve economic organization at this point, attempts a mercantilist power could only consider a threat to its own economic position.

In the second place, the several colonial economies were even less capable of providing their citizens with the standard of living they desired than were European economies. Because land was so abundant and hence cheap, labor for manufacturing enterprises was far more expensive than in England; and skilled labor was for a long time almost unavailable. This, coupled with the scarcity and hence high price of capital, placed colonial manufacturing at a decisive competitive disadvantage. As a result America's only hope of securing the goods necessary to satisfy many cultural wants was to concentrate on the production of the crude goods most suitable to the rugged environment of the New World, and then exchange these goods for finished products overseas.

This factor in turn was most clearly exemplified in the northern colonies, where the difficulty of achieving a satisfactory standard of living was complicated by the pattern of mercantilist regulations already in force. Thus whereas the American colonists preferred to buy most of their imported goods in England because they were superior in quality while being reasonably priced, England in practice refused to import either meat or grain from these colonies—precisely the agricultural staples which could most effectively be produced in such areas as Massachusetts or New York. In part this handicap was overcome by trading with other countries despite higher prices and poorer quality. In part also it was resolved by a series of triangular trading arrangements which made it possible for domestic surpluses to be used in the purchase of British goods indirectly. But whichever approach was taken, an important aspect of the economic adjustment of these colonies was the foreign purchasing power secured through their shipping industries, the building and operation of ships.

This brief account of some of the major economic problems of the colonies will perhaps suffice as a presentation of the theoretical case for the existence of mercantilism in the New World. The crucial test, however, is whether these economies did in fact develop mercantilist control systems, and on this point the evidence is equally unequivocal. New World statesmen were fully as apt pupils of their environment as their European contemporaries.

Many mercantilist restrictions, of course, were aimed at commercial activities.[2] For example, import duties were often levied, not only for the revenue derivable therefrom but as a way of giving preference to goods from certain areas rather than others for balance of payments reasons—or even to encourage importation in domestic rather than foreign vessels. Export duties were also often imposed, again in part for revenue purposes but again also with regulatory ends in view. A representative instance here was a South Carolina duty on lumber exports to prevent the too rapid exhaustion of an irreplaceable raw material and to encourage domestic processing. As with import levies, moreover, duties on exports were also often imposed preferentially in favor of domestic shipping or in favor of trade with some particular area. And when to customs duties are added inspection laws, embargoes, and port controls, it is apparent that colonial commerce was indeed circumscribed by a complex network of domestic regulations.

[2] E. R. Johnson, and Associates, *History of Domestic and Foreign Commerce of the United States* (Washington, D.C.: Carnegie Institution, 1915), chap. iv.

That local governments did not scruple to enact legislation affecting other kinds of businesses is likewise easy to demonstrate.[3] Here the center of attention was manufacturing, a type of economic activity which seemed to have great survival value to seventeenth- and eighteenth-century colonies in America. Massachusetts, Virginia, and Connecticut carried on for a time a program of compulsory textile manufacture. Rhode Island, Maryland, and Virginia established public enterprises to manufacture such products as shoes, textiles, arms and ammunition, and salt. Bounties, premiums, and subsidies were at one time or another standard practice in all the colonies; and land grants, loans, and lotteries were almost as widely used to encourage particular manufactures. Not all such legislation was promotional in nature, either. Prices of items of general consumption (particularly flour) were often closely restricted, and numerous laws were passed designed to guarantee the quality of consumption or export items. But always, and this is the important point, there was in view a purpose closely related to building up the colony as an economic unit.

CONFLICT CONTEXT

Surely this evidence demonstrates that the American colonies were not at all averse to the pattern of government activities then common in Europe. But is it not possible, despite this conclusion, to rescue a large part of American folklore concerning the Constitution? Might it not be that businessmen, though a minority group, did develop an "instinct for freedom," and that motivated by a desire to tear asunder the numerous interconnections between government and business this group led the way to independence? Indeed, this explanation would especially harmonize with the tradition of laissez faire in this country.

No, these long-cherished beliefs cannot be rescued so easily. For a number of reasons American businessmen cannot be made the "heroes" of the Revolution drama.

To begin with, there is no evidence to suggest that business leaders were unwilling participants in American mercantilism. This could hardly be considered surprising, either, in view of the fact that so many governmental activities were promotive of business enterprise; American business interests have never resisted governmental favors of which they were the recipients. But even where direct promotion was not the orientation, the business class as a whole could

---

[3] Victor S. Clark, *History of Manufactures in the United States* (New York: McGraw-Hill Book Co., Inc., 1929), Vol. I, chap. iii.

often justify supporting rather than combating mercantilist policies. For example, legislation to guarantee the quality of export goods was often designed to curb the activities of trade "mavericks" for the benefit of legitimate traders. All in all, it seems safe to say that business accommodated itself comfortably to prevailing governmental practice.

Still more important, it cannot even be argued that businessmen were especially eager to resist British mercantilism. This is not to say, of course, that English legislation did not bear upon the American merchant class.[4] Thus there were laws enumerating certain items which could only be imported or exported by way of England. On three major occasions, furthermore, the mother country passed legislation inhibiting the development of colonial manufactures, the products in these instances being woolen goods, beaver hats, and fabricated iron products. More immediately threatening than any of these measures was the Molasses Act. This enactment sought to protect British West Indian sugar planters by means of duties discriminating against non-British sugar and molasses. Since molasses (to be used in the manufacture of rum for the domestic fur trade and the African slave trade particularly) was one of the most important pillars of the emerging capitalist economy in the North, there was a certain justification for businessmen to look at British regulations with a jaundiced eye.

There is, however, a reverse side to this picture, and when it is taken into account a conclusion quite contrary to American folklore seems unavoidable. The fact is that England's network of mercantilist regulations were not especially burdensome to northern business interests. Legislation prohibiting manufactures certainly had few adverse consequences; economic conditions were not yet conducive to this activity on a sizable scale in any event. No more restrictive were the steps taken to enumerate exports, for until the eve of the Revolution itself northern exports were not enumerated; and as far as the enumeration of imports was concerned, northern merchants developed a network of trading relationships allowing them to operate inside that framework without great inconvenience. Finally, whenever a regulation had threatened to become burdensome (and here the sequel to the Molasses Act is the classic case in point), enforcement had been sufficiently lax and hence evasion sufficiently common to keep frustration well within bounds.

Moreover, membership in the British Empire conferred substantial advantages upon American merchants which went far toward off-

[4] G. L. Beer, *The Old Colonial System* (New York: The Macmillan Co., 1912).

setting whatever inconveniences did arise. Britain's monopoly of the trade of the entire Empire as against foreign ships, for example, had accorded American shipbuilders and ship operators a privileged position of inestimable value. Closely related to this was the protection for American shipping furnished by the powerful British navy. In addition to these advantages, many colonial products (few, to be sure, that were produced in the northern colonies, but a number that were important cargoes for northern ships) were given privileged access to Empire markets. Even the ready availability of British capital and the support of England in disputes with other powers were benefits few northern businessmen did not greatly appreciate.

There is still a third basis for denying businessmen the leading role in America's decisive break with England, and without question it is the most important of all. Not only did they have comparatively less reason for throwing off the yoke of British mercantilism (although admittedly the situation looked fairly grim even for this group for a time after the close of the French and Indian War), but they had a special reason for not wanting this force removed from the American scene. So compelling was this consideration, in fact, that the outbreak of revolt in the American colonies can with much accuracy be traced directly to an inept colonial policy on the part of England.

In order properly to appreciate this aspect of the events leading to the Revolution, it is necessary to understand another dimension of the context within which those events took place. Even more basic than friction with England over commercial policy was the all too often neglected conflict between the upper and lower classes at home.[5]

Early in American history two clear-cut social classes became distinguishable: an aristocracy of large landowners and merchants and a democracy of small farmers and urban laborers. From the beginning a tendency had existed for land holdings to be relatively large along the seacoast. With water transportation readily available there, production for the market could be efficiently organized in large units. The result was that smaller operators were forced by economic pressure to take up land farther back, where, because of the inadequacy of transportation, the type of farming carried on was more self-sufficient in character. Even here, however, the heavy hand of the more wealthy was often felt. Unfortunately even self-sufficient agriculture required tools, seed, and livestock, and these were normally supplied on credit by seacoast merchants. With his farm

[5] Curtis P. Nettels, *The Roots of American Civilization* (New York: Appleton-Century-Crofts, Inc., 1939).

mortgaged to a capitalist, and with his debt stated as a fixed monetary sum, the back-country farmer was compelled to make payments in farm produce at the current market price. When creditors demanded that payments be made at harvest time, when prices were at their seasonal low point for the year, and insisted further that the debtor deliver his produce only to his creditor, it is understandable that debtor-farmers came to think of planters and merchants as enemies.

Two illustrations will make the reality of this conflict in colonial America more vivid. The first took place in an exclusively agricultural context in Virginia; the second was a product of the more advanced, capitalist-type economy of New York.

In Virginia class conflict reached a particularly critical point in 1675 as a result of economic depression and the control of the government by and for the aristocracy. Protesting against a financial system shot through with favoritism and privilege, against a program of taxation which accentuated rather than combated ownership concentration, and against a legal system weighted in favor of aristocratic interests, and having access to no peaceful means whereby their grievances could be forcefully presented, debt-ridden and desperate frontiersmen led by Nathaniel Bacon in that year marched on Jamestown. Encountering little resistance initially, they seized control of the government, burned the capital, and plundered the countryside. In time this rebellion was put down in a summary and hence necessarily brutal fashion by the combined forces of the Crown and eastern planters, although as a consequence a few concessions were made.

Bacon's Rebellion was no doubt the most famous of a large number of essentially similar conflicts. Because the line-up of forces here was farmer against farmer, however, it was less historically prophetic than was a clash between farmers and merchants a decade later in New York. Here, too, part of the problem was the concentration of governmental power in aristocratic hands, but again the crux of the problem was the economic implications of this political fact. The straw that broke the camel's back in this instance was a local regulation decreeing that all flour exported from the province had to be processed in the city. This meant that outlying farmers were compelled to sell their surplus wheat to New York merchants, which in turn meant that the latter group was given an opportunity to monopolize an industry vital to the well-being of a majority of New York farmers. In New York as in Virginia enraged farmers took the road of open revolt, although on this occasion with more success. In 1690 a law was passed declaring that "all towns and places shall have equal freedom to bolt and bake and to transport where they please directly to what place or country they think fit, anything that their places afford. . . ."

To put the matter bluntly, the pervasive and bitter character of these internal conflicts gave businessmen a powerful incentive to maintain rather than destroy British control in the American colonies. The ruling class in Britain was also conservative and hence could be depended upon to stand with colonial conservatives against the radical anticapitalist proclivities of the democratic "rabble." Stated differently, the business interests in America acknowledged themselves to be too weak to maintain control of the domestic governmental machinery without mother country assistance. What were a few clashes of interest between English and American merchants by comparison with this disability?

The parallelogram of forces playing upon the American economy as rebellion came ever nearer can be illustrated particularly well by a crisis that reached a climax in Massachusetts in 1741. Because the scarcity of specie had been a frustrating problem ever since colonial development began, the several colonies had endeavored in a number of ways to improve their money supply through legislation. For the most part this experimentation had not been especially successful, but in the process of trial and error colonial leaders had stumbled upon the institution of paper money. Immediately this device became immensely popular. Not only could the money in circulation be increased in this way, but debtor-farmers could also raise the prices of their produce and hence reduce the burden of their debts.

For the colonial aristocracy this was a most dangerous threat. Much of its economic position rested on its financial hold over the farmer, a hold the farmer seemed about to throw off. As they took steps to challenge this menace before it grew too great, colonial conservatives were promptly joined by the British government. English creditors could no more afford to have the burden of colonial debt tampered with than could colonial ones.

In 1740 an historic land bank was organized in Boston, after England had already demanded that all private-bank notes be withdrawn from circulation. When merchants banded together in refusing to accept currency from this new source, and when farmers endeavored to compel acceptance by force, the Crown was quick to lend a hand. And to make this lesson even harder to forget after this uprising had been put down, Parliament in 1741 outlawed all private banking operations in the colonies. Ironically, the issue arose just when England was making up her mind whether to enforce the Molasses Act rigorously or not. Perhaps this was one reason why she decided that question in the negative.

The New Nation's First Constitution

But if the dynamic force behind the Revolution was not the conservative business group, what was it? And if the motivation was not resistance to Britain's commercial policy, does it follow that mother country regulations were not a causal factor at all? Obviously these are the questions next to be answered, and it is not surprising that the process of answering them leads directly to America's first constitution, the Articles of Confederation.

The first of the problems posed here answers itself. If not the aristocracy, the motive power of the Revolution must have been the democracy. The corollary of this conclusion, however, is more complex; indeed, where motivation is at issue, explanation is never simple.

Why did small farmers and "mechanics" become so determined to press for independence? It would exaggerate to assert that British policy did not enter into the decision. Farmers the country over were thoroughly embittered by the increasing hardness of England's stand against paper money. Laborers, for their part, were not made more fond of the mother country by repeated legislation against embryo manufacturing industries. And both groups were alienated by Britain's policy of restraining the westward movement. Already there had commenced that irresistible expansionism which was to be a fixed factor in American economic development until the Pacific Ocean had been reached.

But it is more than doubtful whether these antagonisms were great enough to explain the upheaval which actually occurred, particularly when it is remembered that England had on numerous occasions intervened in domestic disputes on the side of lower-class citizens— occasions on which oppression by the aristocracy had become so great as to threaten acts of violence which might weaken British control. And this observation is made with a full realization of its implications; it means that *the most fundamental understanding of the American Revolution is not achieved when it is viewed as a rebellion against England as such.*

To state this proposition positively and more concretely, what the majority of militant Americans had come to resent above all else by the early 1770's was minority rule. They were tired of governments run by men who felt so secure against Indian attacks in their seacoast serenity that they refused to vote funds for defense of the frontier—men who were more concerned with furnishing firearms to Indians who might thereby be able to deliver more furs than for the safety of frontier fellow-citizens who might also fall victim to these same weapons. They had had quite enough of government by men who lived so near excellent water transportation facilities that they could not bring themselves to use the public treasury to build the roads and bridges needed by back-country farmers, or who from the pinnacle of their own wealth and privilege did not scruple to secure public lands for purposes of speculation through fraud or corruption while adhering to the letter of the law in foreclosing on their less fortunate neighbors.

In short, the American Revolution may be most constructively viewed as a battle to drive aristocracy from the seats of power.[6] To be sure, patriots made much out of such propaganda slogans as "Taxation without representation is tyranny" directed at the enemy across the water. But these defiances are placed in their proper perspective when it is observed how accurately they applied to the aristocracy in the colonies as well as to England's upper classes. Thus, if a battle against aristocracy did in fact have as its most significant outcome the destruction of British colonialism in much of America, the reasons are at least obvious. On the one hand, causes can often find greater support when buttressed by patriotism; on the other, to get rid of one aristocracy would reduce the other to a size that would permit it to be properly dealt with by less violent means. As someone has so aptly expressed it, the Revolution was fought not so much for home rule as to determine who was to rule at home.

If, now, these observations on the major source of the disaffections which erupted in 1776 are valid, it should be possible to verify them in the sequence of actual events. Briefly, therefore, the high points of the years immediately preceding the declaration of war will be reviewed against the background of this analysis.

In quick succession following the French and Indian War (and in the middle of a painful postwar recession) England passed a number of acts significantly affecting the colonial economy—all these enactments taken together seeming to point to a much more vigorous colonial policy than had been followed theretofore. One of these drew a geographical line beyond which the westward advance was not to go. Another made the ban on the issuance of paper money complete. A Sugar Act was passed designed to enforce the collection of revenues from the importation of sugar and molasses which colonial smugglers had evaded under the Molasses Act. And the climax of this series of measures was reached in a Stamp Act intended to provide a revenue to the mother country from the carrying-on of

[6] Merrill Jensen, *The Articles of Confederation* (Madison: University of Wisconsin Press, 1940).

ordinary business activities by means of stamps which had to be affixed to all kinds of papers and documents.

When colonial tempers first rose to fever pitch in a brief orgy of violence over this new imperial firmness, it was not merchants who led the way.[7] Direct challenges to law and order could never be the method of resistance chosen by conservatives. Only when a more constructive avenue of protest had been mapped out—namely, nonimportation—was the merchant group willing to give support.

Although the most odious of these irritations, the Stamp Act, was withdrawn, matters could scarcely be said to have improved between the time of its repeal and the passage of the East India Act in 1773. Nonetheless during this period the merchants did their best to maintain perspective while endeavoring at the same time to quiet the populace. (As only one indication of conservative fear of unnatural allies at home as compared with anxiety over regulations imposed by natural allies abroad, British troops were first sent to Boston in part at the insistence of highly placed Americans.) It was, in other words, the lower classes that kept the fires of resistance burning while peace was still a possibility. And though businessmen did again join the protest against the later legislation grossly discriminating against them in favor of the East India Company, the property destruction aspect of the "Boston Tea Party" caused them once more to recoil sharply. From this new posture of hesitation, furthermore, they had to be compelled by their more radical colleagues to join in another nonimportation movement.

At this point the march toward war became irresistible, although conservatives continued to drag their feet as long as possible. Unfortunately for their preferences, however, the time soon came when they had to declare themselves either for or against the fight for "freedom" in the face of the already apparent consequences of being in the Tory rather than the Patriot group.

The decision to fight having been made, the internal conflict now centered around the problem of adjusting governmental institutions to the absence of Parliament and the Crown. Here also the constellation of interests involved in the Revolution can be seen in sharp perspective.

The battle was as intense as it was bitter. Conservatives, keenly feeling the need for a power to restrain the anticapitalist proclivities of the democracy, wished to fill this vacuum with a central government which would effectively possess a number of the powers previously exercised by England. Dependent upon the mercantilist

---

[7] A. M. Schlesinger, *The Colonial Merchants and the American Revolution, 1763-1776* (New York: Columbia University Press, 1918).

umbrella to which they had grown accustomed, and fearful lest they prove to be unable to maintain control of local governments without British assistance, these interests hoped to establish a government more fully controlled by them. Lower-class interests, on the other hand, saw in the British government now to be dispensed with precisely the kind of government they were fighting to supplant. Sharing the feeling of conservatives that a central government would be more likely to fall into conservative hands, these interests sought to expand the power of independent and sovereign states.

In this contest resided the genesis of the American struggle over states' rights versus a strong central government which was to be such a fundamental feature of government-business relationships for many years. For the moment, of course, there could be no question where the victory lay. On every count conservatives were defeated. The Articles of Confederation as finally approved provided for a government having neither an executive (in the strict sense of that term) nor a judiciary, possessing no power to levy taxes or to pass laws in conflict with a state law, requiring the approval of the delegations of nine states to exercise the insignificant powers it did possess, and unable to expand its responsibilities except with the unanimous consent of all thirteen state delegations. With small exaggeration it can be said that a government was created which was not really a government at all. To such an organization was now entrusted the destiny of a people precariously balanced between independence and subjugation.

CONSERVATIVE REACTION

It is understandable that the business classes, after having been reversed at all major points, were not disposed to look on the brighter side of unfolding events. Instead they called attention to defects and inefficiencies whenever the opportunity arose, and left no stone unturned to bring about institutional modifications in the direction of their own predilections.

Actually, as long as the war lasted, there was little that could be accomplished on either of these fronts. For one thing, the military struggle continued to be so critical that the rising spirit of nationalism alone dictated a minimum of partisan activity. In other words, once the die had been cast for war, victory was as essential to conservative as to radical well-being; thus powerfully did concensus perform its function despite the existence of fundamental conflict. Moreover, the war-generated prosperity did much to keep business fears at low ebb. And especially when the exigencies of the time did in fact bring about a steady movement toward concentration of the executive power (the outstanding case in point here being the abolition in 1781 of the Treasury Commission and its replacement by a Superintendent of Finance, with Robert Morris, an arch-conservative, appointed to this post to bring a semblance of order into the nation's chaotic finances), the business interests felt there was reason enough for their continued support of the war effort.

As soon as the war was over, however, all this was changed. Without a threatening military struggle in the background, conservatives could be more open in their attacks. Furthermore, the ending of the war brought with it a painful recession which could be conveniently blamed on the ruling administration. Even the trend toward centralization now seemed to have halted. Radicals, too, were responding to a situation less fraught with catastrophe.

Nor would it be argued that the points raised by the outgroup were trivial from its standpoint.[8] Thus on two occasions the Articles of Confederation government requested permission to levy a five per cent import duty to secure the revenue needed to retrieve a financial condition drifting dangerously close to bankruptcy, but was each time thwarted by the action of a single state. Obviously if this situation could not be somehow relieved, conservatives would be left without even a pretense of government centralization. Again when England particularly refused to accord the new nation privileges with respect to empire trade as great as the mercantile class had anticipated, another significant disability came to light. Effective trade legislation, after all, was the most elementary function of an eighteenth-century mercantilist state. As a solution to this difficulty New Englanders would have liked to have seen a firm policy of discrimination against the trade of the erstwhile mother country, but opposition in the nonmercantile states prevented. As still a third problem, when a deluge of British goods threatened to overwhelm an infant, war-engendered manufacturing industry, the so-called central government was helpless to intervene. And finally, when the postwar depression brought with it as serious a problem of pressure for paper money as America had yet seen (a pressure highlighted on the very eve of the Constitutional Convention in 1787 by an armed uprising in Massachusetts, the famous Shays's Rebellion), these groups especially felt that their way of life was in danger.

However, the fact that conservatives had real grievances against their government's weaknesses is no warrant for accepting uncriti-

[8] John Fiske, *The Critical Period in American History, 1783-1789* (New York: Houghton Mifflin Co., 1888).

cally their view that the new power was about to fall to pieces during the 1780's. Impressive evidence can be marshalled in support of the proposition that this was not a particularly "critical" period at all, that many historians have too readily accepted conservative propaganda as historical revelation.[9]

For example, it can be demonstrated that the administration of the Revolutionary War was hardly bungled worse than that of the War of 1812 or of the early years of the Civil War in the North, both latter efforts being under a far more centralized government. The overwhelmingly important fact at this point is that the war was won. The postwar recession, moreover, could scarcely be laid at the door of the government except as a part of the process of political playacting, for an economic let-down after a war is a normal phenomenon. Similarly, much of the difficulty in international economic relations was an only-to-be-expected consequence of a new and uncertain independence. It would in any event have taken time to secure from other powers the deference due an equal rather than the contempt accorded an upstart. From this standpoint the remarkable fact is how quickly the new nation was accepted by other countries (including England), rather than how shabbily it was treated at first. Even with respect to tariff protection for infant manufactures the record is by no means as black as it can easily be painted. One by one, every state that had a significant manufacturing interest developed a protective system. Indeed, it now seems true that this decade saw throughout the entire country a development and a spirit of enthusiastic optimism such as has been experienced in few decades since.

No attempt will be made here to resolve this controversy among historians. Against the background of these opposing views, however, a few comments can be made which will still further assist in placing these momentous happenings in their proper perspective from the standpoint of the problems at issue in this study.

First, however accurate or exaggerated the conservative appraisal of the long-run impossibility of the Articles government, it is all too easy to overlook the tremendous step forward this organization represented. Thirteen sovereign political entities had under it been brought together into a union which no significant interest wished seriously to dissolve. Stated differently, whereas American mercantilism had hitherto been built around the colony as the basic political and economic unit, this emphasis had by the 1780's been decisively transformed. Though the contrast between centralization

⁹ Merrill Jensen, *The New Nation* (New York: Alfred A. Knopf, Inc., 1950).

under Parliament and the King and centralization under the Articles of Confederation was large in one sense, it was relatively small compared with the contrast between foreign rule and self-rule. Before the baby can walk, it must first crawl.

Second, ample allowance must be made for the fact that conservatives were at least as concerned over what the future might bring as they were desperate over the consequences of past and present failures. These groups were in the process of pushing the new economy toward its capitalist-industrialist future[10] (although, of course, they did not interpret their efforts in this way); and their leaders clearly understood that the requisite institutional changes could only be brought about with the tolerance and perhaps even the direct assistance of a national government. From this point it was but a short step to the conclusion that the necessary tolerance and/or assistance would only be forthcoming from a very different kind of government at this level. Critical period or not, who would today argue that their reasoning was fallacious?

Third, note should also be taken of the major factors bringing about the conversion of a majority in favor of the Articles of Confederation into a majority in favor of the Constitution. Here the main points requiring emphasis are the consensus and diversity so indispensable to democratic decision-making.

On the side of consensus, it is important that patriotism (nationalism resulting now especially from the reluctance of foreign countries to admit the United States into the circle of major powers) was at this stage on the side of conservatives; by almost any standard the new government was an ineffective practitioner of the prevailing mercantilist philosophy. Equally significant is the fact that government centralization under England was already beginning to be forgotten. Furthermore, the fact that important provisions of the Constitution did represent basic differences between upper- and lower-class groups must not be taken too seriously. There were numerous other provisions over which no such controversies arose. For example, no substantial segment of the American elite doubted the necessity of replacing the executive committee of the Articles government with a real executive, or of placing control over foreign commerce in the hands of the central government. And finally, there is little doubt but that erstwhile opponents of centralization were beginning now to sense that centralization could be used for lower-class, agrarian purposes as well as for upper-class, capitalist ends.

[10] Charles A. Beard, *Economic Interpretation of the Constitution of the United States* (New York: The Macmillan Co., 1913).

The important fact to remember in connection with all these considerations is that a number of men who later became active Anti-Federalists supported the Constitution both in the Convention and in the struggle for ratification—that no less an Anti-Federalist than James Madison, to mention only a single example, joined with Jay and Hamilton in the propaganda effort designed to "sell" the Constitution to New York voters.

On the side of diversity, the important fact is that there was no all-inclusive cleavage between the "haves" and the "have-nots," or even between capitalists and agrarians. Thus agrarian aristocrats no less than capitalist ones could see the threat implicit in an uprising such as Shays's Rebellion. Moreover, farmers who did not owe substantial sums of money were far less zealous paper money advocates than were their debtor colleagues. By the same token veterans and holders of revolutionary era bonds and paper money, men and women representing every stratum of society, felt that their chances of securing payment would be improved if a stronger central government were created. And not only were there centralist inclinations in lower-class, agrarian ranks, but the Constitution contained several fundamental concessions to the Anti-Federalist viewpoint. The classic instances here were the Bill of Rights and the fact that the central government was to be one of enumerated powers only, all nonenumerated powers to be exercised by the states.

Unquestionably in the replacement of mother country rule by self-rule the pendulum had swung too far in the direction of decentralization, and by the end of the post-Revolutionary War decade it was clearly ready to begin a return sweep. How far would this countermovement go? As of 1787 few men would have been willing to hazard a serious prediction. All that could be said for certain was that conservatives were beginning to organize themselves for the purpose of making the swing as wide as possible, while radicals were becoming alerted to the possibility that care would be required to prevent too great a reaction. The stage was thus set for the battle over the American Constitution which has never really ended.

QUESTIONS FOR DISCUSSION

1. Explain the most important features of mercantilism insofar as it involved business-government relationships.

2. Why were northern businessmen not especially discomfited by British mercantilist restrictions?

3. Defend the proposition that capitalists were not the makers of the American Revolution.

4. What were the main sources of socio-economic conflict within colonial America? What connection, if any, was there between this conflict and the war with England?

5. What were the major economic factors involved in the controversy over money between England and the colonies? Between radicals and conservatives in the colonies?

6. What caused the American Revolution?

7. Was the Articles of Confederation government in the public interest? Why or why not?

8. From the historical situation leading to the writing of the Constitution, pick out the major sources of this policy.

9. Explain the transition from the Articles of Confederation to the Constitution in terms of the earlier discussion of democratic decision-making.

Chapter 4

Triumph for Federalism

THE CONSTITUTION DOCUMENT

Because mercantilism and conflict were the most important mid-wives of the American Constitution, this document unmistakably reflects both forces. Indeed, it can be said without serious exaggeration that its most basic features can be explained in these terms alone.

It could, for example, scarcely be more fundamental that under the Constitution both state and federal governments were to be sovereign. Repudiating alike those extremists who wanted to see the states dissolved in the new union and those who believed the central government should be kept relatively powerless, this determination meant that with respect to some matters the states would continue to be the final authority while within other areas the federal government would have the last word.

Another deeply rooted compromise revealing clearly the conflict context within which the Constitution was written had to do with the division of the federal government's power into an executive, a legislature, and a judiciary, with the idea that each would serve as a check against both of the others. The purpose of this fragmentation of power was to make a strong central government impossible, either for the benefit of the aristocracy or the democracy. On the one hand the "masses" would be given a share in decision-making through Congress, while on the other coordinate subpowers capable of preventing precipitate (anticapitalist?) action were also established. No doubt the analogy uppermost in the minds of the Constitution's authors when this arrangement was decided upon was that between the colonial assembly and Congress on one side and between the mother country's veto power and the President on the other. It is to be especially noted in this connection that the Constitution's framers did not intend for the President to be elected by "the people."

When attention is turned, moreover, from the political aspects of the Constitution to economic content, its mercantilist background can be as clearly seen. Speaking generally, the principle determining the nature of the division of labor between the federal government and the several state governments was this: Where conflicts or non-uniformities between states might prove damaging to the well-being of the nation as a whole, federal sovereignty was provided for; where differences between states did not seem to pose this problem, state control was to be exercised. In other words, the entire nation was to have the same basic economic institutions, whatever peripheral differences might develop from state to state or from region to region. Could there be any other plausible interpretation of the intent of the men who enumerated the following areas within which federal sovereignty was to be exercised?

1. Regulation of commerce with foreign nations and among the several states
2. Establishing uniform laws with respect to bankruptcy
3. Coining money and regulating its value
4. Fixing the standard of weights and measures
5. Establishing post offices and post roads
6. Providing rules governing patents and copyrights

The economic content of the Constitution can be meaningfully discussed in conflict terms, too. Illustrating once again the interest of the business classes in a strong national government, the enumerated powers also coincide with those areas in which conflicts or nonuniformities between states might prove damaging to business development. More specifically, conservatives took care to write into the Constitution a number of provisions designed to correct the most acute deficiencies in their eyes of the Articles of Confederation as these had come to light during the so-called critical period. Thus the new federal government was to have the unquestioned power to tax its citizens, although export duties and direct taxes not levied upon the several states on the basis of population were forbidden. These provisions were designed to assure that the central government would not disintegrate for want of funds, a fate which had almost befallen its predecessor, and to make equally certain that funds were not raised by means of progressive taxation of the wealthy. The inability of the earlier central government to apply economic sanctions against foreign nations was remedied by lodging jurisdiction over foreign commerce with the federal government, while the creditor fear of paper money inflation was dealt with by taking away from the states the power to coin money, to legislate concerning the value of money, or to issue paper money.

This, then, was the foundation upon which this country's economic policy was to be built. It was, however—and this could scarcely be overemphasized—a foundation only; historical hindsight makes it abundantly clear that the American Constitution does not reside within a written document.[1] Rather it is a living, growing thing. On countless occasions it has proved itself capable of meeting the multifarious difficulties that arise in a huge, dynamic economy, while at the same time maintaining enough stability not to become a mere political plaything. Indeed, a substantial part of the study of the evolution of government-business relationships consists of following the twistings and turnings of constitutional interpretation.

But though the written Constitution was fortunately ambiguous enough so that time could play an important role in giving it form, even in 1789 the major questions which would develop in that process could be visualized. They were three in number, each closely related to each of the others. First, precisely where do federal powers leave off and state powers begin, and *vice versa?* Second, how are relationships between the several branches of the federal government to be worked out? Third, how great is the influence of government (federal or state) to be in the country's economic life? Against the background of a vigorously developing economy and a rapidly maturing democracy, these questions were to arise again and again.

HAMILTONIAN CENTRALIZATION[2]

The first answers began to be formulated almost at once as the new nation promptly moved to assert itself in several characteristically mercantilist ways. One of the first laws passed by Congress was a measure denying the use of the American flag to ships not built in American shipyards. An allied discrimination, designed for the benefit of the domestic ship operator, was a reduction of ten per cent of customs duties for all goods imported in American bottoms. And of course a vital continuing activity of importance to both branches of this industry was the endeavor to secure more favorable commercial treaties with foreign nations.

Another type of mercantilist legislation, although one less reminiscent of the nation's mercantile past than prophetic of a manufactur-

[1] W. W. Crosskey, *Politics and the Constitution in the History of the United States* (Chicago: University of Chicago Press, 1953); and Henry Rottschaefer, *The Constitution and Socio-Economic Change* (Ann Arbor: University of Michigan Law School, 1948).

[2] J. S. Bassett, *The Federalist System* (New York: Harper & Bros., 1906).

ing future, was a protective tariff. Because, however, it is so often asserted that America's first tariff was for revenue rather than protection, this measure deserves to be commented upon in some detail.

Consistent with the control over foreign commerce given to the national government, the states had been forbidden to levy import duties. This meant that on the one hand the states would now have to turn to other sources of revenue, and that on the other hand the protection for infant manufactures enacted by the states during the post-Revolution depression would have to be either taken over by the federal government or abandoned.

It is, of course, true enough that the nation's first tariff was the core around which the new government's revenue system was built. The opportunity to make primary use of a tax source which would not conflict with those to be exploited by the states, together with the deep-seated American resistance to internal taxation carried over from the conflict with England, made the customs duty the obvious solution to the central government's major fiscal problem. It is also true, furthermore, that there is to a degree an inherent contradiction between a tariff for revenue and a tariff for protection. But all this to the contrary notwithstanding, it is nonetheless a fact that the nation's first tariff law proclaimed in its very title the purpose of protecting manufactures, and that when the House was confronted with a choice between a revenue measure as such and an avowedly protectionist one it decisively selected the latter.[3] The point to be noted is that even agrarian leaders who had grown up in an atmosphere of foreign relations frictions, which it seemed could be significantly eased by the achievement of a higher level of economic self-sufficiency, were unwilling to compel domestic manufacturing enterprises to stand on their own feet.

To this point legislative endeavors had been relatively harmonious. But that historic conflicts had only been briefly slumbering became abruptly evident when attention shifted from policies concerned essentially with foreign affairs to domestic issues. And perhaps it is in part, at least, a coincidence that conflict reappeared simultaneously with the taking up of his duties as Secretary of the Treasury by Alexander Hamilton.

It is often said that the key to an understanding of Hamilton's economic program is his desire to see centralized government succeed in America, and his consequent interest in seeing the influential classes given a strong vested interest in its continuance. And it

[3] Edward Stanwood, *American Tariff Controversies in the Nineteenth Century* (Boston: Houghton Mifflin Co., 1903), chap. ii.

may be that this is a useful way of viewing the years Hamilton spent as Secretary of the Treasury and as the acknowledged leader of the Federalist party. It is worth observing, however, that an equally useful way of reading the history of this period is to turn this causal relationship around. According to this approach Hamilton did not give the influential classes a stake in the government because it was the kind of government in which he believed; rather he believed in this kind of government because it would so well serve the interests of the influential.

But whichever standpoint is adopted, a glance at the Hamiltonian program will provide ample documentation. Every one of his major policy recommendations was clearly designed to benefit most directly the business classes, and most could with some justification be attacked as discriminating against the less well-to-do. It is therefore not merely a coincidence that virtually all of the conflict over economic policy during the 1790's centered around the personality and the proposals of this genius of young America.[4]

First in point of time was a struggle over the measures suggested for guaranteeing the new nation's credit. The first step in this direction, of course, had already been taken in the form of assuring the new government a dependable income, but of only slightly less importance was the handling of the debts incurred by its predecessor. Hamilton's idea was for the central government to assume full responsibility not only for the debts incurred under the Articles of Confederation but for those incurred by the states during the Revolution and post-Revolution periods as well. This solution would serve the fourfold purpose of giving foreign creditors confidence in the integrity of the American government, providing a more satisfactory medium of exchange for large business transactions, facilitating the accumulation of capital internally, and giving domestic creditors a strong interest in seeing to it that the new government prospered. Agrarians, on the other hand, objected on the grounds that full assumption would give windfall profits to insider-speculators who had bought securities from original purchasers at a fraction of their face value, and that the taxation required to service this huge (by the standards of those days) national debt would fall predominantly on the lower classes. As of 1791, however, agrarian protests were of little avail against the combined strength of Alexander Hamilton's powerful influence and the swinging pendulum. Too many people were eager to establish the nation's credit on a sound footing for assumption to be defeated.

[4] Charles A. Beard, *The Economic Origins of Jeffersonian Democracy* (New York: The Macmillan Co., 1915).

The second great conflict over economic policy during this period involved the creation of a national bank. Hamiltonians were eager to establish such an institution because it could assist the government in financial matters, because it might be able to discipline state banks with their tendency to overissue, because it might help relieve the chronic shortage of specie, and because a well-managed federal banking institution might even facilitate the process of domestic capital formation. Again, however, anticentralists were quick to register disapproval. Farmers were primarily interested in "cheap" money and, hence, were hostile to any attempt to curb their inflationist propensities. However, since such an obviously class interest cannot be effectively argued directly, the attack in this case centered on constitutionality; there was no mention among the enumerated powers of the federal government of authority to establish a bank.

It is a fact fraught with major consequences for the future of government policy in the banking field in this country that, although the Federalists won the parliamentary victory on this occasion, they could scarcely have been said to have defeated their opponents on the constitutional issue. To be sure, a strong case could be and was made to the effect that the power to create a national bank was "implied" in the power conferred on the federal government to coin money and regulate its value. There was clearly the closest connection between bank notes as money and specie as money; and if bank notes were to become an important part of the circulating medium, uniformity in their value was logically a responsibility of the central government. But if by this process of reasoning a national bank could be justified, note-issuing state-chartered banks were *ipso facto* unconstitutional, for the states were expressly forbidden to issue paper money. Yet neither at this nor at any future time was this constitutional issue effectively raised against state banks.

The only other important battle over economic policy during these early years was in the tax field. In 1791 the federal government needed additional funds for frontier defense, and Hamilton proposed a tax on whiskey. A tax source today taken for granted without question, this levy then aroused a violent hostility in the South and in western Pennsylvania.[5] Because transportation facilities back from the coast and the coastal rivers were poor, grain could be marketed far more profitably in the form of distilled spirits. With whiskey the only cash product produced by many frontiersmen, it is not surprising that back-country farmers thought of America's first internal

[5] L. P. Baldwin, *Whiskey Rebels* (Pittsburgh: University of Pittsburgh Press, 1939).

tax as something other than the luxury levy it was considered by Alexander Hamilton. And when the fact that the farmer often sold his whiskey locally to middlemen for half the price currently quoted in Baltimore or Philadelphia (a differential largely explained by the cost of transportation) is taken into account, it is not even surprising that frontier grain producers believed that a per gallon assessment grossly discriminated against them in favor of the larger seaboard refiners who received the full market value for their output. Indeed so intense did feeling become on this issue in western Pennsylvania that an armed uprising resulted, which was only quieted when President Washington with Alexander Hamilton at his side led a body of federal troops into the area. The central government, in short, could and would enforce its centralizing legislation.

JEFFERSONIAN CENTRALIZATION[6]

Smarting from repeated defeats, agrarian radicals intensified their efforts as the decade of the 1790's advanced. If this rush toward centralization could not be checked within the framework of Federalist administrations, a more ambitious technique would have to be used; through democratic means agrarian leaders would have to secure control over the government for the benefit of their own following. By the middle of the 1790's an Anti-Federalist party was in the making; and because America was still overwhelmingly agricultural it could only be a matter of time before the business interests were toppled from power. Thus it happened that on March 4, 1801, Thomas Jefferson, himself an aristocrat yet clearly speaking for "the rabble," was inaugurated as President to the dismay of eastern capitalists.

No doubt it was both the fear of Federalists and the hope of their opponents that prevailing trends would now be reversed, that the pendulum had reached a high point in its swing toward centralization. However, the sequel was not to read that way. A number of factors intervened which compelled the Anti-Federalists to abandon their most fundamental campaign promises.

For example, one of the methods by which the Jeffersonians had intended to resolve the problem of excessive centralization was to reduce both federal taxation and the federal debt. But before plans to achieve these objectives had been more than launched (although the internal taxes were promptly repealed), depredations by pirates from Tripoli on American shipping became so troublesome that the decision was made in Washington to declare war. Furthermore, no

6 Edward Channing, *The Jeffersonian System* (New York: Harper & Bros., 1906).

sooner had the fiscal machinery been set in motion to defray this major cost than Spain withdrew the right of "deposit" at New Orleans and ceded Louisiana back to France. Confronted simultaneously with the threat of having such a powerful nation as France as a border neighbor and the danger of secession from the union by an area thus denied free use of its most effective transportation medium, Jefferson was forced to take a drastic step. Implicitly confessing that there was no constitutional warrant for what he was doing, this strict-constructionist President added $15 million to the national debt by buying Louisiana from Napoleon.

Louisiana was purchased in 1803. In that same year another event occurred which advanced the cause of centralization still further and, in addition, marked a major development in the evolving division of labor among the several branches of the federal government. This time, however, the cause was not external factors over which Americans had no control. The culprit was rather a sordid episode in domestic politics.

In the waning hours of John Adams' administration, an effort had been made to fill as many federal court posts as possible with men of Federalist sympathies. Unfortunately for Federalist plans a few of these last-minute commissions had not been delivered to their recipients by midnight, March 3, and one such disappointed candidate brought suit against Secretary of State James Madison when the latter refused to complete his appointment. And by an ironical quirk of circumstance Federalist John Marshall was Chief Justice of the United States Supreme Court when the celebrated case of *Marbury* v. *Madison*[7] came before that body—the same John Marshall who as acting Secretary of State had countersigned Marbury's commission a few days before he had taken over the Supreme Court post.

The fate of the luckless Marbury is of no concern here. Scarcely more important is the concrete issue he posed for decision by the Court. What is significant is that John Marshall, never more the partisan than in 1803, made brilliant use of this opportunity to declare the Judiciary Act of 1789 unconstitutional. "If, then," he said in his sternest manner, "the courts are to regard the Constitution, and the Constitution is superior to any ordinary act of the legislature, the Constitution, and not such ordinary act, must govern the case to which they both apply." What this meant, in brief, was that the federal courts must exercise a veto power over acts of Congress to prevent that body from violating constitutional principles.

To refer to Marshall as a partisan, be it noted, is not to criticize a

7 1 Cranch 137 (1803).

man rightly regarded one of America's greatest historical figures. Where the fundamental issues of life are at stake there are no neutrals. Nor is it intended to suggest that Marshall manufactured the doctrine of judicial review out of thin air; there are scholars who today insist that the logic of *Marbury* v. *Madison* is unassailable. The important point, rather, is this: although it was several decades before another federal law was declared unconstitutional on the authority of this precedent, Marshall's conclusion was never seriously threatened, and at several critical points in later American history it was to play a vital role in the formulation of economic policy. Whether for good or ill, and on this issue too there is disagreement, a barrier was erected between the expression of public opinion at the polls and the making of policy decisions—although by no means an insurmountable one.

Nor was this the end of an embarrassing series of "betrayals" of Anti-Federalist principles while Anti-Federalists were in control of the government. In 1806, supported by no less prominent an administration spokesman than Secretary of the Treasury Albert Gallatin, the federal government was even making plans to enter the road-building field.

Superficially it would seem that this activity could have been justified by the Jeffersonians. Did not the Constitution confer the authority to establish post roads upon the central government? But in part because strict-constructionists were cautious about embarking upon federal programs which might lead by slow degrees to an over-centralized government, and in part because the motivation behind internal improvements agitation could hardly be identified with an interest in the mail, such a program never became a "platform" item with Anti-Federalists.

The problem here was essentially that America was growing up. With the rapid expansion westward, the need for better East-West transportation was becoming urgent. For a time it had appeared that improved transportation could be made available with private capital; the Philadelphia-Lancaster Turnpike, a road built of broken stone overlaid with gravel which had reduced the cost of carriage between these two points by more than one-third, had returned a profit to its builders from the beginning and had ushered in a turnpike craze resulting in the building of several thousand miles of "first-class" highways. Gradually, however, it became apparent that the successful private-enterprise ventures in this field were to be the exception rather than the rule. From that point forward, as road-building had during the colonial era been a responsibility of the towns, it now fell to the lot of larger governmental units.

But which unit? In 1802, through the legislation admitting Ohio into the Union, an impetus had been given to state responsibility by making available to these governments five per cent of the proceeds of public land sales within their boundaries for the building of roads. Now the federal government proposed to complement these endeavors by building a turnpike connecting East with West, starting at Cumberland, Maryland. And although this broader program was not implemented, Gallatin two years later even suggested that the federal government build an interlocking network of both roads and canals. Indeed it was none other than Anti-Federalist Albert Gallatin himself who expressed most clearly the mercantilist basis of this zeal for improved transportation at federal government expense. Such a system of transportation lines, he said, would contribute "towards cementing the bonds of the Union between those parts of the United States whose local interests have been considered as most dissimilar."

Not quite all the impact of the three Anti-Federalist administrations preceding the War of 1812, however, was on the side of centralization. Emphasizing that constitutional principles are normally subsidiary to the economic interests they protect, many Federalists became quite cool to Anti-Federalist loose constructionism when the central government they had done so much to create began to lean in the direction of a war with their most important trading partner. In fact, when an administration striving to maintain neutrality in the face of the most trying circumstances imposed severe restrictions on American foreign trade as a measure of discipline aimed at Napoleonic War belligerents,[8] and particularly when the war with England they had tried so hard to prevent did break out, many Federalists defied their nation's leadership. They refused to come to the financial assistance of the government during the war, they carried on a thriving commerce with the enemy, and they even threatened to lead their states into secession.

A similar tangle of confused motivations was responsible for the demise of the First Bank of the United States in 1811. When the question of recharter was raised, the administration (and especially the Secretary of the Treasury) pressed for a vote of confidence. The bank had served the government well, and, far more important to Anti-Federalists, it had apparently not been a significant retarding factor in the growth of state banks. However, partly as a consequence of Federalist second-thoughts on centralization (Federalist stockholders in state banks stood to gain substantially from the death

[8] L. M. Sears, *Jefferson and the Embargo* (Durham: Duke University Press, 1927).

of the federal institution), and partly because of Anti-Federalist constitutional objections, the First Bank of the United States was refused a renewal of its charter. Thus, on the very eve of a military encounter during which the services of a national bank would have been most useful, the federal government abandoned this field to the states for the moment.

American Mercantilism at Its Crest

It is a striking although scarcely a surprising fact that government centralization in the new nation correlated closely with the precariousness of her position in the family of nations; the more difficult her situation was the more willing were her citizens to entrust greater responsibilities to the government farthest removed from them. And because of this pattern, it was only to be expected that emphasis upon the nation as an economic and political unit would flourish especially vigorously against the background of a war often referred to as "America's Second War For Independence."[9]

The first of these postwar manifestations of a still more intense nationalism was in the field of banking. With the disappearance of the restraining influence of the First Bank of the United States, state banks had increased greatly both in size and in number. The confusion created by the resultant proliferation of state bank notes, accentuated as it was by a chronic shortage of specie and the absence as yet of effective banking regulation, was then made doubly severe by the suspension of specie payments by the government. Amid the utter chaos that was the nation's financial system at war's end, the carrying-on of ordinary business transactions and the collection of revenue by the government became so difficult that the nation was able to launch another experiment in centralized banking. On April 10, 1816, despite the objections of Federalist banking interests and agrarian strict-constructionism, the Second Bank of the United States was chartered.

No sooner was this problem again temporarily resolved, furthermore, than the question of tariff protection was raised more sharply than ever before. Almost a decade of trade derangement brought about by embargo, nonintercourse, and then war, had stimulated domestic manufactures. Unfortunately for these enterprises, however, the end of the war brought with it a flood of European (especially British) imports. Manufacturers inundated by this tide were quick to appeal to the nation's leaders, and understandably their ap-

9 C. M. Wiltse, *John C. Calhoun: Nationalist, 1782-1828* (Indianapolis: The Bobbs-Merrill Co., Inc., 1944), chaps. viii, ix, and x.

peal contained a strong element of patriotism. Nor were statesmen indifferent to this plea. For three decades the nation had claimed in theory an independence it could not demonstrate in practice, and one of the conclusions drawn from this fact by a majority of America's elite was that dependence upon foreign manufactures was an evil to be overcome as speedily as possible. As a result the demands of manufacturers brought a warm response (over the protest especially of New England shipping interests) in the form of the Tariff of 1816 and the highest level of duties in the young nation's peace-time history.

In the wake of a new war effort, too, it was only to be expected that the question of improved transportation would also be forcefully raised. For one thing the war had demonstrated the inadequacy of existing facilities. For another the American economy was continuing to expand by leaps and bounds, the most conspicuous symbol of that development being the beginning at this time of factory manufactures; and it was plain that a solution to the problem of long-distance, internal transportation was a prerequisite of continued expansion. This time it was John C. Calhoun, the nationalist so soon to turn into an uncompromising sectionalist, who most clearly expressed what was involved. "Whatever impedes the intercourse of the extremes with this, the centre of the republic, weakens the union. The more enlarged the sphere of commercial circulation . . . the more strongly are we bound together—the more inseparable are our destinies."

Because he so thoroughly believed what he was here proclaiming, Calhoun suggested and worked tirelessly to secure the passage of a broad program of internal improvements at federal government expense. Opposed were a number of Anti-Federalists who were not able to overcome their constitutional scruples as easily as men like Calhoun, and New England Federalists who saw little gain for their section from the proposed program. Most strongly in favor were the regions around New York and Philadelphia, where businessmen appreciated the benefits to them of improved communication with the West. So general, however, was interest in a higher degree of economic unification that when the measure was put to a vote in Congress it secured a majority in both Houses. Then, as if to spell out a warning that for the time being the pendulum had now reached its highest point, President Madison vetoed Calhoun's bill.

Actually, no one heeded this warning issued March 3, 1817. The momentum of nationalistic mercantilism was still too strong, and indeed this momentum had yet to run a course that included the delivery of two of John Marshall's most centralizing decisions.

The Second Bank of the United States had a checkered and none too savory career during the first years of its existence.[10] On the one hand it eagerly fell in with the inflation-assisted expansionism of the postwar era and, on the other hand, mingled a too easy money policy with outright fraud and dishonesty. An important consequence was that the Bank never quite succeeded in returning the country to a specie basis, and was itself almost overextended when the "Panic of 1819" struck. Far from being in a position to assist the banking industry (and through it the entire economy) attain a more stable equilibrium, the Second Bank of the United States was compelled to draw the financial noose even tighter in order to extricate itself.

Agrarians long suspicious of this institution were understandably all the more embittered by revelations of gross corruption in the Bank's operations and by the way it sacrificed the well-being of state banks to its own as soon as adversity loomed on the horizon. One of the concrete evidences of this unrest was a series of tax laws passed by a number of southern and western states aimed directly at this federal rival of the banks they had themselves created. Naturally the Bank refused to pay these levies and appealed to the courts for confirmation of its stand. Ironically, the case which reached the Supreme Court first was one involving the Baltimore branch of the Bank, where violation of public trust had unquestionably been carried farthest.[11]

But fraud was not the issue before John Marshall. What the Bank's opponents charged rather was unconstitutionality, and on the question of the powers of the federal government the Chief Justice was always ready to expound. With the air of a man who had made up his mind long before the case came to bar, he declared the measure incorporating the Bank to be valid. It followed of course that the Maryland law placing a special tax on the Bank was not an appropriate use of that state's taxing power. As Marshall put it, a state's power to tax could not legitimately be used to destroy a valid agency of the central government. Thanks to the Supreme Court (no thanks being due to the principal officers of the Bank), the banking field was kept open for federal legislation.

The other Supreme Court decision also involved the constitutionality of a state statute—this time a New York law. That state had granted to Robert Livingston and Robert Fulton the exclusive right

---

[10] W. B. Smith, *Economic Aspects of the Second Bank of the United States* (Cambridge: Harvard University Press, 1953).

[11] *McCulloch v. Maryland*, 4 Wheaton 316 (1819).

to navigate New York's waters by steamboat, a right which had been legally made over to a man named Ogden. In 1818 Ogden brought suit to restrain one Gibbons from operating two steamboats on the Hudson River between points in New Jersey and New York City. When Gibbons claimed the right to operate in the coasting trade under an act of Congress of 1793, a federal question was posed which placed this matter, too, squarely before Chief Justice John Marshall.[12]

Important as this new challenge to the federal government's power was to Marshall, it was even more important to the nation's economic development. Water transportation was the foundation on which specialization and exchange then rested, and the steamboat represented the greatest technological advance in the transportation field since the invention of the wheel. If, now, state governments were to be permitted to pervert the potentialities of this advance by basing regulations concerning it on arbitrary state boundaries, the development of the nation as an economic unit (and more particularly the nation's development of a great manufacturing industry) would be seriously retarded. But John Marshall was once more equal to the occasion. Using language which has perhaps never been exceeded for the finality with which the superiority of the federal government was upheld, he struck down New York's law. "The power of Congress, then, comprehends navigation within the limits of every state in the Union, so far as that navigation may be, in any manner, connected with 'commerce with foreign nations, or among the several States, or with the Indian tribes.'"

THE PENDULUM SWINGS BACK

In retrospect it is apparent that James Madison's veto of Calhoun's internal improvement measure was indeed handwriting on the wall. Although pressure for greater centralization of responsibilities in the hands of the federal government continued, it was to be several decades before so firm a stand on this issue would again be taken. The situation was almost as though, having established its power to govern, the federal government was now content to let someone else do the work of actually governing. For the moment, in other words, developments in the field of business-government relationships were to be carved out in the various state capitols.

The first major indication of this turning of the tide had to do with a legislative program for which Henry Clay, as one of the most able spokesmen for the business community, was largely responsible.

[12] *Gibbons* v. *Ogden*, 9 Wheaton 1 (1824).

Clay believed in protection for America's manufacturing industries, and he believed further that the existing level of protective duties was inadequate. Master strategist that he was, in the early 1820's he devised an interrelated group of policies calculated to win enough support from nonmanufacturing regions to raise the tariff—a program named by him and ever afterwards called "The American System."

The content of the American System indicates clearly where new support for the tariff was primarily to be sought. Western farmers were at this time suffering from depressed economic conditions, partly as a consequence of unfavorable legislation abroad, and hence a program designed to bring new hope to this area could not have been better timed. What Clay proposed was simplicity itself. If the West would support a substantial tariff increase, the East would soon develop into a manufacturing region with a capacity to absorb western surpluses of grain and meat that would make trans-Appalachian farmers independent of European markets. And, to make the bait even more irresistible, Clay promised to use the excessive revenue received from higher duties to build the transportation facilities required to bring western goods to seaboard markets.

The American System was successful enough on the tariff front, although this was primarily because of a dramatic transformation of the New England economy from one built around shipping to one built around manufacturing. But it was singularly unsuccessful in embarking the United States upon a costly internal improvements program at federal government expense. So suddenly, in fact, did the nation's erstwhile interest in activities of this kind now wane that it is worthwhile inquiring into the major factors bringing about this shift in emphasis.

In the background, of course, was the fact that the end of the Napoleonic Wars marked the beginning of the so-called "Hundred Years' Peace." With less pressure on the nation from foreign powers, there was less need to be concerned about the power and prestige of the country as a whole.

This does not tell the full story, however. Had not a number of other conflicts promptly moved into the policy vacuum thereby created, state government powers would surely not have been as decisively aggrandized relative to those of the federal government. These conflicts, then, are the factors to be examined.

It is worth noting, for example, that the reason Henry Clay had to work so hard to secure tariff votes in the West was because the South had recently taken a united stand against protectionism. In part the South's objection was grounded in the fact that the burden of the tariff fell disproportionately on the cotton economy, but in part also it rested on a belief in the unconstitutionality of protection. This conclusion in turn reflected the South's recent discovery that her way of life could very nearly be outvoted in Congress. The Missouri Compromise had given slavery a precarious equality in the Senate, and on this southerners would have to rely to some extent. But few solid hopes could be pinned on so slender a reed. A sounder approach seemed to be to insist on an unyielding strict constructionism; this would prevent issues concerning slavery from being pressed to a vote that might be lost, for the enumerated powers of the federal government included nothing on that subject. It was highly prophetic of the future of Clay's American System when John Randolph of Virginia, speaking of a pending internal improvements measure, uttered these words: "If Congress possess the power to do what is proposed in this bill, they may emancipate every slave in the United States."

But it was not alone in the South that men's faces were turning away from centralization. In New York, where especially strong support for internal improvements had been available a few years earlier, almost no support for such a policy could now be found—and for an obvious reason. Acting on President Madison's decision against the federal government moving in this direction, New Yorkers had taken the initiative. Authorization was secured from the state legislature, public funds were appropriated, and a waterway was built up the Hudson River and across the state to Lake Erie. With an excellent transportation connection of her own to the West, a connection making an important contribution to New York's attainment of undisputed pre-eminence among American cities,[13] her citizens would not be eager to promote transportation facilities benefitting primarily rival urban areas.

Even in the field of banking the principal pressures at work now favored decentralization rather than centralization. One of these, to be sure, was the fact that the Second Bank of the United States was at the moment functioning satisfactorily enough that the need for greater centralization did not seem urgent, but there were other forces in operation here which were of greater importance. Farmers, for example, and especially smaller ones, still had a preference for state banks which the recent inept management of the United States Bank had accentuated, while ambitious New Yorkers wanted nothing better than to inherit for their city some of the business now being done by this Philadelphia giant.

Unquestionably, however, two other factors were still more funda-

[13] R. G. Albion, *The Rise of New York Port* (New York: Charles Scribner's Sons, 1939); and Dorothie Bobbe, *Dewitt Clinton* (New York: Minton, Balch & Co., 1933).

mental. In the perspective of American economic development, it is clear that the 1820's saw a rapid maturation of banking which owed little to activity by the federal government.

For one thing, regulation of banks by state governments became more rigid as increasingly it was realized that banks were performing a quasi-public function. More attention was being given to specie backing for state bank notes, a greater publicity for bank operations was coming to be insisted upon, and more restrictions were aimed against the making of loans on improper security. New York even led the way toward acceptance by state governments of some responsibility for protecting bank customers more directly. Every bank in that state was required to pay each year to the state treasurer a sum equal to one half of one per cent of its outstanding capital stock (until such cumulative payments should amount to 3 per cent), thus creating a fund to be used in reimbursing depositors and noteholders of failed concerns. While it would be too much to say that the end of "wildcat banking" was now in sight, much progress was being made.

In the second place, a centralization was taking place within the banking community which also reduced the necessity of centralization by way of the federal government. About this time Boston's larger banks became concerned about the irresponsibility of bankers in the economic hinterland of that city. Bank notes from out of town tended to flow toward Boston where they circulated at varying discounts, in the process making ordinary business (and especially banking) transactions more difficult and tending to replace in trade channels the notes of the Boston banks themselves. To promote a greater uniformity in note circulation, the major Boston banks banded together to compel their country colleagues to exercise more restraint. Popularly known as the "Suffolk System" (named after the bank that assumed the most prominent role in implementing this arrangement), the technique employed was to compel outlying banks to keep substantial deposits in Boston on pain of having their notes bundled up and sent back for payment in specie. In this way a pattern of concentration of reserves was worked out greatly improving the efficiency with which specie was utilized, and in a relatively short time this device was being copied with variations in other urban centers.

By the end of the 1820's it can be said that the triumph of federalism was complete. To be sure, the term federalism as thus used does not refer to the program of the Federalist party; it means rather a system of government in which the nation shares sovereignty on more or less equal terms with smaller governmental units. It was

characteristic of European mercantilism that the nation-state virtually eclipsed those agencies that had previously exercised the sovereignty it came to possess; only in America did both levels of
government continue to exist side by side.

A sequence of events almost perfectly symbolizing the victory of
federalism took place early in Andrew Jackson's second term as
President. Despairing of securing relief from tariff protectionism in
Washington, South Carolina proclaimed her right to declare the nation's tariff laws null and void within her boundaries. But when the
President defiantly maintained that the nation's laws would be enforced, the country rallied to his side. Even with the pendulum now
swinging against the extension of the federal government's powers,
in other words, the nation was obviously not to be allowed to disintegrate.

QUESTIONS FOR DISCUSSION

1. In what ways did mercantilism and conflict shape the American Constitution?

2. What were the major differences between the Constitution and the Articles
of Confederation?

3. Evaluate the pro and con arguments advanced regarding assumption of
the debt and creating a national bank. Were the right decisions made here?

4. Why was it easier to secure support for America's first tariff than for the
First Bank of the United States?

5. What checks are available against judicial review in the American system
of government?

6. In what ways were Anti-Federalists compelled by circumstances to contribute to the swing toward centralization?

7. Why is road-building so invariably a government function?

8. Enumerate the major items of mercantilist legislation passed during the
period discussed in this chapter. Why are they called mercantilistic?

9. Why did the pendulum begin swinging against centralization?

10. Interpret the evolution of federalism from the standpoint of the concept
"consent."

11. What was the underlying consensus factor so important to government-
business relationships during this period? How did it operate?

Chapter 5

Foundations for Industrialism

THE NEW MERCANTILISM

As long as America's most important nonagricultural industry continued to be foreign trade (shipping and shipbuilding), the government promoted and watched over that activity most zealously. From this standpoint, however, the "Second War for Independence" marked something of a turning point in America's economic history. Prior to that time manufacturing had been a distinctly marginal outlet for capital seeking investment; trade disruptions would be accompanied by a rush of capital into manufacturing pursuits, which would then be as promptly abandoned when opportunities for investment in trade again became available. After the Napoleonic Wars, on the other hand, this "normal" readjustment did not take place.

The explanation for this transformation in economic structure is not difficult to find. Trade could only be a dominant activity in a region whose productive technology was inferior to that of other regions, and the industrial revolution in the western world was now well advanced. Maturing first in England and then gradually spreading to the Continent and later to the United States, techniques for large-scale production were so altering the economic order that historical relationships between Europe and Asia were in the process of being reversed. In America the appearance of the rudiments of the modern factory system was beginning visibly to lessen in importance the building and operation of ships.

It was, of course, only to be expected that a shift in emphasis within the underlying economy would be accompanied by a comparable shift in the focus of government-business relationships. A segment of the economy could scarcely grow significantly in prestige without setting up a flow of pressures favorable to itself in the direction of policy-making officials—the converse of this being a diminish-

79

ing of government solicitousness for other economic endeavors. Thus although government in the United States did not promote manufacturing as extensively as it was customary under mercantilist systems to promote merchant affairs, and although the merchant marine was never wholly abandoned, it is nonetheless true that in a few short years manufacturing enterprises decisively replaced maritime concerns as the favorite object of governmental paternalism. An act passed by Congress in 1817 giving American ships a monopoly of the coastwise trade was the last major piece of legislation favoring that industry until comparatively recent times.

No doubt, too, the transition would have been much less abrupt had not these two types of economic activity become broadly competitive with one another at the public policy level. But when manufacturing and mercantile interests presented mutually exclusive solutions to the problem of trade with the British West Indies, a choice had to be made.

Historically America's trade with the West Indian Islands (particularly those under British control) had been the most important branch of that industry. Indeed so lucrative was it that a running battle between England and this country concerning it had been the order of the day ever since the colonies had won their independence.[1] England, of course, had the advantage in this struggle because she was the sovereign power, but unfortunately for her she could not have her way completely because her own dominions were unable adequately to supply her West Indies outposts with the goods they required.

After the War of 1812 this contest became especially intense. The first gun was fired by England when she prohibited American vessels from entering West Indian ports, thus denying this country's traders access to the profitable triangular trade with that area. The United States struck back by refusing to permit in American ports any British ship arriving from a colony legally closed to our vessels; if Americans could not enjoy these profits, they could at least see to it that Englishmen did not, either.

It was at this point in this historic controversy that the federal government was forced to choose between merchants and manufacturers. It had become apparent to far-sighted British leaders that a policy seriously crippling America's carrying trade would be injurious to England's manufacturing interests. Earnings from the shipping industry in this country were, after all, often spent for

---

[1] F. Lee Benns, *The American Struggle for the British West India Carrying Trade, 1774-1829* (Bloomington: University of Indiana Press, 1923); and George Dangerfield, *The Era of Good Feelings* (New York: Harcourt, Brace & Co., Inc., 1952).

British manufactures. Having already begun to make her own transition from trade to manufacturing, in short, England's next move was conciliatory. She opened up the direct West Indian trade to American vessels.

But if England was willing to sacrifice her merchant marine to the development of her factories, so too was the United States. For if reduced trade earnings for this country would be injurious to British manufacturers, it would by the same token be a boon to American ones. Instead, therefore, of rewarding conciliation with conciliation, America's response was to take an even more intransigeant stand. By demanding the elimination of all Empire discriminations against American ships, a demand to which England could not possibly have been expected to accede, public policy took its stand with the manufacturer.

To be sure, protecting American manufacturers by shackling American ships was both awkward and ineffective, and indeed such a clumsy policy might not have been adopted at all if southerners had not suddenly taken it into their heads to prevent a more direct solution to this problem. Toward such a solution, however, in the form of the American System, statesman Henry Clay was already devoting his best energies. When that objective had been accomplished through the tariff enactments of 1824 and 1828, legislation placing foreign ships in American ports on a full reciprocity basis was the logical sequel. A definitive end was thus reached to traditional mercantilism in this country.

Nor did the "new mercantilism" consist only of tariff legislation. Indeed it can convincingly be argued that American tariff protectionism was not a significant factor in the development of a domestic manufacturing industry.[2] Certainly of greater importance, although this factor would necessarily exercise a more subtle influence, was the protection afforded by the patent-bankruptcy system.

The heart and center of the modern industrial economy is large-scale production. In order to keep its place among other industrial nations, and of course at the time under discussion here the problem was more that of catching up with rivals already out in front, Americans had to turn out an unceasing flow of innovations resulting in lower-cost, better quality output. Furthermore, a goodly portion of these innovations had to be technological in nature, contributing to the transition from hand to machine operations. But herein lay a major difficulty. Machine production requires a heavy outlay of capital—capital, moreover, that is fixed and durable in nature. Under-

[2] F. W. Taussig, *Tariff History of the United States* (New York: G. P. Putnam's Sons, Inc., 1924).

standably men are not willing to convert their liquid capital into illiquid assets unless they feel they have at least a fighting chance to recover the value of such assets by selling their output on the market before they become worthless.

Even in a mercantilist-oriented nation in the early nineteenth century it would obviously not have been seriously proposed that the government underwrite the losses of infant manufacturing concerns. There was available, however, a way by which investment in technical innovations could be protected without creating a system of subsidies so subject to abuse. The first innovator along a particular line, in exchange for making public this particular advance in the arts, could be shielded from imitators until he had had an opportunity to write off the capital required to put the new technique into commercial use—until, in other words, he had been given an opportunity to reap a profit from this contribution to general economic well-being. Here, in brief, is the rationale behind patent protection.[3]

Although America's first patent law was passed in 1790, it should occasion no surprise that inventors and concerns possessing inventions received little protection under it. The nation was, after all, still operating on the basis of pre-industrial premises. As a result for 46 years patent rights were granted without benefit of investigation to determine the novelty of the innovation involved. Such a procedure inevitably created a situation in which conflict and fraud (and hence endless litigation) were the principal components. Finally, in 1836, under the stimulus of the new mercantilism, remedial legislation was enacted. Possessors of valid patent rights were allowed a monopoly of the use of the patented idea for a period of 17 years. From that year dates the patent system which still essentially governs in this country, and from that point forward this public policy played an important role in the development of an industrialized America.

Protection by way of bankruptcy legislation performs a similar function. Men would hardly venture into new fields of endeavor or experiment with better methods of producing standard-of-living items if the result of failure were to be certain economic and social ruin at the hands of a court applying medieval legal concepts. The product of a political coalition between frontier- and labor-based democracy and the rising entrepreneur class, modern bankruptcy rules and procedures were designed to minimize this threat. While being careful not to ride roughshod over creditor (property) rights, thus discouraging the flow of capital without which the economy

---

[3] Floyd L. Vaughan, *Economics of Our Patent System* (New York: The Macmillan Co., 1925).

must lose much of its dynamism, the law sees to it that bankrupts are given an opportunity to make a fresh start. And although this area, which according to the language of the Constitution was to be a federal government responsibility, was dealt with for more than 100 years almost exclusively by the states, apparently the balance struck between creditor and debtor needs was nevertheless highly favorable to American economic development.

In one other way did government directly promote manufacturing activities as such. Beyond their contribution to the creation of an atmosphere favorable to risk-taking, the states took an interest in encouraging manufactures even more forthrightly. In many instances inspection laws guaranteeing quality, in part on the ground that therein resided a major condition for the survival of the new techniques, were re-enacted in almost the identical form in which they had been passed by colonial assemblies. Often also assistance for new enterprises was secured from the public treasury by means of bounties, loans, monopolies, or lotteries. Especially in New England a pattern of tax exemption for a term of years was inaugurated, a practice which occasionally moved local governments to protest vigorously. Prizes and premiums were used by way of state and county fairs to help achieve this same end. Looking at this process from the reverse side, furthermore, it is of some significance that state governments exerted no negative influence; that is, they did not retard industrial development by insisting upon the conservation of natural resources or by regulations designed to protect workers. It was not, in short, owing to any lack of enthusiasm on the part of state government officials that these policies were not an important factor in the nation's manufacturing history.

FIGHTING FOR A MEDIUM OF EXCHANGE

But if the only contribution made by governments to America's emerging industrialism had been these more or less direct encouragements, it could with some force be argued that this country's policy toward manufacturing was one of laissez faire from the very beginning. That this suggestion does not describe the actual situation, however, can readily be appreciated when it is remembered that the government is in fact a partner to every business transaction. Stated differently, the government, and only the government, can maintain the environment within which business is conducted, and therefore upon the government must fall the critical responsibility of seeing to it that environmental conditions are favorable to particular kinds of activity.

As far as American industrialization was concerned, for example, it was of the utmost importance that governmental sanctions stood squarely behind the institution of private property and the sanctity of contract implicit in that institution. The freedom of individuals to do whatever they wanted with their own resources within broad limits no doubt had incalculable consequences for the rapidity with which agrarian America was transformed. Similarly, although perhaps less fundamentally, it was much easier to develop an industrial society on the basis of a uniform system of weights and measures rather than the determination of these standards by individual firms or even by state governments.

But these illustrations of government support for the underlying economic order do not do justice to the subtle ways in which the transition to a manufacturing economy was assisted by government. Actually, in the case of both the institution of private property and the particular system of weights and measures decided upon, no new policies were enunciated after the United States became a nation; all that was required was to confirm and generalize under the new sovereignty practices already being followed. It was, thus, along other lines that governments now made basic contributions to the creation and maintenance of an institutional climate without which modern industrialization could not have become a reality. And in view of the way the centralization pendulum was now swinging, it is not to be wondered at that state governments for a time assumed most of this responsibility.

The first of these developments in point of time was in the money field, where economic evolution was about to take another decisive step forward. Always the problem here had been to develop a money system which would be both adequate and convenient but in which the medium of exchange would not at the same time be subject to severe fluctuations in value. The bank note had proved to be a fairly satisfactory supplement to specie, and by the 1830's much progress had been made toward the creation of an institutional framework which would keep the value of money within reasonable bounds.[4] Now, before this framework had even approached completion, underlying banking evolution itself immeasurably complicated matters.

Viewed from one standpoint, activity on this front was a direct outgrowth of economic dynamics. In a manufacturing economy specialization and division of labor are carried much further than in

---

[4] Davis R. Dewey, *State Banking Before the Civil War* (Washington, D.C.: Government Printing Office, 1910); and Harry E. Miller, *Banking Theories in the United States Before 1860* (Cambridge: Harvard University Press, 1927).

the commercial-type economy now being replaced, and the need for money broadly parallels the complexity of the economic process. On the one hand, production is itself divided into a series of distinct operations—for example, manufacturing, wholesaling, retailing, and so forth—each typically controlled by different economic entities. On the other hand, a vital part of the modern industrial economy consists of specialized and indivisible capital units which are in turn represented by a much larger number of negotiable claims. The exchange mechanism must provide for transfers of goods between manufacturer and wholesaler and between wholesaler and retailer no less than transfers to final consumers, and it must likewise make possible the free circulation of claims throughout the economy.

In other words, not only was the United States entering a period of dramatic increase in what is today called gross national product, but the economy was rapidly becoming one in which a greater quantity of money was required per unit of gross national product. So elaborate, indeed, had the money side of the economy become that evolution in this field was clearly moving beyond the bank note as such. Convenient though folding money is, checks are for many purposes even more so. Thus although the bank note was never to be wholly displaced in this process, deposit credit was already beginning to play an important role in the larger business centers.

The unobtrusive, almost nondeliberate way in which this new device made its appearance is excellently illustrated by one of the ramifications of the Suffolk experiment. A major reason for embarking on this endeavor had been the fact that depreciated notes from hinterland banks were replacing the full-valued notes issued by the more conservatively managed banks in Boston. But when the new Suffolk arrangements had been put into operation it was observed that the notes of Boston's banks did not circulate more freely. Already these banks were making the transition to checkbook money, and this development was not halted when virtually all notes in circulation in the Boston area began to circulate at par.

What was needed, and with all possible speed, was a pattern of banking regulation which would preserve the gains being made at this point and at the same time generalize those advances throughout the economy. Because banking could be made more profitable by the simple expedient of creating more bank credit (at least as long as insolvency could be avoided), and because the practices followed by the more lax members of the banking community tended to become standard for the industry, it was clear that the indicated restraints would have to be imposed by government. It was, therefore, unfortunate for the rising industrialism that this period also saw the most pronounced reaction to date against centralization in this field.

This second dimension of the money problem the nation was now facing arose less directly from underlying dynamics than its companion, although there were significant interconnections. The negative view the federal government took during the 1830's toward a national system of money and credit was part and parcel of a political era often called "The Jacksonian Revolution," and the primary reason for a new "revolution" in American politics at this time was the impact of economic transformation upon large segments of the population.[5] With this development the "era of good feeling" ushered in by the second war with England was ushered out, and the 200 year-old conflict between the classes which had temporarily been in abeyance broke out anew. No policy was more bitterly contested than that involving money—perhaps the only major field in which old wounds had never quite disappeared.

Farmers constituted the largest group actively promoting Andrew Jackson's cause. Under the most favorable conditions the farmer can improve his economic position by producing for the market rather than for himself. Not only is he thus enabled to concentrate productive efforts on a few items which can be produced most economically, but he can then use the proceeds of sales of these products to purchase goods in the production of which someone else is most proficient. There is, however, a price which must be paid for this economic betterment. The farmer thereby loses his economic independence; his standard of living is determined, not alone by how much he produces, but also by how much others are willing to pay for his output. When Jackson was overwhelmingly elected President in 1828 farm prices had been falling for a full decade, and farmers were surely not to be ridiculed for believing that the nation's money system was not functioning satisfactorily.

The other important group reacting vigorously to dynamic changes in the economy was labor. In a commercial-type economy the artisan could at least look forward to attaining the status of a master workman. In this position he was a highly respected member of the community, standing well not only with the journeymen and apprentices whose labor he supervised and coordinated but also with consumers whose preferences he was able to cater to directly. With the passing away of economic organization on a commercial basis, however, various middlemen began to insert themselves between the workman and the consumer, while the keen competition of the new technology

[5] A. M. Schlesinger, Jr., *The Age of Jackson* (Boston: Little, Brown & Co., 1945).

compelled the employer to drive harder and harder bargains with rank-and-file laborers. Squeezed between the machine on one side and the "consumer's man" on the other, workers were soon taking exception to this fall in their social status. The sweeping character of the victory won by Andrew Jackson in 1828 was in part a consequence of the vigor of this reaction.

The farmer's fight at this point was predicated on the belief that the business community was endeavoring to maintain too close a connection between metallic and paper money. Starting from this premise, furthermore, it was not illogical to suppose that the Second Bank of the United States, commissioned as it was to work for uniformity in note circulation and interchangeability between notes and specie, was partially responsible for his difficulties. It was, thus, with the West's interests uppermost in his mind that Jackson in 1832 declared an unremitting warfare against "the monster" which did not end until the banking field had been turned over in its entirety to state institutions. And when Nicholas Biddle, president of the Bank, saw to it that that institution's dying gasps produced as much inconvenience to the economy as possible (this to compel Andrew Jackson to change his mind), farmers were no doubt fully confirmed in their beliefs.

Laborers' thoughts about desirable changes in monetary policy were even more radical. Their most basic grievance against the nation's money mechanism was the fact that wages were often paid in state bank notes at 100 cents on the dollar, which notes were then found to be subject to varying rates of depreciation when the time came to convert them into purchasing power. Had workers been less naive relative to economic matters, they would of course have directed this frustration into solid support for the Second Bank of the United States. Instead, however, of insisting upon the circulation of notes at par, the working man's solution was to abolish bank notes.

As it happened this suggestion fitted in very well both with Jackson's own antipathy toward banks in general, and with the West's resentment against speculation in the public lands. For one brief moment, thus, as time is measured by the perspective of history, the United States flirted with even so backward a step as this. On July 11, 1836, President Jackson issued his justly famous "Specie Circular." Herein it was proclaimed that state bank notes would no longer be accepted as payment for public land purchases; for this purpose only specie money could be used. As the economy struggled to adjust itself to this drastic change in the rules of the game (that is, as specie reserves were withdrawn from eastern banks to serve as hand money

across the Appalachians), no single factor was more important in precipitating the "Panic of 1837."[6]

Obviously a vigorous economy could not long be content with such
anachronistic arrangements. In May, 1838, the "Specie Circular" was
repealed—although the nation was not again to have federal banking
legislation for another quarter of a century. But that state governments would be able to fill a large part of this control vacuum was
made reassuringly clear during the depression ushered in by the 1837
downturn. Both New York and Louisiana, two of the nation's most
prominent commercial areas, took important steps toward creating
a more satisfactory medium of exchange.

In New York the great achievement was the building of a more
secure foundation for a system of crude insurance for noteholders.
The depression had wiped out the safety fund established earlier for
protecting both depositors and noteholders, and the decision was now
made to concentrate upon noteholder protection only.[7] To accomplish this objective, a law was passed in 1838 requiring banks to deposit securities with the state comptroller equal in value to the
amount of notes outstanding. By this device it was hoped to instill
more confidence in note circulation—with the result that specie could
more effectively be concentrated in the banking system as reserves
(because noteholders would be less inclined to insist upon exchanging
notes for specie at the first sign of danger).

Louisiana's contribution to a more effective monetary system lay
in the fact that her banking law of 1842 was the first decisive recognition of the importance of deposit credit in the nation's monetary
mechanism.[8] New Orleans in those days was a commercial community second only to New York, and the "Panic of 1837" had dealt a
heavy blow at that city's financial organization. Determined to avoid
another such setback, business interests in the state moved to bring
their money system more up to date. A percentage reserve was required against all public liabilities; that is, notes and deposits rather
than notes only as heretofore. Furthermore, the reserve required was
100 per cent, although two-thirds of this might be in ninety-day commercial paper. In this way reserves were kept adequate and fairly
liquid, while the amount of money made available (deposits) was related closely to the volume of business being done.

It would be an exaggeration to assert that the nation's money and

[6] R. C. McGrane, *The Panic of 1837* (Chicago: University of Chicago Press, 1924).
[7] Robert E. Chaddock, *The Safety Fund Banking System in New York* (Washington, D.C.: Government Printing Office, 1910).
[8] S. A. Caldwell, *A Banking History of Louisiana* (Baton Rouge: Louisiana State
University Press, 1935).

banking problems were resolved with these developments, even though other states were soon imitating these advances. Indeed until a national system had been established this could scarcely have been the case. The fight, in other words, was to go on as the business interests sought to strengthen this pillar of the economy they were seeking to build. At the same time, however, it is not too much to say that by 1842 the major elements of today's tremendously complex financial organization were already in place. A base of rarely seen specie holding up a superstructure of bank notes and deposit currency, the whole undergirded by a public policy or regulatory framework itself largely hidden beneath the surface of the economic process as long as the mechanism is functioning smoothly, forms the system that has provided one of the most essential ingredients of modern industrialism.

WIDENING THE "EXTENT OF THE MARKET"

Adam Smith, today acclaimed as the greatest prophet of industrialization, made much of the fact that division of labor is limited by the extent of the market. By this he meant that minute specialization of function (as, for example, in a modern factory) is not technologically feasible unless goods are to be produced in large quantities and, hence, is not economically sound unless this great volume of output can then be effectively marketed over a large area. In this characteristically penetrating fashion did the father of economic orthodoxy single out transportation as one of the keys to industrial progress.

In one sense it could be said that American leadership did not need lessons from faraway Scotland on the importance of transportation. Since the appearance of the United States as a nation, improvements in this area of the economy had consistently been a major economic policy issue. However, just as the need for an effective medium of exchange was made much more acute when the nation embarked upon a manufacturing career, so had this development given to transportation a new significance. Whereas during the first quarter of the nineteenth century the central concern had been keeping the new union from falling apart, the problem now became that of providing one of the conditions without which a future so plainly marked out could not be fulfilled.

Yet so abstract a motivation as this would scarcely explain the suddenness with which a new zeal for internal improvements swept over the country. For this another factor was primarily responsible. In 1825 the Erie Canal was completed, joining New York and Buffalo, and from the very beginning it was apparent that that ambitious undertaking was to be crowned with dramatic success. This event stirred men's imaginations as never before with the possibility of creating a network of transportation lines closely connecting every part of the country with every other part. Challenged by this vision, men in all sections of the land set to work to make a nation's dreams come true.

It is worth emphasizing at the outset that few traces of the class conflict so vital in other areas of economic policy became involved in this expansion. Nor was there as yet any significant interference from the sectional clash which was later to extend itself to this field. Indeed, as long as the role of the federal government remained small there was no way in which the slavery controversy could have intervened. The only friction of consequence associated with this movement was a more or less friendly rivalry between the several tidewater areas for advantage in securing an economic hinterland in the Ohio and Mississippi River valleys. Every urban center on the Atlantic seaboard joined actively in this competition, a fact explaining much of the feverishness of this new transportation expansion.[9]

A case in point will illustrate this aspect of the transportation craze which engulfed the country after 1825. Less favored in the terrain available to her than New York, Pennsylvania nonetheless determined to make a bid for the Ohio valley hinterland. Her solution to this problem included a railroad from Philadelphia to Columbia, a canal from Columbia to Hollidaysburg, a railroad equipped with cable cars designed to carry canal boats to traverse the steepest part of the Pennsylvania Alleghenies, and finally another canal terminating at Pittsburgh. Rising to a height of 2,200 feet above sea level as compared with Erie's 650, burdened with 174 locks as against 84 on the Erie, and requiring three transfers of lading en route, it is clear why the Pennsylvania Public Works was never a serious competitor of New York's solution to the same problem.

Equally clear, however, and this is the most important point for present purposes, is another fundamental fact about "the canal era." There was not opened up here a field in which private enterprise could hope to function effectively. On the one hand, whereas the cost of a turnpike would typically be calculated in tens of thousands of dollars, a canal of any consequence at all would run into millions of dollars. The Erie Canal, for example, cost in excess of $5 million, while Pennsylvania's "Main Line" cost $10 million. On the other hand, many of the projects were undertaken largely on the basis of expectations of future development, and even if enough private

[9] Henry V. Poor, *History of the Railroads and Canals of the United States of America* (New York: J. H. Schultz & Co., 1860).

capital had been available this risk would have limited private investment in these operations. It is, in fact, one measure of the risk actually involved that only a small proportion of the internal improvement undertakings during this period actually proved to be economically justified from the standpoint of return on investment.

The obvious consequence of this situation was that the bulk of the financing of canals was done by governments, most typically, perhaps, through the sale of government bonds. This method of financing, moreover, was frequently combined with government ownership and operation, although arrangements were often made to transfer control to private hands when the facility was ready for use. It was, in other words, the rare exception for a canal of this period to be owned and operated from the beginning by private managers, and even in such cases the public credit was often one of the most important resources exploited.

No state in the country escaped this fever; when the canal era came to an end in the late 1830's every state had a burden of indebtedness bearing mute testimony to its involvement. Several states in fact practically bankrupted themselves in this cause, repudiating debts incurred during this decade.[10] In all, $174 million was raised by state governments through bond flotations between 1820 and 1838, chiefly for this purpose, and more than $72 million was borrowed by the three states of Louisiana, New York, and Pennsylvania alone. Even the federal government was drawn into this orgy before it spent itself. To various canal projects in several western states, Congress granted 4,000,000 acres of public lands and, in addition, subscribed more than $3 million to the stock of canal companies, primarily the Chesapeake and Ohio Canal.

It would be putting the matter mildly to say that a large part of this zeal for canals was misguided. Although there were a few instances in which these facilities made a major contribution to America's economic development, it soon became apparent that men had raised their hopes too high in accepting the canal as the solution to the country's problem of long-distance, bulk transportation. Furthermore, the striking success and expansion of the railroad is not as significant a consideration at this point as is often thought. The canal actually retarded the railroad during a period in which too many of those in leadership positions could only see the latter as supplementary to the former, and when canal-building fell victim to depression there were still fewer miles of railroads than of canals.

[10] R. C. McGrane, *Foreign Bondholders and American State Debts* (New York: The Macmillan Co., 1935); and B. U. Ratchford, *American State Debts* (Durham: Duke University Press, 1941).

However, for present purposes little interest attaches to successes and failures of this dramatic era in American economic history as such—or even to the reasons for the large element of failure which did result. Its significance lies rather in what it reveals about the period in which it occurred. So determined were Americans at this time to develop their facilities for transportation as rapidly as advancing technology would permit, and so little impressed were they with the desirability of minimizing the economic functions of government, that in the face of a long succession of frustrations and defeats in the canal field the very governments which had endured these frustrations and suffered these defeats promptly assumed the identical role with respect to the railroad.[11]

The forces behind this alternative approach to a foundation upon which an industrial society might be built were continuous with those behind the canal movement. There was the same intense rivalry between Atlantic port areas for advantage in exchange with the West. In the interior, too, this same insistence upon immediate action was widespread, based upon the (no doubt partially correct) assumption that special rewards would be available for firstcomers. And above all the railroad, even more than the canal, required such a large capital outlay that rapid development on a purely private enterprise basis was quite out of the question.

The wide variety of aids given to the nation's first railroads can be seen particularly in the charters they were given by state governments. Thus, most of these documents included sweeping privileges of eminent domain, and many granted monopoly rights that were even more valuable. (Imagine the value of exclusive rail transportation rights between New York and Philadelphia, as in the case of the Camden and Amboy Railroad in New Jersey.) Railroads were often given tax exemptions of varying degrees, and on occasion the right to raise money by lottery or by going into the banking business. A variation of this latter approach was to require state banks to buy railroad stock as a condition for receiving their own charters.

Not content with the aid which could be rendered these projects through charter provisions, furthermore, state governments even went into the railroad-building business themselves. Pennsylvania, as already noted, included two railroad links in her ambitious push to the West. In the South both Virginia and Georgia entered this field with much success, compensating for private capital shortages which would otherwise have hampered general economic development. To

---

[11] B. H. Meyer, *History of Transportation in the United States Before 1860* (Washington, D.C.: Carnegie Institution, 1917); and J. L. Ringwalt, *Development of Transportation Systems in the United States* (J. L. Ringwalt, 1888).

the west Indiana and Illinois both undertook state projects, although it was left for Michigan to plan a really aggressive program of state railroad construction. The city of Troy, New York, even embarked upon an experiment in municipal ownership. Most governmental railroads soon reverted to private hands, but this is an unimportant detail by comparison with the fact that these lines were added to the rail network under essentially governmental auspices.

And even more important than either charter privileges or direct ownership was the financial aid given private railroad companies by both state and local governments. In Massachusetts, for example, the state in which private capital was most plentiful, the Western Railroad was voted $4,600,000, and a second line across the state was later granted as much if not more. New York issued bonds amounting to $3 million to subsidize the Erie Railroad and advanced $6 million additional to nine other railroad companies, while towns and cities in New York made available some $30 million for railroad projects. Moreover, these are only samples. Throughout the South and the West state and local governments were particularly generous where railroads were concerned. In all it is estimated that perhaps $100 million was borrowed by state governments for this purpose, and that at least one-fifth of the construction cost of the early railroads came from local and municipal contributions.

Again, too, the federal government could not remain completely aloof.[12] Thus a number of railroad surveys were conducted by this agency, such aid proving especially important because of the extreme scarcity of trained engineers at this time. More valuable from a purely financial standpoint was a reduction in tariff duties on iron used in railroad construction—an assistance available, however, only until 1843 when pressure from domestic manufacturers of railroad iron forced a change in policy. But if the role of the federal government during this period did not permit it to do more for the railroads, it is nevertheless true that, speaking generally, government assumed a paternalistic responsibility for the development of this industry— and through it for the development of a manufacturing economy which could never have been created in the absence of the railroad.

A NEW FORM OF BUSINESS ORGANIZATION

One other major development was required before the American economy could be said to have been ready for the industrial future

[12] Lewis H. Haney, *A Congressional History of Railways in the United States* (Washington, D.C.: Carnegie Institution, 1915), Vol. I; and Coordinator of Transportation, *Public Aids to Transportation* (Washington, D.C.: Government Printing Office, 1939), Vol. II.

awaiting it. The proprietorship and partnership types of business organization were a totally inadequate basis on which to build such an economy. Early in the nineteenth century the thoughts and energies of businessmen had begun to wrestle with this problem; and since the federal government exercised no responsibilities in the field of charter granting, these efforts had also necessarily focused upon state legislation.

The principal shortcomings of existing organization types were twofold. First, the death of a proprietor or a partner frequently results in major readjustments within the firm. The heirs of the deceased are normally entitled to make whatever disposition of their inheritance they desire; and if this means that some or all of the firm's assets have to be placed on the market, the result can easily be a serious crippling of its capacity to earn a profit. A closely related difficulty is the fact that the death of a partner legally dissolves the partnership arrangement, which often creates problems over and above those associated with the distribution of resources at inconvenient times.

Second, both proprietorships and partnerships are subject to what is known to the law as unlimited liability, which means that the owner or owners are held legally responsible for the liabilities of the concern to the limit of their own assets. This being the case, a man would go into a business with others only if he had almost as much confidence in their ability and integrity as he had in his own and, what is perhaps more important, only on the condition that he is to have an important share in deciding what is to be done in the name of the concern. Such rigorous conditions attached to business expansion sets fundamental limits to the size of the firm in three ways. In the first place, the number of people in a given individual's circle of friends and acquaintances who meet these rigid qualifications will naturally be small. In the second place, the equal sharing of management responsibilities is apt to create an impossible internal situation as soon as the number of people involved exceeds three or four. And finally, even if this management problem did not create excessive friction, few people would be willing to invest a substantial sum of money under conditions of unlimited liability if management were in fact widely shared.

Of course, these difficulties are inherent in these forms of enterprise; they did not suddenly come into existence. By the same token it does not follow that such disabilities are necessarily fatal, for important public purposes might be served by compelling businessmen to bear with these particular inconveniences. Indeed, it was just this assumption on which early nineteenth-century public policy in this field rested. The problem was rather that underlying economic conditions were changing so drastically that inconveniences which had been tolerable were rapidly becoming intolerable. The forced sale of a firm's assets is one thing when those assets consist primarily of a small ship or an inventory of goods; it is a very different thing when those assets include large quantities of fixed and highly specialized capital as in a modern manufacturing concern or a railroad. Likewise rigid limits on the number of individuals who contribute capital to a given firm was of much less significance before the most efficient technology available dictated production on a large scale. Ways were rapidly being discovered by which scarcity could be turned into, if not abundance, at least a less oppressive scarcity; but if these were to be utilized, economic organization would have to undergo considerable modification.

The need was obvious. A type of business organization would have to be developed which would enjoy a legal existence independent of the individuals who contributed capital to it or gave it direction, and which would at the same time impose upon its owners limited rather than unlimited liability. Fortunately, moreover, the prototype for such an organization already existed as a part of the legal-institutional framework inherited from Great Britain. The difficulty was that the corporate form of business organization was not yet allowed in fields in which private profit was a major consideration. Put differently, corporate charters were typically thought of as a *privilege* available to public welfare enterprises rather than a *right* available for general business purposes. As a result, a limited liability charter could be secured only by special act of a state legislature.

This, therefore, was the obstacle that had to be overcome; special charter acts had to be replaced by the concept of incorporation as a right available to all legitimate businesses.[13] Victory was in time achieved as a result of two primary factors. On the one hand, the legislatures of the several states became burdened with a mass of applications for charters in private profit fields closely identified with the public interest—for example, transportation companies of all kinds and banks. On the other hand, the argument was made that a general law would eliminate the corruption, monopoly grants, and delay in the transacting of other legislative business, inevitable under the special charter procedure.

A glimpse at the major forces involved in this half-century-long struggle is also revealing. Most fundamentally there was here a con-

---

[13] C. C. Abbott, *The Rise of The Business Corporation* (Ann Arbor: Edwards Brothers, Inc., 1936); and J. S. Davis, *Essays in the Earlier History of American Corporations* (Cambridge: Harvard University Press, 1917).

flict between the older agrarian emphasis on a community of independent, self-reliant human beings, and the newer businessman's conception of an individualism centering around independent, self-perpetuating business firms—with the former group interpreting unlimited liability as a device making it easier for the few to exploit the many. After several dozen special charters had been granted within a particular state, however, there invariably developed cross pressures greatly weakening the case of the advocates of incorporation as a privilege. All too often those who had already been accorded this privilege took a stand against granting similar privileges to potential competitors, with the result that those contending against monopoly frequently found themselves fighting side by side with notorious monopolists. To this incongruity another inconsistency was added. The insistence upon special incorporation laws on the ground that charters could thereby be more effectively reviewed from the standpoint of public interest came face to face with the fact that so many charter applications were being made that they could not be properly reviewed. Consequently the opposition to general incorporation laws steadily disintegrated.

TABLE 1. A NEW FORM OF BUSINESS ORGANIZATION

Decade	Number of Corporate Charters Granted in New Jersey
1791-1800	10
1801-1810	42
1811-1820	67
1821-1830	76
1831-1840	178
1841-1850	200
1851-1860	577
1861-1870	1002

Source: J. W. Cadman, *The Corporation in New Jersey* (Cambridge: Harvard University Press, 1949), pp. 206-8. Used by permission.

As could be expected, the bars came down slowly at first. General laws were made applicable to particular fields, often liability was limited only in part, and there were frequent reversals of public policy as partisan politics operated against the background of the special conditions existing within each state. Manufacturing, furthermore, was one of the last major fields to be brought within the scope of these laws. However, by 1837 final victory was in sight; in that year Connecticut passed the nation's first law permitting incorporation for any legitimate purpose. By 1846 this procedure was already so taken for granted that Iowa's constitution of that year contained a clause prohibiting incorporation by special legislative enactment. From that point forward the law of business organization constituted no bar to industrial advance.

The folklore of American economic history has long associated laissez faire with this early period of business development in the United States. It is by now evident how great a distortion this is.[14] Although it is true that the federal government was not deeply involved in business-government relationships during those years, state governments more than made up for this deficiency. Slowly but steadily, subtly, but nonetheless effectively, an environment fully congenial with industrialism was being created; and the active assistance of government was one of the most important single factors in this process. By the time the railroad had established itself, say at midcentury, the necessary framework was essentially complete.

QUESTIONS FOR DISCUSSION

1. Why did manufacturing become more important than mercantile activities after the War of 1812? Could this have happened if public policy had not been favorably inclined?

2. Differentiate between the old and the new mercantilism. How did the problem of trade with the West Indies become involved in this transition?

3. In what ways was manufacturing aided by government directly?

4. Explain the functions of patent and bankruptcy legislation in a dynamic economic system. How are these functions performed?

5. What were the "foundations" referred to in the title of this chapter? Explain why each of these developments can appropriately be so named.

6. Explain the nature of the central problem associated with the creation of a satisfactory medium of exchange. In what ways was this problem being met at this time?

7. Why were private capital and private enterprise inadequate to the task of developing an improved transportation system during this period?

8. In what ways was the corporation superior to alternative types of business organization? Was the corporate form indispensable to the nation's industrial development?

9. Would industrialization have been seriously handicapped if laissez faire had been the underlying public policy toward business during these years?

10. Was the absence of laissez faire a policy hammered out of conflict, or did it reflect a fairly fundamental community consensus?

14 O. Handlin and M. F. Handlin, *Commonwealth, A Study of the Role of Government in the American Economy: Massachusetts, 1774-1861* (New York: New York University Press, 1947); Louis Hartz, *Economic Policy and Democratic Thought: Pennsylvania, 1776-1860* (Cambridge: Harvard University Press, 1948); M. S. Heath, *Constructive Liberalism: The Role of the State in Economic Development in Georgia to 1860* (Cambridge: Harvard University Press, 1954); and J. N. Primm, *Economic Policy in the Development of a Western State: Missouri, 1820-1860* (Cambridge: Harvard University Press, 1954).

Chapter 6

An Edifice Completed

The tendency to identify particular policies with the public interest has given rise to an erroneous conception of nineteenth-century laissez faire. Thus the view is often held that this policy was *the* common good during this era, and that in later years certain modifications of laissez faire then took on this status. A brief recapitulation of one of the more important aspects of the democratic process, however, will put such ideas in a more accurate perspective.

Although there is no desire here to minimize the extent to which it was supported by consensus, the fact remains that laissez faire has always been essentially *a spurious common* good competing for acceptance with other interpretations of the public interest. Stated differently, laissez faire was the policy preference of a group of more or less homogeneous interests that saw in these arrangements an environment especially suitable to their purposes, and which they in consequence endeavored to bring about by presenting in the most glowing terms the values which would accrue therefrom to the community as a whole. And to put this matter still more bluntly, laissez faire seemed by business interests generally to be a philosophy of the relationship between government and business within the framework of which America's vast resources could be most profitably exploited.

INDUSTRIALISM VERSUS SLAVERY

Nor is this the only misunderstanding of that philosophy requiring explicit clarification. Popularly interpreted, laissez faire means "to let alone," in the sense of economic activity uninfluenced by government. But this implies that what was desired was a *neutral* government, whereas in actual fact the government cannot be neutral. In practice a government must support an order approximating the status quo or it must give way to a government which will establish and support a different order. The laissez faire demand, thus, was for a government which would support the kind of economic order most congenial to business profits. Here, in short, is why laissez faire in this sense of minimum government was not insisted upon from the first in this country, why this cry was not loudly heard here for a full half century after it became powerful in England.[1] The necessary economic order had to be created first. A laissez faire government was one thing after the major elements of industrialism had been put in place; such a government would have been intolerable to the architects of the new society in 1800.

The long delay in establishing laissez faire in the United States can be explained in more specific terms, too. It was a significant fact in this connection, for example, that (a phenomenon so characteristic of a vigorous democracy) the business interests themselves were by no means always united on public policy questions. Thus certain kinds of businessmen would have liked to see imprisonment for debt and every other traditional safeguard against property losses through debtor insolvency retained. In the banking field, similarly, one of the major obstacles to a more rapid advance toward the monetary system needed in an industrial society was the vested interest the state banking community had in looser arrangements. Even in the case of corporation legislation, it was most exasperating to businessmen the way other businessmen became aggressively conservative as soon as they had received their own charters.

But this difficulty was minor by comparison with the crucial fact that the United States was still an agrarian society, the consequence of this fact being that the development of the kind of economic order on which a laissez faire system could be built was only possible insofar as the entrepreneur group could find support for the indicated status quo changes outside its own ranks. Indeed, the extent to which such support was available correlates closely with the speed of the institutional evolution in particular fields.

At one end of this scale was the improvement of transportation facilities. With no ideological obstacles intervening here, with little opposition except from enterprises threatened with catastrophe as a result of economic progress, this advance moved forward almost as rapidly as technology permitted. At the other extreme were innovations in banking, where almost no progress had been made in securing monetary uniformity through federal legislation because both farmers and workers were opposed. In between stood bankruptcy and corporation legislation. With respect to the former a slow and

---

[1] Note that the classic statement of the laissez faire philosophy, Adam Smith's *Wealth of Nations*, was published in 1776.

steady progress was maintained by means of a coalition between entrepreneur-debtors, mechanic-debtors, and frontier farmer-debtors, while in the latter case it was in no small part the pressure of special charters in fields agrarian constituencies were actively interested in promoting that broke the back of the resistance to general incorporation laws.

However, the important conclusion to be derived from all this is not that laissez faire was born in this country on, say, January 1, 1850. On the contrary, what must now be emphasized is that in at least one major respect the economic order still fell short of the conditions deemed essential to the success of that policy. Although the business interests had gone far toward committing the several state governments to such of those conditions as these agencies were in a position to guarantee, they had as yet secured few commitments from the federal government. At a number of key points along this front the agrarian line had been stubbornly held, and until a few substantial victories were won in those areas laissez faire could not become a reality. Moreover, the principal antagonist here was not merely agrarianism; it was rather that peculiarly virulent brand of reactionary agrarianism espoused by nineteenth-century slaveowners.[2] Viewed from this standpoint, the significance of the year 1850 is best seen from the vantage point of the "Compromise of 1850," the temporary solution to the first great crisis created by the slavery controversy.

Frustration of the rising industrialism as a result of sectional conflict can be illustrated with respect to several policies. In two major ways, for example, this factor prevented an even more rapid expansion of the railway net. On the one hand federal aid to railroads was kept to the minimum, while on the other hand the long-dreamed-of railroad to the Pacific was delayed for at least a full decade.

For a number of reasons the principal aid the federal government was ultimately to give the railroads was grants of land from the public domain. Here was an asset which, on the side of the federal government, could be made available without making a direct charge on the taxpayer, and which, on the side of the railroad, was extremely valuable in a variety of ways. Timber and stone resources found on such lands could be used in building the line itself; the railroad's proximity to this land would attract settlers into the territory to be served by the road, thus providing the traffic needed to support the

---

[2] R. B. Russel, *Economic Aspects of Southern Sectionalism* (Urbana: University of Illinois Press, 1923); and J. G. Van Deusen, *Economic Aspects of Disunion in South Carolina* (New York: Columbia University Press, 1928).

line when built; and the sale of railroad land to these same settlers would even bring in a flow of cash revenue.

Unfortunately, however, southern defensiveness where its "peculiar" institution was concerned had reached such a peak of intensity that southern leaders saw insuperable constitutional objections to these grants. And since the South during much of this period was in political alliance with the agrarian West through the Democratic party, this policy had to be held in abeyance for the most part. To be sure, the fact that these particular projects would be helpful to the southern economy, coupled with the political genius of Stephen A. Douglas, did permit in 1850 federal land grants for the benefit of the Illinois Central and Mobile and Ohio Railroads. This act in turn furnished a precedent for several similar enactments. But a compromise requiring that such land be first granted to the states with the understanding that they would in turn convey it to the concerns for which it was intended was obviously a major limitation on the federal government's capacity to assist railroad-building in this way.[3]

The Pacific Railroad problem was geographical rather than constitutional. Southerners no less than westerners and easterners were eager to see such a contact with the west coast brought into being, but southerners no less than westerners also wanted this contact to have its eastern terminus in their own economy. A deadlock resulted which neither side was able to resolve in its own favor, and there was possible here no compromise such as was worked out with respect to land grants.

No doubt an even more frustrating consequence of sectionalism for industrial interests was the failure to raise some aspects of the banking question to the level of national policy. Here too, however, southern leadership was unalterably opposed. There was in that section of course the usual nineteenth-century agrarian fear of national banking legislation, a fear the South shared with the West. But the South had other objections as well, and these were if anything even more compelling. One of these was the ever present southern strict constructionism. Another had its origin in the South's resentment against "economic vassalage," a preoccupation now rising to the forefront of southern thinking. A national bank, it was felt, would so distribute its assets geographically as to accentuate the domination of the southern economy by eastern interests, and hence increase the North's capacity to "exploit" its southern partner.

[3] L. H. Haney, *A Congressional History of Railways in the United States* (Washington, D.C.: Carnegie Institution, 1915), Vol. II.

The compromise worked out on this issue, furthermore, was no compromise at all as far as the nation's industrialists were concerned. Reflecting labor's antipathy toward state bank notes (an antipathy much accentuated by the inflation precipitated when Andrew Jackson transferred the government's funds from the Second Bank of the United States to the so-called "pet" state banks), as well as the views of both agrarian groups, the solution effected after one of the most bitter and long-drawn-out political battles of this half-century was a device called the Independent Treasury System.[4] What this innovation was designed to accomplish was no less than the removal of federal government funds from all contact with the money market.

An approach to this problem more unsuited to the needs of a modern economy could hardly be imagined. Moreover, the most important shortcoming of the Independent Treasury from this standpoint was perhaps not even the fact that thereby the federal government forfeited all responsibility for the nation's principal circulating medium. Rather, the more important problem was the consequences for the money market of this attempted withdrawal of the federal government from contact with it. Thus the Treasury Department's disbursements and receipts were rarely in balance; sometimes income exceeded outgo, and sometimes outgo exceeded income. When income was in excess the government would withdraw money from the economy's income stream, in this way deflating the economy, and when outgo was in excess the result of government financial transactions was to create a proportional inflation. Although successive Secretaries of the Treasury did find ways to mitigate the worst of these consequences, there is no doubt that the nation in the Independent Treasury System took a long backward step in the struggle for a more modern monetary system.

But without question the keenest deprivation suffered by industrialists at the hands of the "slaveocracy," at least as industrialists of that day interpreted the situation, was the concerted and highly successful attack launched against the protective system. Gradually the West had slipped away from its close relationship with the East on that issue, and in time much of the protective structure so painstakingly constructed during the 1820's had been chipped away.[5]

There were a number of reasons for this change in political alignments. First, foreign legislation against American exports had not developed to the extent that had once been feared. Second, the west-

---

[4] David Kinley, *The Independent Treasury of the United States and Its Relations to the Banks of the Country* (Washington, D.C.: Government Printing Office, 1910).

[5] Edward Stanwood, *American Tariff Controversies in the Nineteenth Century* (Boston: Houghton Mifflin Co., 1903).

ern grain and meat economy had found a profitable "home market" in the South. Third, as things worked out, perhaps many westerners (in common with many economists both then and now) began to question the close connection between the tariff and a "home market" in the East. However, important though these factors undoubtedly were, the most significant development was probably the line-up of forces on the issue of public land policy. For when the liberalism in this field so desperately desired in the West was unequivocally opposed by easterners who feared the effects of such a policy on the prices of their land and labor, it was especially easy for westerners to help the South reduce the tariff in exchange for southern aid in achieving a more liberal land policy.

For some twenty years this coalition kept the duty level moving generally downward. And when in the late 1850's the union of South with West collapsed (when, in other words, the South became the most determined opponent of a more liberal land policy), the "slavocrats" were still able to win a major victory on this front. With a New Englander (Franklin Pierce of New Hampshire) in the White House, southerners worked out a political trade by which the duty level was lowered while giving New England textile manufactures a higher level of protection. For woolen goods this was accomplished by reducing the tariff on raw wool; on cottons the technique was to put this schedule in a lower rated class. With this success in turning manufacturer against manufacturer, the threshold of tolerance of southern ideals by eastern businessmen surely reached its lowest point.

VICTORY BY CIVIL WAR

But if the industrial East harbored a resentment against the South which had been long accumulating, it does not follow that those interests fanned the flames as the drift toward Civil War became more and more pronounced. Actually northern business firms were torn by a painful ambivalence; offsetting the fact that the South had bitterly and successfully opposed policies felt to be indispensable to business growth and development, it was also true that a profitable economic union existed between northern capitalists and the plantation economy.[6] So exclusively preoccupied was the South with the production of cotton that a very large share of all the capitalist-type services required in that section of the country (that is, banking, factoring, shipping, and manufacturing) were performed by eastern concerns.

---

[6] P. S. Foner, *Business and Slavery: The New York Merchants and the Irrepressible Conflict* (Chapel Hill: University of North Carolina Press, 1941).

Weighing these conflicting interests, businessmen as a group until late in the secession movement stood for a policy of maintaining the union at almost any cost in concessions to slavery.

On the other hand, however, though these interests were late-comers to the ranks of Civil War belligerency, it does not follow that they then accepted that status half-heartedly. Possibly if a basis upon which a secession without bloodshed could have been worked out, businessmen would have lent support to this solution. But it was in fact almost inevitable that the seceding states, whether jointly or separately, would develop a foreign economic policy which would not be pleasing to Boston, New York, and Philadelphia industrialists. Thus when in the course of time the Confederacy enacted a system of import duties (primarily for revenue) substantially lower than those prevailing in the North, the full support of businessmen in the task of coercing the South was at once available. The political alliance between industrial East and agrarian West which had been in process of formation for some time was now complete.

Nor was there any hesitation in these quarters about taking advantage of the dramatically different political situation the withdrawal of the South created. After a lapse of time barely sufficient to permit placing the administration of the war effort on a more or less solid footing, a comprehensive economic program was launched consisting of virtually every piece of legislation for which those interests remaining in the union had been long contending. Clearly there was in both East and West a strong feeling that hay should be put into the barn while the sun was shining.

In May, 1862, the cause of land policy liberalization achieved an unprecedented victory in the passage of the Homestead Act. Henceforth any settler could secure title to 160 acres of ungranted public land simply by cultivating it and residing on it for five years. To be sure, this policy was most immediately designed for the benefit of the agrarian West rather than the industrial East. However, in two ways the latter as well was to benefit from this enactment. First, western farmers were thereby made more willing to help businessmen enact the legislation they especially wanted. Second, the Homestead Act was the initial step in a program of throwing the public domain wide open from which eastern capitalists benefited far more than western farmers.

Two months later, at one fell swoop, the difficulties the slavery controversy had placed in the way of a more rapid railroad expansion were as decisively surmounted. Generous federal government assistance was authorized for the nation's first transcontinental railroad. The aid included large grants of public land, which grants were made directly to the concerns involved rather than through state governments. This achievement established a precedent which was to be followed many times before the nation's zeal for railroad-building began visibly to cool, and in the process set in motion a period of dramatic expansion in the railway net that did not come to end until the entire continent from the Atlantic to the Pacific was interlaced with parallel bands of steel.

Beginning in 1862, also, the tariff was converted into a veritable dream-come-true for protectionists. In mid-1862 a comprehensive internal tax measure was enacted which sought to bring in a revenue from a wide variety of economic activities. Then, in order to be certain that the previously existing margin of discrimination favoring domestic production was maintained, compensating duties against foreign goods were levied. Followed consistently throughout the war, this policy was sound enough in principle. But in the interest of time, as a result of the absence of southern opposition, and because exact compensations for internal taxes were extremely difficult to work out, errors were made in the direction of overcompensation far more frequently than in the opposite direction. By war's end there was simply no explanation but careless indifference if an industry was receiving a level of protection its leaders considered inadequate.

Not until the war was about half over, after the Union's finances had fallen into a most chaotic state, was it possible to make up for lost time in the banking field. When action did become possible, however, the changes brought about could not have been more sweeping. In 1863 the National Banking Act was passed creating the nation's first real national banking system, care being taken in this legislation to incorporate insofar as possible the best of prevailing practices in the states.[7] Thus, borrowing from New York's legislation, national bank notes were to be issued only against federal government bonds as collateral. In addition, this time borrowing from Louisiana (one of the few states in which specie payments had not been abandoned during the "Panic of 1857"), reserve requirements were stated in terms of both deposit and note liabilities. Recognition was also given to the semicentral banking functions being performed by banks in larger cities—by allowing banks in smaller communities to keep a part of their reserves in the larger banks and by requiring the latter banks to maintain proportionately larger reserves. And finally, in order to give the new national banking system every advantage in competition with the now deeply rooted state banking

---

[7] A. M. Davis, *The Origin of the National Banking System* (Washington, D.C.: Government Printing Office, 1910).

systems, a ten per cent tax was imposed on state bank notes with the result that they completely disappeared from circulation.

In one other way did the war period give impetus to the country's industrialization aspirations and proclivities. Manufacturing enjoyed an unprecedented prosperity. Government demand as such was perhaps the most important factor in this development, although the increase in general demand brought about by inflationary methods of war finance was almost as basic. Indeed, even the major economic problems associated with the war had a way of contributing to progress in this sector. Thus the loss of farm labor to the army greatly accelerated the output of farm machinery, while the sharp decline in cotton imports from the South forced a particularly rapid rate of expansion upon woolen textile producers.

Even the ending of the war did not mean an abrupt cessation of the tremendous advantages industrialism was reaping from disunion. Before the South could again wield an influence in national affairs, an influence which would be still greater now that the abolition of slavery had done away with three fifths representation for Negroes in the House of Representatives, she had first to regain her status within the union. Moreover, this could only be granted by her conqueror, and therefore the terms of the South's re-entry had to be determined by majority vote in the North. After a brief interlude known to history as "Presidential Reconstruction" during which Abraham Lincoln and Andrew Johnson endeavored to impose a "soft" peace that would have restored the defeated enemy to citizenship promptly, a Congress clearly dominated by those interests desirous of enacting and maintaining policies the South would be most likely to oppose secured the reins of power in Washington. From this point forward the basic reconstruction strategy was delay—the time thus gained to be used in fixing upon the nation as securely as possible conditions favorable to rapid industrialization.[8]

Whether or not the gains achieved along these lines were worth the bitterness this policy created cannot be determined with assurance. But there were gains. In part they took the form of the haste with which hundreds of millions of acres of the public domain were made available at little or no cost to various types of capitalistic enterprises such as mining, lumbering, ranching, and railroading (squandering the federal government's vast land resources, as the typical summary of this land disposal program expresses it); but perhaps even more important was the progress made on another front.

[8] H. K. Beale, *The Critical Year* (New York: Harcourt, Brace & Co., Inc., 1930).

Prior to the Civil War the federal government had secured most of its revenue from the tariff and the public lands. During that conflict this pattern had been altered drastically, with the result that the wartime tax structure was substantially more progressive and more burdensome to business operations than had been the case in the prewar period. A major task confronting the industrialist group, therefore, was to make federal taxation rest once again primarily on the nonbusiness sectors of the economy.

Repeal of the wartime internal taxes was the first objective. Given the long-standing antipathy to internal taxation in the United States, this goal (with the exception of liquor and tobacco taxes) was readily accomplished. The advantage here was threefold. First, a heavy burden of business taxation was lifted. Second, by insisting that the compensating import duties be retained, the level of effective protection was raised to unprecedented heights. Third, a higher tariff level would even go a long way toward replacing the revenue sources being abandoned—and thus help avoid the danger that replacement taxes would be levied which would also be burdensome to business. The second objective was repeal of the wartime income tax. Although here the opposition encountered was more formidable, success being delayed for several years as a result, this too was accomplished.

With taxation by the states centering around a property tax not yet made applicable to many varieties of business property, these changes in federal taxation gave the nation a tax structure which could scarcely have been more ideally suited to industrial development. Both railroad-building and manufacturing expansion required vast quantities of capital, a fact making extremely important the rate of capital formation and hence of saving. A system of taxation more conducive to capital accumulation than the one that now came to prevail would have been difficult to conceive.

The Last Great Obstacle Surmounted

It might be supposed that by this time every condition for the successful operation of a laissez faire economy had been fulfilled. One link in this chain, however, was still to be forged. And amid the political and social confusion resulting from the Civil War, even this step was taken.

The victory of the corporate form of business organization had left unsettled one major question concerning its legal status—perhaps only another way of saying that this controversy had never quite ended. If the life of the corporation was not bound up with the life of the individuals closely associated with it, was it then to live forever? Was the corporation to become a rival of the state from the standpoint of the right to permanent existence?

Actually, as soon as this question was asked in this way, a far more crucial formulation suggested itself. The fundamental question clearly was not relative longevity; what really mattered was the maintenance of a relationship of superior versus subordinate power. Specifically, what powers was the creator to retain over its creature?

Naturally, the corporation's proponents contended for as little distinction here as possible. Just as naturally those elements in the community that continued to distrust corporations wished to see this distinction maximized. And although in every other major respect the corporation gained steadily in function and prestige, the legal shadow under which it lived hovered constantly in the background.

In 1819 no less a figure than John Marshall had done his best to bring about an improvement in this situation.[9] Dartmouth College, a corporation chartered in 1769 by King George III, had brought to the federal courts a suit against New Hampshire charging that the legislature of that state had violated the Constitution by amending its charter. The Constitution expressly forbade state legislation "impairing the Obligation of Contracts"; if the Supreme Court would commit itself to the proposition that a corporate charter was in fact a contract, the legal position of the corporation might thereby become more securely established.

Of course Chief Justice Marshall could be counted upon to do precisely this—even though such a doctrine was dangerously close to saying that once a corporation was created the sovereign state could not stand between it and the economic and social well-being of the larger community. But since so extreme a view could hardly be tolerated for long, state legislatures were soon finding their way around it. By the simple expedient of reserving the right to amend within the charter document itself, using for this purpose the most general terminology, the intent of Marshall's decision was largely nullified.

Furthermore, the corporation's legal position from this standpoint continued to deteriorate, receiving in 1837 a severe setback administered by the Supreme Court itself.[10] The Charles River Bridge, a corporation, had been chartered by the Massachusetts legislature in 1785 to construct and operate for a period of seventy years a toll bridge across the Charles River between Charlestown and Boston. In

[9] *Trustees of Dartmouth College* v. *Woodward*, 4 Wheaton 519 (1819).
[10] *Charles River Bridge* v. *Warren Bridge*, 11 Peters 420 (1837).

1828 the legislature had authorized another company to erect a bridge only a few rods from the Charles River Bridge property, this new facility to be surrendered to the state and to be free of tolls after a period of time not exceeding six years. Suit was brought by Charles River Bridge, charging that the state had in effect granted it exclusive rights for the term of years specified in its contract.

Chief Justice Taney delivered the opinion of the Court. Coming directly to the heart of the question at issue, he summarily dismissed the exclusive rights contention by a neat use of the *reductio ad absurdum* technique. What if, he asked, such a rule were generally applied? What if the huge sums of capital invested in railroads were now to be placed in jeopardy by the promulgation of this philosophy, or what if the community were denied the benefits of technological advance wherever previously existing corporate charters would be made less valuable as a result? Besides, and this is the pronouncement which gives this case its enduring importance in American constitutional law, a state cannot be presumed to have abrogated a portion of its sovereignty unless that intention has been unmistakably made clear in the charter language. "The whole community . . . have a right to require that the power of . . . advancing the public prosperity, shall not be construed to have been surrendered or diminished by the State, unless it shall appear by plain words that it was intended to be done." Thus bluntly did the Supreme Court insist that the right of a government to govern (the so-called police power) is superior to the rights granted by it to its own subjects.

Unquestionably the Chief Justice was on sound ground here. There was, however, another side to this issue. Corporations with their immense investments in fixed and specialized capital obviously require a stable legal environment; nothing would have destroyed the foundation on which the modern economy was being built more quickly than the subjection of helpless, illiquid capital to the whims of newly elected legislators. But if the required environmental stability could not be achieved by way of the contract clause of the Constitution, as was apparently the case, another approach would have to be devised. By the time the Civil War broke out, conservatives had been genuinely troubled by this problem for a long time.

It will not be argued here, as it is by some students of this period, that the due process clause in the Fourteenth Amendment was the product of a deliberate conspiracy (although it must be confessed that circumstantial evidence supports this conclusion). Suffice it to stress instead the following points regarding this episode in constitutional evolution. First, the wording of the Fifth Amendment could hardly help impressing men searching for a way to protect corporations against arbitrary state action: "nor shall private property be taken for public use [in this case by the federal government] without just compensation." Second, such protection for the nation's corporations, initiated as it was at the height of "Congressional Reconstruction," was so clearly in accord with the spirit of these times as evidenced by the entire pattern of reconstruction legislation. Third, when this amendment was discussed most people were thinking only in terms of protecting Negroes from their erstwhile masters rather than protecting corporations from the sovereignty of state legislatures. Fourth, the first seventy-five years of its life saw the due process clause of the Fourteenth Amendment ("nor shall any State deprive any person of life, liberty or property, without due process of law") used predominantly in the interest of corporations rather than in the interest of the colored race.

With the ratification of the Fourteenth Amendment, it can be said that the last great obstacle to a laissez faire society was surmounted. It is, in other words, no coincidence that only rarely and timidly prior to the Civil War had the business interests attacked the broad conception of positive governmental responsibilities then current, whereas after the war such attacks became frequent and bitter. Having achieved an underlying social order highly consistent with profit-making, and particularly having forged constitutional restraints preventing governments from interfering with such activity, the stage was set for a reversal of the traditional business philosophy toward government. From a view which can with some accuracy be described as paternalistic, businessmen now turned to the idea that government should be kept as aloof from business affairs as possible.

A GLIMPSE INTO THE FUTURE

Perhaps the only way to achieve a realistic understanding of the meaning of laissez faire is to view particular segments of its operation in slow motion. Although it may be fully satisfactory for some purposes simply to use the phrase "to let alone" and inquire no further into details, for other purposes this conception is inadequate. Those people who lived through the years immediately following the Civil War formed their impressions of and reacted to laissez faire on the basis of a few intimate glimpses of its working as events unfolded week by week and month by month. Because the next stage in the evolution of government-business relationships in this country was a consequence of these reactions, it will be appropriate to observe the unfolding scene through the eyes of contemporaries.

The Erie Railroad[11] got its start in life at a time when businessmen were looking to state governments for a variety of aids. It was, therefore, not at all outside the normal course of events that work on this great enterprise began on the strength of $1.5 million in stock subscriptions and a $3 million loan from the state of New York. Nor was there a significant departure from customary modes of procedure when in 1845, the half-completed Erie now bankrupt, the state helped the company back to solvency by converting the earlier loan into a gift.

But that was in 1845. Twenty years later the financial assistance of the government was not needed, and, far more important, it was by that time broadly insisted that corporate affairs were essentially independent of the chartering agent.

In the spring of 1866 the Erie was again in financial difficulty. Assistance on this occasion, however, was forthcoming from a private source—the Erie's treasurer, Daniel Drew. In exchange for collateral security in the form of 28,000 shares of unissued but authorized Erie stock and $3 million worth of unissued but authorized bonds which could be converted into stock at the option of the holder, Drew made available $3.5 million to his company. Then, having laid these plans long in advance, he began to sell Erie short. Immediately Wall Street "bulls" began to tingle with excitement. If this great "bear" could be cornered, millions might be made out of his frantic struggles to extricate himself. These counterstrategies proceeded according to plan, until Drew would indeed have been trapped if he had had to depend upon shares already in the market. But he didn't. As the "bulls" began closing in for the kill, Drew dumped his 58,000 shares of new stock on a totally unsuspecting Wall Street, driving the price from 95 to 50. It was the "bulls" who were trapped.

While this drama was being acted out on "the Street," an event which was to have tremendous consequences for the Erie Railroad was taking place elsewhere in the state. The New York Central Railroad was passing into the hands of Cornelius Vanderbilt. Largely because the Erie was a major competitor of the Central for New York–trans-Appalachian traffic, Vanderbilt had already resolved to secure control of that road as well.

Not being a manipulator of the stripe of his opponents, and having the wherewithal for a direct assault in any event, Vanderbilt quickly set his brokers to the task of buying a controlling interest of Erie common. But the lord of the Central had reckoned without the greedy ruthlessness of the Erie managers. If the "Commodore"

[11] E. H. Mott, *Between the Ocean and The Lakes: The Story of the Erie* (New York: J. S. Collins, 1902).

wanted Erie stock, they determined that he should have it—and from their vantage point in control of the Erie's corporate machinery they prepared to let him have all he wanted. The company's charter forbade the issuance of stock at less than par, and since the market for Erie was well below this figure another stock issue was out of the question. However, bonds could be issued convertible into stock at the market rate. A total of $10 million of such bonds were issued and instantly converted, and soon Vanderbilt's agents were purchasing stock certificates on which the ink was barely dry. As one of the conspirators remarked: "If this printing press don't (sic) break down, we'll give the old hog all he wants of Erie."

To be sure, legal complications did arise from this encounter, but here also the Erie group came out on top. As a precautionary measure they first moved the executive offices of the Erie Railroad to a hotel in nearby Jersey City, later applying for and being granted a New Jersey charter. The main battle was then staged in Albany, where a bill was proposed to the state legislature authorizing the recent issue of convertible bonds and where votes were almost openly for sale at $5,000 to $25,000 each. After this expensive legislative campaign (managed on the Erie side by none other than Jay Gould himself) was won by Drew and his colleagues of high finance, a compromise was worked out through which Vanderbilt was given back most of his money and allowed two seats on the Erie board of directors in exchange for his promise to drop all pending legal actions.

The Erie manipulations were exclusively a state government affair. But that similar operations were also prevalent during these years where the federal government was involved can as easily be demonstrated.

Work on the Union Pacific Railroad[12] had gotten under way slowly at first, one of the primary reasons being the difficulty of finding contractors willing to assume the great risks involved on the basis of unlimited liability. To remedy this difficulty Oakes Ames, a prominent Massachusetts financier and a member of Congress, developed plans to make use of a corporation instead. After investigating a number of available charters, that of the Pennsylvania Fiscal Agency was selected as the most likely candidate. Accordingly, the outstanding stock of this currently inactive concern (chartered in 1859 for the general purpose of building railroads in the South and West) was purchased. The name was changed to the Credit Mobilier of America, a branch office was established in New York where all

[12] H. K. White, *History of the Union Pacific Railway* (Chicago: University of Chicago Press, 1895).

important business was to be transacted, and the brand-new construction company was ready for action.

Note, now, the anomalous situation which was thereby created. Large grants of public land and millions of dollars worth of government bonds had been made available to the Union Pacific Railroad Company. The primary stockholders of that corporation, men whose first concern might reasonably have been expected to be the railroad which was to be built, in turn became the principal stockholders of the Credit Mobilier as well. In this dual capacity these men were forced to choose between their short-term interest in construction company profits and their longer-term interest in railroad company dividends. The former won out, and by the time the Union Pacific and the Central Pacific were joined in 1869 some $16 million had been channeled from the railroad company to the pockets of construction company stockholders, and the completed railroad was left in a precarious financial condition.

What a "reasonable" profit for an undertaking such as this would have been is extraordinarily difficult to say. But that it was recognized by the people involved that what was being done was flagrantly improper is clearly indicated by the precautions taken to prevent Congressional interference. To Ames was entrusted the task of looking after the syndicate's affairs in Washington, and an important part of the strategy adopted consisted of distributing shares of Credit Mobilier stock on highly favorable terms to influential members of the ruling administration. In the Congressional investigation which ensued, this trail of deliberate corruption was found to lead (among other places) to the Vice President of the United States, and Oakes Ames was expelled from Congress.

Now it must in all fairness be conceded that the Erie Railroad and Credit Mobilier cases were on the extreme side. On the other hand, however, it must at the same time be added that, as a type, they were almost routine. And as a society which had by no means adjusted to the new order began to grasp the significance of what was happening, two facts especially stood out. First, it was obvious even to the casual observer how flexible an instrument of business policy the corporation was and, hence, how great a role it was destined to play in creating an industrial civilization. Second, and this is perhaps the more important point for present purposes, it was already becoming clear how fundamental a concept the due process clause of the Fourteenth Amendment was to be in such a civilization.

So brazen in its manipulations was the era dubbed by Mark Twain "The Gilded Age" that historians have all too often become so absorbed in passing judgment that they have neglected their primary task—that is, the problem of understanding what was done in the context of those times. It is for this reason all the more important here to note such extenuating factors as were actually present. For example, it must be remembered that the nation had just ended a bloody civil war; surely it is legitimate to suggest that a little time is required to regain moral perspective after such a gigantic social upheaval. Furthermore, it is also worth emphasizing that a new social and economic order was being born, and that a transformation of this magnitude is almost invariably accompanied by a temporary blurring of accepted standards of behavior.

As a matter of fact, there is even some reason for suggesting that post-Civil War business ethics were not inappropriate to the problems then confronting the United States. With a fabulously rich resource base on which to build, and with an economy expanding both geographically and industrially at an unprecedented rate, perhaps a large degree of unhampered freedom to experiment was desirable. Stated differently, America's margin above subsistence was so great, and the readjustment opportunities for casualties were so favorable, that much flexibility could be permitted without serious damage. The standards of behavior then prevalent would in time become intolerable in a more highly urbanized and less rapidly developing economy, but for the moment they did serve a useful purpose.

This argument in turn must not be misunderstood. The point is not that because such a hugely successful economy was in fact created, the methods used by its creators are of no consequence. Rather, this relationship should be approximately reversed; while we are condemning many of the practices, for example, of the builders of American railroads, let us remember that the railroads did get built.

Questions for Discussion

1. What role was played by government in bringing about the conditions necessary for a laissez faire system?

2. What conflicts developed between businessmen as an environment suitable for laissez faire was being created? How were these resolved?

3. Discuss the early evolution of industrialism in terms of the agrarian-capitalist conflict.

4. In what ways did the South frustrate the emergence of industrialism, and why? How was this problem met?

5. What were the major defects of the Independent Treasury System from the standpoint of the needs of business development?

6. Explain the improvements brought about in the money and banking system by the passage of the National Banking Act.

7. Describe the other economic policies enacted during the Civil War, and indicate what groups primarily benefitted from each.

8. How was the post-Civil War reconstruction period used to advance the cause of industrialization?

9. What was the major problem still confronting the corporation at this time and how was it resolved?

10. What would have been the consequences for the nation's economy if the Dartmouth College decision had been adhered to and the Charles River Bridge case had been decided the other way?

11. Relate the due process clause to laissez faire.

12. What questions about the organization of society were raised by the corporate manipulations of the "Gilded Age"?

Part III
LAISSEZ FAIRE RESPLENDENT

Chapter 7

The First Great Challenge

In the same way that there exists a tendency to date the beginning of laissez faire many years prior to its actual appearance, so is there also a tendency to believe that laissez faire dominated the economy unchallenged for a longer time than was in fact the case. The truth of the matter is that this philosophy never did rule the American scene unopposed. From the first it found itself under attack by those segments of the economy least able to enjoy its fruits, and invariably these attacks were bitterly hostile.

Of course, this observation is in one sense only a repetition of an earlier one: that laissez faire was always only one interpretation of the public interest competing with others for the support of the larger community. However, much more than this is implied. When the success of laissez faire is explained in terms of a victory over active rivals, it becomes apparent that the traditional identification of that doctrine with an ideological position is incomplete. Side by side with laissez faire as a philosophy stands the political process out of which laissez faire policies emerged, and when this dimension is taken into account, a definition more adequate than the orthodox one can be formulated. By equating laissez faire with a government content to do little more than protect private property and enforce contract obligations, orthodoxy has clung to an interpretation unable to accommodate one of the most basic facts about this period in America's economic history—a policy of aggressive tariff protectionism. Note how this difficulty disappears when the following definition is adopted: *laissez faire means that pattern of policies which the business interests after the Civil War were politically powerful enough to establish.*

Lest there be doubt on this point, let it be understood that neither sneer nor facetiousness is intended. All that is involved is an attempt to formulate a definition including everything normally understood

119

to be meant when the concept being defined is used, while excluding everything not understood to be embraced by that concept. Furthermore, when institutional evolution after the Civil War is examined with this definition in mind, it is even more readily seen how appropriate it is. Overwhelmingly during these years successful government policies were those desired by businessmen (typically joined either by farmers or workers), while unsuccessful policies were those opposed by businessmen (again usually supported by other groups).

RATIONALE OF INDIVIDUALISM[1]

But even granting that laissez faire was not *the* public interest during this period, and that the ideological stand taken by that philosophy's proponents is not all there was to laissez faire, it is not to be concluded that the content of this doctrine is of no importance. On the contrary, precisely because it secured so strong a hold on the minds of several generations of Americans that exaggerations concerning it are still the rule rather than the exception, it is even more important to inquire into the sources of its strength. Only after that has been done does it become apparent why laissez faire captured the imagination of a new people in an enormously wealthy new land.

It is, for example, of the greatest significance that laissez faire was able to identify itself closely with democracy. At the heart of democracy lies a belief in the inherent worth of the individual personality, and insofar as this personality is respected the individual must be permitted (within the framework of majority rule) to pursue his own values in his own way. From the standpoint of economic organization, this requirement could plausibly be interpreted to mean that individuals were to be permitted to enter the business or profession of their choice, ally themselves with such other individuals as they cared to in achieving their economic objectives, manage the affairs of their business or professional life as seemed to them most appropriate, and enter into such business transactions with other individuals as were deemed profitable.

On the basis of this simple and obvious technique of relating itself to democracy, moreover, the doctrine of laissez faire was able to build an even more convincing ideological edifice. Different individuals are variously equipped to perform the day-to-day tasks on which the social order depends. Some can do best one kind of work; others perform more productively at another type of endeavor. This being the case, could it be doubted that society's work would be most

[1] John M. Clark, *Social Control of Business* (New York: McGraw-Hill Book Co., Inc., 1939), chap. iii.

efficiently done when every individual specialized in doing what he was able to do most proficiently, and then exchanged the fruits of his labor for the product of the labor of other individuals concentrating on other activities?

Nor does this emphasis upon individual well-being neglect the welfare of the community as a whole. Indeed since society is, to the individualist, only the individual writ large (since, in other words, social well-being is simply the sum of the separate well-beings of the individuals making up society), there is little point to the distinction often made between individuals on the one hand and the community on the other. Even so, however, when attention is focused upon the over-all economy the picture does not change. Economizing consists of allocating scarce resources to those uses in which their productivity will be greatest. If every individual is encouraged to put the resources he commands at work where they will yield him the largest returns, and if he is then allowed to spend these proceeds in those markets offering the best bargains, surely total social product will be at a maximum.

But are individuals not apt to take advantage of one another in the market, and is it not therefore necessary for the sovereign state to exercise some supervisory responsibilities over the exchange process? Not at all, comes back the prompt reply. In the first place, individuals meet in the market as equals; neither party to an exchange transaction has any more power to take advantage of his opposite number than the other. In the second place, every exchange is voluntary. Since individuals are free to commit themselves or not as they choose, it follows that every completed transaction is mutually beneficial or it would not be consummated. In the third place, the individual is the only proper judge of his own interest. If he finds it desirable to enter into a particular business relationship, by what logic can the government superimpose a contrary judgment?

At this point in the argument individualism is forced to make a vital concession, although it must be added that this concession is made without reservation by all but the most intensely business-minded advocates of laissez faire principles. Because in an exchange society everyone is dependent for his economic well-being upon relationships which no one is compelled to enter into with him, it is acknowledged that there must be no monopoly. No individual can be permitted to control so large a portion of the supply of a necessary item that his fellows are in effect forced to conclude bargains which are flagrantly one-sided. And not only must there be competition between the firms already operating within a given trade, but there must also exist a full and free opportunity for outsiders to come in.

All of this can appropriately be summarized in terms of the economist's model-ideal of so-called pure competition.[2] Where a large number of buyers meets in the market a large number of sellers, every member of both groups possessing the market information needed for striking the best possible bargain, an equilibrium will be established having the following characteristics. Every seller willing to sell at the prevailing price can find a buyer, and every buyer willing to buy at that price can likewise find a seller. On the production side all sellers will produce that volume of output consistent with lowest unit cost, while at the same time receiving a price only high enough to reimburse them for the costs incurred including a "normal" profit. Furthermore, this equilibrium will be more or less stable; no one having a desire to alter either output or price will have the power to do so, and no one having the power to make such changes will have the desire to do so. In short, in an individualist social order men are powerless to exploit one another because they are in the fullest sense of the term power-less.

And finally, this philosophy can be presented in an even broader sociological setting. A society must operate to a considerable extent on the basis of personal motivations—that is, self-interest. Always, however, these motivations must be "harnessed" to purposes the community as a whole approves, which means that whenever a serious gap appears between these two things society must either adjust its value system or modify its organization of punishment and rewards in such a way that self-interest dictates a different behavior. The unique feature of laissez faire, therefore, was not that it demanded a social order in which these requirements would be broadly met, but that it felt they would in practice best be met if the *formal* punishment-reward system were held to the smallest possible range of operation.   •

Midwestern Farmers at Bay

Surely this review of the fundamentals of economic individualism makes it clear enough why such a doctrine found ready acceptance in young America. Red-blooded frontiersmen necessarily acted on the belief that they were independent citizens; frontier life did indeed generate a crude sort of equality genuinely congenial with that postulated by laissez faire thinking. Surely, too, it is equally clear why individualism met with a warm response in industrialist circles. Already the seeds of a "big business" economy were being sown, and no forward-looking businessman needed to be told how advantageous would be a social order in which the large, elaborately organized

[2] Frank H. Knight, *Risk, Uncertainty, and Profit* (Boston: Houghton Mifflin Co., 1933), Preface to the Re-issue.

corporation was accorded the same social and legal status as a natural individual.

On the other hand, however, these same considerations make it even less to be wondered at that there were those who from the beginning looked upon laissez faire with frank suspicion. Men engaged in commercial agriculture fifty miles behind the frontier had much less reason than frontiersmen for thinking that their lives were governed by their own decisions. Inextricably enmeshed within the exchange nexus, their standard of living dependent upon railroad concerns and eastern wholesaler-manufacturers, these men felt a great deal less enthusiastic about equality between a person and a corporation than businessmen. Similarly workers, compelled to bargain as individuals with huge aggregations of machinery and real estate, were quick to note the tremendous difference between the bargaining power they possessd and that enjoyed by their employers.

If workers and farmers had joined forces against the new philosophy, laissez faire would unquestionably have had a different history. With the worker group becoming a power to reckon with in direct proportion as industrialization advanced, a political coalition between these two interests would have been irresistible. For a number of reasons, however, such an alignment was not achieved. First, the farmer's economy was built squarely upon private property and the prerogatives of ownership, whereas the success of the labor movement was already beginning to be identified with the establishment of certain human rights on a basis of equality with and often at the expense of property rights. Thus there was here an ideological gap almost identical with that separating workers from employers. Second, organized labor shortly after the Civil War decided that its greatest advantage lay in working within the industrial framework rather than in resisting it. If freedom of association (one of the major ingredients of laissez faire) were to be an important pillar of the new society, workers as well as businessmen could make good use of that fact. Third, because of the fundamental difference between the farmer and laborer economies, the two rarely felt economically oppressed at the same time;[3] the rise in prices which is welcomed by the farmer is a grave threat to the worker, and vice versa. And finally, such a gulf exists between the rural and urban standards of living that farmers could never quite understand why workers already receiving more money income for fewer hours of less arduous toil than characterized their own situation would find it necessary to press for higher wages or better working conditions.

[3] Norman J. Ware, *The Labor Movement in the United States, 1860-1895* (New York: Appleton-Century-Crofts, Inc., 1929).

These relationships, perhaps more than any other single factor, explain the success of laissez faire after the Civil War. The failure of the "enemies" of the business interests to unite against them placed this group in a most favorable balance-of-power position. By carefully choosing their allies as different policy issues rose to the decision level, they could play one adversary off against the other today and then reverse the process tomorrow. It is in fact remarkable, even in historical perspective, how effectively this strategy was used by the Republican party for almost three-quarters of a century.

However, it was not primarily for this reason that the first great challenge to laissez faire was launched by farmers alone, less than five years after the Fourteenth Amendment was ratified. To be sure the bulk of this action did take place in the capitals of several midwestern states, states boasting as yet little industrial development and hence having few laborers. But the reason it was farmers rather than workers who first drew bow is to be explained largely on other grounds. For example, an important point to note in this connection is that midwestern farmers had for half a century enjoyed the same balance-of-power position now being exploited by the business interests. That political advantage was already virtually lost, and this evolution would all the more certainly be soon completed if the pretensions of the corporation were to become the law of the land. Here was undoubtedly one of the primary factors helping the farmer time his first blow, as well as determine his selection of both opponents and weapons.

But great historical movements rarely if ever arise solely out of abstract ideas in the minds of leaders. In addition there must exist widespread discontent among the rank-and-file. From this standpoint especially is it easy to understand why the farmer chose this moment to declare war on corporate individualism.[4]

At the center of a wide circle of farmer grievances stood the railroad. Completely carried away by the possibilities for improved transportation offered by the new medium, the farmer had gone all out to hasten the progress of railroad building. He had made available his own resources in assisting the construction process directly; he had used his hard-earned savings to purchase railroad securities, often even mortgaging his farm for this purpose; he had enthusiastically consented to increases in his own taxes so that state and local governments might also help push this program along a little more rapidly. And all this the farmer had done with the expectation that the betterment of transportation facilities would bring immediate and great returns in the form of lower freight charges.

By 1870 it was apparent that these hopes had been exaggerated.

[4] S. J. Buck, The Granger Movement (Cambridge: Harvard University Press, 1913).

Although in the over-all railroads were being laid in place during this period at an unprecedented rate, very frequently specific projects were either abandoned soon after they were commenced or delayed so long that farmers despaired of ever getting their money back. Even more frequently the projects undertaken were substantially in advance of the availability of traffic which would one day justify their existence, again with the result that expected dividends were not forthcoming. To these difficulties were added the closely related fact that excessive quantities of securities were often issued (a practice known as "stock watering") and the fact that information about the fraud and corruption which surrounded much of the activity of corporations in those days was already becoming common property. As eastern creditors began foreclosing on mortgage debts incurred for the benefit of eastern railroad companies, men in the Middle West who made their living working with their hands were understandably not impressed.

Of course, if the transportation advantages so dearly bought had materialized, these peripheral frustrations would no doubt have been forgiven. Mortgages could then have been paid off, at least. But it was precisely at this point that the farmer suffered his greatest disillusionment. Railroads on the frontier typically enjoyed a monopoly of such traffic as was available, and even where prices were not elevated for this reason they were inclined to be high as a result of the small volume of business available to these high-fixed-cost concerns. Furthermore, wherever competition did promise to develop, it seemed that a business combination was invariably effected which abruptly removed this possibility for relief. Particularly when they became familiar with the generally lower level of rates prevailing to the east and at rail junction points did western farmers feel they were being seriously discriminated against.

TABLE 2. GRIEVANCE AGAINST THE RAILROADS

Representative Railroad Freight Rates in 1873 (cents per ton-mile)		
East of Chicago	1.16	1.26
West of Chicago	1.61	2.17
In the South	1.93	4.21

Source: F. A. Shannon, *The Farmer's Last Frontier* (New York: Rinehart & Co., Inc., 1945), p. 296. Used by permission.

There were, moreover, several ways in which the railroad was thought to be adding insult to injury. For one thing, farmers as yet unaccustomed to the implications of a corporate world were inclined to be suspiciously resentful of absentee ownership. For another, and this was of course closely related to resentment against absenteeism, there was much objective reason for believing that these "foreign" concerns were exercising an undue influence over local governments. And for still another, there was developing a pattern of personal discrimination which not only worked a hardship on those not favored with rate reductions but to an even greater extent contributed to the belief that railroad prices were arbitrary.

One other major source of hostility toward the railroads had to do with the federal policy of land grants to the railroads. These grants had awarded alternate sections of land to a number of western railroads in a strip ten to sixty miles wide depending upon a variety of circumstances. However, in order to make certain that these grants were of maximum value to the railroad, it was also provided that the alternate sections retained by the government would not be available for homesteading until the railroad's land had been taken up. The result was that new settlers had to choose between buying land near the railroad or taking advantage of the Homestead Act many miles away from effective transportation facilities. In a section of the country at a time when roads were almost impassable during certain seasons of the year, this was interpreted in the West as a most unfair procedure.

But despite this accumulation of grievances against a particular industry, there is abundant evidence suggesting that the farmer was not declaring war on the railroad as such but rather on the industrial economy now so rapidly replacing its agrarian precursor. Some of the farmer's wrath, for instance, was also directed against the middleman who stood between him and the consumer of his products, absorbing under the guise of performing essential distribution services what seemed to be an unreasonably large share of the consumer's dollar. Similarly the other side of the farmer's economy, the markets in which he bought for his own use, seemed to be so highly organized that the farmer was again at a disadvantage. Even the money market came in for its share of criticism; farmers compelled to pay the high interest rates which then prevailed, often losing their collateral in the bargain, can perhaps be pardoned for believing that these institutions were designed specifically for their exploitation.

The Supreme Court to the Rescue

Traditionally farmers in the United States had not been addicted to politics, perhaps primarily because political supremacy had historically been theirs without effort. This situation, however, abruptly changed after the Civil War. Aroused as they had perhaps never been before, farmers now began to band together for their own protection. The organization which, more than any other, was responsible for welding the farmer into an effective fighting force was the so-called Patrons of Husbandry or, more popularly, the "Grange," and the fight the farmer now waged is for this reason commonly referred to as the "Granger Movement."

The battle was fought simultaneously in a number of states, especially Illinois, Iowa, Minnesota, and Wisconsin. Here attention will be limited to developments in Illinois; not only was this a fairly typical case, but it was the action taken in that state which was so soon to make history by way of the Supreme Court in faraway Washington, D. C.

For some time public opinion in Illinois had been agitating for legislation subjecting railroads to control by the state government. Finding it difficult to make headway, however, because of prevailing scruples about the constitutionality of such action, proponents in 1869 succeeded in dominating a constitutional convention sufficiently to secure specific constitutional sanction for this kind of legislation. In that document railroads were declared to be "public highways," and the legislature was authorized to "pass laws establishing reasonable maximum rates of charges." A law passed in 1871 implementing this authority was the first enactment in the United States creating a commission armed with positive regulatory powers. This statute shortly became the inspiration and the model for the "Granger" legislation of other states.

Nor were farmers content, inflamed as they were against this their principal "enemy," to limit their political activity to the state level. In Congress in 1871 a law was passed ending grants of land to railroads, although this was clearly a case of locking the barn door after the horse had already been stolen. At this time, too, an investigation was ordered of the need for federal regulatory action in the railroad field. From the standpoint of concrete results, the Windom Committee was abortive, but its report is indicative of the temper of those times. Of the three recommendations made, two were quite radical. First, federal funds should be used to develop waterways where possible as competitors of the railroads. Second, the federal government should itself build and operate a railroad from the Mississippi River to the Atlantic seaboard as another way of maintaining competition in this industry and hence keeping rates at a reasonable level. Third, the government should exercise a degree of control over railway capitalization and financial policies.

Of course, the railroads fought tooth and nail against any and all infringements upon their corporate prerogatives, particularly those emerging from midwestern state legislatures. At the same time, however, taking the longer view, all this hue and cry must have seemed naive to many clear-sighted business leaders. Indeed, what could be more ludicrous than ending land grants at this stage of the game, or the idea of a federally owned and operated trunk line railroad. And as for regulatory legislation in the Middle West, surely the due process clause could be counted upon to stave off that threat. Already the courts were beginning to accept the view that the corporation is an individual for purposes of the Fifth and Fourteenth Amendments, and it seemed elementary that on this basis alone special railroad regulation would be invalidated. With high confidence, some of the leading railroads in the country started test suits on the long road to the Supreme Court.

But if thoughts of the Fourteenth Amendment were comforting to businessmen when the Granger legislation was being enacted, there was reason shortly thereafter for taking a somewhat less optimistic view. In one of the first cases involving the Fourteenth Amendment to come before that body, the Supreme Court handed down an opinion which rocked the world of conservatism to its foundations.

In 1869 the Louisiana legislature, as a police power measure designed more effectively to protect the health of New Orleans residents, had passed a law giving a certain slaughter-house company the exclusive privilege for twenty-five years of all the slaughtering business to be done within that city. A number of butchers whose franchises would now be valueless brought suit against the state, charging among other things that this act was an unconstitutional taking of private property without due process of law.

From today's vantage point it seems obvious that the question raised was a legitimate one, whether the Supreme Court upheld the charge or not. Imagine, therefore, the consternation created when the Court took the position that no federal issue was involved insofar as private property was concerned, because no property had in fact been taken.[5] The aggrieved butchers had been left by the state with every item of their property down to the last whetstone, and hence they had no complaint on that score.

Truly this was a stunning blow—and the shock was not softened by the knowledge that the Court's definition of property would be quite appropriate for the largely self-sufficient household economy which the United States had so recently been. Where goods are produced for use the concept of property is indeed synonymous with physical assets. But America was now clearly an exchange economy, and where goods are produced for exchange value resides

---

[5] *Slaughter-House Cases,* 16 Wallace 36 (1873).

not alone in physical property but also in intangible buyer-seller relationships. In such an economy, indeed, a firm with much costly equipment acquired to produce goods for a market has for all practical purposes no property if access to that market is cut off. A cold chill settled over the business community; on the basis of the Supreme Court's 1873 definition of property even a Fourteenth Amendment could be of small service to laissez faire proponents.

Against this background little encouragement could have been expected from the Granger cases when these reached the Court in 1876. But even though they had no doubt steeled themselves for another blow, there is reason for supposing that conservatives were not prepared for the devastating rebuff on that front they actually received.

The case which reached the Supreme Court first was one involving a Chicago elevator, a type of concern also included in the Illinois law. Obviously the urban elevator occupied a most strategic position in the distribution of western grain. The farmer normally came to the elevator when the supply of his product was most abundant and when his own financial resources were at lowest ebb. In this poor bargaining position he was compelled to take the offered price (and even to accept arbitrary grading standards) because as likely as not there would be only one elevator within reach; or, if more were available, both prices and standards would typically be on a basis agreed upon in advance among these theoretical competitors. Obviously, too, Chicago elevators were in an especially favorable position. Through them flowed a large proportion of the grain produced in several surrounding states, and here perhaps collusion between elevators had been carried farthest.

The brief presented by Munn and Scott attacked the Illinois legislation on four counts, any one of which would have been fatal. First, the regulated concerns were private and not public as asserted in the law. Second, the charters held by these companies contained no reserved right of the state to regulate, and therefore the restrictions in question constituted a flagrant violation of contract obligations. Third, the regulations imposed were contrary to the constitutional requirement that interstate commerce be the responsibility of the federal government. Fourth, the rates actually set were so low as to be a taking of private property without due process of law.

Building on foundations consisting of the nation's English common law heritage (including the concept of "just price" inherited from the middle ages) and the Charles River Bridge and Slaughterhouse decisions, Chief Justice Waite struck down every one of these contentions.[6] "From time immemorial," he said, it had been customary for governments to declare certain industries to be so "affected with a public interest" that special regulations could appropriately be imposed upon them, and the kinds of businesses included in the legislation at bar seemed to qualify for that status. On the matter of reserved rights, furthermore, the Court declared that the power of the state to protect the interests of its citizens is not forfeited by the failure of legislators to anticipate economic and social changes far in advance of their occurrence. Freely conceding that interstate commerce was involved, the Chief Justice even went so far as to assert that until the federal government acted in this field state governments might do so. And finally, echoing the definition of property promulgated in 1873, the Court observed that the remedy for inadequate rates lay at the polls rather than in the courts, for no judicial question was involved.

The Public Utility Concept

Institutional evolution is on occasion a most paradoxical phenomenon, and rarely more so than at this point in American economic development. Thus it can be demonstrated that much of the farmer agitation resulting in the Granger legislation was based on naiveté. Fundamentally the farmer's plight during those years was a consequence of postwar recession complicated by a secular price fall (in turn partially brought about by a remarkable and continuing increase in agricultural productivity); preoccupation with freight rates can to a large extent be reduced to the fact that farm products are bulky relative to their value and therefore expensive to transport (coupled with the fact that the relatively smaller volume of traffic east of Chicago and to the South inevitably resulted in higher rates in those areas); and resentment over the frustration of the Homestead Act by railroad land grants often failed to take into account the question of how else this problem could have been handled. Moreover, with the coming of another major depression after 1873, as experience made it evident that much of this legislation was poorly conceived, and as a result of an unprecedented political campaign by railroad interests, most of these restrictions were soon repealed. It even developed that in *Munn* v. *Illinois* the Supreme Court said some things it was forced shortly to retract. Yet notwithstanding these facts which would seem to point to fiasco rather than fundamental innovations in social organization, this episode was a decisive land-

[6] *Munn* v. *Illinois*, 94 U.S. 113 (1876).

mark in the development of government-business relationships in the United States.

The nature of this achievement can be expressed in several different ways. To begin with it is a significant fact that in the Granger movement the farmer placed his finger upon one of the most vulnerable points in the ideology of individualism. Parties to a bargain must have choices, that philosophy insists, and where choices were not in fact available the farmer was justified in concluding that harnessed self-interest required supplementation by government. Certain businesses, and the railroad is only a conspicuous case in point, are naturally monopolistic. Duplication of facilities would result in social waste on the one hand, and on the other in a situation in which no concern could make a profit. Where such conditions prevail, letting nature take her course may mean the elimination of every firm but one, with the possibility ofttimes that the one firm remaining will charge rates which for one reason or another are unreasonable. Scarcely more than a decade and a half after the inauguration of American laissez faire this weak spot in its armor had been found and successfully attacked.[7]

To put this matter a little differently, what the Supreme Court said in 1876 in language which could not have been misunderstood was that the police power was not to be considered forfeited with the ratification of the Fourteenth Amendment.[8] In other words, the legal philosophy laid down in *Charles River Bridge* v. *Warren Bridge* was in *Munn* v. *Illinois* carried a long step further, and from this new position the Court was never to retreat. And this in turn suggests that it might be more accurate to argue, not that the nation was in 1876 pulled back from total engulfment by laissez faire, but that by this small margin laissez faire failed to be completely established.

As events unfolded in later years, it developed that there were other important dimensions of the doctrine promulgated in *Munn* v. *Illinois*. To begin with, had the Court been loose in its definition of businesses "affected with a public interest," it is clear that governments would have been free to impose restrictions virtually at will. As other cases came to bar, however, it was soon apparent that if due process was to be compelled to come to terms with the police power, the police power was likewise to be compelled to come to terms with due process. And although the Supreme Court never

---

[7] M. G. Glaeser, *Outlines of Public Utility Economics* (New York: The Macmillan Co., 1927); and F. P. Hall, *Concept of a Business Affected with a Public Interest* (Bloomington: The Principia Press, Inc., 1940).

[8] Ernest Freund, *The Police Power* (Chicago: Callaghan & Co., 1904).

stated in unambiguous terms exactly what sorts of industries should be included in the public utility category (maintaining, perhaps, a necessary flexibility at this point), it became increasingly evident that the tests applied would be rigorous. Speaking broadly, the industry had to be one producing a service essential to the life of modern industrial society, and the service had to be produced under conditions of natural monopoly. This, indeed, is the genius of the public utility concept; it permitted regulation without reservation or apology in certain critical cases, without creating anxiety among businessmen lest the entire framework of the order on which they were basing their calculations come crashing down.

There was, furthermore, still another implication of *Munn* v. *Illinois* as it related to due process. Historically that term had referred to the procedures to be followed by the law—due process in this sense being a set of practices designed to prevent the arbitrary seizure and confinement of innocent persons. Due process in the taking of private property, on the other hand, could scarcely have this connotation. If one's property is taken by the government, it hardly matters whether the officials who do the taking are polite or not. Under the Fourteenth Amendment, therefore, a different conception of due process evolved, a conception of *substantive* as contrasted with *procedural* due process. The beginning made in 1876 toward the achievement of this objective was the idea that public restriction of private endeavors had to be oriented toward an appropriate purpose and that legal classifications of citizens (distinctions made between those to whom a given law will apply and those to whom it will not apply) must be related to such appropriate purpose.[9] And of course it goes without saying that the Supreme Court reserved the right to determine as particular cases came before it which purposes were appropriate and which were not.

In one other way did the Granger movement and the adjudication growing out of it contribute to the evolution of business-government relationships. If the states were to exercise a degree of economic supervision over certain industries, how could this best be accomplished? The charter was hardly a fit instrument for this purpose. It is in the first place impossible to anticipate all the problems which may arise in a dynamic society; and even if this were possible, it would still be true that the passage of a charter by a legislature subjects the regulatory instrument to amendment by men who are ordinarily not trained in the economic area involved. Direct and continuing control by the legislature, moreover, offered little im-

---

[9] John R. Commons, *Legal Foundations of Capitalism* (New York: The Macmillan Co., 1924), pp. 342 ff.

provement over charter regulation, because what is thereby gained in flexibility is apt to be lost in the greater element of nonexpert judgment which could easily intervene. An excellent solution to both these difficulties is direct and continuous regulation by a group of experts who devote their full time to this work. Commission regulation in the modern sense may reasonably be said to have originated with the Granger legislation, and few innovations in government in America have proved to be so fruitful.

It would be a mistake, however, to suppose that effective public utility regulation dates from 1876. On the contrary, state regulation of railroads dwindled away to practically nothing during the 1870's, and the electric power and telecommunications industries had scarcely been born at that time. By the same token much further development of the ideas and institutions involved here was necessary before utility regulation as we know it today became a reality. But, and this is the important point, a foundation had been laid on which future developments could be built, and progress was continuous from that point forward.

UPHEAVAL ON THE MONEY FRONT

Side by side with this attack upon the corporation, the business interests were also being harassed by an assault on the monetary adjustment built into the National Banking Act. Here too their principal opponent was the farmer, although many laborers were also in violent opposition to the money-banking policies being followed. Indeed it was no doubt owing to this relatively rare (during those years) coalition between workers and farmers that a minor defeat was administered to businessmen on that front.

In the case of the money mechanism no less than where corporate individualism was more directly involved, the farmer's concern was many-sided; at a number of points current arrangements seemed to deal quite harshly with the agricultural regions of the country, a fact which was all the more galling to farmers because until recently theirs had been the dominant voice in the making of monetary policy.

In the first place, national bank notes had been allocated to the several states on the basis of population and existing banking facilities, with the result that this currency added very little to the circulating medium in the West. And there was an even deeper irony in this situation. In the East checkbook money was rapidly replacing bank notes, and hence it seemed that the national banking system made money available most generously precisely where such generosity was least called for. In the second place, the high rate of interest the farmer had to pay could with some logic be blamed on the operation of the banking system, for under present legislation national banks could not be formed in places having less than six thousand persons and loans on real estate were all but prohibited. A third reason for believing that money policy had recently been deflationary had to do with the fact that the paper money issued during the Civil War had been for use by the North alone. When the South re-entered the Union the money supply was therefore seriously diluted, a consequence which was all the more disturbing because greenbacks were the only effective bank reserves in so many agricultural areas. And, fourth, the national banking system often operated most inefficiently just when the farmer's need for money was greatest, namely, at crop-moving time. Thus at off-seasons money tended to flow to New York where it was likely to become so committed to urban economic activities as to be unavailable to farmers when needed.

To be sure, the farmer's grievances with respect to money were no more fundamental than in the earlier struggle against railroads and middlemen. At this point, too, key facts were a secular fall in the world price level which could scarcely be attributed to American monetary legislation, and the disastrous panic and depression of the 1870's which also had roots much deeper than the monetary institutions of this country as such. But the threat to cherished conservative values implicit in political agitation against the gold standard was nonetheless real despite the element of rural naiveté behind its appearance at this time.

Ever since the end of the war, a running battle had been fought between inflationists and deflationists.[10] The principal focus of attention in this contest had been the war-born greenbacks; businessmen wanted to see these certificates retired, while farmers had pressed for making them a permanent part of the circulation. To date the farmer had been more or less successful in maintaining the status quo, although in 1875 a "lame duck" Republican Congress had passed a law providing for the resumption of specie payments as of January 1, 1879. Fearing that this step would mean a painful contraction of the money supply, inflationists set themselves to the task of thwarting the implementation of that policy.

Here was one reason why the post-Civil War agitation over money reached a particularly intense stage in 1878. Another was the fact that in that year the money supply on a per capita basis reached its

[10] W. C. Mitchell, *History of the Greenbacks* (Chicago: University of Chicago Press, 1903); A. J. Noyes, *Forty Years of American Finance* (New York: G. P. Putnam's Sons, 1909); and F. A. Shannon, *The Farmer's Last Frontier* (New York: Rinehart & Co., Inc., 1945).

lowest point. A secular fall in the long-run rate of interest had pushed the price of government bonds higher and higher, one of the more obvious consequences being a sharp decrease in the willingness of bankers to buy bonds in exchange for the privilege of issuing notes in the amount of 90 per cent of the par value of such bonds.

Still a third factor at work here was labor's willingness to lend powerful support to this assault—a willingness largely explained by the recent drastic change in the over-all performance of the American economy. One of the greatest tragedies which can befall a worker is to become unemployed, and it seemed reasonable to suppose that a looser money policy might help get the wheels of industry turning once more.

However, important though these forces were in stimulating a particularly intense assault on the nation's medium of exchange in the late 1870's, yet another pressure was probably even more decisive. Indeed it seems reasonable to suppose that but for a dramatic change in the value of silver relative to that of gold no money legislation would have been enacted in 1878.

For a number of years the United States had been nominally on a bimetallic monetary standard, with gold and silver theoretically circulating side by side. Because, however, the mint ratio of sixteen ounces of silver to one ounce of gold had long undervalued silver as compared with its value in the market, silver had so consistently gone to the market rather than the mint that in 1873 a routine coinage law omitted the silver dollar from the list of coins to be minted. At the same time discoveries of vast new sources of virgin silver in various parts of the world, coupled with the abandonment of silver in several European money systems, set in motion an increase in the relative supply of silver such as had not been seen for two centuries. When the market value of silver fell below the legal value at the mint, an outcry went up from the silver interests at the discovery that the government would not buy their product as theretofore.

A more fortuitous setting for debtor-farmers to press their age-old demand for cheap money could hardly be imagined. Joined with employment-hungry workers and subsidy-hungry silver capitalists, they now launched the most formidable onslaught against the existing money mechanism most businessmen could remember. Of course, conservatives resisted this fury to the best of their ability (they had worked too hard to create a satisfactory exchange mechanism to lose this battle now by default), but the most they were able to achieve was an unstable compromise. A bill presented by Representative Bland of Missouri calling for free coinage of silver was converted in the Senate into a measure providing for the purchase by the Treasury of not less than $2 million worth of silver each month. Even then President Hayes was prevailed upon to veto the measure, but the two-thirds majority necessary to override was easily secured and the Bland-Allison Act became law.

No one in 1878, and least of all midwestern farmers, would have argued that significant progress was being made toward protecting nonindustrial interests from the excesses of the laissez faire society now growing up so rapidly all around them. Already little remained of the first attempts to bring the railroads under control, and the next decade was to show no more results from the 1878 attack on the money system. Furthermore, even if significant successes could have been pointed to on these fronts, railroads and banking made up only a small proportion of the total economy.

But though achievements had been less spectacular than were at first expected, two things had nonetheless been accomplished. First, notice had been decisively served on industrialists that they were not to have their way unopposed. Second, they had been further informed that their position was far from impregnable. In the years to come, although laissez faire continued to move on to triumph after triumph, these warnings were never to be forgotten.

QUESTIONS FOR DISCUSSION

1. Defend the definition of laissez faire presented in the text. What shortcomings do you see in this definition? What objections do you have to this interpretation?

2. Of what value was the doctrine of individualism during its period of greatest influence?

3. In what ways does the rationale of individualism sound less convincing today than it did one hundred years ago? Is it today an obstacle to appropriate business-government relationships?

4. What grievances did farmers have against railroads? Against other types of capitalist enterprise?

5. Evaluate the validity of the farmers' attack on the railroads.

6. Why was the Supreme Court's decision in the Slaughter-House cases such a blow to conservatives? What do you think of this decision?

7. What did the Granger legislation endeavor to accomplish, how was it attacked, and on what grounds did the Supreme Court repel this attack?

8. What is meant by "the public utility concept"? What is its significance in the government and business field?

9. Explain the significance of the Granger movement from the standpoint of the relationship between the corporation and the community.

10. What were the issues involved in the battle over money after the Civil War? How real was this problem? How realistic was the solution proposed by farmers and their allies?

11. Analyze the first great challenge to laissez faire from the standpoint of the doctrine of individualism.

Chapter 8

Genesis of the Trust Problem

Qualifications must be attached to the designation of a certain period in a particular country as a time of industrial revolution. But if this terminology can accurately be applied to any situation, surely the economy of the United States between the Civil War and the end of the century is an appropriate choice. During these years the entire structure of that economy changed so rapidly that millions of Americans were barely able to make the necessary adjustments. Indeed, as this transformation gathered momentum, citizens who had thought in the early 1870's that they had serious grievances began to feel even more grievously oppressed.

To be sure, the major elements out of which the post-Civil War economy was built had been many years in the making; the economy had long been orienting itself to a machine basis. What happened during the last half of the nineteenth century, thus, was simply that a number of streams of evolution suddenly came together into a rushing torrent. Among the more important of these were the railroad, interchangeable parts, large-sized power units, and the Bessemer process of steel-making. As these several achievements, coupled with a rate of technical innovation unprecedented in human history, began to coalesce, America's small-business society gave way to its big-business successor in an almost unbelievably short time.[1]

MECHANIZATION AND COMPETITION

At this historical distance it is not easy to recapture the profundity of the changes wrought by the machine. Perhaps some comprehension of this phenomenon, however, can be gained by noting its consequences for the primary groups of which the economy was

[1] National Industrial Conference Board, *A Graphic Analysis of the Census of Manufactures, 1849-1919* (New York: National Industrial Conference Board, 1923).

composed; that is, by tracing out some of the more difficult adjustments farmers, workers, and businessmen were compelled to make.

It has already been emphasized that the central problem confronting farmers at this time can best be thought of against the background of the secular fall in agricultural prices, and that this in turn cannot be wholly divorced from the rapidity with which the "farmers' frontier" in the United States was pushed westward. But it is to be noted in this connection that even so rapid an increase in acres under cultivation would not have had as great an effect on prices as it did, had it not been accompanied by an equally rapid increase in the quantity and quality of the machinery used in agricultural production. Of equal significance is the fact that a sort of vicious circle was thereby set in motion which virtually forced the farmer to contribute to his own discomfiture. The more prices fell and hence the more burdensome his debts became, the more did he feel compelled to increase his indebtedness in order to purchase equipment that would enable him to increase production, and in this way depress prices still further. And when in addition to all of this it is remembered that similar developments were taking place throughout all Western civilization, and that improved transportation was bringing farmers from all over the world into competition with one another as never before, it is all the more evident that agriculture's problems were closely related to the progress of mechanization.[2]

The impact of the machine on the laborer was even more direct, and to an even greater extent can it be explained in terms of a sharpening of competitive relationships. Here, however, there was a double-barreled effect: on the one hand, workers were brought into a more intense rivalry with other workers; and on the other, they were brought into an especially keen competition with the machine itself.

Prior to the appearance of factory production, facilitated as this was by the development of a transportation network making possible the distribution of factory output over a large area, the market for labor had been essentially local. Now, in two ways, this isolation of a multitude of separate, tiny markets abruptly ended. Not only could workers more easily transport themselves to another location, but, what was of more importance, the goods produced in one location could with even greater facility invade the territory of far distant workers. When stoves, to take a single example from the many industries rapidly becoming organized in this way, could be

[2] E. G. Nourse, *American Agriculture and the European Market* (New York: McGraw-Hill Book Co., Inc., 1929).

produced in Buffalo and sold in Detroit or St. Louis in competition with locally produced models, workers were quick to feel this enhanced competitive pressure.

Painful though this dimension of the mechanization process was, direct competition with the machine presented workers with a still graver threat. The introduction of machinery meant first and foremost technological unemployment and hence a difficult period of adjustment for the workers so displaced. In turn, the existence of this army of the technologically unemployed tended to push down the wage level for other workers, a result also brought about in part by the fact that machine technology was often if not typically based upon breaking down complex skills into operations which could be performed by less skilled hands. And when workers confronted with this situation sought to organize to protect themselves, they found that members of the army of unemployed could with little difficulty be turned into unwilling strikebreakers.[3]

The "robber baron" approach to this period in American history still frequently encountered implies (where it does not openly assert) that farmers and workers suffered from this economic transformation while businessmen did not. Nothing could be farther from the truth. The selfsame mechanization process which was so distressing to other segments of the community was also creating anxieties within the entrepreneur group.

Here again an important part of the problem can be expressed against the background of changes in competitive relationships. Costly machines could not be effectively employed except as they were operated at or near capacity. From this fact two consequences followed. First, the area over which a given firm's output was sold had to be correspondingly increased, and hence firms previously too far removed from one another to be competitive became active rivals. Second, the character of business competition was strikingly altered. The need to cover the fixed costs associated with specialized, durable capital gave rise to a phenomenon in business decision-making often referred to as "the tyranny of overhead costs."[4] Any weakening of the market in which a high-fixed-cost firm sold its product was apt to create an internal crisis which had to be met by drastic measures—for example, the slashing of prices, often below full cost.

[3] Mary R. Beard, A Short History of the American Labor Movement (New York: G. H. Doran, 1924).
[4] J. M. Clark, Studies In The Economics of Overhead Costs (Chicago: University of Chicago Press, 1923).

The greater intensity of enterprise competition engendered by the machine can be expressed still more strongly, too. It is no careless use of words that applies the term "ruthless" to the business competition of this period. The obverse of the development of an economy consisting of large firms was the disappearance of the small firms which had heretofore reigned supreme. To be sure, if the underlying economy had been expanding rapidly enough, no diminution in number of firms would have been required. In actual fact, however, technological advance was rapidly outrunning sheer growth, with the result that many firms had to be eliminated—in one way or another. It would have been surprising indeed in a society boasting as loudly of its belief in free enterprise as the United States did during this period if a sizeable proportion of these firms had not died violent deaths.

But if these things are true, if the dramatic appearance of the machine enhanced the severity of competition for businessmen as well as for farmers and workers, it is also true that in one respect that situation was reversed in the two cases. For the alert and ambitious entrepreneur there was a way out; adjustments were available by means of which the machine could be turned into fabulous profits. It goes without saying, of course, that such rewards could not be reaped by all. But to those who played the new game most effectively, there seemed for a time to be no limit to what might be achieved. All that was required was to follow the rules, and the riches of a Midas could be had almost for the taking.

And what were these rules? Perhaps the most basic requirement was to be the first to take advantage of the new technology, thus improving the ability of one's own firm to compete by reducing unit costs. But there was also a corollary tactic which was almost as important. A strategy of growing larger that did not directly take competitors out of the field was obviously inferior to one which made a reduction in the number of competitors an automatic by-product of the increase in one's own size. While rivals could just as well be outdistanced through the first approach, it nonetheless had the disadvantage of leaving the loser's facilities still turning out goods for a market often unable to absorb them (without a ruinous reduction in prices). Industrialists quickly learned that the most bitter competition of all came from near-bankrupt firms making desperate efforts to save themselves from disaster.

To summarize, one of the outstanding characteristics of the economy during this period was "cannibalism," the swallowing up of a multitude of small firms by competitors in the process of growing larger. Referred to most frequently as the merger or consolidation movement, this phenomenon was accelerated by a variety of powerful forces. For one thing, there was the dramatic and continuous advance in machine technology. As a second factor, moreover, it would be difficult to over-emphasize the impact of a secularly falling price level, although to a considerable extent this phenomenon must be thought of as one of the principal consequences of the new technology. Still another pressure appeared in the form of a series of down-turns in the level of economic activity—a severe one in the 1870's, a more mild one in the 1880's, and an especially devastating one after 1893. And there were even psychological forces at work. So grim was the competitive struggle that men no doubt developed a fear of competition resulting in more "cannibalism" than was technologically demanded, and it is equally probable that the all-too-human drive to secure power made for still greater excesses. But whatever the causal relationships here, the fact remains that while economic dynamics was so sharply increasing competition in some areas of the economy, it was contributing to an equally decisive lessening of competition in other areas.

COOPERATION IN THE RAILROAD INDUSTRY[5]

So important was this aspect of the relationship between mechanization and competition for government-business relationships over the next several decades that a much more detailed examination of it seems warranted. For two reasons, furthermore, such an examination may appropriately begin with the changing character of competition among railroads. First, the Granger movement can appropriately be thought of as the authentic beginning of popular misgivings about the effectiveness of competition as a protector of the public interest, and subsequent events only accentuated this feeling in the public mind. Second, there was a close relationship between the state of railroad competition and the level of competition in other industries.

The primacy of the technological factor in the formation of larger and larger railroad companies is most easily seen in the early history of that development. At first railroads were typically small affairs, connecting points no farther apart than one hundred miles or so, and the usual situation was the almost complete absence of com-

[5] F. A. Cleveland and F. W. Powell, *Railroad Promotion and Capitalization* (New York: Longmans, Green & Co., Inc., 1909); and S. L. Miller, *Inland Transportation* (New York: McGraw-Hill Book Co., Inc., 1933).

petition between them. As technology advanced, however, and as men began to think in terms of inter-communication over greater and greater distances, it became evident that larger units would both permit more efficient operation and provide a more satisfactory service. Obviously, requiring passengers and freight to make seven changes from one line to another between New York and the Mississippi River (as was for some years the case) was neither demanded in the interest of low-cost production nor the best that could be offered by way of accommodating the public. Consequently the first period of railroad consolidation consisted of end-to-end unions rather than combinations between competing carriers.

By the early 1870's this stage in the expansion of the rail net had about run its course, at which point perhaps the most characteristic feature of this industry became the ruthless, ruinous competition (that is, the reduction of prices below full unit costs) for which this period was so notorious. In 1875 the first-class rate between New York and Chicago fell 60 per cent between January and May, and in the following year the decline between January and July was 80 per cent. During this same period the usual rate of $110 per car for hauling cattle from Chicago to Pittsburgh fell for a time to $5, while grain was hauled from Chicago to the Atlantic seaboard for

TABLE 3. COMPETITION IN THE RAILROAD INDUSTRY

Year Month	New York–Chicago First Class Freight Rates (cents per 100 pounds)
1874—January	100
August	75
1875—January	100
May	40
1876—January	75
July	15
1877—March	75
October	100
1878—February	75

Source: S. L. Miller, *Inland Transportation* (New York: McGraw-Hill Book Co., Inc., 1933), p. 106. Used by permission.

as little as seven and one-half cents per hundred pounds. No doubt this corner would not have been turned as abruptly as it was, had two supplementary forces not contributed an additional impetus— the fact that much railroad building had been speculative construction in advance of economic justification, and the onset of a new

panic and depression in 1873. But the nature of the railroad industry and the dynamic changes taking place in the American economy would have brought about this shift in any event.

In respect of the nature of the railroad industry the case of the
trunkline carriers will illustrate. Certainly two rail lines between
New York and Chicago would not, even at that time, have been
such an excessive number that ruinous competition would have become the normal thing. However, this was not the consideration
which in the final analysis determined the number of routes between these points. Although each of the major trunkline carriers
had common termini, each at the same time served a different set of
intermediate points. Given a system of free enterprise in railroad-
building, in other words, the number of competing lines through this
vast hinterland was a function of the legitimacy of the claims of a
large number of areas for service. It follows that only by the sheerest
coincidence would these claims have resulted in the construction of
that number of through lines which would just avoid excessive competition, and in practice such a nice balance was almost never
struck.

On the side of economic dynamics equally compelling pressures
were at work. Just as railroads came into collision with one another
directly, so also did they indirectly. As the economy grew up, powerful competitive pressures developed between various regions of
the country, a process which caught the railroads squarely in the
middle. Thus the city of Philadelphia could argue for rates on the
Pennsylvania which would give that city an advantage in the running battle between the major Atlantic ports. However, the value of
such concessions to the Pennsylvania could last only until New York
persuaded the New York Central to retaliate in self-defense. Similar
contests produced similar results in the competition between oil production centers, western and eastern packing companies, and Atlantic and Gulf Coast ports, to name only a few specific instances.

What were intelligent businessmen confronted with this difficult
and dangerous competitive situation to do? Surely, there was only
one alternative. Steps would have to be taken to check the severity
of this competition.

It should occasion no surprise, of course, that the elite of the
American railroad community was equal to this contingency, even
though the first attempts at a solution were by no means wholly successful. Here also the trunkline carriers illustrate what was happening especially well. As early as 1854 an agreement for this purpose

among the Erie, New York Central, Pennsylvania, and Baltimore and Ohio Railroads was reached, but new habits were so difficult to establish that this work had to be done all over again in 1858. When that agreement also failed, and particularly when the industry was convulsed between 1868 and 1873 by a series of unusually disastrous rate wars, Commodore Vanderbilt called the famous Saratoga Conference, where the technique of restraining competition was considerably broadened through the establishment of a central board to fix rates and establish certain working rules.

But even this more formal type of price agreement proved not to be sufficiently stable for long-range usefulness. Weaker lines found it too tempting to undercut as a last desperate measure to save themselves from utter ruin. Obviously some way would have to be found to take care of these concerns more satisfactorily. The technique shortly hit upon was the pool, a cooperative arrangement which not only fixed rates but which at the same time did not neglect the needs of the financially least secure cooperators. By the late 1870's this device was being both used and improved upon wherever railroad development had reached a relatively advanced state.

In general pools were of two types. Where the so-called money pool was employed, revenues were distributed among members upon some agreed basis; in the so-called traffic pool, tonnage was distributed in some prearranged manner. Probably the first of these types was the more common, although without question it was the latter which had the greatest influence upon the politico-economic situation as it developed. Arbitrary traffic divisions for pool purposes necessitated using certain large shippers as "eveners," such concerns agreeing to let their tonnage be assigned by the pool in exchange for certain concessions not made available to competitors.

One of the classic examples of the use of the pool in cooperation among railroads was the Chicago-Omaha Pool, a revenue-division arrangement which kept competition within acceptable limits between the Mississippi and Missouri Rivers for almost two decades. However, the most mature expression of this innovation was undoubtedly the Southern Railway and Steamship Association. Here there was established an elaborate organization including a legislative body, an executive committee, a commissioner with broad powers, and a board of arbitrators. Furthermore, this development consisted of a genuine and for the most part effective attempt to secure the best of both worlds. While it was in intent as well as in fact a device to restrict competition, a technique was followed which at the same time fostered the maintenance of a high degree of intermember rivalry. Revenue allotments were made annually on the basis of the preceding year's traffic divisions, and hence there was a constant scramble for the traffic available at the agreed rates.

COOPERATION IN MANUFACTURING[6]

In manufacturing as well as in railroading there was first a period of development of large-scale production as such before these larger concerns began to engage in a warfare with one another so bitter that industrial leaders felt compelled to call a halt. Coming along a little later than the comparable period in railroad history, in part because the rise of a modern transportation network was one of the essential prerequisites, large-scale manufacturing was in its formative stage until after the depression of the 1870's. By 1880, however, the union of limited liability and mechanization was complete enough to permit the next stage in this evolution. Almost simultaneously in a number of fields, businessmen began searching for ways of mitigating the rigors of an uninhibited competition among the as yet untamed offspring of the machine age.

As in the railroad industry, too, this phenomenon at first took the form of simple agreements, evolving from looser to tighter forms of combination. In an incredibly short period of time the implicit understanding that competition was not to be pursued too vigorously had been reached in a wide variety of industries, the details in each case reflecting the peculiarities of the industry involved.

The loosest arrangement of this kind was what was known as the "gentleman's agreement" to maintain prices, a device used perhaps most frequently in various branches of the iron and steel industry and in the mining of anthracite coal. Here, as the name implies, no formal organization was created, no papers were signed, and no penalties were provided for in the event verbal agreements were violated—it being taken for granted that a "gentleman" would keep his word. Unfortunately, however, for the longer future of this kind of cooperation, not every American businessman in the last half of the nineteenth century was a gentleman. At least one renegade was to be found in most such groups (and indeed there were those who entered into these arrangements primarily because an agreement

[6] H. R. Seager and C. A. Gulick, *Trust and Corporation Problems* (New York: Harper & Bros., 1929); and W. S. Stevens, *Industrial Combinations and Trusts* (New York: The Macmillan Co., 1913).

would steady prices while they undercut their gentlemen colleagues), and one determined price cutter might destroy the effectiveness of any such combination.

A second and somewhat more advanced type of cooperation was the agreement to regulate output and hence to control price indirectly. Such programs were developed in a number of industries, the most important being anthracite coal, meat packing, steel rails, cotton bagging, gunpowder, and wire nails. Here the procedure was to secure agreement as to the volume to be put on the market, and then to allot total output among members on some basis agreed upon in advance.

One of the most elaborate output-control arrangements was the wire-nail pool, which is also one of the most historically significant of these early competition-controlling endeavors for an entirely different reason. Here is to be found one of the authentic sources of the so-called "Pittsburgh-plus" method of pricing (basing-point pricing) which has at times been such an important issue between the government and businessmen. The pricing arrangements developed in this industry were as follows. A base cost was first computed, this being as nearly as could be calculated the cost of production at Pittsburgh. Then, since most of the raw material for the industry came from the Pittsburgh area, the cost at any other point was assumed to be the base cost plus freight charges from Pittsburgh. Prices to consumers were then based upon this cost structure. All profits were paid into the pool, which fund was in turn apportioned monthly on the same basis as was used in making production allotments.

Although the output pool did offer advantages over the gentleman's agreement, it too encountered difficulties. Most firms during these dynamic years were eager to expand, which meant that production quotas typically became the center of a continuing controversy. And even where a flexible formula was used, with larger sales being reflected in more generous quotas, firms were given an irresistible incentive to increase capacity (perhaps even shading the group's agreed prices, if a price agreement were involved) in order to receive a quota increase at the end of the agreement period. Frequently the demands then made by various firms were so mutually exclusive that a basis for renewal could not be found—at which point the enlarged capacity might produce an even more destructive competitive situation than that alleviated by the attempt at cooperation.

Another type of pool proceeded by dividing the market among the several producer-members on a geographical basis. This type of arrangement was particularly well suited to international competition, and American concerns producing tobacco, steel rails, glass bottles, aluminum, gunpowder, calcium carbide, and meats during this period entered into many such agreements with foreign competitors. Domestically this approach was more rare, although one classic example did develop. That was the combination entered into by the Addyston Pipe and Steel Company and five other concerns engaged in the business of manufacturing cast iron pipe.

Under this agreement the entire United States was divided into three parts: reserve territory, free territory, and pay territory. Reserve territory was specifically allocated among these several companies. Free territory represented areas in which any concern could engage in unrestricted selling. In pay territory, however, and that designation was given to thirty-six of the forty-eight states, selling was elaborately regulated. All inquiries for pipe from this area were referred to a central board, which group determined prices for all shipments into pay territory. Orders were then allocated among the members in accordance with an agreed procedure, these in turn paying into the pool a bonus on each order, the amount of which being also determined on a prearranged basis. At the end of the year this fund was distributed to the member concerns on the basis of shipments into pay territory.

A third type of pool was the selling agency. With this device manufacturers would turn their output over to a representative organization which would assume responsibility for all sales. Here the outstanding example was the Michigan Salt Association, although the Continental Wall Paper Company was in its day only slightly less famous. In Michigan salt producers made a contract with the association each year, agreeing to turn all their year's output over to the central body. The unique characteristic of this arrangement was the freedom every member retained to produce as much as it pleased; the gain, in other words, came not so much from restricting supply as in preventing buyers of salt from playing one producer off against another. Perhaps partially because of this feature the Michigan Salt Association was one of the most successful of all the pools formed at this time.

The last major variety in this species was the patent pool, in some respects the tightest kind of control developed during the early years of the consolidation movement. By the joint use of major patents, competitors could not only go far toward keeping newcomers out of the field while simultaneously minimizing the competition for and hence the cost of new patents, but they could markedly reduce the costly patent litigation so often an important feature of a technologically dynamic sector of the economy. Such a sector was the electric products manufacturing industry, where General Electric and Westinghouse now joined forces in a patent pool.

THE STANDARD OIL COMPANY[7]

With so much ingenuity going into the details of these devices for bringing competition under control, it might be supposed that it would have been only a matter of time until the pool was adapted to almost any such purpose. The fact is, however, that even as the first pools were breaking down because of the difficulty of building into them the necessary permanence, ingenuity was already beginning to be directed toward the objective of replacing rather than perfecting this technique. Two inherent difficulties plagued this businessman's adjustment to the machine age, and it was soon apparent to the most farsighted that neither of these could be satisfactorily resolved. There was first the fact that the pool allowed member firms to retain so much independence that sharp interest conflicts were practically inevitable. Second, and even more fundamental, there was a serious legal impediment to their successful functioning; pools had to operate essentially outside the law. By this is not meant that the law was actively hostile to these responses to what was widely believed to be excessive competition. Since, however, the common law tended to frown upon agreements inhibiting trade freedom, pooling agreements were unenforceable in the courts.

What was needed, in other words, was a technique of cooperation which would limit the freedom of independent-minded members to deviate from the policies established by the majority, and which would at the same time have the force of law behind it; and by 1879 the wheels of institutional change were already in motion in those directions. Everything considered, furthermore, it is not to be wondered at that a superior approach was built around the corporation; this institution had deliberately been given great flexibility, and hence it was only natural for businessmen now to think about their problems against the background of limited liability and permanent business life. And perhaps it is no more surprising that this new step was first taken in the petroleum refining industry.

From the beginning of that industry's history technological advance had been extremely rapid, with the result that the most effi-

---

[7] I. M. Tarbell, *The History of the Standard Oil Company* (New York: McClure, Phillips, & Co., 1904); and Allan Nevins, *John D. Rockefeller: A Study in Power* (New York: Charles Scribner's Sons, 1953).

cient size for an oil refining concern became larger and larger. Nor was this alone because of technical advances in refining equipment and processes. Another important factor was the discovery of more and more petroleum by-products together with uses for them; only the largest concerns could afford the heavy capital outlay required for efficient processing of these materials which would otherwise have to be thrown away. Understandably the powerful pressure on every producer to grow larger as quickly as possible soon began to generate an intense competitive struggle from which even the stoutest heart was apt at times to cringe.

John D. Rockefeller began his business career at an early age with a produce commission house on the Cleveland docks. However, sensing at an early date the possibilities of the brand-new oil industry, only six years after the first successful oil well was drilled in Titusville, Pennsylvania, Rockefeller sold his commission business assets and invested the proceeds in an oil refining partnership. By 1870 his concern had outgrown this status, and in that year the Standard Oil Company of Ohio was incorporated with a capital stock of $1,000,000—even at this time one of the largest oil concerns in the country. Rockefeller was, after all, an industrial genius, and Cleveland was located very favorably with regard to the major source of raw material at that time.

But these factors were not alone responsible for the Standard's rise to virtual dominance of the entire industry in less than ten years. These were the years during which the railroad industry was in the throes of a savage competition it had not yet brought under control, and hence those concerns were easy victims of the pressure that could be brought to bear upon them by almost any large shipper. The Standard Oil Company was excellently situated for bringing such pressure. Two railroads operated between Cleveland and New York City; and not only could the Erie and the New York Central be played off against one another, but either one or both could be threatened with the use of the Great Lakes and the Erie Canal as an alternative route.

Let it be said for the record that John D. Rockefeller's concern was not the first oil company to browbeat a railroad into granting preferential treatment, and indeed in the 1870's this was a business practice which was often compelled as a defensive strategy where not adopted for offensive purposes. (This, of course, is only another way of saying that cooperation among railroads during these years was also in large part defensive.) But after this has been said, the fact still remains that the brief South Improvement Company episode in the life of the Standard Oil Company was unquestionably one of the most fantastic cases of discrimination in the annals of American economic development.

The South Improvement Company was a Pennsylvania corporation with a charter granting it almost unlimited powers. When it was taken over by certain oil refiners in Cleveland and Pittsburgh under the leadership of the Standard Oil Company, its primary purpose (as a selling-type pool) was to negotiate favorable freight rates with the Erie, New York Central, and Pennsylvania Railroads. This it accomplished with unbelievable success, partially because of the tremendous volume of freight it was able to use as a lever, and partially because the trunkline roads were simultaneously looking for an "evener" in another in the series of pools worked out by those roads. On all oil transported for the South Improvement Company a rebate of approximately one-third was to be allowed, a similar though smaller rebate was to be paid to the South Improvement Company on all oil shipped by competitors, and duplicate copies of all waybills on shipments by competitors were to be furnished to the management of this combine.

Although an intense public outcry against these arrangements put an end to cooperation through this agency in less than three months, the consequences of this episode were nonetheless major. Some twenty of the twenty-five independent refineries in Cleveland sold out to the Standard Oil Company, and that firm's capacity increased from 1,500 to 10,000 barrels of crude per day. Moreover, its enhanced strength and dominant position in Cleveland made expansion elsewhere much easier. Between 1875 and 1877 most of the independent refineries in both Pittsburgh and Baltimore surrendered to this giant, and substantial inroads were made in Philadelphia and New York as well. By early 1879 the Standard Oil group had secured control of 90 to 95 per cent of all the oil refining capacity of the country.

In one sense this represented substantial completion of Rockefeller's long-standing ambition to create a petroleum industry which would not be constantly threatened by outbreaks of destructive competition. In another sense, however, this achievement still hung perilously in the balance. The tie between the various companies which had been brought into the Standard's orbit was only that of a particularly strong gentleman's agreement; if the next turn of the wheel of economic dynamics was not to see this empire shattered, a stronger bond would have to be forged. In order to preserve these gains, in order to protect what had been accomplished from the fate which commonly befell other loose cooperative arrangements, the "trustee" device was inaugurated and the "First Great Trust" was born.

The Standard Oil trust agreement, first drawn up in 1879 and revised in 1882, provided for nine trustees whose responsibility it would be to manage the properties of some forty constituent concerns. Legally the authority on the basis of which the trustees were to act was derived from the possession of a voting majority of the securities of all of the separate concerns, which stock was transferred to them in exchange for the equivalent capital value in so-called trust certificates. Notably the trustees did not take title to the original shares; they were rather accorded what might more precisely be called permanent proxy rights. On the other hand, the original holders lost title to the specific shares they surrendered, retaining title instead to a proportionate share of all stock held by the trustees. In this way ownership of the underlying properties was thoroughly scrambled to make possible the fullest freedom of action by the trustees.

And no sooner had the Standard Oil Company pointed the way than a number of other industries moved to tighten their own organizations along similar lines. In 1884 the American Cotton Oil trust was formed, followed a year later by the National Linseed Oil trust. The Distillers' and Cattle Feeders' Trust was organized in 1887, that year seeing something of a rush to adopt the new technique, as a sugar trust, a lead trust, and a cordage trust were all formed. Clearly the business elite was well along the way toward resolving the special difficulties the machine age was creating for that group.

STIRRINGS OF UNREST[8]

It is often stated that with the rise of the trust, with the adaptation of the now fully accepted corporate form of business organization to the task of reducing industrial competition, a spirit of intense hostility to "big business" arose among rank-and-file citizens which for many years could not be appeased. This is true. Unfortunately, however, that way of putting the matter explains little about the nature of the sentiment which was to play such a vital role in the government and business field over the next quarter of a century. And when the attitudes of the man in the street are examined more carefully, it becomes clear that they were at once more complex and more comprehensive than is commonly supposed.

[8] Henry George, *Progress and Poverty* (San Francisco: Henry George, 1879); Edward Bellamy, *Looking Backward* (Boston: Tichnor & Co., 1887); and Henry D. Lloyd, *Wealth Against Commonwealth* (New York: Harper & Bros., 1894).

To begin with, it is understandable that the trust raised grave problems with respect to the ideology of individualism. If the essence of the good life was the freedom to make uncoerced choices, what chance was there of achieving such a life in an economy blocked off into special preserves marked Standard Oil Company, American Sugar Refining Company, and so forth? What was at issue here, in other words, was the question raised back in the days of the Granger movement, but broadened out in two directions. On the one hand, a wider circle of citizen groups was now aroused as compared with the earlier period. On the other hand, the objects of protest were no longer limited to concerns responsible for distributing the farmers' produce; a number of other sectors of the economy were also now coming under attack.

To bring this consideration down to the level of the concrete world in which the majority lived, there was nothing illogical about the view so commonly held that businessmen were not only making a successful adjustment to the machine but were achieving this success at the expense of other groups in society. Thus farmers could say of the National Cordage Association as accurately as of the Chicago-Omaha Pool or a union of grain elevators in Chicago that the bargaining power of the farmer was hopelessly inadequate alongside that of one of these great combines. Similarly laborers had no difficulty believing that the legal treatment of a huge trust as an individual put the individual workingman at an equally hopeless disadvantage relative to these vast aggregations of buildings, machinery, and working capital—the "soulless" corporation as it was already coming to be called. And finally, many petty capitalists, men whose concerns were a part of the wreckage now littering the path of progress, must have felt that big business was an especially direct threat to them.

As a matter of fact, it is only when these two approaches are in a sense put together that rank-and-file hostility toward industrialism can be fully understood. It could hardly have been more evident that because the rise of big business would have been impossible without the limited liability corporation, businessmen were utilizing an institution created by the community to engage in exploitive practices against that community. Only by making use of the privileges granted by a state legislature through a corporate charter could a concern achieve the great size already attained by a number of industrial and railroad firms, and only through the use of this same instrumentality could a large firm continue to grow from generation to generation as was now possible.

From this standpoint, too, the nature of the unrest against the trust can be made even more specific. All that is required is to focus attention upon the financial side of the corporate-industrial society so dramatically taking form. There was, for example, the widespread practice of stock-watering, that all-purpose technique of issuing securities to insiders, who in return contributed nothing of value to the concern, and hence of diluting the interest of existing security holders. In the railroad industry especially there was the practice of issuing a large number of different kinds of bonds, using the most appealing (and at the same time the most misleading) names for those issues carrying the least attractive provisions for purchasers. There was, moreover, the speculation on the stock market in which valuable portions of the community's productive mechanism were made the plaything of the "fast-buck" operators. And surely no thinking person could have failed to perceive the tendency for corporate management to become increasingly the prerogative of a small group of insiders who were in a position virtually to perpetuate their own control.[9]

Most Americans in the latter part of the nineteenth century believed in private property. At the same time, however, this belief was implicitly grounded in the doctrine that private property is held at the sufferance of society as a whole in order that resources might in this manner serve society's needs most effectively. Few indeed there were (outside the circle of the business elite) who could be persuaded that the nation's resources were being most beneficially used, unevenly distributed as they were rapidly coming to be. Rather there was arising a growing certainty that the philosophy of individualism was only a tongue-in-cheek rationalization by businessmen—that the harness for self-interest which individualists delighted to emphasize was slipping badly. Small wonder that the feeling began to spread that a monster had unwittingly been created, and one moreover already turning savagely on its creator. As a temporary Senate committee expressed the situation: *"No general question of governmental policy occupies at this time so prominent a place in the thoughts of the people as that of controlling the steady growth and extending influence of corporate power and of regulating its relations to the public."*[10]

In summary, the fact throwing citizens everywhere into a panic was that they were losing control over their society, that they seemed to be fast becoming men without a country. Years ago it had become evident that the business interests were firmly in possession

---

[9] H. L. Purdy, M. L. Lindahl, and W. A. Carter, *Corporate Concentration and Public Policy* (Englewood Cliffs, N.J.: Prentice-Hall, Inc., 1950).

[10] Italics in the original.

of the national government; by now there could be no mistaking that this was also true of a majority of state governments. The resources at the command of successful industrialists were proving to be almost irresistible, and the fact that United States' Senators were then elected by state legislatures was only one reason why businessmen found the temptation to dominate these governments so strong. Another was the origin at this time of the public utility industry as we know it today. Loosely written corporate charters governing this development were often immensely profitable. And still a third, of course, was the assistance state governments could render in keeping a rising labor class in check.

If it is true that the soul of a society is mirrored in its literature, surely Edward Bellamy's *Looking Backward* was the definitive expression of the anguish that accompanied the transition from agrarianism to industrialism in America. And although it is futile to try to say what is the central idea of a great literary creation, several emphases in Bellamy's work are especially pertinent to this discussion. First, the striking figure he used to describe existing conditions —a luxurious coach filled with merry capitalists so deep in their cups as not to notice that the combination of heavy vehicle, deep mud, steep hill, and cruel whip was straining the horses (or the masses) beyond their endurance—still creates an unforgettable impression. Second, *Looking Backward* is a Utopia; its author was unable to believe in 1887 that anything short of a basic overhauling of society's institutions would make life with the machine tolerable. Third, the institutional framework he envisaged for the year 2000 had no place for either private property as we know it or competition. Fourth, the world he believed would have to emerge from the dog-eat-dog primitivism of his own time was a communistic one—in the pre-Soviet sense. To be sure, Bellamy's solution was not taken seriously by his contemporaries. To be sure also, these ideas taken as a whole appear even more unrealistic three-quarters of a century later. But that they do accurately portray the torment of a society convulsed by mechanization there can be little doubt.

Not only did the man in the street begin almost immediately to rise up against the trusts, but in this stand he was powerfully supported by the relatively young scientific discipline known as economics.[11] Starting with the classical model of pure and perfect competition, economists clung persistently to the belief that any trace of monopolization is certain to result in resource waste. Thus preoccu-

[11] V. A. Mund, *Open Markets: An Essential of Free Enterprise* (New York: Harper & Bros., 1948).

pied, these men could not bring themselves to give much credence either to the technological basis underlying consolidation or to the equally fundamental fact that competition during this period of transition became almost unbearably intense. With respect to the first of these factors it was emphasized that expansion was frequently carried beyond the point of greatest efficiency, while on the matter of excessive competition the retort came back that industrialists unwilling to compete have no place in an individualist-type economy.

A more mature scholarship, both in the field of economic history and in economic theory, is now spearheading a reassessment of this period. In the first place, it is easy to be too critical of resource waste in a society that ceased being a small-business, low-productivity economy and became a big-business, high-productivity economy so rapidly that observers three-quarters of a century later are still almost bewildered. In the second place, viewing this period from the standpoint of those living in it, it is now clear that the environment within which the businessman operated can realistically be thought of as a hostile one. Then as now the human reaction to such an environment was to endeavor to bring it under control insofar as possible. Given a situation in which a veritable "Sword of Damocles" hung over the head of every industrialist, it is obvious that nice calculations relative to the point of junction between the marginal revenue and marginal cost curves would not be the major determinant of business policy. Obviously it was much safer to be too big than too small, and indeed a concern just the right size from the standpoint of resource use might easily be overpowered by a financially stronger concern. Economists today are becoming increasingly aware of the existence of discontinuities in the economy as a result of which the achievement of the most efficient size by any large proportion of the producers in the major industries would be most unlikely.

QUESTIONS FOR DISCUSSION

1. In what ways did mechanization contribute to an increase in competition? To a decrease?

2. How did mechanization help to bring economic distress to the major politico-economic groups?

3. Explain the impact of the machine upon the economic well-being of businessmen as a class.

4. What economic problem was the pool designed to solve? Was this a problem only for the firms involved, or did society have a stake in it too?

5. Why did business cooperation first become a significant phenomenon in the railroad industry?

6. Explain the connection between the state of competition in the railroad industry and the level of competition in other industries.

7. Distinguish between the major types of pools. What were the principal difficulties confronting this method of inter-firm cooperation?

8. Explain the nature and significance of the first trust agreement?

9. What was the role of the corporation in the so-called consolidation movement?

10. How did the majority of citizens feel about the sudden rise of big business? Were these attitudes justified?

11. To what extent were industrialists justified in cooperating with one another as they did? To what extent was this detrimental to public interest?

Chapter 9

Another Reform Movement Launched

SUCCESS ON THE RAILROAD FRONT

Where to begin? How could frustrated citizens of a newly industrialized society regain control of their economic destiny? Doubtless, there were few who had a clear idea of what should be done, although there was a veritable multitude eager to make an early start.

But if there was legitimate reason to debate whether to move first against industrial or railroad monopoly, there was ample justification for the decision soon made to launch the initial attack against the railroads. For a number of reasons public hostility toward these concerns was just now reaching a particularly intense climax.

One of the important factors here was undoubtedly the publicity which had been given to speculation and fraud in railway affairs. Beginning about the time of the Civil War, these activities had become more and more prominent, reaching a peak in the almost frenzied construction of the 1880's. As early as 1874 the Windom Committee had opined that of all the abuses of the time "none have contributed so much to the general discontent and indignation as the increase of railway capital by stock watering and capitalization of surplus earnings." Five years later a committee of the New York legislature (the famous Hepburn Committee), commissioned to investigate the uses that had been made of New York railroad charters, denounced railroad speculation in even stronger language, and added a similarly emphatic denunciation of railroad pools. Then, in 1884, had come the "railroad panic," so named because it was widely thought to have been brought about by the excesses associated with the railroad building of these years, and because this economic downturn had plunged an unprecedented number of roads into bankruptcy.

157

A second and probably still more important reason for focusing attention first on the railroads was the connection public opinion was certain it saw between the functioning of the transportation system and monopoly in other fields. Who could doubt that the favors secured by large shippers from railroads threatened with or actually in the throes of a vicious rate war were an important factor in the consolidation movement? At this point also the Hepburn Committee had been unequivocal in its conclusions after it made the discovery that on the New York Central one-half of the business out of New York and nine-tenths out of Syracuse moved on special rates, and that few shippers ever saw a printed tariff. Equally extreme cases were revealed in other investigations. Unquestionably, however, the *bête noir* of public opinion in this connection was the Standard Oil Company and the information that had come to light regarding the concessions it had received. Surely no other episode contributed as much to the crystallization of public opinion in favor of railroad regulation as the ill-fated career of the South Improvement Company.

Both of these major grievances were highlighted in an especially forceful way in 1886 when the results of another Congressional investigation were made public.[1] On the matter of railroad financial practices the Cullom Committee had this to say: "This practice [of stock watering] has unquestionably done more to keep alive a popular feeling of hostility against the railroads of the United States than any other one cause." Even more incisive was this group's summary comment on the issue of preferential treatment among shippers: "The paramount evil chargeable against the operation of the transportation systems of the United States, as now conducted, is unjust discrimination between persons, places, commodities, or particular descriptions of traffic."

One other consideration probably helped tip the balance in favor of a first action on the railroad front. Already a substantial success had been achieved in this field, and on the foundations of *Munn v. Illinois* it would perhaps be easy to build further. To citizens beset with a feeling of helplessness amid the forces unleashed by industrialization, this probability of success in another challenge to the railroads was surely a factor of no small importance.

It is worthy of special note, however, that this new campaign for railroad control, continuous though it was with the Granger movement in some respects, was quite different from its predecessor in others. Thus discrimination had replaced the rate level as the pri-

---

[1] Shelby M. Cullom, *Fifty Years of Public Service* (Chicago: A. C. McClurg & Co., 1911).

mary problem to be remedied. Antagonism toward monopoly was central to this endeavor as it had not been earlier, and the monopoly evil here being attacked resided fully as much outside the railroad industry as inside. Even from the standpoint of the railroads themselves the difficulty was now economic disorganization to a far greater extent than the possession of excessive economic power as on the prior occasion. Above all, it was now understood that a large part of this responsibility would need to be shouldered by the federal government rather than the states, although almost everyone still believed that financial practices would have to be regulated by the states through their charter laws.

This shift in the center of gravity of the regulatory problem was itself dictated by a number of factors. Speaking most broadly, what was involved was the increasingly obvious fact that the nation's railroads had outgrown state boundaries. In addition to this general consideration, however, two developments in 1886 suggested an immediate move in the direction of federal control.

The first of these precipitating forces was the report of the Cullom Committee. This group, led, it is significant to observe, by an Iowa Senator, was unequivocal in asserting that federal control was a must, although the specific recommendations made in this report were conservative. Fuller public information regarding railroad operations in general and railroad rates in particular was presented as a fairly adequate remedy. Obviously few ardent reformers could feel that so mild a measure would be sufficient, and in this conclusion they were sweepingly confirmed by the implications of the second crucial event in 1886.

That event was a Supreme Court decision involving a charge of discrimination against the Wabash Railroad.[2] The situation at issue was the following. Between Peoria, Illinois, and New York City, the Wabash had established a rate of 15 cents per hundred pounds for a certain item of freight. On this same commodity, however, the Wabash was charging 25 cents per hundred pounds between Gilman, Illinois, and New York City, the joker here being that the Peoria–New York haul was sixty miles longer than the Gilman–New York distance, trains from Peoria even passing through Gilman on their way to New York. Producers in Gilman, claiming that this discrimination gave Peoria competitors an unfair advantage in the New York market, prevailed upon the Illinois regulatory commission to take steps to equalize these charges.

It is easy to sympathize with the commissioners as this case came

---

[2] *Wabash, St. Louis and Pacific Railway Company v. Illinois*, 118 U.S. 557 (1886).

before them. Of the fact of discrimination, of course, there could be no doubt. Nor was it any more to be doubted that both the city benefitting from and the city injured by this discrimination were in Illinois. The sting came in the fact that New York City was not in Illinois, that the remedy demanded by Gilman merchants clearly involved the regulation of interstate commerce.

Equally easy is it to sympathize with the railroad. The Peoria–New York rate had long since been agreed upon between the Wabash and its trunkline competitors at that point; to raise this rate, in other words, would simply mean relinquishing all thought of securing a share of this traffic. On the other hand, the Gilman–New York rate was not, so the railroad argued, exorbitant; it was calculated only to cover the full cost of performing the service. Wabash officials even pointed out that the lower rate from Peoria did not have an adverse effect upon the rate from Gilman, because the former was high enough to cover all out-of-pocket costs.

Resolving its dilemma by relying on the *Munn* v. *Illinois* assertion that until the federal government enacted needed regulations the states were free to assume jurisdiction over interstate commerce, the commission rejected the railroad's defense and ordered the Wabash to end this discrimination. In turn the brief entered by the railroad specifically attacked the Munn ruling on this point. Such a doctrine, it was insisted, constituted an invasion of federal government powers. Inactivity by the central government means that in its judgment no regulations are required; the clear implication of the Munn view, therefore, was that the fundamental right not to act in a field reserved to the national government could be breached at will.

Confronted thus squarely with what was obviously an absurd earlier decision, the Supreme Court could only reverse itself as gracefully as possible.[3] Immediately the nation was in an uproar. A number of states had recently reactivated their regulatory commissions with the expectation of bringing their railroads more nearly to heel, and unfortunately the issue raised in the Wabash case was characteristic of the cases involving discrimination which had so outraged public opinion. That decision meant, in short, that this problem—the one the Cullom Committee had classified as paramount—could not be remedied by the states.

Probably in appealing to the federal courts for protection against a state statute, the railroad industry did not have in mind the

[3] Albert Stickney, *State Control of Trade and Commerce by National or State Authority* (New York: Baker & Voorhis, 1897).

prompt substitution of federal for state supervision. The idea of laissez faire, by now an integral part of the ideology of capitalism, was intended to apply to governments at both levels. But if this be true, the success of the industry against the Illinois commission was a pyrrhic victory. The following year the Interstate Commerce Act was passed, and the beginning of the end of laissez faire in railroading was in sight.

This enactment was a most comprehensive piece of legislation, for its time.[4] All unjust and unreasonable rates were forthwith prohibited, and the same was true of practically all forms of discrimination. A still more rigorous provision outlawed all pooling arrangements. All rates were to be printed and posted for public inspection, and annual detailed reports on finances and operations were required to be made available to the public. Most significant of all, the new law borrowing at this point from the experience of the states, an Interstate Commerce Commission was established and given the herculean task of seeing to it that the railroads obeyed the law.

It is perhaps typical of the distortions which creep into history that until recently it was taken for granted that regulation of the railroads by the federal government was first and foremost a response to political pressures emanating from agrarian constituencies. The source of this assumption was no doubt the well-authenticated fact that the earlier Granger legislation was so motivated, and indeed it is not now claimed that farmers did not solidly support the new federal measure. However, illustrating once again the complexity of the forces behind particular public policies, by the late 1880's business groups were actually in the vanguard of this movement.[5] Merchants and manufacturers, men whose business was not transportation but who were nonetheless in an exchange society dependent upon an effective, reasonably priced, and regularized transportation system, had in this respect turned traitor to their own class. Probably this was the first major instance of this phenomenon, but in later years it was to be repeatedly demonstrated that the laisesz faire principles acceptable to one segment of the conservative fraternity were not necessarily acceptable to other segments.

[4] S. O. Dunn, *The Regulation of Railways* (New York: Appleton-Century-Crofts, Inc., 1918); and H. S. Haines, *Problems of Railway Regulation* (New York: The Macmillan Co., 1911).

[5] Lee Benson, *Merchants, Farmers, Railroads* (Cambridge: Harvard University Press, 1955).

FOCUS ON ANTITRUST[6]

Having thus made a decisive beginning toward bringing railroad corporations into a more responsible relationship with the larger community, reformers turned to the task of trimming industrial trusts down to size. Here, however, a much different and substantially greater problem was encountered, and as the leaders of this companion movement began to take stock of their resources it was quite evident that this struggle would not soon be ended.

One dimension of the greater difficulty of this problem can be seen by noting at the outset that the controls being developed in the railroad field could not readily be adapted for use against the trusts. Rate regulation was one thing built on a foundation consisting of *Munn v. Illinois* and railroads as common carriers and natural monopolies. It was another thing where manufacturing enterprises were concerned; no one seriously supposed that the Supreme Court would stretch the Fifth and Fourteenth Amendments so far as to permit direct supervision over these concerns. And from a still broader standpoint, the public utility concept would already have outlived its usefulness in an individualistic society were it so soon to be given such a general application.

But if high-fixed-cost manufacturing industries were not to be accepted as monopolies and regulated in the public interest, the alternative was to see to it that competition remained free and open. If the monopolies rising up in every corner of society were not "natural," they must then be "artificial" and would have to be dealt with accordingly. Here the second and by far the most complex dimension of the trust control problem comes into full view. For whereas the legal tradition which existed at the time of *Munn v. Illinois* was directly usable in forging the necessary railroad control tools, where the trusts were concerned the situation was much less fortunate. It was not, of course, that the common law was silent on the matter of competition and monopoly. The difficulty was rather that the economic order had been changing so rapidly that the common law had not yet crystallized its position on that issue.

A brief glance at the evolution of the common law with respect to this problem will make clear what was here at issue.[7] The most important kind of case on this subject that the law had been required to deal with over the past few hundred years was the

[6] Davis R. Dewey, *National Problems, 1885-1897* (New York: Harper & Bros., 1907).

[7] Roscoe Pound, *The Spirit of the Common Law* (Boston: The Marshall Jones Co., 1925).

agreement not to compete as associated with the sale of a business or the practice of a trade—a type of agreement known by the generic name "contract in restraint of trade." At the beginning of modern times, when families seldom moved very far from the locale of their origin and when statuses were ordinarily rigidly fixed, the law took the position that an agreement not to practice his trade might easily make a man a public charge and hence most such contracts were considered contrary to public policy and thus void.

Gradually the underlying economy became more fluid, however, and the courts began to orient their decisions to this change. Where a man did not necessarily give up his livelihood by agreeing to a restraint of trade contract, the earlier uncompromising hostility to such contracts was seen to work a hardship on both buyers and sellers of business goodwill. At this point the attitude of the law became one of judging each case as it arose on its merits, inquiring with respect to each set of facts whether the restraint agreed to was "reasonable" or not. And what was a reasonable restraint? Although trade law was exceedingly complex, and not a little confused, in general the approach of the courts was that restrictions which did not go beyond what was necessary to protect the legitimate interests of the buyer and which at the same time did not bring injury to the public would be permitted.

But scarcely had the law adjusted its thinking to the pre-industrial economic order than further and unprecedentedly rapid economic dynamics posed still different problems. On the one hand, there arose national concerns which could effectively sell their goodwill only by agreeing not to set up a competing establishment anywhere in the country. On the other hand, the recent rebellion of businessmen against competition had brought before the courts the situation in which agreements not to compete were in no way associated with the sale of goodwill. How was the "rule of reason," as it came to be called, to deal with these cases?

The first type of case created few difficulties. Where a particular agreement not to compete left the field fairly open to other actual or potential competitors, and the courts were generally prone to give the contracting parties the benefit of the doubt on this question, restrictions closely related to the goodwill involved were allowed, no matter how large the geographical area included. Where, however, agreements not to compete were not "ancillary" to some other purpose, the questions raised were neither so simple nor so directly answered in terms of evolving legal traditions.[8]

[8] M. A. Handler, *A Study of the Construction and Enforcement of the Federal Anti-Trust Laws* (Washington, D.C.: Government Printing Office, 1941).

The fact is that on this point (precisely where citizens were becoming so concerned) the common law had not yet settled on a pattern of more or less consistent principles. According to the doctrine laid down in some courts (and this view is believed by most students of this subject to have been the dominant one), nonancillary agreements in restraint of trade were to be judged without benefit of any rule of reason; they were *per se* unreasonable. Other courts would uphold such a restraint if the agreeing firms constituted a relatively small segment of the entire industry; while yet others would permit nonancillary restraints covering an entire industry if it could be shown that the resulting market power had not been abused.

FIASCO IN 1890

The confused state of the common law governing trade restraints was only one reason why supplementary tools seemed to be urgently needed. Another was the fact that under the common law only one of the parties to a restriction agreement could bring action against it; neither injured competitors nor consumers had legal rights in this matter. A third was the fact that the common law assessed no penalties against entering into such a contract, except insofar as its refusal to enforce the agreement constituted a penalty. And finally, the common law of course did not provide the basis for a program of public prosecutions.

No sooner was the Interstate Commerce Act out of the way than this companion assault was launched with great vigor. Naturally the primary object of attack was the trust device[9] (and it is perhaps also worth noting in passing that the principal focus of public hostility was the organizations integrating the petroleum and sugar-refining industries). As a House of Representatives committee summarized a feeling now quite widespread: "This form of combination was obviously devised for the purpose of relieving the trusts and trustees from the charge of any breach of the conspiracy laws of the several states, or of being a combination to regulate or control the price or production of any commodity." And when in protest against these findings it was insisted that the several corporations thus combined remained separate and distinct, that stockholders had received only trust certificates and hence had no legal title to the property of the corporations involved, and that the trustees only held stock in the corporations and therefore did not buy or sell or

[9] Eliot Jones, *The Trust Problem in the United States* (New York: The Macmillan Co., 1922).

fix prices or anything of that sort, the House group made it clear that it was not deceived by this maze of legal fictions.

The most immediately successful technique adopted was litigation, these actions in part taking reference from the common law but more fundamentally relating to state incorporation laws. Louisiana had the distinction of originating this line of attack; in 1887 she moved against the cotton oil trust on the ground that its operations in the state were carried on as though it were a corporation when in fact it was not. Shortly thereafter Tennessee took on a "syndicate" in this same industry, the law here basing action on the fact that a Tennessee member of this group had violated its corporate charter by entering into a partnership. In 1888 New York brought suit against one of the members of the sugar trust, this action charging that the concern involved had violated its charter by transferring control over its operations to others. A closely related action in far-off California attacked another member of the sugar trust on the ground that in entering the combine it had forfeited its charter by losing its independence. Nebraska moved against the whiskey trust and Ohio attacked the Standard Oil Company, both of these suits charging *ultra vires* behavior in entering the trust agreement. Clearly the trust method of industrial coordination was under heavy pressure.

This was, indeed, a beginning; if the common law on restraint of trade was not the answer here, perhaps some headway could be made through charter regulations. However, few reformers had any desire to put all of their eggs in one basket, least of all this particular one. Control through corporation charters would be an indirect and slow-moving approach at best, especially in view of the fact that combinations were visibly being formed more rapidly than actions of this sort could be brought against them. A far more satisfactory procedure would surely be to declare illegal by statute the very act of combining, and to set up an enforcement agency to carry on an aggressive prosecution program. Accordingly, a number of states— most notably Kansas, Michigan, Maine, Missouri, and Texas—enacted ambitious antitrust legislation. Within two years one-third of all the states then in the union had passed laws of this kind, and in the next fifty years some thirty-five states in all followed suit.

But just as in the railroad field it was by now understood that the federal government would have to assume a large share of the control responsibility, so also in the case of industrial trusts. Thus even as the states were taking their first tentative steps in this area, agitation for a federal statute as well was reaching fever proportions.

As Supreme Court Justice Harlan later described prevailing sentiment on the trust issue at this time:

All who recall the condition of the country in 1890 will remember that there
was everywhere, among the people generally, a deep feeling of unrest. The
nation had been rid of human slavery—fortunately, as all now feel—but the
conviction was universal that the country was in real danger from another kind
of slavery sought to be fastened on the American people, namely, the slavery
that would result from aggregations of capital in the hands of a few individuals and corporations controlling for their own profit and advantage exclusively, the entire business of the country, including the production and sale
of the necessaries of life.

So powerful was public opinion on this subject that every political
party in the presidential campaign of 1888 declared emphatically
for legislation bearing directly upon it. The business-dominated
Republican party, the organization so soon to have control over the
government in all its branches, expressed itself as follows: "We declare our opposition to all combinations of capital, organized in
trusts or otherwise, to control arbitrarily the condition of trade
among our citizens. . . ." In his first message to that body, Republican President Harrison urged a Republican Congress to give "earnest attention" to the trust problem.

Rarely has a major piece of legislation been so unanimously demanded by all important segments of the population. If this had
been an accurate harbinger of the success a federal antitrust statute
was destined to enjoy, the problem would have been dealt with in
both a summary and a decisive fashion. Unfortunately for the cause
of reform, however, these appearances were deceiving. The businessmen behind the power now in the saddle did not in fact want
an effective antitrust enactment. What they wanted rather was an
increase in the tariff, and they were willing to pay almost any price
to achieve that objective, including putting an antitrust statute on
the books. Their declarations in support of such legislation were
made, in short, with tongue in cheek.

So harsh a judgment should not be advanced, of course, without
supporting evidence. Therefore a few of the major facts on which it
is based will briefly be reviewed. In the first place, simple logic
casts grave suspicion on this performance at the outset. Obviously
the nation's industrial, Republican leadership did not want federal
government interference with their adjustment to the frustrations
of the machine age. When despite this obvious preference the
Sherman Anti-Trust Act passed the House without a single negative
vote and the Senate with only one dissent, what other conclusion
is to be reached than that a political "deal" was in the wind.

Second, a direct connection between antitrust legislation and a new tariff measure at this time can also be clearly seen. For a number of years after the Civil War, not only had the tariff structure levied to finance that conflict been retained almost intact but duties had even been raised on several important products. By 1883, however, public opposition to a tax program regularly taking from citizens far more money than the government needed finally compelled a reduction in most rates. Immediately the business interests determined to repeal these reductions at the earliest opportunity—and perhaps even increase some levies. That opportunity came with the inauguration of Benjamin Harrison in 1889.

There was, to be sure, no difficulty in swinging labor into line behind a tariff increase. Western farmers, however, posed an entirely different problem. Furthermore, if it was the farmer who objected most strenuously to aggressive protectionism at this point, it was also the farmer who was most vocal in his demand for effective federal antitrust legislation.[10] (In this connection, compare the wording of the Republican antitrust plank above with a resolution passed at a Farmers' Congress at Montgomery, Alabama, only a few months before that plank was written: "*Resolved,* That we are opposed to all combinations of capital, in trusts or otherwise, to arbitrarily control the markets of the country to the detriment of producers.") Nor were these two issues separate in the minds of agrarians. "The tariff is the mother of trusts" was becoming a highly popular political slogan, and this belief goes far to explain why many westerners felt that antitrust was only the other side of the tariff question. At the same time, however, it suggested to business leaders how the farmer's attitude toward the tariff might be softened. As one approach he could be offered a protection against trusts which he very much wanted at the cost of a tariff increase to which he was opposed, a bargain which could be made even more attractive by pointing out that the passage of antitrust legislation would also remove one of his major objections to the McKinley Tariff.

Still another indication that the Sherman Anti-Trust Act was primarily the result of backstage maneuvering has to do with yet a third major piece of legislation passed in 1890. Evidently Republican leaders felt that, even with antitrust thrown in, their tariff measure would rest on an insecure political foundation. Accordingly they decided to "sweeten the pot" to an even greater extent. Farmers were still inflation minded, and several western states were eager to expand the Treasury's purchases of silver beyond the

[10] S. J. Buck, *The Agrarian Crusade: A Chronicle of the Farmer in Politics* (New Haven: Yale University Press, 1921).

quantities currently being bought under the Bland-Allison Act. Reflecting these several facts, there now appeared a measure, sponsored by the political party which had always been least inflationist in outlook, calling for the purchase by the federal government of virtually the country's entire annual output of silver. When it is noted that Congressional members of the "party of sound money" voted for the Sherman Silver Purchase Act to a man, there can surely remain no doubt as to the political nature of the Sherman Anti-Trust Act.[11]

It is one of the paradoxes of American economic history that the provisions of the Sherman Act—a measure passed at the cost of the highest tariff the nation had ever had and the most inflationist peacetime federal monetary legislation in the country's history—bore few traces of this suspicious origin. Reformers could have had no reason to be half-hearted in their enthusiasm for a law so sweeping in its condemnation of all organizations designed to eliminate or reduce the rigors of competition. In a surprisingly few words, for an act of Congress, this law said (or so it seemed in 1890) all that needed to be said on this topic:

Sec. 1. Every contract, combination in the form of a trust or otherwise, or conspiracy, in restraint of trade or commerce among the several States, or with foreign nations, is hereby declared to be illegal. Every person who shall make any such contract or engage in any such combination or conspiracy shall be deemed guilty of a misdemeanor. . . .

Sec. 2. Every person who shall monopolize, or attempt to monopolize, or combine or conspire with any other person or persons, to monopolize any part of the trade or commerce among the several States, or with foreign nations, shall be deemed guilty of a misdemeanor. . . .

SHADOWS CAST BEFORE

This language must indeed have been reassuring to liberals. Yet, behind these words, there were several aspects of what had taken place which might well have given reformers pause—if for no other reason than that the victory had been so easy while being at the same time so apparently complete. What did conservatives have in mind that they allowed this measure to become law so obligingly? Surely it is not to be supposed that Republican managers really expected the Sherman Act to become a great success! Taking only a little advantage of the perspective of history, it can be asserted with some confidence that already a few dark clouds could be seen in the background.

[11] T. E. Burton, *John Sherman* (Boston: Houghton Mifflin Co., 1906).

To begin with, there was the fact that, as is now freely acknowledged, the nation's first antitrust law was frankly intended only to declare the common law with respect to this problem. Notwithstanding the tremendous advantages of giving existing law a positive statement (namely, the possibility of a program of public prosecutions, a legal basis for the assessment of penalties, and the right of injured competitors to bring suit), this was a weak foundation on which to build such a vital public policy. On the one hand, as already noted, the common law was not consistent in its handling of the combination problem, this body of doctrine being much less uncompromising, for example, than the language of the Sherman Act. Obviously it would only be a matter of time until the same circumlocutions which were already to be found in common-law decisions began to creep into court interpretations of the antitrust act, until a rule of reason was incorporated in these opinions which might greatly reduce their effectiveness in enforcing competition. On the other hand, the major purpose of statute law is to correct inconsistencies in case law, and above all to compensate for the slowness of case law to respond to changed circumstances. The writing of an antitrust statute in 1890 purporting only to declare the common law was thus in one sense only another way of saying that the process of legal development was not to be hastened—that the law in this field was to continue to evolve by the painfully slow process of piling precedent upon precedent—and this in the face of an extremely rapid accentuation of the problem to be alleviated.

To be sure, the Sherman Act did provide that the Attorney General should institute proceedings to prevent violations; and to whatever extent this was done, the evolution of antitrust legal doctrine would be speeded up. But the sequel to this enactment from that standpoint would seem more nearly to confirm than to counter the view that misgivings were warranted. Notably, a new agency was not created and given broad enforcement responsibilities as in the Interstate Commerce Act; the impetus thus given to legal evolution was, in other words, to be left to the discretion of the President working through an appointed Cabinet official (although suits brought by private parties would also presumably be of some assistance). Under the best of circumstances, of course, this procedure could result in a rapid evolution of case law, but the significant point to note is that in this way the administration was given the best possible opportunity to take advantage of any lessening of the popular clamor against combinations.

However, all the clouds looming on the antitrust horizon were not procedural in character. Several substantive shadows might also have been noticed by the close observer.

One of these was the question of whether or not the Sherman Act could have gone beyond the common law even if that had been its intent. A vital element in free enterprise is and must be freedom of association in business. An individual may establish his own business, or he may go in with someone else. Again, a corporation may be formed which will take over the assets of a partnership (or even another corporation) already in the field. Or still again, two corporations may decide to become a single firm. Out of raw materials such as these has been created a large part of the economic progress the United States has been privileged to enjoy.

No right in a democracy can be unlimited, however. Freedom of association carried too far means monopoly. The two corporations deciding to merge may be competitors, and after the merger competition may be materially reduced. How is this line to be drawn? By the use of what formula can a distinction be made between the association which promotes economic well-being and the one which primarily lessens competition, between the union reflecting only superior business judgment and the one going off rather into that area called exploitation of the consumer? Who is competent to say, thus far you may go but no farther? This is not to argue, of course, that such decisions cannot be made with some degree of reliability. It does suggest the possibility, however, that they can only be made in the process of deciding actual cases. Perhaps, in other words, a rule of reason was destined from the beginning to be an indispensable tool in the battle against the trusts, whatever the complications for antitrust enforcement it might bring in its wake.

Another substantive shadow had to do with organized labor's stand on the trust issue. Clearly a firm policy at this point would have required strong support from laborers as well as farmers. But to whatever extent the reformers of that day studied the implications for their cause of what was happening on the union front, they were surely not comforted by what they saw.

Until recently one of the most fundamental elements in the philosophy of organized labor had been the belief that status as a wage earner was temporary only, that the majority of wage earners might confidently look forward to a mature adulthood as independent entrepreneurs.[12] As long as that view was a dominant labor theme, workers were inclined to look at the growth of big business and the "cannibalism" which accompanied the rise of the machine age as

---

[12] Selig Perlman, A Theory of the Labor Movement (New York: The Macmillan Co., 1928).

a major obstacle to the progression of laborers from dependence to independence. Of late, however, labor had been giving up this emphasis, workers now beginning to resign themselves to a lifetime of wage work. With this transition had come a profound change in this group's outlook on matters of economic policy, and especially the trust issue.

Labor's new position on this question is nowhere better stated than in the memoirs of Samuel Gompers, founder of the first comprehensive national organization of American workers dedicated to economic unionism, the American Federation of Labor.

I have persistently held that economic organizations ought to be free to operate as economic needs developed and that opportunity for initiative is essential to sustained progress. That is why I did not join the hue and cry against industrial combinations that gained momentum in the late 'eighties.[13]

Modern labor unions, in other words, are in their own way trusts no less than are business combinations, and organized labor could ill afford to have the Department of Justice breathing down its neck at every turn. Far better was it for workers to promote their own organizations than to devise a tool to attack business organizations which might then be used against labor groups.

Still another background doubt about the future of antitrust took reference from the campaign against monopoly being waged by the several states. For one thing, it soon became evident that state statutes in this field would not fulfill their initial promise. As a result of a number of factors (including the role of the federal government in this field, and the political coalitions in so many state capitols between farmers and businessmen) these laws were typically neither well enough drawn nor sufficiently well enforced to make much difference. In both the short run and the long run, thus, the history of this legislation closely paralleled the nation's experience with state regulatory laws in the railroad field.

Although for a short time state litigation provided the trusts with a formidable adversary, this approach proved ultimately to be too inflexible for full effectiveness. Two developments will suffice to show what was here involved. The most successful state action of this kind was Ohio's suit against the Standard Oil Company. Agreeing with the state that a corporation must be run by its own directors, the courts in this case forbade the Ohio company from carrying out its agreement with the trust. As a direct consequence of that decision the trust was "dissolved" in 1892, dissolution taking the

---

[13] Samuel Gompers, *Seventy Years of Life and Labor* (New York: E. P. Dutton, 1925), vol. II, p. 225.

form of first distributing the stock of sixty-four of these concerns to one of the remaining twenty, and then distributing the stock of these latter concerns to the holders of the trust certificates. However, since the shares of all twenty companies were to be distributed pro rata to all certificate holders, and since the companies did not pay dividends on fractional shares, small holders were discouraged from giving up their certificates (on which dividends continued to be paid). The nine trustees, therefore, continued to hold not only a majority of the stock of the twenty companies but also such trust certificates as had not been liquidated. Clearly the underlying situation remained unchanged, but this was apparently as far as the law of Ohio could go.

In a superficial sense it could be said that, despite repeated failures of these sorts, litigation initiated by state governments was the destroyer of the trust device. Not only was the Standard Oil trust "dissolved," but when the Nebraska Distilling Company and the North Sugar Refining Company both lost their charters as a result of similar actions this method of combination was abandoned in these industries. By 1892 this form of organization was on the defensive almost everywhere, and by the end of the century it was almost a thing of the past. On the other hand, however, it now seems unlikely that industrialists would have given up so easily if a substitute technique had not been already at hand.

In 1888 a governor of New Jersey, concerned about his state's finances, consulted a prominent corporation lawyer from New York as to how more revenue might be brought into an empty treasury. James B. Dill, perhaps with one eye on the governor's problem but certainly with the other on the needs of his business friends, suggested that New Jersey pass a law permitting concerns chartered in New Jersey to hold stock in other corporations. This New Jersey did, with consequences for the state's treasury the governor had scarcely dared to hope for. For the first time, on any wholesale basis, one company could direct the affairs of another simply by securing a controlling interest in its stock.[14]

The birth of the holding company immediately made the cumbersome trust device obsolete. Not only could all concerns desiring relief from competition go to New Jersey to secure the right to integrate by means of a holding company, but a number of other states quickly followed suit in order to find relief for their own depleted treasuries. A number of the states that imitated New Jersey, incidentally, no doubt concluded they had nothing to lose in any event.

[14] James B. Dill (Compiler), General Corporation Act of New Jersey, With Other General Acts Relating to Business Corporations (New York: Baker & Voorhis, 1903).

With the corporation now fully accepted as an individual in the eyes of the law (the Sherman Act explicitly declaring this relationship), it was only a matter of time before the comity and equal protection of the laws clauses in the Constitution would allow New Jersey corporations freely to come and go as they pleased regardless of state laws—at least within the limits of the prevailing legal definition of interstate commerce. At one and the same time the federal government became the last line of defense against monopoly, and the "common law" was given an even more difficult problem to resolve.

VICTORY ON THE LAND FRONT

Shadows, however, were for the future, and liberals could well pride themselves on a job well done. In two major ways the monster had been humbled. Turning now from this second achievement, reformers gave attention to still a third long-standing issue between the capitalist and the common man.

For several decades prior to the Civil War America's unoccupied public lands had been covetously eyed by the unfortunate from one end of the country to the other. If only they could secure possession of a small portion of this abundance, they thought, their difficulties would disappear. Thus from small, debt-ridden farmers and overworked and underpaid urban workers had come a mounting agitation for a more liberal disposal policy.[15]

No sooner had the Civil War commenced than this agitation was rewarded by a success which could hardly have been more complete—or at least so most people thought at the time. Under the terms of the Homestead Act any individual might become the owner of a 160-acre farm simply by settling on it. Heralded in its own day as the greatest democratic law ever enacted, this measure seemed to mean that henceforth any individual who felt ill-treated in the settled East might achieve a more satisfactory adjustment in the West.

Actually, however, the Homestead Act as enacted was only a promise yet to be fulfilled, and no sooner had the promise been made than the first steps were taken to break it.[16] Legislation was passed making land available in other ways; and since the total amount of land was limited, this meant that the area available for homesteading was correspondingly reduced. Tens of millions of

[15] F. J. Turner, *The Frontier in American History* (New York: Henry Holt & Co., Inc., 1920).

[16] Ray A. Billington, *Westward Expansion: A History of the American Frontier* (New York: The Macmillan Co., 1949).

acres were given to the railroads, and even more went to the states under the Morrill Act. Under the Mineral Land Act of 1866 and the Minerals Act of 1872, land containing valuable minerals was sold in small quantities at from $2.50 to $5.00 per acre. In 1873 the Timber Culture Act was passed, granting to homesteaders an additional quarter of a section on condition that a specified number of acres be planted to trees. The Desert Land Act of 1877 made available at $1.25 an acre a full section of land to anyone who would do irrigation work on it. In 1878 the Timber and Stone Act opened up stone and timber land "unfit for cultivation" in units of 160 acres at appraisal value or $2.50 per acre, whichever was higher. And not only were these new encroachments on the guaranty contained in the Homestead Act authorized, but the purchase of choice lands in advance of survey was still possible under the Pre-emption Act.

In all fairness it must be said that promise-breaking was not the purpose of this supplementary land legislation; a reasonable case can be made for each enactment. Railroad land grants were intended to speed up the westward movement; grants to the states were to help foster education. The minerals acts in turn were for the purpose of securing some compensation to the government for lands often very valuable. Who, moreover, would quarrel with the objective behind the Timber Culture Act? Even the Desert Land Act was in theory little more than an attempt to adapt already established principles to land of a very different character.

If, in other words, all this heterogeneous mass of land legislation had been used for and only for the intended purpose, the average citizen would have had much less ground for complaint. But this was far from the case. In many instances land eminently suitable for homesteading was fraudulently secured under the Timber and Stone Act, while the Desert Land Act was often used to secure a full section of homesteadable land rather than a quarter of a section. Neither the Timber Culture Act nor the Desert Land Act, furthermore, were carefully policed to see to it that recipients of land thereunder lived up to the conditions specified. At one time, indeed, it was possible for a single individual to secure almost two full sections of the public domain without violating the letter of the law simply by taking advantage of the provisions of several acts. Even the Homestead Act was abused; and here of course was the most distressing feature of what was happening from the standpoint of a long-cherished American dream. Again and again a mining or a lumber company would induce dozens of individuals to stake out homestead claims to be later turned over to the company. In short, the public domain, instead of being used to create a nation of small freeholders, became essentially another means whereby the wealth of the nation was concentrated in the hands of a few plutocrats and giant corporations.

Fairness also requires that another observation be read into the record. Due allowance must be made for the unrealism of this particular dream. Even to the extent that free land was available, the western frontier could not have provided a haven for the eastern poor. The real frontier was already the city, and for every urban worker who did in fact go west ten farmers' sons joined the urban labor force. And while the tide of history was militating against this ideal directly, certain other facts of life were operating to destroy it indirectly. The truth is that free land was simply no alternative to the average day laborer possessed of none of the skills required in farming and lacking the capital either to take his family west or to make his operations efficient after he arrived.

What, then, was the issue as reformers squared off to do battle with capitalists at this point? Two things, primarily. First, these developments were an almost perfect symbol of the loss of control of the common man over his society, and no small part of the importance of land legislation from this standpoint was the role often played by the monopoly of raw materials in trust formation. Second, with the end of the western frontier now clearly in sight, the prodigious rate at which the nation was utilizing its tremendous but not limitless resources was beginning to alarm important segments of the population. And of these two interests—control and conservation—there is little doubt but that the most important objective was control.

A first step toward reform in this field had been taken in 1871 with the ending of railroad grants. Since then, but especially during the 1880's, a steady conflict had been waged over efforts to broaden this achievement. In 1891, against the background of the Interstate Commerce and Sherman Anti-Trust acts, another significant victory was attained. A general land reform act was passed containing the following provisions:[17] the repeal of the old Pre-emption Act; a limitation on the amount of the public land that could be granted to one person to 320 acres; repeal of the Timber Culture Act; and a provision authorizing the President to set aside timber areas as national parks. Although not all land abuses were thereby ended, still the chicken-house door was fairly safely padlocked. Unfortu-

[17] B. H. Hibbard, *A History of The Public Land Policies* (New York: The Macmillan Co., 1924).

nately, anyone who had taken the trouble to look inside could hardly have failed to notice that many of the chickens were already gone.

If there was any disposition on the part of reformers to congratulate themselves on accomplishments to date, this activity was soon cut short by the "Panic of 1893" and the severe depression to which it in turn gave way. And when that tragedy had run its course, it was too late. A series of economic forces were set in motion by this downturn which made it unmistakably clear that the task of reform had scarcely begun. Not only did problems arise during the next few years which had theretofore not been pressing, but it even developed that problems to which partial answers had already supposedly been worked out were almost as far from being solved as ever.

QUESTIONS FOR DISCUSSION

1. What was the relationship between the railroad problem and the problem of monopoly?

2. Explain the significance of the Wabash case. Why could the Supreme Court not have made the opposite decision?

3. How accurate is it to refer to the passage of the Interstate Commerce Act as "the end of an era"?

4. Why was the trust problem harder to reach by controls than the railroad problem? Why was the public utility concept not usable here?

5. Describe the evolution of the common law on trade restraints, and its status in 1890.

6. In what ways did state governments attack the trusts? How successful were these efforts?

7. Interpret the McKinley Tariff from the standpoint of accommodation.

8. What were the clouds hovering over the future of the Sherman Anti-Trust Act? Which were the most important?

9. Interpret the rise of big business in terms of consensus.

10. From the standpoint of government-business relationships, of what importance was the 1891 land legislation?

Chapter 10

Conservatism Reigns Supreme

It is often supposed that economic and social reform is more readily achieved in periods of business depression. There is, moreover, an element of logic behind this belief; it is during depression that the intricate mechanism called society shows up at its poorest, and hence it is at such a time that a majority of the people is most apt to feel that changes in the status quo are in order. Yet those who hold to that belief perhaps are too hastily generalizing from the American experience of the 1930's. It was, after all, during the depression of the 1870's that the Granger reforms were largely swept away, while the still more savage downturn of the 1890's produced scarcely a single development which could accurately be labeled reform. And there were a number of other developments during this latter period to which a quite different terminology might appropriately be applied.

At Lowest Ebb

One of the areas in which the patience of liberals was sorely tried was antitrust, where a combination of Congressional laxity and executive caution quickly made it evident that nothing significant was to be expected on this front in the foreseeable future.[1] In part these approaches to the new law may have been the result of a natural (and only half-concealed) administration hostility to its purposes, although in part they were also brought about by the widespread feeling that the act would be self-enforcing. Indeed, it had been to accentuate that feature of the measure that Section 7 with its award of triple damages to injured parties had been included. Whatever the factors involved, however, this part of the story of

[1] Hans B. Thorelli, *The Federal Antitrust Policy* (Baltimore: The Johns Hopkins Press, 1955).

the Sherman Act's early existence is almost completely summed up in a single fact—no additional funds were made available to the Attorney General's office for antitrust work.

Thirty-two months of Benjamin Harrison's term as President remained when the Sherman Act became law. During that period seven cases under it were instituted. One of these was against a group of coal dealers in Tennessee (this case, incidentally, being the only one successfully concluded during Harrison's administration), one involved a number of Minnesota lumber dealers, and one was a labor combination case. The other four were all significant, challenging no less formidable organizations than the whiskey trust,[2] the sugar trust, the cash register monopoly, and the Trans-Missouri Freight Association, but the handling of these "big ones" left much to be desired. The latter three cases were still pending when Harrison's term expired; the whiskey trust case was lost after being developed in a most amateurish way. Instead of bringing suit in the Chicago district, where the trust's main offices were located and where the last independent distillery of consequence had been purchased, action was brought in Boston—because the Assistant Attorney General for the Boston district had first suggested this suit. Thus did the Sherman Act begin to fulfill the hopes of 1890 reformers.

Nor was Democrat Grover Cleveland any more aggressive in this field than Republican Benjamin Harrison. In the course of his full four-year term only eight actions were brought. Of these, four related to labor unions, one was against a group of Kansas City livestock dealers, one involved Salt Lake City coal dealers, and two were of some consequence from the standpoint of the primary objectives of the Sherman Act. These were the celebrated suits against the Joint Traffic Association and the Addyston Pipe and Steel Company.

Reformers would not perhaps have been completely discouraged because the antitrust program was getting off to a slow start. That difficulty, after all, was only to be expected, and time might easily correct it. The antitrust tragedy of this period, therefore, was the Supreme Court's first antitrust decision. Here was an impediment to effective enforcement which liberals could not at the moment see any way around.

The defendant in this case was the sugar trust. Recently this organization (already a New Jersey holding company) had purchased the common stock of four Pennsylvania refining concerns, thereby

---

[2] From this point forward the use of the term "trust" is in the popular sense of any concentration of economic power thought to be excessive.

raising the proportion of the nation's entire refining capacity under its control from 65 to 98 per cent. The government charged violation of the Sherman Act, and asked that these contracts be declared void.

The Court made short work of the government's contention, although in a way that could hardly have been anticipated.[3] No question was raised as to the existence of monopoly; here, at least, the majority was realistic. What was challenged was the federal government's right to seek its suppression. The Constitution, through the Sherman Act, could convey jurisdiction to the Attorney General only in cases involving interstate commerce. But the case at bar, said the Court in all sincerity, concerned manufacturing, not commerce.

The charge has been made that the government wanted to lose this suit—to establish the "right" precedents for future antitrust actions. As evidence it can be pointed out that the case as presented to the Court was poorly drawn, and that the man responsible for its preparation, Richard Olney, a highly successful corporation lawyer and Cleveland's first Attorney General, deferred to no man in his hostility to antitrust. (Olney had shortly before this dropped the government's suit against the National Cash Register Company after the complaining concerns had been brought into this union, and after the sugar trust decision he wrote to a friend as follows: "You will have observed that the government has been defeated in the Supreme Court on the trust question. I always supposed it would be and have taken the responsibility of not prosecuting under a law I believed to be no good. . . .") On the other hand, however, surely the basis on which the Court rested its decision demands another interpretation. Perhaps Supreme Court conservatism would be the kindest way in which this turn of events might be explained; naiveté on matters economic is possibly too harsh. An important point to be remembered is that precedent was overwhelmingly on the side of the majority. Heretofore commerce had always been taken to mean the conveyance of goods from one place to another, and certainly the sugar trust was not engaged in this activity as such. Perhaps, as in its 1873 definition of property, the Court had simply not yet adjusted its thinking to modern conditions.

This event, moreover, was but the first in a series of three 1895 setbacks for late nineteenth-century liberalism at the hands of the Supreme Court. The second involved the distribution of the tax burden, a project almost as dear to the hearts of reformers as the battle against monopoly.

[3] *United States* v. *E. C. Knight Company*, 156 U.S. 1 (1895).

During the Civil War the nation's first income tax had been enacted. Levied expressly as a war tax, its repeal had become one of the first objectives of the postwar, conservative reaction against the wartime tax structure. But so enamored of this type of taxation were the lower classes by war's end that a stiff political fight had to be waged before the conservative position won out, and in the meantime several members of this group had taken the additional precaution of challenging the constitutionality of this type of taxation. In 1872 the Civil War income tax had finally been repealed, an especially gratifying victory for the well-to-do in view of the fact that the Supreme Court had been able to find no constitutional fault with it.

For a long time after the Civil War, reformers had nursed the memories of this defeat, eagerly awaiting an opportunity to reverse this 1872 action. Such an opportunity had not come soon, for the grip of the Republican party on the nation's political machinery had been too powerful. Then, in 1893, had appeared what seemed to be the long-awaited chance. For the first time since before the Civil War the Democratic party was in possession of the Presidency as well as both House and Senate, and Grover Cleveland was not nearly as conservative on the issue of taxation as on antitrust. Fighting against heavy odds the party set out to alter the incidence of the tax structure, beginning with the tariff. Although tariff reduction as such failed for the most part to materialize, an amendment to the tariff law did provide for a moderate income tax.

Immediately another test case was started on its way to the Supreme Court—this time not a Court made up of Justices reared in an atmosphere of agrarianism and appointed (in a majority of instances) by Democratic Presidents, but one composed of men who had lived their adult lives in an industrial environment and who had been appointed to their posts by Republican Presidents. Such a Court had no difficulty reversing the earlier ruling. An income tax, the majority now insisted (and, it would seem in retrospect, quite logically), is a direct tax, and would therefore have to be apportioned to the several states on the basis of population.[4] This decision, of course, meant that no effective income tax could be levied.

And that was that. The nation was thus to continue to have a highly regressive tax structure. During a single year at the turn of the century the Carnegie Steel Works earned a net profit of $40 million, of which Andrew Carnegie's share was upwards of $22 million, without a cent of income tax to pay. Such a tax structure con-

---

[4] *Pollock* v. *Farmers' Loan and Trust Company*, 157 U.S., 429 (1895).

tinued to be most effective in promoting the extremely rapid pace of industrial advance; and no doubt Mr. Carnegie also found it helpful when he built his $5 million castle in Scotland.

The third Supreme Court decision in this series involved organized labor most directly, and from the standpoint of that group was by far the most important of the three. Much earlier in the American labor movement, when employers had had far less to fear from worker organizations than during the 1890's, an excellent technique for countering collective bargaining efforts had been the common-law doctrine of criminal conspiracy. Beginning with an epoch-making decision by the Massachusetts Supreme Court in 1842, however, this device had suffered a drastic decline in usefulness for employer purposes. Feeling keenly the need for a weapon which would cast the shadow of illegality on striking workers, some of the best minds in the country had slowly been perfecting a substitute procedure.

The solution hit upon was the labor injunction. Always the law had recognized the need for legal remedies before the fact in situations in which the damage threatened might prove to be irremediable. Just such a situation was a threatened strike. Business lost by a concern in the course of a strike shutdown might indeed be irretrievably gone. Built upon this time-honored legal foundation, the injunction offered employers a two-sided protection from work stoppages. On the one hand, the very process of enjoining a strike might nip many such actions in the bud; on the other hand, if a strike were called in the face of an outstanding injunction, workers would thereby automatically place themselves on the wrong side of the law—and hence (typically) of public opinion. In short, what the labor injunction meant to laborers was a direct and powerful assault on one of the very foundations of their protective framework.

An excellent opportunity for conservatives to give this recent innovation a major boost appeared in connection with the Pullman strike of 1894. (On labor questions even more than on antitrust, Grover Cleveland was a conservative, particularly as long as Richard Olney was standing by his side.[5]) When railroad workers, in a desperate attempt to help Pullman employees put pressure on their employer, boycotted Pullman cars in and around Chicago, and in the process practically brought railroad transportation in that key area to a standstill, Olney was able to convince Cleveland that the federal government's responsibility for interstate commerce and the

[5] Allan Nevins, *Grover Cleveland: A Study in Courage* (New York: Dodd, Mead & Co., Inc., 1932).

mails demanded intervention. This took the form of injunctions against the strikers, an action speedily converted into contempt of court proceedings when certain of the strikers' leaders openly defied these writs.

One of these men was Eugene V. Debs, president of the American Railway Union. Jailed on a contempt of court charge, he directed his attorneys to seek his discharge on the ground of illegal confinement. Fought all the way to the Supreme Court of the United States, this case was to become a major episode in American constitutional history.

For labor this litigation had two tragic outcomes. First, the Justices unequivocally upheld the validity of the injunction. Thus did "government by injunction" come decisively of age, sanctioned by the highest legal authority in the land, and thus did one of the most fundamental obstacles to labor union progress for half a century become a bitter reality. Second, the lower court had based its validation of the injunction squarely on the Sherman Act. While the Supreme Court preferred to rest its decision on the interstate commerce clause, it explicitly denied that this approach was to be interpreted as an expression of disapproval of the lower court's action.[6] The worst fears of Samuel Gompers were about to be realized with a vengeance, this development also sanctioned by the Supreme Court.

Pollock v. *Farmers' Loan and Trust Company* has often been referred to by constitutional authorities as a "suicidal" decision. By this is meant a Supreme Court pronouncement so contrary to citizen views of fair play and justice as to threaten the prestige of the Court as an institution. How correct that interpretation is can never be ascertained with assurance. To whatever extent this was the case, however, popular resentment was perhaps directed less against this decision as such than against the total effect of these three 1895 pronouncements, i.e., less against the defeat of the income tax than against the way citizens caught between the industrialization process on the one hand and economic depression on the other were being treated by their government. But even on this view the Pollock case was dramatically suggestive of the disabilities under which the common man was now laboring. Thus *United States* v. *E. C. Knight Company* did not seriously trouble organized labor, whereas farmers were not especially concerned about *In re Debs*. But *Pollock* v. *Farmers' Loan and Trust Company*, was a ground on which both groups could stand.

---

[6] *In re Debs*, 158 U.S. 564 (1895).

Growing Pains for the I.C.C.[7]

In the popular meaning of the term there was of course little of the laissez faire spirit in all of this. To be sure, the federal government was in a sense "leaving business alone," but the care that government was taking to see that everyone else left business alone, too, added an extra touch which was not strictly called for by the theory of minimum government. However, when the definition of laissez faire in use here is applied to these phenomena the fit is very much closer. Even the fact that the principal agency responsible was the judiciary, rather than either the legislative or executive branch of the government, is only a detail which does not alter the main configuration of what was taking place.

Nor did these three decisions in 1895 complete the services the Supreme Court felt it necessary to perform for the business community at this time. In the railroad regulation field, where reformers had some reason for believing that significant forward steps had been taken, it had become apparent by the end of the century that most of this work would have to be done all over again.

After a few short years of conformity with the Interstate Commerce Act, the railroads had begun to pine for their lost freedom, this change in attitude being immediately reflected in a determined resistance campaign. The first challenge was purely procedural in nature. In rebate cases key witnesses refused to testify, invoking the Fifth Amendment in justification. When this stand was upheld by the Supreme Court, an amendment to the 1887 act had to be passed affording witnesses absolute immunity from prosecution for the offense about which testimony was to be secured. Closely related to this issue and settled simultaneously with it was the question of whether the Interstate Commerce Commission could legally compel testimony—whether, indeed, the Commission's very existence was constitutional or not. Here the Supreme Court was more amenable, and by 1896 both of these issues had been settled on the side of the Act. But six long years of litigation had been required to achieve this minimal result.

The second great obstacle the new agency was confronted with was its relationships with the federal courts. At first, for example, if a carrier did not choose to conform to a Commission order, the latter was required to secure an injunction from the courts to compel obedience. Not until such a court order was in hand (from the Su-

[7] I. L. Sharfman, *The Interstate Commerce Commission* (New York: The Commonwealth Fund, 1931), Vol. I; and W. Z. Ripley, *Railroads: Rates and Regulation* (New York: Longmans, Green & Co., Inc., 1913).

preme Court if the first court order was appealed, a procedure which became more and more common) did the Commission's order have the force of law. And even then as often as not a new order had to be issued to bring the final decision into conformity with the court's findings. The result was an intolerable delay in settling cases, which by 1900 had almost brought Commission business to a halt.

A still more unsatisfactory relationship with the courts was the refusal of those agencies to accept the Commission's findings of fact. Here the consequence was to turn many of these cases into a ridiculous farce. Since there was little to be gained by making a full presentation to the Commission, carriers often withheld important facts. That body, compelled by law to make decisions based on inadequate information, was then placed in a most vulnerable position when these decisions were taken into the courts. Indeed, the Commission was reversed in fifteen of the first sixteen of its cases appealed. Thus, whether or not this was a deliberate part of the railroad's strategy of resistance (and a good case could be made for such an interpretation), the Commission became to a large extent discredited in the eyes of the public.

But these purely formal difficulties were in the final analysis minor by comparison with a substantive assault on the law which was all this time just under the surface—and which soon virtually destroyed this basic reform. From the beginning it had been understood that the Commission did not have the power to prescribe rates in the first instance. At the same time, however, it was likewise taken for granted that reasonable rates could be prescribed to take the place of rates found to be unreasonable. In fact, not until the law was almost ten years old was this power questioned. Then, in 1897, the most devastating blow yet befell the Commission in the role it was earnestly endeavoring to play. In reviewing on appeal a case in which a new rate had been prescribed, the Supreme Court denied this power to the Commission by means of the following argument:

That Congress has transferred such a power to any administrative body is not to be presumed or implied from any doubtful or uncertain language. The words and phrases efficacious to make such a delegation of power are well understood, and have been frequently used, and, if Congress has intended to grant such a power to the Interstate Commerce Commission, it cannot be doubted that it would have used language open to no misconstruction, but clear and direct.[8]

And even this was not the greatest degradation to which the Commission was subjected during those early years. One of the most

[8] Interstate Commerce Commission v. Cincinnati, New Orleans, and Texas Pacific Railway Company, 167 U.S. 479 (1897).

important evils it had been created to eliminate was so-called long-and-short-haul discrimination—the Wabash type of situation. The law on this point, however, had been rather intricately worded, and had consequently not been easy to enforce at best. Instead of prohibiting such discrimination outright, as had been done with other varieties of this species, a qualification had been attached. According to the law, long-and-short-haul discrimination was to be permitted if the conditions and circumstances surrounding both hauls were substantially dissimilar. This meant, obviously, that someone would have to determine as cases arose what this qualification was to mean. Eager to give a good account of its stewardship, the Commission logically assumed that this would be one of its responsibilities, and forthwith ruled that the fact of competition at one of the two points was not necessarily to be considered such a dissimilarity in circumstances and conditions as to legitimize discrimination. Imagine the frustration of the Commission, to say nothing of the dismay of liberals, when the Supreme Court declared that the carriers were in the first instance to make this determination and that mere rail competition at one of the two points involved would warrant long-and-short-haul discrimination.[9] After this decision was rendered, about all that the Commission could legally do was scold the carriers for violations of the spirit of the Interstate Commerce Act, and report such wrong-doings to Congress and the public.

THE INDEPENDENT REGULATORY COMMISSION[10]

But it would be a mistake to conclude from this account of the Interstate Commerce Commission's early difficulties that the battle being fought out on this front was solely between economic conservatives and economic liberals. Beneath this essentially surface conflict was an institutional rivalry far more important to the evolving relationships between government and business, for on its outcome hinged the answer to the crucial question of whether or not the government would be able effectively to shoulder the responsibilities reformers were desirous of placing upon it. If this were to be done, a way would have to be found to delegate vital aspects of this task to nonconstitutional bodies of experts removed as far as possible from day-to-day political pressures. Such a body would have

[9] *Interstate Commerce Commission* v. *Alabama Midland Railway Company*, 168 U.S. 144 (1897).
[10] Robert E. Cushman, *The Independent Regulatory Commissions* (New York: Oxford University Press, 1941); Ernest Freund, *Administrative Powers over Persons and Property* (Chicago: University of Chicago Press, 1928); and James M. Landis, *The Administrative Process* (New Haven: Yale University Press, 1938).

to find a secure place side by side with those constitutional agencies which had hitherto functioned without assistance. Only in a figurative sense did this mean that the older bodies would have to "move over and make room" for the newer, because the acceptance of broader responsibilities by the government meant that the burden of this work would to that extent become greater. At the same time, however, it is not surprising that a few outcroppings of what can realistically only be termed institutional jealousy would arise to complicate the working out of a division of labor better suited to modern conditions.

All this can be put more pointedly with profit, too. American constitutional theory has it that government consists of legislative, executive, and judicial functions—law making, law enforcing, and law interpreting. While it is difficult enough under the most favorable of circumstances to distinguish clearly between these functions in practice, it was in fact found desirable to turn over to regulatory bodies some responsibilities in each of these areas. Thus the so-called independent commissions make rules for the governance of the industry over which their jurisdiction extends, adopt measures and procedures oriented to the enforcement of these rules, and pass judgment on complaints arising under their operation; and indeed the practice of creating multiple-member commissions rather than agencies headed by a single individual reflects the attempt made at the outset to give the deliberations of these bodies a highly judicial character. But since the Constitution had already vested the legislative, executive, and judicial powers of the government in the Congress, the President, and the Judiciary, respectively, and since the Constitution also explicitly states that these constitutional responsibilities may not be delegated, it is easy to see that integrating nonconstitutional bodies into such a governmental system would cause some difficulties.

In short, the United States Supreme Court, conservative though it unquestionably was, had every reason to raise the kinds of questions it did so as to make absolutely certain that the Interstate Commerce Commission did not exercise more authority than Congress intended. Stated in reverse, the reason the terminology of the 1887 enactment was what it was (declaring, as in the common law, that rates were to be just and reasonable rather than explicitly giving to the Commission the power to prescribe reasonable rates) may well have been because, as the Supreme Court broadly hinted, conservatives had had the greatest influence in its preparation.

Thanks in large part to the growing pains suffered by the Interstate Commerce Commission, reasonably satisfactory relationships between constitutional and nonconstitutional government agencies were in time worked out. Speaking generally, in other words, the regulatory commissions of later years were not subjected to such a rigorous "hazing." And since the pattern of adjustment thus painfully developed has become fairly standard at both the federal and state levels, it is worthwhile pausing here long enough to note some of its most important features.

The keynote of this achievement is that nonconstitutional agencies must be made subordinate to constitutional ones. From the standpoint of legislation this means that Congress (or a state legislature) must determine broad policy, leaving it to the commission to formulate the detailed rules required to apply that policy to the problems arising in a complex and dynamic environment. This insistence, it will at once be noted, reserves to the legislature full control over the direction of policy while simultaneously taking advantage of whatever expertness the commission's membership represents.

Relationships between regulatory commissions and the executive branch of the government are less delicate, but nonetheless important. Typically, the executive retains the primary weapons of enforcement, so that the commission is compelled to look to it for assistance whenever a violation situation cannot be ironed out through moral suasion. Furthermore, the chief executive ordinarily appoints commission members (although a number of states still have elected commissioners). From this latter situation, incidentally, difficulties have often developed; the temptation is great to let political considerations play too large a role in these appointments. Fortunately, however, there are also present defenses against this tendency. Commissioners' terms are staggered, and are usually longer than the chief executive's. More important, the latter cannot remove a commissioner without cause as he is free to do with top officials in the executive departments proper.

But as the Interstate Commerce Commission's early history clearly indicates, the most touchy questions raised by these new agencies pertained to their coexistence with the courts. Hence it was at this point that the greatest precautions had to be taken to provide for subordination without opening the door to complete domination. A few of the major principles adopted were the following.

First, where issues arise with respect to which the commission legally exercises discretion, an aggrieved individual must ordinarily take his grievance to the commission *before* it goes to a court. Second, most commission decisions are subject to review by the courts, but in review cases the commission's findings of fact are generally accepted as conclusive. (The principal exceptions here are two:

negative orders are typically not subject to review, for this would be substituting the court's judgment for that of the commission on matters involving the latter's discretion; facts are reviewed where a constitutional question is raised.) Third, the courts may set aside a commission order: (1) if the statute under which it was issued is unconstitutional; (2) if the commission in issuing it has exceeded its statutory authority; (3) if it is not adequately supported by the findings on which it is based; (4) if it in any way violates constitutional guaranties; (5) if it is based on a mistake of law; or (6) if it is made without evidence or contrary to evidence.

ROUNDING OUT THE PUBLIC UTILITY CONCEPT

While the Supreme Court in tilting with the Interstate Commerce Commission was working out in one direction the implications of the turn the law had taken in *Munn* v. *Illinois*, it was in a historic contest with the State of Nebraska working out these implications in another direction. In the outcome of that encounter, moreover, the Court greatly relieved conservatives by making it clear that a considerable amount of homework was being done by the Justices on the meaning of property in an industrial society. (Note in this connection the definition of property implicit in the use of the injunction in labor dispute cases.)

As a matter of fact it had been becoming increasingly evident that the Court was feeling uncomfortable about the Slaughter House cases pronouncement on this subject. Nor is there anything surprising in the fact that this discomfort seemed most acute where the Court was confronted with that basic corollary of the 1873 definition, the Munn ruling that regulated industries threatened with confiscation must look to the polls and not to the courts. The first strong hint that the Court was about ready to change its mind on this subject came in a railway rate regulation case brought to the Supreme Court in 1890. Petitioners for the railroads asked the Court to reconsider the Munn ruling, and after doing so the Court replied as follows:

This power to regulate [police power] is not a power to destroy, and limitation is not the equivalent of confiscation. . . . (This) is eminently a question for judicial investigation, requiring due process of law for its determination.[11]

What this clearly meant was that exchange-value was to be considered in defining property, and that the Supreme Court would

---

[11] *Chicago, Milwaukee and St. Paul Railway Company* v. *Minnesota*, 134 U.S. 418 (1890).

lead the way in such an endeavor as soon as the question was put squarely before it.

In 1897 such an opportunity was presented in the form of a case involving an insurance company denied the right to continue marketing its service in that state by a Louisiana statute. The company's lawyers argued that property had been taken without due process of law; the attorneys for the state, relying on the Slaughter House precedent, insisted that no property had been taken. The Court minced no words in striking down the state's contention:

The liberty mentioned in that Amendment [Fourteenth] means not only the right of the citizen to be free from physical restraint of his person, but the term is deemed to embrace the right of the citizen to be free in the enjoyment of all his faculties. . . . His enjoyment upon terms of equality with all others in similar circumstances of the privilege of pursuing an ordinary calling or trade, and of acquiring, holding, and selling property is an essential part of liberty and property as guaranteed by the Fourteenth Amendment.[12]

Not only, in other words, is exchange-value a part of property, but liberty of access to markets is an integral part of exchange-value. The Court had, indeed, learned these crucial facts of modern economic life with exemplary despatch once it had set its mind to the task.

With these opinions already in the record, the Supreme Court was well equipped to deal with the Nebraska Maximum Rate case when it appeared on the docket in 1898. At the outset of this decision the Court rejected the state's plea that rate-making was a legislative function, and backed up this reversal of *Munn* v. *Illinois* by laying down some guide rules which would help legislatures in the future minimize their conflict with the courts over that issue. Of the rules actually advanced, one was very general while two were somewhat less so. First, the Court observed that a regulated industry must be permitted to earn a "fair return" on the "fair value" of the property devoted to the public service. Second, two primary considerations in determining fair value were to be the original cost of the property and its reproduction cost.[13]

If these principles did in practice help to minimize friction in this area, it might be pertinent to observe that human imagination could scarcely conceive the amount of legislature-court conflict there would have been if they had not been laid down. In fact, some students of this subject believe that despite this attempt to be constructive the Supreme Court actually muddied the waters. Suffice it

12 *Allgeyer* v. *Louisiana*, 165 U.S. 578 (1897).
13 *Smyth* v. *Ames*, 166 U.S. 466 (1898).

to say here that the Court in *Smyth* v. *Ames* acknowledged that the matter of fair value "will always be an embarrassing question," and that experience has proved this prophecy to be a gross understatement.

Apart from the technical difficulties involved in valuing a complicated business concern on any basis, it can easily be seen why these twin criteria would give rise to special problems.[14] In a dynamic economy powerful vested interests would almost inevitably be found opposing one another from the standpoint of which criterion should be given the greater weight. Consumers as represented by the state would want to emphasize original cost in a period of rising prices and reproduction cost when prices are falling, while the interests supporting the regulated concern would endeavor to reverse these emphases. In the case at bar in 1898 this chronic conflict was plainly foreshadowed. The State of Nebraska desired to take advantage of a long period of falling prices by pushing for a reproduction cost valuation; the companies in turn pressed just as vigorously for original cost.

With this Supreme Court pronouncement on the limits of legislative rate-making, the development of a legal philosophy supporting public utility regulation may be said to have been broadly completed. The contribution of *Smyth* v. *Ames* to that philosophy, to the definition of substantive due process on the one hand and the division of labor between police power and due process on the other, can be summarized as follows.

Where government regulations enforce restrictions based upon public concern over health, safety, or morals, private property may be taken without compensation, provided that due process (with greatest emphasis upon its procedural dimension) is followed in the taking. The assumption here is apparently that such restrictions (as, for example, sanitation requirements in a restaurant) typically involve such an insignificant taking of property that no problem is created from that standpoint. But where government finds it necessary to regulate a concern's prices, private property may not be taken without compensation (that is, a fair return on a fair value). Here the greatest emphasis is upon the substantive dimension of due process which in turn consists of two parts: there are first the precautions required in making certain that the industry or firm under consideration is properly classified as a public utility; and there is second the complex network of premises and calculations which go

[14] John Bauer and Nathaniel Gold, *Public Utility Valuation For Purposes of Rate Control* (New York: The Macmillan Co., 1934); J. C. Bonbright, *The Valuation of Property* (New York: McGraw-Hill Book Co., Inc., 1937); and N. L. Smith, *Fair Rate of Return in Public Utility Regulation* (Boston: Houghton Mifflin Co., 1932).

into determining both fair return and fair value. Where, in short, regulations proceed directly to "the heart of the contract" (that is, prices), the law must recognize that the potential taking of property is very great and place appropriate limitations on this result.

AND CONSOLIDATION WENT ON

For one brief moment in the late 1890's, as time is measured by the perspective of history, it seemed that the tide of antitrust policy was about to turn, that the discrimination with respect to these laws unmistakably in the process of formulation—one principle for labor unions and another for business combinations—was to be repudiated. In a series of decisions the courts laid the foundations for a much stronger antitrust endeavor than had been witnessed to date.

The first of these was in the government's case against the Trans-Missouri Freight Association, a combination of the railroads handling most of the nation's rail traffic west of the Missouri River. Rejecting the government's request that the Association be dissolved, the lower court had contended that the law did not apply to railroads, since these concerns were under the jurisdiction of the Interstate Commerce Commission; and that even if the Sherman Act did apply, there was in this combination no threat of injury to the public. For one thing the rates charged had been filed with the Commission and hence could legitimately be supposed to be reasonable, and for another the purpose behind this integration had been only the elimination of an excessive competition which would itself have been injurious to the public interest. These views the Supreme Court in turn rejected, stating that the Sherman Act did apply and that no appeal to a rule of reason was permissible when nonancillary agreements not to compete were involved. Did not the law prohibit *every* combination in restraint of trade?[15]

This decision was followed a year later by one dealing with an almost identical situation. Here the government's adversary was the Joint Traffic Association, an organization coordinating the affairs of the major rail carriers in trunkline territory. Again the lower courts had held against the government, and again the Supreme Court came to the government's rescue.[16]

In 1898 also an even more significant decision was handed down, this time by the Circuit Court of Appeals, Sixth Circuit. Before the court was the Addyston Pipe and Steel Company pool, and because this was the first major decision involving an industrial trust since

---

[15] *United States* v. *Trans-Missouri Freight Association,* 166 U.S. 290 (1897).
[16] *United States* v. *Joint Traffic Association,* 171 U.S. 505 (1898).

the Knight case, conservatives and liberals alike were awaiting its outcome with great interest.

The importance of this decision delivered by William Howard Taft derives from two facts, apart from its affirmation by the Supreme Court the following year. First, it was here that Judge Taft developed his classic analysis of the relationship between the Sherman Act and the common law. Second, although the Court took pains to distinguish this case from E. C. Knight Company on the ground that a central element in the control exercised here was the allocation of shipments into so-called "pay" territory, the tenor of this decision departed radically from the narrow interpretation of interstate commerce in the earlier case. From this more advanced view the courts were never significantly to deviate in antitrust cases. Unequivocally asserting that the purpose of the Sherman Act had been to give effect to the common law, and that the common law had never tolerated nonancillary trade restraints, Taft ordered the Addyston combine dissolved.[17]

Although superficially these developments were most favorable for the cause of reform, it was not necessary to look far beneath the surface to get an entirely different picture. In the first place, it was evident that the antitrust law had not yet taken the measure of a single important trust. In all of the successful cases thus far there had been involved explicit agreements not to compete. Obviously the crucial test would be the act's effectiveness against the new holding companies or outright mergers where such agreements were not the primary point at issue.

In the second place, the case law that was being developed, favorable though it was in some respects, had its disconcerting side. Slowly but surely the pressure for the application of a rule of reason was building up, and it was becoming ever more apparent how damaging such an innovation might be to the effectiveness of the Sherman Act. The minority opinion in the Trans-Missouri case had relied heavily on this argument. In the Joint Traffic case, counsel for the railroads had included an ex-United States Senator (George F. Edmunds of Vermont) who had participated actively in the writing of the Sherman Act, and that brief had strongly inferred—indeed, had almost openly asserted—that unless the courts interpreted that act in the light of the common law rule of reason it was unconstitutional. Even in the Addyston case this threat had not been wholly absent. Judge Taft's insistence that the common law was to be the standard of interpretation meant that the act was safe from a debilitating rule

17 *United States* v. *Addyston Pipe and Steel Company*, 85 F. 271 (1898).

of reason only until legal talent uncovered a substantial body of evidence showing the use of such a rule in previous decisions dealing with nonancillary agreements not to compete. And such evidence was available.[18]

Third, the nation's antitrust policy could obviously be no stronger than the program of enforcement which was the responsibility of the Attorney General. In this connection, it could scarcely have escaped notice that President McKinley's administration was the most inactive yet on the antitrust front. All the suits won by the government during his term of office had been started by predecessor administrations, and under his leadership only three new cases were instituted. Two of these were against livestock dealers' associations, while the other singled out a coal dealers' combine; not a single suit was commenced dealing with the kind of business cooperation against which the Sherman Act had been directed.

Was this new low in enforcement apathy brought about by such a diminution in consolidation activity that the ordinary citizen had no further fears on this score? Indeed it was not! The turn of the

TABLE 4. AND CONSOLIDATION WENT ON

	Tight Industrial Combinations Effected	
Year	Number	Authorized Stock Capital (millions of dollars)
1890	15	157
1891	16	141
1892	15	192
1893	11	262
1894	3	9
1895	10	112
1896	6	31
1897	8	105
1898	24	548
1899	105	2,201
1900	34	615
1901	23	1,632
1902	26	589
1903	8	137

Source: Hans B. Thorelli, *The Federal Antitrust Policy* (Baltimore: The Johns Hopkins Press, 1955), pp. 294-303. Adapted by permission.

century saw a more fundamental transformation of the economy through the formation of combinations than had to date been seen. Not only, in other words, was enforcement under the Sherman Act

[18] Milton Handler, *A Study of the Construction and Enforcement of the Anti-Trust Laws* (Washington, D.C.: Government Printing Office, 1941).

not lax because this legislation had succeeded in quieting the zeal of businessmen for integration, but the period of America's most active "trustification" took place while the antitrust law lay lifeless in the hands of President McKinley and his Attorney General. Put still differently, at a time when the need to enforce the law was greater than it had ever been, and when the Supreme Court was unusually sympathetic with actions of this kind, the government chose to stand on a policy of uncompromising laissez faire. Here was undoubtedly the most important reason for reformers becoming discouraged.[19]

A few statistics will put these latter observations in even sharper perspective. According to John Moody, a reliable contemporary analyst, the industrial combinations which had been put together prior to 1898 (the year he selected as the beginning of what he called the "modern" trust movement) represented a total capitalization of only a little more than $1 billion, whereas those created during the next six years were capitalized at more than $6 billion. Moreover, in addition to consolidations in manufacturing, Moody calculated that by 1904 some 1,336 telephone, telegraph, gas, and electric power utilities had been drawn together into a handful of consolidations capitalized at $3.75 billion, and that 95 per cent of the nation's railway mileage capitalized at more than $9 billion was as of that date in the hands of six financial groups.[20]

The impact upon popular thinking made by the renewed vigor of these activities can be more fully understood, also, by noting some of the more important interconnections between this development and certain other features of American economic history during these years. It is a most striking fact, for example, that ups and downs in trust building coincided closely with the state of the nation's economic health. Little combining took place during depression years, this activity then burgeoning forth with accelerated intensity as business revived.

Nor was this relationship accidental. Two causal factors were primarily involved. On the one hand, combinations by way of the corporation were dependent upon the ability of the market to absorb the new issues of stock required; and, of course, the money market was weak when economic conditions in general were unfavorable. On the other hand, the disastrous decline in demand which is one of a depression's most fundamental characteristics would precipitate

[19] John Bates Clark, *The Problem of Monopoly* (New York: Columbia University Press, 1904); George Gunton, *Trusts and the Public* (New York: Appleton-Century-Crofts, Inc., 1899); W. Z. Ripley, *Trusts, Pools, and Corporations* (New York: Harper & Bros., 1905).

[20] John Moody, *The Truth About The Trusts* (New York: Moody Publishing Co., 1904).

a wave of ruinous competition in fixed-cost industries, causing great uneasiness in the business community. To be sure, there was little that could be done to remedy this situation while depression lasted, but innumerable resolves were made and plans laid to see to it that such tragedies did not occur again.

A second, closely related feature of this period was the seeming prevalence of what was widely thought of (and almost as often condemned) as unfair competition. Every investigation of trusts (and early in the twentieth century investigation followed investigation with monotonous regularity) piled higher the evidence on the basis of which the public had long ago concluded that monopolies were built essentially by means of these tactics. The methods themselves of course were legion, and many of them were already common knowledge. Thus the exclusion of competitors by monopolizing the source of raw materials had always been a favorite technique where this was possible. In the same category was the securing of freight rate concessions, a practice now almost as common as ever with the emasculation of the Interstate Commerce Act. And the tariff continued in some industries to serve as a monopoly-creating device.

But competitive tactics the public was much less familiar with were coming to light. Of these some of the most important involved the patent system. Designed to help the economy achieve the abundance of which it was capable, patent law suddenly seemed by many to have become a device for the enslavement of the masses by the great corporations. A concern in possession of a basic patent would blanket the technological field around that patent and in this way keep competitors that much farther away from its own preserve. Or all the patents in a technological area might be bought up, this procedure placing the owner in a position to harass competitors with expensive litigation, in addition to making him the only effective market for new patents as technology advanced. Or improvements in a basic patent could be patented at strategic time intervals in order artificially to extend the period of legal monopoly. In these and other equally effective ways were the modern "Frankenstein's monsters" successfully perverting a valuable economic institution (turning what was intended to be a protection for the individual into huge corporate profits), and in the process increasing their economic power at the expense of the less well-organized segments of the community.[21]

No generalized listing of unfair practices, however, can portray this phenomenon quite as vividly as a summary of the most impor-

[21] Walton Hamilton, *Patents and Free Enterprise* (Washington, D.C.: Government Printing Office, 1941).

tant of these techniques utilized by a single concern, the National Cash Register Company under John H. Patterson. National's salesmen endeavored systematically to assemble data relating to competitors' businesses. The employees of competitors were often bribed to reveal trade secrets. Transportation company employees were likewise paid to disclose information about competitors' shipments. Bogus independents were formed to give competitors confidence until the time was ripe to drive them to the wall. Salesmen of the National followed close behind competitors' salesmen, offering their company's machines at below-cost prices to interfere with competitor sales. These key individuals were also instructed to make derogatory statements about competitors' products, character, or ability to meet obligations. At times clients were even induced to break contracts already entered into. Machines cheaply made and deliberately constructed so as to simulate a competitive model were offered to the trade to undermine the goodwill of competitors. Patent infringement suits were used as a basic technique of intimidation. A "graveyard" of defunct machines was even kept at the Dayton plant to impress visitors with the wisdom of staying out of that business. Between 1895 and 1910, 158 new firms entered this competition; all but five failed. This was the concern the government had recently dropped antitrust charges against when the complainant competitors had been absorbed.

Still another important feature of the economy at the turn of the century was the holding company, and especially the New Jersey holding company. Again a few figures can best make clear what was happening. Between 1899 and 1901 New Jersey granted an average of more than 2,000 charters every year to concerns all over the United States, and as a result collected more than $500,000 in each of these years in franchise taxes. In 1901 these receipts soared to more than $1.5 million. According to Moody's listing of all the trusts in existence in 1904, furthermore, two-thirds held New Jersey charters; and of those incorporated in 1898 or after, three-fourths were chartered in New Jersey. Significantly, every one of those combinations referred to by Moody as the "Greater Industrial Trusts" (Amalgamated Copper, American Smelting, American Sugar, Consolidated Tobacco, International Mercantile, Standard Oil, and United States Steel) was a New Jersey holding company.

Even at this historical distance it is difficult to evaluate the nation's first ten years' experience with the Sherman Anti-Trust Act. It is of course clear enough that the most fundamental ideal in the minds of proponents of this measure had originally been what was even then coming to be known as "trust-busting," and obviously from this standpoint the law had thus far been an almost complete failure. But perhaps this is an inappropriate criterion, at least as thus rigidly applied. Perhaps qualification in the direction of greater realism would be a fairer approach.

One point which would particularly have to be made in such a context, for example, would stress that the reform movement had never been quite unequivocal in its antagonism to industrial capitalism. Already there was developing a widespread, if as yet largely unformulated, understanding that there was a close relationship between big business on the one hand and an obviously rising standard of living on the other. In this connection it is to be especially noted that even so radical a reformer as Edward Bellamy had been careful to hold on to the advantages of large-scale production. In other words, in the reform support for the wholesale decentralization of centralized concerns there was undoubtedly a substantial element of that naiveté which often creeps into first proposals for basic institutional change.

But to place the emphasis upon naiveté is to explain the evolution that was taking place in essentially negative terms. A more constructive terminology might simply suggest that the nation was fumbling for a solution to a major problem—and that the essence of fumbling is experimental efforts which in retrospect appear to have been misdirected. How long it would be before the steps taken in this field became more firm and sure, and indeed what kinds of steps these would be when they were finally taken, only the future could ascertain. Clearly no alternative approach had yet begun to command wide public attention. This meant that the atomization of the nonutility business world would continue for a time to occupy the center of the reform stage at this point, even though there was already every objective reason for believing that the clock of time was not really going to be turned back.

QUESTIONS FOR DISCUSSION

1. Defend the Court's position in the sugar trust case. Distinguish between conservatism and institutional lag if such a distinction is possible.
2. What public interest purposes were served by the tax policy implicit in the Pollock decision, and in what ways?
3. What groups of citizens were probably most put out by each of the major decisions of the Supreme Court in 1895, and why?
4. Describe the major difficulties encountered by the Interstate Commerce Commission during its early years.

5. What is the meaning of the term "growing pains" as applied to the Interstate Commerce Commission at this time?

6. Explain the role of independent regulatory commissions in our system of government. How are these bodies fitted into our system of checks and balances?

7. Why would the Supreme Court have been troubled about its earlier definition of property—and why especially so in public utility cases?

8. How else might the problem of public utility valuation have been solved?

9. Explain the fact that with all of this frustration of antitrust proponents no legislation was enacted strengthening this policy.

10. Could the intensive development of trusts after 1896 have been prevented if enforcement policy had been more vigorous? Would this have been desirable?

Part IV

LAISSEZ FAIRE THREATENED

Chapter 11

Girding For Action

Twice since the Civil War unrest against what many people considered to be the evils of industrialism had reached a peak of intensity. On both occasions a flurry of reform activity had resulted; both times the forces of reform had fallen back again, exhausted, without effecting significant changes. Now, with William McKinley taking the oath of office as President for the second time, the tide of unrest was visibly rising again. As liberals began to organize for another try, many no doubt took much comfort from the slogan, "The third time takes the charm." Perhaps, on the other hand, there were others who were occasionally haunted by the equally well-known saying, "Three strikes is out in any league."

If, however, any reliance could be placed on trends in predicting matters of such complexity, the odds should certainly have rested with the more optimistic of these views. The second peak of reform sentiment had clearly exceeded its predecessor in intensity, and (as a result?) the achievement on the second occasion was greater than on the first. By any test the Interstate Commerce and Sherman acts represented a much broader assault on the corporate world than the Granger movement, regardless of the sequel in both cases. And the later reform endeavor was in its turn much more deeply rooted than the one of a decade and a half earlier. Indeed it almost seemed that the intensity of these cycles was growing in geometric ratio. In this fact resided such hope as men were as yet justified in having that the near future might see the new industrial society grow in responsibility to its citizens in proportion as it was growing in productivity and power.

"THE ERA OF THE MUCKRAKERS"[1]

That the new wave of resentment was unprecedented there can be no doubt. This was the "muckrake" period in American history,

[1] C. C. Regier, *The Era of the Muckrakers* (Chapel Hill: University of North Carolina Press, 1932).

an era during which a literature of protest mercilessly exposed skeletons in dark closets in every corner of the economy. (The name, incidentally, originated in the description of the character in Bunyan's *Pilgrim's Progress* who "could look no way but downwards with a muckrake in his hand.") Never before or since in the history of this country have basic social institutions been more comprehensively denounced. One might easily have thought, studying this outpouring of denunciation, that the society against which it was directed was about to be torn asunder by revolution.

An extensive discussion of muckraking would be out of place here. However, a few ramifications of that phenomenon have a special significance for this discussion. For example, this movement was not directly concerned with trusts as such to anything like the extent that is commonly supposed; this misconception probably arises from the fact that one of the first as well as one of the most enduring pieces of muckrake literature was Ida Tarbell's analysis of the Standard Oil Company and its methods. Actually, so catholic was the subject matter of these writings that they cannot be described in terms of any single topic. Corruption in local, state, and national politics, child labor, the commercialization of religion, vice, the prostitution of the press for business purposes, impure foods and drugs, manipulation of the stock market (to mention only the most important subjects)—all these aspects of America's economic life, in addition to big business, were at one time or another during these few years given critical attention.[2]

Another fact worth noting is the powerful support given to the new reform movement by nonfarmer groups. The more important implications of industrialization were at the turn of the century becoming apparent to an ever larger circle of people. One of these was urbanization, the concentration of immense numbers of individuals in small areas—individuals who were then at the mercy of the intricate business mechanism which alone could make city life tolerable. Nor was this awareness limited to workers, organized or otherwise. A white collar class was rapidly developing, and these groups could see as clearly as laborers such things as the corruption of the people's governments for the purpose of exploiting the people through public utility franchises. Amid the rapid formation of trusts during these

---

[2] Louis Filler, *Crusaders for American Liberalism* (New York: Harcourt, Brace & Co., Inc., 1939); Thomas H. Geer, *American Social Reform Movements* (Englewood Cliffs, N.J.: Prentice-Hall, Inc., 1949); C. E. Russell, *Bare Hands and Stone Walls* (New York: Charles Scribner's Sons, 1933); Lincoln Steffens, *Autobiography of Lincoln Steffens* (New York: Harcourt, Brace & Co., Inc., 1931); and Richard Hofstadter, *The Age of Reform* (New York: Alfred A. Knopf, Inc., 1955).

years, it is not surprising that petty capitalists became concerned about their own security in a world of seemingly insatiable business "cannibals."

In the third place, while it is not supposed that a definitive explanation of the appearance of muckraking at this time can be given here, perhaps a few constructive observations on the question of origins can nevertheless be made. Thus it seems clear that to place much significance upon the fact that it was at this historical juncture that the middle-class periodical (magazines such as *McClure's*, *Cosmopolitan*, and *American*) was enjoying a phenomenal expansion is to choose a very superficial ground. Who can be certain that the causal relationship was not rather the other way around: that these journals with their predominantly middle-class appeal were given a vigorous push by the zeal for reform reflected in the muckrake literature? Or who would argue that if denunciation of major social institutions had not struck a responsive chord in the popular mind these magazines would not have turned to other subjects?

Nor does the emphasis upon the disappearance of the frontier at approximately this time strike significantly nearer the heart of the issue, even though as a statement of fact there is an element of truth in this proposition. The fact must realistically be reckoned with that even when the frontier was most accessible it did not provide the economic opportunities for the unfortunate which it is often credited with supplying. To be sure, the credence given to the value of the frontier for this purpose in the popular imagination may have created a psychological cushion against adversity of substantial importance. But that there was such a significant diminution of the absorptive capacity of the American West at this time as to generate a mass reaction as intense and sustained as "muckraking" is to be doubted.

It does not follow from these negative conclusions, however, that though these factors cannot be accorded the status of basic causes they were not intimately related to what was taking place. The middle-class periodical made its dramatic entry onto the stage of American literature at this time largely because it was during the period 1875-1900 that the modern city first came into existence. Stated differently, it was during these years that the American people began decisively to realize that their frontier was indeed the city, and that the American dream would only come true in an urban environment by dint of much hard reform work.

And stating still more specifically what was behind this movement, as one student of the period expresses it, America was undergoing a status revolution; those groups whose status was deteriorating were lashing out in self defense.

The newly rich, the grandiosely or corruptly rich, the masters of great corporations, were bypassing the men of the Mugwump type—the old gentry, the merchants of long standing, the small manufacturers, the established professional men, the civic leaders of an earlier era. In a score of cities and hundreds of towns, particularly in the East but also in the nation at large, the old-family, college-educated class that had deep ancestral roots in local communities and often owned family businesses, that had traditions of political leadership, belonged to the patriotic societies and cultural institutions, and led the movements for civic betterment, were being overshadowed and edged aside in the making of basic political and economic decisions. In their personal careers, as in their community activities, they found themselves checked, hampered, and overridden by the agents of the new corporations, the corrupters of legislatures, the buyers of franchises, the allies of the political bosses. In this uneven struggle they found themselves limited by their own scruples, their regard for reputation, their social standing itself. To be sure, the America they knew did not lack opportunities, but it did seem to lack opportunities of the highest sort for men of the highest standards. In a strictly economic sense these men were not growing poorer as a class, but their wealth and power were being dwarfed by comparison with the new eminences of wealth and power. They were less important, and they knew it.[3]

To be sure, nothing about this literature suggests that the central preoccupation of liberals had significantly altered since the first stirrings of unrest against industrialism. Uneasy and insecure citizens now as then were most desirous of securing control over a "runaway" economy; of finding, for this new society which could apparently not be repressed, a broader foundation than a crass and narrow search for greater profits; of restoring to full vigor the deeply rooted American ideals of equality and individualism; of destroying an economic plutocracy widely thought to be making a mockery out of political democracy. In short, reformers were still seeking a wider diffusion of economic, political, and social power.

But if by 1900 the objective was unchanged, there is nonetheless reason for believing that the adversary had changed its character in the mind of the man in the street. Whereas in 1870 the chief opponent had been the corporation in the form of the railroad, and whereas by 1885 public antagonism was directed principally against the corporation in the form of the industrial trust, the next turn of the wheel of economic evolution brought the helpless citizen face to face with the corporation in the form of an interlocking network of trusts coordinated by the investment banker. Put differently, the

[3] Richard Hofstadter, *The Age of Reform* (New York: Alfred A. Knopf, Inc., 1955), p. 137.

prototype in the public mind of the dragon to be slain had changed from a Commodore Vanderbilt organizing the Saratoga Conference, to a John D. Rockefeller signing the Standard Oil trust agreement, to a J. P. Morgan adding the gigantic U. S. Steel combine to the formidable circle of banks, railroads, and manufacturing concerns already under his control.

Nor was this transformation just a fancy of the popular imagination, for it reflected a revolution in the realities underlying the institution of private property which had been evolving for a number of years.[4] To begin with, one of the inevitable consequences of the corporate form of business organization had been to divorce business ownership from management. Indeed, this had been one of the major reasons for shifting to that form. As corporations had grown larger, moreover, this divorce implicit in their functioning had broadened roughly in proportion. The greater the number of shares, the greater the number of people holding them, and the wider the geographical area over which they were distributed, the smaller the percentage of shares required for effective control. Thus, whereas in the earlier stages of corporate development owners had controlled their concern even though they did not manage it, the time had now come when a sizable fraction of a large corporation's owners neither managed nor controlled their property.

Other aspects of the evolution of business organization had also contributed to this result. To whatever extent preferred stock was issued, stock having no legal right to control, the proportion of total capitalization which would need to be held to maintain control of policy would be correspondingly reduced. This was equally true of the issue of bonds, although here a substantial risk had to be incurred; failure to pay bond interest (as distinguished from stock dividends) would plunge the concern into bankruptcy. (Despite this risk, however, railroad finance had already gone so far in this direction that the recent economic collapse had bankrupted approximately one-third of the nation's railway mileage.) And the perfection of the holding company had carried this process to what might reasonably be called a logical (if somewhat frightening) extreme. By holding closely a small proportion of the shares of the parent concern while at the same time widely dispersing the remainder, and by then causing this organization to purchase a small proportion of the shares of the concerns to be coordinated (the remainder of these being also widely dispersed), a relatively small investment could be made to go a long way from the standpoint of industry control.

[4] W. Z. Ripley, *Main Street and Wall Street* (Boston: Little, Brown & Co., 1929).

And not only was it possible under existing arrangements to buy much more in the way of control rights for a dollar, but the facilities for the concentration of the dollars with which control might be brought into a few hands had also been rapidly evolving. In a society requiring huge amounts of capital, and one in which both the sources of liquid capital and the uses to which it was to be put were numerous, it was inevitable that capital specialists would arise. Furthermore, as the capital requirements of the greatest business enterprises grew greater, the investment houses capable of caring for these needs necessarily decreased in number as they increased in size. It was these great investment banking concerns (commonly referred to as "Wall Street" or "the bankers" in popular discourse) that were now fast becoming the *bête noir* of the frustrated citizens of a vigorous and dynamic industrialism.

FINANCE CAPITALISM[5]

The rise of financiers to such an important position in the economy created what economic historians in America have termed "finance capitalism"—a business environment in which the most basic enterprise decisions were made by bankers rather than industrialists. And so fundamental is this phenomenon to an understanding of evolving relationships between government and business over the next decade and a half that a more extended explanation of how it came about and its impact on public thinking is required.

In theory, of course, it would have been possible for such concerns to have developed and performed their financial functions without maintaining control of the firms to whose capital needs they ministered. If such a pattern of neutrality had been followed, furthermore, it is probable that men like J. P. Morgan, August Belmont, and Thomas Fortune Ryan would not have been the symbols of oppression they in fact became. On the other hand, even to suggest this alternative is highly unrealistic. Powerful forces were at work which in retrospect seem to have led inexorably to the relationships that actually evolved.

For one thing human nature has a way of asserting itself especially forcefully where great temptations arise, and it would be difficult to conceive of greater temptations than were the daily diet of early twentieth-century investment bankers. A value especially easy for these individuals to achieve was the acquisition of power. Another was the receipt of various kinds of "insider" profits. With

[5] G. W. Edwards, *The Evolution of Finance Capitalism* (New York: Longmans, Green & Co., Inc., 1938).

respect to this last, in fact, it is widely supposed that much consolidating was done primarily for the sake of the promoters' profits which could be earned in this process, and here was only one of the ways in which strategically situated insiders could "milk" a great corporation. Of course, it goes without saying that only by retaining control of the concerns thrown on one's doorstep by their need for funds could either of these values be maximized.

Certain of the considerations at issue here can also be stated in less critical terms. An investment banker in command of badly needed financial resources could scarcely have avoided wielding great influence even if he had earnestly endeavored to do so. Where a concern was unable to provide its own capital, two factors especially dictated a close business relationship between supplier and recipient. On the one hand the former would not normally neglect his investment, while on the other hand a management which might need more money at any time would naturally be careful not to make major decisions without consulting its financial backers.

Nor is it surprising that men with money in their control would use the economic leverage thereby placed at their disposal to push forward the work of eliminating competition. When panic and depression during the 1890's renewed the bitter economic warfare between concerns with high fixed costs, with the attendant catastrophic declines in prices, dividend losses, and outright bankruptcies, business leaders were given what seemed to them ample reason for believing that the reduction of competition had not yet been carried far enough. Stated the other way around, men with large sums of money of their own at stake and acting in a more or less fiduciary capacity for others of their own kind were strongly motivated so to rearrange the economic structure as to make these assets as secure as possible. Many financiers of this period, and of these J. P. Morgan was a conspicuous example, sincerely believed that they performed a great service for society by "stabilizing" the economy, by immunizing it against excessive competition. And perhaps they did.

Perhaps, in other words, the legitimate objection of the community at large to finance capitalism was not so much that the economy was thereby made more stable, as the extreme to which this activity was carried and the liberal intermixture of other motives. Both of these latter aspects of what was happening can readily be illustrated.

The lengths to which financiers thought it necessary to go to keep competition within bounds can be seen most clearly in the railway field. Before the railroad consolidation movement launched during the depression of the 1890's had run its course seven financial interests controlled two-thirds of the railway mileage of the country—

mileage generating 85 per cent of the nation's railroad earnings. Moreover, four of these seven interests were so closely related to one another that for all practical purposes the seven groups were only four.[6] Thus a handful of capitalists led by J. P. Morgan dominated the entire Atlantic seaboard area plus the northern transcontinental routes, a "community of interests" controlling the nation's two greatest railroads (the New York Central and the Pennsylvania) so closely as virtually to throttle rail competition in the territory served by them. Even when it is recognized that the Supreme Court had now sanctioned the principle of a fair return on a fair valuation for public utilities, it would be difficult to argue that this much coordination was required by the public interest.

A good case can be made for the proposition that those financial transactions to which J. P. Morgan gave close attention represented finance capitalism at its best[7] (although during his lifetime the popular mind would accommodate few distinctions between "good" and "bad" bankers). But that banker control at its worst cynically exploited the rest of the community can also be conveniently demonstrated by means of a specific instance, this one too taken from the railway field.

Prior to falling into the hands of a group of greedy financiers (of whom a son of Jay Gould was one), the Chicago and Alton Railroad had been both conservatively financed and prosperous. Within a few short years the bankers had increased its capitalization 200 per cent or $80 million, of which only $18 million was invested in railroad property. In this way $66,000 for every mile of its line was added to the Alton's liabilities without adding a dollar to the value of the road's assets. In the series of "deals" by which this was accomplished insiders netted a cash profit in excess of $20 million and secured control of the company's now worthless common stock. And so engrossed were they in financial manipulations that the property itself seriously deteriorated.

But if the threat posed by finance capitalism in general was now becoming a major concern to large segments of the population, two events in 1901 brought this issue sharply to the forefront of public attention. One was the formation of the United States Steel Corporation; the other was the battle between E. H. Harriman and J. J. Hill for control of the Northern Pacific Railroad. Together these episodes illustrate all the important features of finance capitalism in action.

[6] E. G. Campbell, The Reorganization of the American Railroad System, 1893-1900 (New York: Columbia University Press, 1938); and W. Z. Ripley, Railroads: Finance and Organization (New York: Longmans, Green & Co., Inc., 1915).

[7] F. L. Allen, The Great Pierpont Morgan (New York: Harper & Bros., 1949).

The story behind the creation of the great steel combine has been told so often that detailed repetition here is not necessary. A few of the high points only will be related. First, this merger was precipitated by a threat of ruinous competition (between Andrew Carnegie's steel-producing firm and a railroad he was thinking of building on the one hand, and J. P. Morgan's Federal Steel Corporation and Pennsylvania Railroad Company on the other) so frightening as to make even these giants tremble at the prospect. Second, each of the nine concerns put together in this union was a product of numerous prior consolidations, some being already virtual monopolies in a specialized branch of the industry. Third, one-half of the new concern's capitalization was "water" in 1901, although only twice prior to the "Great Depression" did United States Steel miss paying dividends on its common stock. Fourth, the Morgan syndicate of bankers responsible for this achievement received $62.5 million for promotion services. Fifth, this colossus at birth controlled three-fourths of one of the nation's most basic industries.

The prize in the Northern Pacific contest was the Chicago, Burlington & Quincy Railroad, both the rich territory it served and the Chicago connection it offered. Possessed at the moment by Hill's Northern Pacific–Great Northern combine, it was coveted by Harriman's Union Pacific–Southern Pacific interests. The strategy was the purchase of Northern Pacific common stock on the New York Stock Exchange–Harriman (through Kuhn, Loeb & Company with Standard Oil money) to secure control; Hill (side by side with the "House of Morgan") in defense of the status quo. On May 9, 1901, this struggle reached its most dramatic point. It was discovered that both groups held a controlling interest; that is, in the excitement and the accompanying short selling, more shares of Northern Pacific stock had been sold than were actually in existence. In a single hour the price per share skyrocketed from $160 to $1,000, and a compromise was worked out to prevent a financial panic. The compromise consisted of the formation of the Northern Securities Company, a New Jersey holding company controlling both northern transcontinentals and the Burlington, with both Hill and Harriman on the board of directors.

THE MAN WITH THE "BIG STICK"

Prior to September, 1901, there was little evidence that a great reform movement was about to get under way in the United States. Financial capitalism was gathering momentum on every hand, the Republican party was securely in the saddle in Washington, and conservatism in general seemed to hold an almost uncontested supremacy over the minds of a majority of America's leaders. Only the beginnings of muckraking on a large scale suggested the seething unrest just under the surface.

Suddenly, on September 6, all this was changed. On that day a fanatic shot President McKinley twice at close range, and as a result of the wounds he received the President died after serving only six months of his second term. This tragedy catapulted into the White House that rarest of rare specimens in those days, an eastern Republican liberal, a man who had presumably been shunted into the vice-presidency by eastern business interests as a precaution against the reformist inclinations he had evinced while Governor of New York. For the first time since industrialization had commenced in earnest, reformers had their own champion in the office of President of the United States.

Care must, of course, be taken in explaining great historical events in terms of relatively small occurrences. However, it is nonetheless a striking fact that the beginning of twentieth-century economic reform, almost the first real reform achieved since the Civil War, dates from Theodore Roosevelt's accession to the presidency. Almost immediately things began to happen on this front, and from the first Roosevelt's role differed markedly from that of his predecessors.

Nowhere, perhaps, was this difference more dramatically demonstrated than in connection with the first major domestic issue with which his administration was confronted, the anthracite coal strike of 1902. Out of this episode "Teddy" earned a reputation as a liberal which he probably could not thereafter have repudiated even if he had so desired.

On the labor side of this controversy the organization involved was one of the most powerful unions of that day. By now so-called business unionism was the basis on which virtually the entire labor movement was being developed; labor had, in other words, concluded that the best opportunity for asserting control over its environment was to begin with the individual workman and his job. Concentrating their efforts on achieving this objective (by means of collective bargaining and collective bargaining agreements), unions of workers in a number of industries had become formidable employer antagonists.

Equally formidable, of course, were the protégés of the new finance capitalism. Indeed, the brand-new steel trust had the year before overwhelmingly defeated the union speaking for the skilled workers of that industry, and the organization of the anthracite coal industry closely resembled that prevailing in steel. Since coal had become an important industrial raw material, there had been a high level of cooperation between the firms producing coal and those engaged in its transportation.[8] For such transportation companies (whether railroads or the canals that had performed this function before railroads) coal was typically a vital part of total traffic, and it was found highly desirable to secure control over the coal operations in order to be assured of a steady flow of bread-and-butter business.

With the maturation of industrialism, however, it had been discovered that even this precaution was not enough. During periods of declining-demand competition, coal-owning railroads would engage in a ruinous slashing of coal prices in a desperate attempt to cover the fixed costs of their coal and transport operations. Attempts had early been made to put a stop to this practice by organizing traffic pools, but the pressure to increase tonnage still frequently became so great that traffic allotments were not adhered to. To remedy this defect tighter forms of control were developed, until in 1902 the entire anthracite coal industry—producers and carriers—was very closely held. One by one the smaller railroads had become a part of larger properties; slowly but surely independent coal producers had either given up the struggle or merged with financially stronger units; and finally, to cap the climax, the few remaining firms sharing this business had developed a strong community of interest among themselves by interownership of stock and interlocking directorates. It was this network of interests, an important element of which was J. P. Morgan and Company, that in 1902 accepted the challenge thrown down by the United Mine Workers.

What John Mitchell's miners wanted included a reduction in daily hours worked from ten to nine, a 20 per cent increase in wages, payment according to the weight of coal mined, and the recognition of their union. On May 9, the operators having refused to negotiate, this famous strike began. For five and one-half months 150,000 coal miners stayed out of the mines, completely paralyzing the entire industry.[9]

In October, with the nation facing a coal famine, President Roosevelt decided the time had come for the government to take a hand. The action he chose to take, however, was not calling out the troops as Hayes and Cleveland had done before him. Instead he called a conference of operators and union leaders and asked them to agree

[8] Eliot Jones, *The Anthracite Coal Combination in the United States* (Cambridge: Harvard University Press, 1914).

[9] John Mitchell, *Organized Labor* (Philadelphia: American Book & Bible House, 1903).

to arbitration. The union promptly assented, but spokesmen for the industry flatly refused. When the President persisted in his request, and when public opinion sided with the workers against the operators, the latter finally capitulated. A presidential arbitration commission was then appointed and ended the strike, the workers receiving in the ensuing award almost everything they had asked for except official recognition of the union which had on this occasion served them so well.

This was a signal victory for a labor movement that had to date won few signal victories; conversely, it was a dent of some consequence in the armor of finance capitalism. But the importance of this episode for present purposes does not derive from either of these facts as such. The crucial point is rather that for the first time in an issue of consequence the government had stood on the side of workers against the elite of the business community; for the first time the weight of public opinion had helped settle a major strike in labor's behalf. A sharper affront than this laissez faire had not yet received.

Again care must be taken not to exaggerate. One swallow does not make a summer, and much life yet remained in the corporate version of individualism. No doubt President Roosevelt took the stand he did in large part because the public's attitude was what it was. Equally certain is it that the public in turn was less inclined positively toward the embattled workers than negatively against the Wall Street plutocrats and limited liability combinations they were battling. Exactly what was at issue in this controversy from the standpoint of the nonworker public was indicated in the revealing remark of George F. Baer, President of the Reading Railroad:

The rights and interests of the laboring man will be protected and cared for not by the labor agitators but by the Christian men to whom God in his infinite wisdom has given the control of the public interests of the country.

A few more utterances such as this at critical historical junctures and laissez faire would all the more be on the defensive.

THE GREAT BATTLE OPENS

It was almost as if the anthracite coal strike had given a powerful tonic to the forces of reform, releasing pent-up energies which had theretofore been unable to find a constructive outlet. Although no reforms of landmark significance were achieved during Roosevelt's first term, progress was continuous from this point forward for some fifteen years, and during this longer period several basic changes in the economic order were brought about.

Before 1902 passed into history another concrete step was taken on the conservation front. A number of experimental devices had already been tried looking toward the irrigation of millions of acres of fertile and level but too dry western land. However, for the most part these attempts had relied on private enterprise, and it had become increasingly apparent that on this basis little would be accomplished. In 1902, through the Reclamation Act, the federal government embarked on a drastically different approach. A revolving fund was established using the proceeds of public land sales, out of which the first cost of irrigation work was to be financed. To be sure, even this technique was not outstandingly successful. But at the same time it was this enactment which provided the legal foundation for such great projects as the Grand Coulee and Hoover-Boulder dams; and when several decades later the issue of public power became an important aspect of business-government relationships, the existence of such facilities and such enabling legislation was to be of vital significance.

The following year the attention of reformers turned first to the task of rehabilitating the Interstate Commerce Act.[10] In the main the motivation behind this endeavor was the simple fact that it was believed the public interest demanded regulations of the sort imposed in 1887—coupled, of course, with the complete failure of that law to date—but the pressures promoting a reimposition of railway legislation were also accentuated by economic developments during the post-depression years. One such development was the maturation of finance capitalism in the form of the recent reconstruction of the railroad ownership map of the country, the fact that a majority of the board of directors of practically every road east of the Mississippi River could be found in a list of less than forty people. Another was the steady rise of freight rates since the return of prosperity, a phenomenon attributable in part to a general rise in prices, but in part also to the recent elimination of competition in the railroad industry. Still a third was the rapid "trustification" of much of the rest of the economy; the close connection between railroad operations and the creation of industrial monopoly would not yet have been forgotten in any event, but the stream of revelations flowing from muckrake literature and government investigations kept the public's awareness of this relationship even more vigorously alive.

A first step here was formal rather than substantive, and its nature indicated unmistakably the public's preoccupation with the trust

[10] Interstate Commerce Commission, *Interstate Commerce Commission Activities, 1887-1937* (Washington, D.C.: Government Printing Office, 1937).

problem in general as well as the railroad problem in particular. On February 11, 1903, the Expediting Act was passed, an enactment designed to eliminate serious delays in cases involving the Interstate Commerce and Sherman Anti-Trust acts. When the United States was the complainant and when the Attorney General certified the case as being of broad public importance, the circuit courts were to give precedence to and expedite suits brought under these two laws.

A second step, substantive in character, also reflected prevailing antitrust sentiment. Indeed it could even be argued that the railroads were the beneficiaries of the Elkins Act passed only a few days after the Expediting Act.

Not only had little enforcement work with respect to the evil of discrimination been possible under the earlier law, but in addition carriers and their customers had found even more subtle ways of evading the discrimination provisions of that enactment. One of the most ingenious of these, for example, was the so-called "midnight tariff," whereby the carrier would publish a lower rate for a single day so that only favored shippers could take advantage of it. Rates and points of origin were often also cleverly put together in such a way that particular shippers would be preferred, or some concerns were favored over others in the distribution of cars in a period of shortage or given substantial allowances for "services rendered" even though no real service was in fact performed. One contemporary authority estimated that discriminations forced on railroads by large shippers might amount to as much as $1 million a year for a single carrier. Making the carrier as well as its agent punishable in discrimination cases, and making the recipient of a rate advantage equally liable with the giver, the anti-rebate act reduced personal discrimination to a problem of minor proportions.

But the new administration was not content to let the assessment of heavy fines under the Elkins Act against such organizations as the sugar, beef, and oil trusts stand for its full achievement in the antitrust field. Here also 1903 saw drift replaced by decisive movement.

First, a Bureau of Corporations was established in the new Department of Commerce and Labor, the principal work of which was to be investigating trust organizations (except in the business of common carriage) and advising the Department of Justice in antitrust cases. The most notable work of this agency was to come later, in the assistance it was to render the Department in successfully prosecuting the oil and tobacco trusts, but as a straw in the wind this step was most significant.

Even more far-reaching, second, was the explicit recognition given to the by now obvious fact that the Sherman Act would not enforce itself. Private suits were too expensive, and the burden of proof was too great for smaller concerns to make much progress against towering rivals in this way. By means of a special appropriation an Antitrust Division to deal solely with antitrust enforcement was set up within the Department of Justice. It has become the fashion in more recent years to scoff at the idea of five attorneys and four stenographers shouldering such a gigantic responsibility as achieving the ideal set forth in antitrust legislation, but it must not be forgotten how great an advance this was in 1903.

There were conservatives who from the first had realized the great risk involved in making Roosevelt Vice-President. As Mark Hanna, titular boss of the Republican party at that time, had expressed this sentiment: "Don't any of you realize that there's only one life between that madman and the Presidency?" How accurate a prophecy this was from the standpoint of business interests, the extent to which conservatives were now in the hands of the "enemy," was evident enough in general terms long before "the man with the big stick" had held his White House post for a full year. But at the more concrete level which alone has meaning for the majority of individuals this truth probably did not dawn on men of lesser stature until 1904. That was the year Roosevelt's suit against the newly formed Northern Securities Company—one of the first fruits of the conclusion that the only way to enforce the antitrust laws would be to prepare cases and hail offenders into court—was brought to the United States Supreme Court for final adjudication.

The threat to the big business segment of the economy posed by this suit could not have been more direct or more profound. Here was no routine antitrust action. At issue was the crucial question of whether or not these laws could be evaded by adopting the holding company form of organization. Partly because so much was at stake, and partly because he was accustomed to dealing with his fellow "big operators" thus directly, J. P. Morgan had tried to dissuade Roosevelt from taking this step. "If we have done anything wrong," he had said, "why can't you just send your man [the Attorney General] to see my man [a Morgan lawyer], and we will work something out." But the President had refused to be "reasonable," and as a result the question was placed squarely before the Supreme Court.[11]

This case was in every way a sweeping vindication of the govern-

[11] *Northern Securities Company* v. *United States*, 193 U.S. 197 (1904).

ment's decision to enforce the law; the holding company as a device for evasion could not have been more thoroughly discredited. To the argument in the plaintiff's brief that the government was attacking an instrumentality of a sovereign state and hence had no jurisdiction the Court made two retorts, either of which would have been fatal to this view. On the one hand, the instrumentalities of one state government are not to be allowed to violate the sovereignty (the antitrust laws) of a sister state. On the other hand, the form of organization of a creature of a state government cannot determine the extent to which the federal government shall exercise its legitimate powers. The Court even went out of its way to deny, with respect to the facts before it, that the common-law rule of reason was a legitimate defense. As the opinion itself summarized the Court's conclusions: "If Congress has not, by the words used in the [Sherman] Act, described this and like cases, it would, we apprehend, be impossible to find words that would describe them."

THE BITTER WITH THE SWEET

Let it not be supposed that there were now no further difficulties standing in the way of reform, that conservative resistance melted away and a mature industrialism speedily became responsive to the wishes of the ordinary citizen. The momentum of a powerful evolution does not abruptly die away even after it has run its course, and this particular evolution had by no means reached that stage. Nor did liberals of that day with less historical hindsight at their disposal than is available to a later generation make the mistake of becoming overconfident. Fortunately for reform, enough adversity was intermixed with these successes to keep attitudes in proper perspective.

For example, the antitrust achievement that the Northern Securities Company decision unquestionably was, could easily be (and no doubt was at the time) exaggerated. In the first place, it did not escape notice among contemporaries that the Sherman Act was still proving much more effective against railroads than against the industrial trusts it had been primarily intended to subdue. In the second place, although this fact could not have been appreciated until some twenty years later, the greatest era by far for the holding company lay in the future despite the Supreme Court's 1904 pronouncement. And in the third place, even insofar as the Northern Securities Company itself was concerned, it was the considered judgment of no less an authority than J. J. Hill that the readjustments compelled by that decision did not in fact alter the pattern of control of railroads in the Northwest.

Almost simultaneously with the Supreme Court's decision in the Northern Securities case, moreover, liberals, and especially Theodore Roosevelt, were confronted by some basic facts of American political life. In that year a presidential election of critical importance to the cause of reform was held. As weak as the Democratic party was at the moment, the only hope of reformers lay in the re-election of President Roosevelt. And while the temper of the times demanded a reform candidate so that the business interests could probably not have prevented a second term in any event, their active support was still so valued by the President that apparently a political bargain between him and conservative leaders was struck. Students of this period believe that in exchange for his agreement not to interfere with either monetary or tax arrangements, Roosevelt's backers consented to permit "trust-busting" (if not on too vigorous a scale) to go forward and to allow the President to give vent to his conservationist inclinations. To make matters worse from the standpoint of reform, Roosevelt became concerned about the outcome of the election and made a frantic, last-minute appeal for additional funds. Of course, it was to businessmen that he was forced to turn in this situation, and the majority of these supplementary contributions came apparently from the railroad industry. Although it was later bitterly asserted by conservatives that the President did not live up to the promises he had made to his eleventh-hour benefactors (as H. C. Frick put it, "We bought him, but he wouldn't stay bought"), it is understandable that he did not feel as free as would otherwise have been the case when railroad legislation next appeared on the reform agenda. And the crowning irony here was that the sweeping Republican victory in 1904 indicated that Theodore Roosevelt's usual political astuteness had failed him on this occasion.

Not only, furthermore, was less progress being made than reformers would have liked toward reducing the power of the corporation, but at an even more fundamental level labor's struggle to secure social recognition for certain human rights was faring poorly. For some time now labor had been seeking various kinds of legislation in this area, a sociolegal reform program based on the thesis that because the worker's bargaining position is so weak and because the public has a strong interest in seeing to it that the conditions under which the work of the community is done do not fall below certain minimum standards, the machinery of collective bargaining may properly be supplemented by the legal machinery of the state. With respect to certain kinds of government aid for laborers the law had proved to be somewhat flexible, the outstanding cases in point being state child labor laws and legislation giving workers special protection in unusually hazardous occupations. But beyond these obviously narrow limits, the Supreme Court was as yet unwilling to go, feeling that the property of the employer would otherwise be taken from him without due process of law, and/or that such government interference would endanger the worker's freedom of contract.

The major issue at the moment was a New York law limiting bakers' daily hours to ten; and as of 1905 a majority of the Court could not justify maximum-hour legislation in this industry, even though a majority of the workers therein had been pressing for a ten-hour limitation for a number of years, and even though a majority of the states' laborers were already working a ten-hour day or less: ". . . The trade of a baker, in and of itself, is not an unhealthy one. . . . Under such circumstances the freedom of master and employee to contract with each other . . . cannot be prohibited or interfered with, without violating the federal Constitution."[12] Clearly all was still well, in the conservative view, on the Fourteenth Amendment front, and little comfort could be taken by liberals in the only redeeming features of this decision. First, the conservative victory was exceedingly narrow; four Justices dissented. Second, Holmes' sharply worded minority opinion would one day be seen as the truly prophetic utterance it was.

The case is decided upon an economic theory [laissez faire] which a large part of the country does not entertain. . . . The Fourteenth Amendment does not enact Mr. Herbert Spencer's *Social Statics*. . . . I think that the word "liberty," in the Fourteenth Amendment, is perverted when it is held to prevent the natural outcome of a dominant opinion. . . .

The way in which successes and failures were intermingled in these days when the new reform program hung perilously in the balance can be excellently illustrated by a series of encounters between the public and the beef trust in 1905 and 1906. One of these, the first in point of time, was an antitrust suit launched by the new Antitrust Division of the Department of Justice. For more than thirty years the major packers had maintained some form of pooling arrangement, until by the turn of the century a highly formal (and stable) market division agreement with quotas for each company had been developed. Brought to the Supreme Court in 1905, this

---

[12] *Lochner* v. *New York*, 198 U.S. 45 (1905).

case resulted in a permanent injunction against these anticompetitive practices. As in the Addyston case the Court had no difficulty
declaring illegal the price-fixing activities of a number of competitors acting in concert.[13] Even before this decision was handed down
by the Supreme Court, however, substitute arrangements had been
perfected. A new holding company was created, the National Packing Company, which permitted many of the same people to make
the same business decisions that had previously been made by
members of the pool.

This was indeed an ominous turn of events in view of the apparent decisiveness of the Supreme Court's ruling in the Northern Securities Company case. But if liberals were troubled by such considerations they gave no sign, for they were busily engaged in
attacking these concerns on another front, along with other food
processors and drug companies.[14]

In late 1905 and early 1906 *Collier's* carried a series of articles by
Samuel Hopkins Adams, a major item in the rapidly growing volume of muckrake literature, setting forth in sordid detail the sometimes careless and often deliberate use of poisons or other impurities
to make foods and drugs more attractive, to assist in their preservation, or simply to economize on the more expensive materials which
were their basic ingredients. Almost overnight a long-smouldering
resentment against adulterations in commercial foods and drugs
(an agitation rooted to a large extent in dairy farmer opposition to
colored oleomargarine) became a white-hot public indignation. Bills
proposing regulations for this area of industrial life which had long
lain dormant in Congress were revived and started on their legislative way once more.

But such bills had been quietly buried before, and there is reason
for supposing that such would have been the fate of the new crop
if an extremely fortuitous event had not intervened. In early 1906
Upton Sinclair's *The Jungle* was finally published after its young
author had been given a negative reply by three publishing houses.
Almost immediately this muckraking novel, a brilliant exposé of
the conditions under which America's meat was prepared for market,
became a best seller. Simultaneously, public agitation for more effective meat inspection laws both took the spotlight away from the
demand for pure food and drug legislation and assured the satisfaction of that demand, this new struggle soon settling down to a brief
but acrimonious contest between the packers and the general public.

---

[13] *Swift and Company* v. *United States*, 196 U.S. 375 (1905).
[14] Mark Sullivan, *Our Times* (New York: Charles Scribner's Sons, 1927), vol. II.

Much depended, as the battle got under way in earnest, upon the attitude of President Roosevelt. At first he took the position that Sinclair had exaggerated the situations he described. But when a presidential commission turned in an official report corroborating the main features of the novelist's account, Roosevelt was insistent that the federal government take steps to supplement state action in this field. A more rigorous Meat Inspection Act was prepared, this measure jarring loose the major pending Pure Food and Drug Act as it passed through Congress. In vain did food and drug interests in general and the packers in particular bring all the pressure at their disposal to bear upon an aroused body of lawmakers, apparently unaware in their confusion that the stopping of these mild regulations might open the way to far more stringent controls.[15] June, 1906, saw both measures become law—the first carrying much further a responsibility already recognized on a small scale, and the second placing the federal government behind an attempt to prevent either the adulteration or the misbranding of foods and drugs. And while it could hardly be said that the interest of consumers prevailed over the profit motive in this legislation, reformers could at least congratulate themselves on a major task well begun.

The violence, the sheer volume, and the one-sidedness of the muckrake literature have so dominated the view by later generations of Americans of the early twentieth century that it is even now difficult to put these years in proper perspective. How oppressed were Americans at this time? How morally deficient were the forces then guiding the nation's destinies? How completely were citizens in the clutches of a monster industrialism that recognized no rights not reducible to dollar terms?

All that can be said for certain in answer to these questions is that the picture of these times painted by contemporaries was overdrawn. The United States was neither on the brink of revolution, nor visibly moving in that direction. It is indeed one of the paradoxes of American history that in the midst of one of the most intense peaks of muckrake protest the Democratic party was wrested from the Bryan forces, falling so securely into the hands of New York and other eastern conservatives that in 1904 business leaders toyed with the idea of supporting that organization rather than nominating Roosevelt for a second term.

[15] Donald C. Blaisdell, *Economic Power and Political Pressures* (Washington, D.C.: Government Printing Office, 1941).

At the same time, however, there are certain other factors to be taken into account in appraising reform efforts and conservative resistance during this period. For example, to describe the apex of laissez faire industrialism in terms of moral degeneration is in a significant sense to take hold of this problem at the wrong end. With the appearance of the machine, men did not suddenly become mean and vicious; human nature did not abruptly take a sharp turn for the worse. Much of what seems to be explainable in this way, stems rather from what might appropriately be called a breakdown of the preindustrial control system. There had been a time when men were sufficiently closely associated with one another geographically that informal social controls—the ever present and unsympathetic glare of small community public opinion—could be depended upon to keep the worst excesses of power in check. The rise of large-scale production and the city, however, drastically reduced the strength of these controls; consumers and laborers alike were socially far distant from the owners and managers of large business firms producing for a national market. This was the real meaning of the concept "soulless corporation," and the task reformers had set for themselves was that of replacing the checks now available with some more appropriate to the new industrial society.

Looking at this matter from the other side of the fence, moreover, if reformers were desperately seeking to re-establish control over their society, conservatives were endeavoring just as desperately to maintain control over theirs. That is, if liberals felt insecure in the new society because of their powerlessness, the business class felt no less threatened by the prospect that it was about to lose the power and prestige on which its self-respect was based. After J. P. Morgan had failed to talk President Roosevelt out of the decision to prosecute the Northern Securities Company, he asked the President if the latter intended to attack his other interests. Whether he was reassured by Roosevelt's answer we are not told, but there is no mistaking the concern this exchange revealed. Out of the folklore which has since grown up around him, it is difficult to associate "Morgan the Magnificent" with insecurity, but this was unquestionably the central reaction of Morgan and those around him to the reform movement.

QUESTIONS FOR DISCUSSION

1. How does a muckrake literature bemoaning the disappearance of democracy demonstrate the existence of democracy?
2. Explain the muckrake period in American economic history.

3. Why is the growth of the corporation referred to as a revolution in the institution of private property?

4. Defend finance capitalism. Why were many people so upset by this development?

5. Explain the significance of each of the summary comments regarding the formation of the United States Steel Company.

6. Why was it so important to reformers to have a liberal president? Why had Democrats not elected a liberal president instead of Grover Cleveland?

7. Enumerate the major interests involved in the anthracite coal dispute, and explain the outcome of this episode in terms of those interests.

8. Summarize and evaluate the reform achievements of Theodore Roosevelt's first term in the White House.

9. What were the issues involved in the Northern Securities case? Explain the significance of its outcome.

10. Were the business interests wise or unwise to fight so fiercely against any and all changes in the status quo?

11. In what sense was "security" involved in the businessman's fight against government encroachment?

Chapter 12

One Giant Chained

The liberal press of the early 1900's would probably have asserted that President Roosevelt's greatest reform achievement was the dissolution of the Northern Securities Company. With the passing of time, however, this accomplishment has grown steadily smaller in importance while another reform measure has just as steadily grown greater in stature. That measure is the Hepburn Act. As of the end of 1906 there could no longer be any doubt that the federal government intended to follow through on the implications of the public utility concept with regard to interstate railroads. Railroad rates, in other words, were to be regulated in the public interest. Surely this was, in retrospect, the crowning reform accomplishment of Theodore Roosevelt's two terms in the White House.

RAILROADS AT BAY[1]

No sooner had Roosevelt become President, than his administration began to lean toward the Democratic position on this issue rather than the Republican. Thus early were the railroads apprised of their danger, for the primary motive behind this movement was no longer to save the railroads from the trusts or even to save the people from the trusts. The central concern now was to save the people from the railroads. In its most general aspect resentment against the railroad stemmed from railway consolidation, but on a more concrete level citizens could point to rising freight rates and to an unprecedented big-business effort to influence public opinion, launched the moment the seriousness of the President's purpose became widely understood. The principal demand was for Interstate Commerce Commission power to prescribe reasonable rates.

[1] S. L. Miller, *Railway Transportation* (Chicago: A. W. Shaw Co., 1924); and W. Z. Ripley, *Railroads: Rates and Regulation* (New York: Longmans, Green & Co., Inc., 1912).

As early as December, 1904, Roosevelt had characterized legislation in this field as "a paramount issue" in his annual message to Congress. A year later he was demanding "government supervision and regulation of the rates charged by railroads." On the strength of this strong presidential support, a bill was introduced into the House on January 4, 1906, by Hepburn of Iowa, and passed 346 to 7.

But it was one thing in those days to get a railroad regulation measure through the House; piloting it unharmed through the Senate was a very different matter. United States Senators were still elected by state legislatures, an arrangement which made the Senate much more of a tool of wealth than would otherwise have been the case. Branding the President-endorsed proposal as "contrary to the spirit of our institutions" (in the words of Senator Foraker of Ohio), a sizable number of able and powerful Senators set themselves to the task of preventing the passage of Representative Hepburn's measure.

It is interesting to speculate on whether, in the ordinary course of events, the pressure brought to bear by a determined President or that wielded by one of the most powerful lobbies ever put into action against a piece of legislation would have proved to be the more effective. Certainly there are those who even today would predict success for Senators Aldrich (Rhode Island) and Foraker on an "other things equal" basis. Fortunately for reform, however, other things were not equal. At a moment which could not have been more fortuitous a number of events occurred which tilted the balance decisively in favor of passage, and the "Great Debate of 1906" (an even greater one than that concerning the purity of foods and drugs) issued in a liberal victory.

The external factors intervening to produce this result are not without interest in themselves. First, high prosperity during the first years of the century overtaxed the nation's transportation system, and in the resulting breakdown of service grain rotted on the ground and a serious coal famine developed in some parts of the country. Second, an Interstate Commerce Commission report revealed scandalous discriminations against small producers in the distribution of coal cars by the Pennsylvania Railroad. Third, another Interstate Commerce Commission report made public rebates by the Atchison, Topeka, and Santa Fe (in "barefaced disregard of the law") which even implicated a member of the President's Cabinet. Fourth, the results of an insurance investigation in New York were published, showing a cynical carelessness in the handling of funds paid into these concerns which made even many conservatives wince. Confronted with all these incontrovertible evidences that big corporations were often not model citizens, most of the Hepburn Act's opponents in the Senate finally cast reluctant votes in favor of passage.

Although reformers did not get everything they wanted in this measure, what they did get went far toward restoring the Interstate Commerce Commission to a position of substantial influence. Thus the scope of the Interstate Commerce Act was broadened to include private-car lines, express companies, sleeping-car companies, pipelines, and terminal and switching companies. Still more important was the power given the Commission to prescribe just and reasonable maximum rates, to apportion joint rates where the carriers involved were unable to come to an agreement, to establish through routes, and to fix reasonable charges for services and property provided by shippers. And whereas the 1887 law had simply required the railroads to file reports as to finance, operations, and rates in such form as specified by the Commission, the new law empowered the Commission to prescribe a uniform system of accounts for all carriers subject to its jurisdiction and to compel the filing of reports based on that system.

Along with these sweeping new powers for the regulatory agency, the 1906 law imposed one major new prohibition upon the carriers. By means of the so-called "commodities clause," railroads were forbidden to transport in interstate commerce property owned by them except property held for their own use. The primary purpose of this restriction was to separate the nation's companies producing anthracite coal from their close association with transportation concerns (lumber being specifically exempted); it had become increasingly evident that as long as a railroad owned much of the coal it was transporting, a rate structure which would not discriminate against the independent could not be achieved. Yet, clear though this intent was and unyielding though the Supreme Court had been in the Northern Securities case, this evil was not to be so easily uprooted. An early Court decision dealing with this clause drew a remarkably unrealistic distinction between owning securities and owning property,[2] a decision promoting widespread evasion of the law through holding company arrangements. Not until the Hepburn Act had been on the books for almost fifteen years was the commodities clause fully implemented.[3]

[2] *United States* v. *Delaware and Hudson Company*, 213 U.S. 366 (1909).
[3] *United States* v. *Lehigh Valley Railroad Company*, 220 U.S. 257 (1911); *United States* v. *Delaware, Lackawanna and Western Railroad Company*, 238 U.S. 516 (1915); and *United States* v. *Reading Company*, 253 U.S. 26 (1920).

OTHER PEOPLE'S MONEY

While reformers were busily engaged in bringing the railroads to heel in Washington, others of their kind were weighing finance capitalism in the balance in a different area of the economy in the state of New York. For a long time certain financial aspects of limited liability enterprise had disturbed rank-and-file citizens. One dimension of this uneasiness arose out of the sheer mechanics of stock and bond capitalism, together with the abuses to which this mechanism apparently lent itself so readily. Short selling, making a profit from increases or decreases in the prices of shares on the stock market, stock watering, insiders' profits—all these and other common financial operations seemed to men and women who worked with their hands an immoral securing of something for nothing and therefore a fraudulent exploitation of the rest of the community.

More recently, however, these practices had come to be over-shadowed by another dimension of this same threat to peace of mind. Here the focus of attention was finance capitalism proper, the control of the resources of industrial society by tiny minorities of owners. And not only was this excessive concentration of control itself thought to be an evil, but it in turn cast a new light on the financial manipulations about which the public was already upset. What was becoming painfully evident was that the foundation upon which virtually all the undesirable features of the corporate world rested was *other people's money*. To be sure, this was also the basis of most of the desirable features of that world. The limited-liability concern was institutionally grounded in the public benefits to be derived from concentrating the funds of many capital contributors into a single economic entity, and the loss of control by owners over the uses to which their capital was to be put was only a more or less inevitable corollary of that development. But this considera-tion did little to soften the resentment felt by many citizens at the sight of "public" resources being used for the narrowest of private purposes.

Unfortunately, the problem of other people's money was proving to be singularly hard to get at. On one flank the status quo was protected by the Fourteenth Amendment and state incorporation laws. On the other an equally powerful protection was afforded by the common law doctrine of *caveat emptor* ("let the buyer beware"); no one was compelled to buy corporate securities, and those who did should surely be presumed to have done so with full knowledge of what was involved.

Caveat emptor had, it is true, been breached in the case of foods and drugs. Here, however, special factors had been involved. Processed goods in these two categories were often bought under circumstances in which the buyer could not possibly have full enough knowledge to protect himself. Accordingly, the government had taken steps to shift some of this responsibility to the seller. Where could a comparable situation justifying government intervention be found out in the financial world?

The railroad? Hardly! Effective government control in this industry was being exercised only with respect to rates and closely related matters, and few people supposed that the Supreme Court would accept this development as a precedent for federal regulation in the field of corporation charters. Furthermore, even where the new public utilities were concerned there was little chance that effective state restrictions on financial practices could be achieved—if only because such a program in any state would simply drive those concerns over which it had jurisdiction into a more lax legal environment. No, the "Achilles heel" of finance capitalism would have to be found elsewhere. As in the case of food and drugs, an attack on the problem of other people's money would have to await the revelation of flagrant abuses in some area in which the public trust was directly involved.

It was due to no foresight or special efforts on the part of liberals that the golden opportunity on this front arrived long before any but the most optimistic had dared to hope. The responsible factor was rather—and few ironies in American business history exceed this one—a quarrel among the finance capitalists themselves.[4]

At the age of 23 a young man named James Hazen Hyde had fallen heir to the Equitable Life Assurance Society, one of the greatest of America's insurance companies at that time, a concern boasting $400 million worth of assets, custodian of well over $1 billion worth of insurance for almost 600,000 policyholders, and protector of potential widows and orphans numbering 3,000,000. Here was a public trust which seemed made to order for the task at hand. Insurance was a relatively young industry, a distinctive product of industrial capitalism, and as yet little attention had been given to the special problems it raised. No one, to be sure, was compelled to buy life insurance, but the insurance company could still legitimately be expected to manage its affairs so as to be able to fulfill its promises.

[4] Mark Sullivan, *Our Times* (New York: Charles Scribner's Sons, 1930), vol. III.

TABLE 5. A GIANT COMES OF AGE

	Equitable Life Assurance Society	
Year	Number of Policies	Insurance in Force (millions of dollars)
1865	8,097	27.5
1880	52,272	177.6
1890	197,825	720.7
1904	564,594	1,495.5

Source: N. S. B. Gras and Henrietta M. Larson, *Casebook in Business History* (New York: F. S. Crofts and Company, 1939), p. 536. Used by permission.

In those days when capital for expansion and speculation was the *sine qua non* of business prestige, $400 million was a prize well worth possessing. Within a few years young Hyde had been made a member of the boards of fourteen leading railroads, nineteen banks and trust companies scattered all over the United States, and fifteen industrial corporations. Taking alarm at what seemed to them to be the dissipation of the Equitable's assets in unwise investments, a group of men inside that concern took steps drastically to reduce Hyde's influence. This action, primarily because it promised to be highly successful, precipitated a rough-and-tumble war among the minions of finance for control over, or access to, Equitable's resources. The great value placed on this prize in the financial world is indicated by the fact that Thomas Fortune Ryan purchased a controlling interest in Equitable at this time for $2.5 million, in the form of shares from which he was legally entitled to receive a maximum income of $3,514 annually.

It is no wonder that a journalistic world already launched on the muckraking adventure would scent in all this a story worth developing. And it is if anything still less surprising that out of the ensuing publicity there arose a public clamor for a full-dress investigation of the entire insurance business in New York (the home at that time of most of the country's larger insurance companies). A public trust plus an investigation by a legislative committee—this was during those years an almost certain formula for the revelation of flagrant abuses providing the foundation for reform measures.

The following items are a sample of the findings of the so-called Armstrong committee.[5] Nepotism was being practiced on a grand scale. Huge salaries were paid to officers, in addition to which personal expenses of and personal servants for officers had been paid

[5] State of New York, *Report of the Joint Committee of the State and Assembly of the State of New York Appointed to Investigate the Affairs of Life Insurance Companies* (Albany: 1907).

out of company treasuries. Vast sums of money had been kept liquid and idle in affiliated banks and trust companies. Resources had been used to help launch some of the most speculative of the recent new trusts. Investment banking firms had sold huge quantities of securities to insurance companies with which they were interlocked. Intricate bookkeeping devices had been used to conceal transactions already contrary to state law. "Legal expenses" had been very high; to this account had been charged the cost of maintaining a vigorous lobbying program, campaign contributions, retainer fees to several United States Senators, and attempts to influence public opinion.

FINANCE CAPITALISM ON THE DEFENSIVE[6]

The major consequences of New York's exposure of insurance company offenses against common morality were three. First, the management of all these concerns was thoroughly shaken up. The president and two vice-presidents of one company and two vice-presidents of another were indicted. Most of the high officials of the three biggest companies either resigned or were soon forced out.

Second, New York in 1906 enacted a program of legislation governing this industry which not only reformed its operation in that state but which also became to a considerable extent a model for other states to follow in coping with this same problem. By its terms insurance companies were forbidden to hold stock in banks, trust companies, or other corporations, or to participate in security-flotation syndicates. Salaries, commissions, and other expenses were limited, and vouchers were required for all expenditures of $100 or more. Officers and agents were prohibited from having pecuniary interests in transactions with their companies. Policyholders ceasing to make payments on their premiums were to be given a new policy containing the insurance they had to date paid for calculated on a pro rata basis. Insurance companies were forbidden to make contributions to political campaign funds, and their legislative agents were required to register, giving the name of their employer. While this legislation did not explicitly say so, the business of selling life insurance thereby became something of a cross between a bank and a public utility from the standpoint of its relationship to the government, a status the Supreme Court was to confirm a few years later by permitting Kansas to regulate the rates of her fire insurance companies as a protection to the public against monopolistic rate fixing.[7]

6 Henry Clews, *Fifty Years in Wall Street* (New York: Irving Publishing Co., 1908); and John Moody, *Masters of Capital* (New Haven: Yale University Press, 1921).

7 *German Alliance Insurance Company v. Lewis*, 233 U.S. 289 (1914).

The third consequence of this investigation had to do with the Armstrong committee's chief investigator. Before being designated for this task he was a successful enough but quite obscure New York lawyer. Less than a year after the investigation ended, he was elected Governor of New York. Ten years later he missed becoming President of the United States by the narrowest of margins, and a few years beyond that he was appointed to the bench of the Supreme Court. Thus did the people reward Charles Evans Hughes for the part he had played in defending the community against some of the depredations of finance capitalism.

If the attack on finance capitalism by way of the insurance industry resulted from what might be called internal causes, the next challenge it was to meet can as appropriately be thought of as having been brought about by external factors. In 1907 the economy suffered another disastrous financial panic, a fact which must have been especially disconcerting to the masters of finance who had insisted that the country was now immune to those devastating downturns. Although the "Panic of 1907" was not the most severe collapse the nation had ever experienced, its appearance at this time against the background of muckraking and reform made it unusually significant.

For example, the way this panic commenced indicated immediately that something was seriously amiss with the economy's financial organization. On Tuesday morning, October 22, a line began to form at Fifth Avenue and Thirty-fourth Street. All over the city the word began going out "There is a run on the Knickerbocker Trust Company," and the line grew steadily longer. Shortly after noon, after having paid out more than $8 million in cash, this huge institution was forced to declare itself bankrupt. The next day several hundred people were standing in front of the Trust Company of America when that concern opened its doors to begin the day's work. Only with the assistance of a loan from J. P. Morgan and those around him was that firm able to continue in operation until closing time; and after losing $13.5 million in cash in a single day, few insiders were at all sure that the company could weather another such storm.

In short, the trust companies, virtually without exception, were in trouble. A recent innovation of industrial capitalism, and one performing a highly important function (built squarely upon a foundation of other people's money), these concerns were the first to feel the pinch of a new depression. Immediately men began to ask, Why?

The answer was not long in coming—and was absurdly simple in the bargain. Not content with performing the service for which they had ostensibly been created, these firms had gone deeply into the commercial banking business. Understandably the regulations necessary to keep a trust company's operations within reasonable bounds would not suffice for an institution creating a large volume of demand liabilities against itself. Unfortunately, a painful panic was required to bring this weakness to light—a panic which the weakness in turn did much to accentuate. New York moved promptly to correct this difficulty for the future, and of course also other states learned much from that experience. But as far as the "Panic of 1907" was concerned the damage was already done.

It is to the credit of the finance capitalists in general and J. P. Morgan in particular that these men put their shoulders to the wheel and did everything in their power to keep the economy on as nearly even a keel as possible.[8] They made loans to and otherwise supported those institutions that were in the technical sense solvent. They endeavored to limit the decline (or at least the precipitateness of the decline) in the stock market. They worked side by side with the Secretary of the Treasury (who made available $36 million worth of federal funds in this crisis) to shore up the economy at all but its weakest points. And perhaps these efforts did limit the severity of this decline. However, the economy had a certain amount of readjusting to do, and for the most part the downturn continued until this process had been completed.

The moral was obvious, and the business world was quick to take the hint. Not only was the economy not panic-proof, but private citizens even when they had scores of millions of dollars at their disposal could not do much to stem such a tide once it had gotten underway. To a suspicion which had all along been entertained by many that the National Banking Act contained significant defects was now added the eagerness of a thoroughly frightened conservative class (as well as most other segments of the population) to see to it that a like tragedy did not occur again. A more shock-proof economy might be more resistant to reformist pressures. Accordingly in 1908 the National Monetary Commission was created and charged with the responsibility of outlining "an organization of capital and credit by which confidence can be firmly established and credit maintained under all circumstances and conditions." A large order, this, but the group of nine Senators and nine Representatives under the leadership of Senator Aldrich set to work with a will.

---

[8] F. L. Allen, *The Great Pierpont Morgan* (New York: Harper & Bros., 1949).

THE DOUBLE STANDARD

What with new railroad legislation, an insurance investigation, and a major panic, life was anything but serene for businessmen during these years. Haunted on every hand by the threat of basic changes in the rules of the game, they could only wait, watch, and meanwhile play their cards as close to their chests as possible. But that little had as yet been accomplished by way of breaking the grip of finance capitalisim on the economy was soon made clear. In several ways the vigor of that institution largely frustrated all attempts to lessen its influence.

A first case in point here has to do with an event involving the United States Steel Corporation which took place in the midst of the 1907 panic. It developed that a brother-in-law of George F. Baker, a Morgan intimate, was heavily in debt to his firm, which firm was in turn heavily in debt to a number of banks. As a part of the collateral Baker's brother-in-law had left with his firm as security, and which the firm had then used as collateral at the banks, were a large number of shares of stock in the Tennessee Coal, Iron, and Railroad Company, an independent steel concern and the major producer in the Birmingham area.

There was no issue as to whether the brother-in-law was to be saved, relieving a considerable amount of pressure on the banking system in the process. The only question was how. J. P. Morgan's approach was for United States Steel to purchase a controlling interest in the Alabama concern. The great man himself went to Washington to ask the President if the latter would bring suit against him for violating the antitrust laws if he did this, carefully pointing out at the same time how important it might be for a precariously balanced economy to prevent the forced sale of large blocks of T. C. I. stock. Perhaps Morgan got a great deal of personal satisfaction out of putting such a proposition to the destroyer of the Northern Securities Company, and no doubt Theodore Roosevelt reflected briefly on the irony of this turning of the tables. In any event there was really no way out but to approve the transaction once the question had been raised in that form. Thus it was that the greatest consolidation of them all secured control over still another thriving independent, with results that were not always salutary as far as the economy of the southeastern part of the United States was concerned.[9]

[9] George W. Stocking, *Basing-Point Pricing and Regional Development* (Chapel Hill: University of North Carolina Press, 1954).

Another episode involving the United States Steel Corporation also illustrates excellently the strength of underlying trends. No sooner had panic begun to give way to depression than Elbert Gary, chairman of the board, called the leaders of the industry together in the first of the famous "Gary dinners." At this meeting it was agreed that there was no reason why the price of steel should fluctuate with business conditions, and that during this particular change in the economic weather the price of steel would remain constant. And it did. The reason given for taking this step was that it would exercise a stabilizing influence on the economy. Perhaps it did contribute to that end; but it is not without interest in this connection that steel has an inelastic demand, and that as a result under a wide range of conditions profits are higher when prices are higher and vice versa.

Even with respect to financial relationships the inertia of the past fifty years of economic evolution had obviously not been checked. In the first place, the demand that insurance companies dispose of bank and trust company stock did not specify the method of disposal. It was a simple matter, therefore, to sell these securities to the investment companies with which the insurance concerns were already affiliated. The consequence was that no decrease in concentration arising out of past transactions was achieved.

From the standpoint of maintaining or increasing concentration for the future, in the second place, fairly effective substitute arrangements began to be worked out almost immediately. If a close tie was not feasible between investment banking and insurance premiums, why not instead link investment banking with commercial bank deposits?

This was, to be sure, easier said than done. With the rise of checkbook money as a substitute for bank notes, the dominance of the national banks over the country's monetary system which the Civil War legislation had intended to effect had been shattered. At the same time, however, the steady evolution of state bank legislation over the preceding hundred years had built up a fairly comprehensive pattern of control for state banks. With respect to the matter at issue here, for example, banks in most states were forbidden to deal in or hold speculative securities in general and common stocks in particular, with the result that the value of an ownership link between investment banking and commercial banking firms was correspondingly limited. This was the obstacle that had to be surmounted.

Already the elements of what was about to become the standard solution to that problem were visible. As commercial banks became more and more interested in investing their funds in bonds they naturally drew (and were drawn) closer to the concerns whose business it was to find a market for new securities. Similarly, the importance of brokers' loans and of loans to individual investors and speculators to commercial banks tended to create a still more intimate relationship between the major source of funds and the need for such funds in the stock and bond markets. Only one process needed now to be added to make the leading commercial banks full-fledged investment banks, the actual selling of securities. In 1908 this last step was taken. J. P. Morgan's First National Bank organized an investment affiliate, an example soon followed by others. Henceforth commercial banks were free to violate the law in spirit while still observing the letter of its prohibitions—and the unavailability of insurance funds to the investment banking business was more than compensated.

Finally, a number of developments on the trust front itself bore witness to the continuing power of corporate individualism. A succession of reports by the Bureau of Corporations emphasized the steady growth of the largest concerns in some of the nation's basic industries, together with the objectionable business practices which both helped make that growth possible and were in turn made possible by the dominant position thus won. In 1908, by means of an amalgamation of Buick, Oldsmobile, Cadillac, and a number of lesser firms in the young automobile industry, the foundation was laid for the ultimate organization of that industry around a small number of huge concerns. A Supreme Court decision in that same year established the principle that the owner of a patent might, if he chose, utilize his property by withholding it from general use.[10] In 1908 also, trust-buster Theodore Roosevelt halted antitrust proceedings against the New York, New Haven, and Hartford Railroad Company on the latter's promise to be a "good" monopoly. (As things turned out it wasn't, and hence more drastic action was merely postponed.)

And what of the rest of the community? How was it with workers and farmers as big business grew bigger and increased its economic power proportionately? For farmers it was not so bad; prices were rising, and farmers can hold their own reasonably well in an advancing market. But for laborers the situation was about as dismal as it had ever been. A rising price level puts a maximum amount of economic pressure on this group, a challenge much accentuated during these years both by a period of severe unemployment and the grow-

[10] *Continental Paper Bag Company* v. *Eastern Paper Bag Company,* 210 U.S. 405 (1908).

ing power of industrial combinations. Not only, in other words, was labor as desperately in need of organization as ever (and this was especially the case in view of the decision to concentrate on this route to economic betterment), but the obstacles in the way of organization had perhaps never been greater. Even if this had not been true on general grounds, the success with which businessmen now solicited the aid of government in resisting labor organizations would alone make it an accurate description of the prevailing situation.[11]

There were several significant dimensions of this alliance between business and government to challenge the advance of the labor movement. One of these was the use made of the opportunity afforded by a new depression to launch the most intensive "open-shop" drive yet organized by American employers. Backed particularly by the National Association of Manufacturers, this campaign made excellent use of the facilities of state and local governments.

A second major approach was the perfection of the injunction as an antiunion weapon.[12] Here yeoman service was performed by an organization calling itself the Anti-Boycott Association, the principal technique of this group being to carry promising cases into the courts in order to establish favorable legal precedents. A boycott against the Buck's Stove and Range Company, invoked in part because the company had violated an earlier collective bargaining agreement, was successfully met by a federal court injunction demanded by that organization. Written by the company's lawyers and signed by the judge with almost no change in wording, this document has the distinction of being one of the most sweeping orders in the history of American law. Another landmark injunction of this period was granted at the request of the Hitchman Coal and Coke Company, forbidding the United Mine Workers from organizing employees who had signed a "yellow-dog" contract.

Still a third kind of attack on labor's right to organize was the further development of the Sherman Act for this purpose.[13] A strike called against a hat manufacturing company in Connecticut, supplemented by a nationwide boycott, was met by a suit charging violation of the Sherman Act and asking for triple damages. Carried all the way to the Supreme Court by the Anti-Boycott Association, this case issued in a crushing legal defeat for business unionism. For

[11] Charles O. Gregory, *Labor and the Law* (New York: W. W. Norton & Co., Inc., 1936).

[12] Felix Frankfurter and Nathan Greene, *The Labor Injunction* (New York: The Macmillan Co., 1930).

[13] Edward Berman, *Labor and the Sherman Act* (New York: Harper & Bros., 1930).

the first time the Supreme Court stated unequivocally that labor was not exempt from antitrust prosecution.[14]

One other important event of this period will round out this brief account of where labor organizations stood in the eyes of the law. Some years earlier a law had been passed by Congress setting up an arbitration machinery for use in railroad labor disputes, an attempt to give recognition to the public utility status of that industry from the standpoint of capital-labor harmony as well as in the field of economic regulation. Another provision, however, had forbidden railroad employers from discriminating against employees for membership in a union. In 1908 the Supreme Court singled out this provision of the Erdman Act, flatly declaring it to be an unconstitutional interference with the employer's freedom of contract.[15]

By now there could be no doubt about it. The law was unmistakably creating and rigorously maintaining a double standard on the matter of economic organization. Combination was permissible if employers were the ones doing the combining; if it were employees, on the other hand, cooperation was not to be allowed. Here was a cruel impasse for workers. To drift with the status quo as to Sherman Act interpretation was to accept an overwhelming disadvantage in precisely the line of endeavor which now seemed most promising; to push for stronger antitrust legislation would be folly in the face of present legal trends; to demand repeal of the antitrust laws would be to risk giving employers a greater boost in power than employees. It was hard to know what to do, although it was clear that a drive for a stronger Sherman Act was easily the worst possible strategy.

Accent on Taxation

In this, for the moment unresolvable, impasse confronting workers is explanation enough for the fact that antitrust legislation as such was not now a major item on the reform agenda. But though this issue was missing from the liberals' program of legislation at the national level, it does not follow that there was no such program. Indeed a number of items had been growing in importance in the minds of reformers, and there was a determination in many quarters that some of them at least were to be followed through. One of these was taxation. The nation's tax structure continued to be as regressive as ever, and numerous reform groups were still smarting from the tax defeat of the 1890's. Here, moreover, was an issue on

---

[14] *Loewe* v. *Lawlor,* 208 U.S. 274 (1908).
[15] *Adair* v. *United States,* 208 U.S. 161 (1908).

which workers and farmers could join hands despite the fact that the economic fortunes of these interests were poles apart.

William Howard Taft, hand-picked by Theodore Roosevelt to succeed himself as President, was probably as good a compromise candidate as could have been found by eastern conservative leaders of the Republican party and the reformist rank-and-file westerners whose votes were indispensable to Republican electoral success. The fact that he was nominated attests his acceptability to the party's leaders; his election in turn indicates the approval of western voters. Although Taft was known not to have as strong a personality as Roosevelt, and although he was sometimes referred to in labor circles as "the father of injunctions," he was also known to have some liberal tendencies and it seemed reasonable to suppose that on this foundation a few reform achievements might be built.

Another straw in the wind, or at least so it seemed at the time, was the Republican platform. Pledges were made to revise the tariff, to carry railroad regulation still further, and to strengthen the antitrust laws; the presidential campaign of 1908 emphasized these promises in approximately that order. Against the background of a secularly rising price level and the feeling among western farmers that the existing tariff structure discriminated against them in favor of eastern industrialists, the tariff had again become a major political issue. Encouraged by this platform pledge and by the Republican candidate's even more emphatic insistence on tariff revision, reformers prepared to reduce the tariff.

But they had reckoned without the deep roots of aggressive protectionism in the Republican party. No sooner had the intentions of the reductionists been made known (at a special session of Congress called by Taft expressly to revise the tariff downward) than the party's leaders made it clear that they meant to stand fast against the carrying out of this purpose.[16] Eastern businessmen had by now reached the conclusion that tariff protectionism was to be retained for their benefit, even if it did discriminate against western and southern farmers. Thus was touched off an even more bitter debate than had preceded the passage of the Hepburn Act, one which did not end until the Republican party was more sharply divided as between its conservative and liberal wings than it had ever been. The tariff was not significantly reduced.

Perhaps reformers deserved to lose this battle. From the outset they had made no secret of their intent to follow up a reduction in the

[16] N. W. Stephenson, *Nelson W. Aldrich: A Leader in American Politics* (New York: Charles Scribner's Sons, 1930).

tariff by levying an income tax (2 per cent on annual net income above $5,000 for all income receivers). No doubt this fact added much to the strenuousness of conservative resistance to a lowering of duties; a smaller amount of revenue flowing into the Treasury from the customs houses would be an added argument for the tapping of new tax sources.

This consideration operated effectively in reverse, too. The passage of an income tax would of course almost immediately become an argument for reduced protection. And this fact was only one of several reasons why the business interests now fought against a tax on incomes almost as vigorously as against a downward revision of the tariff. In addition to the obvious fact that the new levy would fall disproportionately upon them, there was a widespread fear that another encounter between the Supreme Court and the income tax might have serious consequences. If the Court again declared such a tax to be unconstitutional, public opinion might become so adverse to that body that it would be less effective in protecting business interests in other ways.

Reformers won a partial victory on the income tax,[17] probably because workers could promote that project more wholeheartedly than a reduction of the tariff. With the help of President Taft, conservatives were able to get a mild corporation tax substituted for the income tax proposal as such. However, as a concession to liberals without which this substitution would not have been accepted, the conservatives in their turn were forced to agree to the submission of an income tax amendment to the Constitution to the states. Much to their dismay (and possibly surprise) this amendment was ratified in record time.

THE RAILROADS TAMED

With all pretense of harmony inside the Republican party now shattered, it is not surprising that the next clash between liberals and conservatives concerned an issue almost trivial by comparison with the tax questions which had basically caused the breach. President Roosevelt had taken seriously the 1891 legislation authorizing the chief executive to set aside portions of the public domain for various purposes, withdrawing during his year in office three times as much land as had his predecessors combined (almost 150,000,000 acres). One of the first actions of his successor's Secretary of the Interior was to restore to private entry certain lands which had already been

[17] Kenneth W. Hechler, *Insurgency: Personalities and Politics of the Taft Era* (New York: Columbia University Press, 1940).

reserved, on the (probably technically correct) ground that land had been set aside for reclamation projects where water was not available. Although in historical retrospect Taft's conservation record will withstand scrutiny, his support of Ballinger and dismissal of Pinchot (the liberal-conservationist Chief of the Forest Service who loudly protested the Secretary's action) seemed at the time to be an outright surrender to the monied interests which had always reaped the lion's share of the benefits of a liberal land policy.[18]

The year 1910 saw the battle between reformers and big business return to more familiar territory. So concerned were many citizens by now over the use of other people's money in the building up of vast financial empires that much thought was constantly being given to the question of how this evil might be suppressed. One suggestion, a proposal destined to be strenuously debated before it became law in 1910, was that government owned and operated "postal savings" banks be created in which the man in the street might keep his money. This innovation would serve the dual purpose of keeping some funds out of the hands of the finance capitalists and securing them from dissipation as a result of Wall Street manipulations. These very low-interest depositories for citizen funds did not in fact become a significant factor in the money market, but it is nonetheless easy to understand why the cry of "socialism" was raised against them at the time.

But the establishment of a postal savings system was of little moment by comparison with the next reform venture. The Republican platform had promised railroad legislation, and rebellious midwesterners were resolved to see to it that the party made delivery on the promise. Two major items of unfinished business remained on that front. The long-and-short-haul clause was still inoperative. Even more important, farmers had long wanted to give the Interstate Commerce Commission authority to suspend proposed rate increases until an investigation could be made to determine the necessity for them. After an unreasonable rate has been collected, those injured by it cannot then be compensated with any degree of accuracy. Farmers even now threatened with a general freight rate advance were especially desirous of seeing this matter attended to without delay. (And as soon as the new act was passed, said increase was forthwith disallowed.)

In the event the Mann-Elkins Act almost came to grief. Republican rebels did not prepare their own measure, instead permitting the

18 C. R. Van Hise, *The Conservation of Natural Resources in the United States* (New York: The Macmillan Co., 1910).

administration to take the initiative. Had the bill originally presented been passed, little of consequence would have been accomplished. However, farmer and labor representatives in particular were able to amend it at a number of key points, with the result that a real reform measure emerged. When this work had been completed, the Interstate Commerce Commission possessed full regulatory control over the railroad industry. Almost the only power of significance it did not now have was over the securities issued by railroad concerns, and this power also came close to being included.

For the most part a mere listing of this act's provisions will suffice as an indication of the magnitude of its achievement.[19] Commission control was broadened to include telegraph, telephone, and cable companies, although little actual regulating of these concerns was forthcoming under that authorization. A long-and-short-haul clause which would stand up in court was written; henceforth this kind of discrimination was to be subject to Commission approval. Proposed rate increases could be suspended for a maximum period of ten months, and the burden of proof as to their reasonableness was placed upon the carriers. The Commission was specifically authorized to bring complaints on its own initiative, a power which had heretofore been exercised on the basis of a very shadowy legal foundation. Freight classification was expressly made subject to Commission supervision. And in the place of security regulation a Securities Commission was created to investigate the problem, this group the following year recommending that fullest publicity be given to all such transactions and relationships.

However, two provisions of the Mann-Elkins Act warrant special mention—one because of the institutional changes which might have been introduced into American regulatory practice had it been successful, and the other because of the preoccupation of liberals it symbolized. Due to the fact that the courts were at the moment clogged with railroad regulation cases, the 1910 law provided for the creation of a special Commerce Court. This was to be a body of judicial experts on commerce law, its purpose being the expediting of regulatory work. But an innovation such as this would at best have had to go through a long process of becoming integrated into the nation's constitutional system, as in the case of the Interstate Commerce Commission itself, and in the meantime a major defect in the Commerce Court's underlying philosophy soon brought it to grief. On the one hand, that body raised anew all the questions of narrow

[19] F. H. Dixon, *Railroads and Government* (New York: Charles Scribner's Sons, 1922); and W. Z. Ripley, *Railroads: Rates and Regulations* (New York: Longmans, Green & Co., Inc., 1912).

versus broad judicial review which were now in the process of being harmoniously settled as between the Supreme Court and the Commission. On the other hand, the members of the Commerce Court were to be circuit court judges serving not more than one consecutive year, this requirement effectually preventing a rapid institutional evolution. Actually, the result was sheer chaos. As often as not the Commerce Court reversed the Commission—only to be reversed in turn by the Supreme Court—and after three years of almost unqualified failure, the experiment was abandoned.

For a long time farmers particularly had been much exercised over what they interpreted to be the destruction of many once-serviceable inland waterways by the railroads. This was a gross exaggeration, of course, for the locomotive had replaced the boat largely as a result of technological superiority. But there was a grain of truth in this complaint; the railroads had often used their power to injure water transport rivals. In the Mann-Elkins Act a decisive beginning was made toward an attack on these depredations which was soon to become quite widespread.

The opening gun here was a portion of the wording of the new long-and-short-haul clause. (A prime reason for this kind of discrimination had always been the presence of water competition at certain points.) Where a carrier by rail lowered a rate to meet water competition it could not again raise such rate except upon a showing of the appearance of new conditions other than the disappearance of the water competitor. A second approach, developed in a series of enactments and Commission rulings over a number of years, consisted of broad regulations governing the more general relationships between rail and water carriers. Railroads were on the one hand compelled to establish through routes and quote joint rates with water carriers and in other ways to permit these concerns to play an integral part in providing the nation's transporation service, and were on the other hand forbidden to control their water rivals except where some compelling public purpose demanded such a relationship. And third, it was as a result of this same preoccupation and at approximately this time that the federal government became interested in pushing the development of inland waterways at the expense of the taxpayer. The large sums of money spent in this way are most often spoken of in derisive terms, appropriations for this purpose being commonly referred to as the "pork-barrel." To be sure most of these facilities are of little value relative to their cost, and to be sure also political "back-scratching" does no doubt help to explain this phenomenon. But it is at the same time worth remembering that this policy has deep roots in a far more fundamental fact—public hostility to railroad monopoly.

————

Loud and bitter was the conservative outcry against the comprehensive way the railroads were now controlled by government. Central to these charges was the belief sincerely held by many that this would mean the destruction of one of the nation's greatest industries, that the dead hand of bureaucracy would soon make railroading unattractive to private enterprise. A half-century later it can be said with confidence that these fears were overdrawn. To the assertion that from the time the network of controls over the railroad began to be developed in earnest total miles of road operated did not significantly increase, it can be replied that as a result of a rapid intensification of railway investment the book value of that industry almost doubled over the next two decades.

TABLE 6. AGGRIEVED BUT NOT HURT

| Year | Railway | |
	Book Investment (millions of dollars)	Track Operated (thousands of miles)
1890	8,134	200
1910	14,558	352
1930	26,051	430

Source: Bureau of the Census, *Historical Statistics of the United States, 1789-1945,* pp. 202 and 204.

But this fact was not comforting to many liberals—those who still entertained utopian dreams of fashioning the new industrial society to their own taste. What it seemed to mean was that until the railroad had completed its basic conquest of the continent it had been impervious to reform efforts. If this relationship continued to obtain across the whole reform field (and already insurance regulation and food and drug legislation suggested that this was not idle speculation), reform programs would not be as a mother guiding the new society through its formative years. They would rather play the role of the policeman commissioned to watch, to warn, and to punish the more hardened adult.

It was a disquieting thought. Fortunately, however, it did not trouble men very much in 1910. There was neither opportunity nor energy to spare for worrying about the more fundamental limitations of reform endeavors. The time was now ripe for pressing a number of other reform measures.

QUESTIONS FOR DISCUSSION

1. Distinguish between railroad regulation protecting the people from the trusts and railroad regulation protecting the people from the railroads.

2. Why was a "commodities clause" considered necessary in railroad regulation?

3. What was the problem of "other people's money"? How was the insurance business related to this problem?

4. How accurate is it to refer to banks and insurance companies as public utilities?

5. In what areas did finance capitalism find itself on the defensive during these years? On the offensive?

6. Explain the meaning of the term "double standard" as here used. Is this a manifestation of laissez faire?

7. Was the tax program of reformers or that of conservatives more nearly in accord with the public interest at this time?

8. Why were conservatives so strongly opposed to the establishment of postal savings banks?

9. Summarize the powers over the railroad industry possessed by the Interstate Commerce Commission at the end of 1910.

10. What reforms were accomplished between 1903 and 1910? How significant were these victories?

11. Did America during the first decade of the twentieth century show up democracy more nearly at its worst or at its best?

Chapter 13

More Bonds Forged

All the reforms contemplated by liberals were not centered in Washington, D. C. In a dozen state capitals the resolve to subject the institutions of a mature capitalism to democratic control—to distribute more equitably both the fruits of and the hardships created by industrialism—was now at fever pitch. Nor is it strange that one of these state capitals was Albany, New York, where the insurance scandal had recently added much fuel to the reform fire. And no more strange is it that another one was Madison, Wisconsin, located in the heart of the area from whence came those Republicans so vigorously rebelling against their party's program in the nation's capital.

STRENGTHENING UTILITY REGULATION

It is surely no coincidence that while the Interstate Commerce Commission was winning a secure place for itself in the national government scheme of things, commencing in earnest the complex task of translating broad Congressional directives (for example, assuring the public "just and reasonable" rates) into workable rules and regulations, state governments were also rapidly implementing the public utility concept within their own borders. Almost simultaneously New York and Wisconsin took a long step forward in this field by establishing the first modern regulatory commissions at the state level. To be sure, the motivating force was not the same in the two cases. Governor LaFollette's support came from a public antagonism toward high freight rates and railroad practices inherited from Granger days; Governor Hughes' program, on the other hand, grew out of a popular desire to eliminate the abuses associated with urban utility franchises. But the underlying problem was the same in both states, as were the reform spirit thus given outlet and the approach to a solution.

244

This is not to suggest, however, that the history of the evolution of state public utility regulation was written in approximately equal parts out of experience with railroads and local utilities—gas, electric power, urban transport, water, and telephone concerns. Slowly but surely federal regulation was crowding state agencies out of the railroad field. Thus in a decision rendered about this time the Supreme Court asserted that the Interstate Commerce Commission might regulate intrastate rates whenever such rates adversely affected interstate commerce.[1] When that ruling was followed up over the years with other opinions having the same general import, the states were quick to take the hint. For nearly half a century every phase of railroad regulation has been dominated by the national agency, even though the states do maintain a limited activity in this field.

It was just as well. State regulatory commissions, in Wisconsin as well as New York, have had their hands full with the so-called public service industries. Here has been posed the state regulation problem par excellence. Here, therefore, is where the history of the evolution of this type of government control has been primarily written, at least until relatively recently.

TABLE 7. CHALLENGE TO UTILITY REGULATION

Year	Electric Power Production (millions of kilowatt hours)
1902	5,970
1912	24,752
1920	56,559
1930	114,637
1940	179,907
1950	388,674

Source: Bureau of the Census, *Historical Statistics of the United States, 1789-1945*, p. 156.

Public utility economists are not today especially complimentary in their evaluation of the work of state public utility commissions, and indeed this record cannot be favorably compared with anything approaching ideal results.[2] But it is easy to be unfair in drawing conclusions in this area. On the one hand the state commissions were up against a number of staggering obstacles, and on the other hand the irreversibility of history makes it impossible to draw an

[1] *Houston, East and West Texas Railway Company* v. *United States*, 234 U.S. 342 (1914).

[2] John Bauer, *Transforming Public Utility Regulation* (New York: Harper & Bros., 1950); and Twentieth Century Fund, *Electric Power and Government Policy* (New York: Twentieth Century Fund, 1948).

accurate comparison with the situation which would have existed if the local utilities had not been subjected to control. It follows that the only way to appreciate the achievements of Wisconsin and New York and a handful of other states in the public utility field during the first decade of this century is to review briefly some of the more important problems involved in this endeavor.

It must, in the first place, be remembered that these industries cannot serve the public effectively on a competitive basis. Because they are high-fixed-cost industries full advantage can be taken of economies of scale only to the extent that semimonopolistic rights are granted to particular companies. Similarly, because these operations require the use of the limited space on, over, or under a city's streets, the community must for this reason as well keep the number of concerns to the barest minimum. The result is that a single firm must be given more or less exclusive privileges in the performance of a vital public service, privileges capable of returning the owners of the private property involved fabulous profits for the very reason that the service performed is so vital. Regulatory supervision is then exercised over these operations for the purpose of holding the profits earned by public utility concerns to "reasonable" levels.

Precisely because the difference between the profits which could be earned in the absence of supervision and those available where regulation was effective was so great, the resistance to regulation has been both powerful and unceasing. In fact, the scramble for exclusive franchises by competing firms—franchises to be had only through the assistance of government officials (as was so dramatically emphasized in muckrake literature)—had been the primary cause of the fraud and corruption in places like New York City which had led to the widespread demand for control. Obviously all the greed and chicanery which had earlier gone into the securing of franchises with a minimum of restrictive provisions would now go into the work of frustrating any and all regulatory endeavors.

In the second place, the central task of control, steering a course safely between confiscation of utility property on the one hand and exploiting consumers for the benefit of the utility on the other, raised questions which at best admitted of no simple answers. A regulated industry must in fairness be allowed to earn a return which will at one and the same time protect the value of the property of past investors and attract enough capital from present and future investors to keep the public supplied with a sufficient amount of high quality service. However, when the attempt is made to relate these requirements meaningfully to the complex technological, operating, and financial processes making up the modern business world, the nature

of the regulatory decisions which must be made is often anything
but obvious. For example, it was at this point that the cost of reproduction versus original cost controversy arose to plague regulatory
officials; there does seem superficially to be a close connection
between the valuation of property for rate-making purposes and
dealing fairly with investors. This as well as a number of other ramifications of that phase of public utility regulation have lent themselves all too readily to the minimization of control by highly paid
corporation lawyers and economists and to aggressive propaganda
and lobbying activities.

In the third place, effective regulation demands that the control
agency supervise utility costs. Care must be taken that the books are
not padded, that costs are not incurred which do not contribute to
the service received by the public, and that resources are not used
inefficiently by the utility. With respect to this last consideration especially the commission must, to do its job well, pit the judgment of a
government agency against the judgment of the managers of private
property on purely business matters. Understandably, state public
utility commissioners have operated at a serious disadvantage here
from a technical standpoint, but an even more important factor preventing the implications of the public utility concept at this point
from being carried as far as logic might have dictated has been the
ideological bias of a private enterprise society.

And finally, all these difficulties were accentuated by the hazard
of judicial review (and by this it is not meant to imply that the courts
should have been denied jurisdiction in this field). Side by side with
the Interstate Commerce Commission the comparable state bodies
had to find their place in America's constitutional system, in part
through trial and error. Underpaid, overworked, and sometimes incompetent commissioners, operating under directives which were at
best vague and which were often accompanied by inadequate authority in the bargain (all these conditions roughly reflecting the influence of the regulated over the politico-regulatory process in the
several states), have made mistakes with sufficient frequency to keep
a fairly steady flow of adverse decisions emanating from the nation's
courts. Furthermore, this result has been supplemented by the cor-
poration-private property orientation of a majority of judges in both
state and federal courts. Once again the classic case in point is the
valuation controversy.

These, then, were the obstacles to effective public utility regulation; this was the challenge so forthrightly met by LaFollette in Wisconsin and Hughes in New York. A half century later it is appropriate for some purposes to call attention to defects now visible. In the

present context, however, the remarkable fact is not that these efforts have so far missed being completely successful, but that they have so far avoided being wholly unsuccessful. Rather than criticize the shortcomings of two generations of legislators, judges, and commissioners, let us here simply salute those who took the lead in securing institutional recognition of the public interest implicit in the foundations on which urban life rests. Not only has this recognition become a feature of modern industrial society which is today taken for granted without question, but the specific institution created for this purpose was soon reproduced in virtually every state in the union and still is an important element in government-business relationships.

Some Victories for Human Rights[3]

State legislation significantly altering the status quo was not limited to the public utility field either. Against the background of a more intense period of labor unrest than the nation had ever seen under nondepression conditions, there was now also passed an unprecedented number of state laws modifying customary employer-employee relationships.

Given this controversy in the background, and given the existence in Washington of a fairly effective working coalition of rebellious Republicans and Democrats, it is perhaps a little strange that the federal government did not also join this parade. The only acknowledgment at the level of the national government of the existence of a labor problem at this time was the creation of an Industrial Relations Commission for the not very imaginative or fruitful purpose of determining the causes of labor-capital conflict, and the establishment of a Department of Labor which as yet had few positive functions. But the labor problem was simply not now thought of in national terms, and it is at least a possibility that conservative insistence upon states' rights as a way of warding off federal intervention now boomeranged.

One of the important areas in which state legislation was being used to supplement collective bargaining was child labor. Already laws imposing restrictions at this point existed in some states, but the laws currently in operation were few, and even these often contained little protection for the child worker. Shortly after the turn of the century an aggressive drive to broaden and deepen these protections was launched, promoted by both labor organizations and groups spe-

---

[3] D. D. Lescohier and E. Brandeis, *History of Labor in the United States* (New York: The Macmillan Co., 1935).

cifically organized for this purpose having a predominantly middle-class make-up. Pressed thus concertedly, child labor legislation—whether predicated upon outright abolition or hedging the practice with rigorous restrictions—flowed from state legislatures in a veritable torrent. By 1913 only a tiny handful of states had no legislation on this subject, while several important industrial states had enacted and were enforcing comprehensive child labor laws. In 1911 and 1913 alone, thirty and thirty-one states, respectively, added further restrictions in this field.

Maximum hour legislation for women was another type of labor protective legislation that blossomed during these years, although here as in the case of child labor a considerable amount of preparatory work had been done before the turn of the century. An especially important landmark for this kind of legislation was a Supreme Court decision upholding the constitutionality of a women's hour law in Oregon.[4] Previously efforts along these lines had been under a threatening legal cloud, and the clearing away of that fundamental barrier no doubt accelerated the movement. Again the period 1911–13 saw the most rapid development to date. In these three years no less than twelve states passed their first legislation on this subject while seventeen others substantially improved previously existing statutes.

Minimum wage legislation and laws limiting the number of hours worked by men were not as aggressively pushed at this time as child labor and women's hour legislation. This is not to be wondered at, of course. Regulating the terms of labor contracts in the typical work setting is a far more radical thing than such regulations governing situations which can plausibly be classified as exceptional or peripheral. Despite this greater radicalness, however, so powerful was the impetus behind labor-management reform endeavors that progress was even forthcoming on these fronts. In 1913 alone eight minimum wage laws were passed (though it must be confessed that few measures relating to wages were as yet provided with "teeth"). Legislative intervention in the matter of maximum hours for men was still dominated by *Lochner* v. *New York,* but there was nonetheless a tendency for the definition of the circumstances under which this kind of interference was warranted to become much broader.

The nearest any of this legislation came to "the heart of the labor contract" was in what is today called workmen's compensation, but even here a remarkable progress was being made. Heretofore the American industrial economy had been operating largely on the

---

[4] *Muller* v. *Oregon,* 208 U.S. 412 (1908).

basis of common law rules developed to serve a European handicraft economy. Under these rules a worker injured at his job could collect no damages from his employer if there were adequate grounds for a judicial determination that (1) the worker's own negligence caused the injury, or that (2) the injury resulted from the negligence of a fellow worker, or that (3) the responsible factor was a hazard implicit in the job and known to the worker at the time he accepted employment. The result was that few compensation suits against employers were won; an alert judge could almost always find a basis for denying recovery on one of these bases. As the machine age multiplied many times the number of tragedies arising from work accidents and sicknesses, it became clear that a better way of meeting the social cost involved than placing the burden most directly upon those already in financial difficulty because of the injury suffered would have to be sought. Accordingly the device of "insuring" against these risks on a compulsory basis (with "premiums" assessed ultimately against the consumer, but in such a way that employers were given an incentive to keep this cost as low as possible) was developed. By 1911 the evolution to such a system was well under way, and in that one year ten states enacted modern workmen's compensation laws while twelve others created investigatory commissions.

It goes without saying that businessmen resisted all these innovations with every means at their disposal. Legal limitations on the terms and conditions of the wage bargain are apt to make business less profitable; certainly the philosophy behind these enactments was not the thesis that business also would gain as a result of treating workers more humanely. (Indeed, one of the major reasons workers pushed measures of this kind was to reduce job competition from those groups of laborers, especially women and children, employers had found it easiest to exploit.) But as narrowly circumscribed as most of this legislation still was, it is probable that the reduction of profits was not the major reason for the last-ditch conservative resistance these reforms encountered. The more farsighted business leaders at least were most concerned about two other aspects of what was happening.

First, it was hardly to be doubted that the spirit behind this mass of social legislation reflected a distinct weakening of community support for late nineteenth-century individualism. This concept had originally been based upon the fundamental equality of all adult human beings. Because individuals were basically equal contracts between individuals required no supervision; such contracts as were made could safely be presumed to be in the public interest (in the sense of contributing to the well-being of all parties thereto) because if this were not the case, one or more of the parties would refuse to agree to the terms stipulated. Furthermore, superimposed upon this older approach to individualism, although not directly dependent upon it and at times even contradicting it, there had grown up a supplementary justification for a "hands-off" policy in this area. Grounded directly in "biological Darwinism," a "social Darwinism" had recently become a part of the stock in trade of laissez faire proponents.[5] According to this philosophy it is the fittest that survive. The "best" businesses will flourish, while their "less fit" competitors go bankrupt; the "best" men rise to the top, while their "less fit" fellow-citizens must content themselves with a regime of hard toil and the receipt of only the crumbs which fall from the tables of the elite.

Clearly the assumptions underlying recent social legislation were a far cry from these sentiments. Here was an emphasis, not upon the inherent equality of whichever two individuals happen to negotiate a contract, but upon the realistic fact of inequality—especially where one of those individuals is the bargaining agent for a great corporation. The new approach defined freedom, not as an inherent attribute of all men in a so-called free society, but rather as the possibility of making uncoerced choices from among a number of reasonably good alternatives. Where contracts were entered into, in other words, under circumstances in which one party's choices were not free or where none of the available alternatives could fairly be called good, the new emphasis on human rights would use the power of the state to establish minimum contract terms. And as far as "social Darwinism" was concerned—obviously this concept was being thrown decisively into the discard. A society which would impose minimum wage legislation upon its citizens certainly did not believe that the "law of the jungle" guaranteed the domination of the community by either the most desirable institutional or human specimens.

Second, and equally ominous (although perhaps only saying the same thing in another way), there seemed to be implicit in all this a grave threat to the political foundation on which American laissez faire had traditionally rested. Despite the fact that farmers were still reluctant to see labor organizations usurp the prerogatives of business management or private property, laborers, farmers, and countless middle-class citizens were unmistakably making common cause in the endeavor to clip the wings of big business. And if anyone had been inclined by the end of the first decade of the new century to question this interpretation of what was taking place, two significant events in 1910 and 1911 would surely have clinched the point.

[5] Richard Hofstadter, *Social Darwinism in American Thought, 1865-1915* (Philadelphia: University of Pennsylvania Press, 1944).

In 1910 a crucial Congressional election was held, crucial because its outcome would reveal whether the reforms which had been enacted by the Republican party under pressure would be adequate to maintain nationwide acceptance of conservative management of the country's affairs. The answer was emphatically in the negative. Despite the fact that Republican "Regulars" personally campaigned against party "Insurgents" in the Middle West, it was overwhelmingly "Regulars" rather than "Insurgents" who were defeated—except where this intraparty discord resulted in the election of a Democrat. Moreover, in the industrial east literally dozens of Republicans were defeated by Democrats in one of the most disastrous upsets ever suffered by the Republican party. Obviously reform was still decisively on the march. And here was evidence aplenty that a new and powerful alliance between farmers and workers was in the making in Washington.

As would only have been expected, one of the hotbeds of social reform ideas continued to be Wisconsin. From the standpoint of liberal legislation the Wisconsin legislature of 1911 was one of the most remarkable in the history of that or any other state. Included among the enactments of that single session were the creation of an Industrial Commission with extensive powers in the labor relations field, a workmen's compensation law, a state-operated insurance program, an income tax, limitations governing the labor of both women and children, a state-owned binder-twine plant, and a law sweepingly legalizing the cooperative marketing of farm products. Surely there could be no mistaking the farmer-labor coalition that put this program together.

UNEXPECTED TRIUMPH

A good case can be made for the proposition that William Howard Taft was a more vigorous trust-buster than Theodore Roosevelt, despite the latter's great reputation in that field. Certainly Taft, with half as much time at his disposal, instituted more antitrust suits than his predecessor. Equally certain is it that the opponents he chose on this front were no less worthy than those selected by Roosevelt. And it would scarcely be denied that as many significant antitrust decisions were handed down under Taft's generalship as in the entire previous history of the Sherman Act. But be all this as it may, the most important point to note here is perhaps that Taft and Roosevelt must share on approximately equal terms the credit for one of the greatest antitrust victories ever achieved. In 1911 suits against the oil and tobacco trusts, actions commenced by Roosevelt and prose-

:uted by Taft, reached the Supreme Court. The decisions handed
lown by the Court on that occasion gave liberals already somewhat
lushed from successes in the field of human rights even more cause
:or rejoicing.

The government's most fundamental contention in both these pro-
:eedings was that the Sherman Anti-Trust Act made *all* combinations in restraint of trade illegal, this view being based on the most
explicit judicial precedents. Asking the Court to look beyond the
separate concerns involved in both combines to the fact that the actions of all of them were coordinated through a New Jersey holding
company, the government's brief asked for dissolution.

As of 1911 the Supreme Court needed little prompting when it
came to separating form from substance in the matter of business organization. But as of 1911 the Court had decisively changed its mind
on the question of not applying a rule of reason in antitrust cases.
Since the purpose of the Sherman Act was to give statutory form to
the common law in this area of economic relationships, and since
the common law did distinguish between reasonable and unreasonable trade restraints, it now seemed clear to a majority of the Justices
that judicial discretion would have to be exercised. And this the
Court forthwith proceeded to do.

The judgment of the Court, announced in the bluntest of terms,
was that both these organizations were in violation of the antitrust
laws, and that both should consequently be broken up into a number
of parts just as the government had requested.[6] This drastic conclusion turned on an analysis of the behavior of the two firms: the business practices followed by them while they were in their formative
period, and after they had reached maturity. After reviewing the history of the concentrations of power in the oil and tobacco industries
the Court was unable to believe that in either case the behavior pattern followed was that of a dynamic concern wanting only to compete fairly and openly with all comers. Notice was taken, thus, of the
securing of preferential treatment from railroads, price discrimination in the companies' own price policies, unlawful contracts, local
price-cutting to drive out a particular competitor, espionage, the use
of bogus independents, territorial allocations both at home and
abroad, limitations imposed upon the operation of subsidiaries, and
the buying out of independents for the purpose of closing down their
plants. The Supreme Court summed up this view in its evaluation of
the evidence in the Standard Oil case as follows.

6 *Standard Oil Company of New Jersey* v. *United States*, 221 U.S. 1 (1911); and
United States v. *American Tobacco Company*, 221 U.S. 106 (1911).

We think no disinterested mind can survey the period in question without being irresistibly driven to the conclusion that the very genius for commercial development and organization which it would seem was manifested from the beginning soon begot an intent and purpose to exclude others which was frequently manifested by acts and dealings wholly inconsistent with the theory that they were made with the single conception of advancing the development of business power by usual methods, but which, on the contrary, necessarily involved the intent to drive others from the field and exclude them from their right to trade, and thus accomplish the mastery which was the end in view.

These decisions were only the beginning. Within two years six other important antitrust actions had been decided favorably for the government. The powder trust was dissolved.[7] An organization controlling most of the rail terminal facilities in St. Louis was told that all carriers desiring to use these facilities must be allowed to do so on equal terms.[8] Another major step was taken toward breaking up the combination of railroads still dominating the anthracite coal industry.[9] The Union Pacific Railroad Company was required to dispose of a controlling interest of Southern Pacific stock.[10] A syndicate formed to secure control of practically all the towing and wrecking facilities in fourteen of the principal Great Lakes ports was broken up.[11] And without going to court, the government was able to prevent the American Telephone and Telegraph Company from using its patent position to absorb Western Union and thus include telegraph as well as telephone operations in its monopoly.

Such a concerted assault on the status quo by the Supreme Court must indeed have dismayed business leaders. No longer could any hope be entertained that the holding company device might so confuse the concentration issue in the courts that the Sherman Act could be disobeyed with impunity behind that camouflage. (Note that the Northern Securities Company had been solely a holding company, whereas both the oil and tobacco industries had been integrated by holding companies which were also operating companies.) Still worse, even the judiciary was rejecting the survival-of-the-fittest, law-of-the-jungle foundation on which industrialism had been built. Not content with scrutinizing contracts in restraint of trade and making judgments on monopolies, the courts were now even passing in review the way businessmen conducted their everyday affairs.

On the other hand, however, these antitrust developments were

---

7 *United States v. E. I. du Pont de Nemours Company*, 188 Fed. 127 (1911).
8 *United States v. Terminal Railroad Association of St. Louis*, 224 U.S. 383 (1912).
9 *United States v. Reading Company*, 226 U.S. 324 (1912).
10 *United States v. Union Pacific Railroad Company*, 226 U.S. 61 (1912).
11 *United States v. Great Lakes Towing Company*, 208 Fed. 733 (1913).

by no means as comforting to reformers as they were distressing to
business leaders, even though liberals were in a mood to welcome
assistance from almost any source. Just as the Northern Securities
case was disappointing in its fulfillment of the promise it had originally held out, so too was this group of decisions. To be sure, certain
of the shortcomings of that triumph were not clearly visible until
much later, but even so there was reason for substantial reservation.

For one thing, it had always been supposed by reformers that the
adoption of a rule of reason interpretation of the Sherman Act would
ultimately inure to the benefit of the business side of the economy,
and nothing had yet happened to cast doubt on that conclusion. For
another it was now clearer than ever that antitrust legislation was
being used with greater effectiveness against transportation companies than against industrial concerns. And for still another it was
only now becoming evident to liberals that the view of the economy
on which the antitrust prohibitions had originally been predicated
was naive. Business organizations were rarely classifiable as either
wholly monopolistic or wholly competitive. The majority of cases fell
rather somewhere in between, whereas the entire pattern of enforcement activity to date suggested that the law was reaching only the
most extreme instances of elimination of competition, namely, collusion and single-unit monopoly.

This last point was especially brought home to liberals in the dissolution decrees handed down by the courts in the oil, tobacco, and
powder trust cases. For example, the Standard Oil decree ordered
the holding company to dispose of its stock holdings by distributing
them to its own stockholders, thus creating a community-of-interest
trust to replace the holding company trust being dissolved. The
other decrees were no doubt more successful in accomplishing their
objective than this one. Thus a sincere attempt was made to create
three independent concerns in the gunpowder industry and in each
of the major branches of the tobacco industry. Unfortunately, it was
already becoming evident that the relationship of three firms in an
industry is by no means always and necessarily one of rigorous, bona
fide competition.

"THE NEW FREEDOM"[12]

The election in 1910 of a Democratic Congress, the first in fourteen years, was the signal for a dramatic renewal of reform energies
in the nation's capital. Of course little could be done as yet which
required legislation. The President who had recently encouraged the

---

[12] Woodrow Wilson, *The New Freedom* (New York: Doubleday & Co., Inc., 1914).

formation of the United States Chamber of Commerce in order that the views of business on important matters might be expressed more plainly to government policy-makers was hardly the man to affix his signature to the kinds of measures reformers were eager to enact. Much could be done, however, to lay the necessary groundwork against the time two years hence when (as was confidently believed) a Democrat would be master of the White House.

As is frequently the case in a situation such as this, one of the principal lines of attack was the launching of a full-scale investigation of the problems to be later tackled more definitively. By so doing not only can public support for measures felt to be needed be built up, but additional votes for the next election may also be secured. (And on occasion it even happens that information is gathered which can be used in the actual framing of legislation.)

In accordance with this already familiar political procedure the Democrats now embarked upon an investigation which for sheer drama has perhaps never been surpassed. Steadily in recent years there had grown up in the public mind the idea that there existed in the United States a "money trust" with tentacles reaching into every corner of the economy. Here was an opportunity to place the great magnates of Wall Street under the glare of public opinion before which they would inevitably incriminate themselves—to give these men, in other words, the rope with which they might commit political suicide. Even "Morgan the Magnificent" himself was subjected to a relentless cross-examination on the witness stand as committee counsel and committee members sought to round out the picture of "other people's money and how the bankers use it."[13] When the last Morgan partner had stepped down from the stand, everyone who had been privileged to sit in was agreed that the show had been well worth the price of admission.

It is difficult even at this distance to evaluate the work of the Pujo Committee. If, for example, an important criterion in such an evaluation were tangible legislative results, the conclusion would be forced that this project had few direct consequences. Of all the reform endeavors shortly to be undertaken by a vigorous Democratic administration, none related in any concrete way to the Pujo investigation.

In and of itself this is surprising because the committee's findings were almost as dramatic as the process by which they were made.[14]

[13] Louis D. Brandeis, *Other People's Money and How the Bankers Use It* (New York: Frederick A. Stokes Co., 1914)—a summary of the findings of this committee.

[14] *Report of the Committee Pursuant to House Resolutions 429 and 504 to Investigate the Concentration of Money and Credit* (Washington, D.C.: Government Printing Office, 1912-13).

It was discovered, for example, that the group of men most closely
associated with J. P. Morgan held among them 118 directorships in
34 banks and trust companies, 30 directorships in 10 insurance companies, 105 directorships in 32 transportation systems, 63 directorships in 24 producing and distributing corporations, and 25 directorships in 12 public utility corporations—all these concerns having
a combined capitalization of more than $22 billion. As the committee
summarized its own conclusions:

If by a money trust is meant an established and well-defined identity and community of interest between a few leaders of finance which has been created and
is held together through stock holdings, interlocking directorates, and other
forms of domination over banks, trust companies, railroads, public service, and
industrial corporations, and which has resulted in a vast concentration of control of money and credit in the hands of a comparatively few men—your committee has no hesitation in asserting as a result of its investigation that this
condition, largely developed within the past five years, exists in this country
today.

Surely no one who had the slightest inclination to believe in the existence of a money trust could now have been other than fully convinced.

How is this paradox to be explained, this gap between findings
and reform consequences? Perhaps one result of this investigation
was to make finance capitalists appear more human and hence less
to be feared. Perhaps, too, thinking men and women saw that the
vast majority of wealth controlled by this small group of men was
not money but fixed assets performing a useful public function somewhere in the economy. And perhaps it was even seen by many that
the mere fact of interlocking directorates and interownership of securities does not by itself demonstrate unity of either purpose or
policy. In short, by trying to prove too much it is possible that the
Pujo inquiry ended by proving very little.

But on the other hand, it may be misleading to look only for *direct*
consequences of this episode. It could still be true that these revelations provided an important part of the environment within which
other kinds of reform measures were more easily passed, or that these
other measures were made more comprehensive than would otherwise have been possible.

In this light the money trust investigation can be given a more secure place in the development of government-business relationships.
The election of 1912 was held in the middle of the parade of Pujo
witnesses, and the reform sentiment was unprecedentedly strong.
Eugene Debs, running for the presidency on the Socialist ticket received almost 1,000,000 votes, more than twice as many as four years

earlier. Theodore Roosevelt, heading a third party organization bitterly opposed to Taft-Republican "stand-pattism," won 88 electoral votes as against Taft's 8. And, profiting greatly from this split in Republican ranks, Woodrow Wilson running on an out-and-out reform platform swept the field with 435 electoral votes.

The keynote of the Wilson platform and campaign was "The New Freedom," a term intensively advertised as meaning a pattern of social relationships in which special, unearned privileges would no longer play an important part.[15] Every major aspect of the legislative program submitted to Congress by the new administration, moreover, was ideologically reducible to these terms. Understandably this was an appeal to which numerous segments of the population, feeling disadvantaged in some way, were strongly attracted. One such segment was small businessmen, and here the money trust approach was especially alluring. A fundamental aspect of freedom in a capitalist society is access to capital by the rising generation of entrepreneurs, and the narrow concentration of capital could be plausibly presented as an almost insuperable barrier to independent entrepreneurship.

The first legislative step toward implementing this program was the Underwood Tariff. After driving the protectionist lobbyists out of Washington (no doubt more in a figurative sense than a literal one) by publicizing their endeavors to frustrate this move, the new President was able to push through the first genuine tariff reduction since the Civil War. Here the privilege being combated was the right of tariff-protected domestic producers to "hold up" the American consumer. The second step was to take advantage of the recent ratification of the Sixteenth Amendment by passing a mildly progressive income tax modelled on Wisconsin's brief experience in that field.[16] When to these accomplishments was added the simultaneous ratification of the Seventeenth Amendment providing for popular election of United States Senators, thus giving the average citizen a more nearly even chance to elect his own candidates to this office, reformers could justifiably feel that an excellent start had been made toward weeding out special privileges.

From the income tax, liberals turned their attention to the banking and currency problem, and here the money trust investigation had an influence which was almost direct. Although in the face of recent panics and what by now seemed to be an almost chronic disturbance in the exchange mechanism it was agreed by nearly everyone that

[15] Walter E. Weyl, *The New Democracy* (New York: The Macmillan Co., 1912).
[16] E. R. A. Seligman, *The Income Tax* (New York: The Macmillan Co., 1911).

basic changes would have to be made in this area of the economy,[17] there were nonetheless sharp differences of opinion with respect to some aspects of the necessary modifications. Naturally conservatives believed that changes should be in the direction of a greater centralization of banking operations, and a centralization moreover which would be under the direction of the banker group, while liberals (especially the farmers making up the backbone of the Democratic party) insisted that centralization was a dangerous direction in which to move and that above all banker control must be avoided.

Already the so-called Aldrich bill embodying the ideas of conservatives, the result of the painstaking deliberations of the National Monetary Commission,[18] was before Congress. If, however, there had ever been any thought of giving serious attention to this proposal as a basis for legislation, the Pujo revelations would have decisively intervened. In the event the Aldrich bill was not reported out of committee in House or Senate, and in its place was substituted the Glass bill—named after Democrat Carter Glass of Virginia who had replaced Aldrich as Chairman of the Senate Finance Committee.

CONSERVATIVE TO THE CORE

But even from this standpoint it is necessary to be careful not to exaggerate the impact of the money trust episode. Oddly enough, the most remarkable fact about the Federal Reserve Act of 1913 is much less the anticonservative bias it embodied than its cautious avoidance of the monetary radicalism the Democratic party had historically espoused. Indeed it must have afforded conservatives considerable amusement (as well as relief) to witness the sharp battle within the ruling party over the details of the new law, a battle ultimately won by the more conservative group.[19]

With respect to both organization and substantive provisions this outcome can be clearly seen. On the organization side the principal change now introduced was a greater centralization of bank operations, although this change was carefully hedged about for the benefit of agrarian constituencies. Instead of a single central bank with branches, twelve regional banks were created with a central board to exercise supervisory functions. This board, moreover, was to be a

[17] O. M. W. Sprague, *History of Crises Under the National Banking System* (Washington, D.C.: Government Printing Office, 1910).

[18] *Report of the National Monetary Commission* (Washington, D.C.: Government Printing Office, 1912).

[19] Henry P. Willis, *The Federal Reserve System* (New York: The Ronald Press Co., 1923).

quasi-governmental body, consisting of the Secretary of the Treasury, the Comptroller of the Currency, and six other members appointed by the President. On the other hand, however, two of these six must have had previous banking experience, while one-third of the directors of each regional bank were to be bankers. Another third was to represent agriculture, the remainder the public, and the first two groups were to be elected by the member banks in each region. And finally, state banks and trust companies were not required to join the new system. Surely all this will pass for a well-worked-out pattern of compromises between radical farmers and conservative businessmen.

TABLE 8. THE STRUGGLE FOR MONETARY CENTRALIZATION

	Total Assets (millions of dollars)		
Year	Nonnational Banks	National Banks	Federal Reserve Member Banks
1863	1,192	17	—
1880	1,363	2,035	—
1900	5,842	4,944	—
1915	16,008	11,796	11,887
1930	44,904	29,117	47,349
1945	81,232	81,795	126,436

Source: Bureau of the Census, *Historical Statistics of the United States, 1789-1945,* pp. 263-67.

On the substantive side the conservative-liberal balance worked out is even more striking. At this point, in fact, much of what had been contained in the Aldrich bill passed over almost intact into the Glass bill. Nor is this surprising. The National Banking System had certain key shortcomings, upon the general nature of which the experts were broadly agreed, and any serious reform measure had to come to terms with them. Because the particular measure enacted came to terms with those defects squarely and openly, the result was a banking system much more suitable to a mature capitalism.

Unquestionably the greatest problem here had arisen from the so-called pyramiding of legal reserves. Under the National Banking System small banks had found it profitable to deposit a portion of their reserves in larger banks from which they often found their way into the New York money market. Any concerted withdrawal of reserves by smaller banks, therefore, would necessitate monetary readjustments in New York which might easily reach panic proportions. This difficulty was remedied in the Federal Reserve Act by requiring the deposit of all legal reserves in Federal Reserve Banks, and by forbidding these Banks to do business with anyone except other banks or the government.

A second shortcoming, although one which had grown progressively less acute with the widespread development of checkbook money, had been the inelasticity of the old national bank note. Backed by government bonds, it tended rather to be perversely elastic; in tight supply when business was booming and bankers could secure higher returns by not investing in government securities, and plentiful when the reverse situation prevailed. This problem was corrected by creating the new federal reserve note backed by short-term commercial paper (and gold). At long last the federal government had learned the lesson Louisiana had been trying to teach the nation for seventy years.

The Federal Reserve Act was given to the country shortly before Christmas, 1913, the last major item in a year of reform legislation which for solid achievement broke all records. Before the year was out, however, work had been begun on another reform endeavor high on the list of "New Freedom" enthusiasts, namely, a basic addition to the antitrust laws; and the following year saw this project also successfully completed.

But just as reform in the banking field had resulted in innovations conservatives as well as liberals could classify as an improvement, so was there a complex mixture of motives behind new antitrust legislation. A brief review of the primary considerations at issue on this front makes it quite clear why all the major parties in the 1912 election had included in their platforms antitrust planks which read very much alike.

First, liberals would have been quick to explain their approach in part on the basis of the tongue-in-cheek origins of the Sherman Act and the indifferent enforcement of that statute to date. Here was reason enough to press for supplemental legislation. And that word "supplemental" was important, too. There was no serious thought in any quarter of repealing the Sherman Act.

In the second place, it was by now evident that regulation by litigation possessed grave shortcomings requiring some kind of corrective at the earliest possible moment. On the one hand, reformers considered current procedure too slow and clumsy; on the other hand, businessmen felt (especially after the most recent court decisions) that existing antitrust laws were too indefinite, that men responsible for the affairs of a great corporation were left too much in doubt as to what they might or might not legally do.

But if, third, antitrust regulations were to be speeded up for the benefit of liberals and made more definite for the benefit of conservatives, how might this dual objective be achieved? At this point, too, there was broad agreement upon at least one fundamental step that might appropriately be taken. As Senator Newlands expressed this point:

The railroad question is practically settled; the settlement of the trust question has hardly been commenced. Had we submitted the administration of the antitrust act to an impartial quasi-judicial body similar to the Interstate Commerce Commission instead of to the Attorney-General's office, with its shifting officials, its varying policies, its lack of tradition, record or precedent, we would by this time have made gratifying progress in the regulation and control of trusts, through the quasi-judicial investigations of a competent commission and through legislation based upon its recommendations.

Here, in short, seemed to be an excellent way to hustle history along, to overcome some of the most obvious defects of regulation by litigation. A regulatory commission in this field could promulgate specific rules under the guidance of its Congressional mandate and thereby make antitrust enforcement both more effective and more precise.

Fourth, this possibility in turn led directly to another peg on which an improved antitrust procedure might be hung. An antitrust commission would not of course be concerned with rate regulation —even though some students of this problem (including both liberals and conservatives) advocated permitting businessmen freely to engage in "constructive cooperation" and then rigorously regulating the resulting structures along public utility lines.[20] What then would be the focus of its concern? By now it was almost unanimously agreed among the reform-minded that a basic and hitherto neglected fact about the trust problem was unfair competitive practices.[21] If a regulatory agency could be created and empowered vigorously to attack unfair competition, a wide variety of important purposes could be simultaneously achieved.

As one of these purposes, little businesses could much more effectively protect themselves from the dominant concerns in their field, a result also congenial with the "New Freedom's" emphasis upon the destruction of special privilege. This might be just the "ounce of prevention" needed in view of the difficulty of finding an effective cure once a concern had achieved full-fledged trust status. Moreover, this technique might go far toward making the law more certain.

[20] A. J. Eddy, *The New Competition* (New York: Appleton-Century-Crofts, Inc., 1912); and C. R. Van Hise, *Concentration and Control: A Solution of the Trust Problem of the United States* (New York: The Macmillan Co., 1912).

[21] Commissioner of Corporations, *Trust Laws and Unfair Competition* (Washington, D.C.: Government Printing Office, 1915); and W. H. S. Stevens, *Unfair Competition* (Chicago: University of Chicago Press, 1917).

Finally, since the courts were now embarked on a rule of reason career with respect to antitrust decisions, Congress could in this way supply some of the substance to the "rule" to be utilized by the judiciary.

Still a fifth motivation for what was now done on the antitrust front was actually some little distance removed from the antitrust problem as such. Plain it was by now that competition was a many-sided thing which did not always and invariably produce beneficent results; that even where monopolization was not an issue, care yet needed to be taken to promote legitimate and discourage illegitimate competitive behavior. To be sure, the common law had long endeavored to make such a distinction, seizing upon misrepresentation in all its innumerable forms as central to the behavior to be avoided. But it was becoming increasingly clear that common-law distinctions of this sort were totally inadequate to the modern industrial economy. Stated in ideological terms, what was involved here was this: competition is a major exception to the fundamental rule that property cannot be used to injure others; and where property is used in such a way as to injure others, the social function assigned to competition in a private property society must be fulfilled (i.e., private injury is permissible if social benefit is secured).

And finally, here was an approach to these problems on which even organized labor could conscientiously stand. While workers were not retreating on the organization front, still an emphasis upon fairness in competition could be promoted without serious threat to the longer-range progress of unionization. Not only was this the case taken in and of itself, but the fact that the Clayton Act included a provision intended to provide labor unions and farmer cooperatives a measure of immunity to prosecution under the antitrust laws also operated powerfully in that direction.

In summary, the nation was in the process of acknowledging that its first venture in the antitrust field had been at a time when the problem was bewilderingly new, and that on the basis of subsequent experience a more adequate program could now be devised. The specific conclusions drawn from this quarter of a century under the Sherman Act were embodied in 1914 in two new laws. The first was the Federal Trade Commission Act, establishing a Federal Trade Commission (as a successor to and an extension of the Bureau of Corporations) and giving it broad powers "to prevent persons, partnerships, or corporations, except banks and common carriers subject to the Acts to regulate commerce, from using unfair methods of competition in commerce." The second was the Clayton Anti-Trust Act which specifically outlawed four business practices where their effect was "to substantially lessen competition or tend to create a monopoly in any line of commerce": price discrimination, exclusive dealer and tying arrangements, holding company relationships, and interlocking directorates.[22] Both the Department of Justice and the new agency were given primary jurisdiction under the terms of this statute.

Two aspects of this legislation are particularly to be noted. First, the Clayton Act was intended to be an antitrust statute in the semi-technical sense of that term, although it was understood that the Federal Trade Commission might in addition draw upon the companion measure in antitrust work. Second, however, it was also intended that the Federal Trade Commission would be extensively used in cases fundamentally outside the antitrust area to uplift the level of competition even where no basic threat to competition was involved.[23] What this meant of course was that the new legislation was not as definite as businessmen would have preferred, and perhaps even more important that regulation by litigation would not be wholly dispensed with.[24] On the other hand, however, it also meant that Congress had not made the very grave error of presuming that even a majority of undesirable business practices could be enumerated in a single statute, that the practices which an exceedingly complex business world might devise as substitutes for practices declared illegal could be anticipated in advance. A step had been taken, and that was all. Only the future could say what more might be required—or possible.

An era had ended. The uncomplicated view held by liberals twenty-five years earlier of the inner structure of an adequate reform program could no longer be seriously entertained by responsible, intelligent citizens. To be sure, natural monopolies were still to be regulated and unnatural monopolies were still (in theory) to be outlawed. To this point the earlier philosophy was as vigorous as ever. But it was now also certain that on the one hand a public interest warranting regulatory intervention might be found in situations where natural monopoly was in no way involved, and that on the other hand there are types of competitive relationships other than

22 Elmer A. Lewis, *Antitrust Laws With Amendments, 1890-1945* (Washington, D.C.: Government Printing Office, 1945).

23 G. C. Henderson, *The Federal Trade Commission* (New Haven: Yale University Press, 1925).

24 W. H. Taft, *The Anti-Trust Act and the Supreme Court* (New York: Harper & Bros., 1914).

monopoly in which a reform program might legitimately interest itself. Illustrative of the first of these complications was insurance, processed foods and drugs, and workmen's compensation; illustrative of the second was unfair competition.

Actually this was a logical enough development. If the corporation were to be considered an individual, it was only right that it be treated as a citizen as well. And just as special responsibilities are imposed upon natural citizens wherever the good of the community seems to make that step necessary—just as, for example, fathers are held to the performance of social functions that are not the responsibility of all men—so is it reasonable to fit society's expectations from artificial citizens to the role performed by particular classes of those citizens. Trust companies were to be in one category, tobacco companies in another, but to each was to be assessed responsibilities appropriate to each separate situation.

But, logical or not, conservatives were understandably not impressed. The trouble from their standpoint was that industrialism was creating so many of these special situations—or rather that industrialism was so rapidly mutiplying the proportion of society's citizens eager to broaden the operative definition of public interest.

QUESTIONS FOR DISCUSSION

1. Explain the major obstacles to effective state public utility regulation.

2. Distinguish between human rights and property rights. Why were the former receiving so much recognition at this time?

3. Discuss workmen's compensation from the standpoint of individualism; from the standpoint of "social Darwinism."

4. Why were farmers and workers able to achieve a relatively effective political coalition at this time?

5. Explain the significance of the oil and tobacco decisions of 1911; of the total antitrust program under William Howard Taft.

6. What were the major elements of the reform program of "The New Freedom"? What was the central principle behind this program?

7. Evaluate the money trust investigation. Why in the face of these revelations was nothing of consequence done about the problem of other people's money?

8. What were the most important changes now introduced into the nation's money and banking system?

9. Discuss the Federal Reserve Act from the standpoint of consensus.

10. Why would permitting business cooperation plus an extension of the public utility concept not have been an acceptable solution to the trust problem in 1914?

11. Discuss the 1914 antitrust legislation from the standpoint of accommodation.

12. Relate American conservatism at this time to the concept of public interest.

Chapter 14

Saving the World for Democracy

By October 15, 1914, the date the Clayton Act became law, war had been declared in Europe and the first consequences of world war even for neutral powers were already being felt in the United States.[1] But Americans had been shielded from involvement in European affairs for too long to give up their isolationism easily. Thus it was that after the first humanitarian shock at the horror of what was happening had passed away, and after the first economic readjustments had been successfully made, the United States settled back to watch, to listen, and above all to stay out, meanwhile moving rapidly forward with reform programs calculated to expand still further the government's economic responsibilities.

AN END TO DOMESTIC REFORM

Even before 1914 was over an important measure had been enacted for the benefit of farmers. Under the Smith-Lever Act federal funds were to be turned over to state governments on a matching basis for the purpose of establishing a nationwide agricultural extension service. Through the work of county agents and home demonstration agents, farmers and their wives were to be helped to make a better living for themselves with the resources at their disposal. Three years later this step was followed up by the Smith-Hughes Act providing for federal funds in aid of vocational agricultural training in the elementary and secondary schools. Here the point at issue was the feeling of many farmers that current education programs tended too strongly to take farm boys and girls permanently off the farm.

In 1915 it was labor's turn. Working conditions had always been poorer in America's merchant ships than in most other industries, a fact resulting from a number of circumstances. For one thing

[1] A. J. Noyes, *The War Period of American Finance* (New York: G. P. Putnam's Sons, 1926).

the ship represents the sailor's living quarters as well as his work-place, and at best a vessel has a limited amount of space to use as workers' "homes." Another factor was the close dependence of everyone on board a ship on the high seas upon everyone else and the consequent necessity for unstinting cooperation at certain criti-cal times, these conditions having brought about an almost medieval relationship between ship captains and seamen which still prevailed. A bold attempt to break this vicious circle was now made in the form of the LaFollette Seamen's Act, a dramatically new departure in federal legislation. Under the terms of this law working hours were limited, up to 50 per cent payment of wages was required when the ship was in a non-base port, wage allotments to creditors were abolished, and certain minimum living and working conditions were specified.

By 1916 the nation was ready to indulge in one more reform effort before settling down seriously to the task of finding its proper place in a world at war. For farmers this meant two significant pieces of legislation; for labor it meant one major achievement won partly through legislation and partly as a result of collective bargaining activity; and for the public as a whole this year brought still a fourth new government action.

For a long time farmers had complained bitterly that, as entre-preneurs, they had access to credit facilities which were distinctly inferior. Moreover, this was probably correct, although one of the reasons had unquestionably been the greater risk involved in loaning money to farmers. By now the government was beginning to take this complaint seriously, and indeed the Federal Reserve Act had already somewhat alleviated the problem by permitting national banks to make loans on real estate to a limited extent and by making agricultural commercial paper eligible for rediscount. Now another step was taken looking toward this same objective. Under the so-called Federal Farm Loan Act twelve regional Federal Land Banks were set up and authorized to make long-term (more than five years) capital available to farmers either through farm loan associations organized by farmers or joint stock land banks established by private corporations.

For a long time also farmers had maintained that warehousemen were too often in a position to exploit their farmer clients by under-grading agricultural products and by the use of discriminatory prac-tices. Here too there was much truth in the charge as stated, although again a more or less natural disability of the farmer was also involved. Unfortunately, farmers were often desperately in need of funds when they brought their output to market and hence were easy victims of hard bargaining. What the government now did to help relieve this difficulty, through the United States Warehouse Act, was to license cotton and grain (later extended to many other agricultural items) warehouse operators shipping in interstate commerce so that the farmer might receive a fairer price for his product and in order that warehouse receipts acceptable as collateral for bank loans might be made available. Thus decisively was still another implication of *Munn v. Illinois* carried over into federal law.

Labor's victory was won against the railroads. Demanding an eight-hour day (with no reduction in daily take-home pay), which the railroads refused to grant, the "big-four" brotherhoods set a date on which every railroad of consequence in the country would be closed down. Galvanized into action by this threat, a Congress already concerned about the state of the nation's war preparedness program passed the Adamson Act granting to the belligerent workers the concessions their employers had been unwilling to allow.

A national approach to the problem of an adequate system of highways had been taking shape ever since the automobile had promised to become a major industry. So swiftly was this now coming to pass that a broad expansion of this activity on some basis was fast becoming a "must" item. Since, furthermore, it is not economically feasible to leave road-building to private initiative, the principal question was whether this burden should fall wholly on state and local governments. The year 1916 saw this question answered once and for all in the negative; by the terms of the Federal Aid Road Act of 1916 a policy of federal aid (primarily for through trunk highways in the early stages of this program) to state-administered highway programs was instituted which to this day continues to be the framework within which government responsibility in this field is exercised. Indeed, the most important modification in the approach to this problem has been a persistent tendency for the federal government to broaden its support of highway-building.

TABLE 9. SHARING THE LOAD

Year	State Highway Expenditures (millions of dollars)	Federal Highway Funds to States (millions of dollars)
1915	81	—
1920	321	62
1925	598	92
1930	1,003	94
1940	885	181

Source: Bureau of the Census, *Historical Statistics of the United States, 1789–1945*, p. 221.

Because reform activity as such rapidly fell to negligible proportions as the nation that wanted only to be let alone found itself drawn inexorably toward direct involvement in a foreign war, it has often been concluded that reform sentiment now gave way in the face of a grave national emergency. Although from one standpoint this interpretation does not do serious injury to the facts, there is a sense of vital importance to the present discussion in which it is quite misleading. Two significant considerations suggest that the coming of war to America did not bring an end to reform sentiment in this country.

First, a strong case can be made for the proposition that reform activity ceased primarily because the reformers had achieved their objectives. After all, liberals had been winning victory after victory for almost a decade and a half, and during the most recent four years they had had their way almost unhindered. It is, to be sure, difficult for those living in a later generation, surveying the multitude of responsibilities the government has assumed since 1916, to accept the possibility that at the moment there were no more major reform projects on the agenda, that liberals were now more interested in accumulating experience with the changes already instituted than in formulating a new agenda. However, when it is recalled how cautious even liberals were during this period as measured by today's standards, how insistent reformers were to keep the government as far from actual business operations as possible as they set about altering the status quo, this proposition becomes more realistic.

But this observation that the reform agenda had been basically completed could be only another way of saying that the reform spirit had become quiescent. It is therefore also of importance to note here that in a way which could scarcely have been more fundamental, reform sentiment did not retire from the scene. Rather, it only changed its area of operations. When it became apparent that the days of American neutrality were numbered (even though Woodrow Wilson was re-elected in 1916 in part on the basis of the slogan "he kept us out of war"), all the humanitarian idealism which had kept the reform fires brightly burning on the domestic reform front since the beginning of the century was at once transferred with almost undiminished intensity to the international scene. To an extent which was fully as great as our history books imply, World War I was to Americans a crusade. Strange as this phenomenon now seems, millions of Americans apparently did burn with a genuine desire to "save the world for democracy."[2]

2 F. L. Paxson, *American Democracy and the World War* (Boston: Houghton Mifflin Co., 1939).

INDUSTRIAL MOBILIZATION

Nor is this mere quibbling. Although with this country's entry into the war government and business became suddenly more intimate than they had ever been before, the details of this new intimacy are of no particular importance in and of themselves. The short duration of this experience, its clearly emergency nature, and the sharp conflict between its spirit and the whole temper of American development to date—these factors combined to make the longer-range impact of these years on business-government relationships extremely small. It is only, in other words, when the focus of attention is shifted to short-term outcomes that a significant connection can be seen between this period and the evolution under review here. And when such a shift is made, one of the most fundamental and certainly the most immediate connection observed is the way in which an intense popular reaction against the wartime administration was converted into decisive rejection of reform attitudes.

From this is not meant to be inferred that Americans did not support the declaration of war when it was made, or that they did not respond magnificently when the "call to the colors" came. Neither is it to be supposed that the government insisted upon greater citizen sacrifices than were required to meet the plain demands of the situation. Indeed, the regimentation imposed was if anything too restrained. Rather, the problem was that the change in the nation's way of life occasioned by a modern war (including the creation of some 5,000 different government agencies to implement particular phases of that endeavor) was too abrupt to be taken in stride, and that the resultant frustrations were specifically associated in the public mind with prewar reform.

But this is to anticipate the sequel before analyzing the event. One of the commanding vantage points from which this process can be most clearly seen is the wartime economic activity commonly referred to as industrial mobilization.[3] The keynote of modern warfare is economic scarcity; of almost every one of the literally thousands of products essential to such an effort an exasperating shortage quickly appears. Under peacetime conditions the response of the American economy to shortages was at that time mediated primarily through a nexus of prices and profit margins. With the coming of a major war, however, that method of making the neces-

[3] Bernard Baruch, *American Industry in the War* (Washington, D.C.: Government Printing Office, 1921); and G. B. Clarkson, *Industrial America in the World War* (Boston: Houghton Mifflin Co., 1924).

sary adjustments became inadequate. For one thing, no matter how much adjusting had been done in that way, shortages would have continued to exist; in the twentieth century the demands made by a war economy on a society's productive capacity are simply insatiable. In the second place, price and profit adjustments produce best results when time is not a major factor; in America during World War I time itself was such a scarce resource that supplementary processes were all the more required. Both the magnitude of the economic changes required on this occasion and the speed with which they were brought about can be seen in the fact that for the year ending June 30, 1918, the first full fiscal year of American participation, federal government expenditures were greater than their prewar level by an amount equal to one-fifth of total national income in that year. At its peak the war effort was absorbing fully one-fourth of the nation's real output of goods and services.[4]

The implications of all this for citizens are obvious. Because customary price-profit adjustments were not adequate to the task then confronting the nation, since in any event these processes had to be assisted by others, there were good reasons for preventing them in many cases from operating at all. On the one hand, profits which could easily have risen to exorbitant levels but which could not as such have contributed to the war effort might react adversely upon the attitudes of those whose loved ones were being asked to lay down their lives on the battlefield. On the other hand, price increases, which again might have been very great and which likewise would have contributed little to the effective prosecution of the war, might also have reacted unfavorably upon worker morale as well as considerably increasing the cost of the war to the government.

A thin line separates the compulsory abandonment of the free-enterprise type of economic adjustment and the outright seizure of productive facilities; and perhaps the difference can in the last analysis only be explained in terms of the spirit in which the "taking" is done by the government and hence the way it is received by citizens. Although it is true enough that in World War I such a difference did in fact obtain, it is still not commonly realized how near the United States came to conscripting capital as well as men. When, however, attention is focused upon the work of the major war agencies, little doubt can remain on this point.

The War Industries Board, for example, the central agency in the

---

[4] Simon Kuznets, *National Product in Wartime* (New York: National Bureau of Economic Research, 1945).

network of special control bodies which was created, was given sweeping responsibilities. In a letter to Bernard Baruch, the Board's chairman, President Wilson outlined that group's functions as follows:

(1) The creation of new facilities and the disclosing, if necessary, [sic] the opening up of new or additional sources of supply;
(2) The conversion of existing facilities, where necessary, to new uses;
(3) The studious conservation of existing resources and facilities by scientific, commercial and industrial economies;
(4) Advice to the several purchasing agencies of the government with regard to the prices to be paid;
(5) The determination, wherever necessary, of priorities of production and of delivery and of the proportions of any given article to be made immediately accessible to the several purchasing agencies when the supply is insufficient, either temporarily or permanently;
(6) The making of purchases for the Allies.

Had the War Industries Board been given powers commensurate with these responsibilities, the authority of the government over private property could hardly have been more complete. This, however, was never quite the case (although if the war had gone on for another twelve months it probably would have been). Frequently, therefore, the Board was compelled to rely on the support afforded by a rigorously antiprofiteering public opinion, the superiority of its own knowledge of the over-all economic situation, and the existence in the background of an excess profits tax which would take away from any concern much of the profit accruing to it as a result of defying the Board. But even thus handicapped, this body was able to work its will upon the economic process so comprehensively as to make itself a *de facto* partner to almost every business transaction of consequence.

The authority to issue priorities was, on a comparative basis at least, a mild interference with customary business operations (although the failure to receive priority orders for raw materials resulted for the automobile, construction, and certain other industries in a sharp curtailment of output). What these controls meant, however, was no less than that a government agency rather than the managers of private property would determine which customers were to be served or served first, and which were not to be served or served only if and when an adequate supply was available. Sometimes, to be sure, no more was involved here than the giving of preference to one government agency over another, although it was by no means uncommon for priority orders to run counter to prewar and expected postwar business (i.e., competitive) relationships. As these commands emanated from Washington in ever-increasing numbers, even businessmen inclined to be cooperative were apt at times to be hostile toward the bureaucracy responsible for them.

Closely akin to priorities from this standpoint were the conservation measures undertaken to increase productivity. Products were standardized, the number of styles and designs was reduced, retail customers were asked to carry their merchandise home, paper wrappers were substituted for pasteboard cartons and packing cases, boned corsets were stripped of their steel "bones," and the use of tin to give weight and rustle to silk dresses was prohibited. In more than a thousand different ways, it has been estimated, savings of these kinds were instituted. Again, the way a private property economy goes about its business was seriously contravened.

Direct price control was a more severe technique often adopted to increase the efficiency of war production programs, and no doubt it was for this reason that price-fixing activities were carried on in a cautious manner.[5] Not only was the legal foundation on which these controls rested vague, compelling liberal use of negotiation as a basic procedure, but the sheer magnitude of this task also militated against any significant activity on the price control front other than in the fields of raw materials or quantity-produced intermediate products such as steel. The atmosphere within which price discussions took place, including especially the attitude of businessmen toward this responsibility of the government, could not be better illustrated than by repeating the oft-told tale of the beginning of an important steel price negotiation session. Elbert H. Gary, an ex-judge and chairman of the board of United States Steel Corporation, opened the meeting. "May I ask," he said, "by what authority the War Industries Board has undertaken to fix these prices?" After a brief but ominous silence, R. S. Lovett, speaking on behalf of the Board and hence of the government, replied: "A gentleman of your eminent qualifications in law requires no information from me on that point." And basic steel prices were reduced.

Of the most drastic government weapon, the actual commandeering of facilities, an even more sparing use was made. The War Industries Board itself did not at any time invoke this power, although its existence in the background was a persuasive force of considerable significance. On the other hand, both the Army and the Navy did avail themselves of this device, the army alone issuing 510 requisitions for goods and 996 orders for compulsory production. No argu-

---

[5] C. O. Hardy, *Wartime Control of Prices* (Washington, D.C.: The Brookings Institution, 1940).

ment is necessary to demonstrate how quickly a disruptive influence
so fundamental and comprehensive in nature could have made a
shambles of prewar capitalism.

WAR COMES TO THE MASSES

However, these aspects of the wartime control program impinged
most concretely upon businessmen—citizens who were already convinced that the New Freedom was a grave threat to American institutions. As the demands of war mounted relative to the capacity of
the economy to meet them, and as the network of restrictions designed to cope with this situation broadened, the man in the street
was more and more included within the range of its operation.[6] Before the war ended government supervision was being comprehensively exercised over the supply and distribution of both food and
fuel, the heart and center of the economy of every individual.

One of the first consequences of the outbreak of world war had
been an abnormal demand for American foodstuffs. A number of
factors had contributed to this situation. First, supplies customarily
secured from central and eastern Europe were no longer available
to western Europe. Second, the increased demand for ocean shipping plus the ravages of German submarines compelled the Allies
to substitute nearer sources of supply for more distant ones (such
as Argentina, for example). Third, a war economy creates a greater
demand for some types of food products than exists under more
normal circumstances. When to these structural changes in demand
are added an almost unrestrained competitive bidding for such
American supplies as were available, an inelasticity of supply making for a fundamental rigidity on that side of the market, and two
dry summers in the Middle West, it is easy enough to understand
why economic relationships involving agricultural commodities
rapidly became chaotic. Prices increased by more than 100 per
cent, exports tripled, reserve stocks of bread grains and the hog
population fell to dangerously low levels, middleman margins became exorbitant, and transportation difficulties contributed to violent fluctuations in prices which in turn stimulated an unhealthy
speculative activity.

Clearly the problem warranted strong measures, and those re-
sponsible for the nation's affairs did not hesitate to act accordingly.
A food control act was passed conferring upon a National Food
Administration powers almost as complete as those given the War

[6] W. F. Willoughby, *Government Organization in War Time and After* (New York:
Appleton-Century-Crofts, Inc., 1919).

Industries Board.[7] Having as its general objective increasing production, reducing waste, and controlling the distribution of food supplies, the Food Administration was specifically empowered to make voluntary agreements with producers, to license distributors and to prescribe regulations for concerns operating under license, and to buy and sell foodstuffs. As in the case of the War Industries Board, the power to fix prices was not directly and unequivocally given to the Food Administrator (Mr. Herbert Hoover); and, no less than Mr. Baruch, he preferred to operate on the basis of voluntary cooperation insofar as possible. But within the framework of the national emergency, this organization was given the authority necessary to make every adult American acutely conscious of the existence of the war and his own role in the war effort.

To promote conservation an intensive educational campaign was launched designed to reach every consumer. Eleven million families voluntarily agreed to follow the basic conservation principles set forth therein, of which so-called wheatless and meatless days were the most important, and "Hooverizing" (the popular name for such cooperation) was accepted as a patriotic duty. Whereas at the level of the final consumer these principles were applied on a voluntary basis, enforcement procedures became progressively more severe for earlier stages in the production process. Thus hotels and restaurants were subjected to a certain amount of direct supervision, and producers and distributors of the scarcest food products were even placed under a licensing system involving negotiations between the government and private entrepreneurs on the matter of profit margins.

A number of techniques were adopted for dealing with the most acute difficulties which arose in this area. One of the more important of these was the creation of the United States Grain Corporation, a nonprofit government-owned and -operated corporation, to increase the production and bring order into the distribution of wheat. In order to encourage greater output the Corporation guaranteed all producers a minimum price for their crop. This guaranty in turn was also a stabilizing factor. On the one hand, farmers were discouraged from holding supplies off the market in expectation of a better price; on the other hand, speculators were discouraged from engaging in operations which would have increased the amplitude of price variations. As a further stabilization measure the Corporation made milling agreements with more than 20,000 flour-milling concerns,

[7] W. C. Mullendore, *History of the United States Food Administration* (Palo Alto: Stanford University Press, 1941).

allotting to each one a portion of the available wheat so that these concerns would not be tempted to enter into competitive bidding with one another in the central markets.

Apart from the service it performed in assisting the war effort, the United States Grain Corporation also represented a significant development in its own right. Here was an innovation in government-business relationships destined one day to be much more fully developed. By using the corporate form of organization a government agency can be established free of much of the red tape to which a government bureaucracy is especially vulnerable (for example, the annual struggle for another appropriation). It is an agency which can operate much like a business firm, but for purposes and on a scale which would be impossible for private enterprise.

Another critical food problem was sugar, and here also the approach was by way of a business-type operation. Much of America's sugar supply is imported, and different cost conditions prevail in each of several supply areas. To follow the cue of a more or less free market would have meant paying a price great enough to increase production in the high cost area to suppliers at the lower cost points. The alternative was to centralize dealings in sugar by all the Allies, buying at whatever price seemed appropriate in each separate market and selling on a requirements basis at a fixed price. This was the procedure ultimately followed, a Sugar Equalization Board being created to do the actual buying and selling.

Still a third major problem squarely faced by the Food Administration was pork. The war gave rise to an acute shortage of fats, one consequence of which was a sharp increase in the demand for pork products. In order to stimulate increased production while still keeping prices and profits within bounds, the Food Administration worked out an elaborate control scheme. First, the price of one hundred pounds of pork was pegged at the price of fourteen and one-third bushels of corn, the more customary ratio being one hundred pounds of pork to ten bushels of corn. Then, since the government had no legal authority to fix these prices, centralized buying for the Allies was used as a lever to negotiate profit margin agreements with the packing companies, these agreements providing the mechanism by which the Food Administration could make good on its price promise.

Similar to the food program from the standpoint of the impact of war upon the man in the street was the control which came to be exercised over fuel. In order to expand the output of coal and supervise the distribution of an inadequate supply of that product a Fuel

Administration was created. The most drastic action taken by that agency was a "coal holiday" lasting four days, applied to all industries east of the Mississippi River except the most essential war plants, during which the firms involved were to use no more coal than they ordinarily did on Sundays. This was followed by a succession of nine heatless Mondays, after which time this particular crisis had passed. Only slightly less drastic in the view of free enterprise proponents was a government-imposed system of zone distribution designed to eliminate crosshauling of coal.

But if the war administration's control program found itself on innumerable occasions at cross purposes with the interests of particular citizens or groups of citizens, it does not follow that these endeavors were prompted by anything other than the highest motives. The point is rather that the nation's well-being required the government to travel paths which had previously been not only untrod but strictly forbidden, and that these trail-blazing activities involved the making of decisions which at best could not have pleased everyone.

This impossibility of satisfying both producers and consumers can easily be illustrated. Undoubtedly the Food Administration was successful in keeping pork prices lower than they would have been in the absence of controls. At the same time a liberal profit margin for both producers and packers could be justified on the basis of the need to increase production. But the very fact that profit margins were modified by government action was enough to arouse producer antagonism, while consumers could as reasonably point to profit margin generosity as an indication that they were being discriminated against. (And who is to say whether an allowance of 9 per cent to the packers on invested capital, including borrowed funds, was or was not under prevailing circumstances excessive?) Similarly, price-limiting activities with respect to coal could hardly be wholly pleasing to producers, and consumers would scarcely be inclined to be charitable in the face of an increase in the price of coal sufficient to bring into production mines which could not under more normal conditions be profitably worked.

REVOLUTION IN TRANSPORTATION

Not every aspect of the war control program had as its principal secondary consequence (the primary consequence in all cases being, of course, the assistance thereby rendered the war effort) the heightening of the postwar reaction against reform. Some contributed most directly to the stream of institutional evolution. High on the list of developments in this category was the way the war administration handled transportation problems. First in point of time came the need to increase greatly and with all possible speed the supply of offshore shipping. Second came the crisis precipitated by a near breakdown of the nation's domestic transportation system.

Ever since the Civil War the American merchant marine had been operating at a handicap relative to the ships of much of the rest of the world. Partly as a result of the rise of the iron ship, and partly because the American wage level was so high, both the cost of building ships in the United States and the cost of operating ships manned by American seamen were greater than those incurred by foreign competitors. The response of the industry to these disabilities was more or less naturally to demand government protection, and protection would no doubt have been granted if this issue had not become entangled in a controversy which could never quite be resolved.

The problem here was a conflict of interest between shipowners and shipbuilders. At first owners pressed for what came to be called "free ships," the right to fly the American flag on foreign-built ships. But this would have meant the repeal of the navigation acts, especially the law reserving the coastwise trade to American-built vessels, and of course shipbuilders could not accept that solution.

TABLE 10. AN INDUSTRY ON THE DEFENSIVE

Year	Domestic Merchant Ships Built (thousands of gross tons)
1825	116
1855	583
1870	277
1885	159
1895	112
1905	330
1915	225

Source: Bureau of the Census, Historical Statistics of the United States, 1789-1945, p. 211.

As American shipping operations shrank to the point where they included little more than the coastwise trade, however, owners began insisting that the protective framework be broadened. Accordingly a coalition of forces within the Republican party—a majority of the owners, shipbuilders, and manufacturers of shipbuilding materials —began actively to campaign for subsidies. But because American shipowners still operating in the foreign trade field continued to demand "free ships," and because southern and western agricultural interests in the Democratic party saw in that policy a corollary of their belief in free trade, very little was achieved along subsidy lines. As a result the competitive disadvantage under which the American fleet operated had by the time of World War I reduced this activity to a very small affair. This was the situation confronting the nation's leaders when the need for a bridge of ships extending from Philadelphia to the Marne first became evident.[8]

That the United States must now reverse this long-standing policy of neglect was not questioned. Exactly how this was to be done did, however, occasion sharp debate. But not for long. So urgent was the need, and so conservative was the nation still, that a decision was made to spare no expense in getting the job done quickly and at the same time minimizing the government's role. The result was a subsidy program which far overshadowed anything the most ardent proponents of protection had ever suggested.

Responsibility for a gigantic program of wartime shipbuilding was vested first in a United States Shipping Board. This body in turn created the Emergency Fleet Corporation, still another government-owned and -operated corporation, to be responsible for the detailed administration required. Then in the face of an elaborate report-recommendation prepared by President Manson of the Pacific and Eastern Steamship Company showing that the government could build its own ships in small shipyards at a cost of $75 per deadweight ton, the Fleet Corporation proceeded to develop plans for the building of large shipyards and letting contracts to private concerns to build ships in these yards. These ships were then sold to the government at a price of $140 per deadweight ton and up (or at cost-plus, with all the padding of costs implicit in that arrangement). A number of the concerns thus commissioned to build ships for the government had never before built a ship, being organized for the sole purpose of taking advantage of these lush contracts. When the ships had been delivered to the government they were immediately leased to private operators under contracts which included little incentive for economical operation but which forced the government to bear the burden of all operating losses, and contracts for repair work were similarly generous. Finally, to cap the climax, when the fighting ended the Fleet Corporation dared not close down operations in a large shipyard abruptly because of the adverse effect this would have had upon the community in which it

[8] J. A. Salter, Allied Shipping Control (Oxford: Carnegie Endowment for International Peace, 1921).

was located, with the result that the keels of one-third of the vessels built under this program were laid after the Armistice was signed.

It is of course possible that the procedure suggested by Mr. Manson would have failed, and certainly a nation is justified in making some sacrifices even in wartime to preserve free enterprise if this is one of its important values. Above all, in the case at hand, the ships so critically needed did get built. At the same time, however, there does seem to have been about this aspect of America's World War I ship-production program a disregard of considerations broader than sheer private greed, which places this episode in a class apart from almost every other phase of that war effort.

Side by side with this emergency shipping legislation there was also enacted a law designed to meet the merchant marine problem on a longer-range basis. On the surface the approach taken at this point was to place common carriers by water in the public utility category, but in numerous ways the analogy with rail regulation (and hence identification of this development with the reform movement) is clearly inappropriate. In the first place, only carriers on the high seas were to be regulated, and even then so-called "tramp" vessels were excluded. A second indication that the motivation here was more promotional than regulatory was the fact that the only rate powers of consequence given the United States Shipping Board was the authority to prevent discriminatory practices, a device (as in the Elkins Act) more oriented to the elimination of ruinous competition among carriers than to the protection of shippers. And most revealing of all, these concerns were explicitly permitted to enter into cooperative agreements with one another without fear of the antitrust laws if only such agreements met with the approval of the Shipping Board. This, in the face of virtually no effective control over rates, was the equivalent of an announcement that only the welfare of the ship companies themselves was to be considered.

The wartime domestic transportation problem arose as much from defects in the government's own control program as from either a deficiency on the part of the railroads or the sheer magnitude of the task they were now asked to perform.[9] As a result of a lack of coordination between domestic transport and either offshore shipping or east coast factories, hundreds of loaded cars were consigned to eastern destinations which could not be unloaded on arrival. This difficulty was, in turn, accentuated by the fact that transport priorities (created on an uncoordinated basis by a number of different

[9] Walker D. Hines, *War History of American Railroads* (New Haven: Yale University Press, 1928).

agencies) had been greatly overissued to the point that a large proportion of all freight was legally required to be moved immediately. When an attempt was made to alleviate these difficulties by sending government "expediters" to help the railroads do their job more efficiently, mere confusion often gave way to sheer chaos. The backing up of freight cars in the East became so serious that essential traffic could hardly move at all, and a complete breakdown of railroad service was imminent.

The first attempt to remedy this situation was a voluntary cooperation among the railroads themselves designed to make possible their operation as a single integrated unit rather than as a number of independent, competitive organizations. Unfortunately, however, deeply ingrained habit patterns proved to be so tenacious that this step failed to bring about the desired result. Without further ado the government stepped decisively into the breach, operating the railroads on its own account for a period of twenty-six months. This expedient made it possible gradually both to work off the tie-up of cars at the ports and to eliminate the use of railroad cars as warehouses in industrial areas, with the result that the threatened disruption of essential traffic did not occur.

By common consent this was one of the great successes of the entire war period. Yet, ironically, this episode has from that day to this been singled out by conservative propagandists as a particularly telling illustration of the adverse consequences of government intervention in business affairs.

Superficially this case can be made. Certainly the government did lose money, in the sense that the revenue received for the service rendered was not sufficient to pay the earnings guaranty without assistance from the Treasury. And, depending upon what is included in this calculation, the deficit amounted to at least well over $1 billion. But that this fact demonstrates the inefficiency of government operation is a proposition which cannot be considered proved by mere assertion.

The fact of the matter is that the financial results of a business operation do not in and of themselves shed any light on the efficiency with which it is conducted. On the one hand, an inefficient concern may earn net profits under certain easily conceivable conditions. On the other hand, if a concern decided to give away its output, its net monetary losses would obviously be no measure of its productive efficiency. In the case of the railroads during World War I the government probably raised wages to a greater extent than private managements would have done, while raising rates to a smaller extent than could have been justified by advances in cost. Both these things, however, were done as a part of the government's over-all responsibilities—the first to avoid work stoppages, the second to diminish to that extent inflationary pressures—and neither had anything to do with inefficiency as such.

A New World for Labor

Just as the three blind men were unable to agree on what an elephant was like by feeling its ear, leg, or trunk, so is it necessary to look beyond particular problems and policies to form an accurate picture of the American economy during World War I. How did the various segments of the community fare against the background of economic mobilization? Who gained and who lost, both absolutely and relatively?

It is important in this connection to bear in mind that major wars are typically financed, in the nations waging them, by inflationary means, and that the United States during World War I was no exception to this general rule.[10] That being the case, the crucial test of relative well-being is the behavior of different types of income by comparison with changes in the purchasing power of the dollar.

As would only have been expected, business concerns in general profited substantially from the war. This broad conclusion must, to be sure, be qualified in several important ways. Thus the gain in business profits was much more pronounced before the United States entered the war and embarked upon a comprehensive economic control program than afterwards. Moreover, those industries whose output was not essential to the war effort increased the purchasing power of their dollar profits by much less than did more strategic industries. Third, there was a marked contrast between the purchasing power gains made by business concerns taken as a whole and the gains passed on by those concerns to their owners; as a result of a widespread policy of retaining earnings, the purchasing power of total business disbursements to owners remained roughly constant throughout the war period. But gains there were in this sector of the economy, and very substantial ones, and it was largely because of these that the number of American millionaires increased during these years severalfold.

Farmers perhaps even more than businesses made economic gains during the war. Because the supply of agricultural commodities is

---

[10] E. L. Bogart, *War Costs and Their Financing* (New York: Appleton-Century-Crofts, Inc., 1921); and J. M. Clark, *The Costs of the World War to the American People* (New Haven: Yale University Press, 1931).

highly inelastic, the increase in demand for these goods brought about by a major war tends to be absorbed in higher prices rather than in greater output. Comparing 1918 with 1913, the after-taxes real income of farm operators and agricultural wage earners increased a full 25 per cent. Again these gains were unevenly distributed; cotton farmers especially suffered from wartime economic maladjustments as the war on the high seas interfered with the normal relationship between southern cotton farms and British textile mills. Here to an even greater extent than in the case of business operations, furthermore, some of the gains registered were more apparent than real. So powerful was the farmer's urge to own his own land that many invested these newly earned profits in the purchase of farms, more often than not heavily supplementing their own capital with mortgage loans in this process, and these investments all too soon proved to be disastrously speculative. But for all this farmers did improve their economic position during the war period; while the war lasted and even for some months thereafter this group had no reason for feeling that the wartime prosperity had in any sense passed it by.

But economic benefits from war for both businessmen and farmers was by the early twentieth century a historical relationship of long standing. On the contrary, however, it was no part of the established pattern that workers also reap some of these rewards. Here, indeed, did World War I see economic history written in the grand style. For although the wartime gains of laborers were neither as large nor as widely diffused as those of society's other great interests, this was the first major war in American history during which laborers as a group had not seen their standard of living seriously reduced.

A first factor in labor's favor was the ready availability of jobs. This meant not only employment for all who desired to work, but competition between employers for competent workmen. Thus whereas war orders did not find their way equally to all industries, labor mobility was sufficiently high to permit a sizable shift of workers from less vital to more vital activities. As a result of this shift, the great improvement in employee bargaining power during the war, a tremendous increase in overtime hours worked at enhanced wage rates, and government cost-plus contracts, no large body of day laborers was seriously injured by the rising cost of living, and large numbers actually increased their real earnings. Statistically these developments can be summarized in the fact that the index of average hourly earnings approximately kept pace with the index of consumer prices, which means in turn that about as many workers achieved wartime economic gains as suffered losses during this period.

But if labor's wartime accomplishment on the real income front was in its way spectacular, certain other worker achievements during these years were even more so. From its inception the modern labor movement had concentrated first upon its own organizational integration with the rest of the community and only secondarily upon pressure for wage increases as such. In this connection, furthermore, it is of great significance that the New Freedom was the first administration in Washington, D.C., that had ever been aggressively friendly to labor; insofar as its other responsibilities permitted, the government during these years did everything in its power to encourage collective bargaining. During World War I these two facts helped bring about a remarkable advance for organized labor.

One way in which this advance can be seen is in the growth of labor unions themselves. The high demand for labor made possible the strengthening of union membership drives without a corresponding increase in employer resistance. At the same time the rising cost of living provided a powerful motivation behind organizational work, as did also the pressure for production leading to long hours, speed-up, and other working conditions aggravating discontent. Although both the American Federation of Labor and the Railway Brotherhoods joined with big business in giving the nation a no-strike–no-lockout pledge, and although the strikes which did take place were typically of little consequence, the fact is that both the number of strikes and the number of persons involved in strikes increased significantly during the war years. In such an environment it is of course not surprising that union membership increased by one-fourth.

Another aspect of this development was the unprecedentedly close cooperation between labor and the government which characterized the World War I period,[11] a cooperation motivated in part by the administration's innate sympathies, and in part by the importance to the war effort of worker goodwill. To a limited extent labor was given a voice in the operation of the major war agencies. To a much greater extent labor was given representation on those agencies created for the express purpose of helping maintain harmonious employer-employee relationships, including numerous special agencies designed to eliminate substandard working conditions in a num-

[11] G. S. Watkins, *Labor Problems and Labor Administration in the United States During the World War* (Urbana: University of Illinois Press, 1919).

ber of conspicuous instances. A government agency (the United States Employment Service) was created to facilitate the shift of workers from less to more vital, and hence usually higher-paying, jobs. The government as the economy's most important purchaser of the output of industry broadly utilized this opportunity to enforce improved working conditions of various sorts upon a large number of concerns and industries. In the extreme case of the Adamson Act government legislation was the instrument for bringing about an improvement in wages and hours, thus establishing a precedent which became a fundamental goal of other government agencies working in this field, while the Railroad Administration went out of its way to deal with railroad workers generously enough that no work interruptions would occur in that industry. Here, in short, was one front on which it could not accurately be said that reform ever ceased during the entire war period.

With businessmen and farmers achieving substantial economic gains, and with workers making up in organizational advances what they were failing to achieve on the wage rate front, it would almost seem that everyone benefited from the war economy. This, however, could hardly be; a nation already at full employment could not divert one-fourth of its productive capacity to the turning out of war goods without depriving some segments of the economy of a portion of their accustomed standards of living. By this time industrial America had built up a sizable urban middle class, its largest single element being a white-collar worker group, and the incomes received by this group proved to be highly inflexible in the face of the rising cost of living. Government employees, for example, are estimated to have lost approximately one-third of their prewar level of real income, while salaried workers in private industry lost about one-fourth. Moreover, those people ordinarily receiving a substantial proportion of their income directly from property also suffered from income erosion.

Insofar as the war and its aftermath did contribute to a popular revulsion against reform, a revulsion aided and abetted by Republicans and conservatives, here is certainly one of the paradoxes of American history. The central fact about resistance to reform in the United States, after World War I no less than before, was the energetic leadership given that cause by Republican businessmen. Yet one of the striking facts about the war administration was its dominance by Republicans drawn from the business world—and this despite the fact that the ruling group in Washington was politically

Democratic. Throughout the entire War Industries Board only one policy-making position was held by a Democrat, and that one by Bernard Baruch who had made a fortune in the stock market. The head of the Food Administration was a confirmed Republican (ten years later to become a Republican President) and he naturally gathered around him men of like sympathies. Likewise, decision-makers in the Fuel Administration, the Shipping Board, and the Railroad Administration were typically men whose prewar life had been anchored deep in private business operations.

QUESTIONS FOR DISCUSSION

1. In the new coalition between workers and farmers what were the major benefits each received?

2. Why did reform activity virtually cease as the war began to drift toward this country?

3. Why are adjustments by way of changing prices and profit margins most effective over longer than shorter periods?

4. What were the responsibilities of the War Industries Board, and how did it go about the task of meeting them?

5. Explain the economic bases underlying the wartime food and fuel control problems.

6. What were the responsibilities of the Food Administration, and how did it go about the task of meeting them?

7. Explain the role of the government in resolving the most acute offshore shipping problem of the war years.

8. Explain the role of the government in resolving the most acute domestic transportation problem of the war years.

9. How were economic gains and losses resulting from World War I distributed, and to what extent were these particular results intended?

10. What aspects of the wartime control program (if any) could appropriately be classified as reform? To what extent was domestic reform an objective of the controls developed?

Chapter 15

Return to Laissez Faire

If the blowing of bugles in April, 1917, resulted only in a shift in the center of gravity of reform endeavors from domestic issues to the international scene, the signing of the Armistice in November, 1918, was the signal for a repudiation of reform in all its ramifications. With this retreat to the other shore, and particularly with the wholesale burning of bridges accompanying it, the nation gave itself over to a laissez faire as unrestrained as any it had ever seen—a relapse lasting for a full dozen years and coming to an end only under the impact of the most savage economic depression in the history of civilization.

FAREWELL TO REFORM

So decisive was this turnabout, so intense the spirit with which the New Freedom was trampled under foot, that an understanding of the evolution of government-business relationships from this point forward requires a thorough examination of this phenomenon. Where did the forces of reform go? Why did the zeal to transform the status quo evaporate so suddenly? Only in a context consisting primarily of answers to questions such as these can post-World War I America be comprehended.

Let it be remembered, to begin with, that by 1918 conservatism had been on the defensive for some fifteen years, and that every one of those years had seen another nail driven into the coffin of the way of life conservatives were so eager to preserve. Furthermore, whereas at first reform activities had constituted only a peripheral threat to the philosophy upon which a laissez faire society must be built, in more recent years this threat had greatly widened in scope. During the war especially the idea that the government is to interfere with business operations only occasionally, only where a particularly great need arises, seemed clearly to have been abandoned. Confronted with the war emergency, the gravest crisis the new industrial nation had yet faced, every major aspect of the economy had become "affected with a public interest" sufficiently to warrant intervention.

To be sure, businessmen were not so far removed from reality as to believe that wartime controls had been unnecessary. Indeed, their wholehearted and active support of the control program is dramatic evidence to the contrary. Nor is it to be supposed that conservative leaders gave credence to the view that Woodrow Wilson and his administration could in any legitimate sense be held responsible for America's participation in the war, however much they may have utilized that interpretation for political purposes in later years. What was involved was rather that the war administration had demonstrated the wonders centralized planning in an economy could accomplish, and it was feared that this lesson might encourage citizens to push more rapidly along the reform road the nation had been travelling when the war had interrupted normal pursuits.

Two closely related phases of the wartime control network highlight conservative concern on this score. Because the war effort required the construction of facilities of little use in ordinary times, and which consequently would not have been made available by businessmen making decisions on the basis of prospective profits, a War Finance Corporation had been created. The task of this organization had been to provide the capital with which such facilities were constructed, to use government investment as a device to "socialize" certain basic risks. And just as it was essential for the government to put capital into the economy at strategic points, so did it seem appropriate for the government to see to it that capital did not flow into the system for purposes which would not contribute to the main business then before the country. This was the function of the Capital Issues Committee, a group authorized to pass upon all new security issues. It is readily understandable that when conservatives reflected on innovations such as these against the background of the recent bitter reform attack on finance capitalism, they would feel very uneasy about the future of their world.

However, the repudiation of reform is not to be explained wholly on the basis of conservative anxiety. Out of this sentiment there did no doubt emerge an eagerness to fan whatever fires of discontent might be arising in other parts of the community, but it could not itself have been the primary conflagration. Businessmen naturally would avail themselves of whatever opportunities were available for making a "comeback" onto the power stage; as a minority group, they would just as naturally have found little support for an endeavor so oriented. The question thus remains: where did the main body of the reaction against reform come from?

Here the important point to remember is that the reform achievements of prior years had been the work of a political coalition consisting of farmers, workers, and the urban middle class; that while the reform battalions were strong enough to do great things as long as these three groups were all pulling in the same direction, there had never been any reason for supposing that a significant part of this cooperation could be sacrificed without at the same time shattering the very foundations of the New Freedom. Indeed Woodrow Wilson's administration was the visible embodiment of this coalition; these interests spoke through it insofar as they were able to speak at all, and it in turn spoke with authority only to the extent that these three interests were in agreement about what was being said. As a result of these relationships the cause of reform was now doubly vulnerable. On the one hand, any adversity befalling the Wilson administration could not but react unfavorably upon reform endeavors. On the other hand, any weakening of the ties binding farmers, laborers, and the white-collar group together could not but threaten the political instrument through which this union had achieved its victories.

It would have been impossible in any event for the Wilson administration to have retained its prestige intact in the face of such an intense national experience. At best mere men have difficulty maintaining a perspective from which to view great events, and this failure is all the more certain where personal interests are also at stake. Entirely apart from the question of reform, thus, many citizens would have harbored resentment against the nation's leadership because of the loss or crippling of loved ones or simply the frustrations and inconveniences growing out of the war effort. But when propagandists hit upon the theme that the tragedies and hardships of war were imposed upon the people in the interest of reform, and especially when Woodrow Wilson himself enhanced the plausibility of that argument by devoting the last years of his presidency to an idealistic endeavor designed to bring permanent peace to the world (the ill-fated League of Nations), the inevitable reaction against the war was converted into antagonism for reform.

Viewed from the standpoint of the coalition itself, similar forces were at work. Farmers had not entered into cooperation with workers in order to attack the rights of private property. Significantly, with a single exception no reform legislation had been oriented to that end, and the exception was protection for labor from the operation of the antitrust laws which farmers were anxious to achieve on their own account. It was, in other words, no part of the original agreement that the government in Washington would make a major project out of assisting laborers to improve their ability to usurp management prerogatives through collective bargaining. It is not of course to be concluded that this development was the result of a political double cross, either. The need for an uninterrupted flow of goods from the country's major industries created a situation which had not been contemplated when the coalition had originally been put together, and underlying administration sympathies had done the rest. At the same time it is not in the least surprising that this stepping out of bounds, coupled with high agricultural prosperity, went far toward putting an end to a type of political alignment which had been extremely rare in American history.

The urban middle class likewise began during the war to have misgivings about one of its major allies, and here too the principal causal factor was undoubtedly the progress being made by labor. Fixed income receivers would not have been happy in any case to bear the largest share of the economic burden of the war. But when this happened side by side with labor's sweeping advances on the collective bargaining front, it would have been little short of miraculous if a political alliance could have withstood the strain. Men and women not closely associated with the labor movement have a difficult enough time fitting the strike into their philosophy of a harmoniously functioning society under peacetime conditions. How could they possibly have rationalized these activities in wartime, especially when their own standard of living was being steadily chipped away in part as a result of the concessions for workers thus won. And this breach was if anything even more injurious to the cause of reform than that between workers and farmers, for whereas the alliance between labor and agriculture had been based largely upon expediency, cooperation between workers and the urban middle class had been based upon some very basic common attitudes.

Sowing the Wind

If, when the war ended, all or even a majority of the forces operating to weaken reform had promptly vanished the nation might still have been spared so sharp a swing toward reactionism as in fact occurred. In the event, however, the die was cast as surely against liberalism after the war as during America's involvement in it; in almost every particular, postwar readjustments took a form unfavorable rather than favorable to a continuation of prewar trends. And after the war no less than during it, organized labor was at the vortex of a circle of developments which could not have avoided injuring the cause of reform.

In the first place, although workers had achieved a great deal in recent years, their leaders still felt that much unfinished business remained in the collective bargaining field. Little progress had as yet been made in mass-production industries such as steel and automobiles, and many of organized labor's newly acquired members were in war-expanded industries which were rapidly releasing workers. At the same time full union treasuries, a virtual (if temporary) guaranty by the government of the right of collective bargaining which would almost certainly be less valid under Woodrow Wilson's successor, the fact that many employers were known to have tolerated the wartime enhancement of labor's bargaining strength only because it was thought to be a short-term phenomenon scheduled for prompt reversal after the war, and the continuance of inflation for a year and a half after the Armistice—all these factors

TABLE 11. FORMULA FOR LABOR UNREST

Year	General Price Index (1913 = 100)
1914	100
1916	117
1918	157
1920	193

Source: Department of Commerce, *Historical Statistics of the United States, 1789-1945*, p. 231.

guaranteed that labor-capital relationships in the immediate postwar period would be stormy.

From the standpoint of an economic program designed to alter the status quo, a worse time for labor unrest could hardly have been chosen. A rising nationalism in the United States was already beginning to believe that everything in this country was superior to everything outside it, and the postwar propaganda against Wilsonian internationalism was finding a multitude of uses for that theme. For example, American participation in the war, and more particularly her active cooperation with other nations in seeking the foundations for a lasting peace, were being advertised as an anti-American surrender of domestic virtues in exchange for foreign vices. Against such a background it was inevitable that economic pressure by laborers against employers would be portrayed to the public as an importation of the Bolshevik Revolution into the United States. In Russia the workers had risen up and overthrown their masters, destroying private enterprise and private property in the process. Was it not obvious that American workers were endeavoring to duplicate that performance here?[1]

To make matters worse certain of the developments now taking place on the labor front played directly into the hands of anti-union publicists. Thus it is not to be denied that radicals in the United States had been heartened by revolutionary success in Europe, and that as a result many labor disputes were either engineered or taken over by a revolutionary element in the labor movement which had been repudiated by the nonradical majority. Fuel was also added to this propaganda fire by the fact that one of the first major labor disputes of the postwar period was a semirevolutionary one: a general strike called for the purpose of benefitting workers in the Seattle shipbuilding industry and with the idea of prostrating the entire city if necessary. And no sooner had public opinion begun to recover from that outrage to conservative attitudes than the specter of American bolshevism was again raised, this time by an action of the unquestionably conservative American Federation of Labor. A strike of Boston's policemen was called to compel city officials to recognize the Federation as the policemen's bargaining agent. The resulting orgy of pillage and destruction, ended by the appearance on the scene of the National Guard, convinced even many of labor's most confirmed supporters that the situation was getting out of hand.

In a somewhat different category was the so-called Plumb Plan, although the public relations consequences of this episode fit into the same pattern. It was agreed on all sides that one of the pressing problems of the day was railroad legislation, that when these concerns were turned back to their owners, a fairly fundamental rethinking of the nation's policy toward that industry would be required. Furthermore, it is understandable that the favorable treatment railroad workers had received under government operation would have colored their outlook with regard to the public policies which should be forthcoming from such a re-examination. The result of these two considerations was the advancement by representatives of organized labor in the railroad industry of a proposal that the railroads be taken over by a government corporation on a permanent basis.

[1] H. W. Laidler, *A History of Socialist Thought* (New York: The Thomas Y. Crowell Co., 1927).

Given both the wartime experience and the legislation which was ultimately passed in the railway field, this suggestion was not nearly so radical as the conservative press of that day maintained. The new corporation would have been controlled by a board of directors made up of management, government, and employee representatives in equal proportions, the water currently contained in railroad securities was to be squeezed out, railroad rates (still to be supervised by the Interstate Commerce Commission) were to be set so as to permit a 5 per cent return on investment, and a neutral machinery for settling labor disputes was to be established. A far cry this, surely, from the class struggle portrayed in *Das Kapital*. But all the same it was not an appropriate time for workers to recommend nationalizing the railroad industry.

The moral in all of this is obvious. Whatever the reasons particular segments of society might otherwise have had for restraining their impatience with workers, they were, as these events unfolded, strongly counterbalanced. Businessmen who wanted nothing quite so much as an opportunity to stem the tide of labor's advance found ready at hand a weapon made to order for this task. Farmers who had always been a little reluctant to join forces with a group refusing to pay unqualified obeisance to the institution of private property as that institution was then functioning were given a basis for confirming their worst fears and repudiating erstwhile allies. The urban middle class, watching aggressive postwar unionism turn the full force of postwar inflation against the white-collar group (just as it had earlier done with wartime inflation), was all the more certain that in breaking with the reform coalition it was making the right decision.

And Then the Harvest

Given these circumstances, it was only to be expected that the hand of reaction would fall most heavily upon organized labor; a rejuvenated laissez faire was naturally most anxious to preserve the prerogatives of management against further encroachment, and even to set back the clock a little at this point if possible. Accordingly, sometimes with the government's active assistance but more often only with the tacit approval of government, a campaign was launched to reduce drastically the economic power accumulating in the hands of labor.

As long as the postwar prosperity lasted, business efforts in that direction had to be primarily defensive. This limitation was not a major handicap, however, because as workers had long since learned to their sorrow big business was not without defenses, especially when the government was willing to use its resources to tilt the balance of power in favor of the employer. In 1919 the first attempt in almost twenty years was made to organize the steel industry. The disastrous defeat suffered by unionism at this point illustrates particularly well the relative strength of workers as compared with their opponents as the postwar struggle began in earnest.[2]

By modern humanitarian standards the union was overwhelmingly right in this encounter. The men operating blast furnaces, for example, had not only a twelve-hour day and a seven-day week, but were required to do an 18- or 24-hour stint once every two weeks when the shift was changed. Moreover, workers' housing and general living conditions were often deplorable.

But right did not make for might on this occasion. For one thing the bargaining position of the union was weakened by two major difficulties. The first of these was the fact that steel towns often contained many immigrant groups speaking a dozen different languages. The second was the type of organization work being carried on; instead of a single union embracing all employees, a number of independent American Federation of Labor crafts were carrying on very poorly coordinated efforts.

For another, once the fabulous assets of the steel industry were mobilized against this unionization drive, even such force as resided in the workers' case was quickly dissipated. Control over local newspapers made it exceedingly easy for conservatives to deny the union an adequate forum whereby to carry its side of the dispute to the public. Conversely, these resources were valuable in soliciting moral support for the employers' stand. (And of course an important element in both these endeavors was the presentation of this strike to the public as the work of foreign-inspired revolutionaries.) Espionage was employed on a large scale for the purpose of creating disunion among rank-and-file workers, and of accumulating additional material for propaganda use. Innumerable ingenious devices were utilized for turning the unskilled worker against his more skilled colleague. And at every opportunity strikebreakers were brought into the struck plants to absorb the jobs of striking employees.

So effective was this anti-union campaign, indeed, that a Senate investigating committee was prompted to deplore the workers' "Red" leadership—although that group did also censure the companies for their intransigency. Without significant exception, furthermore, governments threw in their lot with employers. Mounted state troopers dispersed gatherings of strikers in city streets, and in Al-

---

[2] William Z. Foster, *The Great Steel Strike* (New York: B. W. Huebsch, 1920).

legheny County, Pennsylvania, meetings of more than three persons
were outlawed. In fact, the only nongovernment organization openly
sympathetic to the workers' cause was the Interchurch World Movement.[3] With public opinion so universally aroused in its behalf, the
industry could well afford to take refuge in its past profits and wait.
And this it did.

The new laissez faire appeared in a somewhat different, although
scarcely an unfamiliar, form in connection with another major labor
dispute in 1919. Bituminous coal miners, complaining about the high
cost of living, demanded a substantial wage increase and struck
when their employers refused even to discuss the matter with them.
One week before the strike was scheduled to begin, the President declared that the country was still at war, thus appealing to patriotism
and the needs of national defense as a means of preventing the walkout. When the workers ignored the President's declaration, on the
grounds that the Fuel Administration had long since ceased to function and the price of coal had sharply risen in recent months, he had
a drastic injunction drawn up forbidding any action whatsoever
which would aid the strike. Although the strike went on for a time
on an unauthorized basis, this step by the principal architect of the
New Freedom effectively broke its back at the outset.[4]

It was at this point that the vicious circle operating against both
organized labor and Woodrow Wilson took still another decisive
turn. Prior to this a single remnant of the earlier reform coalition
had remained—the tie between labor and Woodrow Wilson's administration. Now that the President had seen fit to turn against the
workers by utilizing the most reprehensible tactic in the lexicon of
unionism, laborers clearly had no choice but to repudiate Wilson. In
a very real sense, in other words, both organized labor and Woodrow
Wilson now lost their last friend. And when strikes in the country's
two most basic industries created reconversion shortages and contributed to inflation, current propaganda about the close relationship between the labor movement and revolutionism was still more
widely believed.

Even the Supreme Court was to make a major contribution to this
aspect of the new laissez faire, and in several different ways. A first
opportunity presented itself when a case came before it involving the
constitutionality of a law passed by Congress to prevent interstate

[3] Interchurch World Movement of North America, *Report on the Steel Strike of
1919* (New York: Harcourt, Brace & Co., Inc., 1920).
[4] John L. Lewis, *The Miners' Fight For American Standards* (Indianapolis: Bell
Publishing Co., 1925).

commerce in goods produced in commercial establishments by children. Taking an extremely narrow view of the meaning of interstate commerce, one painfully reminiscent of that used in the E. C. Knight Company case, the Court in a 5–4 decision declared that statute void:

The act in its effect does not regulate transportation among the States, but aims to standardize the ages at which children may be employed in mining and manufacturing within the States. The goods shipped are of themselves harmless. The act permits them to be freely shipped after thirty days from the time of their removal from the factory. When offered for shipment, and before transportation begins, the labor of their production is over, and the mere fact that they were intended for interstate commerce transportation does not make their production subject to federal control under the commerce power.[5]

To be sure only federal action in this field was here outlawed, and the Court had the year before approved a state law limiting factory employees to ten hours of work per day.[6] Unfortunately, however, it was the very fact of interstate competition (interstate commerce) which made state action in the child labor field especially ineffective.

From child labor legislation, the Supreme Court turned to the protection for organization and collective bargaining by workers that Congress had sought to write into the Clayton Anti-Trust Act. In the first of a series of cases on this subject, the issue presented involved an attempt by a mechanics' union to unionize a nonunion printing company, an attempt which had depended largely on the refusal of union men to repair or work on this company's presses or to work for anyone using them. Relying on Section 20 of the Clayton Act, the union resisted an injunction intended to put an end to this uncomfortable pressure. On appeal, the Supreme Court took it upon itself to rule that the Clayton Act did not exempt secondary boycotts from legal action.[7]

This narrowing of the Clayton Act as a protection to labor organization rights was shortly carried still further in a case involving picketing. Here the Court ruled that neither mass picketing nor picketing by outsiders was protected by Section 2.[8] Then, having thus prepared the way for this larger step, the Court virtually nullified the intent of that wording. Arizona had passed an anti-injunction law closely modeled after the Clayton Act exemption. When the Arizona courts refused to issue an injunction in a picketing case on the ground that state law forbade such action, the Supreme Court was asked to render judgment on the issues involved. The high

[5] *Hammer v. Dagenhart,* 247 U.S. 251 (1918).
[6] *Bunting v. Oregon,* 243 U.S. 426 (1917).
[7] *Duplex Printing Company v. Deering,* 254 U.S. 443 (1921).
[8] *American Steel Foundries v. Tri-City Trades Council,* 257 U.S. 184 (1921).

Court's opinion was that the Arizona (or any other similar) statute could exempt only *legal* picketing from judicial restraint.[9] Since the Supreme Court's definition of legal picketing was a narrow one, workers were left with little of what had so shortly before been considered a sweeping legislative victory.

In a way there was an ironic appropriateness in what was here happening. Labor had set out to destroy a legal double standard operating to its disadvantage by substituting in its place a legal double standard operating in its favor. With one hand the courts were now making it clear that they were as reluctant as ever to exempt workers from antitrust penalties; with the other they were soon indicating an equally great reluctance to alter the status of business relative to the antitrust laws.

Throughout the war a softened attitude toward big business had been evidenced by the administration. This was only to be expected, of course, with so many top government positions filled by business leaders. But even apart from that fact the government had discovered, both in its capacity as a buyer of the output of industry and as a regulator of business activity, that working with a smaller number of larger firms made for more efficient government operations than dealing with a larger number of smaller firms. Furthermore, the government had even gone a long step farther down this road by encouraging the organization of the firms in a number of industries into associations through which the government might transact its business with those industries more expeditiously. It goes without saying that in the face of preferences of this sort antitrust activity was all but suspended for the duration.

The most tangible wartime consequence of this reversal of attitude was the passage of the Webb-Pomerene Act in 1918. For a number of years concerns engaged in the export trade had complained that the centralized market power possessed by their customers and competitors abroad, a power made possible by the tolerance of cartels by foreign governments, put firms in the United States at a decided disadvantage. During the war, moreover, this difficulty had become even more acute when the Allied governments themselves formed monopolistic agencies for the purpose of buying in this country. To remedy this situation, an antitrust exemption for concerns producing for export was made law. Henceforth such firms could cooperate on export trade matters to the fullest extent without fear of prosecution, provided a copy of their

9 *Truax v. Corrigan,* 257 U.S. 312 (1921).

agreement was filed with the Federal Trade Commission, and provided that this privilege was not used to evade antitrust restrictions.

With these things taking place on the administrative and legislative fronts, it was only to be expected that the Supreme Court would soon be getting into this act. As a matter of fact as early as 1918 this body had termed as reasonable and hence not illegal the acquisition by the United Shoe Machinery Corporation of every major concern producing shoe machinery. The government had maintained that this company had utilized its patent holdings and an elaborate system of leasing to compel the country's shoemakers to do business with it, and that this situation had indirectly coerced its competitors to enter into an illegal combination. But the Court took a different view. United's machines were used by others, said four out of seven Justices, because they were superior, and hence the combination was to be thought of as a series of acquisitions designed to bring about a more effective use of patents in this field, even though entry into the business by new firms was restricted.[10]

It puts the matter mildly to say that this decision gave big business the benefit of every doubt. And it is merely a truism to suggest that this use of the rule of reason went far to confirm the fears liberals had long had that such an interpretation would one day emasculate the Sherman Act. In any event this was the judicial environment within which an antitrust suit against the United States Steel Corporation came before the highest tribunal in the land in 1920.

The prayer of the government for dissolution of this combination was based squarely on the evidence, such items as the dominant position of the Corporation in the steel industry as demonstrated by the Gary dinners being stressed. Without disputing the main facts brought out by the government, however, the Supreme Court took a basically different approach to the issues presented. Thus Justice McKenna, speaking for the majority, took judicial notice of the lack of evidence showing that the Corporation had at any time behaved aggressively toward its competitors, the fact that its illegal price leadership activities had ceased before action was instituted by the government, and a decline in the percentage of the nation's steel business done by this concern from two-thirds to one-half. Put differently, an original intent to monopolize had obviously been abandoned, and the present position of the company apparently resulted primarily from efficient operations. Summarizing its views, the Court uttered these classic sentences:

[10] *United States* v. *United Shoe Machinery Corporation,* 247 U.S. 48 (1918).

The corporation is undoubtedly of impressive size, and it takes an effort of resolution not to be affected by it or to exaggerate its influence. But we must adhere to the law, and the law does not make mere size an offense, or the existence of unexerted power an offense. It, we repeat, requires overt acts, and trusts to its prohibition of them and its power to repress or punish them. It does not compel competition, nor require all that is possible.[11]

In this way was the abuse theory of mergers born; in the absence of unworthy motives, predatory behavior, and an overwhelmingly large proportion of the industry under a single management, the Court will be inclined to let sleeping dogs lie. In this way also did the rule of reason decisively come of age.

Surely little could have been added to these decisions which would have contributed to the frustration of antitrust reformers in the immediate postwar period. But if anything of this sort was missing, it was soon supplied in the outcome of the first case involving the work of the infant Federal Trade Commission to reach the Supreme Court.

Obviously if that agency were to play a positive role in elevating the level of competition, apart from actions relating to practices in the antitrust area, it would have to do so under the broad authorization written into the Federal Trade Commission Act. Equally obviously the possibility of making such a contribution hinged in turn upon a reasonably liberal interpretation in the courts of the concept of unfair methods of competition. As early as 1920, notice was served on the Commission that a sympathetic hearing by the conservative judges then on the federal bench was not to be taken for granted.

In one of its earliest actions the Commission had brought suit against a concern refusing to sell steel ties for use in bailing operations to firms that did not also buy the necessary bagging from it. Apparently it was not felt here that this practice threatened competition within the meaning of the Clayton Act, hence the ground argued was the meaning of unfair competition under the companion measure. Not only did the Supreme Court insist that in the case at bar arrangements of this sort did not constitute unfair competition (actually this reversal was based on what might almost be termed a technicality; the Commission had not introduced specific evidence showing injury to competitors), but Justice McReynolds made some fundamental (if also obiter dicta) comments which ran directly counter to the most basic purposes reformers had had in mind when the Federal Trade Commission Act was passed.

11 *United States* v. *United States Steel Corporation,* 251 U.S. 417 (1920).

The words "unfair competition" are not defined by the statute and their exact meaning is in dispute. It is for the courts, not the commission, ultimately to determine as a matter of law what they include. They are clearly inapplicable to practices never heretofore regarded as opposed to good morals because characterized by deception, bad faith, fraud, or oppression, or as against public policy because of their dangerous tendency unduly to hinder competition or create monopoly. The act was certainly not intended to fetter free and fair competition as commonly understood and practiced by honorable opponents in trade.[12]

Obviously such an approach would not make the antitrust laws more definite or minimize government by litigation in this field. The Court in this decision repudiated not only the guidance of the legislative branch of the government on the matter of definition but also assistance from the administrative body established by the legislature for that express purpose. Furthermore, the definition of unfair competition to be used was at the same time essentially limited to the common law meaning (that is, "passing off," simulating a competitor's product) which the 1914 legislation had sought to expand, plus the Sherman Act prohibitions which had been broadly attacked as excessively vague. Indeed, the Court even came close to defining acceptable business morality as synonymous with existing business mores. Evidently the Federal Trade Commission was in for a period of "hazing" similar to that which had complicated the work of the Interstate Commerce Commission during its early years.

RAILROAD REGULATION TURNS RIGHT

Not all the early postwar developments in the field of business-government relationships were as aggressively antireformist as those involving organized labor and business consolidations. In some areas there was also a further building on foundations laid in prior years, foundations which in their origin had been reformist in character. Even in these situations, however, the fact most worth noting is the absence of the reform spirit which had marked the laying of these foundations—the conservative pall that hung over virtually every change of consequence in the status quo. This process of pouring conservative wine into liberal bottles can be seen particularly clearly in the Transportation Act of 1920.[13]

With the single exception of the Plumb Plan for which there was substantial although minority backing, all the proposals offered for dealing with the railroads required first and foremost their return to

[12] *Federal Trade Commission* v. *Gratz*, 253 U.S. 421 (1920).

[13] Rogers McVeagh, *The Transportation Act of 1920* (New York: Henry Holt & Co., Inc., 1923).

private operations. This, therefore, was the first business to be attended to. And, as would only have been expected in the politico-economic atmosphere of 1920, care was taken to do generously by the carriers in this transfer of control, a central concern here being the need of these concerns for a good credit rating if they were to remain in a position to provide an adequate service to the public. Because government operation had (deliberately) broken the connection between the rates charged by the carriers and their need for net profits, and because during these months traffic had been routed with no thought of competitive relationships or the postwar positions of particular private enterprise units, the wartime earnings guarantee was extended to September 1, 1920, to ease the difficulties of readjustment to peacetime conditions. Later in the year a one-third increase in rates was allowed to restore the carriers to a paying basis.

But there were a number of reasons why the country was not content with a mere return of the railroads to their private owners. One of these was the conservative bent of the times; another (although this is in part only saying the same thing in a slightly different way) was the fact that a number of interests had special axes to grind.

Most notably in this connection it is to be observed that the law now enacted reflected a basic shift in the public's attitude toward these concerns. Heretofore the spirit behind regulatory enactments had been almost exclusively restrictive, emphasizing only the responsibility of the railroads to the public. Now, for the first time, there was embodied in a railroad control measure a recognition of the responsibility of the public to its common carriers. It was almost as if the railroad industry, having accepted regulation as an unavoidable fact of life, was now determined to play a major role in determining its character.

In two ways the step that was here taken derived directly from *Smyth* v. *Ames*. That decision had, in the first place, unequivocally stated that a regulated public utility must be allowed to earn a fair return on a fair value. It had, in the second place, put particular stress upon the difficult task of valuing utility property. Against this background, but also with a view to taking steps to remedy the evil of watered stock supposed by reformers to be very widespread, Senator La Follette had pressed hard for an enactment requiring a physical valuation of all railroad assets. Such a law had been passed shortly before the war, and this prodigious labor was now getting definitively under way.

Building on these preliminaries, the Transportation Act of 1920 specifically acknowledged the public's affirmative responsibility to see to it that the railroads were given the opportunity to earn a fair return on the value of their property, if a schedule of rates could be found which would yield so favorable a situation. Accordingly the Commission was instructed so to fix the rate level that the

. . . carriers as a whole (or as a whole in each of such rate groups or territories as the Commission may from time to time designate) will, under honest, efficient, and economical management . . . earn an aggregate annual net railway operating income equal, as nearly as may be, to a fair return upon the aggregate value of the railway property of such carriers, held for and used in the service of transportation.

Closely related to this new over-all approach was a group of provisions concerning cooperation among rail carriers. For some time doubts had been developing as to the wisdom of an insistence upon unilateral decision-making by these companies. For one thing, the war experience had demonstrated the superiority of a degree of integration by comparison with complete atomism. For another, the freight rate structure is a complex interrelated whole; an individual rate published by a single carrier may be the key to a hundred important rates on the books of a dozen carriers. Since, furthermore, the railroads were now fairly thoroughly regulated (and hence tamed) it seemed that no harm could come from allowing a certain amount of interrailway cooperation under the supervision of the Interstate Commerce Commission.

And still another factor suggested that a second look might appropriately be taken at intercarrier relationships. It had recently been observed that, although railroads competitive with one another had to charge the same rates, a rate level which would bring a fair return to one railroad would financially starve another, while a level which would enable the latter to earn a fair return would produce extortionate profits for the former. This was the famous weak-and-strong-road problem which has from that day to this remained a sore point in railroad regulation.[14]

Out of this complex of factors there emerged in 1920 a number of sweeping changes in the public attitude toward carrier cooperation. First, the thirty-year ban against pooling was lifted (it will be recalled that this step had already been taken in the offshore shipping field), although all pooling arrangements had to be submitted to the regulatory agency for approval. The Commission was authorized

[14] I. L. Sharfman, *The American Railroad Problem* (New York: The Century Co., 1921).

:o approve other types of unification arrangements, up to and in-
:luding outright merger; and where such approval had been obtained,
antitrust prosecution was to be waived. The Commission was also
lirected to prepare and publish a plan for the consolidation of all
of the nation's railroads into a limited number of groupings, each
one capable of earning a fair return upon its total property.

The most epoch-making of all these changes, however, was a set
of provisions designed to alleviate the weak-and-strong-road problem until such time as it was more permanently resolved through
consolidation. Under this statute any carrier earning a rate of return greater than 6 per cent was required to place one-half of the
excess in a reserve fund which would then be drawn upon in years
when it earned less than 6 per cent, the remainder to be put into a
revolving fund under the jurisdiction of the Commission for loans
to less fortunate railroads. In rationale, this move was only the obverse side of the positive responsibility of the community toward
its utility concerns; if the regulated company is as a matter of right
entitled to a fair return, the public is in turn entitled to impound
for its own use earnings in excess of those considered fair. Known
as the recapture clause, this extremely rigorous application of the
public utility concept was to be bitterly contested in the courts
until its validity was upheld by the Supreme Court.[15]

A third major departure now taken in the regulation of the nation's railroads was the broad power given the Interstate Commerce
Commission over the issuance of securities. For almost fifty years
federal control in this field had been urged in some quarters, and
over a somewhat shorter period several state governments had been
experimenting with this type of regulation. But it is essential to add
that authority over security issuance was not in 1920 the same
control which had first been recommended by reformers at intervals ever since Granger days. On the one hand, from the standpoint
of real reform it was now too late to accomplish much in that way.
On the other hand, the principal beneficiary of this step was the
security holder, and a more conservative interest group could
hardly be found.

Still another major feature of the Transportation Act of 1920 was
the provisions included therein for resolving railway labor disputes.
For some time the nation had been seeking a way of avoiding these
disruptions of service in that vital industry, but with little success.
Unfortunately, moreover, the problem was becoming increasingly
urgent as both carriers and workers found themselves more and

15 *Dayton-Goose Creek Railway Company* v. *United States*, 263 U.S. 456 (1924).

more hemmed in with respect to labor-capital relationships by the growing effectiveness of regulation. The innovation now launched consisted primarily of the creation of a Railroad Labor Board of nine members representing equally management, labor, and the public, commissioned to investigate and make recommendations with respect to the settlement of any labor dispute threatening the flow of commerce.

In addition to these more important provisions, the Transportation Act of 1920 also contained a number of more or less routine extensions of the principles of utility regulation in the railroad field. Thus the Interstate Commerce Commission was given power to approve or disapprove all new construction projects and proposals to abandon service. Power to prescribe minimum as well as maximum rates was granted the Commission, as well as authority over the division of joint fares, rates, or other charges among the carriers. And the Commission's control over the routing of traffic and matters relating to car service and joint use of facilities was very greatly extended.

MERCANTILISM REVISITED[16]

In the field of merchant shipping as with rail transportation it would be misleading to classify immediate postwar developments as either reformist or antireformist as such. Here, too, the principal task was to work out a peacetime policy to replace emergency wartime legislation. For example, it was essential at the earliest possible moment to stop the administrative machinery which had so effectively been producing additional tonnage on government account, and a closely related problem was what to do with the huge fleet now in the hands of the United States Shipping Board. Again, in other words, the most important aspect of what was taking place was not so much the direction now taken by the nation's leaders as the spirit behind these actions.

From this standpoint an excellent point at which to begin an examination of the Merchant Marine Act of 1920 is the process by which it was enacted. On November 8, 1919, the House by an overwhelming vote passed a bill designed only to put an end to the wartime shipping program. In the Senate, however, it occurred to some (and lobbying activities by the shipping interests no doubt contributed heavily to that result) that the opportunity now afforded

[16] Paul M. Zeis, *American Shipping Policy* (Princeton: Princeton University Press, 1938).

for passing basic promotional legislation in this field could hardly be improved upon. Advantage could be taken both of the need for haste (to stop the building of more vessels on the one hand, and to get Congress adjourned on the other) and the freshness of the war experience in the public mind. Following through on that determination, the Senate Commerce Committee wrote and secured the passage of a bill which could not have favored the shipping industry more if this latter group had written the measure itself— and indeed it may have done just that.

A second indication of the motives behind this enactment is its own preamble which declared:

That it is necessary for the national defense and for the proper growth of its foreign and domestic commerce that the United States shall have a merchant marine of the best equipped and most suitable types of vessels sufficient to carry the greater portion of its commerce and serve as a naval or military auxiliary in time of war or national emergency, ultimately to be owned or operated privately by citizens of the United States: and it is hereby declared to be the policy of the United States to do whatever may be necessary to develop and encourage the maintenance of such a merchant marine, and, in so far as may not be inconsistent with the express provisions of this Act, the United States Shipping Board shall, in the disposition of vessels and shipping property as hereinafter provided, in the making of rules and regulations, and in the administration of the shipping laws keep always in view this purpose and object as the primary end to be obtained.

Third, the new merchant marine legislation even sought to reestablish a pattern of preferential treatment for American vessels as against foreign ones which the world had not seen since the repeal of the British trade and navigation acts. Thus it was provided that the special, low domestic freight charges on import and export freight which had long since received Interstate Commerce Commission sanction were not to apply unless the goods involved came in or went out in American bottoms. A more important provision commanded the President of the United States to abrogate and rewrite every treaty renouncing this country's right to impose higher import duties on goods brought to this country in foreign vessels. Still another mercantilist twist was the extension of the monopoly of the coastwise trade long enjoyed by American shipowners to include all the insular possessions of the United States. Actually every one of these policy declarations was soon nullified by administrative inaction, but these later consequences do not alter the clear intention of those who wrote this statute.

Fourth, the United States Shipping Board was specifically directed to use its regulatory authority to protect the American fleet. In the words of the law, the Board was:

To make rules and regulations affecting shipping in the foreign trade not in conflict with law in order to adjust or meet general or special conditions unfavorable to shipping in the foreign trade, whether in any particular trade or upon any particular route or in commerce generally and which arise out of or result from foreign laws, rules, or regulations or from competitive methods or practices employed by owners, operators, agents, or masters of vessels of a foreign country. . . .

But without doubt the clearest expression of the deeper meaning of this law was the policy followed by the Board in disposing of the government fleet. According to the law it was to be turned over to private citizens of the United States "as soon as practicable, consistent with good business methods and the objects and purposes to be attained by this Act"; and in selling government property to private operators the seller was to be guided by the same considerations "that would influence a prudent, solvent business man in the sale of similar vessels or property which he is not forced to sell." In the event, however, these injunctions were given little heed. Sales were made as though this program had to be completed before the next election, and as though the seller were in fact insolvent and forced to realize what he could on his assets.

A few figures will illustrate. After paying private concerns $140 or more per gross ton to have cargo ships built, the government sold out to private operators in the early 1920's for $17 and $18 per gross ton. To a single management interest, the Dollar group, the Board sold for less than $14 million seventeen magnificent passenger liners which had cost the government more than $90 million; and Dollar's company thought so well of these transactions that it paid Dollar a commission of $635,000 for negotiating them. In addition to these sales, furthermore, the Shipping Board followed a policy of withdrawing the government fleet from actual operation in other ways: by selling vessels for scrap and simply by withdrawing them from service. And throughout this period other government property associated with the emergency shipbuilding program was disposed of in a similarly profligate manner.

In all fairness, of course, it must be recognized that ship sales by the government after the war were made under vastly different price conditions than those which had prevailed during that conflict. Moreover, it must also be noted that these sales to private operators were to a degree an alternative to the losses being steadily incurred under government operation. But even at this latter point the case for what was done is by no means clear-cut; the losses under government operation were in almost every instance in part the result of the type of lease contract in use, a contract which by no stretch of the imagination could be termed an instrument designed to protect the Treasury's funds. Over-all, it is difficult to escape the conclusion that the government's disposition of its war-built fleet was carried out with no more regard for the interests of the nonshipping public than the wartime building program.

Only an imperfect impression of the completeness of the nation's turn from reform can be conveyed when attention is directed primarily toward economic policies as such. The full picture does not emerge until the consequences of the postwar reaction for civil rights are brought to the center of the stage. This was a period during which the American people grimly insisted that the social philosophies of their fathers and their grandfathers were good enough, that the new-fangled ideas being brought into this country from Europe as a result of the war were to find no haven here. Nor was this hostility limited to ideas which were really radical. It applied equally to the logical next steps along the road the nation had long been travelling, as, for example, the evolution of business unionism. The result was a phenomenon almost unknown in this country since the days of the burning of witches in old New England; men and women were quite literally persecuted for their beliefs, beliefs which contemplated no graver crime than changes in the status quo to be brought about by democratic processes.

Perilous days were ahead for the American way of life. There is no greater denial of the most fundamental premises of democracy than the insistence that particular policies are to be accepted as Absolutes. Repudiation of reform as such was only a surface manifestation of the problem now confronting the nation. The real challenge lay much deeper.

Questions for Discussion

1. Outline the major factors bringing about the downfall of the prewar reform spirit. Could this result have been avoided?
2. Why were conservatives so eager to discredit the Wilson administration?
3. How radical was organized labor immediately after World War I?
4. Was labor justified in its unionization campaign after World War I? How intelligently did it seek to advance that cause?
5. In what ways did the Supreme Court contribute to the frustration of labor in the post-World War I period?

6. State the rule of reason as of 1920. How careful did industrialists now have to be to avoid violating the antitrust laws?

7. Comment on the problem of regulating the fairness of competition as of 1920.

8. Enumerate the ways in which the Transportation Act of 1920 departed from past precedents in this field.

9. State the weak-and-strong-road problem, and explain how the Transportation Act of 1920 proposed to resolve it.

10. How valid do you consider the rationale behind the recapture clause? Do you think the Supreme Court should have upheld it?

11. What was the central purpose of the Merchant Marine Act of 1920, and how was that objective to be attained?

12. Interpret the 1920 shipping legislation from the standpoint of public interest.

13. Why is an attack on civil rights so threatening to a democratic way of life?

Chapter 16

New Problems for a New Age

Conservative though it was, however, the government had no choice but to grapple as best it could with the major problems of the postwar period. Partly as a result of the war itself, and partly because of the stage of economic evolution the United States was now passing through (and, indeed, insofar as the war was a factor here, it did little more than telescope changes which would have come about in any event), the nation was confronted with several difficult situations it had never had to contend with before.

THE RIDDLE OF MONETARY POLICY[1]

One such situation, the first to put in an appearance, was the problem of monetary management posed by the existence of the new Federal Reserve System. Note that no particular problem of this kind had been contemplated when the money and banking mechanism had been revolutionized just prior to the war. Rather a central banking organization had been created to resolve specific difficulties—those created by financial panics—and it had been confidently supposed that these gains would virtually all be net. It was, therefore, somewhat disconcerting to learn that the new instrumentality itself raised important public policy questions.

The problem was this. In order that it might effectively serve the purpose for which it was created, the Federal Reserve System had been equipped with several basic tools. It could raise or lower the rediscount rate, the charge assessed against member banks who deposited commercial paper as collateral for central bank loans; it could raise or lower the reserve requirements, the proportion of loans and discounts member banks were required to hold in the form of cash; it could engage in open market operations, adding to

[1] Paul M. Warburg, *The Federal Reserve System* (New York: The Macmillan Co., 1930).

or reducing the quantity of securities held in its own portfolio. One set of these tools (raising the rediscount rate, increasing reserve requirements, and selling securities) would tighten the money market and hence operate to restrain the level of business activity. The other set (lowering the rediscount rate, reducing reserve requirements, and buying securities) would make money easier to obtain and hence tend to expand business activity.

To be sure, these tools were as yet fairly blunt and unwieldy, in large part because they had been placed in the hands of thirteen different groups of people geographically distributed over the entire country rather than a single group located in Washington. But even so the situation now was in marked contrast with that which the Federal Reserve Act had replaced. Then the availability of money and credit had been the outcome of the uncoordinated decisions of so many bankers that under normal circumstances no one of them had felt any over-all responsibility. In the "Panic of 1907" J. P. Morgan and those around him had made a valiant attempt to create a higher level of integration, but had discovered that the weapons then at hand were inadequate. What men in high places were now learning was that the price which had to be paid for the tools needed to combat (or prevent) monetary emergencies was the responsibility for managing them in the public interest when no emergency was in sight.

The power of the controls at the disposal of the Federal Reserve System was first demonstrated during the war. Prior to this, every major war in which the United States had been involved had been financed in substantial part by the issuance of paper money. But so effective was the new banking mechanism at creating credit that in World War I, the most strenuous war effort in the nation's history to date, no paper money at all was issued. On the one hand the Federal Reserve Banks loaned citizens many of the funds needed to buy war bonds, and on the other hand these organizations bought large quantities of government bonds on their own account. In these two ways the central bank helped the Treasury get the money it needed over and above the amount it secured from taxation and selling bonds to nonbank investors.

The war period presented one kind of a test for the new banking system. No sooner was the war over than a challenge of a different order appeared.[2] Whereas during the war federal reserve credit had contributed to a situation agreed by everyone to be inflationary but broadly countenanced in the interest of the war production

[2] P. A. Samuelson and E. E. Hagen, *After the War, 1918-1920* (Washington, D.C.: National Resources Planning Board, 1943).

program, after the signing of the Armistice (although inflation continued for a time unabated) it was by no means agreed that this condition should continue to be tolerated. The question was raised, in other words, whether the Federal Reserve System should not use the power at its disposal to dampen down the postwar boom enough to check the upward spiral of prices.

It is characteristic of decisions in this as well as many other areas that they cannot be postponed. Life has a way of going on, and to a considerable extent it must be lived one way or another as it goes along. In the field of monetary policy steps are either taken to curb an inflation or that state of affairs is permitted. Whichever approach is taken, a decision has been made. In the case at hand, two successive policy lines were followed. For some twelve months after the cessation of hostilities, little restraining influence was exerted. Then, early in 1920, restrictive measures were instituted. And therein lies an interesting, if somewhat tragic, story.

Whether the central bank authorities would have acted sooner if they had been free to do so is a moot question. The fact of the matter is, however, that they were not free. Because armament expenditures did not end abruptly, and because the federal government felt it necessary to extend large credits to our erstwhile allies abroad, the Treasury continued to run a sizable deficit after the

TABLE 12. A MAJOR COMPLICATION

Fiscal Year	Federal Deficit (−) (millions of dollars)
1916	+48
1917	−853
1918	−9,033
1919	−13,371
1920	+212

Source: Bureau of the Census, *Historical Statistics of the United States, 1789-1945*, p. 296.

war. As a result monetary policy could not be decided apart from grave issues of fiscal policy; steps could not be taken to restrain the boom without at the same time running the risk that the government would have difficulty selling its securities. The men then in charge of the nation's banking policy were unwilling to assume this responsibility, and it is probable that no group of men competent to function at this level would have done so.

Late in 1919 the rediscount rate began to rise, and this trend continued until mid-1920 when the New York rate stood at 7 per cent. While this development was under way the forces making for inflation began to weaken, and the level of economic activity commenced to slacken. For a time this movement was gradual, but as it gained momentum it turned into one of the most violent downturns in the nation's history. Thanks to the new money and credit structure this decline was not accompanied by panic; obviously much had been achieved from that standpoint. But it was nonetheless a bitter lesson for the nation's leadership. Not only was there a necessity for constant management of the country's monetary affairs, but even with such supervision the economy might still go into a tailspin.

Of course, there were the inevitable post mortems and recriminations. On a *post hoc ergo propter hoc* basis there was reason for charging that the Federal Reserve authorities had caused the collapse. A more mature judgment, however, based on additional years of experience with the central banking device as well as a fuller experience with economic depressions, suggests that this causal relationship was overdrawn. There seem, on the one hand, to have been enough deflationary forces at work to explain what happened on different grounds. And it is now well understood, on the other hand, that the rate of interest standing alone is not a particularly significant determinant of business activity. At the same time it was another very sobering thought to those who held this power in their hands that, though they were compelled to use it, its use could boomerang.

With this episode a new major function of government may be said to have been officially launched. Never again would the heretofore sacrosanct gold standard be the primary arbiter of monetary affairs. Never again would it be questioned that the federal government must assume a large share of the responsibility for the effective functioning of the exchange mechanism. It was a task neither demanded by liberals nor relished by conservatives. No group had either pressed for or fought against its acceptance. For more than a century the United States had lived under a Constitution commanding the central government to manage the nation's money supply. At long last the requirements of a maturing capitalism was giving substance to a provision which had never before been taken especially seriously.

ENTER THE FARM BLOC

It was in the middle of the most painful part of this economic downturn that the nation was given the opportunity to make official its judgment concerning the Wilson administration. There was really never any doubt about what that judgment would be. Two years earlier, in the off-year elections, voters had given the President a Republican Congress with which to finish out his term of office. This halfway measure was now broadened by giving these legislators a man of their own political persuasion to sign the bills they passed. From this point forward (for a while, at least) conservatives were to have complete freedom to continue the policies which eight years earlier had been a major cause of their crushing electoral defeat.

It was Warren G. Harding himself who more accurately than anyone else put his finger on the pulse of the postwar public. "America's first need," he said, "is not nostrums, but normalcy." Immediately that term became one of the watchwords of the day, and millions of citizens all over the country bent their efforts toward finding a way to "return to normalcy."

For conservatives, now in full charge of the nation's affairs after a long period of sitting on the sidelines, it was especially easy to give content to this idea. Normalcy meant laissez faire, and although the drift in that direction before Harding's inauguration had been unmistakable, the time had obviously come to move even more rapidly along that road. Unfortunately for these interests, however, this proved to be more easily said than done. No sooner were the Republicans firmly in power than there arose a number of other problems, and in grappling with these difficulties the restoration of government by and for businessmen was delayed.

One of these had to do with the farmer. For two reasons, furthermore, this challenge was particularly frustrating. In the first place it was as true during the 1920's as during the nineteenth century that the Republican party could not remain in power without the support of the agricultural Middle West. This meant that enough concessions would still have to be made to farmers to convince them that supporting Republican candidates for office was in their best interest. Still worse, in the second place, the farmer was rapidly becoming a much more effectively organized interest group. The recent innovation of the county agent, a competent government employee paid to look after the farmer's interests in virtually every agricultural county in the country, had been largely responsible for the creation of a nationwide farmers' organization of unprecedented effectiveness. This was the American Farm Bureau Federation, long to be the most powerful agricultural pressure group in the country. To the intense dismay of laissez faire enthusiasts, the rise of such a group meant that the concessions which would need to be given to farmers would have to be substantial; token concessions offered with tongue in cheek would clearly not suffice.

The farmer's problem, the reason it was so certain that substantial concessions would be demanded, grew most immediately out of the war and its aftermath. Abnormal war conditions had on the one hand resulted in a considerable expansion of the output of most agricultural commodities, and on the other hand pushed the prices of these products extremely high. As a result American agriculture was vulnerable to any weakening of demand for its output, a state of affairs bound to appear sooner or later. For a time after the Armistice, farm prices retained their wartime relationship with other prices; Europe could not quickly return to her prewar sources in any event, and American foreign policy also contributed to this situation in the form of liberal reconstruction loans to European allies. But as world economic conditions improved, and particularly when the United States abruptly terminated government loans abroad, the prices of American farm products began to fall off sharply.[3] The signal for the beginning of this painful contraction was the ending of the government's guaranty of the price of wheat in the middle of 1920.

TABLE 13. ORIGIN OF THE FARM BLOC

Year	Gross Farm Income (billions of dollars)	Index of Prices Paid by Farmers (1910-14 = 100)
1915	8.0	105
1917	13.1	149
1919	17.7	202
1921	10.5	152

Source: Bureau of the Census, *Historical Statistics of the United States, 1789-1945*, p. 99.

All this, be it noted, took place before the general economic downturn overwhelmed the rest of the economy. With that development agricultural well-being received another severe setback, and by the spring of 1921 the farmers of the country were in as unfavorable a position relative to the rest of the nation as ever before in the country's history. The prices of most farm products fell to between one-third and one-half of the postwar high, and

[3] Edwin G. Nourse, *American Agriculture and the European Market* (New York: McGraw-Hill Book Co., Inc., 1924).

some items became almost unsaleable. Given this underlying situation, and adding to it the role of the Federal Reserve System in the postwar inflation and the subsequent collapse, and the fact that it was at this critical time that the freight rate increase allowed under the Transportation Act of 1920 went into effect, it is understandable that farmers felt they had legitimate grievances against their country's economic organization.

This, then, was the context within which the newly-formed Farm Bureau began to organize for action in the farmer's behalf, even before Woodrow Wilson's administration was replaced.[4] Two pieces of legislation in particular were pushed. One looked toward the revival of the War Finance Corporation for the purpose of financing exports of farm products; the other provided for substantial tariff increases for a long list of agricultural products. In the waning days of his administration, President Wilson vetoed both measures. He was a trade liberal to the core, and was unwilling to be responsible for creating major obstacles to the free flow of goods across national boundaries. Especially, moreover, did he feel that these actions would not be appropriate to America's new status as a creditor nation.

But desperate farmers were not to be deterred by the disapproval of a repudiated and ailing President. The War Finance Corporation measure was passed over his veto; the agricultural tariff was put before President Harding, who signed it without a murmur of protest. Regrettably, however, both for farmers and for those eager to get on with the business of placing the nation once again on a laissez faire basis, neither of these steps was particularly beneficial. This was in part because they did not strike at the heart of the farmer's problem, but there were special factors at work as well. For its part the War Finance Corporation was not given sufficient funds to accomplish stated objectives. And on the tariff side, two major disabilities stood in the way of the results sought. First, most agricultural staples were on an export basis, and could hence not be aided by import duties. Second, the farmer's insistence upon a tariff was utilized by manufacturers to secure the passage of the Fordney-McCumber Tariff containing the highest general duty level in the nation's history. What some few farmers gained from protection for their own products was more than counterbalanced by the burden imposed upon all other farmers by this increase in the industrial tariff.

[4] D. F. Houston, *Eight Years With Wilson's Cabinet* (Garden City: Doubleday, Page & Co., 1926).

In May of 1921 the organization of farmers to secure relief from economic distress took on an even more ominous form. A bipartisan group of powerful Senate leaders first met in the office of Senator Kenyon of Iowa to consider ways of expediting legislation designed to aid agriculture. Significantly, one of the sponsors of this meeting was Gray Silver, legislative representative for the Farm Bureau, and much of the discussion consisted of an exposition by Silver of the farmer's problems and needs as seen by his organization. Joined later to a limited extent by a bipartisan group in the House having similar sympathies, the so-called "Farm Bloc" was a link between agricultural leaders which could hardly have been more direct—or more powerful.[5]

Somewhat awed by this aggressive show of farmer strength, conservative leaders pressed hard for an early adjournment of Congress. But farmer aspirations were not to be so easily sidestepped; these men could recognize the "bum's rush" as quickly as anyone. When they made it clear that they could prevent adjournment, and that they proposed to do so until certain of the farmers' demands were met, the Harding administration quickly came to terms. And as a result of this kind of pressure politics, the Farm Bloc over the next two years succeeded in getting passed an unbelievable volume of legislation benefitting agriculture.

The first major item on this list consisted of converting an important phase of the meat packing industry into a public utility. For a long time farmers had felt that these concerns ran their businesses to suit only themselves, and that they cooperated with one another in order more effectively to exploit the farmer in the bargain. Over the years, too, the possibility of bringing effective antitrust action against these giants had gradually ceased to be considered as a workable alternative to the status quo. One of the first investigations undertaken by the Federal Trade Commission had indicated that most of the collusive practices the Supreme Court had enjoined 15 years before still persisted, and this body had suggested that only public ownership and operation would constitute an effective reform. Although so extreme a remedy was not seriously considered, steps were nonetheless taken to trim these concerns down to size. First, through a decree arising out of another antitrust action, the packing end of this business was separated from the stockyard end. Second, the Packers and Stockyards Act of 1921 required every stockyard facility operating in interstate com-

[5] Arthur Capper, *The Agricultural Bloc* (New York: Harcourt, Brace & Co., Inc., 1922).

merce to register with and submit to regulation by the Secretary of Commerce. Under this supervision these concerns are expected (just as any other public utility) to furnish reasonable service upon request at just, reasonable, and nondiscriminatory prices.

Nor was the contribution of this enactment to evolving government-business relationships limited to its success in overcoming a critical bargaining disability of the livestock producer. When this statute was challenged in the courts, it was decisively upheld in a way which went far beyond the case at bar. Counsel for its opponents, taking their cue from the judicial attitudes implicit in *Hammer* v. *Dagenhart,* argued that the activities placed under control were not interstate commerce, and hence were not a proper subject for federal regulation. The Supreme Court, however, would not have it so, applying instead concepts already implicit in a steadily lengthening list of antitrust cases.[6] To be sure, the Justices were not yet ready to use the interstate commerce clause as a basic "police power" for the federal government, but the concept of a "stream of commerce" vitally affected by concerns not themselves engaged in commerce in its traditional meaning as developed in *Stafford* v. *Wallace* provided a most useful precedent when that time did come.

As a second major Farm Bloc achievement grain exchanges were given a similar treatment. Although futures markets perform a function of vital significance to a modern economy, they also provide opportunities for manipulation which may operate to the disadvantage of the larger public. To minimize these results (for example, to prevent speculators from rigging the market to the detriment of the price received by the farmer), the Grain Futures Act of 1922 was passed. Under its terms all futures markets which affected interstate commerce were required to submit to regulation by the Secretary of Agriculture, whose responsibility it was to see to it that all traders received full information about market conditions and to prevent unfair and deceptive practices. This regulation was neither as comprehensive nor so rigorously enforced as that over the packers, but here again an important grievance was laid to rest. And on this foundation fourteen years later a much more impressive structure was to be built.

Still a third key item had as its principal purpose assisting farmers to deal with middlemen more effectively. Because so many farmers believed that cooperation offered a way out of their distress (and indeed encouraging the cooperative movement was the most im-

[6] *Stafford* v. *Wallace,* 258 U.S. 495 (1922).

portant nonlegislative objective of the Farm Bureau at this time),
a law was passed in 1922 bestowing special privileges upon these
organizations. Where a cooperative was genuine—as distinguished
from the cooperative so called only to attract custom from farmers
who would otherwise have traded elsewhere, or organized for the
purpose of securing Capper-Volstead benefits for free enterprise
operations—it was to be free from prosecution under the antitrust
laws (the Clayton Act exemption was, in other words, strengthened)
and relieved of the necessity of paying federal income taxes. The
law's definition of a genuine agricultural cooperative was a concern
organized to process, handle, or market farm products, which limited voting power to one vote per person, paid no more than 8 per
cent dividends on membership capital, and did as great a volume
of business with members as with nonmembers.[7]

And still a fourth important piece of legislation was enacted in
the farmer's behalf. Here the focus of attention was his long-standing complaint about the inadequacy of the credit facilities available
to him. The Federal Reserve Act and the Warehouse Act had made
short-term credit more easily obtainable by farmers by making crop
harvest paper a more valuable credit resource. Under the terms of
the Federal Land Bank Act the farmer's need for long-term credit
to purchase land and to make permanent improvements thereon
had been recognized. Now the in-between situation was made the
subject of special legislation, the need of farmers for six-month to
three-year capital for the purchase of livestock and equipment. The
Intermediate Credits Act of 1923 created federal intermediate credit
banks in each city already containing a federal land bank, both types
of banks to be under the same management. Here also credit was
to be extended either through the medium of private banking organizations or through farmer cooperatives.

In addition to these larger changes in the status quo, farmers
succeeded during these years in turning several smaller situations
to their advantage. An adjustment was forced in the thinking behind federal aid to road-building in the direction of more federal
funds for farm-to-market roads. The life of the War Finance Corporation was extended for still another year, although by now the
principal function of this agency was rescuing illiquid banks in
farming areas from bankruptcy. An amendment to the Federal Reserve Act stipulated that at least one member of the Federal Reserve
Board was to be an agricultural representative. And largely at the

[7] Edwin G. Nourse, *Legal Status of Agricultural Cooperation* (New York: The
Macmillan Co., 1927).

instigation of farmer groups a 10 per cent reduction in freight rates was ordered.

THE FIRST "SICK" INDUSTRY[8]

Another problem growing most directly out of the war experience but more fundamentally due to certain underlying economic trends had to do with bituminous coal. This industry, to an extent even more pronounced than agriculture, suffered readjustment difficulties after 1918. When this segment of the economy failed to reorient itself to the return to peace as "normalcy" failed to reappear, the nation was confronted with another situation resembling that which now plagued the farmer.

Although this terminology did not become current during the "roaring 20's," when it was the fashion not to concede that anything was wrong with the American economy, bituminous coal production became during that decade what has since come to be known as a "sick" industry. This designation is applied to those branches of the economy which are overextended but which for some reason are unable to get rid of the excess resources invested therein. A review of some of the major economic characteristics of the bituminous side of the coal industry will make it clear why it has become by common consent the outstanding example of that phenomenon.

First and foremost, here is an industry which satisfies almost all the requirements of what economists have termed pure competition. The product cannot be differentiated; there is no reason for preferring the output of one producer over that of another. At the same time, there is such a large number of producers that no one firm or group of firms can exercise any significant influence over price. Deposits are widely scattered, and mining operations can be commenced on a small scale at relatively little expense. There is, therefore, a high degree of freedom of entry.

By contrast, in the second place, the other side of this market is highly organized. Major customers are railroads, public utilities, and steel manufacturers, concerns possessing enough bargaining power to keep the price of coal at a minimum level. Furthermore, the demand for coal is relatively inelastic—in large part because the demand for the products of major users is also inelastic. The result is that to whatever extent oligopolistic buyers depress coal prices, the gross revenues of producers are reduced, for a lower price results in a less than proportionate increase in volume.

[8] W. H. Hamilton and H. R. Wright, *A Way of Order for Bituminous Coal* (New York: The Macmillan Co., 1928); and E. E. Hunt, F. G. Tryon, and J. H. Willets, *What the Coal Commission Found* (Baltimore: The Williams & Wilkins Co., 1925).

But if unprofitable operations arise in a free enterprise economy, it is the function of the price and profit system to bring about the necessary adjustments. Factors of production which are poorly paid relative to rewards elsewhere are supposed in theory to seek alternative employment, this shift continuing until the factors remaining in the low-paying industry are better paid. In the production of bituminous coal, however, this tendency is not strong enough to offset several powerful forces working in the opposite direction. A mine once put into production commits its owner to certain fixed costs which must be met even if output ceases. Property taxes are typically assessed on the basis of the estimated value of deposits. Even a closed mine must be ventilated to prevent the accumulation of dangerous gases, pumped to prevent damage by flooding, and timbered to avoid costly cave-ins. Coal that has been mined, moreover, can not be stored except at substantial cost, if only because it must be moved away from the vicinity of the mine to permit operations to continue. As a result of such factors producers are impelled to produce at capacity and to sell all that they produce.

It can readily be seen how profound would be the consequences of a World War I for an industry so organized. While the war lasted

TABLE 14. A SICK INDUSTRY IS BORN

Year	Value of Bituminous Coal Production (billions of dollars)
1914	.5
1916	.7
1918	1.5
1920	2.1
1922	1.3
1924	1.1

Source: Bureau of the Census, *Historical Statistics of the United States, 1789-1945*, p. 142.

there continued to be a tremendous pressure upon bituminous producers to expand output, a pressure arising both out of the increased demand at home and the immobilization of producing resources in Europe. As was to be expected, in other words, an increase in the price of coal from $1.25 to $9.50 a ton brought about a substantial increase in production. But when the war ended, simultaneously allowing domestic demand to taper off and overseas production to be resumed, disaster struck almost at once. The price fell abruptly to one-third of the wartime peak, falling in this process much farther than the industry's cost of production, while output remained more than 100,000,000 tons per year above the prewar production rate. Worst of all, this situation did not improve during a decade of post-war prosperity. The price of coal continued to fall, production levels refused to adjust themselves to the new conditions, and by the end of the 1920's three operators out of five were producing at a loss.

No matter how tragic their consequences, developments such as these, however, would not necessarily be important to a discussion of government-business relationships. Only insofar as the government elects to intervene does that issue arise. But neither bituminous coal miners nor their employers were politically powerful enough (as farmers had been) to force their problem to the forefront, and business leaders had no great interest in taking steps either to advance the price of coal or to reduce the resources engaged in its production. Thus this problem might have limped along indefinitely without any action on the part of the government if another consideration had not also been involved. Bituminous coal was then as it is today an indispensable industrial raw material. When, therefore, the economic difficulties of the industry began to appear in the form of a chronic labor problem (by far the largest single cost of production in this industry is wages), it was apparent that serious attention by the public might be necessary.

During the coal strike of 1919 wartime regulatory powers over the industry were reinstituted, and a Bituminous Coal Commission was created to arbitrate this labor dispute. Then, when this crisis had passed, these government responsibilities were speedily terminated; an age struggling to minimize government activities would naturally lose no time ridding itself of such obvious remnants of the wartime government expansion. In 1922, however, after the operators had refused to renew the 1920 agreement, another strike made re-institution of some controls to insure an equitable distribution of a limited coal supply almost mandatory. And this time, after the crisis was over, public responsibility was not immediately abandoned. A United States Coal Commission was created to investigate conditions in the industry and make recommendations concerning a permanent government control program.

The report of the Coal Commission was conservative in the best tradition of that day, although it did suggest that a modicum of stand-by control should be established. Thus it believed that a broadening of the Interstate Commerce Commission's authority over coal distribution would be appropriate, and that an investigation of all labor disputes in the industry should be made and a full report thereon presented to the government. But conservative though these proposals were, they were too liberal for the 1920's; the Commission's recommendations were a dead letter almost before they had been prepared. And of course while conservative proposals were being thus ignored, there could be no hope of a public hearing for a suggestion put forward by coal miners' groups that the mines be nationalized. During this era such an idea (along with the Plumb Plan in the railroad industry) was simply treated as an offshoot of the Communist Revolution.

CONSERVATION FOR THE MACHINE AGE[9]

For an entirely different set of reasons the nation found itself during this decade also on the verge of adding the drilling end of the petroleum industry to its lengthening list of specially supervised segments of the economy. Because of the unique character of this branch of production, it was becoming apparent that operation on a purely free enterprise basis had grave shortcomings.

Crude petroleum is found in its natural state in irregularly-shaped reservoirs between layers of rock. With the oil in these nature-made storehouses are also deposits of natural gas under heavy pressure. When the upper fold of rock entrapping gas and petroleum is penetrated, the gas expands forcing the oil to the surface. If wells draining from a given pool are spaced according to the dictates of modern science, maximum advantage can be taken of this natural propellant. If care is not taken, however, improper drilling methods will result in a loss of the gas as it escapes, this being a valuable product in its own right, and the wastage of gas pressure to push the oil out which in turn means that expensive pumping equipment must be installed and that much oil otherwise obtainable will mingle with the surrounding water and be lost.

Unfortunately, too, property law in America has operated to maximize this difficulty. An individual putting down an oil well on his own land is considered the owner of all oil obtainable through it regardless of how much of that oil actually comes from beneath the land of his neighbors. This arrangement encourages the first individual to put down numerous wells instead of the number best calculated to make most efficient use of available resources, while his neighbors are virtually compelled to put down wells of their own in order to get in on the quick wealth thus obtainable. In other words, whereas the conservation of an irreplaceable resource demands that

[9] M. Murphy Blakeley (ed.), *Conservation of Oil and Gas* (Chicago: American Bar Association, 1949).

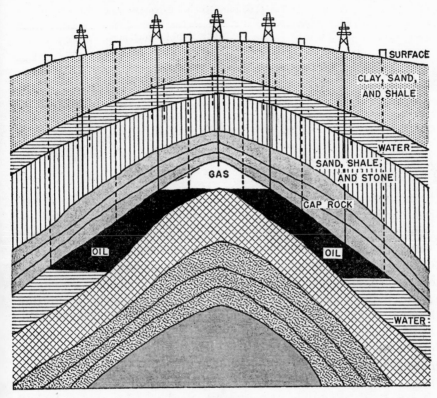

SURFACE

CLAY, SAND, AND SHALE

WATER

SAND, SHALE, AND STONE

GAS

CAP ROCK

OIL

OIL

WATER

Fig. 2

the takings from a pool be managed as a unit, American law puts a premium upon an extreme atomization.

Because American property law is so written, furthermore, other types of waste appear. An excessive amount of oil is brought to the surface (that is, more than can be sold at remunerative prices) where it must be either stored at great cost or sold at a loss to be used in ways that would not be economical if more scientific methods of extraction had been used.

Little thought had been given to this problem in the early days of the industry, particularly after the smaller pools in Pennsylvania were supplanted by the fabulously rich fields in the Southwest. But it was now evident that the era now dawning was to be in a significant sense a gasoline age. The tractor, the automobile, and the airplane were all now obviously destined to have a great future, and to contribute much to the life of the people in the process.

TABLE 15. THE GASOLINE ENGINE COMES OF AGE

Year	Petroleum Production (millions of barrels)
1895	53
1905	135
1915	281
1925	764
1935	997
1945	1,714

Source: Bureau of the Census, *Historical Statistics of the United States, 1789-1945*, p. 146.

Equally important, perhaps, was the fact that the United States had just participated in a world war demonstrating how vital the internal-combustion engine was to be in modern warfare. These considerations, plus the fact that petroleum reserves were not only irreplaceable but exhaustible, began to turn men's minds in the direction of enforced conservation.

But these considerations were in one sense only the supporting framework for the tentative, halting measures now taken in this field. Furthermore, the significance of the war at this point was by no means limited to its decisive launching of the "automobile age." A more important fact here is that the petroleum industry, in much the same way as the bituminous coal industry, was in a seriously disorganized condition. Here, too, both demand and supply had been tremendously increased by the war effort. And here also resource investment did not respond promptly to the much altered postwar conditions. On the other hand, however, one important difference did obtain. Oil producers were in a much more favorable position than their bituminous coal counterparts to bring about appropriate changes in public policy, perhaps in large part because there were so many fewer of them.

Understandably, the first steps taken were by the states; Texas took the lead, passing a law in 1919 giving her Railroad Commission authority to prevent physical waste. This example was followed by others, until today all the important oil-producing states have conservation statutes. Regulations cover such diverse matters as well-spacing, methods of drilling, casing, shooting, and plugging wells, the flaring of gas, open storage, oil-gas and oil-water ratios, and the repressuring of pools for secondary recovery. By careful attention to such factors much progress has been made, although full unitization is not compulsory and is hence quite rare.

So critical was this problem felt to be in the early 1920's that for a time the federal government toyed with the idea of taking a major part in petroleum conservation. Fuel conservation is not, after all, far removed from water power and lumber conservation, although this concern about the nation's petroleum supply by the administration even then reeling from the Teapot Dome scandal did have its humorous side. In 1924 a Federal Oil Conservation Board was established to study the problem. Deeply conservative but at the same time unwilling to take a stand against post-World War I conservationism, this group did go so far as to propose interstate compacts as a supply control technique, on the ground that action by the states would be at once easier and more effective if these separate efforts were coordinated. (No interstate oil compacts were negotiated in the 1920's.) And when the industry, fully in the spirit of those times, suggested that a quota and market-sharing system be worked out with foreign producers, the Board saw no objection. However, the Attorney General ruled that such a plan would be a violation of the Sherman Act, and therefore nothing came of this either.

The "American Plan"

Not only were conservatives and the governments they controlled leaning over backward to keep government from exercising responsibilities that might adversely affect private property rights, but they were also working actively to see to it that threats to property rights did not develop in other quarters.

For example, the greatest of care was required during these years to prevent radicals from imposing greater tax burdens on the well-to-do. To be sure, the battle launched on this front was offensive rather than defensive, for the income tax amendment together with the problem of financing a major war had already brought into being a less regressive tax structure than conservatives deemed desirable, but protective action was no less necessary for this fact.

To remedy this situation President Harding pressed into service as Secretary of the Treasury none other than Andrew Mellon, perhaps the richest man in the country and certainly one of its greatest financiers. Mellon set to work with a will to eliminate as many upper-bracket taxes as he could, substituting for these where necessary more and higher excises. The result was a tax structure excellently adapted to rapid capital accumulation and hence economic development but less well suited to the needs of what many would have termed equitable distribution. (It was, by the way, during this decade that the idea of income filtering down from higher- to lower-income receivers was first widely used in this country as a justification for income concentration.

However, it was not taxation which posed the gravest threat to property rights during these years. That distinction must surely be reserved for the labor movement. One of the dominant ideas behind business decision-making now became the proposition that the progress labor had made during the war would have to be dealt with soon and drastically or those advances might solidify into permanent gains. Accordingly a more formidable assault was launched against the workingman's organizations than had ever been seen in the United States.

A first attack here, and one of the most fundamental, was a concerted drive to eradicate the union shop, a program especially appropriate for the early years of this decade when economic depression had already put the nation's workers on the defensive.[10] The keynote for this drive was struck in 1921 at a meeting of the National Conference of State Manufacturers' Associations which went on record as demanding that workers "have the right to work when they please, for whom they please, and on whatever terms are mutually agreed upon between employee and employer. . . ." Note especially here the use of the word "employee," carefully stated in the singular. Taking advantage, furthermore, of the antiforeignism of the times, this assault by Americans on other Americans was widely advertised as the "American Plan." Before the decade was over almost every conceivable resource, private and governmental, had been utilized to root out and destroy as many nests of "revolutionary" union shopism as possible.

Another important way in which the government could assist businessmen with their labor problems was to stand by them in time of strike.[11] Thus in the coal dispute of 1922, the President offered the full cooperation of the federal government (and of course the state governments involved could also be counted on at such a time) in protecting property or workers desiring to work. In connection with a railroad shopmen's strike in the same year, President Harding indicated even more clearly how helpful the United States government could be on such occasions, and simultaneously made

10 Savel Zimand, *The Open Shop Drive* (New York: Bureau of Industrial Research, 1921).

11 Edward Berman, *Labor Disputes and the President of the United States* (New York: Columbia University Press, 1924); and E. E. Witte, *The Government in Labor Disputes* (New York: McGraw-Hill Book Co., Inc., 1932).

plain to laborers how little assistance they were to receive from the recent Railway Labor Act. Just prior to the depression the Railway Labor Board had awarded railroad shop workers a 22 per cent wage increase. When, after the economic decline, the railroads objected to these gains, the President appointed a different slate of public representatives, thus paving the way for a downward adjustment. The resulting strike was then met with an injunction based on the government's power over interstate commerce and the antitrust laws.

While the federal government was operating so successfully on this front in Washington, state legislators in faraway Kansas were experimenting with a different technique for accomplishing an almost identical objective. Here a number of basic industries (for example, food processing) were declared to be public utilities, and compulsory arbitration of labor disputes therein was decreed as a substitute for strikes. (How characteristic of this era that an instrument for reform was in this way employed in the interest of an almost reactionary conservatism.) So sweeping was this innovation, and so readily might it have been utilized in other states, that labor was most fortunate to be spared this anguish by the intervention of the Supreme Court. A majority of the Justices refused to concede that the meat packing industry was a public utility; indispensable though it was, it was not the natural monopoly type of operation that had heretofore been considered to have the status of a public utility.[12]

But though the Supreme Court took a position on this occasion which coincided with labor's preferences, this was the exception rather than the rule during the 1920's. In quick succession that body delivered a series of blows at the labor movement which were as crippling as those received from any source.

The first of these was a judgment by the Court on Congress' second attempt to bring an end to child labor. Carefully avoiding the constitutional pitfalls of the earlier endeavor, the new act provided for a 10 per cent tax on the net profits of any person or firm employing children as workers. The result was that when the law was attacked as a regulation of interstate commerce, the government was compelled to take the naive position that the measure was actually only a tax. The Court made short work of this subterfuge:

In the light of these features of the act, a court must be blind not to see that the so-called tax is imposed to stop the employment of children within the age limits prescribed. Its prohibitory and regulatory effect and purpose are

[12] *Wolff Packing Company* v. *Court of Industrial Relations*, 262 U.S. 522 (1923).

palpable. All others can see and understand this. How can we properly shut our minds to it?[13]

It is perhaps not inappropriate to wonder if a frontal assault on this problem based squarely on *Stafford* v. *Wallace* in defiance of *Hammer* v. *Dagenhart* would not have had a better chance of success.

A similar opportunity was given the Court in connection with a law specifying minimum wages for women employed in the District of Columbia. Attacked as an abrogation of the freedom of contract guaranteed by the Constitution, this measure too was speedily condemned by the nation's highest judicial tribunal. And after unequivocally declaring the law invalid, the Supreme Court proceeded to add insult to injury by moralizing as follows:

> To sustain the individual freedom of action contemplated by the Constitution, is not to strike down the common good but to exalt it; for surely the good of society as a whole cannot be better served than by the preservation against arbitrary restraint of the liberties of its constituent members.[14]

But an even more telling blow on behalf of private property was yet to come. The sickness of the coal industry resulted early in the 1920's in a plea to the United Mine Workers from unionized operators that an active campaign be launched to organize unorganized coal producing firms. This was done by means of an organization strike, and as one consequence the Coronado Coal Company brought an action against the union demanding triple damages under the Sherman Act. The offense charged was the prevention of shipments to other states of that coal which was not mined because of the strike.

The issue here posed for the Court could not have been more farreaching. A decision upholding the company would in effect make illegal virtually every important strike. And while the Supreme Court, speaking through Chief Justice William Howard Taft, was not eager to take so drastic a step, neither was it willing to give workers and their organizations a clean bill of health.

A neat judicial strategy was employed to resolve this dilemma. The interruption of commerce claimed by the company was held to be indirect only, and hence not illegal. However, the Court went on to say, if it could be demonstrated that the primary intent of the strike was to keep coal out of interstate trade channels, a case along the lines desired by the company could perhaps be made.[15] Ac-

[13] *Bailey* v. *Drexel Furniture Company*, 250 U.S. 20 (1922).
[14] *Adkins* v. *Children's Hospital*, 261 U.S. 525 (1923).
[15] *United Mine Workers* v. *Coronado Coal Company*, 259 U.S. 344 (1922).

cordingly a new suit was brought, charging this time that the central purpose of the strike had been to keep coal produced by nonunion men from reaching markets supplied with coal produced by union miners. A little fanciful, perhaps, when viewed in terms of the fundamental realities involved, but the company got its triple damages.[16]

In one way only was labor benefitted by a deliberate public policy during this period. The doors of America, always heretofore open to oppressed and aggrieved people from Europe, were now tightly closed. Henceforth American workers would not have to contend for jobs with destitute immigrants accustomed to working for low wages; never again would employers be able to hire almost any number of strikebreakers that might be wanted simply by going to one of the nation's great ports. But this change of policy was not inaugurated because of the benefit to be derived therefrom by labor. Rather conservatives were so convinced that un-American ideas were coming into the country with these newcomers that they were willing to give up the benefits they were deriving from free immigration.

Thus scourged on all sides, labor was no doubt tempted to join

TABLE 16.   FRUITS OF THE AMERICAN PLAN

Year	Labor Union Membership
1900	791,000
1910	2,116,000
1920	5,034,000
1930	3,632,000

Source: Bureau of the Census, *Historical Statistics of the United States, 1789-1945*, p. 72.

the union of town and country offered by third-party candidate La Follette in 1924. If, furthermore, such a cooperation could have been worked out, it is likely that the New Deal (speaking figuratively) would have started the following year. But the times were not yet quite right. The low agricultural prices which it would be the farmers' first objective to raise were the principal advantage many workers could see in the prevailing situation, while farmers were as opposed as ever to the extension of bargaining rights which would be the major item on labor's agenda. And perhaps there still remained a residue of the ill-will which had grown out of the prewar attempt at cooperation. In any event, both La Follette and the Democratic candidate were roundly defeated, and the architects of a status quo

16 *Coronado Coal Company* v. *United Mine Workers*, 268 U.S. 295 (1925).

operating to the disadvantages of these two great groups of citizens were authorized to continue managing the nation's affairs.

————

It has for a very long time been a part of the thinking of political scientists that power can only be dealt with by power in other hands. Only recently has this proposition become an explicit part of economics.[17] By now, however, it is broadly conceded that one of the major ways other social groups can hold their own against the power concentrated in the hands of big business is to accumulate power in their own hands.

It need scarcely be emphasized that this concept was not strange to the thinking of workers in the 1920's. This, indeed, had by then been the central feature of their program for a third of a century. The trouble was that they were not being permitted to implement their philosophy. Along every approach they had tried they had encountered a traffic policeman in the form of the judiciary, and had pulled up to the curb at his command.

Nor did this fact go wholly unnoticed by influential people even in its own time. Indeed, an eminent Supreme Court Justice himself protested bitterly against what a majority of his colleagues was doing, in the process calling explicit attention to the double standard the Court was developing in the fields of business combination and labor organization. In this connection Justice Brandeis made two major points. First, he suggested that labor's collective bargaining endeavors were just as clearly reasonable restraints of trade as were such business operations as the United Shoe Machinery Corporation and United States Steel. Second, after making a pointed reference to the tremendous aggregations of power the Court had tolerated in these two concerns, he concluded on the following note:

It would, indeed, be strange if Congress had by the same Act willed to deny to members of a small craft of workingmen the right to cooperate in simply refraining from work, when that course was the only means of self-protection against a combination of militant and powerful employers. I cannot believe that Congress did so.[18]

But for the moment, Congress had for all practical purposes done precisely that.

[17] J. K. Galbraith, *American Capitalism: The Concept of Countervailing Power* (Boston: Houghton Mifflin Co., 1952).

[18] *Bedford Cut Stone Company v. Journeymen Stone Cutters' Association of North America*, 274 U.S. 37 (1927).

Questions for Discussion

1. What was the riddle of monetary policy?

2. Explain and insofar as possible justify the course followed by the Federal Reserve authorities after the war.

3. Enumerate the major factors contributing to the postwar agricultural depression.

4. How appropriate to the farmer's problem were the measures insisted upon by agricultural leaders?

5. In terms of what aspect of the democratic process might the farm legislation of the 1920's be called laissez faire as that concept is defined here?

6. Explain the concept "sick industry," and show why it is so descriptive of the bituminous coal mining industry.

7. What was the connection between the "sickness" of the bituminous coal industry and labor problems in that industry?

8. Why can a pool of oil reserves be most economically exploited as a unit?

9. How did the business interests use government to keep labor in its place during these years?

10. What was the status of labor's right to bargain collectively after the second Coronado Coal decision?

11. Evaluate Justice Brandeis' criticism of the line his colleagues were taking in labor cases.

12. Looking back on these early postwar years, to what extent would you say they were characterized by laissez faire?

Chapter 17

Big Business in the Saddle

With the inauguration of Calvin Coolidge on March 4, 1925, the postwar readjustment can be said to have been substantially completed. Virtually all vestiges of the recession had disappeared, and most of the problems inherited from the war had either been resolved or lost from sight amid the signs of high prosperity now visible on every hand. No longer, in other words, was it necessary for the resurgence of laissez faire to restrain itself. No longer did men need to hold themselves back instead of giving their energies over to the task of money-making with full abandon. In short, normalcy had returned.

DISILLUSIONED AGAIN

The implications of this transition were apparent in almost every corner of the economy. However, by common consent among students of this period in American history, the hallmark of what was taking place was evolution on the big business front: to an extent matched on only one previous occasion (if at all) men in high places in the business world were calling the tune. As an inevitable consequence, and to the great dismay of liberals, literally every safeguard erected to prevent public exploitation at the hands of trusts seemed in the process of being swept away. And at no point was this more true than in connection with the antitrust legislation the "New Freedom" had launched with such high hopes ten years before.

Thus Section 7 of the Clayton Act had prohibited intercorporate stock ownership wherever it threatened to lessen competition. But by the time aggressive businessmen and a conservative Supreme Court had subjected this provision to the treatment appropriate to the 1920's, little remained of it. If the acquiring company used its stock control to bring about a merger of the assets of the two concerns, the law would not intervene.[1] In like manner the Clayton Act proscription of interlocking directorates in Section B brought about only a small number of resignations, and a prohibition of this sort is so easy to evade by the use of dummy directors that little energy was spent trying to enforce it.

The situation was hardly better with respect to Section 3. To begin with, the new legislation did not add as much to previously existing law as had been supposed at the time; the courts had already developed ample precedents for frowning on exclusive dealing, even if they did not always do so. Perhaps as a result of the statutory prohibition the judiciary became a little more sceptical of these kinds of arrangements,[2] although there was still no willingness to condemn this practice wherever found.[3] The Act had said "where the effect may be substantially to lessen competition or tend to create a monopoly in any line of commerce," and here as elsewhere the courts saw to it that qualifying phrases were broadly interpreted.

This same history of an occasional success matched by frustrating defeats also characterized the antitrust attack on tying contracts. The principal achievement here was an action compelling the United Shoe Machinery Corporation to cease requiring its lessees to lease all the machines they used from it as a condition for leasing any.[4] On the other side of this ledger, however, was another rebuff handed the Federal Trade Commission by the Supreme Court. An order which would have prohibited major gasoline refiners from leasing roadside pumps to filling stations on condition that only their own product be sold therefrom was here set aside, Justice McReynolds taking the position that there remained a substantial degree of competition in the petroleum distribution business and that the public might legitimately be protected from deception in this way.[5]

Nor were reformers boasting of progress in the field of price discrimination. Two factors explain the meager results obtained under Section 2. First, this section had been written primarily to curb predatory price cutting of the sort which had at one time been a major factor in trust formation. Unfortunately for that objective, however, this practice was not now a prominent feature of the in-

---

[1] *Federal Trade Commission* v. *Western Meat Company; Thatcher Manufacturing Company* v. *Federal Trade Commission; Swift and Company* v. *Federal Trade Commission,* 272 U.S. 554 (1926).

[2] *Standard Fashion Company* v. *Magrane-Houston Company,* 258 U.S. 346 (1922).

[3] *Federal Trade Commission* v. *Curtis Publishing Company,* 260 U.S. 568 (1923).

[4] *United Shoe Machinery Corporation* v. *United States,* 258 U.S. 451 (1922).

[5] *Federal Trade Commission* v. *Sinclair Refining Company,* 261 U.S. 463 (1923).

dustrial scene; more subtle forms of competition had largely obviated the necessity for using such a crude device. Second, even to the extent that there was still a problem this kind of a prohibition might have done something to alleviate, legal interpretation would still have created a fundamental obstacle. In quick succession two cases were decided in which the phrase "in any line of commerce" was interpreted in such a way that discrimination by a manufacturer against some of its own distributors (in one case a retail cooperative, and in the other an association of retailers) was not included.[6]

Far removed from the original purpose of this section, however, the Federal Trade Commission did find a use for it, though at the moment very little was accomplished even in that direction. In the steel industry especially, but also in a number of other industries producing commodities on which transportation costs were a substantial proportion of total price, a system of delivered pricing had matured over the years. Under these arrangements price to the consumer was a certain base price plus cost of transportation to the purchaser from the nearest so-called basing point. This pricing technique almost necessarily involves what can only be described as discrimination against purchasers near producers a long way from a designated base point, and this was particularly true in the steel industry where Pittsburgh was at this time the only location so favored.

In one of the few major antitrust actions taken during the decade by any group, the Federal Trade Commission found the United States Steel Corporation and its subsidiaries guilty of violating Section 2 of the Clayton Act and ordered the abandonment of "Pittsburgh-plus." Without contesting this order in the courts the corporation announced its intention of complying "in so far as it is practical to do so." The net result was the substitution of a multiple basing-point system for a single one, with base prices at the new base locations higher than at Pittsburgh.

Not only was antitrust progress painfully slow on the side of the substantive law changes introduced by the recent reform movement, but a similar fate was gradually overtaking the procedural innovation from which so much had at one time been expected. On every side the Federal Trade Commission was being overwhelmed with a conservatism quite inconsistent with the intentions of its creators.[7]

---

[6] *Mennen Company* v. *Federal Trade Commission*, 288 F. 774 (1923); and *National Biscuit Company* v. *Federal Trade Commission*, 299 F. 733 (1924).

[7] D. C. Blaisdell, *The Federal Trade Commission: An Experiment in the Control of Business* (New York: Columbia University Press, 1932).

To begin with, successive Republican administrations lost no time in making conservative appointments to that body whenever an opportunity arose (and who would criticize them for this?). Not a single Wilson appointee to this agency was reappointed, and by 1925 successor administrators were in the majority. From that time onward little was to be expected in that quarter by way of significant attempts to check tendencies toward concentration.

An episode in point will illustrate. In 1925 William E. Humphrey, a man noted for his aggressive conservatism, became chairman of the Commission and at once set about introducing appropriate changes into its operations. When he was at one point chided for thus perverting the agency's original objectives, he is said to have retorted: "What do you think I am here for?"

Somewhat surprisingly, this steady accretion of conservatism did not completely destroy the effectiveness of the Federal Trade Commission, even in the 1920's. One of the responsibilities it had been given was to conduct investigations of the "organization, business conduct, practices, and management of any corporation engaged in commerce . . . ," and much valuable work was done in this field. Thus the Packers and Stockyards and Grain Futures acts had both been based on data developed by Federal Trade Commission investigations, although these investigations had been conducted prior to the onset of Commission conservatism. But even thereafter numerous investigations were carried out, frequently as a result of Congressional mandates accompanied by special appropriations, and some of the more important of these greatly aided the writing of other items of reform legislation after this series of business-oriented administrations had passed from the scene.

From another standpoint, however, the atrophy of its initial promise overtook the Commission at this point as decisively as at any other. One of the purposes for which this investigative power was provided had been to raise the moral level of business behavior through "pitiless publicity." Almost at once the appearance of insuperable obstacles made it clear that such an objective could not even approximately be attained. On the one hand, the courts made it difficult for the Commission to secure the necessary information. With respect to an investigation launched at the request of Congress early in the 1920's, the Supreme Court maintained that private papers could not constitutionally be demanded unless the governing Congressional Resolution specifically charged violation of the law.[8] On another occasion the Commission was denied the right

[8] *Federal Trade Commission* v. *American Tobacco Company*, 264 U.S. 298 (1924).

to require the furnishing of information for an investigation commenced on its own initiative on the grounds that it could legally only request the Attorney General to demand the needed data.[9] On the other hand, the amount of investigating that would have been required to carry out this purpose effectively would have made necessary much larger appropriations than Congress was willing to make available.

And finally, on the unfair competition front, where the new agency had originally been expected to make an especially creative contribution, the story was but little different.[10] Thus after the Gratz decision the Commission was reluctant to develop a definition of this concept differing from common law and Sherman Act interpretations, and after a few new appointments had been made there was little interest in accomplishing much of anything along that line. Only one important success was achieved in this field. The Supreme Court upheld a Commission order directed against resale price maintenance,[11] thus building further on a number of prior legal precedents on that point. In addition, there was an indication that one day the courts might allow the Commission to assist in the working out of a more constructive definition of unfair competition. When an order was entered against the common practice of labeling clothing made of mixed materials as "wool," the Supreme Court upheld the Commission.[12] But despite these glimpses of the sun through the dark, low-hanging clouds, no liberal would have argued that anything significant was happening in this field either.

All in all it is easy to understand why the reputation of the Federal Trade Commission had by the end of the decade fallen to a low level, and why this development is not to be explained solely in terms of the common tendency for a regulatory agency to become a friend of the concerns it was created to regulate.[13] At the same time, however, fairness requires that one further consideration be thrown into the balance. The question must be seriously raised if this group was not in fact given an impossible task. What the Commission was asked to do was no less than to devise for all of industry a plane of competition which would represent a happy medium between a level of industrial concentration widely considered dangerous to the

[9] *Federal Trade Commission* v. *Claire Furnace Company*, 274 U.S. 160 (1927).

[10] N. B. Gaskill, *The Regulation of Competition* (New York: Harper & Bros., 1936); and J. P. Miller, *Unfair Competition* (Cambridge: Harvard University Press, 1941).

[11] *Federal Trade Commission* v. *Beech-Nut Packing Company*, 257 U.S. 441 (1922).

[12] *Federal Trade Commission* v. *Winsted Hosiery Company*, 258 U.S. 483 (1922).

[13] M. H. Bernstein, *Regulating Business by Independent Commission* (Princeton: Princeton University Press, 1955).

underlying community and the economic war of all against all which the consolidation movement had replaced. And, looking at this question from a slightly different point of view, it must be kept in mind that whereas the Interstate Commerce Commission was at this time expected to be an expert body only in the railroad field, the sphere of operations of the Federal Trade Commission was a hundred major industries. Since the 1920's the Commission has done much to enhance its stature, but it is important even now that mere men not be judged by too rigorous a set of criteria.

ANOTHER DOUBLE STANDARD

With Republicanism choking the life out of the Federal Trade Commission and otherwise emasculating the New Freedom attempt to invigorate antitrust policy it would scarcely be expected that the over-all administration of these laws would be especially aggressive. It would perhaps do the nation's leaders an injustice to say that antitrust prosecution was lax during this period. Certainly, there were suits enough. But all too often the defendants were building-material rings, food racketeers, or labor unions, with the result that the impression was conveyed to the public of great activity on this front whereas in reality no significant changes in the basic structure of industry were ever officially contemplated.

Even where basic antitrust actions were launched, furthermore, the ingenious conservatism of this era was able to devise a method of procedure which enabled the administration to build an even more impressive paper record of accomplishment with little risk. One of these was the expanded use of the consent decree, a technique whereby antitrust cases can be settled out of court. The parties come together informally to discuss terms, no outsiders being present and no record being kept for examination later by experts, and an agreement is reached which can be understood only by a close student of the industry in question. A consent decree settlement, of course, is not necessarily a lax antitrust procedure, but its wide use during these years placed it under deep public suspicion.[14] It is surely no coincidence that after the middle of this decade court action was almost never resorted to in antitrust cases.

In the Federal Trade Commission, too, procedural innovations were making their appearance as government cooperation with business became the order of the day. Closely analogous with the antitrust consent decree is the unfair competition stipulation, a settle-

[14] W. H. Hamilton and Irene Till, *Antitrust In Action* (Washington, D.C.: Government Printing Office, 1941).

ment out of court which does not require making public the names of respondents. Similarly oriented was the cessation of an earlier practice of releasing a public statement whenever a complaint was issued. And still a third technique designed to help the Commission get along more amicably with its business friends was the so-called trade practice conference.

One of the more enduring consequences of World War I had been the impetus given the formation of trade associations as the government found it necessary again and again to sit down with a representative group from an entire industry. The Federal Trade Commission now built further on these foundations by calling industry representatives together and agreeing, on a wholly extra-legal basis, on a pattern of trade practices which would henceforth be considered acceptable in that industry. This agreement then became the standard used by the Commission in "regulating" these concerns, and they in turn were assured of freedom from prosecution as long as they adhered to the rules thus laid down.[15]

Undoubtedly the trade practice conference technique has its uses. For one thing, harmony between a regulatory body and those it regulates is of value in and of itself—if only this objective be not carried too far. Moreover, trade practices which are objectionable to a majority of the leaders in an industry may become standard as the result of the competitive behavior of an unethical fringe group. Industry-wide agreement can often isolate this element, and compel it to fall into line. But there are dangers here as well. Profitable practices will not often be given up voluntarily, and the policy of lending official sanction to these agreements may well put the government behind practices which in fact involve restraint of trade. The general tenor of antitrust administration and the regulation of competition at this time did not instill confidence that great pains were being taken to achieve the valuable outcomes of such a policy while rejecting those less capable of withstanding scrutiny.

But despite the efforts thus made to keep activity on this front to a minimum without creating a public scandal, a number of significant cases were processed and a few important court decisions were handed down. By now, furthermore, a large enough accumulation of such decisions was available to show more clearly than ever before the pattern they were following. And while this pattern taken as a whole was by no means as anti-antitrust as was the 1920's in general, there was about it much that was disquieting to liberals.

[15] Federal Trade Commission, *Control of Unfair Practices Through Trade Conference Procedures* (Washington, D.C.: Government Printing Office, 1941).

A first, and perhaps the clearest, trend now visible was the rigorous way these laws were still being applied to the railroad industry, despite the comprehensive economic regulation to which these concerns were otherwise subjected. In two decisions rendered during this decade the Supreme Court, using both the antitrust laws and the Hepburn Act, largely completed the task of separating the railroad and anthracite coal industries by means of the most drastic dissolution decrees yet handed down.[16] Shortly thereafter the Southern Pacific Railroad Company was forbidden to retain a controlling stock ownership in the Central Pacific Railway Company.[17] In view of the fact that the Central Pacific had been under lease to the Southern Pacific for fifty years this latter decision was by no means an obvious one, and the Interstate Commerce Commission through its power to approve railroad consolidations a few years later in effect reversed the Supreme Court. Perhaps, however, this incident helped bring home to the public the implications of the antitrust exemption for railroads written into the Transportation Act of 1920. In any event there were to be few more important antitrust cases involving railroads.

A second basic element visible in antitrust decisions was the almost invariable condemnation of price-fixing activities by a number of separate and distinct firms. The classic case during the 1920's in which this situation arose was a price agreement by concerns manufacturing four-fifths of the vitreous pottery bathroom fixtures produced in the entire country, and the Supreme Court has never stood firmer in outlawing that kind of an agreement.

The aim and result of every price-fixing agreement, if effective, is the elimination of one form of competition. The power to fix prices, whether reasonably exercised or not, involves power to control the market and to fix arbitrary and unreasonable prices. The reasonable price fixed today may through economic and business changes become the unreasonable price of tomorrow. Once established, it may be maintained unchanged because of the absence of competition secured by the agreement for a price reasonable when fixed.[18]

Nor did the courts stop with direct price-fixing as such in applying that philosophy. An analogous reasoning was used during this decade to outlaw agreements to restrict output on the ground that output control is one method of price control.[19] By the same token agreements to divide markets also fell under the ban, for market sharing can hardly avoid being the other side of output control.

16 *United States* v. *Reading Company,* 253 U.S. 26 (1920); *United States* v. *Lehigh Valley Railroad Company,* 254 U.S. 255 (1920).
17 *United States* v. *Southern Pacific Railroad Company,* 259 U.S. 214 (1922).
18 *United States* v. *Trenton Potteries Company,* 273 U.S. 392 (1927).
19 *American Column and Lumber Company* v. *United States,* 257 U.S. 377 (1921).

Even the newly developed trade associations felt the effects of this position. Wherever the collection and dissemination of trade statistics and/or open price systems (the practice of making available to every firm in the industry information concerning prices charged by every other firm) bore any overt traces of a price agreement the Supreme Court emphatically objected,[20] although such programs not evidently so oriented were typically approved.[21]

But was not the 1920 United States Steel decision an exception to these generalizations? Is it not true that this giant concern had for years been the price leader for the entire steel industry, and that the basing-point system of pricing was in effect a subtle form of price agreement? To be sure, these things are true, but the steel opinion is not made thereby an exception to the basic rules now being broadly followed. On the one hand, the Court distinguished carefully between the situation in which a dominant concern sets the price for an industry and one in which the smaller fry only follow the price the leader sets for itself. In this connection judicial notice had pointedly been taken of the fact that United States Steel had, before the suit against it was commenced, ceased to set prices for the industry. On the other hand, basing-point pricing was not yet as well understood as it was one day to be, and the Federal Trade Commission in its basing-point action had not charged price conspiracy against the industry.

No doubt the Court may legitimately be accused of being a little unrealistic in its approach to some of these problems. There are situations in which lesser concerns in an industry "follow" their leader because they feel they dare not do otherwise, and there are other situations in which innocent-appearing trade association activities are merely the façade behind which illegal activities are covertly carried out. But the judiciary's philosophy and intentions in these cases were nevertheless sound, and it is probable that little damage to an effective antitrust program came from this source. Where the Court did fail, however, the point at which its thinking most conflicted with the ideas of reformers, was the freedom from prosecution enjoyed by combinations of firms joined together by outright merger of physical assets.

At no point was this double standard more apparent than the way the Supreme Court handled cases coming before it under Section 7 of the Clayton Act, forbidding the looser holding of stock but toler-

---

[20] *United States* v. *Linseed Oil Company,* 262 U.S. 371 (1923).

[21] *Maple Flooring Manufacturers' Association* v. *United States,* 268 U.S. 563 (1925); and *Cement Manufacturers' Protective Association* v. *United States,* 268 U.S. 606 (1925).

ating the union of concerns brought about by means of this same stock ownership. Unfortunately, however, the matter went deeper than this. In other kinds of cases as well the Supreme Court gave approval to actions by a single firm which it would have forbidden were they carried on by the concerted action of a number of firms wielding an equivalent economic power. The outstanding illustration of this during the 1920's was a suit brought against the International Harvester Company.[22]

The history of this concern paralleled that of the United States Steel Corporation in a number of ways important to this antitrust proceeding. It had always been a "good" trust; no long list of predatory practices was alleged against it as in the oil and tobacco cases. Its proportion of the total business done by the industry of which it was a part had steadily declined from eighty-five per cent to sixty-four, as compared with a drop from two-thirds to one-half for the steel concern. For a number of years the smaller firms in the industry had followed International's lead with respect to prices. Perhaps, indeed, the parallel was sufficiently strong in and of itself to justify the Court's repeating in this case the argument against dissolution advanced in the earlier decision.

The law, however, does not make the mere size of a corporation, however impressive, or the existence of unexerted power on its part, an offense, when unaccompanied by unlawful conduct in the exercise of that power.

But the Court went still farther in its 1927 opinion. Price leadership was much more decisively accepted than it had been seven years before.

And the fact that competitors may see proper, in the exercise of their own judgment, to follow the prices of another manufacturer, does not establish any suppression of competition or show any sinister domination.

Just as in an earlier stage of the battle against big business successes against the trust form of organization had driven men to use the tighter form of control offered by the holding company, so now was public policy forcing consolidations into the still tighter mold of outright merger.[23] As a protection to the community against business organizations thought to be potentially dangerous, the government seemed in reality to be only putting sheep's clothing on the same old wolf. How much and what might have been accomplished by a rigorous antitrust policy under the most favorable circum-

---

[22] *United States* v. *International Harvester Company,* 274 U.S. 693 (1927).

[23] National Industrial Conference Board, *Mergers and The Law* (New York: National Industrial Conference Board, 1929).

stances must remain a conjecture, but it is not to be doubted that as long as this new double standard developed by the Supreme Court continued to hold the field other antitrust policies would be much like pounding sand in a rathole.

A NEW CONSOLIDATION MOVEMENT[24]

The proof of the pudding, it is said, is in the eating. If this be true, if antitrust activity during the 1920's can accurately be likened to pounding sand in a rathole, the period should have been outstandingly favorable for the rapid growth of big business. And this it was. Plants dramatically increased in size as mass production methods spread from industry to industry, and as equally dramatically

TABLE 17.   BIG BUSINESS ON THE MARCH

	Net Income of Nonfinancial Corporations (billions of dollars)			Per Cent of Total	
Period	All	200 Largest	800 Next Largest	200 Largest	800 Next Largest
1920-1923	6.0	2.0	1.1	33.5	18.9
1926-1929	8.5	3.4	1.6	40.7	18.7

Source: A. A. Berle and G. C. Means, *The Modern Corporation and Private Property* (New York: The Macmillan Co., 1933), p. 37. Used by permission.

separate plants were gathered up into larger management units. In the short space of ten years some 15,000 business firms disappeared as a result of being acquired by other firms. By the time this new wave of combinations had passed its crest, it has been estimated that the 200 largest nonbanking corporations in the country possessed nearly one-half of the nation's corporate wealth, 40 per cent of its business wealth, and one-fifth of total national wealth.[25]

It is tempting to say that not since the turn of the century had such a phenomenon been witnessed. But this is too mild a comparison. A more nearly accurate statement would be that never before, in any country's history, had there been such a spectacular business development. Even if we include the consolidation movement climaxed by the formation of the United States Steel Corporation, there had not been previously a decade in which so much institutional evolution had taken place in this field.

[24] A. R. Burns, *The Decline of Competition* (New York: McGraw-Hill Book Co., Inc., 1936); and Myron Watkins, *Industrial Combinations and Public Policy* (Boston: Houghton Mifflin Co., 1927).

[25] A. A. Berle and G. C. Means, *The Modern Corporation and Private Property* (New York: The Macmillan Co., 1933).

For example, it was during this decade that big business began decisively to invade retailing. Barely out of its infancy prior to World War I, the chain store ten years thereafter was selling approximately one-fourth of all the food, drugs, tobacco, apparel, and general merchandise entering retail channels. This encroachment of big business upon the domain of independent middlemen understandably aroused bitter resentment among the vested interests already in these fields. To a degree the latter were able to fend off this attack by organizing cooperative chains of their own. Furthermore, it was to become clear at a later date that the chains would not soon (if ever) wholly eliminate their smaller rivals. But the encroachment nonetheless continued, and resentment mounted in proportion, until it became virtually inevitable that a reaction would one day set in which would have much significance for government-business relationships.

Another area of the economy in which consolidation was only now making its way was the relatively young electric utility industry. And even more significant than the fact that another major industry was being thus "modernized" was the fact that the principal technique whereby this result was being achieved, the holding company, was a device supposed long ago to have been rendered quite harmless.

There were a number of reasons why electric utilities and holding companies were finding one another so compatible. Individual electric light and power companies are by nature monopolistic, and hence combinations of such concerns risked little from the standpoint of antitrust prosecution. Moreover, because these enterprises had a high percentage of mortgageable property and because their earnings were relatively stable, they especially lent themselves to holding company control. A high bond ratio supported by mortgageable property and stable earnings meant that control could be secured with a smaller investment than would otherwise be required. As a result the formation of utility holding companies became a favorite method of making fabulous promotion and other profits.

So profitable, in fact, were transactions of this kind that holding company was even pyramided on holding company until three layers of holding companies above an operating company were not at all unusual. The extreme case of Samuel Insull's empire saw as many as eight holding companies pyramided on top of one another, an empire controlling $2.5 billion worth of wealth and responsible for the production of one-eighth of all the electric power generated in the entire country. In the railroad field, where similar conditions also favored the holding company device, two brothers named Van Sweringen built a $1 million investment into the control of a dozen Class I railroads with assets of approximately $1 billion.

And not only were new industries being consolidated with the aid of old techniques, but in addition basically new devices were also being perfected. One of the most important of these was the trade association.[26] In peace as in war it was apparent that such an organization could perform many useful functions for its members, not the least of these being to increase the degree of cooperation within an industry and hence to help keep competition in check. Given a legitimate reason for bringing together representatives from the major units of an industry, in other words, it would be a dull-witted group indeed that could not also transact a little illegitimate business on the side. At this point, in fact, the government was carrying its policy of noninterference a long step farther. As Secretary of Commerce, Herbert Hoover was doing all that one man in a high office could do to encourage the spread of these activities, while the trade practice conference technique of the Federal Trade Commission was no doubt also an important promotional force.

But all of these aspects of consolidation during these years were relatively minor by comparison with still another. That was the Delaware corporation. Just as one of the keys to the preceding combination movement thirty years before had been the holding company innovation in New Jersey, one of the central facets of this one was the wide variety of still more wonderful things that could now be done under the auspices of a Delaware charter. The following is a partial indication of how far the corporate form of business organization had evolved since the first general incorporation laws were passed.[27]

Corporate directors, for example, did not need to live in Delaware, nor did either directors' or stockholders' meetings need to be held there. Directors of a Delaware corporation, furthermore, did not need to own any stock in their concern; they could issue stock in exchange for services at whatever ratio they saw fit; they could arrange (or even rearrange) the voting rights of the various classes of stock in whatever way they deemed best (and indeed this latter privilege could even be carried to the point of issuing common stock

[26] National Industrial Conference Board, *Trade Associations: Their Economic Significance and Legal Status* (New York: National Industrial Conference Board, 1925), and Charles A. Pearce, *Trade Association Survey* (Washington, D.C.: Government Printing Office, 1941).

[27] R. C. Larcom, *The Delaware Corporation* (Baltimore: Johns Hopkins University Press, 1937).

which had no voting rights whatsoever); and the validity of contracts entered into, in which the interests of the corporation and one of its directors was in conflict, was not in any way affected by that conflict.

Obviously it was no coincidence that the Du Ponts were very influential in Delaware politics at this time. With such a hospitable political atmosphere it is not to be wondered at that in a single small building in Wilmington, Delaware, no less than 10,000 sizable corporations made their home—and all of them on the tenth floor. The entire history of the corporation and hence consolidations had been a record of the progressive dilution of the relationship between property owners and their property, but even the architects of the holding company would scarcely have recognized this relationship at the end of the 1920's.

RULE OF REASON IN PERSPECTIVE

It has been somewhat the fashion among liberals and economists (and by this is not meant that these two terms are mutually exclusive) to look upon the 1920's as a period of exploitation of the masses by business and financial interests. Although there is nothing to be gained by denying that conservatives were in control of the nation's decision-making machinery and that they did not use it for philanthropic purposes, it is well worth emphasizing that what was happening in the antitrust field did have its other side.

A considerable proportion of the liberal-economist criticism of antitrust policy during the 1920's focuses upon the damage supposed to have been done to antitrust objectives by the rule of reason. This insistence is difficult to evaluate because its meaning is not always clear, but the representative interpretation given at this point seems to have been that the Supreme Court should have applied the Sherman Act as it was written rather than modified it with a principle arbitrarily extracted from the air.

There are at least two reasons for believing that this approach to the evolution of American antitrust policy is misleading. First, it is now clear, if there was ever a time when it was not, that in this respect the Court did apply the Sherman Act as it was written. On the one hand, that statute was written for the purpose of making explicit common-law principles on the subject of trade restraint which definitely included a rule of reason. Nor, on the other hand, is William Howard Taft's solution of this difficulty, the proposition that in the common law nonancillary trade restraints were allowed the benefit of no such interpretation, to be accepted at this point. Mature scholarship seems to leave no doubt that, great jurist though he was, Taft was simply in error in presuming to declare *the* common law with respect to combinations in restraint of trade.

In the second place, it is surely not inappropriate to ask what the consequences would have been if no rule of reason had been allowed to enter into antitrust adjudications. Once the judiciary had adopted a realistic definition of commerce for this purpose, what contracts of significance between two business concerns could reasonably be said not to have restraint-of-trade consequences? Every such contract has as its central objective making certain that a given transaction takes one form rather than another, that business relationships flow in particular directions and not in others. If, in other words, *every* contract in restraint of trade were illegal, virtually all business activity in an industrial society would be proscribed. In short, when this matter is thought of against the background of the elementary facts of modern economic life, it is evident that a rule of reason was indispensable.

If this be granted, next, the charge against the rule of reason changes its character. The accusation must now emphasize the Supreme Court's failure to develop an adequate (a more reasonable?) rule of reason. It may well be that a different, a more rigorous, rule of reason would have more effectively protected the public interest. Moreover, economic science may indeed hold the key to the framing of such a rule. But this is a far different thing from the proposition that the rule of reason was an arbitrary creation of the Supreme Court.

Nor is it even to be accepted without question or qualification that the particular rule of reason applied in the 1920's was responsible for much of the weakness of antitrust policy during that era. Would it not be more realistic to suggest that the difficulty here was rather that the Court was endeavoring to find solutions to problems which with every passing year became still more complex. To be sure, the Justices were often enough naive, from the standpoint of historical hindsight. At the same time, however, it is to be doubted that, considered in the main, antitrust decisions after 1920 were less rigorous in the reform sense than theretofore. If by inconsistent is meant unpredictable, the chief limitation of the courts in this field has been inconsistency; but this has surely resulted far more from the dynamic character of the economy and hence the prevailing definition of the problem to be resolved than from conservative bias.

If one were inclined to be even more charitable toward the judiciary, furthermore, the double standard developed in antitrust cases can readily be seen to have a much more solid justification than is typically conceded by critics.[28] On the one hand, a strong presumption necessarily operates against agreements governing the "heart of the contract" by separate firms. The very fact that these concerns are separate rather than integrated indicates the presence of factors other than the productive efficiency available from larger decision-making units. On the other hand, a much different presumption must surely operate where the courts are confronted with an outright consolidation, a firm that has over the years demonstrated its ability as a single entity to hold its own in the economic maelstrom. (It is instructive, incidentally, to think of a merger in this connection as an *ancillary* agreement not to compete, and one that does not at all preclude the entry of other firms into the industry.) Now, to be sure, there is such a thing as financial strength enabling a large concern to exist despite operating inefficiencies, an economic domination of smaller concerns by larger ones which has the effect of "holding an umbrella" over the heads of the latter. But this is only to suggest again that perhaps the courts did not devise the best possible rule of reason, that they presumed too great a difference between these two types of situations. Surely, moreover, some allowance was appropriately made for the difficulty of rebuilding an industry pulled up by the roots as a result of an antitrust action. Dissolution experience—the success with which these economic eggs had in practice been unscrambled—was certainly not wholly reassuring here.

Another point of view from which can be justified a cheerful tolerance of the uncertainties engendered by a regulation through litigation which does not go out of its way to minimize the use of discretion by regulatory agencies takes reference from the basic alternative to such a policy. Although that technique is indeed subject to numerous shortcomings, as was amply demonstrated during this period, at the same time it has the very great advantage of not putting the industries thus regulated into a strait-jacket. This, however, is precisely the consequence of the public utility type of regulation, the promulgation and enforcement of a comprehensive set of rights and responsibilities. Even businessmen pressing for a higher degree of certainty as to what could or could not be done under the law assuredly did not want to achieve that objective at so high a price, and it is only slightly less obvious that the larger public was no more ready for such a step. Not only would this have been more regimentation than a people pledged to give private enterprise the benefit of most doubts could accept, but the success of public utility regula-

[28] Twentieth Century Fund, *Big Business, Its Growth and Place* (New York: Twentieth Century Fund, Inc., 1937).

tion to date was scarcely an argument in favor of vastly extending that type of control.

For yet another important reason, too, the interpretation of anti-trust policy during these years advanced by many economist-critics cannot be accepted as the last word on that subject. Thus one of the most serious charges brought against a concentrated industrial struc-ture is the loss to society of the fruits of competition which is thereby brought about. One of the principal benefits emphasized in this connection is the relationship between competition and techno-logical advance, the fact that firms under severe competitive pres-sure are more apt to introduce productivity innovations and in this way maximize the advantages of private enterprise for the commu-nity as a whole. Paradoxically, however, when this decade—and in-deed the entire period during which there had existed a trust or monopoly problem—is measured with this yardstick, it is difficult to make the criticisms leveled by liberals square with their ideals.

An outstanding case in point is the huge and distinctively Ameri-can automobile industry. During the 1920's consolidation in this new area of the economy was brought to at least a temporary climax, a situation in which the industry was dominated by three major con-cerns. Yet simultaneously with this development automobile manu-facturing was completely revolutionized, and these firms pioneered the application of mass production techniques to heavy industry. Moreover, this was not an isolated phenomenon. These years saw the advance of the use of science in industrial production on a scale hitherto undreamed of. And although it is quite true that this prog-ress was built primarily on private profit foundations, it is of signifi-cance that the United States became at this time the only nation in the world in which an automobile, a radio, a telephone, and a refrig-erator were all common household items.

It can be argued, of course, that if trusts had not literally run away with the economy as they did, progress might have taken place still more rapidly. To this contention two responses may be offered. First, with the economy and through it the entire social scene being trans-formed so drastically that hundreds of thousands of individuals were barely able to make the necessary personal adjustments, it can surely not be regarded as a tragedy that technical advance did not proceed at an even swifter pace. Let it not be forgotten that this decade saw in this country a larger and more persistent pool of technologically unemployed persons than at any previous time.

A second approach to this question is even more fundamental. Consolidation in the 1920's, no less than 50 years earlier, was in large part motivated by the desire to modify the rigors of unchecked competition, to achieve in the midst of swirling, bustling change a degree of economic security; that is, freedom from the tyranny of overhead costs. The suggestion has been advanced that only insofar as businessmen were able to achieve a minimum of this kind of security could they have participated as actively as they did in the introduction of economic changes. And this result is no more paradoxical than the fact that automobiles can travel faster than would otherwise be the case because they are equipped with brakes.[29] In other words, it is possible that the existence of some checks to competition speeded up rather than slowed down economic development.

The concept of security in turn suggests another angle from which the so-called failure of antitrust can profitably be viewed. It is today acknowledged that the provision of security for citizens is a valid as well as a valuable test of the effectiveness of an economy's operation, and the time was to come (much sooner than those living through these dynamic years would have supposed) when a major objective of the American economy was to be the level of security it provided for its people. Judgments may differ on whether recent generations of Americans have come to want too much security. By the same token, there is room for difference of opinion on whether business in the United States has overprotected itself. The important point, however, is that businessmen are entitled to a share in whatever security their society is able to provide.

And finally, in interpreting this period the important fact must not be lost from sight that antitrust policy was already understood to be much less basic than had at one time been anticipated. Whereas a third of a century earlier it had been supposed that government interference with business operations would for the most part consist of a narrow area within which regulation would substitute for competition and a very broad area within which competition would be enforced, by the middle of the 1920's these expectations had been materially revised. On the one hand, the public utility category was outgrowing the bounds that had originally been set for it; on the other hand, in between these polar approaches to the problems created by an industrial society there was developing a wide variety of other types of business-government relationships. In the face of these developments it is all too easy to overemphasize the rule of reason as an explanation of underlying trends.

[29] J. A. Schumpeter, *Capitalism, Socialism, and Democracy* (New York: Harper & Bros., 1947), p. 88.

THE NEW COMPETITION

But be all this as it may, the fact remains that the 1920's saw a development which had long been in the making reach a high degree of maturity. During the earlier phases of the industrial revolution the most dynamic aspect of competition had been with respect to prices. By the 1920's this dimension of competition had been relegated to a distinctly inferior position, the most active dimension now taking the form of product differentiation and service rivalry. Here, in other words, was the most fundamental reason why the Federal Trade Commission had found little to do under Section 2 of the Clayton Act along the lines contemplated by that law's creators. Instead of engaging in predatory price cutting to eliminate competitors, the preferred approach now was to reach increasingly subtle understandings with them on the matter of prices, and then to make a big show of being competitive in less dangerous ways. Often referred to as "the new competition," this development marked a change in the operation of the economy that could hardly be overemphasized.

A number of factors explain this shift in emphasis. First, while the transition to big businesses from smaller ones was taking place, the fact that not all of the concerns in the field could become large meant that the adjustment process would have to be a violent one. Perhaps, the only way the necessary changes could have been brought about was by way of the bankruptcy route. It is interesting to reflect in this connection that to a significant extent the unfair competitive practices which figured so largely in the antitrust debate had perhaps made their principal contribution in determining who won and who lost in the bitter struggle for existence rather than in altering the structure of the nation's productive organization.

This consideration suggests that the new competition arose because the old had essentially accomplished its purpose. Closely related to this possibility is the unquestionable fact that the old competition was frankly inappropriate to the economic environment it had done so much to create. When there had been dozens of firms in an industry, a policy of rigorous price competition could be safely followed, for the output of a single firm was not so great that every competitor would at once know what was going on and follow suit. By the time the field had been narrowed to not more than five or six major firms, however, a policy of securing custom by means of price reductions was likely to be simply suicidal. "Live and let live" now seemed the more intelligent approach.

Perhaps, too, antitrust policy, however poorly implemented, is entitled to a share of this responsibility. Certainly the way the public persevered in its attempt to do something about this problem might well have convinced business leaders that public tolerance was not without limits. From the standpoint of the old competition, moreover, the outcome of the oil and tobacco antitrust suits was also most instructive. The straw in the wind here may well be a striking change in business attitudes toward society at large and particularly apparent during these years. Almost totally reversing the extreme indifference to public opinion which became fairly general shortly after the Civil War, highly placed businessmen were now endeavoring with all of the skill and talent money could buy to clothe their institutions in the regalia of public service.

For many years now the debate has gone on between advocates and opponents of the new competition. The former insist that this is the only realistic procedure for a huge concern under modern conditions, while the latter maintain that what is now called competition is actually only a cheap imitation of the real thing. Nor is there any sign that this issue is about to be resolved. Happily, it is not for this discussion to attempt a definitive statement on this point. All that is of importance here is the vital fact that in the years to come the relationships between government and business were again and again to reflect this controversy.

Arbitrarily dating the beginning of industrialization from the Civil War, the new economy in the United States was now a full two-thirds of a century old. Throughout that entire period the growth of big business had had to contend with a strong undercurrent of public hostility (although that current was never weaker than under Harding, Mellon, Coolidge, and Hoover), but the adjustment to modern conditions had gone on nonetheless. Now, with the ending of another accelerated evolution along familiar lines, the structure of the American economy became approximately what it has since been. Stated differently, industrialism in the United States had turned a crucial corner—or, more accurately, it had come of age. Reformers of a later day would make much capital out of a number of phases of these fabulous years, but short of revolution there could be no doubt that big, very big, business was here to stay.[30]

[30] Walter Adams (ed.), *The Structure of American Industry* (New York: The Macmillan Co., 1950).

Questions for Discussion

1. How sympathetic was the Supreme Court toward the antitrust legislation of the New Freedom?

2. Evaluate the work of the Federal Trade Commission through the 1920's.

3. In what ways did the nation's leadership during this decade sabotage the antitrust activities of erstwhile reformers?

4. How does basing-point pricing lead to price discrimination? Why would that method of pricing be objectionable to liberals?

5. Why would a conservative administration emphasize such devices as the consent decree, the stipulation, and trade practice conferences?

6. How was the Interstate Commerce Commission able to overrule the Supreme Court in the case of Southern Pacific control over the Central Pacific?

7. Apply the quotation from the Trenton Potteries decision to price leadership in the steel and farm machinery industries.

8. Distinguish between and evaluate the two double standards in the field of antitrust policy.

9. Why was the holding company such an excellent device for consolidations in the electric light and power and railroad industries?

10. How was consolidating made easier by the use of a Delaware charter?

11. In what ways do traditional criticisms of antitrust policy fail to do full justice to the problems involved?

12. Explain what is meant when it is said that businessmen in consolidating their firms were seeking security.

13. Distinguish between the new competition and the old. Why did this change take place?

14. What economic responsibilities had the government assumed to date that were designed neither to regulate monopoly nor to enforce competition?

Chapter 18

Behind the Mask

In 1927 there was published a book written by an outstanding British economist under the title *The End of Laissez Faire*.[1] In a sense the theme of that volume did not fit the American scene at the time it was written, however appropriate it might have been to the situation in England. Indeed, the very idea of the end of laissez faire was apt in the United States of the latter 1920's to be met in most quarters with an air of tolerant amusement. Had not the leadership of the nation just ushered in a "new era" of "perpetual prosperity"? Who could so much as think of ending an economic system capable of performing that feat?

The point need not be belabored that perpetual prosperity proved to be far less than perpetual, and that as a result government responsibilities were soon to broaden greatly. What is less clearly realized, however, is that in a variety of ways this country, while the new era was still at its height, was continuing to drift unmistakably away from laissez faire. On a number of fronts problems were arising which, if (or when) they were met in ways already well marked out, would significantly expand the functions of American governments. This does not mean that problems were recognized as problems during the 1920's, for of course that was in general not the case, and little was done about most of these situations at the moment. But the fact remains that perspectively if not prospectively Professor Keynes' book contained an important message for this country.

UNFINISHED BUSINESS—TRANSPORTATION

Note first in this connection what was happening in that chronic trouble area, railroad transportation. Central to this situation was the fact that the Transportation Act of 1920 was failing in several

[1] J. M. Keynes (London: Leonard and Virginia Woolf).

basic ways to accomplish its objectives. For one thing, voluntary consolidation along lines proposed by the Interstate Commerce Commission was not proceeding at all satisfactorily.[2] Following through on the principles set forth in its legislative mandate, the Commission had developed a plan of consolidations intermingling weak and strong roads in such a way that each of the several systems could earn a fair return. Quite understandably, however, railroads that were doing well would not of their own volition saddle themselves with the burden of averaging earnings with one or more unprofitable concerns.

This failure necessarily gave the recapture clause a more fundamental role in resolving the weak-and-strong-road difficulty than had originally been intended. Although that provision had been projected as only a temporary expedient, it was emerging as the only major line of attack on the problem. It was therefore unfortunate that signs of breakdown began also to appear at this point. A part of the difficulty here was the fact that all too few railroads were earning enough to provide recapture funds, despite the general prosperity of the period. Still more important, too few needy railroads were eligible to borrow such funds as were available, so rigid were the security and interest requirements fixed by law. And, most important of all, it was rapidly becoming apparent that the railroad problem could not be solved by means of loans.

Not only, furthermore, were there too few consolidations following the plan enunciated by the Interstate Commerce Commission, but there was too much combining motivated by other considerations. The critical development here was the revived use of the holding company, particularly the Van Sweringen empire and the circle of interests being built up around the Pennsylvania Railroad. As a consequence of this evolution, Congress' intention to give the Interstate Commerce Commission full jurisdiction over railroad integration bade fair to be frustrated, and it was by no means certain that even a highly conservative legislative body would tolerate open defiance of its will for very long.

The inadequacy of railroad earnings, too, was a problem in its own right. But when serious thought was given to lifting the level of rates as a solution, a major obstacle intervened. All of a sudden a dynamic new competitor of the railroads, the motor truck, had emerged, making the demand for rail freight service so elastic that it was doubtful if a higher rate level would add significantly to railway net operating

---

[2] W. N. Leonard, *Railroad Consolidation Under the Transportation Act of 1920* (New York: Columbia University Press, 1946).

TABLE 18. ANOTHER SICK INDUSTRY

Year	Railroad Rate of Return (%)	Motor Truck Registrations (000's)
1910	5.66	10
1915	5.23	159
1920	3.04	1,108
1925	5.12	2,483
1930	3.62	3,519

Source: Association of American Railroads and Department of Commerce.

income. Moreover, the new medium had naturally endeavored most aggressively to secure that traffic on which rail rates were already highest. This taking of the railroads' most profitable business, leaving them with a proportionately larger volume of traffic carried either at a loss or without profit, has been termed "skimming the cream," and unquestionably this practice was helping put the railroads under financial pressure.

It was perhaps a foregone conclusion from the outset that highway transportation would become a regulated industry, if for no other reason than to maintain safe conditions on the highways and to protect the highways themselves. By the 1920's, moreover, regulation in a number of states was already being extended to economic control for common carriers along familiar public utility lines, a complex pattern of regulation in which contract carriers were treated differently than common carriers and private carriers than either of the other types. But just as at the state level it was necessary to prevent private and contract carriers from destroying the more valuable (from the public's point of view) common carriage, so was it growing increasingly evident that regulation of interstate motor transportation would have to be prevented from destroying the indispensable rail transportation industry.

One other problem involving the railroad industry lingered just beneath the surface, and indeed at one point this situation even erupted on a minor scale. Largely as an outgrowth of labor dissatisfaction with the operations of the Railroad Labor Board, still another attempt was made to legislate away the labor-capital problem in that industry. This consisted of a still more elaborate procedure which had to be followed before a strike could be called.[3] A permanent Board of Mediation was created whose function it was to

[3] Harry D. Wolf, The Railroad Labor Board (Chicago: University of Chicago Press, 1927).

assume first responsibility for settling any dispute threatening to disrupt commerce. If this effort did not succeed, the Board was to urge the parties to submit to arbitration, the outcome of which would be legally binding. Should this fail also, the President was to appoint an emergency board to investigate the dispute and report to him concerning it, and during this entire procedure and for thirty days thereafter a strike could not be called. Throughout this process of negotiating, mediating, and investigating it was hoped that public opinion would compel a settlement without shutting down the industry.

There was perhaps reason enough for the feeling of railroad workers that the cards were now less decisively stacked against them. On the one hand, the procedure to be followed seemed to give the labor side of disputes a broader opportunity to exert an influence on public opinion. Far more important, on the other hand, the Railroad Labor Act of 1926 contained the first guaranty of labor's right to bargain collectively to be found in a federal statute, and one of the most fundamental such guaranties to be found in any American statute to date. But if labor statesmen could only have peered far enough into the future they would have seen in this legislative endeavor portents of things to come which might have partially offset' these favorable factors in their minds. For while the law was now moving at a snail's pace to accept one basic weapon of the modern labor movement, it was simultaneously broadening the restrictions surrounding an even more basic tool. Already the pattern was beginning to be established of matching collective bargaining gains with restrictions on the right to strike. Moreover, labor-capital relationships in the railroad industry were not significantly improved by these innovations.

And outside the railroad field other transportation problems were building up to the point of requiring the exercise of additional governmental responsibilities. The situation in the motor transportation industry has already been noted in this connection. Three other similar cases were pipeline transportation, the brand-new aviation industry, and the merchant marine.

The motivation behind oil pipeline regulation arose less out of the needs of the transportation than the petroleum industry, the pertinent relationships here paralleling those which had grown up between railroads and the anthracite coal industry. Pipelines provide an inexpensive method of transporting this product where water facilities are not available, and integration in this industry had always included ownership of the pipelines required to carry petroleum from the oil fields to refineries or to portside. At the same time, however, the independents who could not afford to duplicate existing pipeline facilities desired to take advantage of this mode of carriage. The problem here was that the power of the large, integrated firms to set the price on the pipeline haulage of competitors' oil gave them a leverage within the industry which had long been considered unfair.[4]

The Interstate Commerce Commission had been slow to utilize the authority conferred upon it by the Hepburn Act to regulate in this field. When action was first taken, moreover, the oil companies did everything in their power to evade regulation. The first step in that campaign had been to refuse to accept oil not belonging to themselves, and then defying the Commission by maintaining that they were private carriers. When this position was rejected by the Supreme Court on the grounds that since a pipeline is a natural monopoly, Congress was within its rights in declaring these concerns to be common carriers,[5] they continued to exclude the independents by refusing to accept shipments smaller than an amount few of these firms could supply at one time and by charging high rates. The result was a tendency for the majors to build their refineries near the market for the finished product and for the independents to locate their refineries near the fields. To date all that the Interstate Commerce Commission had done about this problem had been to reduce minimum tender requirements, but it was obvious to anyone not wholly dazzled by the exterior brilliance of the new era that much remained to be done on this front.

The rapid development of the airplane, in large part as an outgrowth of World War I, had convinced many that this mode of transport deserved substantial federal government encouragement. At first the principal way in which this consensus was implemented was through the inauguration of an air mail service operated by the Post Office Department. By 1925, however, it was felt that the time had come to transfer this administrative responsibility to private hands, and a system of generous mail subsidies to private commercial operators was worked out and given the force of law in the Air Mail Act of that year. But relieved now of this phase of aviation development, the federal government promptly took on another. Under the terms of the Air Commerce Act of 1926 the Secretary of Commerce was charged with the task of promoting air commerce and with maintaining the safety of air travel.

---

[4] William Beard, *Regulation of Pipe Lines as Common Carriers* (New York: Columbia University Press, 1941); and Federal Trade Commission, *Report on Pipe-Line Transportation of Petroleum* (Washington, D.C.: Government Printing Office, 1916).

[5] *The Pipe Line Cases*, 234 U.S. 548 (1914).

Thus far no steps had been taken to subject private air transportation firms to economic regulation. Already, however, there were indications that the achievement of maximum public benefits from this new mode of transportation would involve the maintenance of a degree of order in the industry by government edict. In other words, there could even at this stage in the airplane's development have been little doubt that one day it would be the focal point of still another great public utility industry, and that since this industry would not fit inside state boundaries such regulation would have to be under the supervision of a federal agency.

Although the Merchant Marine Act of 1920 had dealt kindly with the domestic shipping industry, little had been accomplished at that time in the way of permanent subsidies for these concerns. However, agitation pointed in that direction had continued, and by the end of the 1920's it was evident that without such assistance this industry would again shrink to the insignificant dimensions which had characterized it at the outbreak of World War I. Finally, in 1928, the resistance of agrarians and liberals to further steps along this line weakened, with the result that the Jones-White Mail Subsidy Act was passed. Ironically, however, despite the fact that construction aid and mail payments to ship operators were greatly liberalized, and that the new law did nothing to bring the public interest closer to the forefront in the administration of these programs, the American merchant marine was not thereby rescued from the threat of extinction.

UNFINISHED BUSINESS—PUBLIC UTILITIES

Nor was it only in the transportation field that more government activity was required on the basis of the implications of policy decisions already made. All across that broad area known as public utility regulation a similar situation prevailed.

At no point was this more strikingly illustrated than in the control of electric utilities, where state regulation was unable to deal with certain of the problems that were arising. This does not mean, of course, that there was much sentiment favoring the replacement of state utility regulation by federal control. Although the states were having their troubles in the sphere of operation reserved to them—political and other pressures from the regulated concerns and the cumbersomeness of the fair value rule, for example—few would have seriously suggested an expansion of federal responsibilities to remedy these difficulties. The problem here arose rather from two other sources.

In the first place, the dramatic growth of this industry was rapidly making it an interstate business with all of the complications for regulatory jurisdiction implied thereby in America's federal system. By 1928 more than 10 per cent of all the electricity consumed in the country crossed a state boundary, and five years later this proportion was to approach one-fifth. Already, moreover, state utility commissions had made attempts to extend their authority into this no-man's land, with the idea of at least steadying the situation until such time as the national government saw fit to act, but had been decisively rebuffed in these endeavors by the Supreme Court. First, a state on the receiving end of such an interstate transmission had attempted to regulate the wholesale rate on the imported product, only to be told that this would place an unconstitutional burden on interstate commerce.[6] A little later a forwarding state sought to break this deadlock, but was bluntly informed that the prior case governed that situation also.[7] And all the while the National Electric Light Association was carrying on one of the most comprehensive propaganda campaigns ever launched to see to it that this regulatory gap was not filled by federal action.[8]

In the second place, an even more compelling fact was giving this industry a national character. That fact was the holding company. The excited accumulation of utility properties into gigantic empires by means of that device had by the end of this decade created structures towering far above the pygmy state utility commissions which alone had regulatory jurisdiction in this field. An indication

TABLE 19. FINANCIAL GENIUS RUNS WILD: ASSETS OF
UTILITY HOLDING COMPANY (Sept., 1934)

	(billions of dollars)	(per cent of total)
Electric Bond and Share	2.6	19
Standard Power and Light	1.2	9
Commonwealth and Southern	1.2	9
North American	1.2	9
Associated Gas and Electric	1.2	9
Five largest systems	7.4	55
Fifteen largest systems	12.5	90
All systems	13.9	100

Source: Securities Exchange Commission, *Fourth Annual Report*, pp. 7-8.

[6] *Missouri* v. *Kansas Natural Gas Company*, 265 U.S. 298 (1924).

[7] *Public Utilities Commission of Rhode Island* v. *Attleboro Steam and Electric Company*, 273 U.S. 83 (1927).

[8] D. C. Blaisdell, *Economic Power and Political Pressures* (Washington, D.C.: Government Printing Office, 1941).

of the extent to which the industry had been taken over by these gargantuas can be had from the fact that at the height of this movement 15 holding company groups controlled concerns receiving more than 90 per cent of the nation's gross electric power revenues.

It is of course not to be supposed that this development was wholly artificial. Holding companies could point to solid justification for their existence. Thus in this decreasing-cost industry with its complex load factor important operating economies can be achieved through increased size, not the least of which being the possibility of improving the management of local utility concerns. Holding companies, furthermore, could often aid their charges in securing the large quantities of capital required to keep abreast of technological advance and sheer expansion. This was especially the case with smaller operating utilities which would have had a very limited access to the capital market without the assistance of these foster parents. And finally, holding companies often performed valuable engineering or other specific services for the concerns under their control.

If, in other words, the holding companies now taking over in this field had limited their influence to activities of these kinds, no holding company problem would have arisen. But everything financial in the 1920's was carried to excess, and the public utility holding company was a particularly excellent illustration of that tendency.[9]

To begin with, most of the major public utility empires were built far beyond any advantages of large-scale operation. Indeed there were instances (most notably, Samuel Insull himself) in which the men at the top did not even understand the structures they had created, to say nothing of managing these systems in a superior way. Viewed from another standpoint, moreover, the complexity of these organizations contributed to the speculative fever of the new era by preventing the stockholding public from knowing what it was buying in a public utility security. The pyramiding of concern upon concern also made the firms at the top exceedingly unstable financially, in addition to increasing beyond all reason the differential between the amount of money invested by those at the top and the value of the properties they controlled. In order to acquire a particular property excessive prices were often paid. Outrageously high service fees were not uncommon, and other devices were perfected for "milking" the operating companies (the most nefarious perhaps

---

[9] Federal Trade Commission, *Utility Corporations* (Washington, D.C.: Government Printing Office, 1935).

being calling on firms lower down in the hierarchy to loan money to those above them).

Although it was soon apparent that state commissions would be unable to deal adequately with a Delaware holding company doing a local utility business in Minneapolis, some of these bodies nonetheless at first made a valiant effort to expand their powers with that end in view. By the end of the decade, however, the hopelessness of this endeavor was widely understood. The complexity, the political and financial power, and the interstate nature of these organizations coupled with the interstate transmission of electricity, in short, were rapidly advancing the day when the nation would act to restore the private property–public interest equilibrium in this field that economic evolution was fast destroying.

In one other way the role the federal government was one day to play in the electric light and power industry was beginning to take on a more definitive form at this time. In part as an outgrowth of official Washington's interest in conservation, attention had long ago been directed to its strategic position in the area of hydroelectric power generation; in perhaps a majority of instances water power resources were available on streams that were also either navigable or in a federal forest preserve. Shortly after World War I a first halting step had been taken to utilize this position to best advantage. A Federal Power Commission was created to look after the community's interest in this area. Composed of the Secretaries of War, Interior, and Agriculture, however, little came of that innovation, and it was hence only a matter of time until the federal government would stake out its rights in this field more decisively.[10]

By 1928 one aspect of the federal government's future plans on this front was made clear, although in a very small way. Responding primarily to the demands of Californians for an improved water supply, irrigation facilities, flood control, and additional electric power, Congress authorized the construction of a huge dam on the lower Colorado (the Hoover-Boulder Dam). Although power generation was a secondary rather than a primary motive behind this project, and although great care was taken to hedge it about with restrictions calculated to keep government enterprise in the power business to the barest minimum, this was nonetheless the first stage of a development which was one day to be a crucial issue in government-business relationships.

What was true of electric power, next, was true also of natural

[10] Robert D. Baum, *The Federal Power Commission and State Utility Regulation* (Washington, D.C.: American Council on Public Affairs, 1942).

gas. Here too was a product under the control of state commissions from the standpoint of local distribution, but which frequently (indeed, in this case typically) passed over one or more state boundaries before it reached local distribution. Here too, moreover, was a business offering an excellent opportunity for holding company promoters, who made excellent use of the possibilities thus afforded. With the vast network of natural gas pipelines from the oilfields in the Southwest to the great consuming centers of the North and East still under construction this problem had not yet reached as critical a point as in the case of electricity, but it was even so quite evident that this situation also was building up to federal action.

Still a third public utility industry around which problems that state commissions could not wholly resolve were accumulating was telecommunications, and especially the telephone industry. The American Telephone and Telegraph Company has the distinction of being the first major holding company in the public utility field in point of time, and even at the peak of the holding company movement could with some validity have claimed to be the greatest of them all. From the headquarters of this giant concern in New York the vast preponderance of local telephone service was (as indeed still is) indirectly controlled, while virtually all the nation's long distance telephonic communication came (and still comes) under its direct supervision. And not only was the parent concern obviously beyond the reach of state commissions, but a number of American's subsidiary operating organizations were regional (rather than statewide) in character.

Four problems in particular were arising in this area which would apparently require action by an agency capable of looking at these operations as a whole. First, American Telephone and Telegraph controlled its own "manufacturing department" (the Western Electric Corporation), and the absence of arm's-length bargaining in the purchase of telephone equipment of all kinds was beginning to raise eyebrows in a number of quarters. Second, there seemed to be a tendency for the Bell System to charge excessive depreciation, thus inflating operating expenses, and then to demand a rate base from which only observed physical depreciation had been deducted. An increasing number of people were of the opinion that this "have-your-cake-and-eat-it-too" depreciation policy needed to be comprehensively examined. Third, American regularly charged each of its subsidiaries a percentage of its gross revenue for services rendered, and in the absence of knowledge about the cost of those services to the holding company local regulation had to be to that extent in the dark. Fourth, accurate regulation of local and long distance (intrastate and interstate) rates would clearly have to await a reliable allocation of costs between these two types of services.

For almost twenty years now the Interstate Commerce Commission had theoretically exercised jurisdiction over this business on behalf of the federal government. However, for a number of reasons little had been either attempted or accomplished by that body. For one thing, the training and experience of these commissioners had invariably been in railroad transportation, and therefore they felt neither competent enough nor inclined to regulate the telephone and telegraph industries as aggressively as the situation demanded. For another, the complexity of telephone regulation had by no means been fully appreciated when the Mann-Elkins Act was passed, and the Interstate Commerce Commission's legal foundation was extremely weak. Obviously before problems of the sort now confronting regulatory authorities in the telephone industry could be resolved, further legislation would have to be enacted.

The need for regulation in the radio broadcasting industry is so unique that it is perhaps stretching a point to refer to it as a public utility at all. A wireless transmission station requires the use of a specific portion of the so-called radio spectrum. Furthermore, unless in a given geographical area a particular portion of this spectrum is used by only one transmitter the result is mutual interference and extremely poor service. It follows that in the absence of a coordinating authority this medium of communication would be severely handicapped.

As this new industry mushroomed into prominence during the 1920's (the first presidential election campaign carried to the country by radio was in 1924) these facts became evident. In order to create some kind of order out of the rapidly developing chaos Secretary of Commerce Hoover unearthed an old statute having nothing whatever to do with radio broadcasting (a radiotelephony, maritime statute) and endeavored to use it as a basis for assigning frequencies by negotiation. When regulation by such haphazard methods broke down, as it did almost immediately, pandemonium broke loose in the industry and the value of radio communication was for a time almost destroyed. As a result the Radio Act of 1927 was passed giving a Federal Radio Commission the authority to approve applications for broadcast licenses, assign wave lengths, fix hours of operation, and limit station power.

In this area, in other words, the inherent conservatism of the national government was relaxed sufficiently to permit action even before the decade of the 1920's was over. However, the action taken was strictly minimal, and the industry regulated thereby continued to be exceedingly dynamic. It was, in short, not difficult to predict even in 1927 that this timid extension of federal government power would one day be carried much farther.

UNFINISHED BUSINESS—AGRICULTURE

It might be supposed that with all the legislation passed in the farmer's behalf in the early years of this decade, no further action would have been required on that front. Such a supposition, however, would reckon without the fact that the painful postwar recession developed in agricultural areas into chronic depression. Agriculture had also become a "sick" industry.[11] Thus farm representatives who had earlier pressed for emergency measures were by now demanding major changes in the status quo on a more permanent basis.[12]

A glance at the major forces behind this agricultural depression will make plain why the programs being proposed were long-run in character, and therefore why conservatives were so alarmed by them. First, the United States was fast becoming such an excellent

TABLE 20.   PRODUCTIVITY WITHOUT PROSPERITY

Year	Exports		Tractors on Farms
	All	Crude Foodstuffs	
	(millions of dollars)		
1915	2,716	507	25,000
1925	4,819	318	549,000

Source: Bureau of the Census, *Historical Statistics of the United States, 1789-1945*, pp. 100 and 246.

place for foreigners to buy manufactured goods that there remained abroad too little purchasing power with which to buy American agricultural exports. Second, because the demand for products of the farm is inelastic, an increasing per capita income at home does not result in a proportional increase in the consumption of agricultural staples. Third, rapid technological progress in agriculture plus the high rural birth rate was keeping output up despite the difficulty

[11] United States Department of Agriculture, *Farmers in a Changing World: 1940 Yearbook of Agriculture* (Washington, D.C.: Government Printing Office, 1940).

[12] Theodore Saloutos and John D. Hicks, *Agricultural Discontent in the Middle West, 1900-1939* (Madison: University of Wisconsin Press, 1951).

with both foreign and domestic demand. And finally, the substitution of gasoline for grain as a source of power on the farm, and the substitution of rayon for cotton, were especially putting pressure upon the Middle West and the South.

In part the legislative demands now made by farmers were only a continuation of the types of government activities which had seemed to provide some relief in the past. Thus in 1924 the Inland Waterways Corporation Act was passed, another episode in the Midwest's age-old attempt to develop water transportation as a way of keeping the railroads in line. During the war the government had operated a barge service on the Mississippi, Missouri, Illinois, and Warrior rivers in order to supplement rail transportation, and, essentially perhaps because the nation's leaders had not yet gotten around to this problem, that facility had since the war continued to operate under the general supervision of the War Department. Now a government corporation was created to take charge of this responsibility, the thought being that private capital might thereby be encouraged to enter this business. The results were quite paradoxical. Although the Corporation lost money, often quite heavily, more than one hundred private barge lines did begin service on inland waterways over the next quarter of a century.

Freight rates, too, came in for their share of attention, and in as naive a way as at any previous time.[13] The so-called Hoch-Smith Resolution of 1925 declared it to be Congressional policy for the Interstate Commerce Commission to consider in the fixing of rates "the conditions which at any time prevail in our several industries . . . insofar as it is possible to do so, to the end that commodities should freely move." In accordance with that policy the Commission was directed to investigate the railway rate structure to determine how it affected different regions and products, making such changes as seemed to be thereby indicated, and to put rates on agricultural products at the lowest lawful level. This attempt to revise the rate structure for the benefit of the farmer by legislative fiat ended as ignominiously as had every one of its predecessors, although it did perhaps result in the ironing out of a number of minor inequities. The first time the Commission specifically cited the Hoch-Smith Resolution in support of a reduction in an agricultural rate its decision was appealed, and the Resolution was no more. The Supreme Court held that this mandate was nothing more than the expression of a Congressional hope.[14]

[13] D. P. Locklin, *Railroad Regulation Since 1920* (New York: McGraw-Hill Book Co., Inc., 1928).
[14] *Ann Arbor Railroad Company* v. *United States*, 281 U.S. 658 (1930).

There was, in the third place, continued emphasis upon cooperatives throughout this decade. The idea was now becoming firmly fixed in the minds of farm leaders that the farmer's great problem was his lack of bargaining power, his economic impotence in dealing with the great organizations which commanded the gateways of commerce whenever he endeavored to buy or sell. The cooperative seemed to many to be a solution to this difficulty. If the farmer could only organize his side of the markets in which he operated (and especially those in which his goods were sold), so this thinking ran, surely he would be that much less at a disadvantage. This point of view, in fact, was so doggedly held, and conservatives were so eager to divert the farmer's attention from more radical measures, that further legislation was passed promoting these organizations. The Cooperative Marketing Act of 1926 established a division in the Department of Agriculture the sole responsibility of which was to foster and assist farm cooperatives. A year later legislation was passed forbidding boards of trade from discriminating against such organizations in establishing membership requirements.

But precisely because these steps did secure grudging support from conservatives (perhaps precisely because they took their cue from past endeavors to help agriculture), they did not long satisfy farmers confronted with a far more serious problem than ever before. They were, in other words, trivial by comparison with the agricultural depression, and, knowing this, farmers early in the 1920's set their sights much higher.

What kind of a policy did agricultural leaders think would solve their difficulties? The problem seemed simple enough to men with a powerful vested interest in its solution. If at base one of the primary forces behind chronic agricultural depression was the falling off of sales abroad, it seemed obvious that a fundamental part of the remedy should be the subsidizing of exports. This was to become during the 1920's the central objective of farm leaders,[15] and no aspect of those years made more of an impression upon the people living through them or is better remembered by later generations than the so-called McNary-Haugen movement.[16]

Although the strategy initially decided upon for achieving this goal ultimately failed, it was nonetheless a strategy well calculated to keep opponents on the political defensive.[17] Thus on the one

[15] M. K. Kile, *The Farm Bureau Through Three Decades* (Baltimore: The Waverly Press, 1948).

[16] Gilbert C. Fite, *George N. Peek and the Fight For Farm Parity* (Norman: University of Oklahoma Press, 1954).

[17] John D. Black, *Agricultural Reform in the United States* (New York: McGraw-Hill Book Co., Inc., 1929).

hand, no charge upon the Treasury was proposed. An equalization fee assessed against that portion of various farm products sold domestically would be used to finance the operation. On the other hand, a vigorous effort was made to identify this program with the protective tariff, both to legitimize it in the public mind and to secure support from those interests which had in the past been so successful in getting tariff legislation passed. The two most common slogans of the movement were "equality for the farmer," and "making the tariff effective for the farmer."[18]

Representative Gilbert Haugen of Iowa first presented this proposal to Congress, and the appeal to the spirit of fair play could not have been more plainly expressed.

All will agree that it is unfair to continue a policy which protects one and not the other. What is good for the goose is good for the gander. Such a discriminating policy cannot long continue.

But that the strategy first adopted by the bill's proponents could not succeed, and why, was made equally plain two days later by Representative Luce of Massachusetts.

You are asking that as an inevitable result of an increase in the cost of living our employers be forced to pay still higher wages, while employers in Europe, as an inevitable result of a lowered cost of living, can pay still smaller wages. As the sure sequence, you are asking that the prices of all American-made articles shall be raised, while the prices of all foreign-made articles are lowered. So you are asking us to help those against whom we raise our tariff wall.

If industrialists could not support McNary-Haugenism because discrimination against the farmer was essential to the effectiveness of their own protection, laborers found themselves in essentially the same situation. In a decade which could hardly have been more filled with frustrations for workers, this group could point to only two major aspects of the status quo offering it aid and comfort. One was the low prices of agricultural products (to put it bluntly, the agricultural depression); the other was the protective tariff on industrial products. What the farmer now wished to do was to eliminate both of these pillars of the worker's economy in the process of improving his own position.

Forced thus to fight their battle alone, farmers abruptly altered their strategy. In order to make the best of an admittedly bad situation, the tariff was moved off the center of the stage while cotton was brought in to take its place. When this "marriage of corn and

[18] George N. Peek and Hugh Johnson, *Equality For Agriculture* (Moline: Moline Plow Co., 1921).

cotton" was finally consummated, a McNary-Haugen bill was twice pushed through both Houses of Congress. Both times, however, that measure was prevented from becoming law by a Coolidge veto. (Be it remembered that this was the same man who had a number of years earlier endeared himself to conservatives by saying, "The business of the United States is business.") Then, to complete this painful circle of frustration, in the presidential election campaign of 1928 both major parties pledged themselves to do something *else* for the farmer.

It is not to be wondered at that when almost simultaneously with Coolidge's second veto generous subsidies for the merchant marine became law, farmers were not impressed. Still less enthusiastic were they when one of the first major items placed on the agenda of Herbert Hoover's first Congress was another across-the-board increase in customs duties, the Smoot-Hawley Tariff. But when it became apparent what the new administration's idea of adequate farm legislation was, it is especially understandable why farmers felt that insult had been added to injury.

The Agricultural Marketing Act of 1929 created a Federal Farm Board to assist in the "more orderly marketing of farm products." Equipped with a $500 million revolving fund, this agency was to loan money to cooperative marketing associations and to conduct its own direct "stabilization" operations. In either case the philosophy behind the new program was that farm surpluses were only temporary phenomena, and that all that was needed was a mechanism making it possible for these products to be held off the market until their price improved.

The farmer by now knew better, and hence it was not seriously supposed among agricultural leaders that anything more than a palliative had been enacted. Here, in other words, was still another area in which unresolved problems were accumulating, problems which would one day have to be given more serious attention. It would be incorrect to suggest that, as with the transportation and public utility problems in this same category, the principles around which a more satisfactory solution could be built were already on the statute books. Indeed, as of 1929 there were few who even pretended to know what a satisfactory solution to the farm problem might be, and it was equally uncertain what changes in the political status quo would have to take place before such a solution could become law. But it was clear enough that at this point as at so many others the decade of the 1920's was maintaining its reputation by passing its problems along to its successor. And certainly no problem thus passed on became more intractable.

"Main Street and Wall Street"[19]

In one other major area of the economy was laissez faire riding for a very painful fall. To be sure, in the matter of the financial organization of American society there was not, as in the case particularly of the farm problem, a contemporary realization of something drastically wrong. For this, unfortunately, the beginning of the most savage economic depression in all history had first to be endured. In a more sober environment, however, it was difficult to look back at the financial practices common during the latter 1920's without a feeling of shame that they were not suspect at the time. And it was precisely because great evils could flourish so widely unnoticed that it was deemed necessary a little later to erect safeguards in the public interest.

It is not, of course, to be supposed that now, any more than at the time of the Pujo investigation, popular antagonism toward finance capitalism was directed against the corporate form of organization as such. To be sure, many reformers still retained the historic liberal attitude of suspicion regarding the operation of such enterprises, an attitude finding much to feed upon in what was happening in the field of limited liability in Delaware and in other states endeavoring to outdo the Du Pont political machine. But now, as earlier, the insoluble problem at this point was how to sustain the desirable features of a modern industrial society without this institution. As a result reforms when they came were once again oriented to specific abuses that had suddenly become apparent.[20]

Only a few illustrations of the worst of these abuses can be included here. One of the classic cases in point had to do with the operations of the National City Bank of New York, a commercial bank, and the National City Company, the National City Bank's investment affiliate. The Company had been organized originally out of the proceeds of a 40 per cent dividend on the Bank's own stock, and it was supervised by a group of three trustees, all of whom were officers or directors of the Bank. In everything but name, therefore, the two institutions were one—and this despite New York laws forbidding commercial banks to sell securities and the strong probability that this arrangement was also illegal under the National Banking Act. The National City Bank was the second largest commercial bank in the entire country, and the National City Company was the nation's largest distributor of securities.

[19] Title of volume written by W. Z. Ripley (Boston: Little, Brown & Co., 1927).
[20] F. L. Allen, *Lords of Creation* (New York: Harper & Bros., 1935); and Ferdinand Pecora, *Wall Street Under Oath* (New York: Simon & Schuster, Inc., 1939).

Among the securities sold by the Company were the bonds of foreign governments. One such issue accepted for distribution was a bond flotation of the State of Minas Geraes. A report from one of the Company's foreign agents had stated that the financial laxness and administrative ineptitude of that state's leadership "borders on the fantastic." When translated into prospectus language, this analysis became: "Prudent and careful administration of the State's finances has been characteristic with successive administrations in Minas Geraes." The bonds sold very well.

As would be expected, too, some of the securities marketed by the Company were holdings which for some reason or another the Bank wanted to take out of its own portfolio. At one point, for example, the Bank wanted to dispose of 300,000 shares of Anaconda Copper. The price of copper had just fallen 25 per cent in a single month (and the chairman of Anaconda's board was also a member of the board of directors of the National City Company). Accordingly, these 300,000 shares were transferred from the Bank to the Company, and so successful were the latter's salesmen in selling them to the public that an additional 1,000,000 shares were purchased for resale to the Company's own customers.

A similar procedure was followed on another occasion when the Bank found itself sustaining heavy losses on several large Cuban sugar loans, although the technique used here was more complicated. First, stockholders were asked to subscribe to $50 million in additional capital stock, the proceeds of which were divided equally between the Bank and the Company. Second, the Company used its share of these funds to buy all the securities of a newly organized concern known as the General Sugar Corporation. Third, this company then bought the Bank's bad loans for $25 million. This circle of transactions was then closed when the Company subsequently wrote down its investment in General Sugar to $1.

Not content, furthermore, with the profits to be made from buying and selling in an unmanipulated market, the Company on numerous occasions participated in "pools" designed to create an even more favorable market for stocks in which it was interested. One such pool dealt in the stock of three copper-producing concerns. Out of these manipulations the Company made a profit of just under $10 million, and at virtually no risk, for all these concerns were subsidiaries of Anaconda Copper and the chairman of the board and the president of that company were National City's fellow pool members.

Still other interesting features of the operation of this immense institution can be seen in the way members of its management team were reimbursed for their services. To begin with, each man in this group received a base salary of $25,000. Over and above this each member of the executive group was given a handsome incentive to increase profits in the form of a proportionate share of a so-called management fund ($1 out of every $5 of net earnings above 8 per cent on invested capital). Still more "compensation" was available in the form of blocks of securities at extremely favorable prices, shares held back out of an issue to be sold to the public at much higher prices. A fourth way of remunerating members of this group was to loan them large sums of money with which they could increase the volume of speculating they were doing on their own account.

The Chase National Bank of New York was larger than the National City Bank as a commercial banking institution; the Chase Securities Company, on the other hand, was somewhat less impressive than the National City Company. Little difference would be claimed as between the behavior of these two great concerns, however, although it is possible that the record of the Chase bank was even more flagrant than that of its rival from the standpoint of the exploitation of outsiders by insiders. One instance will suffice as an indication of this difference. The president of Chase National during the early months of the stock market crash made the astonishingly large sum of $4 million by selling short the stock of his own bank all the while the bank itself was endeavoring to support the market, which meant that he was in effect making short sales to his own institution. When the time came for him to cover these purchases, furthermore, he borrowed the necessary funds from his bank. And when the time came to pay income taxes on these earnings he so juggled these profits among members of his family and several personal corporations that not one cent was collected by the federal government.

Although by now far from the largest, J. P. Morgan and Company was still the greatest banking concern on Wall Street. Moreover, the Morgan firm was during the 1920's (as always) a relatively conservative organization, and hence there was here less giving in to the temptation of the times than at many other Wall Street addresses. But even in this pillar of America's financial mechanism the speculation poison was clearly working. Thus it was this house that launched the United Company, a key element in one of the most complex public utility holding company pyramids of the day. It was J. P. Morgan and Company also that gave birth to the Allegheny Corporation and other important units in the Van Sweringen brothers' railroad holding company empire. And in distributing the common stock of such concerns (J. P. Morgan and Company had historically been almost exclusively a bond house), the method adopted was allocation to a "preferred list" of Morgan's own customers at very favorable prices. Allegheny common, for example, was made available to such a group at $20 per share at a time when its market value was $35 per share.

Still another way in which this aspect of the new era can be visualized is to note its influence on one of the most basic institutional evolutions of that period. At base the investment trust was a most useful device by means of which small investors could enter the securities market without running the almost intolerable risk of nondiversification. In other words, this type of organization was first and foremost a custodian of the investment funds of men and women who could not afford to lose their savings, and therefore bore a relationship to the community at large not unlike commercial banks and insurance companies. Yet, despite the fiduciary nature of this relationship, these organizations were freely used to participate in market pools, to launch speculative new corporations, and to favor insiders at the expense of outsiders.

And finally, no account of the financial orgy of the period 1927-1929 would be complete without reference to the stock market boom as such. In this connection would have to be mentioned the reckless

TABLE 21. WHO'S AFRAID OF THE BIG BAD WOLF?

Year	Capital Issues of Corporations (millions of dollars)	Broker's Loans Outstanding on September 30* (millions of dollars)	Stock Exchange Transactions* (millions of shares)	Average Stock* Prices† (dollars)
1926	3,644	3,219	451	186
1927	5,970	3,915	577	247
1928	7,191	5,514	920	333
1929	7,217	8,549	1,125	470

* New York Stock Exchange.
† Dow-Jones high for 25 industrials.
Source: Bureau of the Census, *Statistical Abstract of the United States, 1930*, pp. 312-13.

abandon with which the buying of securities on 90 per cent margin was encouraged; the channeling of unbelievable quantities of commercial bank credit to support the purchase of questionable stocks at ever higher prices; the use of the investment trust device to bring the stock market more or less legitimately within reach of millions of smaller-income receivers; the siphoning off into securities markets of hundreds of millions of dollars of liquid capital by industrial concerns that had either completed expansion plans for the time being or felt that the purchase of claims was a more lucrative investment opportunity than capital formation; and the way in which exaggerated expectations pushed this market up and up, thus creating still more exaggerated expectations and still higher prices. It was as if every part of the nation's entire complex financial mechanism, in the manner of the legendary Pied Piper of Hamelin, had been deliberately oriented to the task of luring innocent victims to wholesale disaster.

There is no way of knowing to what extent the pattern of practices suggested here contributed to the anguish suffered when this top-heavy edifice came crashing down, or even to the height of the speculative boom and hence to the violence of the ensuing decline. It is easy to understand, however, why citizens turned bitterly against the men and organizations that had so abused them. The lifeblood of a modern industrial society is the flow of money and capital through the various mechanisms created to facilitate this circulation. If those responsible for their operation could not be depended upon to deal fairly with the people whose money they were responsible for, here was reason enough for imposing burdensome government restrictions.[21]

Nor is it any answer to what is involved here to say that a citizenry gets the leaders it deserves—that, in the case at hand, the gullibility of the man in the street was a prime factor. This is true, of course, in a sense. But in a democracy citizens expect their leaders to live by a higher standard than they apply to their own behavior. As this is expressed in a well-known proverb: "If gold rusts, what can poor iron do?" And the important implication of this is that in a democracy leadership is held and institutions exist at the sufferance of the mass voter.

All this can be put still differently with profit. A surprisingly small number of people went to jail for their part in the debacle of the late 1920's, although the heads of both the National City Bank and the Chase National Bank (to mention only two such instances) resigned under pressure of an aroused public opinion. But from a more fundamental standpoint a punishment far more appropriate to the crimes committed was meted out to those who perpetrated them. Although unfortunately, as so frequently happens with general retributions, the innocent had to suffer along with the guilty, the financial reforms of the New Deal as society's most basic reaction

[21] M. E. Dimock, and H. K. Hyde, *Bureaucracy and Trusteeship in Large Corporations* (Washington, D.C.: Government Printing Office, 1940).

to "finance capitalism gone wild" could hardly have been more fitting.

Unquestionably the laissez faire of the 1920's was a brazen camouflage. Conservatives, of course, are not to be blamed for pretending that no fundamental changes had been wrought by economic evolution and prior reforms. But they could not have been more wrong. America would never be the same again; the government had decisively entered the lists in a broadly responsible capacity, and would never be ousted from that role. Furthermore, every year that passed was revealing new areas in which the government would one day play a vital part. From one end of the economy to the other, from labor's demand for a guarantee of the right of collective bargaining to the resounding cry for regulation of the New York Stock Exchange, fields for new government activities were being built up. And, unfortunately for conservative preferences, the head-in-the-sand approach to this fact during the 1920's probably only accentuated that development when it came.

QUESTIONS FOR DISCUSSION

1. In what sense can the decade of the 1920's be referred to as the end of laissez faire in the United States?

2. What is the meaning of the term "unfinished business," as used in this chapter? How accurate is that description?

3. Describe the difficulties being encountered at this time in the solution of the weak-and-strong-railroad problem.

4. Explain the connections between the rise of the gasoline engine and the plight of the railroad industry.

5. Why was the regulation of pipelines proceeding no more rapidly than it was?

6. In what ways was state regulation of the electric light and power industry becoming inadequate?

7. Explain the depreciation problem associated with telephone regulation.

8. Why did the public utility holding company pose such difficult problems from the standpoint of regulation?

9. What were the major factors responsible for depression in agriculture during the 1920's?

10. Describe and evaluate McNary-Haugenism as a solution to the problem confronting American agriculture.

11. Discuss the strategy used in the attempt to pass the McNary-Haugen bill, including the reasons for its failure.

12. What was the problem of "insiders" versus "outsiders" as it developed during this period?

13. Why were the financial practices of this decade so certain to be at least partially remedied in the forseeable future?

14. At what price was the laissez faire of the 1920's purchased?

Part V

LAISSEZ FAIRE REPLACED

Chapter 19

"The Years of the Locust"[1]

Too Little and Too Late

Even as American leadership was ignoring questions of public policy soon to become quite grave, in one area of the economy there had arisen a problem which did not lend itself to such casual treatment. A speculative boom, of course, could not flourish without an abundant supply of money, while the money supply could not be large enough to support a speculative inflation without the more or less active cooperation of the newly created Federal Reserve System. Thus it was that one group of the nation's financial leaders had to give constant attention to the policy course to be pursued.

Now it must be acknowledged at the outset that in a number of respects Federal Reserve authorities were placed by unfolding events in a most unenviable position. First and foremost, although the public thought of these people as a single, monolithic entity when things went wrong, they in fact wielded a highly fragmented power. The System's control over the money supply was still split thirteen different ways; and although from the beginning the New York Bank had exercised a leadership most of the other Banks had been happy to follow with modifications, the System did not possess an authority commensurate with its responsibilities.

In the second place, the men in charge of the nation's money supply had to make their decisions in the face of the studied indifference of many other policy-making officials.[2] On one side the desire on the part of most of official Washington to ignore this issue resulted in the appointment to Federal Reserve posts of men more recommended by their political and economic philosophies than by

---

[1] Title of volume by Gilbert Seldes (Boston: Little, Brown & Co., 1933).

[2] William A. White, *A Puritan in Babylon: The Story of Calvin Coolidge* (New York: The Macmillan Co., 1938).

their competence in the money field. Thus in early 1929 Charles S. Mitchell, head of the National City Bank, became a director in the New York Federal Reserve Bank. On the other side the attempt by a few conscientious and able Federal Reserve policy-makers to make the underlying health of the American economy in the late 1920's a major concern was like trying to swim against a strong current. The nation's political leadership persistently refused to acknowledge that the new era's perpetual prosperity might be getting out of hand, that men of property might need restraint. As strong a statement of criticism as was ever elicited from a high government official was the judgment expressed by Andrew Mellon at a press conference in answer to a question about excesses in the stock market that now would be a good time for the prudent investor to buy bonds. Against such an attitude of unbounded optimism, apprehensions about the country's money supply would obviously receive little heed.

There were, in the third place, technical difficulties associated with the effective use of monetary controls at this time. To begin with the new money and banking system had not at all been created with the idea of using it on occasion to hold a boom in check. It would, therefore, at best require much experimentation and practice to have accomplished this task well—to say nothing of the mental adjustment that would be required before such an endeavor could have received the requisite public support. It must not be forgotten, in this connection, that the stock market boom was exceedingly profitable while it lasted. Furthermore, an inflation taking primarily the form of soaring security prices was a sufficiently unique phenomenon that men would have been all the more nonplussed to know how to restrain it with the tools at hand. The restrictive techniques available to monetary authorities were all purely quantitative in nature, making no distinction between funds flowing into productive business activities and those serving only to push the prices of securities higher and higher.

And fourth, perhaps the most crucial difficulty of all was the fact that the economic environment was most uncongenial to the steps real restriction would have demanded. Thus, after provoking the wrath of almost the entire politically organized population by their action at the peak of the post-World War I boom, Federal Reserve leaders were now understandably gun-shy. During the early part of the decade, moreover, the struggle the Western world was making to re-establish a full gold standard greatly weakened the case for inaugurating an inhibitory policy. A tight money condition, a raising of the domestic interest rate relative to the foreign rate, would

have had the effect of slowing down the flow of American investment abroad and hence of accelerating the importation of gold into
the United States. With this country already in possession of a
larger share of the world's stock of monetary gold than was considered desirable from the standpoint of the international gold
standard, these interrelationships between the domestic and foreign
money markets substantially prevented adoption of a more appropriate monetary policy.

Notwithstanding all these difficulties, however, it was finally decided that action would have to be taken. Toward the end of 1928
and in early 1929 Federal Reserve officials began a reversal of the
easy money policy which had prevailed to date, although in March,
1929, this effort was essentially abandoned largely as a result of the
efforts of Charles S. Mitchell.

It would be "Monday morning quarterbacking" of the most indefensible sort to assert that the Federal Reserve System's course
throughout this decade was a misguided one.[3] At the same time, it
would be difficult to conceive of a policy followed by more perverse
consequences. Thus the ready availability of credit early in the
decade contributed to a stock market boom of such proportions that
in the end American capital would have deserted foreign money
markets quite apart from a tightening of the money market here at
home. Not only, furthermore, was the earlier policy in this sense
self-defeating, but its more restrictive successor came no nearer to
accomplishing its objective. By this time the rate of real capital
formation had begun to taper off, one corollary of this being that
surplus corporation funds were now finding their way into the
market even more rapidly than Federal Reserve policy was succeeding in withdrawing commercial bank funds. By this time, too,
the boom was broadly feeding on itself; for example, the popular
enthusiasm for securities was so great that the new investment trusts
were also able to help compensate for credit withdrawals at other
points. And of course the climaxing tragedy was the fact that when
the crash came, the central bank authorities could with superficial
plausibility again be charged with "pulling the trigger."

It was another sobering experience for the makers of monetary
policy. All the more was it apparent what a difficult responsibility
resided in the Federal Reserve System. But this was neither the only
nor the most fundamental lesson implicit in this sequence of developments. Also apparent was the need to put better tools in the hands

[3] Paul M. Warburg, *The Federal Reserve System* (New York: The Macmillan Co.,
1930).

of those wielding this responsibility. In other words, it was becoming clear that here was an area in which a *little* control could not be effectively exercised in a modern economy, that the control pattern would have to be broadened and deepened before it could be said to be adequate to its task. In short, here was yet another important area in which laissez faire was being subtly undermined.

First Reaction[4]

October 24, 1929, fell on a Thursday. On that day neither the first nor the greatest of the October, 1929, stock market tragedies took place. Nevertheless, there is good reason for referring to it as "Black Thursday." Then it was that men first began to understand that the bottom might really drop out of the world as they knew it. Thus belatedly did it register with Americans that perpetual prosperity had no more been achieved than perpetual motion.

A part of what is meant by the name "Black Thursday" is of course obvious. As a result of this, the most drastic decline in share prices in a single day in the history of the New York Stock Exchange, thousands upon thousands of small and large market operators were literally wiped out. But another and a much deeper meaning is also suggested by that terminology. Although it is misleading even to try to attach an exact date to major historical developments, a defense can be made of the proposition that on October 24, 1929, the mask behind which the 1920's had insisted upon hiding was torn away. Suddenly, and even more bitterly, the realization was driven home to conservatives that the nineteenth century was over, that the sociopolitical environment within which business had then operated could not be recreated, that, in short, the New Freedom lived on in spirit despite its untimely physical death.

Understandably, this realization was not at once (if ever) communicated to the public. Too much was at stake to permit a confession of failure to be broadcast to the world. On the one hand, conservatives had justified their leadership in large part on the basis of "a chicken in every pot, and a car in every garage," with the result that even the bare admission of the fact of depression would have asserted the bankruptcy of the nation's leadership as eloquently as wholesale resignations from public office. On the other hand, it was apparent that little was to be gained while perhaps much was to be lost by openly acknowledging what the average citizen was rapidly coming to sense anyway. It is, in other words, to the great credit of

[4] Irving Fisher, *The Stock Market Crash—And After* (New York: The Macmillan Co., 1930).

those in high places in 1929 that they did not lose their heads as they were losing their fortunes.

Put positively rather than negatively, the first concern of those in charge of the nation's affairs was to reassure the fearful, to convince the people that nothing had really happened. As the New York banking community had endeavored to stem the tide of deflation in 1907, so did another generation of Wall Street bankers embark upon a similar project in 1929. At about 12:00 noon on "Black Thursday" the president of the New York Stock Exchange personally transmitted the bankers' orders for 25,000 shares of United States Steel at the latest recorded price and for varying quantities of a dozen or so other stocks. With that development the market steadied, remaining in a fair state of order through the following day, at which time the Treasury officially announced that the collapse had been checked. On October 26 this encouraging word was carried to every corner of the land in the form of a pronouncement from the White House to the effect that "the fundamental business of the country—that is, the production and distribution of commodities—is on a sound and prosperous basis."

If the underlying structure had been sounder, if a little more attention had earlier been given to the fundamentals of financial organization, all this might have been much more than whistling in the dark. As it was, unfortunately, the dominoes kept pushing one another down with systematic thoroughness. Thus the newly organized investment trusts, having so far departed from the functions in the performance of which they were to make their primary contribution as to be themselves deeply involved in the call loan business, made haste to withdraw the funds entrusted to them which were being so used. Industrial corporations likewise, almost frantically began extricating from the stock market the funds they had invested therein. In the holding company field, moreover, the financial leverage which under favorable circumstances can generate fantastic profits now began to operate in reverse. In empire after empire the uppermost concerns began to topple, often pulling much sounder subsidiaries down with them. And then, of course, there were the many operations financed on a 10 per cent margin. As plunger after plunger was forced to sell some of his holdings in order to "feed the kitty" on the rest, the wave of retrenchment could only reach tidal proportions. When to these organizational defects is added the far more basic fact that the "Mellon Plan" of taxation had contributed to a one-sided distribution of the nation's income, it can be seen how futile were such steps as supporting the market and counseling citizens to be of good cheer.

Confronted with these inexorable realities, the attitude of open defiance of the forces which had been unleashed and let loose upon an unsuspecting economy did not last long. On Tuesday, October 29, the greatest wave of selling yet engulfed the Exchange, and it was apparent that the efforts of the giant banks of New York were as nothing by comparison with the power of the forces now on the loose. A Federal Reserve report in mid-November indicated that the readjustment was far from over, and at approximately this point the new President concluded that more than a stock market decline was involved, and hence prepared to adopt more drastic measures.

Even this conclusion, however, did little to loosen the powerful hold of the past on Herbert Hoover and those around him. Government responsibilities beyond those involved in protecting and at times promoting property rights had become such a deeply ingrained taboo among conservatives that the long-standing policy of "letting nature take her course" insofar as economic conditions were concerned was still given the benefit of almost every doubt. Where private enterprise activities could speed up nature's own healing process well and good, but the government (and especially the federal government) was not directly to intervene.

Quite in accord with the best thinking on business cycle theory today (but also quite in accord with the instincts of a 1929 conservative), the administration's first thought in this connection was to stimulate investment. Pointing to the fact that of late capital had been diverted into the securities market, the President on November 15 suggested that businessmen of all types could not better demonstrate their faith in America's future than by rejuvenating the nation's lagging construction program. On November 21, both a stronger and a broader appeal was made directly to business and labor leaders at a conference called for that purpose. Here an agreement was arrived at under the terms of which employers agreed to maintain employment as far as possible and more especially not to cut wages, in exchange for which promise labor representatives pledged their members not to interfere with this holding operation by demanding pay increases.

Two days later another appeal was made. In telegrams to all state governors and to a large number of mayors, President Hoover asked for fullest cooperation in a program of public works expansion. No suggestion was contained therein that the federal government would also participate in such a project. Indeed, in his first annual message to Congress, the President even made this omission explicit. It was, he said, of the first importance in this crisis not to upset business confidence by threatening the federal government's balanced budget. Social services, therefore, including relief payments, must necessarily remain in the hands of private charitable organizations assisted by local and state governments.

Unfortunately, these first thoughts on appropriate governmental policies in the midst of an especially acute modern economic downturn bore little fruit.[5] It is simply not in the pattern for private enterprise to expand its facilities, maintain employment, and keep the rate of wages intact in the face of a serious decline in aggregate demand. Just as the bankers had been inadequate to the task they had set for themselves, so were industrialists inadequate to the task now

TABLE 22. EXIT BUSINESS CONFIDENCE

| Year | Gross Private Domestic Investment (billions of dollars) | |
	New Construction	Durable Equipment
1929	7.8	6.4
1930	5.6	4.9
1931	3.6	3.2
1932	1.7	1.8
1933	1.1	1.8

Source: Department of Commerce.

entrusted to them. These years recorded few episodes of steadfast courage more heart-warming than the last-ditch honoring of this agreement by United States Steel and Henry Ford's valiant attempt to *raise* wages in the automobile industry, but the hole in the dike was already so large that these few small fingers could not hold the angry waters in check. And as for coordinated public works expansion at the state and local levels, the depression was clearly a *national* phenomenon and could hence only be effectively dealt with on a national basis.

OBSTINACY OF ORTHODOXY[6]

As one by one the champions sent forth to do battle with the enemy returned from the lists defeated and dispirited, allies already in the field were being similarly turned back. Immediately after the first hint of major trouble the Federal Reserve System had taken steps to reverse the tighter money policy inaugurated so shortly be-

[5] J. K. Galbraith, *The Great Crash* (Boston: Houghton Mifflin Co., 1955).
[6] R. G. Tugwell, *Mr. Hoover's Economic Policy* (New York: John Day Co., Inc., 1932).

fore. The rediscount rate was substantially lowered, and a vigorous campaign of open market security buying was launched. It was at this point that still another sobering lesson about monetary policy was learned the hard way. While it is easy enough to restrict business activity by making energetic use of the tools available to money and banking authorities, it is a far different thing to bring about an economic expansion by reversing this process. Stated differently, banks can in this way be forced to tighten credit, but central bank decisions cannot compel cautious businessmen to apply for loans. Because, in short, "one can pull but not push with a string," excess reserves simply piled up in the banks and the deflationary spiral went on its way unhindered.

Meanwhile the newly created Federal Farm Board had been jousting with the foe on a quite different basis. And whereas doubts had existed in many minds whether this agency was competent to bring real aid to the farmer under the best of circumstances, it was in the event expected to do its bit under the most adverse conditions imaginable. The outcome was not long in doubt. Having determined that the price line on agricultural staples had to be held at some point at whatever cost, the Board began to buy especially wheat and cotton from all comers at officially determined prices. The cost proved to be too great. In an amazingly short time the $500 million revolving fund was gone, and Congress persistently refused to send good money after bad. Most of the rest of the Federal Farm Board's active and impotent life was spent in disposing of the stocks of farm commodities this abortive action had placed in the government's hands.

If it be supposed that the administration in Washington was encouraged by these failures to take a second look at its tenacious clinging to economic conservatism, a glance at the further policies adopted will dispel that illusion.[7] Actually official attitudes were if anything hardening as a federal budget deficit loomed on the horizon for the first time in a dozen years. This was perhaps the major reason supplemental funds were not made available to the Federal Farm Board. Here too was the principal explanation of President Hoover's veto of a special loan program for veterans—a program, however, which was passed despite the veto. The depression was having its inevitable consequences on government income, and it seemed obvious to a business-oriented officialdom that reduced revenues must be accompanied by reduced expenses.

[7] W. S. Myers and W. H. Newton, *The Hoover Administration: A Documentary Narrative* (New York: Charles Scribner's Sons, 1936).

But much more was at stake than the budget. Also involved was the moral integrity of the American people, a virtue the reeling administration proposed to protect come what may. This meant that unemployed, underfed citizens must be prevented from succumbing to the temptation to "go on the dole." The feeling of uselessness which goes along with the inability to find work, the undernourishment which arises out of the need to concentrate food expenditures on low-cost-per-calorie carbohydrates, the social degradation associated with moving "across the tracks" where rents are cheaper— these and other depression tragedies were simply not to be thought of as in the same category with the loss of individual initiative which would be engendered by the acceptance of relief. Thus did conservatives rationalize their mortal fear lest the discipline of the industrial labor force get out of hand.

It is both interesting and instructive to watch this struggle as it unfolded, incredible though it now seems that men would take such a stand so aggressively. Inevitably this citadel was breached, but even as a more realistic outlook evolved strange mental and policy contortions were indulged in order to keep modifications of this fundamental principle to the barest minimum. Of these contortions the central one was the grading of different kinds of doles in the order of their perniciousness. Least evil in its consequences was private relief. Most to be avoided was federal assistance. Somewhere in between stood aid by local and state governments. This hierarchy of evils is the most important key to an understanding of the Hoover administration's approach to the human problems of deep depression.

Compelled by the very existence of 4,000,000 unemployed people, the President in October, 1930, organized the so-called President's Emergency Relief Organization for the purpose of coordinating local, private relief work. Through the governors of the several states some 3,000 relief committees were created to relieve the distress now visibly growing acute. Unfortunately, the funds available to private and even nonfederal governmental relief agencies were already so nearly exhausted that there were too few resources to be thus coordinated. As stated by the first director of this organization, $40 million worth of relief was not an effective substitute for $20 billion worth of wages.

But if the President's Emergency Relief Organization in 1930 was ludicrously inadequate, the work relief program suggested by the administration in 1931 was almost criminally so. This was the famous "Give-a-Job" campaign, in which private citizens were asked to put the unemployed to work mowing lawns, washing cars, and doing other types of odd jobs. With unemployment now at 7,000,000, this appeal was unquestionably the most absurd step of all in a series of measures history has branded as tragically incompetent. The very triviality of this approach to social disaster was one of the primary reasons for the appearance in 1931 of the first loud outcry against Washington "indifference."

Nor does this item represent the height of economic orthodoxy's attempt to keep its head buried in the sand. In 1931 a small area in the Southwest was devastated by what the Secretary of Agriculture called the worst drought in the country's history. When Congress seriously began considering a $60 million relief measure, after the President had suggested $25 million, Mr. Hoover publicly rebuked the legislative branch of his government. Two points were made in his chastisement. First, Congress was being careless with funds. Second, food for human beings—the horrid dole—was to be provided as well as feed for livestock. Feed, fertilizer, and seed were of course not subject to opprobrium. Farmers, after all, were businessmen, and these items were a part of their stock in trade.

So bitter did this controversy become that the Red Cross had to be used as an intermediary to resolve it. But even with this assistance only an unsatisfactory compromise could be achieved. The Red Cross, of course, could have given food to human beings without raising broad philosophical issues, as long as it used donated funds. Unfortunately, however, the Red Cross' own funds would have been inadequate to this task, and hence a Congressional appropriation was necessary. But with government funds (and especially federal government funds) involved, it became unthinkable to *give* food to human beings. (Citizens hungry as a result of unemployment might see in this step a precedent applicable to their situation and lose interest in looking for work.) As a result all these drought relief funds were *loaned*—whether for buying feed, fertilizer, seed, or food—on almost prohibitive security. The President, in thanking the Red Cross for its assistance, said that in avoiding free distribution of government money "You have renewed and invigorated the spiritual life of the nation."

One other important technique was utilized during the early years of the depression for avoiding federal government relief appropriations. At one point several thousand veterans (the Bonus Expeditionary Force) camped near Washington to add their presence to the pressure on Congress to pass a bonus measure. With the outbreak of a "riot" precipitated fully as much by the authorities as by the bonus marchers, troops from nearby Fort Meyer were ordered to the scene.

TABLE 23. THE OBSTINACY OF ORTHODOXY

Year	Government Purchases of Goods and Services (billions of dollars)	
	Federal	State
1929	1.3	7.2
1930	1.4	7.8
1931	1.5	7.7
1932	1.5	6.6

Source: Department of Commerce.

When these arrived (after a delay of one hour while an orderly returned to the Fort to get General MacArthur's tunic, service stripes, and English whipcord breeches), the bonus army was soon dispersed and their headquarters and living facilities burned to the ground. This episode in mid-1932, the "shame of Anacostia," might perhaps be said to have been the dying gasp of an approach to industrial depression by now outmoded.

THE CLIMATE SOFTENS

Care must be taken not to condemn Mr. Hoover and those around him too unequivocally for their stubborn orthodoxy. In the first place, it is only fair to emphasize that the President and his colleagues believed profoundly in the material and moral superiority of the world they were bending every effort to preserve against the concerted assault of the unemployed, the weather, and reformers. It is often bemoaned that all too frequently in a democracy men in leadership positions are willing to sacrifice whatever principles are necessary in order to get re-elected. If this be true, Herbert Hoover symbolizes democracy at its best. Never did a President of the United States (or, for that matter, a political party) so obviously accept in advance an overwhelming political defeat rather than compromise cherished ideals. Hoover's administration has repeatedly been charged with callous unconcern for the people whose destinies he helped to shape during several critical years. This is almost slanderously untrue. The fact is that in conservative circles it was conscientiously believed that depression sufferers would be better off if compelled to endure this suffering rather than being relieved of it at the cost of surrendering their precious individual independence.[8]

[8] Herbert Hoover, The Challenge To Liberty (New York: Charles Scribner's Sons, 1934).

And if, in the second place, it is argued that this was an unrealistic approach to modern industrial society, that increasing industrialization breeds interdependence almost more rapidly than men can adjust to its implications, there are yet other things to be said on behalf of these men. The inertia exhibited on this occasion is, after all, the principal source of that institutional stability which keeps the centrifugal forces within a society from battering it to pieces. Conservatism's social function is to fight with some success for the preservation of past achievements, for it is only on such a foundation that harmonious social change can be built. To be sure, there are rare occasions (and this was surely one of these) when social inertia prevents the making of changes as rapidly as the smoothest functioning of the social order demands, but that is only the price which must be paid for avoiding the much more frequently recurring danger of inaugurating changes too rapidly for the health of the community.

Let it not be forgotten either that in the context of Hoover's four years in the White House the enemy at the gates was not the "Great Depression" that citizens later saw in looking back at the decade of the 1930's. The phrase "prosperity is just around the corner" became popular in 1930 and continued to be so for many months. In other words, although it is obvious in retrospect how premature this thinking was, it must at the same time be recognized how genuine it was. The principle of avoiding the dole must necessarily have looked much larger in terms of a relatively short depression than if it had been measured against the situation actually developing.

And it is perhaps also worth noting that this Republican administration in its reaction to deep depression differed in no significant way from that of a predecessor Democratic administration some forty years before. In the 1890's as in the early 1930's men in want were treated shabbily while property was treated most solicitously. To be sure, this does suggest that men had learned little in the interim, but far more important it makes clear one of the most important facts that had to be learned before a different outlook could prevail. At the level of the structure and strategy of democratic government, the central point at issue was the greater proportion of the population now in the industrial labor force, and a conservative Republican leadership would naturally be the last to learn this lesson.

To bring all these considerations into sharper focus: when it is asked who during those years had any better understanding of what should be done than those history now condemns for inaction and error, there is no convincing answer. On every previous occasion the nation had recovered from depressions without artificial respiration;

is it to be supposed that Democrats more quickly than Republicans would have concluded that the Great Depression was different from this standpoint? Furthermore, who is today willing to assert that a society is not required to pay a price for wholesale government intervention—or that the price exacted is of no significance? Unquestionably the time came when the nation was more than willing to take whatever risks resided in forthright action, but it is by no means obvious that the American people were ready for bold experimentation significantly before there was a New Deal prepared to give it to them.

Against the background of these observations, the most remarkable fact about the early years of the Great Depression is perhaps less the persistence of past attitudes than the slow but steady undermining of those attitudes even before the Republican administration was replaced, together with the way in which policy erosion blazed trails aggressively followed by succeeding Democratic administrations.[9] In part this was because the Democrats won control of Congress in 1930, but in even larger part it reflected the tremendous pressure against the status quo generated by the economic breakdown (and indeed changes in the political complexion of the government at this point were primarily a consequence of economic distress). With respect to the modifications in policy brought about by this last factor, it has been said with some justification that the conservatives were compelled to preside at their own funeral.

The first faint trace of unorthodoxy in the federal government's depression program was an almost infinitesimal public works effort. A considerable program of new governmental building was already under way, and this enabling legislation was now altered to allow the expenditure of as much as $65 million in a single year rather than $35 million. Simultaneously federal grants to states for highway construction and rivers and harbors expenditures were likewise increased. (More along these lines was not attempted because a Hoover-appointed committee to investigate the value of this type of anti-depression government activity brought in a negative report.) But note that not only were these funds hopelessly inadequate, but the emphasis even here was upon *work* relief and projects which were to be undertaken anyway. And note also that until the depression was a full two years old this is virtually the only item of its kind to be found.

January, 1932, saw the administration's policy of drift decisively

9 R. L. Wilbur and A. M. Hyde, *The Hoover Policies* (New York: Charles Scribner's Sons, 1937).

replaced by a program of positive action. The first item on this agenda was the creation of the Reconstruction Finance Corporation, a government concern charged with the responsibility of making "fully and adequately secured" loans to banks (as well as insurance companies and railroads) threatened with bankruptcy because of the low value and illiquidity of their assets.[10] Here too the conservative component of what was being done almost overshadowed the progress being made, and the President was as a result vigorously attacked for setting up a "bread line" for business while refusing aid to the unemployed. Of course the administration denied this charge, falling back on the time-worn conservative doctrine that economic well-being for the masses is a function of the economic well-being of such basic social institutions as these. And while in a modern economy there is much justification for giving special attention to banks, insurance companies, and railroads on precisely this ground, the use of such an argument in the face of widespread suffering no doubt helped deepen popular resentment against Hoover's administration.

In February another positive step was taken, although perhaps more out of necessity than choice. With the decline in business activity had come a corresponding decline in the volume of commercial paper available for use as backing for federal reserve notes. Until now this deficiency had been made up by the use of gold, a procedure fully legal under existing law, but the country had in the course of the deflationary spiral become a large net exporter of gold. Rather than tolerate the withdrawal of currency from circulation as gold reserves became inadequate, which possibility was now threateningly imminent, the law was amended to permit the substitution of government bonds for commercial paper as backing for federal reserve notes.

By mid-1932, perhaps in part under pressure of the impending presidential election campaign, this retreat was beginning to turn into a rout. In June a last desperate effort was launched to preserve the precious conservative ideal of a balanced budget. On the one hand an act was passed designed to reduce expenditures, while on the other Congress enacted the largest peacetime tax increase in the nation's history. In addition to this highly orthodox purpose, one important reform objective was also achieved by this revenue measure. The tax rates applicable to those in the higher income brackets which Andrew Mellon had so successfully assailed were for all practical purposes restored. At a time when one of the economy's most

---

[10] Jesse H. Jones, *RFC, Seven Year Report to the President and the Congress* (Washington, D.C.: Government Printing Office, 1939).

vital needs was to force more of the resources of higher income citizens out of private hoards, it was at least fortunate that new taxes rested especially heavily on that group.

In July the Reconstruction Finance Corporation principle was applied to concerns in the home finance field. Twelve regional Home Loan Banks were established with authority to rediscount first mortgages for these institutions. Again sound financial principles were written into the law (that is, the requirement of full and adequate security), but there was also that same broad hint of a softening of the hard crust of conservatism.

In July also came the first major breach in established fiscal policy. For some time the federal government had been promising that when the resources of state and local governments became inadequate to the relief demands made upon them, federal assistance would be proffered. After two and one-half years of depression, and with some 11,000,000 persons walking the streets in search of employment, the time had clearly come to make good on that promise. This was done through the so-called Emergency Relief and Reconstruction Act. By the terms of this law the Reconstruction Finance Corporation was authorized to make $300 million worth of loans to states financially unable to take care of their distressed citizens with their own resources. Loans up to $1.5 billion were also authorized to states and municipalities for self-liquidating public works, $300 million more was made available for non-self-liquidating public works, and still other funds were appropriated for an emergency relief and public works grant-in-aid program. Although the administration continued to pay lip service to the dictum that "though the people support the government, the government should not support the people," this law forever ended the stubborn doctrine that welfare payments were outside the federal government's sphere of responsibility.

Nor was this all. Not only was the cherished hope of a balanced budget now only a memory, but there was arising to torment the public conscience the thought that perhaps a sound fiscal policy in this sense was not even an appropriate objective under present conditions. Thus it was being pointed out that to levy additional taxes only transfers purchasing power from the people to the government and hence contributes nothing toward remedying deflation. More important at the moment, moreover, was the converse of this argument: that only the federal government possessed the resources needed to restore the economy to full-scale operation. With a Stuart Chase to give ideas such as these effective popular expression (as a John Maynard Keynes was soon to give them scientific plausibility),

TABLE 24. EXIT FINANCIAL ORTHODOXY

Year*	Federal Government Debt (billions of dollars)
1929	16.9
1930	16.2
1931	16.8
1932	19.5
1933	22.5

* As of June 30.
Source: Treasury Department.

this was excellent campaign material as the nation prepared to make official its repudiation of the men who never quite seemed to understand that the victims of a modern industrial depression are not necessarily either shiftless or incompetent.

SIGNS OF THE TIMES

While the nation was in these ways wrestling with itself over anti-depression policy, economic evolution was grinding out numerous changes in government-business relationships in other ways. In a number of areas, in other words, the leaven that had been working throughout the decade of the 1920's was now beginning to bear fruit.

One such development was a strengthening of the Federal Power Commission, as for the first time users of the nation's water power resources were subjected to a significant degree of public regulation.[11] The agency headed by three members of the Cabinet was abolished in 1930, and in its place was created a bipartisan commission composed of five full-time commissioners with authority to employ an expert staff to assist them. To this group was then given the responsibility of granting licenses for the development of power on navigable streams. In the making of these grants the Commission was to consider how proposed projects would affect the use of water for such other purposes as irrigation, flood control, and navigation—preference to be given to those projects allowing fullest use of the water resources involved. For the same reason, the Commission was required to give priority to applications by state and local governments, and forbidden to grant licenses for a longer period than five years.

Progress on that front could, to be sure, easily be exaggerated. The first appointees to the new Federal Power Commission were of

[11] E. R. Abrams, *Power in Transition* (New York: Charles Scribner's Sons, 1940).

course highly conservative. Moreover, few regulatory powers such as were now taken for granted in the public utility field were yet given to the revitalized Commission, the only exception of consequence being authority to prescribe and police conformance with a uniform system of accounts. In all other regulatory areas the federal body was required to defer to state commission jurisdiction. But for all these shortcomings a noteworthy beginning had been made, one on which future administrations could readily build as occasion dictated. And although such was not one of the primary purposes involved, another move was here made in the direction of a full-fledged public power program.

In 1930 also commercial aviation moved one long step nearer full public utility status. Ostensibly, and perhaps most fundamentally, the Watres Act of that year had as its purpose the liberalization of the Post Office Department's air mail subsidy, and indeed this was accomplished so successfully that within a few years a number of scandals were broadly hinted with respect to it. But even more important from the standpoint of the longer-range evolution of American aviation policy was the broadening of regulatory authority included in this law. By its terms the Postmaster General was authorized to order extensions or consolidations of mail routes, specify the type of passenger service to be performed by mail planes, prescribe accounts and accounting practices, and establish safety requirements for airline equipment and personnel. These specific powers, coupled with the more subtle authority wielded by anyone who has favors to bestow, made the federal government a full partner of the rapidly developing aviation industry from this point forward.

Still another peripheral development during these gloomy years had to do with the holding company in general and the American Telephone and Telegraph Company in particular. Prior to this time the Supreme Court had been exceedingly cautious about accepting the view that a regulatory commission must have sufficient authority to investigate and if necessary disallow a portion of certain operating expenses where arms-length bargaining between the utility and some outside concern does not prevail. And although this reluctance on the part of the judiciary imposed a general disability upon state commissions, it was especially a handicap where local utility concerns received services from parent holding companies.

During the period under review here this problem was nowhere more important that in connection with relationships between state and regional telephone operating companies and their gigantic holding company mother. Not only did these upstream payments affect a huge number of telephone users, but the close relationship between Western Electric and American made these payments a substantial item. It was therefore an achievement of no little moment when in 1930 the Supreme Court agreed with the Illinois public service commission that the burden of proof as to the reasonableness of these intrasystem payments should be on the holding company.[12] On the one hand, this meant an important move toward more effective regulation in the telephone field. On the other hand, it meant that state regulation could now begin to combat the circumvention of utility control through the holding company device, and a number of states promptly took advantage of this new freedom.

The coming of depression also gave a new twist to relationships in the petroleum industry. Although the central motivation behind conservation measures had thus far been to guarantee an adequate future supply of an exhaustible and irreplaceable resource, there is at best a thin line of demarcation between conservation in this sense and cartelization for the benefit of private producers.[13] To date this line, however thin and delicate, had been kept reasonably intact. With the fading away of the "Model-T prosperity," a series of developments transpired which destroyed the distinction heretofore successfully maintained.

First in point of time was the collapse of demand for the finished products of this industry. Almost simultaneously with this disastrous change, furthermore, came one still more devastating. In 1931 the East Texas field was brought into production so rapidly that the collapse of prices became nearly complete. Immediately the primary orientation of interest in conservation shifted to the protection of the economic well-being of producers.

Several steps were taken in quick succession. First, Oklahoma, Kansas, and Texas made a compact with one another to restrict production, and established an interstate advisory committee to allocate total output among the three member states. Second, Oklahoma put into effect an old prorationing law allocating her own production to particular producers. Third, Texas enacted a prorationing law based upon the Oklahoma model. Fourth, in both states these statutes were enforced by declaring martial law.

Of course, the authority of state legislatures to thus alter the emphasis of these programs was challenged by a few discomfited pro-

---

12 *Smith* v. *Illinois Bell Telephone Company,* 282 U.S. 133 (1930).

13 M. W. Watkins, *Oil: Stabilization or Conservation?* (New York: Harper & Bros., 1937).

TABLE 25. MOTIVATION FOR CONSERVATION

	Petroleum Output	
Year	By Quantity (millions of barrels)	By Value (millions of dollars)
1929	1,007	1,280
1930	898	1,070
1931	851	551

Source: Bureau of the Census, *Historical Statistics of the United States, 1789-1945*, p. 146.

ducers. As a defense, however, the states argued that prorationing (preventing economic, as distinguished from physical, waste defined as production in excess of "reasonable market demand") is a method of conservation. When the Supreme Court upheld this interpretation in 1932,[14] and when as a result most of the other important oil-producing states embarked upon prorationing careers, this relationship between business and government became a permanent feature of the American economy.

In the bituminous coal industry an analogous evolution was taking place. Although that industry had not shared in the prosperity of the preceding decade, the coming of depression here also precipitated a major crisis. Since the structure of the industry did not lend itself to cartelization under government auspices, however, an ambitious private cartelization program was undertaken. Calling itself Appalachian Coals, Incorporated, a common sales agency was set up by 137 producing companies and given the responsibility of allocating orders among members and determining whether the price was so low as to require a limitation of output.

This time it was the Department of Justice that brought suit, the charge being violation of the Sherman Act. Again the Supreme Court found in favor of the cartel. Stressing the fact that this organization, although handling three-fourths of the coal produced in Virginia, West Virginia, Kentucky, and Tennessee, controlled less than 12 per cent of the coal mined east of the Mississippi River and was hence not in a position to control prices, the Court held that Appalachian Coals was a reasonable limitation on competition in an industry in great distress.[15] Interestingly enough, this decision has the distinction of being the classic exception to the rule that the

[14] *Champlin Refining Company* v. *Corporation Commission of Oklahoma*, 286 U.S. 210 (1932).

[15] *Appalachian Coals, Incorporated* v. *United States*, 288 U.S. 344 (1933).

Supreme Court has never upheld a price-oriented combination of
rival firms.

In one other major way was the internal disintegration of laissez
faire now becoming general, even before the leadership of the nation
was entrusted to other hands. The plight of organized labor, the
tragic consequences of falling wages and widespread unemployment added to the havoc that had been wrought among labor unions
by the "American Plan," was by 1932 so desperate that it was even
possible to secure the passage of an act giving to workers in general
a stronger guarantee of the right to bargain collectively than had
ever before been written into an American statute.[16] Specifically, the
Norris-La Guardia Act fundamentally weakened the use of federal
injunctions as a strike-breaking or strike-prevention technique. First,
such injunctions were not thereafter to be issued at all except after
the hearing of witnesses in open court and after formal court findings of certain specified kinds. Second, yellow-dog contracts were
made unenforceable in federal courts. Third, injunctions under the
antitrust laws might be no broader in scope than under the common
law. Fourth, in no case might a federal injunction prohibit acts of
the sort by now commonly associated with routine business unionism.

It was all very ominous to once-proud upholders of the conservative tradition. But it was not merely these more or less isolated
breaches in the laissez-faire wall as such which concerned them.
Rather the problem was that these seemed so clearly to be but the
advance guard of what was obviously a basically different way of
thinking about socio-economic affairs. Looking behind these superficial symptoms, the nation's erstwhile leaders (for these men had
lost their following long before they did their offices) could see
three broad evidences of the existence of what to them was the most
dreaded of all diseases.

They could see, in the first place, a shift in the center of gravity
of American government from the several state capitals to Washington, D.C.

In the second place, it was plain that throughout all governments
in the United States there was henceforth to be a much broader
representation for those groups that had to this point taken little
part in basic policy formulation—and therefore a narrower representation for conservatives. What this meant, the anticonservative spirit

[16] Lewis L. Lorwin, *The American Federation of Labor* (Washington, D.C.:
Brookings Institution, 1933).

beginning to run rampant throughout the land, was especially forth-rightly set forth in 1932 by a Justice of the Supreme Court.

The Oklahoma legislature had declared ice companies to be public utilities, and, on the ground that this industry was already over-crowded, had required that no new firms of this kind might be established without first securing a certificate of convenience and necessity. When this statute was challenged by one Liebmann as an improper use of the police power, a majority of the Supreme Court concurred. Justices Brandeis and Stone, however, took exception to their colleagues' reasoning in an unusually sharp dissent written by Brandeis.[17] Taking note of existing economic conditions, the de-mands for stabilization being made on every hand, the current development of prorationing in the oil industry, the fact that econ-omists and statesmen did not fully understand the depression or how the economy might best be extricated from its grip, this famous dissent ended as follows:

To stay experimentation in things social and economic is a grave responsibility. Denial of the right to experiment may be fraught with serious consequences to the nation. It is one of the happy incidents of the federal system that a single courageous state may, if its citizens choose, serve as a laboratory; and try novel social and economic experiments without risk to the rest of the country. This Court has the power to prevent an experiment . . . But in the exercise of this high power, we must be ever on our guard, lest we erect our prejudices into legal principles. If we would guide by the light of reason, we must let our minds be bold.

And, in the third place, in a still more specific way could con-servatives see in recent events the handwriting on the wall, or, quite literally, the threatening program of the New Deal. The Norris-La Guardia Act began with an exceedingly pointed declaration of policy which read in part as follows:

Whereas under prevailing economic conditions, developed with the aid of gov-ernmental authority for owners of property to organize in the corporate and other forms of ownership association, the individual unorganized worker is commonly helpless to exercise actual liberty of contract and to protect his freedom of labor, and thereby to obtain acceptable terms and conditions of employment, wherefore, though he should be free to decline to associate with his fellows, it is necessary that he have full freedom of association, self-organi-zation, and designation of representatives of his own choosing, to negotiate the terms and conditions of his employment, and that he shall be free from the interference, restraint, or coercion of employers of labor, or their agents, in the designation of such representatives or in self-organization or in other concerted activities for the purpose of collective bargaining or other mutual aid or pro-tection.

[17] *New State Ice Company* v. *Liebmann*, 285 U.S. 262 (1932).

QUESTIONS FOR DISCUSSION

1. What were the major obstacles to the more effective use of monetary policy during the 1920's?

2. In what ways did the monetary policies actually followed operate perversely?

3. Why were the stock market crash, and still more the ensuing depression, a tragedy for conservatives?

4. It has been said that President Hoover did not seriously expect any results to follow from his November 21 conference. Can you explain why this might be true? Why, then, was the conference held?

5. Enumerate the antidepression steps taken by the government in the first two years of the depression, and explain the purpose and outcome of each one.

6. Explain the significance of the struggle during these years over the dole.

7. Would the country have been better off if the Hoover administration had been less stubborn than it was, or if the New Deal had taken over two years sooner?

8. If, by some chance, Hoover's term of office had had four more years to run in 1933, how far do you think he would have gone in New Deal directions during that time?

9. What changes in business-government relationships were taking place outside the field of depression policy proper?

10. In what major areas was the center of gravity of American government shifting to Washington? In each case explain why this development was taking place.

11. Why is a philosophy such as that expressed by Brandeis in the ice company case properly considered anticonservative?

12. What is the message that the declaration of policy in the Norris-La-Guardia Act endeavored to get across?

Chapter 20

Orthodoxy in New Hands

No one more than Franklin Delano Roosevelt would have wanted to make a dramatic entry onto the national scene. Here was a man who thrived on drama, who functioned at his best only under the pressure of swiftly moving events. No one, furthermore, was ever accorded the opportunity of stepping into the limelight under more dramatic circumstances. Indeed, it is conceivable that the situation which prevailed in the United States on March 4, 1933, was even more tense than the architect of the New Deal would voluntarily have chosen.

TRIAL BY FIRE

If there had existed the slightest inclination during the 1920's to seek out weak spots in the economy in order to keep a continuous shoring-up program in operation, one of the facts which would have been under scrutiny was an unprecedented number of bank failures. In all, nearly 7,000 banks went under during this decade of high prosperity. To be sure, these were preponderantly smaller banks, and a majority of these bankruptcies seem to have been a consequence of lax state banking laws and depression in agriculture. Still, almost one-fifth of these failing institutions were Federal Reserve members, a circumstance which should have lent even greater significance to what was happening.

With the banking system already evincing weakness, it was only to be expected that deflation would accentuate this difficulty. Hazardous banking practices and illiquid investments could only become fatal as assets of all kinds steadily shrank in value. Whereas in 1928 the number of bank suspensions had been 659 by 1931 this figure had reached the truly shocking total of 2,298. Over-all, the

TABLE 26. A SYMPTOM OF ILL-HEALTH

Year	Bank Suspensions
1918	47
1920	167
1922	367
1924	775
1926	976
1927	669
1928	499
1929	659

Source: Bureau of the Census, *Historical Statistics of the United States, 1789-1945*, p. 273.

30,000 banks operating in the United States in 1920 had been reduced by almost exactly one-half fifteen years later.

Perhaps it could not have been predicted that the nation, having escaped financial panic at the time of the stock market crash, would nonetheless have to contend also with that dimension of economic crisis at a later date. Perhaps, in other words, it was felt that the precautions taken in the form of Reconstruction Finance Corporation legislation were adequate. But such optimism reckoned without both the precarious nature of a modern banking system in the face of a general deflation and the catastrophic breakdown of the international financial mechanism. Already the abandonment of the gold standard was in full swing; already the central banks of several European countries had collapsed, and the debilitating consequences of these failures were spreading outward in ever-widening circles.

In any event, it came as a surprise as well as a shock to a nation that considered itself well insulated from the backwash of Europe's troubles when the worldwide pressure for liquidity began to overwhelm America's banking system.[1] Between February 8 and March 3, 1933, member banks were compelled to withdraw $1.7 billion from the Reserve Banks to meet the needs of their own customers, the greater part of this withdrawal occurring in the last week of this period. During these same weeks, out-of-town banks withdrew $800 million from New York City banks, leaving financial leaders in the nation's money capital uncertain and fearful of the future. The excess reserves held by Federal Reserve Banks fell in a little over a month from $1.5 billion to $400 million. On the day of March 3 alone New York banks were required to pay out to banks in the

[1] C. C. Colt and N. S. Keith, *28 Days, A History of the Banking Crisis* (New York: Greenberg, Publisher, 1933).

interior and to their foreign customers $300 million. The great lesson learned during these anxious days was that even a central banking system is not proof against a major liquidation.

The first bank "holiday" (a general closing of banking institutions in order that officials and the public alike might assess the situation) was declared by the Governor of Nevada in October, 1932. Early in February, 1933, a shorter holiday brought temporary relief to New Orleans banks. However, these were seemingly unrelated phenomena, and would hence not have been a cause for general uneasiness in and of themselves. Thus it was only when on February 10 it developed that banks in the great city of Detroit were in difficulty that close official attention began to be given to all the nation's banks.

A special interest attaches to the bank holiday now proclaimed throughout the entire state of Michigan. In the first place, the date of this proclamation coincided closely with the beginning of the intensified demand for liquidity which can realistically be referred to only as a run on the American banking system. On February 23 Indiana's banks were closed, Maryland's on the 25th, Arkansas' on the 27th, and Ohio's on the 28th. Between the last day of February and March 3, 17 other states closed their banks, and it was evident that it was only a matter of time until every bank in the land would be shut down.

However, since it is not possible to establish a clear causal connection between these events so closely associated in time, a second aspect of the Michigan holiday is perhaps of greater significance. Behind the failure of Detroit's banks was a record of bank empire-building through the medium of holding companies and "trustee shares," the speculative use of commercial bank resources, and a general cumulation of shockingly bad bank management liberally mingled with activities that were clearly illegal. This record deserves to rank with the most notorious instances of financial recklessness for which the decade of the 1920's is now so well remembered. Repeatedly bank examiners had warned of shoals ahead for these concerns, but, as was also typical of those years, such warnings had gone unheeded.

Unfortunate though the banking crisis was on its own account, that misfortune was accentuated as a result of a unique feature of American politics. In those days, a period of four months ensued between the time one administration was repudiated at the polls and the time its already elected successor took over the reins of office. It was during such an interregnum that the greatest challenge of the entire Great Depression period rose to crisis proportions. (Largely because of the difficulties which developed out of that situation, incidentally, this period was reduced officially to less than two months and is coming unofficially to be of even shorter duration.)

Inevitably, in a vigorous democracy, this critical issue was caught in the crossfire of partisan politics. Republicans insisted that the pressure for liquidity reflected the fear of citizens that the new administration intended to tamper with the currency. Democrats countered with the charge that it was the weaknesses in the nation's financial structure currently and dramatically being revealed by two Congressional investigating committees which were injuring public morale. And to prove this contention it was pointed out that only a small proportion of current bank withdrawals was in gold. In the midst of these recriminations, a regrettable incident occurred which still further broadened the political overtones of this debate. As a result of a misunderstanding on the part of the Clerk of the House the names of those banks which had received Reconstruction Finance Corporation loans were made public. Understandably Republicans would prefer to think that this was part of a deliberate opposition attempt to embarrass the incumbent administration, while Democrats insisted that their intention had been only to have this information available to those soon to be responsible for the making of difficult decisions. Before this painful period ended, its political dimension had even descended to the sordid level at which President Hoover sought to compel his successor to repudiate his own program or to take full blame for the banking crisis, and President-elect Roosevelt refrained from joining his predecessor in the action he had himself already determined to take lest his political opponents receive credit for relieving the situation.[2]

"Action, and Action Now"

The step decided upon was to shut the doors of all banking institutions until such time as public confidence had been restored sufficiently to permit them to function effectively. Moreover this step had already been taken as far as state banks were concerned (New York's governor having finally been won over by the pleadings of Roosevelt's lieutenants at midnight, March 3) when the new President took the oath of office on the afternoon of March 4, 1933. It was, therefore, an important part of a strategy already decisively marked out when in his inaugural address President Roosevelt

[2] Raymond Moley, *After Seven Years* (New York: Harper & Bros., 1939).

endeavored to reassure a thoroughly frightened people by asserting that "the only thing we have to fear is fear itself—nameless, unreasoning, unjustified terror which paralyzes needed efforts to convert retreat into advance." By the same token he was as much fitting words to deeds already performed as making a promise for future fulfillment when he said, "The people of the United States have not failed. In their need they have registered a mandate that they want direct, vigorous action," and when still more emphatically he said, "This nation asks for action, and action now."

TABLE 27. THE CROWNING TRAGEDY

Year	Unemployed
1929	429,000
1930	2,896,000
1931	7,037,000
1932	11,385,000
1933	11,845,000

Source: Bureau of the Census, *Historical Statistics of the United States, 1789-1945*, p. 65.

These were bold words, spoken as they were while the nation's economic heart lay almost lifeless on the operating table. (And not only was the banking system completely paralyzed, but during the week just ended the steel industry had operated at only 12.5 per cent of capacity.) But the American people were by now too numbed by depression to be impressed by words alone, and this the new administration well knew. Accordingly there followed in quick succession a number of government actions which in a few days did more to win public confidence in the nation's leadership than President Hoover had accomplished in more than three years.[3]

Inauguration day fell on a Saturday. Before bank opening time on Monday the bank holiday already declared by the governors of all of the states was made complete by the closing of all federal banking institutions. On Thursday, March 9, Congress was convened in special session, passing on that same day the Emergency Banking Act setting forth the procedure by which sound banks would be allowed to reopen and unsound ones liquidated.

Two days later the new Congress passed the Economy Act. The campaign pledge of the new President which had pleased conservatives most was his promise to put an end to Hoover deficits, to balance the federal budget by reducing government expenditures.

[3] L. M. Hacker, *A Short History of the New Deal* (New York: Appleton-Century-Crofts, Inc., 1934).

Over the protests of a small group of progressives who objected to this catering to millionaires, the administration now made a vigorous attempt to fulfill that pledge.

With the passage of this measure, a bare week after President Roosevelt had taken his oath of office, the New Deal had successfully met its first crisis. Slowly at first, but with gathering momentum, the confidence of the country in itself began to return. Within three weeks a large number of banks were once more carrying on normal business activities, $1 billion had been returned to circulation from private hoards, and there was never again a question as to the soundness of the banking system. And although the new administration had been confronted at the outset with a more dramatic situation than it might have preferred, it was now well rewarded for the courageous way this crisis had been vanquished. Prior to this, countless thousands of citizens had stood with Roosevelt chiefly as a way of standing against Hoover. By mid-March, however, a majority of Americans was ready to support the new President on a much more positive basis.

This was indeed fortunate, for the program of action of the new leadership had only begun. Before the pattern of policies now beginning to take shape had been completed, the President was to need all the support he could muster.

It has been aptly said that the program of the New Deal rested on the three foundations of relief, recovery, and reform. Although, to be sure, all three of these objectives can be seen at every stage of the program's development, and although it is even difficult on occasion to distinguish these several elements in particular pieces of legislation, it was only to be expected that speaking broadly, first priority was granted to the problem of relief. Moreover, if the term relief is given a fairly broad interpretation, the action already taken on the banking front clearly belongs in that category. Just as relief in its more common meaning has to do with maintaining and rehabilitating human resources, so did these steps have to do with maintaining and rehabilitating institutional resources.

Probably no special significance is to be attached to the devotion of first energies to the nation's institutions rather than to its people as such. An issue of the gravest kind had arisen which demanded immediate attention. At the same time, however, the New Deal would have forfeited much of its right to proclaim humanitarian sympathies had it not turned abruptly from this work to the needs of those to whom depression had brought the greatest suffering. Furthermore, the new administration had been swept into office largely on the basis of its promise to remember "the forgotten man," and unquestionably the great army of unemployed workers was the group most needing to be remembered.[4] Before the end of March, the administration was busily engaged in improving upon the Hoover record in this field.

Three kinds of unemployment relief programs were promptly inaugurated. The first of these was the justly famous Civilian Conser-

TABLE 28. ACTION, AND ACTION NOW

Fiscal Year	Federal Government Emergency Expenditures (billions of dollars)
1933	1.3
1934	4.0

Source: Department of Commerce, *Statistical Abstract of the United States, 1934,* p. 158.

vation Corps. Because the depression had fallen on young workers, those just entering the labor market, with particular severity, it was most appropriate that the first such relief measure put into operation by the New Deal was one designed to meet that problem at its source. Under the legislation more than 2,000,000 young men in 1,500 camps in every state in the union were put to work on public projects such as erosion and flood control, the construction of recreation facilities, forest fire prevention, conservation of wild life, and the building of landing fields for the new aviation industry.

The Civilian Conservation Corps alone among the New Deal's first approaches to the tragedy of unemployment was an innovation. Neither of the others added significantly to the principles already developed by the Hoover administration. One of these was the Federal Emergency Relief Administration, a program by means of which the resources of the federal government were even more definitively placed at the disposal of state governments, although now wholly in the form of grants-in-aid rather than loans. The other was the Public Works Administration, a federal public works program of somewhat larger proportions (although not yet strikingly so) than those grudgingly developed under Hoover.

SALVAGE OPERATIONS IN THE RAILROAD INDUSTRY

If steps to rehabilitate the banking industry can appropriately be classified as relief, this designation also fits the next major item on

[4] E. W. Bakke, *The Unemployed Worker* (New Haven: Yale University Press, 1940).

the New Deal agenda. With an importance to the economy rivaling that of the banking system, the nation's railroads were a vital part of the institutional structure to be maintained at almost any cost.

Taken as a whole, the railroads had never quite achieved during the 1920's the prosperity of which so many industries were able to boast. Furthermore, as one of the most highly fixed cost industries in the economy, that industry was virtually prostrated by the drop-off in business activity. Freight revenue declined approximately 50 per cent while passenger revenues fell even farther, and net operating revenue after payment of fixed charges fell from almost $1 billion to an amount which failed to meet fixed charges by more than $150 million. Railway employment shrank from 1,661,000 to 1,000,000, the railroads' ability to secure capital almost disappeared, and maintenance expenditures fell to the danger point.[5]

Attempts had of course been made to retrieve this desperate and still deteriorating situation. A petition to the Interstate Commerce Commission for a 15 per cent rate increase had been turned down on the ground that still more railroad traffic would thereby be diverted to other media. A few strategic increases were permitted, however, with the understanding that the revenues thus made available would be pooled for the benefit of needy carriers; and in all, loans of some $75,000,000 were made from this fund. Wage rates were reduced 10 per cent, along with drastic cuts in the number of employees. And when all these steps proved inadequate to stem the rising tide of institutional disintegration, the Reconstruction Finance Corporation had loaned to railroads one-third of a billion dollars to relieve the most intense pressures.[6]

But even the aid forthcoming from this great, new government corporation proved in the end to be insufficient. When the Roosevelt administration first turned seriously to this problem in late March, 1933, it was apparent to any competent observer that wholesale bankruptcies could not be avoided much longer. It was against this background that legislation was developed to salvage as much as possible from this inevitable financial wreckage.

The first step here was to introduce a number of major changes into bankruptcy procedures in the railroad industry, where the operation of existing laws had revealed a number of serious shortcomings. In part these resulted from the inappropriateness of the gen-

[5] H. G. Moulton and Associates, *The American Transportation Problem* (Washington, D.C.: Brookings Institution, 1934).

[6] Herbert Spero, *Reconstruction Finance Corporation Loans to Railroads* (New York: Bankers Publishing Co., 1939).

TABLE 29. RAILROADS IN DISTRESS

| | Railroads Placed Under Receivership | | |
Year	Number	Miles Operated	Capitalization (thousands of dollars)
1929	3	624	30,981
1930	4	4,752	277,324
1931	19	5,195	432,152
1932	13	11,817	626,577
1933	32	25,124	1,750,397

Source: Department of Commerce, *Statistical Abstract of the United States, 1934,* p. 366.

eral bankruptcy laws to firms which in any event must be kept going on some basis rather than summarily closed down, and in part they reflected the facility with which American finance capitalists had been able under those laws to "milk" bankrupt railroads. More specifically, the following criticisms had persistently been leveled against railroad reorganization law in recent years. First, the management of properties in receivership was typically in the hands of minority security interests who used their position to pay excessive fees to receivers, protective committees, reorganization managers, and lawyers. Second, these same groups were often able to block reorganization plans which did not accord them preferential treatment. Third, the natural reluctance of security holders to see their paper assets extinguished frequently resulted in the approval of reorganization plans which did not cut deeply enough into existing equities and hence launched concerns which would soon have to go through the "wringer" all over again. Fourth, the Interstate Commerce Commission had no authority over any part of the reorganization process except the power to withhold approval of the new securities to be issued. This the Commission hesitated to do, even where the new capital structure raised doubts in the minds of its members, in view of the great cost to all parties which would have been involved in starting over from the beginning.

Section 77 of the Bankruptcy Act of 1898, first passed in March, 1933, but since then extensively amended, was designed to remedy these defects. The basic change in procedure incorporated in this legislation was to give the Interstate Commerce Commission broad responsibilities at every stage of the railroad reorganization process. Sufficient power was granted this body to enable it to eliminate most of the abuses common under the old procedure.

Helpful though it was to protect the public interest in cases of actual railroad receivership, this legislation did not purport to go to the heart of the problem against which it was aimed. The most vital need obviously was to prevent this situation from arising in the first place. To this end the Emergency Transportation Act was passed hard on the heels of the bankruptcy legislation.

The philosophy underlying this enactment was the notion that the competition still remaining in the railroad industry was extremely wasteful. If only all barriers to cooperative action among these carriers could be removed, so this thinking went, cost savings could be found which would go far toward putting this industry back on its feet. In accordance with these ideas the Transportation Act of 1933 authorized the creation of regional coordinating committees consisting solely of carrier representatives and the appointment of a Federal Coordinator of Transportation. The regional committees were to inaugurate whatever cooperative, cost-saving steps they could devise on their own initiative; the function of the Coordinator was to order such innovations where private negotiations were unable to effect them.[7]

For three reasons this approach to the problem of the railroad industry bore little fruit. To begin with it can be argued that the thinking behind it was not wholly sound, that the wastes of railroad competition were less of a financial burden than was commonly supposed. Another difficulty was the inability of carrier representatives to agree on the cooperative measures to be taken.[8] As the Coordinator put it: "Their habit of mind is intensely individualistic and suspicious of collective action." Still another explanation of the meager results obtained, and perhaps the most important, was the labor-protective provisions included. The New Deal would not, of course, have permitted sweeping changes in railroad operating practices at labor's expense. Labor's influence on New Deal policies was already strong enough to see to that. Furthermore, there was no reason for supposing that improving the position of railroad investors at the cost of a serious deterioration in the position of railroad workers would have assisted in conquering the depression. It was therefore provided in this law that neither the number of railway employees nor their compensation was to be reduced as a result of changes brought about under its provisions. In the face of so bind-

---

[7] Federal Coordinator of Transportation, *Regulation of Railroads*, Senate Document 119, 73d Congress, 2d Session, 1934.

[8] Claude M. Fuess, *Joseph B. Eastman: Servant of the People* (New York: The Macmillan Co., 1952).

ing a restriction there was little that could be done along these lines.

Looking beyond the immediate depression situation, the new transportation legislation also made several changes in the basic law controlling government-railroad industry relationships. First, it recognized the failure of the recapture clause to achieve its purposes by retroactively repealing that provision. Second, holding company combinations were unequivocally placed within reach of the Interstate Commerce Commission.[9] Third, the earlier rule of rate-making requiring the Commission to fix rates calculated to yield a fair return on a fair value was replaced by the following paragraph:

In the exercise of its power to prescribe just and reasonable rates the Commission shall give due consideration, among other factors, to the effect of rates on the movement of traffic; to the need, in the public interest, of adequate and efficient railway transportation service at a cost consistent with the furnishing of such service; and to the need of revenues sufficient to enable the carriers, under honest, economical, and efficient management, to provide such service.

SALVAGE OPERATIONS IN AGRICULTURE

While the nature of the rescue work to be undertaken in the railroad field was still under discussion, plans were being drawn up for rehabilitating another huge sector of the economy. Here, moreover, the atmosphere of urgency within which preliminary debate and negotiation were taking place was even more compelling. To be sure, farmers had a place to live and land on which many food needs could be directly supplied. Nevertheless, this group was taking a terrific beating from the depression,[10] and its reaction to this fact was much more ominous than that of unemployed workers. Here, in other words, was another great group of citizens appropriately referred to by the term "forgotten man."

This observation can readily be made specific. In the four years immediately preceding, cash farm income had fallen from $13 billion to $5 billion, and the one-third of the nation's population living on farms was currently receiving only 10 per cent of the national income. Stated differently, the index of prices received by farmers had fallen more than twice as far as the consumer price index. Inevitably the farmer's ability to keep up the payments on a mortgage debt incurred when times were much better was disastrously af-

[9] House of Representatives, *Regulation of Stock Ownership in Railroads,* House Report 2789, 71st Congress, 3d Session, 1931.
[10] M. Ezekiel and L. H. Bean, *Economic Bases for the Agricultural Adjustment Act* (Washington, D.C.: Government Printing Office, 1933).

TABLE 30. FARMERS IN DISTRESS

Year	Agricultural Production (1919-1927 = 100)	Farm Prices (1923-1925 = 100)	Gross Farm Income (billions of dollars)
1928	111	101	11.7
1930	107	86	9.5
1932	104	44	5.3

Source: Department of Commerce, *Statistical Abstract of the United States, 1934*, pp. 570 and 573.

fected by this change in the price structure, and thousands upon thousands of farms were threatened by foreclosure proceedings. This threat to what is perhaps the American farmer's most profound aspiration put many farmers, particularly in the Middle West, in a very ugly frame of mind. Crowds of armed farmers began to attend sheriff's sales, bidding on auctioned property at trifling prices for return to the original owner. Farmer strikes were organized for the purpose of preventing (by force, if necessary) the sale of farm output at prevailing prices. On May 4 a conference of farm leaders drew up plans for a nationwide strike, a decision which was abandoned only at the request of the President that the new agricultural legislation be first given a trial.[11]

Against the background of this dangerous situation, a full-scale farm relief program would have been enacted sooner than was actually the case if those responsible could have agreed more quickly on the provisions to be included. Where agreement was reached, immediate action was taken. Thus because the first need was to stem the tide of farm foreclosures, prompt action was possible at that point. As an emergency measure, farmers were invited to wire the White House collect for assistance when (literally) they saw the sheriff turning in at their gates. On March 27 an executive order was issued providing that the various federal farm credit agencies be more adequately integrated with one another through a new agency to be known as the Farm Credit Administration. And when the new farm legislation was passed a little later, broad provision was made for refinancing farm mortgages by the federal government on highly favorable terms.

There was also agreement that the more fundamental problem to be confronted in this area was a better price adjustment for agricul-

[11] Grant McConnell, *The Decline of Agrarian Democracy* (Berkeley: University of California Press, 1953).

tural products. But here a variety of alternatives, each with its special advocates, was available, with the result that a number of compromises had to be worked out before this objective could be implemented.

First and foremost, for example, there was a bitter debate over the matter of production control, whether the farmer was to be thus regimented or not. Understandably, of course, farmers generally would have preferred to have their cake and eat it too. On the other hand, a most persuasive argument against such an approach was the tragedy which had recently befallen the Federal Farm Board. The Board had itself repeatedly insisted that it could not accomplish its purposes without authority over output, and elementary economics strongly supported that view.

Closely related to this controversy was the inevitable contest between the McNary-Haugenites and those supporting a different approach—one aspect of this difference in viewpoint, obviously, being simply another dimension of the production control issue. Whereas the use of export subsidies would not (in theory) have required controls over production, acceptance of a one-price system almost automatically demanded this further step. But those who continued to press for the program so prominent in the 1920's had another major reason for their insistence. Their way was the *American* way, as opposed to an un-American internationalism. A one-price agricultural relief program would hold an umbrella over foreign producers, and might even invite them to compete in the American market.

And finally, there was the most basic dispute of all—that between small, diversified farmers and larger producers of staples over how farm prices were to be raised. The former believed passionately in the age-old farmers' utopia of relief through inflation; the latter felt that a direct government price support program was the more practical method. Here again the problem of production control was implicitly raised. Clearly elevating the price level for the benefit of debtors would not generate nearly as much pressure for output restriction as a direct price-fixing operation.

Although in the end of course these underlying issues did have to be compromised, the Agricultural Adjustment Act of May 12 was a characteristic early New Deal measure in that it made as few clear-cut decisions as possible. Instead, its language was made extremely broad, leaving to future administrators and future political pressures the drawing of the final lines. Thus did this administration feel its way over treacherous terrain cautiously and experimentally. Nowhere is this better illustrated than in the so-called Thomas

Amendment to the Agricultural Adjustment Act. Giving in to irresistible pressure from agricultural areas, the President assented to legislation authorizing him to embark upon a variety of highly inflationary ventures, including the outright issuance of $3 billion in greenbacks. Then, because it would have been unthinkable for an administration speaking for workers as well as farmers to try to resolve the farm problem through inflation, he let most of these powers lie idle.

But though the Emergency Farm Relief Act left much to the arbitrament of time (and indeed time has wrought many significant changes in this program), certain basic directions were visible from the outset. Most conspicuous from this standpoint was the statement of purpose which prefaced this enactment's more detailed provisions. That purpose was no less than to "re-establish prices to farmers at a level that will give purchasing power . . . equivalent to the purchasing power of agricultural commodities in the base period." And as if this were not an ambitious enough task, the base period was taken to be the five highly prosperous years immediately preceding World War I. Here, in short, was born the concept of parity which has played such a central role in the federal government's farm program ever since. Here too is found the most important element of continuity in farm legislation from McNary-Haugen days.

Only slightly less fundamental was the emphasis upon production control written into this law (although, ironically, the first Administrator of the new Agricultural Adjustment Administration was George N. Peek, a prominent McNary-Haugenite who perhaps more than any other man abhorred that technique). So flexible, however, were its provisions that the basic purpose announced could be in principle (and in practice actually was) accomplished in a variety of ways.[12]

A first and no doubt the most important approach was benefit payments to farmers in exchange for (voluntary?) acreage restrictions, the necessary funds to be derived from a tax on the processing of the commodities on which such payments were being made. Another technique was price-pegging (nonrecourse) loans by a new Commodity Credit Corporation, this device representing the principal carry-over from the brief experience of the Federal Farm Board. Still a third was a system of marketing quotas to be enforced by means of a tax on all sales in excess of the quota assigned; here the

[12] E. G. Nourse, J. S. Davis, and J. D. Black, *Three Years of the Agricultural Adjustment Administration* (Washington, D.C.: Brookings Institution, 1937).

objective sought was typically to force more farmers into the "voluntary contract" system. Marketing agreements were authorized as a market stabilization measure, entirely apart from government-sponsored production or marketing limitations. Under this law, too, export subsidies on a small scale were possible, as was the direct purchase of surpluses by several government agencies. At first only seven "basic" commodities (cotton, corn, hogs, wheat, dairy products, rice, and tobacco), products whose prices were especially depressed by the existence of large export surpluses, were to be subject to production control. Later nine additional items were placed in this category, although some of these were basic only from the standpoint of political expediency.

KEYSTONE OF THE ARCH

It is perhaps misleading to classify the New Deal's early agricultural policy as salvage work. To many people much more was involved. What the depression-ridden American economy seemed to need more than anything else was purchasing power, and it was reasoned that a gain in economic well-being for farmers could not but be reflected in an upturn in business generally.[13] In other words, the farm program was to be thought of as a recovery as well as a relief measure.

While such an analysis had merit as far as it went, there was good reason for not taking it too seriously. For one thing, the experience of the 1920's suggested that this causal relationship could easily be carried to an unwarranted extreme. For another, it was inevitable that public attention would focus upon unemployment as the central problem to be combated on this front, the corollary of this fact being the determination that it was more important to get men back to work than to put them on relief.

Ever since the beginning of the depression each of the groups most intimately involved in this phase of economic breakdown—workers and businessmen—had been pressing for its favorite formula for recovery. With the weakening of bargaining power which invariably accompanies mass unemployment, worker groups were insisting upon the need for minimum-wage–maximum-hour legislation as the key to greater purchasing power. Manufacturers, on the other hand, were looking in a different direction, the feeling in that group being that excessive competition was the principal cause of business prostration, and that if only a way could be found to check this

[13] Albert L. Meyers, *Agriculture and the National Economy* (Washington, D.C.: Government Printing Office, 1949).

evil the economy would quickly work its way off dead center. To be sure, there already existed numerous trade associations and other organizations through which this problem might be approached, and the idea of fair trade practices on an industry-wide basis had of late been spreading rapidly throughout the major manufacturing and service industries. The difficulty here was that the antitrust laws were most restrictive at precisely those points at which agreement was most thought to be necessary if the depression were to be thus conquered. In short, what businessmen wanted was the suspension of the antitrust laws to permit a greatly broadened self-government in industry.

These two approaches to the most critical problem of deep depression were not wholly incompatible with one another. The maintenance of purchasing power would indeed give a "shot in the arm" to business, and destructive competition does have a way of extending to the wage structure. Stated differently, wage maintenance is a safeguard against price-cutting, and price maintenance is a safeguard against wage-cutting. All the same, there was an important sense in which these alternatives were appropriately thought of as mutually exclusive. Wages are a cost as well as purchasing power, and excessive costs can stall the economic mechanism as quickly as inadequate purchasing power.

Because of the traditional antagonism between employers and employees on the subject of labor legislation, as well as because of the difficulty of finding a common meeting ground, these two solutions had to this point been pushed separately. One of the most interesting as well as most significant developments of the entire New Deal period was their merging into the new administration's most basic initial assault on the depression, the National Industrial Recovery Act.[14]

With the American Federation of Labor, speaking at this time for some 80 per cent of all the organized workers in the United States, threatening a general strike to compel the adoption of a 30-hour week as a work-sharing device, Senator Black of Alabama introduced a bill designed to make 30 hours the standard work week in manufacturing industries in interstate commerce. Shortly after Roosevelt's inauguration his Secretary of Labor explicitly placed the administration's seal of approval upon this approach to the problem at hand. At this stage in the Act's evolution there was added to it a minimum wage provision as a guaranty that shortening the work

[14] Basil Rauch, *The History of the New Deal* (New York: Creative Age Press, Inc., 1944).

week would not leave some workers without a living wage, and an explicit guaranty of collective bargaining rights to insure against the minimum wage becoming also the maximum.

To conservatives the prospect of such a measure becoming law was little short of appalling, and they began to organize a concerted opposition to its passage. In a number of cities all over the country leading industrialists met together for the purpose of preparing formal protests. Leaders of national business organizations appeared before the appropriate Congressional Committees to register business' objections more directly. Faced with this resistance by an important segment of the underlying community, President Roosevelt withdrew administration support from the labor bill as such. But when business sought to induce the President to substitute its version of antidepression policy, he appeared personally before the annual Chamber of Commerce convention in Washington to appeal for concessions to labor in return for government assistance in the suppression of unfair competitive practices. When that group responded favorably to this proposal, the way was opened for final passage of the Recovery Act.

This law as signed by the President on June 16[15] specifically provided for maximum hours, minimum wages, and collective bargaining rights for labor generally, and for the elimination of child labor in interstate commerce. In all other respects associations of producers were given virtually a free hand to agree with one another on matters of industry coordination. All such agreements (codes of fair competition, as they were called) had to be approved by the President, but once approved they were not only exempt from antitrust prosecution but were in addition enforceable in the federal courts. Called by the President "the most important and far-reaching legislation ever enacted by the American Congress," the National Industrial Recovery Act was a fairly satisfactory compromise of conflicting objectives. But the conflict was not removed by the enactment of the law, and the President clearly stated the delicate balance which would have to be achieved if it was to be successful:

I am fully aware that wage increases will eventually raise costs, but I ask that managements first give consideration to the improvement of operating figures by greatly increased sales to be expected from the rising purchasing power of the public. . . . If we now inflate prices as fast and as far as we increase wages, the whole project will be set at naught. We cannot hope for the full effect of this plan unless, in these first critical months, and even at the expense of full initial profits, we defer price increases as long as possible.

[15] L. S. Lyon and Others, *The National Recovery Administration* (Washington, D.C.: Brookings Institution, 1935).

Although the expectation of greater sales volume as a result of increased purchasing power was realistic enough (in addition to wage maintenance, there was also the new role of the federal government in the field of relief; indeed, the Public Works Administration enactment was actually Title II of the Recovery measure), only the future could tell how effectively such a balance could be achieved.

The National Industrial Recovery Act has appropriately been called "the keystone of the arch" of the New Deal's first full-scale challenge to the depression. But this is only to view its significance in the context of its time from a single standpoint. At a somewhat more fundamental level this enactment can be viewed as the definitive measure of the despair into which the country had fallen. For more than 40 years liberals had been waging a bitter battle against the trusts. During most of that period the replacement of a conservative administration by a less orthodox one had been the signal for renewed efforts on that front. On this occasion, however, the most decisive defeat of a conservative leadership in the nation's history was followed by an abrupt reversal of a policy now almost half a century old. Such was the confusion of these times when 11,000,000 people were unemployed and hunger stalked the land.

A Glimpse into the Future

But though the New Deal gave first attention to relief and recovery, it does not follow that its other dimension was wholly neglected. In three important areas the proclivities for which this leadership was one day to be primarily remembered broke through the relief-recovery emphasis of these anxious weeks.

During World War I a major dam at Muscle Shoals (Wilson Dam), a steam power plant, and two nitrate plants had been constructed on the Tennessee River by the federal government to supplement private enterprise output of explosives. Ever since these facilities had lain idle, although a number of leaders including especially George W. Norris of Nebraska (a Republican) had urged their operation by the government for the further development of the resources of the Tennessee River Valley. Bills to bring about that result had been vetoed by both Coolidge and Hoover, and thus matters stood when a new set of sympathies began to dominate the Washington atmosphere.

On May 18 the Tennessee Valley Authority Act was passed,[16] a victory for those who had long insisted that the nation's water re-

[16] David Lilienthal, *TVA: Democracy on the March* (New York: Harper & Bros., 1944).

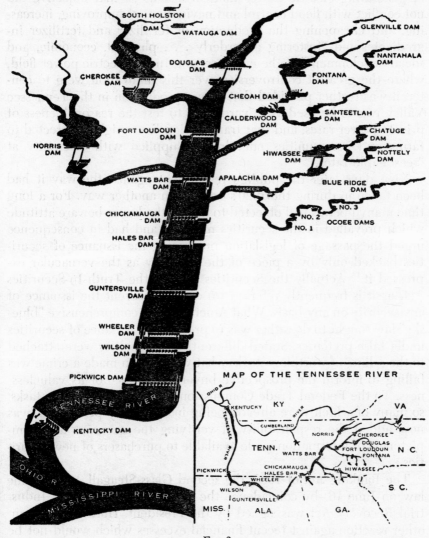

FIG. 3

sources should be developed under close government supervision (and an aftermath of the depression collapse of the fantastic utility holding company structures built up during the preceding decade). To a government corporation[17] was given the responsibility of developing flood control and navigation facilities along the Tennessee;

[17] C. H. Pritchett, *The Tennessee Valley Authority: A Study in Public Administration* (Chapel Hill: University of North Carolina Press, 1943).

of generating electric power thereon insofar as that objective did
not conflict with flood control and navigation; of improving, increasing, and cheapening the production of fertilizer and fertilizer ingredients; and "fostering an orderly . . . physical, economic, and
social development" of the entire region. In the electric power field,
where the greatest controversies over this innovation were to center, it was further provided that power production in the Tennessee
Valley was to be used as a "yardstick" to test the reasonableness of
private power rates, and that transmission lines might be erected to
farms and communities not already supplied with electricity at
"reasonable rates."

Nine days later the public's resentment against the way it had
been taken in during the 1920's erupted in another way. For a long
time many liberals had objected to the let-the-buyer-beware attitude
which prevailed in the securities markets, and had in consequence
urged the passage of legislation preventing the issuance of securities backed only by a piece of the blue sky as the vernacular expressed it.[18] Actually the Securities Act (or the Truth-In-Securities
Act, as it is frequently referred to) did not prevent the issuance of
any security on any basis. What America's first comprehensive "blue-
sky" law sought to do rather was to prevent the issuance of securities
under false pretenses. Stated differently, no penalties were attached
to the selling of worthless stock; what was therein made a crime was
failing to inform the prospective buyer in advance of its valueless-
ness. To the Federal Trade Commission's multitudinous other tasks,
so many of which were already being inadequately performed, was
now added the responsibility of verifying the accuracy and completeness of information made available to purchasers of new securities.

The Banking Act of 1933, the second Glass-Steagall Act, became
law on June 16—by coincidence the same day the National Industrial Recovery Act was signed by the President. Here was still another reaction against recent financial excesses which would not be
postponed until relief and recovery policies had been more thoroughly worked out.[19] And perhaps the most significant fact about
this enactment was that, although it brought about several sweeping
changes in banking organization, it by no means completed the reform program directed at this segment of the economy set in motion

[18] Twentieth Century Fund, *The Security Markets* (New York: Twentieth Century
Fund, Inc., 1935).

[19] F. A. Bradford, *Monetary Developments Since 1932* (New York: Longmans,
Green & Co., Inc., 1934).

by recent revelations before Congressional investigating committees.

The most widely discussed innovation now introduced was the insurance of bank deposits, the creation of the Federal Deposit Insurance Corporation, to lessen the danger to the economy of a run on the banking system such as had caught the nation so seriously off guard a few months before. A second change, one which was both widely discussed and at the same time almost unanimously taken for granted, was the separation of investment from commercial banking. But since both provisions were primarily locks for doors to already empty stables, the most important feature of this law was the beginning it made toward what was to become a series of enactments increasing and centralizing the power residing in the Federal Reserve System. Thus open market operations were no longer to be carried on by the regional Federal Reserve Banks, becoming rather the responsibility of an Open Market Committee consisting of one representative from each region. In addition the Federal Reserve Board was given authority to limit the use of commercial bank credit for speculative purposes.

By almost any standard it was a remarkable achievement. With the new President's oath of office only 104 days behind it, the incoming administration had passed major legislation in a dozen different fields. The monster which had so shortly before held the nation by the throat, was now feeling strong fingers tightening around its own neck. In less than four months the country had seen more decisive action taken than in the forty months preceding.[20]

One of the observations commonly made about the New Deal is that its first principle was action, any action, right or wrong. And there is some merit in this characterization. The nation's new leadership did believe that the morale of the people, against the background of three years of letting nature take her own good time in generating recovery, would be best served if the government seriously endeavored to bring about improvements. Moreover, a willingness to experiment with alternative ways of resolving depression problems inevitably resulted in ineffective actions. Such failures lend credence to the charge that mere action was a fundamental end in itself.

On the other hand, however, to place much emphasis upon this description of the New Deal's first challenge to the depression would almost surely be wrong. Actually the most striking single aspect of the lines of policy laid down during these early months is the clear-

[20] Schuyler Wallace, *The New Deal in Action* (New York: Harper & Bros., 1934).

cut pattern they followed. Oddly enough, too, this pattern ran basically counter to the philosophy which is today most closely associated with the New Deal. During "the hundred days" the new administration was least interested in pleasing "the forgotten man," most interested in courting the support of the business community.

An abundance of evidence is available to document this conclusion. Who would argue, for example, that President Roosevelt could not have found support for the nationalization of both the banking and railroad industries had he been so inclined? And how else is the futile clinging to the doctrine of a balanced budget which had already been abandoned by an almost reactionary Republican administration to be explained, especially when the new President even went so far as to suggest separating regular from emergency expenditures in order to hide the actual deficit? This orthodoxy in turn relates closely to the fact that first thoughts in the field of relief involved expenditures which were relatively small by comparison with those later deemed necessary. Note, furthermore, how carefully agricultural legislation avoided the solution conservatives had so desperately resisted during the 1920's, how masterfully the President sidestepped the inflation conservatives believed would have meant "the end of western civilization," and how a large part of the emphasis in the new railroad legislation was directed toward the protection of owners of railroad securities. And finally, it would be difficult to conceive of any measure more oriented to the preferences of businessmen than the National Industrial Recovery Act.

To be sure, there were reforms. But the impact of these on the conservative mind can easily be exaggerated. Thus the Securities Act must surely be thought of as little more than a minimum adjustment in that area after the earlier orgy of security speculation. This was if anything even more the case with the new banking legislation, quite apart from the fact that any amount of reform legislation would in fact have seemed conservative in outlook by comparison with the alternative of nationalization. Indeed, some of the leading figures in the banking fraternity actually welcomed a stiffening of standards by government edict. Illustrative of this attitude is the following statement by Winthrop W. Aldrich, the successor of the notorious Albert Wiggins at the Chase National Bank:

No one who has observed recent events . . . can have failed to be impressed by the necessity of change. . . . The officers of our commercial banking institutions should have constantly before them a realization of their great responsibilities to the public. The bank officer's usefulness to his bank and to the community is dependent upon public confidence in his integrity of purpose.

His actions must be of such character that when they are fully exposed to public view, no doubt can arise as to his motives. If our financial institutions are to be preserved, the public is not only entitled to expect, but it must have absolute assurance that the business of our commercial banks is being carried out in a manner which commands complete confidence.

Of all the early New Deal reforms, in other words, a conservative could take serious exception only to the Tennessee Valley Authority experiment. But that few conservatives would in fact do so was ensured by the relief of a majority of these individuals that the departure from "sound principles" was no greater than it was.

QUESTIONS FOR DISCUSSION

1. Why can a modern banking system not withstand a run? Why was a banking holiday a successful way of dealing with this crisis?

2. Explain why a balanced federal budget continued to mean so much to conservatives.

3. Distinguish between relief, recovery, and reform. Why is it difficult to draw clear-cut lines of demarcation between these things in practice?

4. Why is reorganization procedure such an important matter in a regulated public utility industry?

5. Compare the Emergency Transportation Act with the National Industrial Recovery Act from the standpoint of basic philosophy.

6. Why was violence nearer the surface in depressed agricultural communities than in industrial areas where unemployment was especially acute?

7. What was the nature of the debate over agricultural legislation? Were the right decisions made?

8. What was the conflict between the recovery formulas of employers and employees? To what extent were these solutions not in conflict?

9. Outline the major provisions of the National Industrial Recovery Act, and explain the contribution each was supposed to make to recovery.

10. Explain the early development of the New Deal program in general, and the National Industrial Recovery Act in particular, from the standpoint of accommodation.

11. Which features of the New Deal's earliest reform measures were most radical?

12. Explain the meaning of the title of this chapter.

13. Who were the principal beneficiaries of the first few months of the New Deal?

14. Would any administration coming into power in the United States in March, 1933, have done less than the New Deal did?

Chapter 21

End of the Honeymoon

The "hundred days" is also often referred to as the "honeymoon" of the New Deal, a period during which the blushing bride (the people) and the swashbuckling groom (the government) lived together in almost complete harmony. Without in any sense neglecting "the forgotten man," the high success with which the new administration sensed the importance to recovery of maintaining the confidence of the business community and for that reason avoided alienating that group would seem to make this parallel most apt.

Nor does the analogy stop here. A honeymoon period is considered a thing apart, not merely because of the harmony enjoyed therein, but even more because of the contrast between that situation and the frictions which begin soon to push their way to the surface. So was it with the New Deal. Such close cooperation between the diverse elements making up a modern economy did not last long. Before Franklin Roosevelt had been in the White House four months cooperation was already beginning to give way in the face of deep-seated conflicts.

The question is properly asked why the honeymoon had to end, why harmony could not have continued to characterize a regime now so enthusiastically supported. Most fundamentally the answer to this question is that the public interest narrows greatly in time of stress. Just as self-preservation is the first law of human existence, so is it the first law of institutional existence. Confronted with a crisis which might destroy their society as a going concern, men and women have a way of abandoning differences in order to concentrate their efforts upon destroying the common enemy. But since crises do not last forever, there will sooner or later come a time when citizens will again feel sufficiently secure in their institutional environment to reassert the conflicting objectives temporarily put aside.[1] When that time comes their government must choose which of several alternative clusters of interests it will primarily support.

The New Deal that went out of its way to maintain the goodwill of businessmen is also frequently called the "First New Deal." However, by mid-1933 the defeatist psychology which had pervaded the land in early March was already beginning to evaporate, and an administration that had reveled in the adulation of all major segments of the population was compelled to decide which of these segments it least minded offending. It was at this point that the "First New Deal" began to retreat in favor of the much better known "Second New Deal."

FIRST FRICTIONS

Admittedly this exaggerates. There had of course been controversy inside the New Deal from the outset. Nonetheless there did come a time when this factor became so pronounced as to justify thinking of it in qualitatively different terms. And it is even possible to point with a fair degree of precision to those spots which first gave rise to widespread tension.

There was, for example, the situation that developed almost immediately in connection with the farm program.[2] Although George Peek, its administrator, disapproved of production controls, while his boss, Henry Wallace, Secretary of Agriculture, believed such restrictions would have to be employed, there was nevertheless agreement that during this first season farmer regimentation would be necessary. Furthermore, as a result of the delay in passing farm relief legislation and readying the required administrative machinery, crops had already been planted before the government was prepared to implement its new program. This meant that to restrict output in 1933 would involve the actual destruction of growing crops.

To their credit or not, depending upon the point of view, the men of the New Deal did not flinch before the obvious logic of their position—and indeed there is after all little difference between deliberately not planting corn in order to raise its price, and plowing under corn already planted to accomplish the same purpose. In all, 10,000,000 acres of cotton, 12,000 acres of tobacco, 10,000,000 acres of corn, and 6,000,000 little pigs were destroyed, and several thou-

[1] A. M. Schlesinger, *The New Deal in Action, 1933-1939* (New York: The Macmillan Co., 1940).
[2] Joseph S. Davis, *On Agricultural Policy, 1926-1938* (Palo Alto: Stanford University Press, 1939).

sands of acres of peaches were not harvested. By an interesting quirk of fate a similar destruction of growing wheat was avoided because of a devastating drought in Kansas, Nebraska, and the Dakotas. Ironically, what was normally considered a tragedy came on this occasion as a relief to Washington administrators.

The public outcry against the destruction of food in the face of widespread want can readily be imagined. Certainly, moreover, such behavior does seem on its face to outrage common sense. The fact is, however, that what was now being done for the benefit of farmers was not significantly different from what businessmen and workers had been doing for themselves for many years. One by one the major economic groups in American society had discovered that the foundation of private well-being in an exchange economy is, in a highly significant sense, not abundance but scarcity.[3] It is certainly regrettable that the farmer first achieved the requisite power to implement his awakening to these fundamental facts of modern economic life in the middle of deep depression, and it was extremely embarrassing that the implementation of such a decision at such a time was under the leadership of the federal government. But there is surely no logical ground for preventing the farmer from adjusting himself to the economic system as it in fact operates, and the only way this adjustment could have been made was with government assistance.

Even more deep-seated was an opposition to the National Recovery Administration program which also began to arise almost immediately. In the first place, this approach to recovery got off to a start which ran precisely counter to its underlying philosophy. Anticipating the recovery which was in theory to flow from this program, entrepreneurs set in motion an inventory accumulation and a production for inventory which by July had taken on boom proportions. Then this bubble burst leaving the situation much as it had been before except that prices continued at a markedly higher level. Thus whereas it had been intended that purchasing power be increased while prices remained constant, the problem now became that of increasing *real* purchasing power in the face of a price level already much advanced.

This fundamental obstacle was in turn complicated by the tremendous administrative difficulties confronting the attempt to expand purchasing power as such. On the one hand, public works projects on a scale adequate to make a dent in the unemployment

[3] J. R. Smith, *Abundance: The Devil of the Machine Age* (New York: Harcourt, Brace & Co., Inc., 1941).

TABLE 31. THE HEIGHT OF FRUSTRATION

1933 Month	Industrial Production[*]	Prices[‡] Wholesale Farm	Prices[‡] Wholesale Other[†]	Consumer	Factory Weekly Earnings[‡]
March	60	70	91	96	75
July	100	100	100	100	100
November	73	93	107	104	97

[*] Federal Reserve Board.
[†] Other than farm products and food.
[‡] Department of Labor.

problem could not be gotten under way quickly.[4] On the other hand, the actual working-out of the complex agreements contemplated by the national recovery legislation (and through them an increase in labor purchasing power) proved to be so gigantic a task that the limited number of competent personnel in Washington was simply unable to proceed as rapidly on this front as had been hoped.

In some respects closely related to the initial failure of the National Industrial Recovery Act were dirt-farmer grievances directed against the first season's operations of agricultural relief. Perhaps the leading complaint here was the continued weakness of farm as compared with other prices. After the mid-year pricking of the speculation bubble, agricultural commodities slowly fell in price while other wholesale prices and the consumer price index continued to rise. In addition, however, the charge was made that it was only the large landowner who received significant benefits from relief payments. Smaller operators often could rent only a portion of one small field to the Triple-A, and as likely as not they would not find it worth their while to do so. And finally, farm workers, tenants, and sharecroppers not only received no share of relief payments, but frequently found themselves off the land in the bargain as acreage was reduced and as employer-owners used relief payments to buy tractors.[5] In the fall of 1933, as in the spring, farmers in the Corn Belt were flirting with open violence.

BRINGING UP REINFORCEMENTS

An administration thus pressed understandably began to be concerned about the popular support it had so painstakingly built up. The fickle public of the politician does not long revere heroes who

[4] National Resources Committee, *Public Works Planning* (Washington, D.C.: Government Printing Office, 1935).

[5] A. F. Raper, *Preface to Peasantry* (Chapel Hill: University of North Carolina Press, 1936).

for any reason fail to "deliver the goods." In order to maintain its hard-won esteem in the minds of citizens, therefore, the New Deal now brought into action a basically new set of antidepression weapons—weapons used with a varying degree of success, and having an equally varying impact on the mood of conservatives.

The first major new line of attack, as was only to be expected, was on the National Industrial Recovery Administration front. In late July a campaign was launched to accelerate the purchasing power consequences expected to flow from the codes. This took the form primarily of the so-called President's Reemployment Agreement, an urgent appeal to all industry for immediate compliance with minimum wages of thirty cents per hour, maximum hours of thirty-five per week, and the abolition of child labor. Every firm voluntarily acceding to the President's request was authorized to display in a prominent place a paper-picture "Blue Eagle," the symbol of compliance with the "Blanket Code."[6]

Insofar as the purpose of this step was to hasten the formulation of specific industry codes, it was outstandingly successful. The Blue Eagle campaign, an attempt to arouse the consuming public sufficiently that it would boycott noncomplying concerns, was so effective that there was a rush to join up; and having committed themselves to these cost raising concessions, employers were naturally under considerable pressure to complete code arrangements permitting more adequate price maintenance activities. On the other hand, to whatever extent this procedure was designed to promote recovery it was scarcely more than a futile gesture. Despite widespread adherence to the President's request, the index of industrial production continued to fall throughout the remainder of the year.

It is perhaps worth noting in passing that this drive to make the National Industrial Recovery Act effective did not merely fail. It was in addition far less an emphasis upon the legitimate demands of labor than appears on the surface to be the case. In the first place, the Blanket Code specifically permitted price increases if these were "necessary," and the administrative machinery available was never able to prevent this provision from being abused. In the second place, labor was asked to refrain from "aggression," to give up its most powerful tool in the collective bargaining field. In the third place, employers finding the Blanket Code too severe for their particular industries were invited to submit their own codes containing alternative provisions. And fourth, the very prodigiousness of

[6] Committee of Industrial Analysis, *The National Recovery Administration* (Washington, D.C.: Government Printing Office, 1937).

the task of approving and supervising the inauguration of some 600 codes in so short a time still further guaranteed that trade association views would be predominantly reflected therein.

But there was never any disposition on the part of the New Deal to carry all its eggs in a single container. Partly because purchasing power did not seem to be increasing by way of the code route, partly because the Public Works Administration was handicapped by the requirement that only conventional types of projects were to be undertaken by it, and perhaps partly because the fifth winter of the depression was rapidly approaching, the President announced on November 8 the creation of the Civil Works Administration.[7] The foremost objective of that agency was the employment of 4,000,000 unemployed persons on federal "make work" projects. In this it enjoyed a complete success, although it is understandable that the $1 billion thus spent would not be interpreted in the same way by all segments of the population.

TABLE 32. CHALLENGE TO DESTITUTION

Month and Year	Federal Government Emergency Expenditures (millions of dollars)
1934: October	104
November	293
December	463
1935: January	808
February	447
March	449
April	370
May	350

Source: Department of Commerce, *Statistical Abstract of the United States, 1935*, p. 162.

Two other measures were also adopted to help minimize suffering during that fifth winter of heavy unemployment. The first, a program actually more significant for its longer-range consequences than for its aid to the unemployed during the 1930's, had to do with assisting unemployed workers to find jobs in private industry. An important result of the rise of a laboring class dependent upon job opportunities provided by others had been the rise of labor exchanges; that is, employment agencies. At first, although some

[7] National Resources Planning Board, *Security, Work, and Relief Policies* (Washington, D.C.: Government Printing Office, 1942).

states had accepted this as a direct public responsibility, most state governments had been content to establish regulations preventing the worst abuses of private concerns in this field. This adjustment, however, had recently been seriously upset by a Supreme Court ruling to the effect that the prices of private employment agencies could not be regulated[8] (a decision, incidentally, which has long since been repudiated[9]), with the result that this function was more and more becoming a public one. In 1933, recognizing simultaneously the importance of this responsibility, the even greater need for such a service in the midst of economic depression, and the inadequacy of state funds, Congress passed the Wagner-Peyser Act making federal funds available to the states for this purpose on a matching basis, and recreating, to coordinate these activities, a United States Employment Service such as had functioned briefly during World War I.

Fundamentally different in orientation was the creation of the Federal Surplus Commodities Corporation for the purpose of making surplus food available to the needy. For some months a program along these lines had been in operation, using Agricultural Adjustment Administration and Federal Emergency Relief Administration funds, but this work was now formalized and greatly expanded.

Probably more important than any of these endeavors in the minds of the nation's top political leadership, however, and certainly the step least calculated to make conservatives happy, was still another device now employed to give the economy the "shot in the arm" it still so clearly needed. Actually the United States had in effect joined the nations that had already abandoned the gold standard, in the Presidential Proclamation declaring the national banking holiday, by forbidding the export of gold and putting an end to the redemption of other money in gold or gold certificates. An apparently emergency measure and intended primarily to offset the disadvantages created for American exporters by foreign devaluations, this step had aroused little opposition at the time it was taken —at least from the standpoint of domestic policy. Only as it became increasingly evident that the government intended to move in the direction of a government-managed currency system domestically on a more or less permanent basis did serious objections begin to arise.

Cut loose from the dollar, gold rose in price from $20.67 per ounce on March 4 to $29.01 on October 21. In retrospect it seems that

[8] *Ribnik* v. *McBride*, 277 U.S. 350 (1928).
[9] *Olsen* v. *Nebraska*, 313 U.S. 236 (1941).

stabilization at this level would have approximately offset the currency deflations of other countries, and certainly further devaluation did not have international trade benefits as its major purpose. Thus when on October 22 it was announced that the dollar was to be depreciated even more in terms of gold, it was admitted by the administration that the intent was domestic price inflation.[10] The Reconstruction Finance Corporation was directed to buy large quantities of gold at higher and higher prices, until the decision was made (by the Gold Reserve Act of January, 1934) to stabilize at $35.00 per ounce—an over-all devaluation of approximately 40 per cent.

But though this step (or experiment, as it was frankly conceded to be) loomed large in the thinking of the administration, it did not prove to be of significance as an antidepression measure. The reason, moreover, is not far to seek. Its basis was the "commodity-dollar" theory proclaimed by several academic economists, the most serious shortcoming of which being that it was based on the quantity theory of money in its most primitive form. Instead of relating the price level to the quantity of all types of money in actual use, this approach professed to see a close relationship between prices and the quantity of gold alone. The naiveté of this way of thinking was soon apparent, for there was no discernible change in the domestic price level as a result.

INDECISION IN TRADE POLICY

Having thus made another sweeping attempt to conquer the depression, and resting from those labors while at the same time anxiously awaiting their outcome, the administration had for the first time an opportunity to take significant steps in the reform field. Whereas previous measures of this kind had been slipped in, so to speak, between moves of a clearly emergency nature, it was now possible to make solid progress toward a full-fledged reform program. With the same grim determination and easy self-assurance that had thus far characterized relief and recovery efforts, the nation's leaders now turned to this other dimension of their contribution to American history.

One of the first items on this agenda, and one destined to have a long and fruitful life, was a basic shift in tariff policy. Ever since the passage of the Smoot-Hawley Tariff four years earlier, a strong public reaction to Republican protectionism had been developing. In part this was because international trade had declined so drastically,

[10] A. W. Crawford, *Monetary Management Under the New Deal* (Washington, D.C.: American Council on Public Affairs, 1940).

this in turn resulting to a considerable extent from numerous acts of retaliation by various foreign nations. No doubt it also reflected in part the feeling which had for some time been growing more insistent that an international creditor nation must welcome imports rather than discourage them if it desires to receive payment for its own exports as well as interest and principal receipts on account of foreign investments. There was even a mounting unrest against the way the American tariff had historically been made; the setting of rates by Congress had seemed to encourage a log-rolling type of procedure which made almost impossible the development of what many were coming to think of as a rational tariff policy.

The administration's response to these sentiments was the Reciprocal Trade Agreements Act of June 12, 1934.[11] By its terms the President was given the authority to raise or lower any tariff rate by as much as 50 per cent. However, in order to be certain that concessions were not given to foreign competitors without corresponding concessions for the (direct as well as indirect) benefit of American exporters, it was stipulated that Presidential adjustments might not be made except as a result of bargaining negotiations out of which broadly equivalent reductions in trade barriers were accorded this country's businessmen.

Let it not be supposed, however, that this change in American tariff policy was either abrupt or complete. There was here no sudden abandonment of the practice of protecting domestic producers from foreign competition, no sweeping acceptance of the doctrine long advocated by economists that the common denominator of a modern economy is the consumer and therefore the only tariff policy which can serve the interest of the entire public is free trade. Indeed the remarkable fact about the reciprocal trade agreements program during the depression was not that it made so much difference in American foreign economic policy but that it made so little.

For example, the official (and no doubt sincere) justification given for the new legislation had little in common with standard economic doctrine on this subject; rather it was urged that men and women were involuntarily unemployed, and that one way of putting them back to work would be to increase exports by reducing import barriers. Furthermore, it is now widely agreed that Smoot-Hawley rates were in many instances higher than was warranted even by the desire to afford a high degree of protection, and that in consequence much of the rate-lowering of the early years of reciprocity consisted

[11] J. C. Pearson, *The Reciprocal Trade Agreements Program* (Washington: The Catholic University of America Press, 1942).

merely of squeezing the water out of existing rates. And it is also to be noted that no tariff reduction negotiations were scheduled with the most aggressive competitor of American manufacturers during this entire decade, little Japan.

TABLE 33. A HISTORIC POLICY REVERSAL

Fiscal Year	Average Tariff Rate on Dutiable Imports
1929*	40
1930*	45
1931†	53
1932†	59
1933†	54
1935‡	43
1937‡	38
1939‡	37

* Before Smoot-Hawley Tariff.
† Smoot-Hawley Tariff.
‡ Reciprocal Trade Agreements Program.
Source: United States Tariff Commission.

Not only was the Reciprocal Trade Agreements Act as such less unorthodox in practice than it seemed to be in theory, but it was at the same time made a part of an over-all trade policy which itself operated to dilute its impact considerably.[12] Thus, on the one hand, both the Agricultural Adjustment Act and the National Industrial Recovery Act commanded the President to impose import barriers to whatever extent was necessary to keep the benefits of the recovery program within this country. On the other hand, the forced devaluation of the dollar (that is, artificially raising the price of gold from, say, $29.00 or $30.00 per ounce to $35.00) did so much to promote American exports while inhibiting American imports that there was much less need to promote exports by encouraging imports.

This same phenomenon can be even more clearly seen in several items of legislation passed almost simultaneously with the reciprocal trade enactment. There was, first, the creation of the Export-Import Bank. This organization was not, as its name implies, designed to encourage impartially both imports and exports. Its purpose was rather to make government credit available to foreign nations that would thereby be enabled to purchase more American exports. To be sure, this was an objective for which no apology needs to be made. At the same time it did savor more of this country's traditional preoccupa-

[12] Alonzo E. Taylor, *The New Deal and Foreign Trade* (New York: The Macmillan Co., 1935).

tion with exports than it did a recognition of the importance of imports to a creditor nation.

Although it was not in any sense an administration measure, the Silver Purchase Act of 1934 was nonetheless also an integral part of the foreign economic policy the Roosevelt government was putting together piece by piece. If economic orthodoxy in this field be defined as a nationalistic disregard of the impact of unilateral decisions on other nations, this was American orthodoxy with a vengeance. Once again a coalition of farmers and silver producers prevailed upon the government to create an artificially high price for silver, a procedure which in a few short years forced a China, in need of all her resources to repel the aggressions of an expansionist Japan, off the silver standard and into a period of financial chaos.

But even this does not fully illustrate the lengths to which men were willing to go in 1934 to keep the break with the past, which the Reciprocal Trade Agreements Act undoubtedly was, to the smallest possible proportions. Price-support operations under the Agricultural Adjustment Act for the benefit of domestic sugar producers were complicated by the fact that a large quantity of that product was regularly imported, and it would obviously not have done to permit Treasury outlays to redound to the advantage of foreigners. Accordingly, the Jones-Costigan Sugar Production Act was passed in early 1934 stipulating the shares of the American market to be furnished by domestic and the several foreign suppliers. The basis for these quotas was, of all things, actual market shares under the Smoot-Hawley Tariff.

June, 1934

The Reciprocal Trade Agreements Act was not the only piece of reform legislation first promulgated in June, 1934. Indeed, so much activity of this kind reached a climax during those thirty days that by mid-year no thinking conservative could have doubted that his group had slipped considerably on the administration's priority list.

Before this month had hardly begun, on June 6, another major step was taken to make certain that the stock market never again got as out of hand as it had in the preceding decade.[13] After all these years of futile protest against finance capitalism, recent events had at last provided a basis for asserting the public interest implicit in a modern nation's financial organization in broader terms than had ever before been possible—and reformers were determined to strike

[13] United States Senate, *Stock Exchange Practices* (Washington, D.C.: Government Printing Office, 1934).

before this iron cooled off materially. More specifically, the Securities and Exchange Act was passed: (1) "to make available currently to the investing public information regarding the affairs of the corporations whose securities are traded in the securities markets"; (2) "to prevent the diversion into security transactions of a disproportionate amount of the nation's credit resources"; and (3) "to eliminate manipulation and other abuses in the security markets."[14]

To carry out the first of these purposes, the Act required that all securities traded on national exchanges as well as these exchanges themselves be in effect licensed by (technically, registered with) the federal government. To carry out the second the Federal Reserve Board was empowered to fix margin requirements, and a newly-created Securities Exchange Commission was given authority to limit borrowing by security dealers, brokers, and exchange members. In recognition, furthermore, of the desirability of placing similar powers in the hands of a single group (as well as the improbability of effective enforcement of the earlier Securities Act by the Federal Trade Commission), the stock market responsibilities of this latter body were also lodged with the new agency.

Fullest detail in this enactment, however, was reserved for the implementation of its third purpose. All directors, officers, and owners of 10 per cent or more of a registered security were required to report monthly all personal transactions in the securities of their own company, and were forbidden to keep profits made on such transactions unless the securities involved had been held for more than six months. A number of especially notorious manipulative devices, for example, market pools and the dissemination of false or misleading information, were specifically proscribed; and the new Commission was given broad authority to issue rules governing the use of other market practices.

While the government was timidly but nonetheless unmistakably imposing public utility status upon the nation's securities markets, the aviation industry was finding itself being elbowed unceremoniously farther and farther in that same general direction.[15] By 1934 the Watres Act had proved to be both too generous and too loosely written with respect to mail subsidies, and a reformulation of these provisions became suddenly an extremely urgent matter. And when the Air Mail Act of 1934 was passed on June 12, it included a num-

---

[14] W. E. Atkins, G. W. Edwards, and H. G. Moulton, *The Regulation of the Security Markets* (Washington, D.C.: Brookings Institution, 1946).

[15] P. T. David, *Economics of Air Mail Transportation* (Washington, D.C.: Brookings Institution, 1934).

TABLE 34. TOO MUCH FOR TOO LITTLE

	Air mail service		
Year	Length of Routes (miles)	Mail Carried (thousands of pounds)	Cost of Service (millions of dollars)
1930	14,907	7,720	14.6
1935	28,884	10,775	8.8

Source: Department of Commerce, *Statistical Abstract of the United States, 1937,*
p. 339.

ber of paragraphs broadly expanding the role of government in relation to commercial air transportation.

By comparison with the regulations to be imposed upon this industry a few years later, the regulatory innovations of 1934 were indeed mild. But it was no comfort to the business community as of
June, 1934, to reflect that the government might soon expand its
powers still further. Quite the contrary. Thus when the Interstate
Commerce Commission was now given authority to fix fair and reasonable rates for the transportation of air mail and to prevent the
earning of unreasonable profits by any air mail carrier, and when the
Postmaster General was authorized to take a number of drastic
steps to prevent the concentration of this industry into the hands of
a few large operators (such as prohibiting the transfer of air mail
contracts, and separating the manufacturing and transportation
branches of the aviation industry), conservatives were understandably not pleased.

The Communications Act of 1934, passed on June 19, was also cut
from this same pattern. Here too was an area of the economy which
public utility status had been fast overtaking. The primary difference was that in this instance the chase very nearly ended in 1934.

Few basic changes were now introduced into radio regulation
except that to a new Federal Communications Commission were
transferred the responsibilities in this field which had hitherto been
exercised by the Federal Radio Commission.[16] The regulation of telecommunications, on the other hand, was decisively intensified.[17] Not
only were the powers in this field which the Interstate Commerce
Commission had not in fact used given to a new agency specializing
in the problems thus raised, but these powers were also brought

16 Llewellyn White, *The American Radio* (Chicago: University of Chicago Press,
1947).
17 Federal Communications Commission, *Investigation of the Telephone Industry
in the United States* (Washington, D.C.: Government Printing Office, 1939).

more nearly up to date. Thus the Federal Communications Commission was unequivocally given public utility rate-regulating authority over telegraph carriers and long-distance telephonic communication, and broad flexibility was allowed for the cooperation of state and federal agencies in resolving problems arising in the constitutional no-man's land created by the nature and organization of the telephone industry.

But if conservatives could console themselves that thus far these June twists of the knife in an old wound were after all only applications of principles of government-business relationships already well established this rationalization soon proved erroneous. Before June, 1934, had passed into history there were also enacted a number of laws which clearly blazed new trails.

There were, in the first place, several changes in the railroad labor legislation then in effect. And of these a still more outright recognition of labor's right to organize and bargain collectively was not the principal case in point as far as conservatives were concerned. After the Norris-La Guardia and National Industrial Recovery Acts this was by now an easily discernible if highly regrettable trend. In a significantly different category, however, was a law setting up a retirement fund for all railroad workers accumulated from contributions made by both carriers and by their employees—the definitive beginning of a federal social security program in this country. To be sure, conservatives did not object to their workers' looking forward to a comfortable old age. It was only that the invasion of private rights to the extent of compelling individuals to prepare financially for this contingency in a certain way and as a part of an immense group effort seemed to have vaguely sinister implications.

At least equally sinister to conservatives but much less vague were the implications of the Frazier-Lemke Farm Bankruptcy Act. Under the provisions of this legislation the terms of many farm mortgage

TABLE 35.. PLIGHT OF AN AMERICAN DREAM: MORTGAGED FARMS IN 1930

Number	Per Cent of Total	Farm Mortgage Debt
2,350,313	40.1	$9,214,278,000

Source: Department of Commerce, *Statistical Abstract of the United States, 1937*, p. 593.

contracts already in force were summarily altered. Payments were scaled down or postponed, certain procedures by which foreclosed property was to change hands were expressly stipulated as a protection to debtors, and farmers who had lost their farms were required to be given first opportunity to buy them, and at a price fixed by district court. This sort of thing, of course, was "old stuff" to property owners as far as state governments were concerned. Every major depression in the history of the country had seen its flurry of state mortgage moratoria. Moreover, the federal government had the year before put the Treasury's resources behind the transfer of mortgages from private to government hands. But the 1934 innovation was far more ominous than either of these approaches. For the first time since laissez faire had become an important feature of American ideology the national government had been instrumental in abrogating on a wholesale basis contracts between private individuals. No breach in the principles of historic American laissez faire could have been more profound than this.

And still one more blow was given to the discredited business community in June, 1934. The one saving feature of the Frazier-Lemke Act was that once existing contracts had been terminated, all future contracts of the same sort could at least be written with this kind of government intervention in mind. But when the new administration began to finance new homes in the mass market as well as refinance old residential mortgages for would-be home owners unable in the depression to make the payments stipulated in their loan agreements, it was easy to see that the federal government was entrenching itself on a much more permanent basis in a field which had heretofore been the undisputed province of private enterprise.

Here as elsewhere drastic steps were not taken without justification in existing realities. Indeed in the housing field as at so many other points the first halting innovations had already been taken by the preceding administration. But the Federal Home Loan Bank System of Hoover days had proved no more successful in accomplishing the task set for it than the Reconstruction Finance Corporation in stemming the tide of railroad bankruptcies and bank failures. By mid-1933, as a result of optimism in home-buying during the 1920's coupled with shrinking purchasing power after 1929, the rate of foreclosures on homes was more than 1,000 every working day.

The new administration moved to halt this devastation in several different ways. First, the Home Owners' Loan Corporation (1933) was created to carry on outright salvage operations. In all, this agency acquired more than 1,000,000 mortgages having an aggregate face value of $3 billion, almost one-fifth of the entire urban home mortgage debt in the country. Second, the Federal Home Loan

Banks, allied with their member savings and loan associations and assisted by a newly-created federal home finance agency, were instrumental in basically reforming the way in which private residential construction was financed to the end that like catastrophes might not occur in the future. And third, the National Housing Act of June, 1934, in order to stimulate new construction as well as reform home finance techniques, established the Federal Housing Administration to develop in cooperation with private lending agencies a system of mutual insurance for loans for the building of new homes or the modernization of old ones.

Looking back on this development years later most far-seeing businessmen were to concede that in this area private enterprise had blundered badly. Prior to this, residential mortgages were typically of the lump-sum variety; at the expiration of a certain period of time (for example, 5, 10, or 15 years), no payments on principal (and often not even interest payments) having been required in the interim, large sums of money became due and payable. The result was a method of financing which on the one hand greatly narrowed the possibility of most Americans owning their own homes, and which on the other hand could only operate to intensify a deflationary spiral. Once the federal government had devised an instrument by means of which principal and interest were paid as regularly as rent and in comparable sums (as well as providing home-builders with a higher degree of protection from exploitation at the hands of local contractors and real estate agents), this innovation was promptly acknowledged as far superior and was taken over by private operators. But of course this retrospective judgment did nothing to calm conservative fears at the moment.

DEEPENING SHADOWS

With the reform fever now running so high, it was almost inevitable that it would begin to intermingle to a greater or lesser extent with the New Deal's recovery program itself. Since there already existed a growing groundswell of opposition to the National Recovery Administration, there arose an abundance of opportunities for alterations in that program.[18] When the government in fact began to utilize these opportunities to develop nonconservative solutions to the problems thereby raised—when, in other words, steps were taken to resolve conflicts in favor of nonbusiness groups—the dismay of the business community knew no bounds.

[18] Simon N. Whitney, *Trade Associations and Industrial Control: A Critique of the NRA* (New York: Central Book Co., 1934).

Of course, too, businessmen were not inclined to be charitable, and therefore there was no disposition to look at extenuating circumstances. Had there been, they would have seen at once that much of what the government was now doing to alter the direction of National Recovery Administration operations was motivated less by a desire to "stack the deck" for the benefit of consumers, workers, and small businessmen as such than by the need to counterbalance the stacking big business had already done in favor of itself. Thus it was by now apparent that overwhelmingly the heart and center of the code effort was the variety of techniques employed to control prices, whether directly or through allocation of markets, control of production, limitations on productive capacity, or control of the channels of distribution. Although the legislation setting up this program had stipulated that its provisions were not to be used to establish monopoly, it was plain that in practice the government was becoming a promoter and protector of monopoly on a gigantic scale.

The principal grievance of small businessmen against the developing system could hardly be more obvious. At any time in a private enterprise system there will exist a large number of small concerns which could not exist if required to pay the same wages and charge the same prices as their larger colleagues. A brief mental comparison of the economic position of the corner grocery store with a downtown chain is all the documentation needed on this point. In a situation in which the larger firms wielded the greatest influence in working out uniform prices and wages for an entire industry, the temptation deliberately to squeeze these smaller and typically less efficient producers just a little was almost irresistible. (And of course the other side of this issue was the undesirability of fixing uniform wages, for example, substantially below the level already prevailing in the larger concerns.) The question posed for the administration when this process became apparent was not merely whether it should give in to the political pressure of the larger group of small operators, but whether a painfully constricted economy would be better off if a sizable number of these concerns were forced into bankruptcy.

Labor's objection to the recovery program as it was working out in practice was twofold. First, the maximum hours provision in this legislation was to promote work-sharing, and with this end in view labor representatives had contended for a 30-hour week. Primarily to avoid compelling too abrupt an adjustment too quickly the President's Reemployment Agreement had specified 35 hours. But when the individual codes began to be formulated, for one reason or another 40 hours per week became standard. Second, employers continued to fight bitterly against the collective bargaining rights written into Section 7A of the Act, and a strenuous drive to substitute company for independent unions was accordingly launched. This threat was quite naturally met by a wave of strikes called for the purpose of preventing labor's organization guaranty from being

TABLE 36. LABOR'S CHALLENGE TO THE NIRA

| Year | Number | Work Stoppages | |
| | | Workers Involved | |
		Number (thousands)	Per cent
1932	841	324	1.8
1934	1,856	1,470	7.2

Source: Bureau of the Census, *Historical Statistics of the United States, 1789-1945*, p. 73.

thus sabotaged, and hence here also the government was confronted with a problem which far transcended the question of how the fruits of the recovery program were to be divided. To an extent difficult to realize at this historical distance, recovery was itself being directly threatened.

The first step taken to adjust these inequities (as well as to introduce a few ideological changes into the system) had come on October 22, 1933. On that date businessmen in small towns were exempted from the Blanket Code, price increases were required to be investigated, and a machinery for handling specific complaints arising under the program was established. December 16, 1933, saw a second small modification, a broadening of the responsibilities of the Act's administrators to preserve industrial peace to include mediation, conciliation, and arbitration.

By early 1934 these tendencies were beginning to form a consistent and distressing pattern from the standpoint of conservatives. On January 20 the President issued an Executive Order designed to strengthen the Act's provisions against monopoly. At this point the ambiguity inherent in the recovery enactment from the beginning stood out in particularly bold relief. The law stated emphatically that monopoly was not to be permitted in the codes, but that code provisions were to be exempt from the antitrust laws. Here was an exceedingly fine point in logic. If monopoly did not result, the antitrust exemption was meaningless; while if exemption was really intended, the Act did not quite mean what it said about steering clear of monopoly.

This ambiguity in turn now gave rise to a painful though short-lived intra-administration tension.[19] With Hugh Johnson, administrator of the program, arguing vehemently that price-fixing and production-control practices were not monopolistic but were instead indispensable to price maintenance, Congress bluntly demanded an investigation. This was narrowly avoided by the creation by the President on March 7 of a non-Congressional investigatory group, the National Recovery Review Board; but when this body brought in an adverse report, the administration refused to admit that a fair evaluation had been made and General Johnson became exceedingly bitter. Despite these denials, however, a number of steps were now taken, suggesting that the Review Board's report had been taken seriously after all. On May 9 a Policy Board was created to formulate "acceptable, desirable policies as to code provisions." Two weeks later an Executive Order was issued bringing to an end code regulation in the service industries. In June price-fixing provisions in new codes were prohibited. On July 14 an Industrial Appeals Board was organized with power to grant relief to small businessmen seriously disadvantaged by the Act's administration. In September Johnson resigned his position, and was replaced by a five-man commission. On October 22 it was announced that code provisions limiting production would no longer be enforced.

Broadly paralleling these developments, although not closely related to them, was an equally clear-cut shift in the administration's emphasis with respect to labor's interest in the recovery program. Reacting against employer attempts to frustrate Section 7A guaranties, the President on March 5, 1934, pulled no punches in asserting that the term "free choice" written into that Section meant exactly that. "I ask that the letter and the spirit of free choice be accorded to its workers by every corporation in the United States." Thus encouraged labor leaders organized recognition strikes in such numbers that both total strikes and workers involved were in 1934 at a twelve-year peak. So difficult did this situation become that 19 states took the extreme step of calling out the militia on one or more occasions during that year, and almost 50 workers were killed by company guards.

ANOTHER NAIL IN THE COFFIN

It is to be doubted that very many conservatives in 1934 either discussed or thought about the sweep of current events in philo-

[19] Hugh S. Johnson, *The Blue Eagle From Egg to Earth* (Garden City: Doubleday & Co., Inc., 1935).

sophical terms. The business mind is above all practical, and human beings under stress are especially unlikely to deal in abstractions. But for those whose minds did have and maintain through this difficult period a theoretical bent, there occurred an event which no doubt provided considerable food for thought.

In 1933 the New York legislature had created a Milk Control Board with the power "to fix minimum and maximum . . . retail prices to be charged by . . . stores to consumers for consumption off the premises where sold." As one of its first actions this newly created regulatory agency had fixed 9 cents as the retail price of a quart of milk. One Nebbia, proprietor of a grocery store in Rochester, had defied the Board's order by selling two quarts of milk and a 5-cent loaf of bread for 18 cents. When this defiance was challenged in the courts by the Milk Control Board, Nebbia through his lawyers maintained that the New York statute contravened the equal protection and due process clauses of the Fourteenth Amendment, and that therefore the Board's order was null and void.

If ever during these trying years conservatives felt confident, it would certainly have been when they read Nebbia's brief in this proceeding as presented to the United States Supreme Court. Surely here was an impregnable position. Many years ago this body had given birth to the public utility concept, the doctrine that private enterprise prices could not be regulated by government unless the concerns involved possessed certain narrowly prescribed characteristics. Although one effect of this innovation had been to permit intensive regulation within a relatively small area of the economy, its more important consequence had been to prohibit price regulation over a far broader range of economic activities. By no stretch of the imagination could the milk industry be classified as a public utility in this traditional sense.

But whatever comfort was drawn from a study of Nebbia's presentation was completely shattered when Justice Roberts, speaking for a divided Court, delivered an opinion denying every one of Nebbia's contentions. And so fundamental are the implications of this opinion for the evolution of government-business relationships that it is appropriate to review this landmark decision and its meaning in some detail.

The Court first reviewed the legislative history of the act creating the Milk Control Board. Milk is a product the demand for which is highly income-elastic, which means that a decline in aggregate purchasing power throughout the economy as a whole will be accompanied by a particularly sharp decrease in the demand for milk.[20] When in the Great Depression this state of affairs developed, the price of milk in New York declining much more than prices gener-

TABLE 37.   NEBBIA V. NEW YORK

Year	Average Price of Fluid Milk in New York (dollars per barrel)
1929	3.997
1932	2.379

Source: Department of Commerce, *Statistical Abstract of the United States, 1937*, p. 303.

ally, a committee of the state legislature had made an investigation of the industry.

It was against the background of the findings of this committee that the New York regulatory statute had been written. The major conclusions had been as follows. First, milk is an essential item of diet, it cannot be stored, and it is an excellent medium for the growth of bacteria. In consequence, failure of producers to receive a reasonable return for their labor and investment threatens a relaxation of vigilance against contamination. Second, in order to be able to meet the public demand for drinking milk, this industry must ordinarily turn out some 20 per cent more milk than will in fact be used in fluid form. This surplus, which often amounts to much more than 20 per cent, must in turn be used in the manufacture of other dairy products, and the price to the farmer of this portion of the supply is substantially less than his receipts from fluid milk. Unless the burden of this surplus is equitably distributed among all producers, the pressure to convert surplus into fluid milk is apt to result in a destructive competition which may have very serious consequences for both the quantity and the quality of this basic food. The purpose of price-fixing by the Milk Control Board, in other words, was to prevent this kind of market instability.[21]

Justice Roberts first and quite summarily dealt with Nebbia's contention that he had been denied equal protection of the laws.[22] Since the act in question placed every seller of milk under the same restrictions, the Court could see no basis for this complaint. Indeed,

[20] R. W. Bartlett, *The Milk Industry* (New York: The Ronald Press Co., 1946).
[21] W. P. Mortenson, *Milk Distribution as a Public Utility* (Chicago: University of Chicago Press, 1940).
[22] *Nebbia* v. *New York*, 291 U.S. 502 (1934).

the majority opinion even went so far as to suggest that if the law had in its terms applied different rules to retailers than to wholesalers, it would not necessarily follow that the legislation was for that reason arbitrary and hence invalid.

The Court was less curt, although not less emphatic, when it turned its attention to the question of due process. Here the first major point made was that with the single exception of the railroad industry, "no business has been so thoroughly regimented and regulated by the State of New York as the milk industry." To be sure, this regulation had not heretofore included price control, and the Court was well aware that this fact brought it face to face with the basic distinction, which was by now settled doctrine, between concerns "affected with a public interest" and other types of businesses.

There was no hesitation in meeting this issue and no mincing of words:

We may as well say at once that the dairy industry is not, in the accepted sense of the phrase, a public utility. . . . But if, as must be conceded, the industry is subject to regulation in the public interest, what constitutional principle bars the state from correcting existing maladjustments by legislation touching prices? We think there is no such principle. . . . It is clear that there is no closed class or category of businesses affected with a public interest, and the function of courts in the application of the Fifth and Fourteenth Amendments is to determine in each case whether circumstances vindicate the challenged regulation as a reasonable exertion of governmental authority or condemn it as arbitrary or discriminatory. . . . So far as the requirement of due process is concerned, and in the absence of other constitutional restrictions, a state is free to adopt whatever economic policy may reasonably be deemed to promote public welfare, and to enforce that policy by legislation adapted to its purpose. . . . Price control, like any other form of regulation, is unconstitutional only if arbitrary, discriminatory, or demonstrably irrelevant to the policy the legislature is free to adopt, and hence an unwarranted interference with individual liberty.

Freely translated into nonlegal terminology, this epoch-making decision seemed to mean this. Property is not a physical object that an owner may do with as he pleases. Property is rather an abstraction, a bundle of rights; some things an owner may do with his property, and some things he may not do. The make-up of this bundle, the nature of the things that an owner may do with his property, is in the final analysis always determined by the laws in force within the community, and in a democracy there are few changes in this bundle which may not be made if the duly elected representatives of the people believe them to be in the best interest of society as a whole.

Actually, this development hardly came to alert businessmen as a surprise, distressing though it unquestionably was. Ever since the New Freedom era it had been widely understood that the pattern of government-business relationships built around the public utility concept was eroding badly in favor of expanded government responsibilities. By the same token, the nation did not (contrary to the fears of conservatives while these developments were taking place) rush pell mell into a wholesale repudiation of historic private property rights, even though this upholding of New York's 1933 legislation regulating the price of milk did stimulate the spread of similar controls in virtually all states having one or more large urban areas (controls, however, closely resembling the National Recovery Administration codes in that they most favored businessman-producers at the expense of consumers).[23] But all the same there were few who doubted that in *Nebbia* v. *New York* the demise of laissez faire had moved still another long step nearer.

———

The die was now cast. An administration that was apparently no longer able to make decisions receiving general approbation was more and more espousing new and threatening doctrines rather than established and long-accepted ones—more and more orienting its program toward the needs of the "forgotten man." And, what was even more ominous, the voting public seemed to approve. In November, 1934, the ruling group in Washington received a vote of confidence almost unprecedented for a nonpresidential election year. For the first time in the experience of most men then living, the administration in power gained strength in both House and Senate in a by-election. Here was reason enough for the plea to General Smedley D. Butler by Wall Street representatives in December that he lead a fascist march on Washington—an episode later related under oath to a Congressional committee by the General himself.

QUESTIONS FOR DISCUSSION

1. Why did the New Deal honeymoon come to an end?
2. Was the destruction of food in 1933 justifiable? Why or why not?
3. What were the first problems to arise in connection with the National Industrial Recovery Act, and how were they met?
4. In what ways did the farm relief program fail to satisfy its beneficiaries in 1933?
5. Explain the purpose of raising the price of gold in late 1933. How was this supposed to operate, and why did it fail?

[23] Warren C. Waite, Don S. Anderson, and R. K. Froker, *Economic Standards of Government Price Control* (Washington, D.C.: Government Printing Office, 1941).

6. Enumerate the major changes in trade policy incorporated in the Reciprocal Trade Agreements Act. How fundamental were these changes during the depression?

7. What other reforms were promulgated in 1934? Were any of these either ill-conceived or poorly timed?

8. In what respects did labor feel the recovery program was discriminating against its needs? Was it?

9. Explain and evaluate the steps taken to modify the National Recovery Administration.

10. Could a program such as that contemplated in the National Industrial Recovery Act have been worked out without giving rise to the problems our own National Recovery Administration created?

11. What were the characteristics of the milk industry thought to justify regulation? Do these characteristics justify regulation of that industry in time of prosperity?

12. Why may *Nebbia* v. *New York* be appropriately thought of as a point of demarcation between two eras?

13. What elements of the "First New Deal" (if any) still remained at the end of 1934?

Chapter 22

The New Deal Shows Its Colors

CANNON TO THE RIGHT OF THEM

But if by the end of 1934 the business community understood that the New Deal was changing its character, it had still to be furnished with a coherent statement of the philosophy which was now to govern the Washington scene. If, in other words, conservatives now knew that the "First New Deal" was a thing of the past, they were as yet not wholly clear as to the nature of the "Second New Deal."

However, just as June, 1934, had provided the key to the first of these realizations, so did January, 1935, furnish the key to the second.[1] In his annual message to Congress on the fourth day of the new year, the first major White House pronouncement since the new leadership had been so resoundingly approved the preceding November, President Roosevelt stated in unequivocal terms the principles by which his administration would now be guided. Whereas to this point the first emphasis had been relief and recovery, with reform measures sandwiched in only when it seemed that conservatives would not be unduly frightened thereby, henceforth reform was to be moved to the center of the stage.

This did not mean that recovery was considered to have been achieved, for there were still some 10,000,000 people involuntarily unemployed. Nor did it mean that the government's interest in recovery was waning. Rather the President's new emphasis was predicated upon the proposition that the attempt to achieve recovery by pursuing it directly had failed. And although it can be argued that the administration in this conclusion somewhat belittled what had been accomplished to date, it is true that the National Recovery Administration's answer to the devastation created by a modern depression had to date fallen short of expectations.

[1] Ernest K. Lindley, *Half Way With Roosevelt* (New York: The Viking Press, Inc., 1937).

Stated still more bluntly, and certainly the President spared no feelings in his presentation, the thesis on the basis of which the national government was now prepared to act was this. Thus far the attack on depression had been overly solicitous of existing institutions, and had in consequence inadequately cared for the needs of the human beings institutions are created to serve. In other words, the New Deal had not been sufficiently daring, sufficiently experimental, in devising new institutional arrangements to bring an end to the human tragedy now growing intolerable.

Thinking people in almost every country of the world have come to realize certain fundamental difficulties with which civilization must reckon. Rapid changes—the machine age, the advent of universal and rapid communication and many other new factors—have brought new problems. Succeeding generations have attempted to keep pace by reforming in piecemeal fashion this or that attendant abuse. As a result, evils overlap and reform becomes confused and frustrated. We lose sight, from time to time, of our ultimate human objectives.

It must have come to American conservatives with a considerable shock that the ruling administration felt it had not been flexible enough in working out changes in the status quo. The fears thereby raised, moreover, were accentuated rather than mollified by the chip-on-the-shoulder terminology the President saw fit to use in setting forth social justice as the keynote of a new approach.

We find our population suffering from old inequalities, little changed by past sporadic remedies. In spite of our efforts and in spite of our talk, we have not weeded out the overprivileged and we have not effectively lifted up the underprivileged.

To be sure, President Roosevelt did take some pains to sugarcoat this bitter pill, to maintain contact with America's ideological past at every possible point. But what businessman would be deceived by the following use of one of the most basic symbols of laissez faire?

No wise man has any intention of destroying what is known as the profit motive; because by the profit motive we mean the right by work to earn a decent livelihood for ourselves and our families.

And what conservative would fail to see the threat lurking in the background of the following discussion of economic equality?

We have . . . a clear mandate from the people, that Americans must foreswear that conception of the acquisition of wealth which, through excessive profits, creates undue private power over private affairs and, to our misfortune, over public affairs as well. In building toward this end we do not destroy ambition, nor do we seek to divide our wealth into equal shares on stated occasions. We continue to recognize the greater ability of some to earn more than others. But we do assert that the ambition of the individual to obtain for him and his a proper security, a reasonable leisure, and a decent living throughout life is an ambition to be preferred to the appetite for great wealth and great power.

Of course social justice is not a self-defining concept, and therefore the President gave a brief explanation of the definition his administration would primarily endeavor to implement. And it is not surprising that the central emphasis here was the personal, human security which the depression had virtually destroyed for so many people.[2]

The security of the men, women and children of the Nation . . . remains our first and continuing task; and in a very real sense every major legislative enactment of this Congress should be a component part of it.

In defining immediate factors which enter into our quest, I have spoken to the Congress and the people of three great divisions:

1. The security of a livelihood through the better use of the national resources of the land in which we live.
2. The security against the major hazards and vicissitudes of life.
3. The security of decent homes.

I am now ready to submit to the Congress a broad program designed ultimately to establish all three of these factors of security—a program which because of many lost years will take many future years to fulfill.

It is understandable that custodians of the faith of private enterprise capitalism would consider a governmental program built around such a philosophy to be an outright repudiation of the principles which had made America great. Furthermore, there is a significant sense in which this evaluation was quite accurate. There are, however, other points of view from which this turn of events can be examined, and from several of these there is at least another side to this matter.

First and foremost, when the "Second New Deal's" major premise is viewed on its merits, it is seen to be not wholly fanciful. Although economists are not agreed as to the causes of depressions in general or the Great Depression in particular, and although it would oversimplify to suggest a single cause for such a complex phenomenon, retrospective analyses have more and more stressed in this connection the concentration of wealth and income in the higher income

[2] Abraham Epstein, *Insecurity: A Challenge to America* (New York: Random House, Inc., 1938).

brackets during the 1920's—the failure of real wages to rise proportionately with an almost unprecedented increase in productivity. An exchange mechanism functions smoothly only insofar as a proper balance is maintained between mass spending power and capital accumulation. If the former is inadequate, the latter becomes to that extent pointless, and a serious deflation may easily develop as a result. To this point recovery efforts had been broadly governed by the orthodox insistence that purchasing power filters down to the poorer classes of society from the hierarchy above (the only major exception being the Civil Works Administration); in a democratic society it was fitting that the opposite approach should now be given a chance to show what it could do.

In the second place, the harshness of the criticism directed against those elements in American society said (at the present time as well as in the 1930's) to be overemphasizing security is in several respects overdrawn. First, those groups that were helped by the "Second New Deal" to find a greater degree of security during that decade, and that have since been keenly interested in maintaining and expanding these gains, were not the first interests in the country to make security a major value. The entire history of the protective tariff, successive waves of business consolidations, and the trade association movement then reaching something of a climax in the National Recovery Administration, are all indicative of a conservative orientation in this same direction which had long been a fixed feature of economic organization in the United States.

Second, what has seemed to be an insistence upon achieving a greater and greater degree of security is in large part only an attempt to provide citizens of an exchange, interdependent economy with as high a level of security as citizens enjoyed before their lives fell so overwhelmingly under the influence of impersonal and often harsh supply and demand factors. Because, in other words, modern economic life consists to a considerable extent of forces so huge and powerful that the average individual is helpless before them, modern democracies have decided that certain basic threats to individual well-being are to be absorbed by the group as a whole rather than allowed to fall with crushing weight upon a part of the group only.

And finally, to those who argue that an excessive emphasis upon freedom threatens both economic progress and traditional freedoms there are still other observations to be made. On the one hand, the antithesis between security and progress has not as yet been demonstrated to be as complete as it has often been presumed to be; to this point a satisfactory rate of economic progress has proved possible despite a program guaranteeing what has come to be called minimum individual rights for every citizen. Stated differently, because of the exceptionally high rate of productivity already achieved in America, this economy can afford to provide its citizens with a higher level of security without destroying its ability to develop further than would otherwise be the case. On the other hand, it is scarcely necessary to remind lovers of freedom that that cause is often best served by limitations of freedom, even though it is extremely difficult to know precisely where to draw the line in specific instances.

Cannon to the Left of Them

The "Second New Deal" was thus decisively launched in January, 1935. True to his promise the President did develop a legislative program designed to implement the new philosophy, and by April this program was beginning to take definitive form.

The first item on this agenda was the Resettlement Administration. From the beginning the administration's agricultural endeavors had been severely criticized as discriminatory against the large number of farmers who for one reason or another were either just barely holding on or had already succumbed to the rigors of depression, a criticism statistically supported by the fact that 1,000,000 farm families were actually on relief. The central interest of this new agricultural agency was farmers whose land was not quite productive enough to repay cultivation. Loans were made to farmers on submarginal land by means of which they could resettle on land capable of yielding a more adequate return for labor expended (or make capital expenditures on the land they were now using to increase its productivity), and a variety of other rehabilitation devices was developed. While these activities never advanced farther than what might be called an experimental stage, such a revolutionary assumption of strictly paternalistic responsibilities by government went far to confirm the fears already aroused.

In May a second part of this program was ready to be put into operation. In a sense it too was a part of the over-all planning now being done in Washington for the benefit of the farmer. By contrast, however, the Rural Electrification Administration was not oriented to rural destitution, but reflected rather the widespread feeling that farmers were not receiving their fair share of the comforts a modern economy is capable of providing its citizens because of the reluctance of private utility companies to extend their lines into low

TABLE 38. RURALIZATION OF ELECTRICITY

Year	Number of Farms Electrified on December 31	
	By Private Companies	By Public Authorities
1930	649,000	—
1940	1,448,500	601,500
1950	1,998,000	2,426,000

Source: Department of Commerce, *Statistical Abstract of the United States, 1955*, p. 535.

population density areas. It follows that the primary justification of this program as a security measure had little to do with the depression in agriculture as such. Instead government loans at low rates of interest to rural electrification cooperatives were designed to promote a considerable amount of work relief activity, while the farmer demand for appliances which would thereby be stimulated was expected to bring about a mild chain reaction also beneficial to the general economic situation.

In theory at any rate the Rural Electrification Administration was a less extreme departure from orthodoxy than the Resettlement Administration. Yet it is probable that the former activity aroused a more intense opposition than the latter. A number of factors lay behind this violent reaction. For one thing, this undertaking seemed clearly to be an extension of the public power policy already symbolized by the Tennessee Valley Authority; the new agency was directed to give preference to projects distributing power generated by publicly owned plants. Furthermore, although like the Federal Housing Administration government activity in the rural electricity field was an encroachment on private enterprise, unlike the housing activity (except in the low cost housing and slum-clearance areas into which the government had not yet extensively intruded) rural electrification seemed sure to involve a direct subsidy from the United States Treasury. And it is also to be remembered in this connection that the Resettlement Administration never really "got off the ground." Perhaps, in short, the best indication of the validity of the reaction of conservatives to the Rural Electrification Administration is to be found in a few relevant statistics: over the next 15 years this agency was directly responsible for carrying electricity into 2,500,000 farm homes, and by reason of its very existence stimulated private concerns to intensify their efforts in this field to such an extent that the percentage of American farms wired for electricity increased from 10 to 90.

But neither the Rural Electrification Administration nor the Resettlement Administration are to be discussed in the same breath with the next major item on the administration's agenda, whether from the standpoint of its importance in the thinking of the nation's leaders, the bitterness of the criticisms it aroused, its sheer magnitude as measured by the sums of money required to implement it, or its place in the broader history of the federal government's long battle against the Great Depression.[3] The tragedy confronting the nation was still the millions of unemployed, and it was therefore only logical that the greatest effort would continue to be turned toward that problem. However, when President Roosevelt's new emphasis upon security made contact with this problem to the tune of many billions of dollars, the result could hardly have failed to keep such hostility toward the administration as actually existed at white heat.

The role of the Works Progress Administration after its inception in May, 1935, until its activities began to taper off several years later can be described in a number of different but closely related and overlapping ways. It can in the first place be thought of in contrast to the work relief programs that had preceded it and for which it was essentially a substitute. The first program of this kind had been the Public Works Administration, the object here being to absorb the unemployed in public works projects of a basically conventional nature—projects that would have been done by the government in any event, although anticipating future needs on this front. When it developed that there were simply not enough such projects to make a respectable showing in these fields, the Civil Works Administration had been organized to create immediate relief work for a large number of workers during the winter of 1933-34. Although the usefulness of the work done under that program was not a minor consideration, the need to emphasize speed did operate to the disadvantage of the utility principle. The Works Progress Administration was designed to make possible acceptable compromises at both of these points. On the one hand, activities were to be found which were not in all cases wholly conventional public works projects; on the other hand, as much long-range planning was to be done as the situation permitted in order to keep "boondoggling" to a minimum.

In the second place, the new work relief program can be viewed

[3] Donald S. Howard, *The WPA and Federal Relief Policy* (New York: The Russell Sage Foundation, 1943).

against the background of its more detailed objectives as set forth by President Roosevelt himself:

But the stark fact before us is that great numbers still remain unemployed.

A large proportion of these unemployed and their dependents have been forced on the relief rolls. . . . The lessons of history, confirmed by the evidence immediately before me, show conclusively that continued dependence upon relief induces a spiritual and moral disintegration fundamentally destructive to the national fibre. To dole out relief in this way is to administer a narcotic, a subtle destroyer of the human spirit. It is inimical to the dictates of sound policy. It is in violation of the traditions of America. Work must be found for able-bodied but destitute workers.

Starting from these premises the President suggested that the new program of "emergency public employment" should be governed by the following principles:

[1] All work undertaken should be useful—not just for a day, or a year, but useful in the sense that it affords permanent improvement in living conditions or that it creates future new wealth for the Nation.

[2] Compensation on emergency public projects should be in the form of security payments which should be larger than the amount now received as a relief dole, but at the same time not so large as to encourage the rejection of opportunities for private employment or the leaving of private employment to engage in Government work.

[3] Projects should be undertaken on which a large proportion of direct labor can be used.

[4] Preference should be given to those projects which will be self-liquidating in the sense that there is a reasonable expectation that the Government will get its money back at some future time.

[5] The projects undertaken should be selected and planned so as to compete as little as possible with private enterprise. . . .

[6] The planning of projects would seek to assure work during the coming fiscal year to the individuals now on relief, or until such time as private employment is available. . . .

[7] Effort should be made to locate projects where they will serve the greatest unemployment needs as shown by present relief rolls. . . .

These principles in turn suggest still a third vantage point from which the Works Progress Administration can constructively be viewed, namely, the major criticisms offered against it, these having their origin primarily in the administrative problems involved in endeavoring to carry out stated objectives to the satisfaction of all concerned.[4] For example, the sheer pressure of time, the need

⁴ National Resources Planning Board, *Security, Work and Relief Policies* (Washington, D.C.: Government Printing Office, 1942).

to make a maximum contribution as rapidly as was humanly possible, could not but make this organization vulnerable to the charge of incompetent administration even in the vast majority of cases in which graft and corruption were avoided.

Second, the problem of reconciling the demand for useful projects with the requirement that the realm of private enterprise be not invaded created further difficulties. Insofar as usefulness was defined as the ability to earn a return on capital invested (and there was during these years a strong tendency to adopt just such a definition), to that extent virtually all government projects would have been classified as useless. Even when self-liquidation was made the test at this point the question immediately raised was whether enough such projects could be found to accomplish the task which had now to be accomplished. And if more or less objective criteria such as these were not adopted, there was room for a very wide divergence of opinion as to what constituted "useful" employment—a controversy this program's administration in practice tended to resolve by

TABLE 39.   HEART OF THE NEW PROGRAM

Month and Year	General Relief Cases	Works Progress Employees
January, 1935	5,276,000	—
July, 1935	4,369,000	70,000
January, 1936	2,616,000	2,798,000

Source: Department of Commerce, *Statistical Abstract of the United States, 1938*, p. 162.

defining as useful any activity taking a citizen off relief and putting him to work.

Third, the emphasis upon projects requiring the use of as much direct labor as possible also came into conflict with other principles on the President's list. It was of course obvious why this requirement was included; the object after all was to put people to work, not machines. Unfortunately, however, in an economy based upon capital to the extent the American economy was at that time, this stress on human labor could only add up to gross inefficiency in terms of the standards in most common use. Particularly when, in addition, rates of wages higher than relief payments were insisted upon for "inefficient" production, this endeavor went sharply against the grain of traditional economic relationships in the United States.

Indeed, fourth, this matter of rates of compensation perhaps stirred up more controversy than any other single aspect of the Works Progress Administration program. In any community wages in private employment vary from just above the relief level to levels substantially higher than this. Wages for work relief lower than the average of prevailing private wage scales would result in a discrimination against public employees inconsistent with one of the most fundamental purposes of these expenditures, while work relief wages at this level would result in government wage rates higher than those paid by some private employers. There was, in other words, much substance to the charge that work relief "ruined" many workers for private employment, even though this complaint was often made by employers whose primary objection was the government employment obstacle to beating down the prevailing wage scale.

And there is, finally, one other useful frame of reference for looking at the Works Progress Administration as a whole. No doubt it would be fair to say that top officials in Washington were by 1935 less concerned with the details of this huge new spending program than with the fact that billions of dollars of new purchasing power would thereby be created. Under the stimulus of the depression and the problems it had created economists and politician-statesmen had been critically examining the relationships involved in a serious deflation. By the middle of 1935, furthermore, the rebellion against balancing the federal budget which had only just begun to make Herbert Hoover uneasy at the time he relinquished his office to Franklin Roosevelt had achieved a much higher level of intellectual respectability.

For approximately a century it had been broadly accepted by political economists that a *general* deflation in an exchange economy was a contradiction in terms. In such a society, so this analysis went, receipts from the sale of current output are paid out to the owners of the factors of production, who in consequence have in their possession the purchasing power with which these goods can be taken off the market. From this it was concluded that production creates its own demand and that a general overproduction of goods in the depression sense was not possible.

Faced now, however, with a situation in which just this was obviously happening, economic scientists had been compelled to re-think the fundamentals of their discipline at this point. More and more it was being accepted that the receipt of money income does not automatically create effective demand, that hoarding on a significant scale can create a condition more or less accurately described as general overproduction.[5] When this happens, the new economics was insisting, the government must take responsibility for supplementing private spending sufficiently to restore the balance between production and consumption which has for some reason been lost.

Furthermore, the contribution to gross national product of thus "priming the pump" would not be limited only to the new purchasing power directly injected by the government. As a result of the so-called circular flow of money, the passing of purchasing power from one spender to another all the way from the consumer to the producer of basic raw materials, the nation's income could be increased by an amount far greater than the quantity of purchasing power thus introduced. Nor was it thought to be an especially difficult task to create new purchasing power. All that was required was to run the budget into the red by the desired amount in financing some such program as the Works Progress Administration, taking care that insofar as possible money was paid out to individuals more likely to spend than save it. There was, however, one condition that had to be met. If businessmen became concerned about such unorthodox behavior on the part of their government, and in consequence reduced their own spending programs, the Treasury's efforts would be to that extent nullified. (Unfortunately, this strange, new doctrine proclaiming a virtue for government deficits was apt to produce just such a reaction.)[6] Here, indeed, was another major source of the bitter conservative opposition to work relief as a fundamental attack on the depression that began to develop almost immediately.

It is academic to attempt to give a definitive judgment on what became easily the most controversial aspect of the New Deal's anti-depression activities. On the one hand few would today challenge the purposes this program was intended to achieve, while on the other hand not many would undertake to defend everything that was done in the name of those purposes. But a retrospective judgment of this kind is beside the point in any event. Suffice it, therefore, to limit over-all comments here to these two. First, it was at this point that the United States government first came decisively to grips with the implications of mass unemployment in an industrial society; no society can maintain its existence as a going concern unless its citizens are given constructive functions to perform

[5] J. M. Keynes, The General Theory of Employment, Interest, and Money (New York: Harcourt, Brace & Co., Inc., 1936).

[6] Dudley Dillard, The Economics of John Maynard Keynes (Englewood Cliffs, N.J.: Prentice-Hall, Inc., 1948).

therein.[7] Second, were a similar catastrophe to strike the country again, this New Deal program would again be a primary point of departure in government policy-making.

A SILVER LINING

As the administration's new program, the "Second New Deal," began thus to unfold, and as conservatives began to feel more and more hopelessly ensnared in a net from which there seemed to be no escape, an opposition movement began simultaneously to form. And as in the days of old, just when it seemed that no one dared to stand against the giant a champion was already advancing, sling in hand.

Prior to 1935 there had been no indication that the Supreme Court would erect constitutional roadblocks in the way of the New Deal's advance. If anything, in fact, the decisions of this body had been encouraging. Thus a Minnesota statute providing for a moratorium on mortgage foreclosures had been upheld,[8] and *Nebbia* v. *New York* had sustained an even more sweeping exercise of governmental powers for emergency purposes.

Scarcely had the year 1935 opened, however, than the Supreme Court made it unmistakably clear that it was to be a major factor to be reckoned with on the reform front. The signal here was a case involving the petroleum industry. This area of the economy, like so many others, had for some time been essentially dominated by National Recovery Administration codes. But because of the special conditions prevailing in that industry, the basic code legislation had included a special provision relating to it. Section 9(c) of the National Industrial Recovery Act declared the shipment across state boundaries of oil produced in excess of quotas allowed by state regulations to be in violation of federal law.[9]

On January 7, three days after the President had announced to the country his new reform-recovery philosophy, the Supreme Court pronounced this clause in the recovery legislation unconstitutional. The power given the President in this instance was, said the Court, a legislative power. And while it had long since become settled doctrine that Congress might within limits delegate its authority to the Chief Executive, the courts had insisted that these limits be

[7] Harry L. Hopkins, *The Realities of Unemployment* (Washington, D.C.: Government Printing Office, 1937).

[8] *Home Building and Loan Association* v. *Blaisdell*, 290 U.S. 398 (1934).

[9] J. E. Pogue, *Economics of the Petroleum Industry* (New York: Chase National Bank, 1939).

carefully observed. Specifically, it was insisted that reasonably clear-cut standards be laid down to guide the President in his use of such powers. Section 9(c), according to Chief Justice Hughes speaking for the majority, contained no such standards.[10]

From the standpoint of the petroleum refining industry and its regulation, this decision was no tragedy. Before the year was out an effective substitute control mechanism had been created. In February the so-called Connally Hot Oil Act was passed, adding the necessary standards and safeguards to the language of the now defunct Section 9(c). Later in 1935, moreover, the network of control over this industry was still further broadened (while at the same time a powerful pressure for still more federal government intervention was defeated) by the formation of the Interstate Oil Compact Commission. This was a cooperative endeavor participated in by 20 (almost all) of the nation's oil-producing states and designed to work with the Bureau of Mines in developing state quotas on the basis of the national situation. (Traditionally individualistic state governments were being led to compromise their sovereignty in this instance by their interest in the tax revenues available from the oil industry.) But from certain other viewpoints the import of this development was a major threat to reform progress. Most immediately it meant that the entire National Recovery Act was in mortal danger, for no greater care had been taken to insert guiding criteria at a dozen other points. Even beyond this consideration, moreover, it meant that bold unorthodoxy in several other major legislative areas might collide with an unyielding judicial orthodoxy.

The next major court test to which the New Deal was exposed involved one of the actions taken incident to going off the gold standard. An essential procedure in implementing that policy had been to call gold in from circulation and to prohibit payments in gold. The effect of this had of course been to abrogate all contracts specifying payment in gold, and it was inevitable that test cases would forthwith be launched. In the so-called Gold-Clause Cases the Supreme Court handed down a 5–4 decision which, although it did no damage to the administration's currency program, in no uncertain terms challenged the government's right to make gold payments illegal insofar as past contracts were concerned.[11] This paradoxical result came about as follows. Payees under abrogated gold contracts (government or private) were told on the one hand that their valid right to receive gold was in fact meaningless because the gov-

[10] *Panama Refining Company* v. *Ryan*, 293 U.S. 388 (1935).
[11] *Norman* v. *Baltimore & Ohio Railroad Company*, 294 U.S. 240 (1935).

ernment unquestionably had the power to forbid the possession of gold, and on the other hand that the Court would not pass on their right to receive currency in settlement of their contracts according to the post-devaluation dollar value of gold rather than the pre-devaluation value because it had not been shown that any injury had resulted from repayments on the first of these bases.

By early May the contest between the New Deal and the Supreme Court had become virtually open warfare. On May 6 the Court handed down its verdict on a challenge brought against the Railroad Retirement Act by 134 Class I railroads. In another 5–4 decision which in recent years at least is almost unique in the ferocity with which a Congressional statute has been invalidated, Justice Roberts made short work of this enactment.[12]

To begin with, on three counts it was declared that this law contravened the Fifth Amendment. First, the group entitled under the Act to receive pensions included almost 150,000 workers who had severed their connections with the railroad industry during the year preceding its passage. The Court considered this "arbitrary in the last degree" and "without support in reason or common sense." Second, it had been provided that the pension plan was to go into effect immediately, with results that the Supreme Court could not bring itself to approve. Many retired employees would receive payments to which they had contributed nothing. Such payments would in other words have to be supported by younger workers who would in consequence receive smaller benefits when they retired, and by carriers that had already fully compensated such retiring workers for services rendered. Third, the fact that the railroads were in this law treated as a single employer was criticized on the same general ground. For example, all employees aged 70 or over were required to retire immediately, which meant that the 56 respondent carriers having no workers in that age group would be unreasonably burdened.

These findings of course would alone have been sufficient to destroy the Railroad Retirement Act. At the same time, in and of themselves they would have caused relatively little concern in high administrative circles. The points raised could be corrected, and it would therefore be only a matter of time until a new law was written correcting these defects. In an entirely different category, however, was another part of the Supreme Court's view of this legislation.

We are of the opinion that it is also bad for another reason which goes to the heart of the law, even if it could survive the loss of the unconstitutional features

[12] *Railroad Retirement Board* v. *Alton Railroad Company*, 295 U.S. 330 (1935).

we have discussed. The Act is not in purpose or effect a regulation of interstate commerce within the meaning of the Constitution.

If so narrow an interpretation of the commerce clause were to stand, if the *Hammer* v. *Dagenhart* rather than the *Stafford* v. *Wallace* interpretation of interstate commerce were to be consistently relied upon, then little of the basic reform program of the "Second New Deal," much of which was already on the legislative drawing boards, could survive a legal assault.

On May 27 the Supreme Court bull had a veritable field day in the New Deal china shop. Three adverse decisions were rendered on that one day, two of these declaring an act of Congress unconstitutional.

The first of these decisions invalidated the National Industrial Recovery Act.[13] In part this was on the same grounds that had been so vigorously presented in the earlier decision on Section 9(c). Actually such a decision was at this point little more than routine, for the Court had so unequivocally expressed itself on this particular issue that no other outcome could reasonably have been expected. Furthermore, the administration was not especially inconvenienced by this development, as the sequence of events between the January 7 and May 27 decisions suggests. The ease with which the oil code was in effect re-enacted in such a way as to remove the Court's objections indicates that the entire law might similarly have been rescued, and legislation designed to do just this was proposed by the party in power. Opposition was too strong to permit its passage before the court test was concluded, however, and the unfavorable decision markedly weakened the measure's support. In this limited sense the Supreme Court can be said to have defeated the administration in this matter, although there are those who argue that if the President had not been deterred by his experiences with the National Industrial Recovery Administration to date, he would have pressed harder for a revised law and would have won out. The fact is that by early 1935 it had become clear to most liberals that this program had all along been an attempt to reconcile the irreconcilable, that competitive industry is inherently incapable of regulating itself in the public interest.

But because the administration was certainly expecting and probably more than half hoping that this "First New Deal" experiment would fall by the wayside, the significance of this decision lies elsewhere. Here also the Court based its conclusions in part on an interpretation of interstate commerce on which fundamental reforms

---

[13] *Schechter Poultry Corporation* v. *United States*, 295 U.S. 495 (1935).

at the level of the federal government could not be built. In the Schechter case the government had defended its jurisdiction on the grounds that paying wages below the code minimum and engaging in trade practices forbidden by the code "affected" interstate commerce under depression conditions. This argument the Court tersely rejected, remarking that if the federal government possessed the power to regulate every matter indirectly affecting interstate commerce, "there would be virtually no limit to the federal power and for all practical purposes we should have a completely centralized power."

Shortly after President Roosevelt took over the reins of office, he had asked arch-conservative William E. Humphrey to resign from the Federal Trade Commission on the grounds that the views he held would make it impossible for him to carry out the policies of the new administration. When Humphrey refused to resign, the President summarily removed him and appointed a replacement. This step was challenged in the courts on the ground that the Federal Trade Commission had been purposely set up by Congress so that it would be free from just this kind of executive domination. In upholding this contention against the views of the President the Supreme Court did not succeed in altering the personnel of the Federal Trade Commission since Humphrey had died in the meantime, but it did strike a major blow for the cause of retaining for regulatory commissions a fairly high degree of the political independence Congress had intended them to have.[14] (On the other hand, however, it is probable that the Federal Trade Commission did suffer from neglect by the President being thus thwarted in putting it to work early in his administration.)

The third May 27 Supreme Court decision of importance here declared the Frazier-Lemke Farm Bankruptcy Act unconstitutional. In a Kentucky farm foreclosure proceeding the operation of this Act had resulted first in a reduction in the mortgage of 50 per cent, and then in a 5-year stay of payments under its terms when the creditor had refused to accept the new appraisal. Said the Court:

For the Fifth Amendment commands that however great the nation's need, private property shall not be thus taken even for a wholly public use without just compensation. If the public interest requires, and permits, the taking of property of individual mortgagees in order to relieve the necessities of individual mortgagors, resort must be had to proceedings by eminent domain; so that through taxation, the burden of the relief afforded in the public interest may be borne by the public.[15]

[14] *Humphrey's Executor* v. *United States*, 295 U.S. 602 (1935).
[15] *Louisville Land Bank* v. *Radford*, 295 U.S. 555 (1935).

In short, whereas in the Minnesota mortgage moratorium law case the Supreme Court had been willing to justify emergency powers in terms of the national crisis, this consideration was apparently no longer as compelling as it had then been in the thinking of the Justices.

In the strictest sense of the term it is not entirely accurate to refer to the Supreme Court and conservatives as allies in the drive to blunt the edge of the New Deal's assault on the status quo. For one thing, there were here none of the joint councils for strategy planning which would be implied by this terminology. For another, the invalidation of the National Industrial Recovery Act was scarcely an act of friendship as far as conservatives were concerned. But in the broader sense that "whoever is an enemy of my enemies is a friend of mine," American businessmen were more than willing to accept aid from almost any source. And in a situation in which those in power seemed for the time being to be immune to attacks by way of the ballot box, assistance from a quarter not handicapped by the current frightening voting trends was especially welcome.

CANNON IN FRONT OF THEM

Unquestionably the administration was wounded by these repeated thrusts, and indeed it made no secret of the fact. Much to the dismay of believers in the America that was, however, there was as a result no let-up in the development of the legislative program essential to the implementation of the philosophy espoused by the "Second New Deal." In fact, the nation was at this very moment about to plunge into a reform campaign such as has rarely been seen in the history of civilization.

June, 1935, saw the first step taken along this road. That was the National Youth Administration, another device for removing younger workers from the labor market and compensating them for the disproportionate burden of unemployment falling upon them.[16] In two respects, however, the new technique went beyond the objectives contemplated by the Civilian Conservation Corps. Girls as well as boys were to be eligible for assistance, and an important new purpose was to give a "shot in the arm" to an educational endeavor hard hit by the depression. By making funds available for the education of needy youth, not only were the individuals thus aided helped to achieve the "equality of opportunity" about which we

[16] Lewis L. Lorwin, *Youth Work Programs, Problems and Policies* (Washington, D.C.: American Council on Education, 1941).

so like to boast, but many educational institutions were themselves greatly assisted in the process.

In July the most anticapitalist measure to date was passed. Called by various names—the National Labor Relations Act, the Wagner Act, "Labor's Magna Carta"—this enactment had as its primary objective the re-enactment of the collective bargaining guarantees which had been written into Section 7(a) of the National Industrial Recovery Act and had so recently fallen victim to judicial interpretation.[17]

Three points are to be especially noted about the new labor law. First, five specific activities were declared to be "unfair labor practices" when engaged in by employers. These were: (1) interfering with employees in the exercise of guaranteed rights; (2) supporting a company union; (3) firing or hiring workers on the basis of their union status or activities; (4) discriminating against workers for invoking the provisions of the new law; and (5) refusing to bargain collectively with properly designated employee spokesmen. Second, a machinery was set up for the purpose of determining employee representatives for collective bargaining. Because there had understandably developed considerable competition between different worker organizations as to which was to speak for a particular group of workers, and because effective collective bargaining requires a high degree of unity among the workers involved, a mechanism for adjudicating such rival claims had to be provided for in a measure designed to facilitate this phase of labor's century-old struggle for self-determination in an industrial society. Third, a National Labor Relations Board was created to administer the new Act. Intended to be politically independent in the same sense as previously established regulatory agencies, this body was given full discretion to determine the appropriate bargaining units in particular cases (in practice procedures in this area have revolved around majority rule) as well as wide powers to interpret and prosecute under the unfair practices sections of the statute. Never again was it to be seriously doubted that group as distinguished from individual labor bargaining would be fully protected by the federal government—which is of course reason enough for the last-ditch hostility aroused by this statute.

And then came "Black August." Surely never before in history had a government introduced so many reforms in so short a time, except, perhaps, a government created by revolution. Certainly, be-

17 Harold W. Metz, *Labor Policy of the Federal Government* (Washington, D.C.: Brookings Institution, 1945).

lievers in individualistic laissez faire in the United States had never before and have not since been exposed to such a concentrated dose of new supervision and restraint. By comparison with August, 1935, June, 1934, was almost a trivial affair.[18]

Not all of these August innovations were completely anathema to businessmen. There was for example the Alcohol Control Act re-enacting the National Recovery Administration liquor code. Under the terms of this law a Federal Alcohol Administration was created in the Treasury Department to administer the code provisions.

Little uneasiness was created either by the Motor Carrier Act. Behind this statute stood the stubborn fact that the internal-combustion engine had created a powerful competitor of the railroads, and that this unregulated competitor was widely thought to be threatening serious injury to the public interest. Stated differently, one of the principal pressures behind the beginning of comprehensive public utility control of motor carriers by the federal government was the desire to protect the common carrier service performed by railroads (just as in the substantive portions of this law common motor carriers were protected from injury by contract motor carriers), a fact which goes far toward explaining why the railroad industry was itself one of the most important groups pressing for this legislation.

Similar in its impact on conservative thinking was the Bituminous Coal Conservation Act, another re-enactment of N.R.A. code provisions as the return of price-cutting and competitive wage reductions reminded the nation that this industry was still in dire economic straits. Here a National Bituminous Coal Commission with

TABLE 40. AN INDUSTRY STILL SICK

| Year | Bituminous Coal Mine | |
	Wage Earners	Wages (thousands of dollars)
1919	545,798	682,601
1929	458,732	574,800
1935	435,426	402,677

Source: Department of Commerce, *Statistical Abstract of the United States, 1938*, pp. 708 and 709.

wide powers to regulate the soft coal industry was created; and a tax of 15 per cent on all bituminous coal sales was levied on pro-

[18] Robert E. Lane, *The Regulation of Businessmen* (New Haven: Yale University Press, 1954).

ducers, of which complying firms were allowed a drawback of 90 per cent.

And even the Banking Act of 1935 did not arouse intense opposition in business circles. It had been well understood on the one hand that most of the New Deal banking legislation had to this point been of an emergency character, and that consequently many of the banking lessons learned in the 1920's and early 1930's still had to be embodied in permanent form. On the other hand, it was more than ever obvious that with the abandonment of gold as the regulator of domestic monetary affairs some other regulatory mechanism would now have to be substituted in its place.

As a result of these factors primarily the new banking legislation went much farther toward centralizing money and banking control than had ever been possible before, both in the hands of the Federal Reserve System as contrasted with member banks and in the hands of the System officials located in Washington as contrasted with the several regional banks. Specifically, the major provisions of this law were the following. First, state banks having $1 million or more in deposits were required to become members. Second, the old Federal Reserve Board was replaced by a Board of Governors, and this body was not to include either the Secretary of the Treasury or the Comptroller of the Currency. And third, to this group was given a wide variety of new, key powers. The president of each regional Federal Reserve Bank had to be approved by the Board before he could be appointed; this agency was made the dominant element in the Open-Market Committee; control over reserve requirements was given to it (together with the power to approve the rediscount rate established by the regional Banks); and it was given authority to regulate the rate of interest paid by member banks on time deposits.

It was not until, in other words, the administration began concentrating its attention upon security, the correction of private enterprise abuses, and weeding out the overprivileged, that this August became "black." On the security front, for example, no less than three important measures were enacted in this single 31-day period. A new farm mortgage law was passed, carefully rewritten to avoid constitutional objections but still heavily weighted on the side of debtors. In like manner the Railroad Retirement Act was carefully revised in the light of the Supreme Court's objections to it and re-enacted. (It was no doubt particularly exasperating to conservatives the way legislation favoring other groups was being painstakingly rescued from the Supreme Court's veto, while laws favoring business were simply abandoned as soon as the judiciary raised its voice against them.)

Far transcending these security measures in long-range significance, however, was the Social Security Act.[19] Here not a mere handful of workers in a single industry but millions of workers in dozens of industries were placed under a compulsory security program. Moreover, whereas the separate railroad law (at this time) protected its beneficiaries only against the hazard of old age, the Social Security Act provided insurance against involuntary unemployment as well.

Broadly speaking, three types of programs were provided for. The first of these was a contributory old-age and survivors' insurance program, in which covered citizens become eligible for retirement and survivors' benefits on the basis of (but only in part quantitatively proportionate to) payments into a fund accumulated for that purpose. A second consisted of federal supplementation of state old-age pensions—an emphasis reflecting the fact that the far more desirable contributory retirement arrangement could not, for the moment at any rate, be made available to all citizens, and one which has greatly improved state old-age pension systems. The third was a limited but nonetheless epoch-making unemployment insurance program.

A variety of techniques was called for by this legislation. Thus the contributory retirement program was to be an out and out federal activity, financed by payroll taxes supposed theoretically to be borne equally by employers and employees. Federal support for state systems of noncontributory old age pensions, on the other hand, although drawing funds from social security payroll tax resources, was of course to be administered by the state agencies which had long been operating in this area. In this latter device, already coming to be referred to as "the new federalism," legislators had borrowed heavily from the arrangements previously worked out in the road-building and employment service fields. But it was perhaps not primarily to maximize government decentralization, as in the case of these other programs, that state administration was insisted upon. Possibly even more important in the minds of legislators at this point was the objective of reducing the risk of court invalidation.

However, the greatest complexity of institutional arrangements, the most intricate interweaving of state and national government

---

[19] Paul H. Douglas, *Social Security in the United States* (New York: McGraw-Hill Book Co., Inc., 1939).

responsibilities, was reserved for the unemployment compensation legislation. Here also the finances required were based upon a national government payroll tax, although in this case, for the purpose of strongly encouraging state governments to assume this responsibility, the federal law permitted state unemployment insurance taxes to be subtracted from liability under its own tax program up to 90 per cent of the latter. Another different twist incorporated into this new activity (although this feature was largely taken over from workmen's compensation practice) was the technique of levying taxes for this purpose on employers only, the point here being a not wholly successful attempt to give employers an incentive to minimize unemployment by relating tax contributions to the unemployment experience of the particular concern.

But if these approaches to the objective of greater citizen security met with much resistance, the storm they created at the time of their passage did not begin to compare with the antagonism aroused by an administration measure designed to correct private enterprise abuses in the electric light and power industry. Almost never has a legislative proposal been opposed by as many powerful and varied pressure groups or by as formidable an array of financial resources. Included in the former were such groups as the American Bankers' Association, the Investment Bankers' Association, the Association of Life Insurance Presidents, and the Edison Electric Institute. Indicative of the latter was the $700,000 spent for this purpose by the Associated Gas and Electric Company alone, and the $300,000 spent by the Committee of Public Utility Executives.

However, the New Deal, apparently knowing exactly what it was doing from both a technical and a political standpoint, was not to be deflected on this issue even by a lobbying campaign of this magnitude. On the technical side it was fortified by an exhaustive investigation of the electric and gas utility industries recently concluded by the Federal Trade Commission;[20] politically the strength of its position came primarily from the public's memory of the recent catastrophic crash of the great holding company empires. Thus when in protest against government regulation of public utility holding companies it was argued that the life savings of widows and orphans would thereby be destroyed, pointed references to the tragedy which had befallen the means of subsistence of countless widows and orphans under unregulated private enterprise in this field made a highly effective counterargument. And when in the

[20] Federal Trade Commission, *Utility Corporations* (Washington, D.C.: Government Printing Office, 1935).

course of debate on this bill the prodigious propaganda-lobbying effort against it came to light, passage of a regulatory measure was all the more assured.

As its main purpose, Title I of the Public Utility Holding Company Act of 1935 gave to the new Securities Exchange Commission considerable powers over electric and gas utility holding companies. The most severe of these provisions was the requirement that all third-level and higher holding company organizations be dissolved, and in addition to this so-called "death sentence" the Commission was directed to simplify the remaining holding company structures to a point where they could be broadly comprehended by the average investor, and at the same time be justified in terms of operating economies.

Underlying this sweeping assumption of jurisdiction by the federal government in a field which had long been outgrowing the exclusively state regulation of the past was the desire to eliminate such holding company integration as benefitted primarily the promoter-insider, while retaining that which enabled a complex, heavy capital using, and fixed cost industry to serve the public more effectively. To this end numerous other regulatory powers were also conferred upon the Securities Exchange Commission—Congress taking care here, however, not to allow the federal agency to encroach upon the activity of state commissions in this field. Thus holding companies subject to Securities Exchange Commission were henceforth forbidden to acquire either the assets or the securities of any other business concern without approval; all transactions between companies in the same holding-company system (including the payment of dividends) were subjected to comprehensive regulation; accounting methods prescribed by the Commission were to be followed; officers and directors were required to keep the Commission informed of their transactions in their companies' own stock; bankers were forbidden to sit on holding company boards of directors without approval; and lobbying activities by these concerns were severely circumscribed.

Title II of this same Act went even farther toward correcting the disabilities of state regulation in the electric power field. Here the Federal Power Commission was the recipient of added powers. Henceforth this body was to have comprehensive public utility regulation powers over electricity moving across state boundaries, although here also this law was so written as not to threaten the work of state regulatory bodies. Among the important powers henceforth to be exercised by the Federal Power Commission in this area were regulation of interconnection, security issuance, consolidation, accounting practices, interstate rates, and interlocking directorates. No longer was this body to be primarily a conservation agency.

And if the political storm created by the Public Utility Holding Company Act was the most intense at this time, the reaction to President Roosevelt's next reform item was at least not far behind. That was the so-called Wealth-Tax Act, the administration's principal 1935 approach to the objective of weeding out the overprivileged.

It is not easy to identify, or at least to be certain about the identity of, the principles behind so basic an economic policy. In the case at hand, however, a few clues can be pointed out with a reasonable degree of confidence. It is, for example, a fact that there existed a widespread resentment against the unequal distribution of wealth and income currently prevailing, a fact attested by the immediate and sweeping success of Huey Long's Share-Our-Wealth Clubs. Surely the President in his address to Congress recommending changes in the nation's tax laws had this restlessness very much on his mind when he said: "Social unrest and a deepening sense of unfairness are dangers to our national life which we must minimize by rigorous methods." Quite possibly, furthermore, he offered his own program as a specific antidote to the "Kingfish's" much more radical proposal. Certainly the administration was much concerned about the political prestige those around Long were achieving on the basis of their highly equalitarian philosophy.

Three proposals were made by the President. The first was an increase in inheritance and gift taxes, a change broadly explained in the following language:

Great accumulations of wealth cannot be justified on the basis of personal and family security. . . . Such inherited economic power is . . . inconsistent with the ideals of this generation. . . . Creative enterprise is not stimulated by vast inheritances. . . . A tax upon inherited economic power is a tax upon static wealth, not upon that dynamic wealth which makes for the healthy diffusion of economic good.

The second was a steeper progression of rates on individual incomes, about which the President had this to say:

Wealth in the modern world does not come merely from individual effort; it results from a combination of individual effort and of the manifold uses to which the community puts that effort. . . . As Andrew Carnegie put it, "Where wealth accrues honorably, the people are always silent partners." . . . The disturbing effects upon our national life that come from great inheritances of wealth and power can in the future be reduced . . . through a definite increase in the taxes levied upon very great individual incomes.

The third was a scaling downward of the federal income taxes currently imposed upon small corporations, and a scaling upward of the rates then being applied to larger concerns.

Furthermore, the drain of a depression upon the reserves of business puts a disproportionate strain upon the modestly capitalized small enterprise. Without such small enterprises our competitive economic society would cease. Size begets monopoly. Moreover, in the aggregate these little businesses furnish the indispensable local basis for those nationwide markets which alone can ensure the success of our mass production industries.

It was perhaps only fitting that "Black August" was ushered out with the enactment into law of a tax revision measure based squarely upon these recommendations.

It is still something of a mystery why businessmen chose to make such an unyielding stand against the Public Utility Holding Company Act. If any measure during that entire period was designed almost exclusively to alter practices which virtually every thinking American would have agreed were indefensible, this was that measure. And yet conservatives did in fact reserve for that piece of legislation their most concerted opposition. Now to be sure, allowance must be made for an element of sincere belief that this step by the government would be injurious to the public interest. But this factor would scarcely explain the violence of the campaign actually launched. There must, in short, have been other forces at work. And perhaps a major one of these was sheer panic.

This is not mere speculation, either. Shortly after "Black August" passed into history Roy W. Howard, owner of a chain of newspapers that had generally supported the New Deal, wrote to President Roosevelt that his administration was rapidly losing the support of many businessmen who had earlier been on his side. One of the principal reasons given for this wavering of support was the Wealth-Tax Act, the insistence of the government upon "soaking the rich" rather than broadening the tax base. Mr. Howard's suggestion to the administration was that it allay business fears by refraining from further experimentation, by allowing a "breathing spell."[21]

As to broadening the tax base, the President in his reply to Mr. Howard placed primary emphasis upon the regressive nature of non-income taxes. Then, intending to be reassuring, he addressed himself to the heart of the issues his correspondent had raised as follows:

[21] Edwin Rozwenc (ed.), *The New Deal, Revolution or Evolution* (Boston: D. C. Heath & Co., 1949).

This administration came into power pledged to a very considerable legislative program . . . This basic program has now reached substantial completion and the "breathing spell" of which you speak is here—very decidedly so.

QUESTIONS FOR DISCUSSION

1. Distinguish between the "First" and the "Second" New Deals.

2. Explain President Roosevelt's approach to the problem of security as contrasted with the attitude of conservatives toward that concept.

3. What were the principal items in the new security program, and what was the specific role of each?

4. Which of the principles underlying the Works Progress Administration should have been given the most weight? The least?

5. Was there an alternative to some such program as the Works Progress Administration? Explain.

6. Make out as strong a case as you can against the Works Progress Administration approach to unemployment.

7. Which elements in the Supreme Court's attack on the New Deal were most damaging, and why?

8. How valid was the position of the Supreme Court in the series of cases reported in this chapter?

9. Should the Supreme Court have the power to defy the elected representatives of the people in this way?

10. Which parts of the Administration's 1935 legislative program were most vulnerable to legal attack, and why?

11. In terms of the depression on the one hand and problems which had long been in the making on the other, how radical was the 1935 New Deal?

12. Evaluate the Wealth-Tax Act.

13. Was the New Deal an evolution or a revolution?

Chapter 23

A Crisis Met and Mastered

There were other points the President might also have raised in his letter to Roy W. Howard concerning New Deal legislation—points which while they might not have gone far toward putting conservative fears to rest, would at least have placed these anxieties in a more realistic perspective. The New Deal was undoubtedly altering drastically the face of America's politico-economic structure. But when this fact is laid side by side with certain other equally unquestionable facts, it is clear that the impact of the New Deal can be exaggerated.

THE NEW DEAL IN PERSPECTIVE

To begin with, it is necessary to think about New Deal relief and recovery innovations in the light of available alternatives. Starting from the simple and unequivocal proposition that no society can permit a tragedy such as the Great Depression to have its way with citizens unhindered,[1] it is a noteworthy fact that Roosevelt's anti-depression policy moved from the conservative to the radical rather than in the opposite direction. And when it is recalled how surely (if not so swiftly) Hoover orthodoxy was itself shifting toward the ground ultimately occupied by Roosevelt, this fact becomes still more noteworthy.

But even so, with the possible exception of the Works Progress Administration, it was probably reform measures rather than relief and recovery programs which disturbed conservatives most. Here the first important point to be observed is that for a considerable period prior to the depression reform had been systematically suppressed. That is, there had been arising numerous situations which, in retrospect if not during those years, obviously required a gov-

[1] Paul H. Douglas, *Controlling Depressions* (New York: W. W. Norton & Co., Inc., 1935).

ernmental activity which could be postponed but not for an indefinite period. Furthermore, although this is perhaps only saying the same thing in a different way, it is worth emphasizing that a sizable number of fairly fundamental items of New Deal legislation —for example, the elimination of child labor, the guaranty of collective bargaining, social security, and minimum wage-maximum hour limitations—involved problems which had been increasingly resolved in an essentially similar way both by the more advanced industrial states in this country and by foreign countries which had been industrializing over a longer period of time than the United States. In other words, this country was to a considerable extent during the 1930's only coming to grips with some of the major problems of an industrial civilization.

Against the background of these observations, too, a brief review of American reform history is instructive. If 1860 or thereabouts is accepted as marking the beginning of American industrialization, it will be recalled that some 10 years elapsed before a significant reform sentiment developed. Then the Granger movement had set in, lasting some 3 or 4 years, reaching a climax in, say, 1871, and achieving little of permanent significance. At this point, for another decade and a half, reform could again make no headway. About the middle of the 1880's, however, reformers began to find a more responsive socio-political atmosphere, and reform projects were again strenuously pressed. This reform era lasted longer than the Granger movement and accomplished much more. But after this second period of reform came to an abrupt end around 1891, another reform hiatus set in which again lasted 12 or 14 years. About 1903 or 1904 still a third reform period was ushered in—a reformist endeavor which was not to be concluded until Woodrow Wilson had been President for several years, and which was to bring about unprecedented changes in the status quo before it merged with World War I.

In short, economic and social reform in America has progressed in distinct cycles. Periods of conservatism have been followed by periods of liberalism ever since the beginning of American industrialization, with each liberal period exceeding its predecessor in intensity and hence in accomplishments. When Franklin Roosevelt was inaugurated on March 4, 1933, it had been some 15 years since the first strong reaction against the New Freedom had appeared, and thus a new period of reform was only to be expected, even apart from the fact of deep depression. And the New Deal era also followed the established pattern with respect to the extent of its achievements.

It is not easy to explain these cycles that have repeated them-selves with such regularity. A few suggestions in this connection may, however, be hazarded. First, every smoothly functioning so-ciety is fundamentally conservative, and therefore it is not normally possible to initiate reforms until the problems these are designed to solve have become inescapable. By the same token, second, after making what might reasonably be termed minimum adjustments to difficulties which cannot be wished away, this inherent con-servatism then insists upon waiting as long as possible to see how these innovations are going to work out before proceeding further. In the third place, it is possible that conservative resistance is most easily broken down after the lapse of sufficient time to demonstrate that the last group of reforms did not bring intolerable consequences in its wake, and this possibility becomes even stronger when it is remembered that a period of 15 years brings to positions of leader-ship large numbers of men more familiar with the reformed situa-tion than with the "good old days."

All this strongly suggests that far too much emphasis has been and still is given to the motives of those responsible for New Deal policies, by defenders as well as by attackers.[2] Just as these men were not engaged in carrying out a sinister conspiracy against any and all American institutions, just so were they not embarked upon a crusade to inaugurate sweeping social changes wherever a case for reform could be made. The New Deal can best (and indeed only) be understood when it is thought of as a human response to basic environmental forces, as mediated by the ballot box of a modern democratic state. In other words, if Franklin D. Roosevelt is to be called a statesman because he harnessed a nation's unrest and guided it in directions consistent with powerful historical and socio-logical forces, he must also be referred to as a politician in that his every move was carefully considered from the standpoint of elec-tion-day consequences.

Spectre of Defeat

Early in 1936, the battle between the President and the Supreme Court was unequivocally joined. Shortly after the decision invali-dating the National Industrial Recovery Act was rendered, the President explained at length in a series of press conferences the implications for the New Deal's reform program of the narrow inter-

[2] George A. Steiner, *Government's Role in Economic Life* (New York: McGraw-Hill Book Co., Inc., 1953).

pretation of interstate commerce which seemed now to be dominating the thinking of the Court.[3] Referring to that decision as the most important "of my lifetime or yours," and stressing how painfully this restricted the sphere of operation of the federal government in attacking the grave problems then confronting the country, the President unburdened himself of several remarks which could only be interpreted as critical of the nation's highest tribunal.

We have forty-eight Nations from now on under a strict interpretation of that decision . . . [which is] a perfectly ridiculous and impossible situation. . . . There are former decisions of the Supreme Court which have held much more liberally in . . . cases where people were trying to get an injunction against labor. . . . We have been relegated to the horse-and-buggy definition of interstate commerce.

No one of course would argue that when on January 6, 1936, the Supreme Court declared the Agricultural Adjustment Act unconstitutional, there was in this act any spirit of defiance of the President. But in certain of the remarks Justice Roberts included in the majority opinion there was clear evidence that the President's comments and the ensuing wave of criticism directed against the Court had cut deep.[4]

It is sometimes said that the court assumes a power to overrule or control the action of the people's representatives. This is a misconception. . . . When an act of Congress is appropriately challenged in the courts . . . the judicial branch of the Government has only one duty,—to lay the article of the Constitution which is involved beside the statute which is challenged and to decide whether the latter squares with the former. . . . This court neither approves nor condemns any legislative policy. . . . The question is not what power the Federal Government ought to have but what powers in fact have been given by the people.

(It is perhaps not inappropriate to observe that few constitutional lawyers even in 1936 believed this matter to be as simple as Justice Roberts' summary statement made it appear.)

The constitutional defect found in the Agricultural Adjustment Act had nothing in common with those responsible for the demise of the National Industrial Recovery Act. Statutory amendments made the preceding year in the light of the earlier decision had forestalled the Court on these points. The standards to be used by administrators were made more specific (in many cases, however, by giving legislative sanction to policies already developed by these

[3] Edward S. Corwin, *The Commerce Clause Versus State Rights* (Princeton: Princeton University Press, 1936).

[4] *United States* v. *Butler*, 296 U.S. 1 (1936).

same administrators), and the products covered were limited to those directly entering into interstate commerce. But if New Deal leaders were ingenious in finding their way around judicial obstructions, the Supreme Court was equally ingenious in finding new ways to frustrate those efforts.

This first price-support program worked out by the New Deal had been largely financed by a processing tax imposed at the manufacturer's level. A cotton textile mill had gone bankrupt after paying out to the government a substantial sum in processing taxes, and its receivers had sued for recovery on the grounds that the levy was beyond the powers of the federal government. With this a majority of the Justices agreed. Because the Constitution had not specifically granted regulatory power over agriculture to Congress, "Congress has no power to enforce its commands on the farmer to the ends sought by the Agricultural Adjustment Act. It must follow that it may not indirectly accomplish those ends by taxing and spending to purchase compliance."

The direct damage done to the administration's agricultural program by this turn of events was slight and of short duration.[5] There was, to be sure, much initial confusion—the inevitable consequence of the Court's demand that the government return to taxpayers money illegally taken from them, but which the Agricultural Adjustment Administration was obligated also to pay to farmers. To be sure also, the administration had to develop a substitute agricultural program. But both of these problems were as easily and quickly resolved as numerous others that had been created by adverse Supreme Court decisions. On the one hand, an "unjust enrichment" tax was levied upon those concerns to which tax repayments were made; much of this tax of course had been passed on to consumers. On the other hand, a 1935 measure designed to help farmers reduce soil erosion on their farms (a more or less routine response to years of agitation on this front, recently accentuated by the "dust bowl" experience in the Southwest[6]) was rewritten to serve as a vehicle for the nation's agricultural production control program.

Because the prevention of erosion required interstate control, this activity had long been accepted as being within the power of the federal government. Accordingly a Soil Conservation and Allotment Act was passed in February, 1936, authorizing the government to make payments to farmers for diverting land from soil-depleting to

[5] National Industrial Conference Board, *American Agricultural Conditions and Remedies* (New York: National Industrial Conference Board, 1936).

[6] John Steinbeck, *The Grapes of Wrath* (New York: The Viking Press, Inc., 1939).

soil-building crops, for increasing the area planted to soil-building crops, and for adopting soil-building practices. The way these two very different purposes were tied together was exceedingly simple, although perhaps a little crafty. Those crops designated as soil-depleting were made identical with those currently being overproduced. Still further to protect this measure from judicial interference, arrangements were also made gradually to turn its administration over to the several states. And in recognition of the criticism of the earlier program that tenants and sharecroppers had been discriminated against, provision was now made for channeling a larger share of the program's benefits to those groups.

Because the Supreme Court did time and again strike down a prominent New Deal measure, it is commonly supposed that during this period every court test issued in a decision adverse to the administration. Actually this is a misconception. Although almost every New Deal innovation of consequence was challenged in the courts, the fact is that a dozen new programs were given a clean bill of health from the beginning, items in this category including regulation of securities and security markets, transportation legislation, alterations in the banking system, and a wide variety of new public utility regulation functions.[7] At the moment, February 17, 1936, the great administration victory, the concrete evidence of the Supreme Court's impartiality, was a favorable decision involving the Tennessee Valley Authority.

It is easy enough to understand why the center of the controversy that has raged around this agency has been its activities in the electric power field; it is at this point that its operations have most directly threatened private enterprise. It does not follow, however, either that electric light and power was intended to be or has in fact been the primary business of the Tennessee Valley Authority, or that (as much popular opinion still insists) this activity has been gradually and perhaps even surreptitiously added by administrative decision to the statutory responsibilities given to that organization. The Tennessee Valley Authority program has from the outset been a comprehensive whole, an attempt to develop the Tennessee River Valley economy in its entirety.[8] Indeed this conservation objective has consistently been the most fundamental fact underlying all major federal government activities in the public power field—as well as the source of a large proportion of the difficulties encountered by such

[7] Franklin H. Cook, *Principles of Business and The Federal Law* (New York: The Macmillan Co., 1951).

[8] Gordon R. Clapp, *The TVA* (Chicago: University of Chicago Press, 1955).

projects. The principal reason a huge government program was organized in the Tennessee River Valley area was because no private concern could afford the outlays required for flood control (and other governmental) facilities, while much of the private-enterprise complaint against the government's power operations in this area has had its roots in the difficulty of finding a satisfactory formula for allocating costs between the power and the various other operations.

In broad outline, these were the problems which came to a focus in the Tennessee Valley Authority's first major court test. Of course the government agency could have sold the power it generated to those private concerns already operating in that region, but against the background of the recent public disillusionment with the private power industry this would have been too much to expect. The alternative was for the government to transmit its own power and sell to ultimate consumers. But since the electric light and power business is naturally monopolistic, this meant that the private concerns in the area had to go. When, however, the Tennessee Valley Authority endeavored to purchase for its own use the transmission facilities already available in the area, court suits were instituted by utility stockholders to prevent their sale to the government. In the first such case to reach the Supreme Court it was ruled that the power generated at government-owned Tennessee River dams belonged to the government, and that the government had the right to dispose of this property by selling it.[9]

On the basis of this and other favorable developments on the legal front, the Tennessee Valley Authority became *the* supplier of electricity over a wide area. And while it has also been engaged in a wide variety of other projects, one of its great achievements has un-

TABLE 41. IMPORTANT SECONDARY REACTION

Unit	Average Residential Rate (cents per kilowatt-hour)	
	1933	1937
United States' Average	5.49	4.39
Tenn. Elec. Power Co.	5.77	2.86
Georgia Power Co.	5.16	3.04
Alabama Power Co.	4.62	2.97
Tenn. Valley Authority	—	2.41

Source: Senate Document No. 56, 76th Congress, First Session, Part I, p. 151.

[9] *Ashwander* v. *Tennessee Valley Authority*, 297 U.S. 288 (1936).

questionably been in this field. Although these operations were never able to provide a "yardstick" by which regulatory bodies could judge the reasonableness of private power rates (because of the cost allocation problem, the difficulty of arriving at an appropriate tax equivalent, and the complication of low interest rates as a result of utilizing the federal government's credit), government competition did compel private concerns in neighboring territories to experiment intensively with the economy of low rates. A major consequence of this development has been that the Southeast, the poorest economic region in the entire country, boasts the highest per capita consumption of electricity.

But from the standpoint of the administration's larger problems, *Ashwander* v. *Tennessee Valley Authority* was no turning of the tide. On May 18 the Bituminous Coal Stabilization Act was invalidated on the same ground which had been used in destroying the Agricultural Adjustment Act.[10] A tax had been levied on all coal producers, and then refunded to those who complied with code provisions governing such matters as wages, hours, working conditions, and collective bargaining rights. The Court maintained again that this kind of levy was not truly a tax but a coercive device to give the federal government powers denied it by the Constitution. And lest it be erroneously concluded that the states might exercise jurisdiction in this field even though the federal government could not, the Court on June 1 flatly declared that the State of New York could not legally fix minimum wages for women.[11] As in the case of the District of Columbia law of 15 years earlier, the Court believed such legislation deprived citizens of the freedom to make contracts guaranteed them by the Fourteenth Amendment. Four Justices dissented.

In this uncompromising attitude of the Supreme Court, the "Second New Deal" clearly met its greatest crisis, roughly comparable with the banking crisis met by the "First New Deal." If the federal government did not possess the power to legislate on behalf of labor, the Wagner Act was already a forlorn hope. So much comfort was in fact taken from this turn of events in conservative circles that lawyers by the score assured employers that "Labor's Magna Carta" could be violated with impunity. Furthermore, if the Wagner Act were destroyed, the Social Security Act would surely go soon thereafter. The loss of these two measures would mean no less than the complete disintegration of the most important principles on which

[10] *Carter* v. *Carter Coal Company*, 298 U.S. 238 (1936).
[11] *Morehead* v. *New York ex rel Tipaldo*, 298 U.S. 587 (1936).

the administration was now standing. Already the President's fertile brain was exploring avenues of counterattack.

One Thing at a Time

That vigorous defensive operations were not commenced at once may have been due in part to the fact that the appropriate strategy had not yet been worked out. But there is also another, and perhaps a more important, reason. By mid-1936 the President's first re-election campaign was beginning to get under way, and it was no doubt felt that to challenge the Supreme Court openly at such a time would be unwise. Taking a chance that the really critical decisions would not be issued yet awhile, the New Deal decided to concentrate at the moment on the program of legislation which had gotten off to such a dramatic start the year before. Stated slightly differently, the "breathing spell" given conservatives lasted almost exactly nine months.

The first product of this new reform effort was a measure designed ostensibly to strengthen the antitrust laws—specifically Section 2 of the Clayton Act. The 1914 ban on price discrimination had, it will be recalled, gotten off to a slow start as a result of an exceedingly narrow judicial interpretation of the phrase "in any line of commerce." Although the Supreme Court had in 1929 broadened the meaning of these words in the direction of the intentions of their authors,[12] a new stumbling block was now appearing. The original legislation had permitted exceptions to its blanket prohibition where there were "differences in the grade, quality, or quantity of the commodity sold," and where the lower prices made "only due allowance for differences in the cost of selling or transportation." When the federal courts indicated a tendency to interpret these two clauses as independent of one another, when in short there developed a judicial disposition to permit almost any difference in grade, quality, or quantity to justify almost any difference in price,[13] it was clear that something would have to be done.

But it would be a mistake to identify the Robinson-Patman Act exclusively with a need felt by antitrust reformers to plug a loophole in the Clayton Act. Side by side with that objective was another one, a purpose difficult to explain in terms of a zeal for spirited competition. Indeed it is supposed by most students of the subject that this other purpose was really the dominant force behind this measure.

---

[12] *Van Camp Company* v. *American Can Company*, 278 U.S. 245 (1929).

[13] *Goodyear Tire and Rubber Company* v. *Federal Trade Commission*, 101 F.2d 620 (1939).

When left to its own devices the distribution of goods is a highly competitive field, a fact that had perhaps never been more true than in recent times in the United States. In the preceding two decades channels of distribution in the American economy had been undergoing profound alterations. Thus the traditional separation of manufacturing, wholesaling, and retailing into distinct stages in the distribution process had been severely challenged by the mass distributor whose economic effectiveness depended in large part upon his success in combining two or more of these operations. As a result, tens of thousands of small retailers whose position had been much more secure under the older system were beginning to feel painfully squeezed, and of course a long depression would be precisely the time when such pressure would be most intense.[14]

It was only natural for the men and concerns most discomfited by these trends to fight back. One obvious countermeasure was to subject the integrated distributor to discriminatory taxation. Beginning in the 1920's, a substantial number of specially written state income tax laws were placed on the statute books, all intended to bear more heavily upon the chain store than upon single-unit operators.[15] During the depressed 1930's this device was even more widely used, and it was not until some years later that the movement began to recede.

Another way of achieving the same objective was to use the law to reduce the competitive advantages of the mass distributor in a more direct fashion. A first step in this direction had been taken in a number of National Recovery Administration codes, wherein wholesalers' discounts were denied to retailers and quantity discounts and advertising allowances limited. Now much more along this line was accomplished by means of a federal law drafted in all major particulars by counsel for an association of wholesale grocers.

The two purposes intended to be served by this statute signed by the President on June 20, 1936, are plainly apparent in its provisions.[16] On the price discrimination front proper it explicitly confirmed the position taken by the Supreme Court in the Van Camp case, and at the same time tightened up the wording of the general prohibition in Section 2. Henceforth price differentials between customers must "make only due allowance for differences in the cost of manufacture, sale, or delivery resulting from the differing methods

[14] United States Federal Trade Commission, *Relative Efficiency of Large, Medium-Sized, and Small Business* (Washington, D.C.: Government Printing Office, 1941).
[15] *The Great Atlantic and Pacific Tea Company* v. *Grosjean*, 301 U.S. 412 (1927).
[16] Wright Patman, *The Robinson-Patman Act* (New York: The Ronald Press Co., 1938).

or quantities in which such commodities are . . . sold or delivered."
Other provisions, however, also demonstrate how this genuine antitrust reform was intermingled with an objective less readily defended.

In the first place, sellers were forbidden to pay broker's commission to a buyer. Furthermore, sellers were also forbidden either to
make a price allowance for services rendered by a buyer or furnish
him services, unless these services are available to the latter's competitors "on proportionally equal terms." To be sure, these clauses
are in part safeguards against evasion of the central discrimination
provision, but there is at the same time no mistaking the ease with
which this terminology could be brought to the defense of traditional distribution methods against large-scale innovators. And with
respect to the latter point one other change introduced into the
Robinson-Patman Act is surely conclusive. Heretofore a legitimate
defense against the charge of price discrimination had been that the
price complained of was quoted "in good faith to meet competition."
This wording was now altered to read "in good faith to meet an
equally low price of a competitor."

The contrast between the new enactment and the spirit of the
antitrust laws can be conveniently summarized in several ways. To
begin with, although the existence of discrimination proves that the
market in question is "imperfect," it does not follow that the eradication of the symptom will improve the condition. Thus whereas the
Clayton Act had been concerned primarily with the consequences of
discrimination for competitors of the firms doing the discriminating,
the new law was primarily concerned with consequences for competitors of the firm receiving preferential treatment—and in the
latter type of case discrimination is as apt to strengthen as to weaken
competition. Put differently, the purpose of the antitrust laws had
been to preserve competition, while that of the Robinson-Patman
Act was to preserve particular, small competitors. In order to serve
as a stimulator of competition in today's complex business world,
antitrust legislation must be able to adapt itself to evolving business
practices. The rigid prohibitions of the Robinson-Patman Act operate in a precisely opposite fashion.

The second item in this new series of reform measures was an undistributed profits tax, the most revolutionary tax innovation of the
entire New Deal era. Here too the purpose was, in part at least, to
give special protection to small businesses. On the one hand the
imposition of higher taxes on firms retaining rather than distributing

their earnings was thought of as an antimonopoly measure, while on the other this enactment also carried farther the 1935 Wealth-Tax Act principle of levying lower tax rates against smaller concerns. But another purpose was also to be served by this device—and perhaps at this point an even more important one.

By late 1936 the feeling that one of the principal causes of continued hard times was the withholding of income from the purchasing power stream had become more powerful. Of course business leaders were not especially impressed by this argument and were still less enthusiastic about the administration's interest in wooing the small business group. According to their version of what was happening out in the over-all economy, it was actually the unfolding of new and radical tax policies which was contributing more than any other single factor to the current propensity to hoard.[17]

Still another front which saw action during the latter part of 1936 was the field of labor legislation. The Walsh-Healey Government Contracts Act established minimum wages and maximum hours and prohibited child labor in firms working under government contract. Here was at least a small step in this direction that the federal government could take without fear of a Supreme Court veto. Under the terms of the so-called Strike-Breaker (Byrnes) Act, too, employers were prohibited from transporting in interstate commerce persons intended for use in strike-breaking activities, a technique of anti-unionism rapidly becoming "big business." The Merchant Marine Act carried labor protection still farther in one industry. By requiring three-fourths of the men working on American ships to be American citizens, ship operators were prevented from using foreign workers to force low labor standards upon American seamen, and in addition all such concerns receiving assistance from the United States Treasury were required to meet minimum wage and other working conditions standards.

But protection for the American workingman was neither the only nor the most important reason for passing a new Merchant Marine Act in 1936.[18] The most fundamental factor involved here was a growing tension in international affairs suggesting the importance of not permitting the American flag fleet to deteriorate too drastically. However, this factor might even then not have been effective in reversing traditional Democratic antisubsidy policy if an important

[17] Editors of the "Economist," *An Analysis and Appraisal of the New Deal* (New York: Alfred A. Knopf, Inc., 1937).

[18] Paul M. Zeis, *American Shipping Policy* (Princeton: Princeton University Press, 1938).

reform issue had not also become entangled with it. For some time evidence of a scandal in the mail subsidy program then in operation had been developing, and the administration vigorously embarked upon a campaign to create a more wholesome system.

Suggesting that existing policy had been especially subject to abuse because an attempt had been made to conceal its subsidy implications, the President said in his message to Congress calling for new legislation:

I propose that we end this subterfuge. If the Congress decides that it will maintain a reasonably adequate American merchant marine I believe that it can well afford honestly to call a subsidy by its right name.

In the completed measure not only was a new, "scientific" assistance program inaugurated, consisting of both construction and operation

TABLE 42. CALLING A SPADE A SPADE

Fiscal Year	Merchant Marine Subsidy (millions of dollars)
1938	1
1939	44
1940	99
1948	183
1950	100
1952	230
1954	153

Source: Department of Commerce, *Statistical Abstract of the United States, 1941,* p. 180; *ibid., 1955,* p. 353.

subsidies, but a new agency was created to administer merchant marine legislation. This was the Maritime Commission, to which organization were given all the functions heretofore performed by the United States Shipping Board as well as other responsibilities under the new law.

One last measure completed the administration's pre-election reform program. That was the Commodity Exchange Act which put the finishing touches on the process of converting the nation's commodity exchanges into public utilities which had been started in the early 1920's, and at the same time broadly completed a government program of supervision for markets for agricultural products which had been on the reform agenda ever since Granger days. Indicative of the expanded regulatory responsibilities written into this measure is the fact that whereas the Secretary of Agriculture had heretofore exercised most of these powers, there was now created a Commodity

Exchange Commission in the Department of Agriculture to perform this function. All commodity exchanges and all traders in these markets were required to register with the Commission and to submit complete, periodic reports covering their operations. The dissemination of false and misleading information was prohibited, together with a formidable list of manipulative devices. Power to limit speculation was also conferred upon the Commission, this taking the form of limits on the futures transactions of individual traders and on the amount the price of a particular commodity might fall in a single day.

As Maine Goes

Standing thus astride a great reform program offered to a people grown weary of stubborn adherence to the status quo in the face of deep depression, the New Deal had reason to feel highly confident of success as election day drew near. To be sure, not every group in the economy had directly benefited from these reforms; whereas business interests had initially been an integral part of the New Deal coalition, they had by now been unmistakably dropped out. At the same time, however, the administration could point to evidences of a sound economic recovery on every hand, and businessmen were in a position to benefit from that side of unfolding events.

TABLE 43. PROGRESS ON THE RECOVERY FRONT

Year	Industrial Production* (1947-1949 = 100)	Factory Weekly Earnings†	Unemployment† (thousands)
1933	37	$16.73	11,842
1934	40	18.40	9,761
1935	47	20.13	9,092
1936	56	21.78	7,386
1937	61	24.05	6,403

* Federal Reserve Board.
† Department of Labor.

These two broad facts—a reform program designed to benefit all nonconservative groups and a steady upward movement of the major economic indices—provided the context within which one of the most interesting and dramatic presidential campaigns in the history of the country was fought out. This interest and drama, be it noted at the outset, did not arise because the electoral contest itself had anything in particular to do with its outcome. Perhaps few such campaigns do; and in the 1936 struggle for votes especially, Democrats probably never had a moment's doubt but that they would be victorious, while Republicans probably never entertained serious expectations of winning. Indeed, it is precisely because the result was assured from the beginning that the conduct of this campaign is so significant.

In his annual message of January 3, 1936, the President first revealed the major features of his re-election campaign. On the domestic front the most important of these was to be a direct attack on big business, with the result that this contest was waged along overt class lines to an extent rarely recorded in the annals of constitutional government. The following items will illustrate the tone of the President's thinking at this time.

First, and this was perhaps the most damaging accusation of all, the big-business opponents of the New Deal were identified with the forces of fascism abroad. The nation was just now becoming alarmed over the rise of Hitler in Germany, Mussolini in Italy, and Franco in Spain, and was therefore the more readily alerted to this danger at home.[19] Elaborating upon this theme, the President asserted that a small but powerful group of business leaders had dominated the government under successive Republican administrations and had then abdicated these responsibilities with the coming of the depression: "but now with the passing of danger they forget their damaging admissions and withdraw their abdication. . . . They steal the livery of great constitutional ideals to serve discredited special interests"; they divert the national resources entrusted to them to the purposes of partisan politics; "they engage in vast propaganda to spread fear and discord among the people—they would 'gang up' against the people's liberties."

More specifically, the President charged his opponents with hostility toward democracy. The principle of government in which they believed, he observed, could readily be seen in the principles used in conducting their own affairs; "autocracy toward labor, toward stockholders, toward consumers, toward public sentiment." What these people want in securing control over the government, he added, is not to turn back the hands of the clock but to use for their own purposes the new instruments of public power which are dangerously vulnerable to abuse if not kept in the hands of "a people's government."

[19] Sinclair Lewis, *It Can't Happen Here* (Garden City: Doubleday & Co., Inc., 1935).

In the hands of political puppets of an economic autocracy such power would provide shackles for the liberties of the people. Give them their way and they will take the course of every autocracy of the past—power for themselves, enslavement for the public.

Nor did the President's temper improve between January 3 and late June, at which time in the process of accepting his party's nomination as their candidate for the presidency he delivered his famous "economic royalist" speech.

The royalists of the economic order have conceded that political freedom was the business of the Government, but they have maintained that economic slavery was nobody's business. They granted that the Government could protect the citizen in his right to vote, but they denied that the Government could do anything to protect the citizen in his right to work and his right to live. . . .

These economic royalists complain that we seek to overthrow the institutions of America. What they really complain of is that we have taken away their power. . . . In their blindness they forget what the Flag and the Constitution stand for. Now as always they stand for democracy, not tyranny; for freedom, not subjection; and against a dictatorship by mob rule and the overprivileged alike. . . .

Governments can err, Presidents do make mistakes, but the immortal Dante tells us that divine justice weighs the sins of the cold-blooded and the sins of the warm-hearted in different scales. . . .

This generation of Americans has a rendezvous with destiny . . . here in America we are waging . . . a war for the survival of democracy. . . .

I accept the commission you have tendered me. I join with you. I am enlisted for the duration of the war.

If, apart from the policies developed during this period as such, an explanation were sought of the deep distrust of the New Deal by businessmen long after the death of the principal New Dealer, it would surely be found in this deliberate and almost ferocious attack on the motives of conservatives. Interestingly enough, however, the most painful aspect of this choice of a ground on which to fight a presidential election campaign was not so much the attack in and of itself as the fact that there was available no successful defense.

Let it be granted, of course, that in the tradition of partisan politics in an effective democracy the President's charges were exaggerated. Nonetheless there was behind this attack a solid foundation of scarcely arguable fact. The government had for some years prior to the advent of the New Deal been controlled by conservatives for the benefit of a fairly narrow circle of interests. With the coming of depression that government had indeed been slow to assume responsibility for the relief of wholesale suffering. Then, when the worst of the crisis had passed, these groups had fought tooth and nail against policies designed to provide citizens with more adequate protection from the insecurities accompanying industrialization. And perhaps most frustrating of all from the standpoint of conservatives was the fact that the President could not be seriously damaged by being accused of "setting class against class," a device usually not politically profitable in a cohesive democracy. It could too convincingly be argued that this "class warfare" had actually been inaugurated by the New Deal's opponents in, for example, the "American Plan" and successive McNary-Haugen vetoes.

No more successful was an attack on administration unorthodoxy, the charge that New Deal reforms were creating an institutional environment in which private enterprise could not continue to function effectively. Here also was an accusation which was difficult to deny categorically, but administration proponents could at this point too easily blunt their opponents' attack by simply calling public attention to the fact that private enterprise capitalism minus recent reforms had actually broken down and by suggesting that the introduction of carefully calculated reforms could hardly make the system perform any more ineptly.

Denied the use of such obvious weapons, New Deal critics were virtually reduced to contesting the administration's claim that its efforts had routed the forces of depression. Two arguments to this effect were advanced. First, it was asserted that after four years of deepening depression the economy had been so thoroughly liquidated that an upturn would have developed in any event. Second, it was broadly hinted that had a radical government not adopted measures which inhibited business expansion recovery would by this time have advanced much farther. While neither of these propositions was demonstrably wrong, it is at once clear why they did not rally the nonconservative voter around the antiadministration banner. On the one hand, they were too hypothetical and abstract to have the kind of mass appeal required to reverse current voting trends. On the other hand, the administration could plausibly argue not only that there was no evidence that the passage of time would have brought recovery, but that from the standpoint of business conditions alone (even if no other purposes were taken into account), the radical "Second New Deal" had succeeded where the conservative "First New Deal" had failed.

The poverty of the Republican party's appeal was pathetically demonstrated on election day. In a victory more sweeping than in any election since George Washington ran for the presidency unopposed, Franklin Delano Roosevelt was returned to office. Only two states cast their electoral votes for his opponent. For a long time it had been said with some truth that, in national elections, "As Maine goes, so goes the nation." For many months after the 1936 election Democrats lost no opportunity to say in derision "As Maine goes, so goes Vermont."

CRISIS CONFRONTED

As of January, 1937, it had been a full year and a half since adverse decisions by the Supreme Court had first dangled a sword of Damocles over the head of the "Second New Deal." This meant that court tests of fundamental New Deal reforms had for some time now been running the judicial gantlet, and indeed lower court opinions had already been rendered against both the National Labor Relations Act and the Social Security Act. In other words, while the administration was waiting until the "Second New Deal" had been validated at the polls before attacking this problem, the problem itself had been growing increasingly critical.

Unfortunately, however, the mere passage of time was not the only reason why this issue was becoming more acute. Within three months after organized labor had been given its "charter of liberties" in the form of the Wagner Act, the first steps had been taken to organize labor in a number of mass production industries on an industrial basis.[20] For almost 50 years labor organizations had been frozen into a craft mold, a type of institutional structure most unsuited to industries such as steel, automobiles, oil, cement, chemicals, electrical appliances, aluminum, and textiles; and by the middle of the 1930's it was evident that the next major step on this front would necessitate a fundamental break through this institutional crust. By early 1937 the brand-new Committee for Industrial Organization was already an accomplished fact and showing promise

TABLE 44. LABOR ON THE MARCH

| Year | All unions | Number of Workers Enrolled (millions of workers) | |
		The Committee for Industrial Organization	The American Federation of Labor
1929	3.6	—	2.9
1936	4.2	—	3.4
1937	7.2	3.7	2.9
1940	8.9	3.6	4.2
1945	14.8	6.0	6.9

Source: Bureau of the Census, *Historical Statistics of the United States, 1789-1945*, p. 72.

[20] Herbert Harris, *Labor's Civil War* (New York: Alfred A. Knopf, Inc., 1940).

of becoming the greatest forward stride for the labor movement since the turn of the century.

The danger here was that if the National Labor Relations Act foundation on which industrial unionism was being erected were to be destroyed, this vital development might easily abort. And if this were to happen the labor movement might not recover from this shock for a quarter of a century. It was no longer, thus, a question of whether collective bargaining guaranties were to be found valid this year or two years from now. An institutional momentum had gotten under way which, if broken, might not be restored intact merely by a favorable decision two years later. Unless, in short, the Wagner Act received Supreme Court approval at the first test, an historic opportunity might well have been irretrievably lost. That the Committee for Industrial Organization was "playing for keeps" is sufficiently attested by the fact that early 1937 saw this group become almost overnight an equal of the American Federation of Labor in numbers as a result of the use of the famous but semirevolutionary "sit-down" strike.

These were the pressures on President Roosevelt when, almost immediately after his election, he began to direct his most creative efforts toward resolving this crisis.[21] On January 6, 1937, notice was served on the country that the President meant seriously to attack this problem—and in a head-on fashion. In his annual message to Congress on that date he said:

The Judicial branch also is asked by the people to do its part in making democracy successful. We do not ask the Courts to call non-existent powers into being, but we have a right to expect that conceded powers or those legitimately implied shall be made effective instruments for the common good.

The process of our democracy must not be imperiled by the denial of essential powers of free government.

There was in these comments of course no indication of the strategy the administration planned to follow. But on February 5, the day the President sent his momentous proposal for reorganizing the judiciary to Congress, this too was made plain. Although this proposal included suggestions which had long had the backing of competent authorities interested in speeding up and in general streamlining the judicial process, its most fundamental feature was a plan for reorganizing the Supreme Court. What was requested here was the authority to appoint one new Supreme Court Justice for

[21] Charles G. Haines, *The American Doctrine of Judicial Supremacy* (Berkeley: University of California Press, 1932).

every Justice in this Court over seventy years of age. There were six of these.

In a majority of the discussions of this episode in American history, the President comes off second best. Perhaps, furthermore, this is as it should be. The picture customarily drawn of a President (often presented as a "would-be dictator") so anxious to complete his program as to be willing to turn his back on a century and a half of constitutional tradition unquestionably contains an important element of truth. And because the President, at least in the technical sense, lost his fight, America's "crime does not pay" philosophy tends to accentuate in the public mind the sins he is so strongly felt to have committed.

In any event, so well remembered is the case for the plaintiff that no recapitulation of it is necessary here. What is needed rather is a short resumé of the defendant's brief, now so generally forgotten.

It is of some interest to recall, first, that in 1869 a law had been passed allowing Federal Justices to retire without compensation at the age of 70. The thought had evidently developed thus early that there was such a thing as a Justice who was too old to do his work well. There was, moreover, another precedent for the step the President wanted to take. A 1919 law had authorized the President to appoint an additional district or circuit court judge whenever one did not retire at the voluntary retirement age—but only after making a finding that the incumbent was unfit to carry his full share of his court's workload by reason of mental or physical impairment. Surely few would need to stretch their sympathies to appreciate the essential soundness of Roosevelt's view on this point: "No President should be asked to determine the ability or disability of any particular judge."

Apart from precedent, next, there was a valid basis for maintaining that the federal courts were undermanned. Overcrowded dockets were undoubtedly creating delays and hence greatly increasing the cost of litigation, with the result that lawsuits were tending to become a luxury which only the wealthy could afford. As the President expressed it, a speeding-up of justice was necessary to "eradicate the growing impression that the courts are chiefly a haven for the well-to-do." To be sure, these facts do not prove that this problem was wholly caused by the age of some Justices, but it was certainly not fantastic to suggest that this was one of the factors involved.

Nor was it fantastic to believe that, on the bench as well as in other walks of life, hardening of the arteries is accompanied by a hardening of mental processes, and that conditions during the 1930's made those years a particularly unfortunate time for this phenomenon to be accentuated.

A lowered mental or physical vigor leads men to avoid an examination of complicated and changed conditions. Little by little, new facts become blurred through old glasses fitted, as it were, for the needs of another generation; older men, assuming that the scene is the same as it was in the past, cease to explore or inquire into the present or the future. . . .

A constant and systematic addition of younger blood will vitalize the courts and better equip them to recognize and apply the essential concepts of justice in the light of the needs and the facts of an ever-changing world.

And finally, it was possible for many citizens who did not at all approve of "packing the Court" as such to agree that the Court was threatening the country's economic and social future. Such citizens could enthusiastically echo these sentiments expressed by the President:

If by that phrase "packing the Court" it is charged that I wish to place on the bench spineless puppets who would disregard the law and would decide specific cases as I wished them to be decided, I make this answer: that no President fit for his office would appoint, and no Senate of honorable men fit for their office would confirm, that kind of appointees to the Supreme Court.

But if by that phrase the charge is made that I would appoint and the Senate would confirm Justices worthy to sit beside the present members of the Court who understand these modern conditions, that I will appoint Justices who will not undertake to override the judgment of the Congress on legislative policy, that I will appoint Justices who will act as Justices and not as legislators—if the appointment of such Justices can be called "packing the Courts," then I say that I and with me the vast majority of the American people favor doing just that thing—now.

With respect to the nation's most conservative Justices, moreover, it is well worth emphasizing that this issue was not drawn between the President and the Supreme Court. Oft-repeated official utterances of Supreme Court Justices could be quoted in support of President Roosevelt's position. In the words of Justice Holmes, beyond a doubt one of America's truly great jurists:

Great constitutional provisions must be administered with caution. Some play must be allowed for the joints of the machine, and it must be remembered that legislatures are ultimate guardians of the liberties and welfare of the people in quite as great a degree as the courts. . . .

I have not yet adequately expressed the more than anxiety that I feel at the ever-increasing scope given to the Fourteenth Amendment in cutting down what I believe to be the constitutional rights of the states. As the decisions now stand, I see hardly any limit but the sky to the invalidating of those rights if they happen to strike a majority of this Court as for any reason undesirable. I cannot believe that the Amendment was intended to give us *carte blanche* to embody our economic or moral beliefs in its prohibitions. Yet I can think of no narrower reason that seems to me to justify the present and the earlier decisions to which I have referred.

In this same connection, too, it is to be remembered that most of the decisions to which President Roosevelt took exception were split decisions, some of them even being decided by the narrow margin of five votes to four, and that members of this very Court had often spoken quite sharply to their colleagues along the same lines as those set forth by Justice Holmes. For example, the following from Justice Stone's dissent in the recent New York minimum wage case:

There is grim irony in speaking of the freedom of contract of those who, because of their economic necessities, give their services for less than is needful to keep body and soul together. But if this is freedom of contract no one has ever denied that it is freedom which may be restrained, notwithstanding the Fourteenth Amendment, by a statute passed in the public interest.

Clearly there were two issues here, and unfortunately they had gotten inextricably confused. There was first the question whether a President should be permitted to stack the judicial deck to secure decisions upholding his legislative program, and there was second the question whether this particular Supreme Court was insisting upon an interpretation of the Constitution injurious to the nation's well-being. If, as in retrospect seems highly probable, a majority of citizens would have answered the first of these questions in the negative and the second in the affirmative, it must surely be marked down as a major achievement of a virile and dynamic democracy that this tangled web was unravelled along precisely those lines.

This result was not of course merely fortuitous. Powerful forces had been activated to compel just such a result. To begin with, a bitter rebellion broke out in the ranks of the President's own party which might have prevented acceptance of the reorganization proposal in its original form in any case. This defection was then greatly strengthened when on March 29 the Supreme Court (in another 5-4 split) flatly reversed itself on the subject of state minimum wage legislation by upholding such a law passed by the legislature of the state of Washington,[22] and unanimously upheld the revised Frazier-Lemke Farm Mortgage Act.[23] And when two weeks later, in the most surprising development of all, the Court unequivocally upheld

---

[22] *West Coast Hotel* v. *Parrish*, 300 U.S. 379 (1937).

[23] *Wright* v. *Vinton Branch of Mountain Trust Bank of Roanoke*, 300 U.S. 440 (1937).

the Wagner Act,[24] so much pressure had been taken off the administration to make possible the complete abandonment of the "packing" proposal. In its place was substituted a bill providing for full pay for Justices retiring from the Supreme Court bench at or after the age of 70. And when on May 18 archconservative Van Devanter did retire under the provisions of the new law, and especially when on May 24 the Social Security Act was upheld (on the grounds, among others, that these federal tax rebates to states constituted an incentive rather than coercion),[25] the crisis was over. During the next four years President Roosevelt was given the opportunity of appointing no less than seven Supreme Court Justices.[26]

Validated in the courts as well as at the polls, the "Second New Deal" was now a reality. But something more than whether or not this reform program would stand had been at issue in this battle— and to this other question an equally decisive answer had been given. For many years the desirability of judicial review (the right of the courts to declare laws passed by state and federal legislatures unconstitutional) had been hotly debated. Now more clearly than ever before it could be seen how academic much of this argument had been. In point of fact this power of the courts is far from complete; that is, it has obviously been tolerated because it has been exercised with caution. As long as the courts follow the injunction laid down by Justice Washington in 1827, this power is apparently secure in their hands:

It is but a decent respect due to the wisdom, integrity, and the patriotism of the legislative body, by which any law is passed, to presume in favor of its validity, until its violation of the Constitution is proved beyond all reasonable doubt.

But let them seriously disregard this plea for judicial self-restraint, as they clearly did in the 1930's, and it is almost mathematically certain that this power will not long remain intact. It is thus no casual use of words by the students of the Supreme Court that refers to "suicidal decisions." In short, the Justices do, because they must, watch the ballot box. If it is true, as many insist that the Supreme Court has since the 1930's tended to watch the ballot box too closely, it is at least not surprising that the reaction to the crisis of those years took that particular form.

[24] National Labor Relations Board v. Jones and Laughlin Steel Corporation, 301 U.S. 1 (1937).

[25] Helvering v. Davis, 301 U.S. 619 (1937).

[26] C. Herman Pritchett, The Roosevelt Court: A Study in Judicial Politics and Values, 1937-1947 (New York: The Macmillan Co., 1948).

QUESTIONS FOR DISCUSSION

1. What were the problems which arose during the 1920's, but which received little or no attention until the 1930's?

2. Can you name any New Deal reform policy which you think would not have soon appeared in essentially the same form quite apart from the depression and the New Deal?

3. How valid do you consider Justice Roberts' views on the function of the Supreme Court as expressed in the *United States* v. *Butler* decision?

4. List the New Deal enactments which were invalidated by the Supreme Court alongside another list of those which were not invalidated.

5. What were the fundamental factors involved in the controversy between the Tennessee Valley Authority and private power companies in that area?

6. Why were the Wagner Act and the Social Security Act considered especially vulnerable to Supreme Court attack?

7. Explain the purpose and describe the provisions of the Robinson-Patman Act.

8. Distinguish between maintaining competition and preserving particular small competitors.

9. How was it supposed that an undistributed profits tax might improve the general economic situation?

10. In the 1936 presidential campaign, was President Roosevelt's major emphasis "hitting below the belt"? Explain.

11. Why was the court issue considered so critical that drastic measures had to be taken?

12. Was the President justified in the position he took regarding the Supreme Court?

13. What is your opinion of the American institution of judicial review?

14. It is often said that the New Deal developed a new concept of government in a democracy. How would you describe this change?

15. Did the New Deal "rewrite the Constitution" through an expansion of the interstate commerce clause?

Chapter 24

Recession and Stagnation

After the administration's struggle over reorganizing the Supreme Court, the New Deal was never quite the same. This battle, moreover, was no doubt one of the important reasons why some of the old "vim and vinegar" was visibly lacking from this point forward. Many there were, and within the President's own party, who were now inclined to be suspicious of the motives of the man who had tried so desperately to tamper with one of the country's oldest government traditions. And among those holding such sentiments were of course many who in addition felt that reform had gone far enough for the moment—including a number of southerners who were beginning to recoil from efforts to improve the lot of the Negro sharecropper and other gestures threatening the race adjustment worked out in the South.

ANOTHER CRISIS

But this was by no means the only factor contributing to the relative listlessness of the Washington scene after mid-1937. Another was the frustratingly perverse behavior of the economy. No sooner had the smoke of the court contest begun to lift than one of the

TABLE 45. A RUDE INTERRUPTION

Month and Year	Industrial Production*	Prices†		Consumer	Factory Weekly Earnings†	Factory Employment†
		Wholesale				
		Farm	Other‡			
July, 1937	100	100	100	100	100	100
June, 1938	68	77	94	98	85	74

* Federal Reserve Board.
† Department of Labor.
‡ Other than farm products and foods.

sharpest declines in business activity in the nation's history set in. Instead, therefore, of dramatically broadening and deepening the reform program claimed to have been so instrumental in achieving recovery, a considerable energy had to be directed toward resuscitating an economy which had obviously not righted itself after all.[1]

It is no more possible to state with certainty what caused this catastrophe than to explain why other such downturns have come about. Enough is known about economic downturns, however, to make it reasonably certain that no single cause is ever responsible, and against the background of that probability a few of the forces believed in retrospect to have been at work in 1937 can be suggested. Although there is much disagreement about the relative weight to be assigned to each of these, there is nevertheless a substantial consensus as to their nature.

First attention here can appropriately be directed toward fiscal policy. Beginning in the middle of the preceding year, the government's net contribution to the income stream had begun to fall precipitately.[2] From a high of $4.1 billion in 1936 this figure fell to less than $1 billion in 1937. For this turn of events, three factors seem to have been primarily responsible. First, the administration was inclined to be overconfident about what had already been accomplished by way of building a solid foundation for full prosperity. Second, there seems also to have been reflected more than a trace of the old balanced-budget orthodoxy. Third, the new social security taxes just now striking the economy with all their force were a deflationary factor of significant proportions.[3]

But even the drastic falling off of "pump-priming" expenditures which set the multiplier to operating in reverse tells little about the onset of this recession-in-the-middle-of-a-depression. Although this development does represent one side of the coin, a major step toward transferring control over the economic mechanism from the government back to private enterprise, it does not explain why that move failed so completely. Why did the big-business critics of the New Deal not seize this opportunity to make good their campaign claims and promises of the preceding year?

At this point a prime factor seems clearly to have been monetary policy; the money and credit environment was made anything but

[1] Kenneth D. Roose, *The Economics of Recession and Revival* (New Haven: Yale University Press, 1954).

[2] Laurence R. Klein, *The Keynesian Revolution* (New York: The Macmillan Co., 1947).

[3] A. G. Hart, *Debts and Recovery, 1929-1937* (New York: Twentieth Century Fund, Inc., 1938).

conducive to the re-establishment of private enterprise initiative. One of the principal objectives of the Board of Governors of the Federal Reserve System in recent years had been the promotion of fuller employment, and toward that end its central policy had been the maintenance of easy credit conditions to help the economy get off dead center. During 1936 and the early part of 1937, however, more preoccupied with the technical fact of high excess reserves than with the level of unemployment as such and in consequence fearing an inflationary price spiral, the Board had first increased margin requirements for the purchase of securities and then, in a series of steps, raised commercial bank reserve requirements 100 per cent. Meanwhile the Treasury, also eager to reduce excess reserves, had taken action to prevent incoming gold from being added to the nation's credit-expansion base by sterilization operations. The result of these moves was to bring about a firming of interest rates, one of the worst conceivable policies from the standpoint of encouraging an increase in private investment.

But, as with fiscal policy, monetary policy as a factor in precipitating the 1937 decline in economic activity can easily be exaggerated —and the fact that the rate of interest is a much less significant determinant of business policy than was once supposed is only one explanation of why this is so. Another is that there were several additional reasons why private enterprise did not promptly take over where the government was leaving off. Thus price-cost relationships had for a number of months been moving in a direction adverse to profit expectations, and one of the most important factors behind this development was no doubt the strengthening of collective bargaining which New Deal legislation had encouraged. Furthermore, conservatives made a considerable point of the fact that in their opinion the New Deal in a variety of other ways as well had created a sociopolitical environment which had so shaken business confidence that much more than a reduction of the federal government's deficit would be required to restore the nation to a sound private enterprise equilibrium. Especially included in this category were such items as undistributed profits taxation, the social security program, public power projects, financial regulation, the Wealth-Tax Act, and the eclipse of orthodox economic thinking relative to the national debt.[4]

These then are the most important factors behind the 1937 recession. But it is not these forces in and of themselves that are important to this discussion. The more significant fact is rather that out of

[4] Harold G. Moulton, *The New Philosophy of Public Debt* (Washington, D.C.: Brookings Institution, 1943).

this experience emerged a number of implications vital to evolving government-business relationships.

In the first place, the growing realization that the task of stabilizing a complex, modern economy is both delicate and difficult was again given a sharp impetus. On three different occasions since the Federal Reserve System had been created, since economic stabilization had become an overt policy objective, the efforts of those whose task it was to manage the nation's antidepression weapons had been woefully inadequate. Nor was this, with respect to a single one of these occasions, because those officials had been caught napping; each time they had been endeavoring to read the situation accurately and to guide the economy intelligently on the basis of those readings. Furthermore, these successive failures had occurred despite a progressive sharpening of the tools available for this work—by legislation as well as by use. Evidently, considerable homework still remained to be done on this subject.

That this point was quickly grasped in the present instance is amply demonstrated by the promptness with which actions were taken to give the economic mechanism freer rein. As soon as the fact of collapse became apparent, several of the policies which had been most immediately responsible were reversed. The undistributed profits tax and the assessment of heavier federal income taxes against

TABLE 46. ACTION AND REACTION ON THE FISCAL POLICY FRONT

| | Federal Government | | | |
Year	Receipts	Expenditures (millions of dollars)	Deficit	Employment Taxes
1936	4,116	9,069	4,953	—
1937	5,029	8,281	3,252	266
1938	5,855	7,304	1,449	743
1939	5,165	8,765	3,600	740
1940	5,387	9,127	3,740	834

Source: Department of Commerce, Statistical Abstract of the United States, 1941, pp. 178-79 and 194.

larger concerns were both summarily repealed, the federal government's budget deficit was greatly increased, and the monetary measures inaugurated in such naive fright were hastily revised. And probably in part as a result of these prompt actions, by the middle of 1938 the downward trend had halted and several key indexes of economic activity were beginning to turn up.

In the second place, several painfully concrete aspects of the stabilization problem itself were also being brought home. For example, it was now more evident than ever before how crucial is the factor of timing in both fiscal and monetary policy, and hence how vitally important is an intimate understanding of underlying economic relationships. (And as a more or less obvious corollary of this conclusion, it was already becoming apparent that monetary policy would be a much more useful antidepression weapon than fiscal policy.) Moreover, it was now even clearer than it had been in National Recovery Administration days that to focus attention upon either aggregate purchasing power or business costs to the exclusion of the other can be fatal. And finally, it was being learned that every significant government decision (as, for instance, the new social security taxes) may be potentially of great importance for over-all stability—whatever the more immediate purpose.

But if as a result of this experience a consensus was developing with respect to a number of the problems created by a modern industrial depression, the same could not be said about one of the issues thus raised—and this unquestionably the most important one of all. That was no less than the question of whether the business community or the government should accept the largest share of the blame for what had happened.

Nor was this merely a political matter. There were vital technical issues at stake in this puzzle as well. If, thus, private enterprise had (as government spokesmen together with a number of liberal leaders maintained) instigated a capital strike in order to bring discredit upon the administration, one set of policy conclusions could appropriately be drawn. But if, on the other hand, the government had instead (as many highly-placed conservatives preferred to believe) created conditions incompatible with private business decisions (and there were even those who insisted that the government was doing this deliberately to discredit business leadership as a justification for the extension of government power), a quite different set of policy inferences would be in order. To be sure, much of the controversy which now raged over this issue was politically oriented. To be sure, also, arguments on both sides were, as always in political debate, exaggerated. But with all these overtones there was nonetheless a desire to penetrate deeper into the mysteries of the business cycle from the standpoint of government-business relationships. And because there was here a sincere quest for answers to important questions, it is unfortunate that no consensus was forthcoming at this time in regard to them.[5]

[5] A. H. Hansen, *Economic Policy and Full Employment* (New York: McGraw-Hill Book Co., Inc., 1947).

LIMPING ALONG

It was not, however, so much that a new business downturn brought reform activity to a standstill. The legislative program of the New Deal still went on. Rather the change from this time onward consisted primarily of the fact that so few of the things that were done, by comparison with earlier years, were new and different. Thus although conservatives continued to think of the administration as dangerously revolutionary, the remarkable fact about the New Deal during and after 1937 was how tame it had really become —a fact even more remarkable in view of the glare of public opinicn turned at approximately this point on the "one-third of a nation" which was, according to the report of a presidential commission, "ill-fed, ill-clothed, and ill-housed."

The record of legislation passed in 1937 demonstrates this fact especially well. Although a number of important laws were enacted, most of these did little more than build on foundations already in place.

One of the more significant pieces of legislation enacted during that year, for example, was the rewriting of the bituminous coal measure the administration had been trying to make constitutional for several years. This new effort, moreover, succeeded where its predecessors had failed. By omitting the labor provisions of the old law, those parts which the Supreme Court had objected to most strenuously but which were now to a limited extent at least taken care of through the Wagner Act, a regulatory enactment was now passed which placed this industry under a set of very comprehensive controls.

The declaration of policy in the new law is highly suggestive in this regard.

That regulation of the sale and distribution in interstate commerce of bituminous coal is imperative for the protection of such commerce; that there exist practices and methods of distribution and marketing of such coal that waste the coal resources of the Nation, and disorganize, burden, and obstruct interstate commerce in bituminous coal, with the result that regulation of the prices thereof and of unfair methods of competition therein is necessary to promote interstate commerce in bituminous coal and to remove burdens and obstructions therefrom.

Under this law a new National Bituminous Coal Commission—composed of two persons with experience as coal mine operators, two with experience as mine-workers, and three whose background was not specified—was established and authorized to set minimum prices for all coal moving in or affecting interstate commerce and to police the industry against 13 specified unfair methods of competition.[6] So stringent was this new stabilization measure that persistent violators were made subject to a fine of 20 per cent of the market value of all coal sold by them. And when the constitutionality of this measure was challenged in the courts, Justice Douglas, speaking for eight of the Supreme Court's nine Justices, answered as follows:

If we undertook to narrow the scope of federal intervention in this field . . . we would be blind to at least thirty years of history. . . . If the strategic character of this industry in our economy and the chaotic conditions which have prevailed in it do not justify legislation, it is difficult to imagine what would.[7]

Interestingly enough, although having nothing whatever to do with the New Deal's reform program as such, the anthracite end of the coal industry was simultaneously undergoing an evolution having much in common with these developments in the bituminous field—and even more with conservation-stabilization efforts in the petroleum industry. Because almost all the hard coal mined in the United States comes from a small area in northeastern Pennsylvania and because that economic activity is dominated by a small number of firms, federal assistance was not needed. A committee composed of three representatives each of the operators, the United Mine Workers, and the Commonwealth of Pennsylvania was established to agree on the total amount of anthracite coal to be mined, a total then allocated among the participating firms in accordance with a formula agreed upon in advance.

Another step taken in 1937 designed solely to remedy damage done to the New Deal program by the Supreme Court was the passage of a new Railroad Retirement Act. Even though the Social Security Act was now safe from legal attack, railroad workers still insisted upon a program of their own. The principal reason for this, of course, was that prior to the framing of the more general legislation these workers had settled upon a schedule of benefits substantially more favorable than that written into the Social Security Act, and it is quite understandable that they would not willingly have accepted an inferior program. Furthermore, this confusion in social security legislation and administration was compounded the following year when a special unemployment insurance act covering railroad workers was passed, that program also to be administered by the Railroad Retirement Board.

[6] R. H. Baker, *The Bituminous Coal Commission* (Baltimore: Johns Hopkins Press, 1941).

[7] *Sunshine Anthracite Coal Company* v. *Adkins,* 310 U.S. 381 (1940).

A development which would have been quite radical, although not strictly new, was the President's 1937 proposal that "seven little TVA's" be created. These, he felt, together with the government power facilities already in operation or in process of construction, would complete the task of blanketing the nation with agencies "to conserve and safeguard the prudent use of waters, water-power, soils, forests, and other resources of the areas entrusted to their charge." However, so great was the storm of protest against this suggestion that nothing came of it, and the President therefore had to be content with the progress already being made in this field.

But if this setback meant that the cause of public power would not advance as rapidly as the administration might have wished, it does not at all follow that progress on this front was not quite rapid

TABLE 47. PUBLIC POWER ON THE MARCH

| | Electric Power Production by | | |
Year	Private Utilities	Municipal Utilities (thousands of kilowatts)	Federal Government
1920	12,023	601	10
1925	20,045	1,125	198
1930	30,285	1,601	226
1935	31,820	2,001	300
1940	34,399	2,977	1,944

Source: Department of Commerce, *Statistical Abstract of the United States, 1941*, p. 436.

even so.[8] Construction of the series of dams which was required by the Tennessee River Valley development blueprint was proceeding apace. In the lower Colorado River Valley, Hoover–Boulder Dam had been completed in 1936, and other projects in this area were in the planning stage. On the Columbia River, Bonneville Dam was completed in 1937, and Grand Coulee Dam was scheduled for completion in the near future.

An essentially new way of tackling an old problem was authorized in the Bankhead-Jones Farm Tenant Act. The continuity here was particularly indicated by the fact that the new agency thereby created, the Farm Security Administration, was given supervisory powers over the older Resettlement Administration, even though the new legislation did take up the cudgels for the farmers at the lowest end of the income scale on a far broader scale than had ever been done before. In part because it was widely believed that the

[8] J. C. Bonbright, *Public Utilities and the National Power Policies* (New York: Columbia University Press, 1940).

original Agricultural Adjustment Act had actually contributed to the growth of tenancy (although in part also as a result of a concern over the growth of farm tenancy now three decades old), the Farm Security Administration was given funds with which to make loans to farmers desiring to purchase farms. Moreover, the new agency was also commissioned to take steps toward ending the worst exploitation of migrant farm labor. Opposition from the "fruit and vegetable crowd," the major employers of migrants, and from southerners objecting to the rehabilitation of Negro sharecroppers, kept the effectiveness of this program far below the high hopes of its sponsors, but it was nevertheless considered by the administration an integral part of the "Second New Deal."[9]

A measure containing even more that was new was the Wagner-Steagall Housing Act. Although slum-clearance projects had been under way ever since Public Works Administration days on an emergency basis, this was the first attempt to implement the President's ideal of "the security of decent housing" for everyone. The United States Housing Authority was created and empowered to loan money at low interest and for long periods of time to local public housing groups (and in extreme cases even to make outright gifts) to make possible the erection of low-rent dwelling units into which slum-dwellers would then be transferred. And to introduce a greater degree of order into the federal government's now far-flung housing activities, the new Authority was given the task of coordinating them all.

Ironically, in short, the only major item on the 1937 legislative agenda which was almost wholly new was the Miller-Tydings Act—a law which would have been called a reform measure in the "Second New Deal" tradition by few liberals of that day.

The Robinson-Patman Act had sought to hamper the operations of large distributors in a subtle, indirect way. For some time, as still another aspect of the defensive reaction of smaller retailers to the telescoping of distribution channels, attempts had gone forward to accomplish this same end more directly and hence more effectively. The approach on this front which by now seemed most promising was resale price maintenance.[10]

Actually, it was manufacturers who had first begun experimenting with this device. Success, however, had not crowned that effort. Increasingly, insistence upon setting a price below which retailers

[9] Donald C. Blaisdell, *Government and Agriculture* (New York: Rinehart & Co., Inc., 1940).

[10] E. T. Grether, *Price Control Under Fair Trade Legislation* (New York: Oxford University Press, 1939).

might not sell a particular product had been held to be both a violation of the Sherman Act and an unfair method of competition under the Federal Trade Commission Act. Furthermore, a substantial proportion of output in so many lines had come to be distributed by chain operators who might raise objections to resale price maintenance arrangements in the very tangible form of marketing their own private brands.

At that point the initiative in this struggle passed to the National Association of Retail Druggists. With this organization taking the lead, a concerted assault was made against the resistance of state legislatures to so flagrant a breach of the nation's antitrust traditions. And under the special circumstances prevailing during the 1930's, that objective was achieved. In part by means of a carefully prepared "public education" campaign, designed to identify resale price maintenance in the minds of citizens with the concept of fair competition, "fair trade" legislation began to make rapid progress.

The first great success in this endeavor was the passage of enabling legislation in California. From the beginning that law was a center of controversy. Obviously it would have been unrealistic to require a separate contract between the manufacturer and every retailer of a fair trade item. At the same time it seemed clear both that the legal basis of this undertaking would have to be a written contract and that unless virtually all sellers of the product in question were bound by the same rules little could be accomplished. This nice problem in legal strategy the California law neatly solved by declaring that an agreement between a manufacturer and one retailer would be binding upon all retailers (within the state).

Of course, this statute was challenged in the courts. Somewhat surprisingly and most paradoxically, however, the Supreme Court sweepingly upheld it. The paradox was this. Justice Sutherland approved resale price maintenance on the ground that manufacturers were entitled to take this step to protect the goodwill embodied in their trade marks.[11] In other words, a measure written to protect retailers was justified in terms of the property rights of manufacturers—and in fact it is argued by many that the principal beneficiaries of that policy have been the manufacturers rather than the retailers.

Once this hurdle had been surmounted, it was only a matter of time before a majority of the states had enacted similar statutes. But another problem still remained. Where interstate commerce was

[11] *Old Dearborn Distributing Company* v. *Seagram Distilling Corporation*, 299 U.S. 183 (1936).

involved, federal rather than state law governed, and ordinary business operations were by now more often interstate than intrastate
in character. Therefore, the lobbyists of retailer associations turned
their attention to Congress—and with full success. To be sure, the
ruling administration never did support the Miller-Tydings Act,
perhaps primarily because it did not (as the Robinson-Patman Act
had) even pretend to be a contribution to antitrust reform. But so
determined was a majority in Congress to exempt resale price maintenance agreements from the antitrust laws, despite the known
objections of President Roosevelt, that this law was attached as
a rider to the District of Columbia appropriation bill just prior to
adjournment.[12]

One feeble attempt was made in this enactment to maintain in it
some consistency with antitrust traditions. No product could be fair-
traded unless it was branded and sold in competition with essentially similar products put out by other manufacturers. In practice,
however, this safeguard cannot mean very much. Obviously no
manufacturer will consent to fair-trade his commodity unless he is
assured that his competitors will be doing likewise. Not only, in
other words, did this law accomplish its primary purposes of inhibiting competition in retailing and freezing the distributive
mechanism against the innovations of an advancing technology, but
it even facilitated price-fixing agreements among manufacturers.
Happily, therefore, from the standpoint of reform, most products
entering into the American standard of living are for one reason or
another not amenable to the fair trade technique.

THE LAST BIG YEAR

In 1938 there was again little that was new, although that year
also chalked up an impressive list of achievements. Again, too,
the reform work done included items in a wide variety of fields.

As one important item on this agenda, it was perhaps only to be
expected that the reforming zeal of the 1930's would at some point
fasten upon the (inherent?) conflict between consumers and the
purveyors of foods and drugs. For a number of years criticisms of
the limitations of the old legislation in this field had been mounting,
the Food and Drug Administration itself leading this attack, and in
1933 a comprehensive revision had been presented to Congress.

Until 1936 it was widely considered unlikely that any such
measure could be passed, so powerful was the resistance movement

---

[12] M. W. Watkins, *Public Regulation of Competitive Practices* (New York: National Industrial Conference Board, 1940).

launched against it. At a critical moment, however, almost 100 persons died from the aftereffects of using the new drug sulfanilimide, and much of the last-ditch opposition forthwith melted away. As a result the Food, Drug, and Cosmetic Act of 1938 was placed on the statute books.[13]

A number of important changes were herein introduced into the law governing these relationships, in addition to a general tightening of the language used to make it more appropriate to a modern industrial society. For the first time cosmetics (with the exception of soap) and therapeutic devices were included in its provisions. The prohibitions against misbranding were greatly strengthened. And, on the enforcement side, penalties for violation were made much more severe.

Closely related to the Food, Drug, and Cosmetic Act both in time and subject matter was the so-called Wheeler-Lea Amendment to the Federal Trade Commission Act. By means of this measure, furthermore, a long step was taken toward restoring to that agency the power and prestige its New Freedom sponsors had intended it to have.

To be sure, the Commission had won a signal victory when the Supreme Court upheld its political independence against the Chief Executive. To be sure also, the Court had at long last reversed the restrictive rule laid down in the Gratz case. According to the view now taken by the Justices:

We cannot say that the Commission's jurisdiction extends only to those types of practices which happen to have been litigated before this Court. Neither the language nor the history of the Act suggests that Congress intended to confine the forbidden methods to fixed and unyielding categories.[14]

However, this latter success had been largely nullified by another Supreme Court pronouncement. In 1931 the Commission was denied jurisdiction under the Federal Trade Commission Act in situations where consumers and not competitors were the injured parties[15]—the reasoning here apparently being that consumers need no other protection from business practices than competition.

Categorically denying this thesis, and understandably anxious to take advantage of both its political independence and its hard-won freedom from the Gratz limitation, the Federal Trade Commission had for some time now been pressing for an alteration of its basic

---

[13] Stephen Wilson, *Food and Drug Regulation* (Washington, D.C.: American Council on Public Affairs, 1942).

[14] *Federal Trade Commission* v. *R. F. Keppel and Brothers*, 291 U.S. 304 (1934).

[15] *Federal Trade Commission* v. *Raladam Company*, 283 U.S. 643 (1931).

legislation prohibiting "unfair or deceptive acts or practices in commerce" as well as "unfair methods of competition." In 1938 this request made contact with the forces locked in bitter combat over the Food, Drug, and Cosmetic Act. One result of this development was a revision of the Federal Trade Commission Act along the lines requested by the Commission. The other major provision of the Wheeler-Lea Act gave the Commission (largely because industry leaders preferred regulation with respect to this matter by that body rather than by the Food and Drug Administration in the Department of Agriculture) authority to police special prohibitions against the false advertisement of foods, drugs, cosmetics, and therapeutic devices.

The Fair Labor Standards Act, the second major reform accomplishment of 1938, was concerned primarily with enacting into law those provisions of the National Industrial Recovery Act pertaining to labor which had not been embodied in the Wagner Act.[16] Or, to put the matter slightly differently, what was now done was to generalize for application to all interstate commerce operations the main provisions of the Walsh-Healey Public Contracts Act. No longer fearing a Supreme Court reversal on these points, the federal government undertook in 1938 to outlaw child labor, to place a floor under hourly wages (at 25 cents per hour at first but gradually rising to 40 cents), and to put a ceiling of 40 on weekly hours without overtime (although here also a transition period was allowed).

Not only, moreover, did this enactment go far toward standardizing basic elements in the wage contract (for the benefit especially of workers who were not yet members of a strong collective bargaining agency), but when a test case involving this statute reached the Supreme Court, that body handed down an historic decision upholding it. Specifically repudiating *Hammer* v. *Dagenhart*, a majority of the Justices (4 Justices dissenting) supported perhaps the most basic transfer of power from the states to the federal government ever effected—and at the same time defended in principle a definition of interstate commerce which would be repeatedly used in upholding other Congressional grants of power.[17]

The power of Congress over interstate commerce is not confined to the regulation of commerce among the states. It extends to those activities intrastate which so affect interstate commerce . . . as to make regulation of them appropriate means to the attainment of a legitimate end, the exercise of the granted power of Congress to regulate interstate commerce. . . . Congress, to

[16] Orme W. Phelps, *The Legislative Background of the Fair Labor Standards Act* (Chicago: University of Chicago Press, 1939).

[17] *United States* v. *Darby*, 312 U.S. 100 (1941).

attain its objective . . . recognized that in present day industry, competition by a small part may affect the whole and that the total effect of the competition of many small producers may be great. . . .

In 1938 also an act was passed extending the responsibilities of the Federal Power Commission into the last remaining major public utility no-man's land—the interstate transmission of natural gas. Although the powers given that agency in this area were somewhat less extensive than those it already possessed in the electric power field (authority over financial practices and combinations being particularly significant omissions), and although here also the greatest care was taken not to encroach upon state sovereignty, the Commission was given a fairly complete agenda of public utility regulation powers—and the courts early adopted an especially liberal view of its jurisdiction in a series of key court tests.

Very much in the spirit of this extension of federal powers in the utility regulation field was the Civil Aeronautics Act of 1938, wherein the vigorous trend in the direction of conferring full public utility status upon the commercial aviation industry, reached its climax.[18] Under the terms of this law a Civil Aeronautics Board was created as an independent regulatory agency to supervise the economic aspects of this industry's operations, while to another agency (the Civil Aeronautics Administration, loosely attached to the Department of Commerce) were given the broad promotional responsibilities the federal government had for a number of years been assuming in this area.

It was in 1938, too, that the nation's farm program was again basically rewritten. The law of two years before had been drawn up in haste in order to meet a crisis situation, to say nothing of the fact that experience with this program to date had by this time done much to crystallize the thinking of the nation's leaders on these problems. Put differently, the time seemed clearly to have come to give this policy a more permanent form. However, while a number of changes were made, few of these were in any way fundamental. By now the parity concept had become the key element in this effort, and under the new law this fact was recognized by putting parity payments on a direct appropriation basis—although the use of non-recourse loans was not abandoned, and although there was at this point little thought that 100 per cent of parity could even approximately be achieved in this way. By the same token production controls moved much closer to the center of this program, and the legal

18 Lucile S. Keyes, *Federal Control of Entry Into Air Transportation* (Cambridge: Harvard University Press, 1951).

TABLE 48. A BIGGER SHARE FOR THE FARMER

Year	Government Payments to Farmers (millions of dollars)
1933	131
1934	446
1935	573
1936	287
1937	367
1938	482
1939	807

Source: Department of Agriculture, *Agricultural Statistics, 1946*, p. 563.

relationship between conservation payments (which were to be continued) and the parity side of this endeavor was considerably loosened.

And finally, there were in 1938 two important developments in the government–business field which had little to do with legislation as such. One of these primarily involved the Federal Communications Commission; the other was most closely associated with the work of the Securities and Exchange Commission.

Shortly after its creation the Federal Communications Commission had launched a full-scale investigation of the telephone business, an activity which was completed in 1938. Although one result of this study was the submission to Congress of a number of recommendations for additional legislation which were not acted upon, the important consequence was the accumulation of a mass of information which has been invaluable in improving the effectiveness of regulation in that industry—state as well as federal.

One of the first major decisions of the Securities and Exchange Commission after its creation had been to permit maximum scope for self-regulation of the New York Stock Exchange rather than to impose rules from without.[19] This was not, incidentally, a concession to Wall Street in the technical sense of that term. The Exchange had always been a strictly private operation, never having even been granted a charter by the State of New York, and those in charge of the new regulatory agency felt that best results might therefore be obtained by giving it an opportunity to mend its ways without interference by outsiders. At the same time, on the other hand, government officials made it clear that if, after a reasonable time, the Ex-

[19] Twentieth Century Fund, *The Security Markets* (New York: Twentieth Century Fund, Inc., 1935).

change had not itself taken steps, the government would undertake to initiate a reform agenda.

In the event, the strategy of the Commission was vindicated. The bitterness of many members of the Exchange toward government interference, a bitterness clearly demonstrated by their stubborn resistance to the invitation to submit a reorganization proposal for Commission approval, makes it even more obvious what the response of the Exchange would have been to a government proposal. Unfortunately for all concerned, however, the Commission's decision coupled with Wall Street defiance meant that progress on this front would be difficult and long delayed.

In late 1937, the government made its first decisive move. Against a background of Exchange ineptness in dealing with irregularities incident to the stock market collapse of that year, William O. Douglas, Chairman of the Commission, in a fighting speech declared that that agency's patience was now at an end. Thus stimulated, Exchange leaders submitted to the membership a proposal for a thorough reorganization. Amid serious doubt as to whether even under these circumstances such a report would be approved by a majority, a former president of the Exchange (Richard Whitney) was arrested for grand larceny for diverting to his own uses funds and securities entrusted to him by customers. With this development in early 1938, resistance to reform disintegrated. A leading reformer (William McChesney Martin, Jr.) was elected president, and a series of round-table discussions with Securities and Exchange Commission representatives was begun to work out a more satisfactory set of trading rules.

STRANGE INTERLUDE

But it would be grossly misleading to leave the impression that these more or less tangible developments wholly exhausted the 1938 news on the reform front. Indeed, by far the most dramatic item on this list has been reserved for separate treatment. This special emphasis, be it noted, is not to be understood as indicating any profound consequences flowing from the administration's comprehensive study of the concentration of economic power, for it would be difficult to point to anything of this sort. But in spite of extremely limited results, that paradoxical episode in the life of the New Deal is so full of implications important to an understanding of recent government–business relationships in the United States as to warrant particularly careful study.

A common interpretation of this episode has it that when the 1937 recession ground to bits the New Deal's claim that fundamental economic reforms had generated a gratifying recovery, the nation's leaders were powerfully motivated to find a "scapegoat" upon whose shoulders the responsibility for this new catastrophe could be shifted —and that "big business" was selected to perform this function. However, although the case for such an interpretation is persuasive, there is perhaps here a little of what is often referred to as trying to prove too much. While it would hardly be denied that the timing of this onslaught was strongly influenced by the economic downturn, and possibly much of its fierce intensity as well, there is an abundance of evidence suggesting that the roots of this campaign lay much deeper.

In the first place, for example, it must be remembered that hostility to trusts (big business) had for more than half a century been a fundamental article of faith in the liberal creed. Not always on the surface, but never far beneath, this attitude could be depended upon as an avenue of approach to the mass voter under almost any circumstances. Furthermore, for obvious reasons citizens would look especially to the Democratic party when it was in power for protection from these "monsters." And finally, there could be no denying that during the 1920's both administration prosecution under and judicial interpretation of the antitrust laws left much to be desired from the standpoint of liberals, and that little had as yet happened during the 1930's to reverse these trends. In short, this endeavor is probably to be explained in considerable part as both a natural response to the business excesses of the 1920's, and a more or less logical outgrowth of (reaction to) the ill-fated National Recovery Administration experiment.

Nor is it particularly surprising, in the second place, that a new antitrust drive in the late 1930's would have a different orientation than any such campaign in the past. Keynesian economics had by this time secured a powerful hold both on the mind of official Washington and on much unofficial thinking. An important aspect of that system of thought revolved around the necessity of maintaining a sufficient purchasing power at the lower end of the income scale to enable consumers to buy the goods industry is capable of producing at full employment. When to this general proposition was added the growing conviction that the Great Depression had itself been brought about by an excessive concentration of income in the upper brackets, it would have been an unresponsive leadership indeed which would not have begun linking together two such attractive popular appeals.

Still a third way in which a new antitrust drive fitted neatly into the trend of events during these years had to do with the President's recent electioneering attack on the "economic royalists." Given this emphasis in the thinking of the administration—and note in this connection the strongly worded plank in the 1936 Democratic platform directed against "monopolies and the concentration of economic power"—no urging was necessary to move top government policy in the direction of such a made-to-order opportunity to carry the fight to the enemy. In other words, although the appearance of a new economic downturn may well have made an open attack on big business much more politically urgent than would otherwise have been the case, it probably did little to put ideas in the heads of administration leaders.

And at one other, even more concrete, point is it evident that these ideas were taking shape even before the downturn began. In May, 1937, Leon Henderson, an administration spokesman destined as a consequence of this event to rise to a much higher level in those circles, specifically, unequivocally, and most dramatically predicted a business recession within six months—and gave as his reason for so believing a rise in the price level with which general purchasing power was failing to keep pace. When within six months the predicted recession did develop, the stage could not have been more perfectly set for what was about to happen.

These facts, then, make up the essential background against which the "greatest economic study in American history" was launched.[20] On April 29, 1938, the President sent a special message to Congress requesting a comprehensive investigation "of the concentration of economic power in American industry and the effect of that concentration upon the decline of competition." Almost exactly seven weeks later the President signed into law the measure creating the so-called Temporary National Economic Committee. Composed of members from the Senate, the House of Representatives, and the Executive Branch of the government, this group was for two full years to hold the spotlight position in the unfolding New Deal drama. The "Investigation of Concentration of Economic Power," extending over an extremely busy eighteen-month period, consisted of 775 hours of hearings in which 552 witnesses were heard and 3,300 technical exhibits submitted, and was made available to the

[20] David Lynch, *The Concentration of Economic Power* (New York: Columbia University Press, 1946).

public in the form of 31 large volumes of hearings supplemented by 43 analytical monographs—this mass of material constituting perhaps the most complete factual description of any complex economy in the history of civilization.

But though the Temporary National Economic Committee did in some respects turn out a prodigious performance, though it must be conceded that its labors were not (in the words of the President) "confined to the traditional antitrust field," and though it did furnish a valuable point of departure for much effective antitrust work in later years—it nonetheless seems appropriate to refer to this episode as a strange interlude.[21] There are several reasons for this. First, the new program represented a complete about face from one of the most basic policies followed by the "First New Deal." Not only, thus, had the administration heretofore avoided any trace of historic American "trust-busting," but it had launched its attack on the depression by encouraging businessmen to collaborate with one another. Now the nation's leaders were embarking upon a diametrically opposite policy without publicly acknowledging that any change was involved or that the previous approach had been a mistaken one.

And this point can be made even more strongly, too. Attacks on the concentration of economic power had prior to this never produced dramatic (some would even say significant) changes in the structure of industry,[22] and there was really no objective reason for supposing that the New Deal would be successful at this point where previous endeavors had failed. On the other hand, however, the federal government had during the 1930's been instrumental in altering the structure of the economic system in a fundamentally different way. This was by helping to organize labor in the mass production industries—perhaps the only basic change in the power structure of a modern economy which can be achieved apart from direct government controls.[23]

From a still more fundamental standpoint, the new orientation must be thought of, in retrospect at least, as strange because of the assumptions on which it rested. To begin with, whatever agreement there is on the proposition that maldistribution of income may have important business cycle consequences, this agreement does not

---

[21] John Scoville and Noel Sargent, *Fact and Fancy in the T.N.E.C. Monographs* (Washington, D.C.: National Association of Manufacturers, 1942).

[22] Walton Hamilton and Irene Till, *Antitrust in Action* (Washington, D.C.: Government Printing Office, 1941).

[23] Frank Tannenbaum, *A Philosophy of Labor* (New York: Alfred A. Knopf, Inc., 1951).

extend to the further proposition that the perverse behavior of the economy during the 1930's was due to an income maldistribution attributable to the concentration of economic power. Here again, in fact, the New Deal had along other lines—through its tax policies —taken steps far more appropriate to the end of correcting income maldistribution than the Temporary National Economic Committee approach.

Much the same thing can be said of another thesis prominent in administration circles during those years. Price inflexibility may indeed have significant economic consequences throughout the business cycle, especially in view of the fact that in some major price areas flexibility rather than inflexibility is the rule,[24] but it does not follow from this (and scholars are becoming less and less convinced of this once so highly advertised relationship) that price inflexibility is a prime cause of either income maldistribution or cyclical business downswings.

And perhaps the most ironical fact of all is that whereas the administration was operating on the assumption that undesirable monopolistic rigidities in industry as such were an important cause of the recession, probably a more potent factor operating here was the monopolistic rigidities in the labor bargain which this same administration had done so much to promote. This is not of course to say that the New Deal erred at this point, but the abstract desirableness or undesirableness of the encouragement given to labor organizations does not alter the ramifications of that development for economic dynamics.

"BATTLE OF THE PH.D.'S"

Because the new antitrust drive was so unsound, the surprising thing is that it created the long-sustained stir that it did. Moreover, this becomes an even more pertinent question when it is remembered that this program was not in fact formally launched until the 1937-38 recession had almost run its course. The Temporary National Economic Committee, in other words, might easily have sunk into the quicksand of historical oblivion. That it did not, that this implausible approach to a basic economic policy became for a time a dominant feature of government–business relationships, is due primarily to another characteristic of the American economy during this period which will not soon be forgotten.

Paradoxically, when toward the middle of 1938 the economic downturn ground to a halt, instead of resuming the recovery so

[24] United States Senate, *Industrial Prices and their Relative Inflexibility*, Senate Document 13, 74th Congress, 1st Session, 1935.

drastically interrupted the economy stubbornly hovered around a level of activity far below what it could theoretically have achieved. Whereas the index of industrial production had reached 65 at its prerecession high, it was almost three years before it rose consistently above that point. Industrial production, prices, and factory earnings were all lower in 1939 than they had been two years earlier, and unemployment was more than 2,000,000 greater. After ten full years of depression the economy had still not regained the level of performance from which it had fallen.

TABLE 49. ON DEAD CENTER

Year	Industrial Production* (1947-1949 = 100)	Factory Weekly Earnings†	Unemployment† (thousands)
1929	59	$25.03	429
1936	56	21.78	7,386
1937	61	24.05	6,403
1938	48	22.30	9,796
1939	58	23.86	8,786

* Federal Reserve Board.
† Department of Labor.

Understandably, this development precipitated a long-drawn-out discussion of the soundness of the underlying economy, a discussion which (also quite naturally) took as its point of departure the controversy over the factors responsible for the 1937–38 recession. Put differently, because the "Investigation of Concentration of Economic Power" emerged directly from this earlier discussion, it could not but figure significantly in the new debate. Waged as heatedly in academic as in political circles, this discussion has often been referred to as the "Battle of the Ph.D.'s." Indeed, it could perhaps be said without misleading exaggeration that the focal point of this give and take was the relevancy and implications of the new Keynesian economics for government economic policy. And while it must be confessed that the professors did not add to their prestige by failing to agree on the reasons for the perverse behavior of the American economy, it can at least be said that it was at this time that Keynesianism became an integral part of all macroeconomic thinking.

Central to this argument were the intricate interrelationships between saving, investment, and consumption. Neither saving nor investment can take place in the absence of the other, but neither can investment increase without an increase in consumption.

Furthermore, an increase in investment directly contributes to an increase in consumption (through the multiplier), and an increase in consumption directly contributes to an increase in investment (through the acceleration principle). Out of these self-reinforcing interconnections both the upward spiral of recovery and the downward spiral of collapse must come.

Building on this foundation, the more enthusiastic Keynesians explained the weakness of the American economy in the late 1930's along the following lines.[25] As a society becomes more wealthy, its people tend to save more of their income. Saving in a modern economy, however, can become effective only if capital is thereby accumulated. But since the point of investment is the sale at a profit of the goods it is capable of producing, the fact that citizens are saving rather than spending prevents savings from being transformed into capital. The result is that money income is simply hoarded rather than being returned to the income stream, and a portion of the labor force is thereby denied employment.

Here, in barest outline, is the reasoning behind the more pessimistic conclusions being drawn relative to the performance of the economy at this time. Not only, furthermore, were many economists coming to believe that economic equilibrium at less than full employment might be theoretically possible, but some there were who believed that the American economy was actually suffering from what came during these years to be known as secular stagnation. As a result of the closing of the frontier, a decline in the rate of population increase, a tapering off in the tempo of technological advance, and a high propensity to save (rate of capital formation) inherited from the days when a burgeoning industrialization made this an absolute necessity—it was thought that major structural changes might be required before the economy could again achieve an equilibrium without a substantial amount of uncomfortable and embarrassing unemployment.

Economists who were more orthodox in their thinking denied that the economy might bump along at substantially less than full employment for a long period of time as a result of more or less natural factors—that the American economy was beginning to suffer from "economic maturity."[26] They insisted rather that if a large

[25] W. H. Beveridge, *Full Employment in a Free Society* (New York: W. W. Norton & Co., Inc., 1945); and Alvin H. Hansen, *Full Recovery or Stagnation* (New York: W. W. Norton & Co., Inc., 1938).

[26] E. W. Swanson and E. P. Schmidt, *Economic Stagnation or Progress* (New York: McGraw-Hill Book Co., Inc., 1946); and George Terborgh, *The Bogey of Economic Maturity* (Chicago: Machinery & Allied Products Institute, 1945).

number of workers continued to be involuntarily unemployed, the explanation could only be that labor as a group was demanding excessive wages. If, in other words, powerful labor organizations with their stubborn resistance to wage reductions had not been encouraged by the government, there would not be this difficulty of employing those desiring to work. Furthermore, so this argument ran, capital accumulation is closely related to the advance of technology; as innovations are introduced costs and therefore prices are reduced, and in this way capital accumulation itself directly creates the purchasing power with which an increased output of goods can be bought.

To this analysis the Keynesians in turn reacted with great vigor. In the first place, they said, while it is true that wage reductions would reduce costs and to this extent improve the business outlook, it is also true that wages are the purchasing power without which the output of industry cannot be sold. It does not, in short, follow that a wage level adjustment would be a stimulant in the net. In the second place, whereas it might work out that technology, falling costs, and price reductions would create a self-equilibrating system of relationships, the fact is that with business decisions concentrated in a very few hands, competition is not strong enough to push prices down as rapidly as the needs of equilibration would require. And, as evidence on this point, it was urged that the experience of the economy in the 1920's should be conclusive.

From these theoretical foundations, the economists turned next to the policy implications of their views. Here the most unorthodox position was that the government must take responsibility for creating enough purchasing power to keep its citizens employed to whatever extent private business does not. If, thus, the American economy was suffering from stagnation, short-term pump-priming would logically have to give way to pump-priming on a longer-term basis. Along with this approach, it was suggested, a government program designed to redistribute income in favor of those who spend rather than save would minimize the need for long-range government intervention of this sort.

There were other liberals, however, who, although also unorthodox in their thinking, were unwilling to concede so broad a role to the government. This group insisted that the essential first step should be to restore a competitive economy. In all probability, so this view went, nothing more would be needed, but certainly nothing more should be attempted until the healing force of "old-fashioned competition" had been allowed to work itself out. Here, of course, was the point at which the Temporary National Economic Committee and its work held the center of the stage.

To more orthodox, conservative economists both of these approaches were not only error but heresy. The clue to proper government policies, these economists believed, was the profit expectations so crucial to the successful functioning of a private enterprise system. Because employment in such an economy depends upon the production of fixed, long-lived capital, and because the willingness of investors to tie up their resources in nonliquid assets therefore hinges to a large extent on an underlying confidence that the "rules of the game" will not meanwhile be changed, it was argued by this group that government policies had themselves brought about the economy's present stagnant condition. Changes in the rules of the game had in fact been introduced into economic institutions by the New Deal on such a wide front that uncertainties had been created which had seriously impaired the willingness of business leaders to employ society's citizens. The economy's difficulties, thus, were not to be remedied by more pump-priming; what was needed was rather major repairs for the "pump" the New Deal had so badly damaged.

Thus it was that a lively and at times bitter argument about stagnation led essentially to the same impasse which had emerged from the debate precipitated by the recent recession. But though the policy deadlock was in one sense no nearer a resolution than ever, two important points with respect to it were by this time beginning to impress themselves upon the nation's most thoughtful citizens.

On the one hand, it now seemed clear enough that the factors which determine an economy's performance include subjective as well as objective considerations. For example, an undistributed profits tax may in 1935 have been theoretically fully appropriate as a device to limit hoarding, and by the same token it may have been wholly correct (as administration spokesmen insisted) that interest rates were sufficiently low that business concerns were not as compelled to rely on reinvested earnings as industrial executives typically believed. Over and above these objective facts, however, there was also the crucial question of how entrepreneurs felt about these and many other matters—and the raising of this question was now understood to imply nothing whatsoever about the motives of businessmen.

On the other hand, while it had long since been agreed that the government must take a greater responsibility for the over-all performance of a modern economy than had historically been supposed, what was now becoming clear for the first time was that for this very reason business must also shoulder special burdens in the interest of greater economic stability. Precisely because the government must endeavor to keep the over-all economy on an even keel, coupled with the fact that these efforts can easily be sabotaged by business fears of intervention, an obvious requirement at such times is that conservatives take a realistic view of the need for government action. Not only, in other words, must government give businessmen the benefit of the doubt as to the motives behind their behavior, but businessmen must be similarly charitable about the motives of government.

Unfortunately, however, until these crucial understandings became far more general than was as yet the case, the impasse would remain as a self-reinforcing threat to the American economy. The poorer the economy's performance, the greater the responsibility that would have to be assumed by government; the greater the responsibility assumed by government, the poorer the economy's performance was likely to be. If (as seemed clearly to be the case) a majority of citizens believed that greater governmental responsibilities were either necessary or desirable under depression conditions, and if businessmen were inclined to react unfavorably to major extensions of government authority (which also now seemed quite evident), here was a politico-economic vicious circle from which there could be no easy escape.

TWILIGHT OF THE NEW DEAL

Of course the most desirable solution to this difficulty from the standpoint of the administration would have been for conservatives to revise drastically their ideas about the limits of government responsibility. But this was apparently not to be—at least not for the immediate future. And perhaps one of the principal reasons why this way out seemed so remote was that southerners were more and more seeing in the New Deal's emphasis upon human as contrasted with property rights a dangerous undermining of Dixie institutions. But this was only one of the factors involved. The painful truth was that, for a number of reasons, Congress was growing steadily more conservative—so much so that it was fast becoming obvious that a continuation of present trends would bring an end to reform activities long before conservatives became tolerant of this reform administration.

Perhaps the administration was at this point unduly concerned about its place in history, which was surely by now quite secure. In any event the President, as was his wont, met this new problem head-on. Arguing that if the voting public still had confidence in his leadership it should in the 1938 Congressional elections return Senators and Representatives more in tune with his philosophy, President Roosevelt campaigned actively against several incumbents in his own party. Whether the indifferent success accruing to this endeavor meant simply that the people were no longer willing to follow the administration down the reform road, or that the White House "purge" itself antagonized and frightened voters, is not easy to determine. Suffice it to say here only that because the President achieved so little along this line during that period the last two years of his second term were to add little to the New Deal's reform achievement.

Furthermore, what little was accomplished on this front was now still more directly continuous with the past rather than creatively new. Thus, as one example, the Wool Products Labeling Act was passed in 1939 giving the Federal Trade Commission special authority to eliminate misrepresentation of the wool content of most textile products. (Indeed, it may even stretch a point to refer to this as reform legislation at all, for its primary purpose was to protect wool and woolens producers from the competition of other fibers.)[27] The Investment Company and Investment Advisers acts in 1940 similarly built on old foundations. Here the Securities and Exchange Commission was given special powers to protect individuals doing business with either investment banks or investment trusts.

Still a third late New Deal development was a further lowering of the barriers against branch banking. For a long time the feeling had been growing that commercial banking decisions in this country were being made by too many people. To be sure, much had been done to correct this situation by arranging for a high degree of centralization through the Federal Reserve System. However, it was not felt that government centralization was the full answer to this problem, a conclusion especially prevalent in a Washington environment growing more conservative with every passing day. During the 1920's the first concession had been made when city-wide branch banking was first permitted for national banks. In 1940 the

[27] A. L. Edwards, *Product Standards and Labelling For Consumers* (New York: The Ronald Press Co., 1940).

next logical step was taken—the authorization of branch banking on a state-wide basis.

And finally, mention must be made of the Transportation Act of 1940, still another in the long series of enactments broadening the responsibilities of the Interstate Commerce Commission.[28] Two things primarily were accomplished by this law. First, the Commission was given regulatory authority over common and contract carriage by water in interstate commerce—the Maritime Commission losing in this process all regulatory powers except those exercised over carriers on the high seas. Second, the broad legislative policy by which the Commission was to be guided in its work was amended to take into account the addition of motor and water carriers to the list of Commission-regulated transportation agencies.[29]

It is hereby declared to be the national transportation policy of the Congress to provide for fair and impartial regulation of all modes of transportation subject to the provisions of this Act, so administered as to recognize and preserve the inherent advantages of each; to promote safe, adequate, economical, and efficient service and foster sound economic conditions in transportation and among the several carriers; to encourage the establishment and maintenance of reasonable charges for transportation services, without unjust discrimination, undue preferences or advantages, or unfair or destructive practices; to cooperate with the several States and duly authorized officials thereof; and to encourage fair wages and equitable working conditions;—all to the end of developing, coordinating and preserving a national transportation system by water, highway, and rail, as well as other means, adequate to meet the needs of the Commerce of the United States, of the Postal Service, and of the national defense. All of the provisions of this Act shall be administered and enforced with a view to carrying out the above declaration of policy.

It is a commonplace, although not less true because commonplace, that it was World War II which brought the United States out of the Great Depression. For that reason the nation was not at this time compelled to work through to a definitive settlement the most difficult problem which had emerged from that experience. But only a temporary stay was thus won; the economic policy impasse which had been reached did not thereby disappear. And when the military interruption was over some six years later, it returned with something akin to a vengeance—accentuated in intensity in part because it had persisted for so long.

[28] Federal Coordinator of Transportation, *Regulation of Transportation Agencies*, Senate Document 152, 73d Congress, 2d Session, 1934.

[29] C. L. Dearing and W. Owen, *National Transportation Policy* (Washington, D.C.: Brookings Institution, 1949); and C. S. Duncan, *A National Transportation Policy* (New York: Appleton-Century-Crofts, Inc., 1936).

QUESTIONS FOR DISCUSSION

1. Why did the New Deal lose momentum after 1936?
2. What factors precipitated the 1937-38 recession?
3. Why is stabilization policy in a modern exchange economy so difficult?
4. Was the Bituminous Coal Act of 1937 more of a "First New Deal" or a "Second New Deal" measure?
5. Explain the purpose and describe the provisions of the Miller-Tydings Act.
6. Is the conflict between consumers and sellers of foods and drugs really inherent? Explain.
7. Why is competition not an adequate protection for consumers in a modern industrial society?
8. What were the historical roots of the "Investigation of Concentration of Economic Power"?
9. State and evaluate the major assumptions behind the Temporary National Economic Committee episode. Why is this episode appropriately referred to as a strange interlude?
10. Explain the relationship between the "Battle of the Ph.D.'s" and the problem of the government's role in the functioning of the economy.
11. Did President Roosevelt stand to gain enough from a successful "purge" of conservative Democrats to make this a sound step to take? Explain.
12. By 1940 what industries were being regulated as public utility industries by the federal government?
13. Contrast the 1940 declaration of national transportation policy with that enunciated in 1933.
14. Putting yourself in the position of an ardent reformer in 1940, can you think of any area requiring reform which was not the subject of basic New Deal legislation?
15. To what extent was the "Second New Deal" a "labor" government?
16. How accurate do you think it is to say that between 1929 and 1940 laissez faire was replaced?

Chapter 25

War Takes Command

It was not an inept political judgment which led the President to base his claim to a vote of confidence in 1938 on reform grounds even after the nation's reform ardor had begun unmistakably to cool. The fact is that an incumbent administration must make a positive appeal of some kind, and, at the moment, reform seemed to be the only available possibility. To be sure, effective national defense in the face of a seriously deteriorating international situation could in theory have provided an acceptable substitute. But the President had for many months been endeavoring to shift policy emphasis in that direction, only to be met with a persistent public apathy making such a transition impossible. Not until after Hitler invaded Poland in September, 1939, did public sentiment become sufficiently aroused to permit President Roosevelt to begin relinquishing the political capital he had for some seven years been making out of institutional change.

A DEMOCRACY GOES TO WAR

It is temptingly easy to suppose that once a nation is confronted with a security crisis domestic animosities are at once forgotten and all energies promptly turned to the destruction of the common enemy. To a degree, moreover, this does explain what takes place in a society thus threatened. However, for two reasons so simple a description exaggerates the ease of the political adjustment of the United States to World War II. First, even though Germany, Italy, and Japan were all engaged in aggressive expansionism, there continued to be many Americans who insisted that the war had no real relevance for this country. Second, despite powerful motivations in the direction of full cooperation among all segments of society when external danger threatens, no important group will wholly disregard

524

the question of how the burdens imposed by war are to be allocated
—or how the fruits of victory will be distributed.

The passage of time alone sufficed to remedy the first of these
difficulties. As Hitler in quick succession invaded Scandinavia, over-
ran the Low Countries, prostrated France, and launched a war to
the death against Russia, and especially when Japan climaxed a long
series of belligerent moves in the Pacific with the attack on Pearl
Harbor, public indifference dramatically faded away. The second
problem, however, could only be resolved by the administration
itself. Slowly but surely the ruling power in Washington had become first and foremost a labor government. Before wholehearted
support from the rest of the community could be expected, other
groups would have to be assured of equitable treatment as to both
the sacrifices and the benefits of a major defense effort.

It cannot be said that the success with which the administration
undertook this task was due entirely to the political skill of the
President and those around him, for luck and a highly favorable
international environment no doubt also contributed. At the same
time, it can be asserted that this necessity was promptly recognized
and a campaign to meet it vigorously launched. The carrying out of
this project, the conversion of a government from a predominantly
labor orientation to a much broader base, constitutes one of the
most significant developments in the government–business field in
recent years.

A first obvious move on this front was to let it be known that
further reform endeavors were to be foresworn for the duration of
the defense emergency. The simplest way of accomplishing this
was to devote legislative and administrative energies exclusively to

TABLE 50. ABOUT FACE

Fiscal Year	Works Progress Administration Expenditures (millions of dollars)	War Department Expenditures
1939	2,162	490
1940	1,478	667
1941	1,285	3,636
1942	882	14,070

Source: Treasury Department.

the war production program. This the administration proceeded to
do so zealously that little doubt about its intentions could have
remained in any event. And when as a part of his second re-election

campaign the President symbolically proclaimed the replacement of "Dr. New Deal" with "Dr. Win-the-War," this first step could be chalked up as completed and completely successful.

But conservatives could scarcely afford to be content with the knowledge that the New Deal's reform program was no longer to be aggressively pressed.[1] Of equal importance was it to receive assurance that the government policies incident to the war effort would not run rough-shod over business interests. As early as September, 1939, a preliminary gesture in this direction was made by the administration. The first agency created for the purpose of assuming responsibility for mobilizing the nation's productive power (although the responsibility given this group was only the making of an over-all survey) was the so-called War Resources Board. At the head of this organization, with full freedom to choose his own associates, was placed Edward R. Stettinius, Jr.—a progressive business leader, to be sure, but one also closely connected with both the United States Steel Corporation and the House of Morgan.

Just what the President hoped to accomplish by this move cannot be known for certain. But that it far more than achieved whatever political purposes he had in mind is not to be doubted. On the one hand, big business was notified that it was not to be left out of the councils guiding the new economic orientation, and compelled as the price of being thus included to accept a large share of the responsibility for an internationalism not yet accepted by the voting public. On the other hand, the business community, momentarily drunk with its new prestige, embarked upon a pattern of behavior which could have had no other result than to humble its representatives in relationships with other important political groups.

What Stettinius did, no doubt after extensive collaboration with members of his own circle, was to select as co-workers on this first emergency agency five other conservatives. No one who could by any stretch of the imagination be thought of as a spokesman for either agriculture or labor was named. Of this incredibly naive blunder, this direct and overt confirmation of the New Deal accusation that businessmen were unable to think beyond the interests of their own class, there were two major consequences. First, the President was given an opportunity to abolish the War Resources Board and begin all over again the task of creating a defense production administration. Second, the next step in this evolution could

[1] Eliot Janeway, *The Struggle For Survival* (New Haven: Yale University Press, 1951).

be (and was) heavily weighted in the direction of other interests with far less protest than would otherwise have been possible.

From this point onward progress toward an administrative mechanism for giving over-all direction to war production having the broadest possible foundation out in society at large was slow but sure.[2] In the late spring of 1940 the National Defense Advisory Commission was created to take over this task where the War Resources Board had left off. At the head of that body was placed William S. Knudsen, another big business representative, and to assist him in various aspects of the task at hand two other business leaders were named (including Stettinius), together with an agricultural spokesman, a prominent labor leader, a New Deal administration man, and a woman to speak for both women and consumers. And when early in 1941 the requirements of the situation became more demanding, and in consequence authority had to be more concentrated, the Office of Production Management was created with only Knudsen and laborite Sidney Hillman sharing power at the top.

This process of broadening the political base of the nation's defense government can be seen also at the still higher level of party strategy as such. In mid-1940 President Roosevelt appointed to the position of Secretary of War Henry L. Stimson, a leading corporation lawyer from New York and an ex-Secretary of State and Secretary of War under Republican presidents, and to the position of Secretary of the Navy Frank Knox, a well-known newspaper publisher and the most prominent Republican in Illinois. In the face of these nods in the direction of conservatives as a group, the Republican party was hard put to find a suitable candidate to place in the field against Roosevelt in the fall of that year. When the best that they were able to do was Wendell Willkie—the conservative's hero of the battle against public power in the form of the Tennessee Valley Authority, but a man who could nonetheless find little to criticize from the standpoint of issues then current—they were doomed to another overwhelming defeat.

From another fundamental standpoint, the transition of the federal government from a labor-oriented New Deal to a war government for all the people is visible in a number of concrete policies adopted early in the defense effort. For example, when businessmen seemed reluctant to undertake expansion programs lest these new facilities become of no use before their cost had been recovered out

[2] Robert E. Sherwood, *Roosevelt and Hopkins* (New York: Harper & Bros., 1948).

of earnings, the government did not press for investment outlays backed by nothing more substantial than patriotism. On the one hand, many needed facilities were developed outright by the government (although typically then leased to private firms for operation), and many others were developed with the aid of government loans so written that the financial risk rested with the Treasury rather than the firms involved. On the other hand, plant capacity created specifically to take care of defense needs was permitted to be depreciated over a period of five years for income tax purposes (or the duration, whichever time period was shorter) rather than the much longer period ordinarily insisted upon. Furthermore, when an excess profits tax was enacted to keep profiteering to a minimum, a special provision was added permitting net profits to be averaged against net losses for tax computation purposes.

And finally, a preliminary glimpse at the balance struck between reformism and conservatism during the war years can be had by noting a few of the major implications for the United States of a war economy at this particular time. On the reform side the most fundamental fact was the speedy return of full employment, a de-

TABLE 51. END OF UNEMPLOYMENT

Year	Armed Services	Civilian Employment (millions of persons)	Unem- ployment
1940	0.4	47.5	8.1
1941	1.5	50.4	5.6
1942	3.8	53.8	2.7
1943	8.9	54.5	1.1
1944	11.3	54.0	0.7

Source: Department of Commerce.

velopment which went far toward creating directly the security the "Second New Deal" had been endeavoring with little success to bring about indirectly. On the conservative side, this same prosperity made the erstwhile ideological battle with the New Deal mainly academic. Moreover, the very nature of the controls exercised over an economy by the government during a modern war made it certain that (in World War II as in World War I) the administrative mechanism would in fact be controlled by businessmen. Indeed, the preference of procurement agencies for dealing with a few large concerns rather than a multitude of smaller ones (to say nothing of the outright granting of legal immunity from antitrust prosecution for cooperative endeavors "requisite to the prosecution of the war") even contributed to the concentration of economic power against which the New Deal had so lately declared open warfare[3]—and this despite thunderous verbal attacks on "creeping giantism" by the Department of Justice, broadly tolerated and perhaps actively encouraged by the President.[4]

AN ALPHABETICAL JUNGLE

This deliberate widening of the circle of interests participating in the administration's decision-making suggests one way in which World War II had a profound impact on business–government relationships. An equally important aspect of this development, however, is the process by which the government became not only a party to almost every economic transaction of consequence, but also a sort of super-entrepreneur itself creating in detail the environment within which every important business decision was made. World War II, far more than World War I, required a total effort by the United States, and the responsibility assumed by government was correspondingly more comprehensive.

There was of course no question that the government would need to supplement and often even supplant private enterprise decisions on a considerable scale.[5] A fundamental characteristic of a major war effort is a scarcity of almost everything, and it is therefore vitally important to make sure that first things are put first. Furthermore, this task cannot for a variety of reasons be left to the market mechanism. The price system brings about economic adjustments effectively under a wide range of circumstances, but it functions poorly when broad structural changes must be made in a short period of time. An even more telling consideration here is the fact that the values at stake in a war are values not readily reducible to dollars and cents terms. Thus, although it is equally essential not to try to do away with the price mechanism entirely, the decision to fight could only mean an expansion of government responsibilities to an extent never before experienced by Americans.

This phenomenon of a government-directed economy did not arise at once.[6] For one thing, a full understanding of the effort which

[3] Smaller War Plants Corporation, *Economic Concentration and World War II* (Washington, D.C.: Government Printing Office, 1946).

[4] Thurman Arnold, *Bottlenecks of Business* (New York: Reynal & Hitchcock, 1940).

[5] L. V. Chandler and D. H. Wallace, *Economic Mobilization and Stabilization* (New York: Henry Holt & Co., Inc., 1951).

[6] Civilian Production Administration, *Industrial Mobilization For War* (Washington, D.C.: Government Printing Office, 1947).

would ultimately be demanded could not in any event have developed except as prompted by the unfolding of events abroad. For another, powerful vested interests form behind the idea of "business as usual," interests which refuse to be dislodged except as compelled to do so by the sheer force of circumstances. And for still another, the conversion of an economy from peace to war production can proceed a little farther without government interference when commenced with a considerable reserve of idle resources (although it was startling how quickly bottlenecks began to develop even in an economy as seriously underemployed as the United States was at the outbreak of World War II). But as the need did arise, as more and more people in leadership positions recognized that need, and as the approach to full employment made it frustratingly apparent that total war requires more of practically everything than can be produced, a nation already accustomed to the proliferation of government agencies brought about by the Great Depression was again bewildered by the mushroom growth of new alphabetical organizations.[7]

The War Resources Board episode, it is of interest to note, took place even before Hitler invaded Poland. This early, in other words, did the United States officially determine that unsettled conditions abroad contained some threat to this country. Also significant, however, is the fact that this debacle was not corrected until after the "phony war" (the so-called "Sitzkrieg") during the winter of 1939-40 had erupted into a series of major moves by Germany climaxing with the fall of France. At this point the National Defense Advisory Commission was created, empowered to do something more than study the situation but as yet without power actually to direct economic activity. Its primary method of operation was to secure industry cooperation with respect to the most important next steps through moral suasion backed by the prestige of the federal government and its own membership.

It was at this point too that several other basic steps were taken. During the last half of 1940 the wheels were first set in motion to create a tax structure more appropriate to a defense economy. On July 25 the Rubber Reserve Company and the Metals Reserve Company were organized as subsidiaries of the Reconstruction Finance Corporation for the purpose of acquiring a stockpile of rubber, tin, and other metals vital to an expanded program of war production. One month later the Defense Plant Corporation, another Recon-

[7] John R. Craf, *A Survey of the American Economy, 1940-1946* (New York: North River Press, 1947).

struction Finance Corporation subsidiary, was set up to build and own defense plants which could not conveniently be financed in other ways. In late August also the Reconstruction Finance Corporation established the Defense Supplies Corporation, an agency commissioned primarily to take whatever actions were deemed necessary in making a long list of critical and strategic materials more readily available. (It is to be noted, incidentally, that in all more than 100 new government corporations were created to assist with various phases of the war emergency.)

Thus far virtually everything that had been done had proceeded on the assumption that few if any sacrifices would actually be required. By late 1940, however, despite the fact that there were still some 9,000,000 people unemployed, the "guns *and* butter" emphasis which had to date characterized the preparedness effort was beginning to run into difficulty.[8] Already it was apparent that choices

TABLE 52. "THE MIRACLE OF PRODUCTION"

Year	Ships Constructed	Automobile Production (millions)	Aircraft Production (thousands)
1940	319	3.7	12.8
1941	703	3.8	26.3
1942	1,108	0.2	47.8
1943	1,901	—	85.9
1944	1,723	—	96.3

Source: Bureau of the Census, *Historical Statistics of the United States, 1789-1945*, pp. 211, 223, and 224.

would have to be made between the civilian and defense economies —and even between various parts of the defense program itself. Indicative of this development was the creation on August 28, 1940, of the Supply Priorities and Allocations Board. At once more specialized and more concrete in its responsibilities than any agency yet created, this body—although still lacking the statutory authority to function as effectively as many would have liked—was asked to determine policies and make regulations governing allocations and priorities with respect to the procurement, production, or transportation of any and all commodities important to the nation's security.

Against the background of Hitler's all-out bombing of Britain preparatory to invasion, the pace at which the government was closing in on normal business operations was greatly accelerated.[9] On Jan-

[8] Office For Emergency Management, *Conversion: America's Job* (Washington, D.C.: Government Printing Office, 1942).

[9] Bureau of the Budget, *The United States at War* (Washington, D.C.: Government Printing Office, 1947).

uary 7, 1941, the National Defense Advisory Commission was replaced by the Office of Production Management. Here the specialization theme a little later to be such an important characteristic of the war administration was still more apparent. Three operating divisions within this new organization were initially specified in the Executive Order creating it—production, priorities, and purchases—and other sub-groups (such as materials, labor, contract distribution, and civilian supply) were administratively added later.

Prior to this no great concern had been expressed about the problem of inflation, although it was understood that the more nearly the economy approached full employment the more critical would that matter become. By the spring of 1941, however, it was agreed by the nation's policy-makers that the time had come to commence action on this front. Thus it was that on April 11 there was created the first specialized agency for dealing with prices, the Office of Price Administration, another government body expected to achieve great things despite the almost complete absence of statutory authority.

So abruptly did the war effort of the United States become all-important after the surprise attack by the Japanese that it is often overlooked how far along the preparedness road the nation already was. The fact is that even before priorities, conservation measures, and maximum price orders became legal in the technical sense they were becoming an integral part of American economic life—this development roughly coinciding with Germany's first great push into Russia. Indeed, it would exaggerate little to suggest that the most important single consequence of America's declaration of war was the availability from that point forward of all the statutory power needed to enable the government to impose its will upon private enterprise wherever necessary—which was virtually everywhere.

The attack on Pearl Harbor came on December 7, 1941. Of course, the alphabetical jungle brought about by the war then became even thicker, and this despite the fact that "old-line" government agencies were now especially turned to the service of a nation fighting for its very existence. The first post-Pearl Harbor agency of major importance to businessmen was the Board of Economic Warfare established on December 17. As one approach to the grave necessity of putting all resources to the most helpful use, this body was given the responsibility of supervising both export and import activities to make sure that these transactions best served the war program.

On the following day the tremendous strain an all-out war would put on the nation's transportation facilities was recognized by the creation of the Office of Defense Transportation. Speaking broadly, the task of this agency was to devise and implement plans to make the transportation resources available adequate to the demands being made upon them. In the event, however, the largest share of this body's energies was absorbed in the motor transportation field —both because of the grave shortage of rubber, and because the supply of trucks, buses, and taxicabs could not be significantly increased.

The War Production Board, successor to all agencies heretofore charged with the responsibility of facilitating production, came into existence January 7, 1942.[10] Here was what might appropriately be called the nervous system of the wartime control network. The crucial position held by this agency can best be visualized by noting that at the height of its power and influence, through the so-called Controlled Materials Plan, it supervised the use of virtually every pound of steel, copper, and aluminum used in the entire economy. On the assumption that other materials could be made to go as far as these items, they were made the focal point for most decisions involving priorities and allocations. And the implication of this, of course, was that everyone using any significant quantity of one of these products had to secure approval for that use from the War Production Board —and the control exercised over a long list of other critical and strategic materials was only somewhat less complete.[11]

On January 12, the War Labor Board began its active and controversial career. Both labor and management had given their pledge that war production would not be halted on account of labor disputes, but it was nonetheless deemed wise to keep this problem under surveillance. This Board, therefore, was granted power to "finally determine all controversies which might interrupt work which contributes to the effective prosecution of the war." With such a charge, and with a membership consisting of two Congress of Industrial Organizations representatives, two American Federation of Labor spokesmen, four representatives from management, and four members representing the general public, it was a foregone conclusion that this agency would have a hectic existence. But even more important is the fact that it did an effective work—considering the odds against which it struggled.

[10] Donald M. Nelson, *Arsenal of Democracy* (New York: Harcourt, Brace & Co., Inc., 1946).

[11] D. Novick, M. Anshen, and W. C. Truppner, *Wartime Production Controls* (New York: Columbia University Press, 1949).

Operating also in the labor field, although in a fundamentally different way, was the War Manpower Commission. Here the emphasis was upon assisting the transfer of workers from less essential to more essential areas of the economy (and, conversely, preventing movements in the opposite direction) insofar as wage differentials alone could not achieve the desired results. A number of devices were employed to accomplish this tremendous task—these including the Selective Service System, the United States Employment Service, and the so-called National Roster of Scientific and Professional Personnel. Limited though it was by dependence upon voluntary cooperation, this agency nevertheless gave a good account of itself before the war ended—and in the process became intricately enmeshed in ordinary business operations.

Because of the vital importance of food both to America and to her allies, the production and allocation of this resource was next made the responsibility of a separate agency. At first this work was delegated to the Department of Agriculture, but a little later the War Food Administration was created for that purpose. Shipping and shipbuilding was another critical area in view of the gigantic task of adequately supplying, in addition to critical needs within the domestic economy, the armed services and our Allies in Europe and in the Pacific simultaneously. Here the Maritime Commission was retained as the principal shipbuilding agency, but a new group was designated to be responsible for the most effective operation of vessels on the high seas. Established February 7, the War Shipping Administration for many months supervised the use of every vessel in the American merchant fleet except those operating exclusively on the Great Lakes.

To provide the housing required by war production workers, as well as to better coordinate the efforts of all federal agencies in the housing field, the National Housing Agency was organized on February 24. A Smaller War Plants Corporation was created in June to help smaller businesses secure war contracts, to assist larger firms to broaden the base of their subcontract network, and to loan money to smaller concerns to enable them more effectively to participate in war work. In September the rubber situation became so dangerous that a specialized agency—the Office of Rubber Director—was formed to take the leading part in the making of a number of important decisions involving that product, and in the ensuing months both a Petroleum Administration for War and a Solid Fuels Administration were established to perform a similar function for oil and coal.

Fight Against Inflation[12]

This account of the ways in which the government extended its influence to the most remote corners of the economy is of course illustrative only. None but the most important agencies could, in so brief an account, even be mentioned, and in no case could details of the evolution of policy or of operation be included. A more concrete picture of this phenomenon, therefore, may be had from a microscopic-type survey of one basic part of this control program. In part because of the drama inherent in the regulation of prices, and in part because of the special relevance of that program to the problem of postwar readjustment, the area which might most appropriately be subjected to intensive scrutiny is the struggle to keep the price level within bounds.

The control of inflation during wartime serves a variety of purposes. Thus supervision at this point will help minimize the monetary cost of war and hence ease the financial problem associated with it. Price control can also aid a war effort in a more direct way, by removing the incentive producers under government contract would otherwise have to hoard vital materials which might soon go up in price. Probably more important than either of these functions, however, is the need to distribute the burdens of war as equitably as possible. (And it might parenthetically be added that this relationship operates also in reverse; little success is apt to be achieved in the control of prices except as the burdens involved are equitably distributed.) Maximum production depends upon the unstinting cooperation of millions of individuals, and the incentive for such cooperation is vulnerable to feelings that the socio-political environment is biased.

Prior to Pearl Harbor the price problem was not confronted on any over-all basis. Specific maximum price orders had been issued whenever a bottleneck situation developed, this approach proving to be reasonably satisfactory until a large proportion of the slack in the system had been taken up and government deficit spending reached astronomical figures. How sporadic this early effort was can be seen in the fact that no attempt whatever was made at this time to control prices at the retail level.

By early 1942, however, it was apparent that an attack on inflation on a much broader front would be required. Accordingly, on January 30 the Emergency Price Control Act was passed, giving

[12] Seymour Harris, *Price and Related Controls in the United States* (New York: McGraw-Hill Book Co., Inc., 1945).

the Office of Price Administration extensive powers to keep the wartime price level in hand.

There were many who argued that this first serious attempt to control prices during World War II was a typical "Second New Deal" performance. Superficially, furthermore, a case can be made in support of that proposition. Control of wages was not explicitly demanded, and farm prices were specifically not to be checked until they were 10 per cent above parity.

But this analysis takes an unduly narrow view of the complexities of managing an economy engaged in total war. Thus from the standpoint of equity it can not readily be maintained that this legislation was discriminatory. With a rapidly swelling flood of purchasing power generated by the government literally exploding throughout the economy, businessmen were not prevented from profiting from the war expansion by ceilings on their own prices in the face of a steady rise in wages and the prices of farm products. In fact, it could

TABLE 53. PRICE CONTROL PROBLEM

Year	National Defense Expenditures (billions)	Price Indexes	
		Wholesale	Consumer
		(1947-1949 = 100)	
1940	$ 1.7	51.1	59.9
1941	6.1	56.8	62.9
1942	26.0	64.2	69.7
1943	72.1	67.0	74.0

Source: Treasury Department and Department of Labor.

more convincingly be argued that higher wages and farm prices were necessary to balance off the greater volume of goods businessmen would now be able to sell. And with respect to the prices of agricultural products especially, to tell the farmer he must be content with parity or less after he had suffered from chronic depression for some twenty years was scarcely an obvious move.

A more serious criticism levelled at this January 30 enactment was that with such major gaps in coverage it could not effectively control inflation. This was true enough—as far as it went. But here again certain of the complexities involved make it necessary to qualify the accusation derived from this statement of fact. As far as wages were concerned, with 4,000,000 persons still unemployed and the necessity of making many employment adjustments which would be greatly facilitated by wage flexibility, the case for tight wage controls this early in the war effort was by no means compelling. Nor was the case for stringent farm price controls at this point any more clear-cut. Because agricultural output does not respond readily to an increase in demand the prices of these products are placed under a particularly intense inflationary pressure at the outbreak of a war, and it was therefore not simply foolish to let more of this pressure spend itself before endeavoring to bottle it up.

In short, a step only had been taken, one which would require supplementation after the process of conversion had advanced several more strides. Greater sales volume would not indefinitely permit business concerns to absorb cost increases without injury, whereas the need for internal flexibility would grow less and less important as the conversion process moved toward completion. The only question, thus, was how long this problem could be dealt with in so loose a fashion.

During the first few months of 1942 the over-all index of prices rose more than 2 per cent per month, a rate which if continued would have approximately doubled the price level in three years. Believing that the time had come to tighten up on this front, the President on April 27 outlined a comprehensive anti-inflation program and demanded prompt action with respect thereto.

The first response to this appeal came from the Office of Price Administration. Although prior to this retail prices had been subject to virtually no controls, that situation was now abruptly ended by the issuance of the famous General Maximum Price Regulation. Under this order the highest price charged during the preceding month was made the legal maximum price for nearly everything purchased by ultimate consumers. Simultaneously more than 300 defense areas (later broadened to include the entire nation) were designated as critical from the standpoint of housing and rentals therein frozen.

Of course the decision to control prices carried with it the need to ration important items available in insufficient quantity to satisfy demand at artificially low prices.[13] The alternative was to allocate scarce goods on a first-come-first-served basis, and a surer way to injure a war effort either directly or by way of civilian morale would be difficult to devise. Before this part of the control ordeal was over, the Office of Price Administration had created an administrative framework for rationing which included 8,000 local rationing boards.

[13] Victor A. Thompson, *The Regulatory Process in OPA Rationing* (New York: King's Crown Press, 1950).

A third concrete step toward inflation control was taken on May 6, when the Board of Governors tightened consumer credit controls—although an unprecedented flow of cash income generated by the government's procurement program made this move less effective than was perhaps hoped. Two months later, on July 16, it having been determined that the time had come to call a halt to the sabotage of price control through wage inflation, still another skirmish in this campaign was blueprinted. Under the terms of its famous "Little Steel Formula," the War Labor Board decreed that hourly wage rate increases would not be permitted beyond those necessary to match the rise in the cost of living since Pearl Harbor. To be sure, this prohibition was not completely airtight; among other things, exceptions were allowed for the purpose of correcting serious inequities. Furthermore, the use of hourly wages as the unit of comparison, rather than weekly earnings, was highly favorable to workers under war conditions. But despite these "loop-holes," July 16 was recognized as marking a genuine turning point in the battle against inflation.

On October 2 the screws were tightened still further. Apparently feeling that limitations on wage increases should be accompanied by similar controls over farm prices, the President demanded a strengthening of the statutory power then available to him in this field. The result was the Stabilization Act, the most important provision of which was the stipulation that in the case of both wages and the prices of agricultural products the highest prices to date were made the maximum permissible by law. Although a limited administrative discretion was still retained by both the War Food Administration and the War Labor Board, and although prices in both of these categories had already risen sharply, this was nonetheless a stringent measure.

As an indication of how delicate the political balance was now becoming, President Roosevelt also took the drastic step on October 3 of creating a super-agency called the Office of Economic Stabilization whose major responsibility was to settle disputes arising between agencies—including disputes in the price control field. But even with this innovation the price "freeze" was somewhat less rigorous than appears on the surface. Several exceptions still continued to be the law of the land, chief of these being high farm price guarantees where necessary to increase production vitally needed for the war effort—despite the fact that most farmers were in fact already receiving the 110 per cent of parity stipulated earlier. At the same time, however, this steadily increasing firmness did stand as a terse reminder to the nation of the administration's determination to keep a heavy hand on this throttle.

At this point only one more step remained to be taken on the price control front. To whatever extent people could be induced not to spend the purchasing power the war economy was so abundantly generating, the price control problem would obviously be to that extent relieved. One way in which this could be accomplished was to

TABLE 54. FINANCING TOTAL WAR

Year	Domestic Investment	Personal Saving	National Debt	National Debt Held by Banks
			(billions of dollars)	
1940	13.9	3.7	50.9	19.5
1941	18.3	9.8	64.3	23.7
1942	10.9	25.6	112.5	47.3
1943	5.7	30.2	170.1	61.4
1944	7.7	35.4	232.1	96.5
1945	10.7	28.0	278.7	115.1

Source: Department of Commerce and Treasury Department.

compel citizens to part with purchasing power by taxing it away from them. And although there were many who argued that far too little was done along this line, it is nonetheless true that in 1942 there was passed "the greatest tax bill in history" (including income tax rates even more steeply progressive than in the late 1930's) and that vast sums of money were taken away from citizens in this way. Moreover, heavy taxation was broadly supplemented by voluntary saving—another technique for keeping the level of spending well below the level of available purchasing power. Never have the American people been so willing (eager?) to accumulate liquid assets. Whether this was primarily the result of patriotism, or of the success with which prices were in fact controlled, or of the scarcity of consumer durable goods, the fact remains that it greatly assisted the fight against a dangerous upward price spiral.

With a single exception, these developments in 1942 completed the list of major episodes associated with this phase of the World War II period. April, 1943, saw labor growing restive as the cost of living continued to inch upward, and it was determined in Washington that an even more decisive action should be taken. Accordingly, on April 8 the President issued his celebrated "Hold-the-Line" order, requesting all price control administrators virtually to abandon the use of discretion with respect to price increases. At the same time a subsidy program was inaugurated under which processors of meat, milk, bread, coffee, butter, sugar, and certain other food items were reimbursed by the government for the expense involved in not passing cost increases along to consumers in the form of higher prices.

Between the "Hold-the-Line" order and the end of the war, roughly two years, the cost of living in the United States rose only 2 per cent. By any standard this was a remarkable achievement. No doubt a number of factors in addition to the control program as such helped to make this achievement possible. High on such a list of course would be the tremendous productive power of the American economy, the fact that the farmers' parity ratio trended slightly downward from mid-1943 onward, and the high level of patriotic fervor prevailing throughout the war period. But with all these factors, it is still a tribute to the statesmanship of Franklin Delano Roosevelt that he was able to abandon New Deal partisanship sufficiently to achieve this kind of a balance among normally antagonistic forces.

TABLE 55. PROSPERITY FOR EVERYONE

Year	Farmers' Parity Ratio (1910-1914 = 100)	Factory Weekly Earnings	Corporate Profits (billions)
1940	80	$25.20	$ 2.9
1941	94	29.58	7.8
1942	106	36.65	11.7
1943	119	43.14	14.4
1944	116	46.08	13.5

Source: Departments of Agriculture, Labor, and Commerce.

AND THE BAND PLAYED ON

While it is true that many and certainly the most important developments in the field of government–business relationships during these years arose directly out of the war effort, it does not follow that World War II saw the continuity of economic evolution on this front completely broken. The fact is that during this period a number of significant steps were taken in this field which had little connection with the war as such.

The first item in this category was the achievement by labor of the crowning success of a full decade studded with dramatic successes.[14]

[14] Glenn W. Miller, *American Labor and the Government* (Englewood Cliffs, N.J.: Prentice-Hall, Inc., 1948).

For almost half a century now, labor organizations had been seeking immunity under the nation's antitrust laws. At one point, moreover, sufficient pressure had been exerted on Congress to secure the passage of a law designed to meet this worker demand. But in the frustrating sequel to that accomplishment the judiciary had seen fit to exercise a veto which robbed this exemption of most of its effectiveness.

No legislation remedying this situation was ever made a major part of the program of the New Deal—although it is clear that the reason for this omission was not a lack of sympathy with labor's desires at this point. Rather it was apparently felt that existing legislation was adequate, that what the courts had done the courts would have to undo. Stated differently, further progress was made dependent upon getting on the bench men whose thinking was more in tune with that of the voting public.

Simultaneously with the beginning of serious defense preparations, the judicial victory won by the President began to bear fruit on this front. A suit against a union asking for treble damages under the Sherman Act was in 1940 decided in favor of labor. Despite the fact that some 80 per cent of the output of the company involved moved in interstate commerce, the Supreme Court in a 6-3 decision refused to find the union guilty.[15] Said Justice Stone on this occasion:

The Sherman Act was directed only at those restraints whose evil consequences are derived from the suppression of competition in the interstate market, so as "to monopolize" the supply, control its price, or discriminate between its would-be purchasers.

The following year the Court went even farther in a case involving a strike at the Anheuser-Busch brewery in St. Louis.[16] This time it was Justice Frankfurter who enunciated the Court's philosophy:

So long as a union acts in its self-interest and does not combine with non-labor groups, the licit and the illicit . . . are not to be distinguished by any judgments regarding the wisdom or unwisdom, the rightness or wrongness, the selfishness or unselfishness of the end of which the particular union activities are the means.

It cannot of course be known for certain just how far Congress had intended to go in the antitrust exemption written into the Clayton Act. Surely it is not to be doubted, however, that it meant to go farther than the Supreme Court of the 1920's permitted. But on the

---

[15] *Apex Hosiery Company* v. *Leader,* 310 U.S. 469 (1940).
[16] *United States* v. *Hutcheson,* 312 U.S. 219 (1941).

other hand, it can also be plausibly argued that Congress' intention had not been to write so sweeping a protection as the Roosevelt Court insisted—a proposition to which many students of this subject still subscribe. Perhaps, though, the point most worth noting is that since 1941 Congress has had every opportunity to set this record straight, but that it has instead been allowed to stand.

A second wartime but nonwar development was in the field of telegraph communication. Prior to 1943 this industry had been composed of two concerns, Western Union and Postal Telegraph, with the former enjoying substantial advantages over its rival. It and it alone operated the stock market ticker service, and it also had exclusive rights to the use of railroad facilities in performing its responsibilities. But even with these advantages Western Union was barely able to earn a fair return for investors (and certain of its exclusive arrangements were also under attack by the Justice Department), while Postal Telegraph was currently in receivership. As a partial solution at least to a number of difficult problems, the Federal Communications Commission recommended that these firms be allowed to merge. At the very peak of the war production effort, Congress enacted the necessary enabling legislation and this combination was promptly effected.

Unfortunately, the primary problem of this industry remains.[17] The telegraph business is being subjected to a more and more vigorous competition from other communication media—such as air mail, two-way communication, and teletype. Partly as a result of this intense competition Western Union's equipment has not kept pace with technological advance and its service consequently leaves much to be desired, these shortcomings in turn accentuating its financial problem. Furthermore, although some three-fourths of the company's income comes from its operations in 150 cities, it is still compelled to maintain service in 4,000 smaller places where operations are typically carried on at a loss. What the next steps for this public utility are to be cannot accurately be predicted, but it has become increasingly clear that some are in the offing.

Two other developments during this period involved public utility industries. In the first place the generation and distribution of public power was given a tremendous impetus.[18] On the one hand, not only did the demand for power grow by leaps and bounds with the return

[17] President's Communications Policy Board, *Telecommunications: A Program For Progress* (Washington, D.C.: Government Printing Office, 1951).

[18] Twentieth Century Fund, *The Power Industry and the Public Interest* (New York: Twentieth Century Fund, Inc., 1944).

to full employment, and with it the demands made on those facilities in public hands, but in the absence of the generating plants recently erected at government expense electric power might easily have been one of the critical wartime shortages. In short, by its contribution to the war effort, public power so to speak "won its spurs" in the public mind. And although this result in one important sense did relate to the war as such, it can also appropriately be thought of in terms of the growth in power consumption in public power areas which would have accompanied the return of prosperity and economic expansion in any event.

Nor, on the other hand, was the development of facilities already in existence the only victory achieved by public power at this time. In addition, a huge and basically new endeavor comparable with the Tennessee Valley Authority was commenced. This was a comprehensive plan for the development of the Missouri River Basin prepared jointly by the Corps of Army Engineers and the Bureau of Reclamation and enacted into law in the Flood Control Act of 1944. Involved were 138 major projects for hydroelectric power, flood control, and irrigation, including five large dams, hundreds of smaller dams, 1,500 miles of levees, plus innumerable navigation, recreation, conservation, public health, and other facilities. Repeatedly since 1944 a Missouri Valley Authority more adequately to coordinate these far-flung responsibilities has been proposed, but to date opposition from public power opponents and states jealous of their own sovereignty have succeeded in thwarting this step.

In the second place, significant progress was made during these years in the field of public utility regulation. The recently revitalized Federal Power Commission had tackled the responsibilities placed upon it competently as well as enthusiastically. Although focusing its primary attention upon those concerns and those activities it was required by law to supervise most directly, the Commission was nonetheless not unmindful of the services a strong federal regulatory body might perform in strengthening the work of state commissions.[19] Particularly was this group aware of the problem that had been introduced into utility regulation by judicial insistence upon the fair value criterion for judgments about rate reasonableness.

Almost immediately the Federal Power Commission in effect declared war on this doctrine—by the simple expedient of ignoring it and then defending that procedure in the courts. The first major test of the new approach came in 1942. Although the issue was not

[19] Robert D. Baum, *The Federal Power Commission and State Utility Regulation* (Washington, D.C.: American Council on Public Affairs, 1942).

sharply raised, and although the Supreme Court did not yet unequivocally abandon the *Smyth* v. *Ames* rule, in rejecting the company's contention that an amortization allowance for wasting gas reserves should be based on "present value" the Court said:[20]

The Constitution does not bind rate-making bodies to the service of any single formula or combination of formulas. Agencies to whom this legislative power has been delegated are free, within the ambit of their statutory authority, to make the pragmatic adjustments which may be called for by particular circumstances.

But if the Court in 1942 was unwilling explicitly to repudiate this ancient precedent, that tenderness did not long stand in the way. Two years later a Commission valuation based on "actual legitimate cost" came before the Supreme Court. Emphatically reiterating what it had said two years earlier, and accepting a responsibility for the judicial self-restraint public utility students had long been demanding, this body now went further as follows:[21]

. . . And when the Commission's order is challenged in the courts, the question is whether that order "viewed in its entirety" meets the requirements of the Act. . . . Under the statutory standard of "just and reasonable" it is the result reached not the method employed which is controlling. . . . It is not the theory but the impact of the rate order which counts. If the total effect of the rate order cannot be said to be unjust and unreasonable, judicial inquiry under the act is at an end.

And with these words, the ghost of *Smyth* v. *Ames* was laid to rest—perhaps forever.[22]

It was during these years, too, that regulation of the air waves by the Federal Communications Commission took on at least a semblance of maturity. At first this work had been all but overwhelmed by the sheer mechanical details of allocating air space among a multitude of rival claimants. After this pressure began to taper off somewhat, however, time and energy could more generously be devoted to certain broad policy questions.[23]

One such question was whether local radio stations were to be granted exclusive rights to broadcast in their own locality, an issue the Commission settled in the negative with the full approval of the

[20] *Federal Power Commission* v. *Natural Gas Pipeline Company of America*, 315 U.S. 575 (1942).

[21] *Federal Power Commission* v. *Hope Natural Gas Company*, 320 U.S. 591 (1944).

[22] John Bauer, *Transforming Public Utility Regulation: A Definite Administrative Program* (New York: Harper & Bros., 1950).

[23] Charles A. Siepman, *Radio, Television, and Society* (New York: Oxford University Press, 1950).

Supreme Court.[24] A second was the extent to which this body would concern itself with the control of radio by the major networks. This decision was to assume considerable responsibility—not only in the form of a set of rules governing relationships between networks and stations, but also by compelling the National Broadcasting Company to dispose of its so-called "Blue Network" thus bringing to this field a more open competitive situation. Here too, incidentally, a nudge from the Supreme Court was necessary to make these new rules of the game "stick."[25]

A third problem raised in this area had to do with Commission jurisdiction over program content. Although that agency is specifically forbidden to censor the broadcasting industry, it is required to develop public interest concepts relative to the granting and renewal of licenses. In general the Commission has moved hesitantly with respect to this issue. Beyond establishing a few broad rules of fair play, it has left licensees to their own consciences in serving the public. In 1946 a special report was issued complaining that program content often does not correspond closely with the promises made when licenses are applied for, but even here it was decided that the power to revoke licenses alone was too blunt an instrument for successful use in combating this difficulty.

And finally it was at this time that the Federal Communications Commission first began to grapple with a responsibility which gives it a unique position among regulatory agencies—the need to supervise the rate of technical change. Television was just becoming commercially feasible, and the Commission's task of allocating air space to the new medium would of course be a decisive factor in this development. Actually at this point the war effort so delayed the need for major decisions that the Commission did not become a bottleneck, and it was not therefore until the arrival of color television that this body found itself caught in the middle of a technological tug-of-war. Even here the requirements of war (the Korean conflict) ultimately saved the day, with the result that the Commission's first 20 years of existence saw a fabulous advance in the science of air broadcasting which its activities had done little if anything to retard.

Still another important item in the evolution of government–business relationships during World War II was the abandonment of an innovation the "Second New Deal" had worked particularly hard to bring about—the Bituminous Coal Commission. The insatiable de-

24 *Federal Communications Commission v. Sanders Brothers Radio Stations,* 309 U.S. 470 (1940).
25 *National Broadcasting Company v. United States,* 319 U.S. 190 (1943).

mand of the war economy for power soon converted that industry from a condition of painful surplus to one of exasperating scarcity. With this transformation prices rose, ruinous competition became a thing of the past, and reasonably favorable wages and working conditions were no longer dependent upon the holding of a regulatory umbrella over the industry. Then, because both labor and management had from the outset considered the Commission a necessary evil, advantage was taken of the new situation to step out from under this network of regimentation—and after World War II as after World War I the soft coal industry was thereby committed to make its postwar adjustments on a more or less laissez faire basis.

As this industry successfully reduced the role of government in its operation, however, two other industries were now becoming more deeply enmeshed in the regulatory network. One of these was the insurance industry; the other was the pipeline end of the petroleum industry.

For some thirty years now the right of the states to regulate insurance company rates had been an accepted fact. In actual practice, however, very little had yet been done in that field. So lax were most state laws that quite typically insurance rates were set by "rate bureaus" composed of representatives of a number of competing firms with little or no supervision by state officials.

This comfortable equilibrium was in 1944 abruptly shattered when the Supreme Court, reversing an earlier decision of 75 years' standing, ruled that insurance was commerce.[26] The most important immediate result of this reversal was to make insurance companies liable to prosecution under the Sherman Act. For a time there was serious thought of establishing a new equilibrium by placing the larger insurance companies under federal control, but, as perhaps an indication of the decline in New Deal sentiment in Washington the decision was made instead that the federal government bow out in favor of state regulation. This was done in the McCarran Act of 1945. Under this enactment the antitrust laws were to be held in abeyance for insurance companies for a transition period of three years, after which time they were to become operative only "to the extent that such business is not regulated by state laws." Although this solution did, as intended, cause the enactment of more rigorous statutes in all states having any considerable insurance business, it cannot be said that that industry is yet controlled as conscientiously as the local utility industries.

Prior to World War II the Interstate Commerce Commission had

[26] *United States* v. *Southeastern Underwriters' Association*, 322 U.S. 533 (1944).

done little about regulating oil pipeline transportation in the public interest. It had, to be sure, reduced minimum tender requirements on two different occasions. In the middle of the 1930's, furthermore, it found in the course of an investigation of this business that the rates of 21 companies were excessive—with the result that most of these concerns reduced their charges. Because, however, there was in all of this no serious attempt to hold earnings in that field to a fair return, the Department of Justice in 1941 brought suit against the major integrated companies charging that the receipt of dividends from pipeline operations constituted acceptance of rebates in violation of the Elkins Act. This proceeding was concluded a little later when the companies involved accepted a consent decree in which they agreed to restrict dividends to 7 per cent of the valuation of pipeline properties—in this way largely eliminating the incentive to charge high rates.

One other matter of some importance made the transition from debate to decision during the war. With the mushroom growth of new government agencies possessing substantial powers over persons and property, there naturally arose a great deal of criticism of their operation.[27] Much of this antagonism, of course, reflected only the resistance of vested interests to new controls, but important questions of principle were also being raised. As a relatively new government institution, the administrative (quasi-legislative, quasi-judicial) agency had to be fitted into the American system in such a way that cherished individual rights were not neglected in the process. To be sure, much water had gone over this dam since the creation of the Interstate Commerce Commission, and indeed that body's procedure was in many respects adopted as a model for the legislation on this subject soon to be enacted. But it was nonetheless thought to be important to formalize the procedural due process requirements of these agencies—if only to make them more uniform from one to another.

Several types of situations will illustrate the problem now rising to the forefront of public attention. First, although from the beginning persons whose lives and property placed in jeopardy by a commission action had been entitled to a hearing before that action was taken, the hearing process itself was found to be so expensive and so cumbersome that principles were required setting limits to the kinds of proceedings which had to involve this step. Second, where hearings are to be held there seemed to be a need for a generalized state-

27 J. M. Landis, *The Administrative Process* (New Haven: Yale University Press, 1938).

ment as to what should be considered due notice to those having a right to be heard. And third, because the burden of work in many administrative agencies was so great that a degree of delegation of top-level responsibility was indicated, principles had to be worked out determining when a hearing might be conducted by a Civil Service Examiner rather than an appointed policy-making official without endangering fundamental rights.

Work on legislation setting forth minimum requirements in this area went through a number of stages. The first was the work of the President's Committee on Administrative Management which made its ground-breaking report in 1937. Next the problem was turned over to the Attorney-General's Committee on Administrative Procedure for study, this group concluding its labors in 1940–41 with the publication of a series of studies on the work of the major administrative bodies.[28] Meanwhile, however, a number of interests had grown impatient, and had banded together to pass the so-called Walter-Logan bill in 1940. This first attempt at formulating the principles henceforth to govern in this field ended when the President sent this measure back to Congress without his signature. The President felt on the one hand that legislation was inappropriate while the problem was still under study by the Attorney-General's Committee. Still more important, on the other hand, it was his (undoubtedly quite accurate) conviction that this bill was motivated more by a desire to thwart the work of administrative bodies than by an interest in their more effective functioning. At that point this issue became so overshadowed by the war that it was all but abandoned, and only toward the end of the conflict was it reactivated. Early in 1946 the Administrative Procedure Act was passed, a measure allowing the new governmental technique to retain considerable elbow room while still maintaining the shield guaranteeing traditional liberties.

It would be misleading to suppose that virtually all Americans—conservatives no less than liberals—did not applaud the steps taken by the government to make the nation's war effort fully effective. There was, in other words, no "dragging of feet" motivated by a fear of encroachment by government on the operations of private enterprise. But it is at the same time not to be imagined that this acceptance of the facts of life associated with modern warfare made con-

---

[28] Attorney General's Committee on Administrative Procedure, *Administrative Procedure in Government Agencies* (Washington, D.C.: Government Printing Office, 1941).

servatives any more happy with the longer range tendencies toward paternalism and socialism they were certain they could already see on the horizon. Put differently, there was never any real doubt but that the ideological battle pushed aside by the war would be resumed at the earliest possible moment. And it was. Indeed, that controversy was now to become again and for a number of years remain the central issue on the government and business front.

QUESTIONS FOR DISCUSSION

1. What was the political problem of the New Deal as the nation turned its energies to world war? How was it resolved?

2. How was the tax structure altered in preparation for a major war effort?

3. Why is comprehensive government control of the economy an essential part of a major war production program?

4. Explain the failure of the price mechanism to operate as efficiently over short periods of time as over longer ones.

5. Why is it not desirable to dispense with the price system altogether during a major war?

6. List the major control agencies, and state the principal function of each.

7. What particular purposes does a price control program serve in a war economy?

8. Explain the slow pace at which an effective wartime price control program was developed.

9. What are the connections between government spending, saving, and price control?

10. How might the bulwarks erected against inflation have been strengthened?

11. Do you think labor was at this point made too safe from antitrust attack?

12. What were the major consequences of the war for the public power program?

13. State and explain the significance of the philosophy enunciated in the Hope decision.

14. What is your opinion of the way the federal government met its new responsibilities in the insurance industry?

15. Explain the nature of the principal issues involved in the debate over administrative procedure.

Part VI

A MIXED ECONOMY

Chapter 26

Aftermath of Total War

No doubt this renewal of ideological hostilities at home was undertaken with a great deal of confidence by conservatives. As the New Freedom had been repudiated after World War I, so now would the New Deal be similarly dealt with. Enthusiastically, therefore, leaders of this persuasion turned to the first step in this program—reversing the process by which the government had during the war assumed unprecedentedly comprehensive economic responsibilities.

Unwinding the Control Mechanism

Nor did this objective meet with opposition on the liberal side of the fence. No one proposed that the government continue to dominate the economy to the extent deemed necessary during wartime, and hence it was understood by all that emergency controls were to be ended very soon after the fighting stopped. The only caveat interposed by anyone was that this be accomplished responsibly rather than recklessly—with due regard to reorienting production to a peacetime basis as smoothly as possible. But here again there was no controversy; no group had anything to gain by pushing the economy "off the deep end." Thus it was that by common consent preparations for reconversion began simultaneously with the attainment of the maximum rate of arms output.

This coincidence in time of the climax of the war production program and the subtle but unmistakable shift in emphasis toward postwar planning can readily be demonstrated.[1] Just as in the fall of 1942 the coordination of agencies dealing with price control had become imperative, in early 1943 the most pressing need seemed to be an agency superior to all war agencies. To accomplish this task

[1] War Production Board, *Wartime Production Achievements and the Reconversion Outlook* (Washington, D.C.: Government Printing Office, 1945).

an Office of War Mobilization was created in May. Two months later the President first requested Congress to begin formulating demobilization legislation. November saw the creation by the Senate of a Special Committee on Post-War Economic Policy and Planning, and the Chairman of the War Production Board testified before that group that his agency had already begun blueprinting for reconversion. Almost simultaneously the Director of the Office of War Mobilization announced that elder statesman Bernard Baruch had been asked to study the problems of reconversion for his agency, this group thereby securing leadership among government agencies in transition planning, and the first cut-back in the war production program was made—the closing down of four aluminum potlines.

From this time onward reconversion preparations rapidly gathered momentum as virtually every government agency began to devote some of its resources to that task.[2] In January, 1944, the President in his annual budget message dealt with this problem in some detail, calling for "concerted efforts by industry, labor, and Government." This statement was followed within only a few weeks by the so-called Baruch-Hancock report setting forth a number of fundamental principles to guide reconversion policies.[3] The issuance almost at once of three Executive Orders implementing certain of the recommendations embodied in this document gave it enormous prestige, and it soon became the core around which the reconversion program was ultimately built. By October, 1944, the war in Europe seemed so nearly over that legislation was passed creating the rudiments of an administrative organization more competent to act in this field. The foundation on which that structure was erected was a new Office of War Mobilization and Reconversion, essentially the old Office of War Mobilization with somewhat altered responsibilities.

The strategy underlying the thinking being done on reconversion logically took reference from the nature of the military conflict then still raging. It was anticipated that the Allies would achieve victory in Europe early in 1945, and that the war in the Pacific would go on for many months thereafter. Such a sequence of events would have had the advantage of allowing transition adjustments to be made by stages over a relatively long period of time rather than all at once. And as late as mid-December, 1944 this highly favorable expectation seemed fully realistic.

[2] Twentieth Century Fund, *Postwar Planning in the United States* (New York: Twentieth Century Fund, Inc., 1944).

[3] B. M. Baruch and J. M. Hancock, *Report on War and Postwar Adjustment Policy* (Washington, D.C.: Government Printing Office, 1944).

Unfortunately for these plans, however, the fates decreed differently. At both ends of this projected time schedule the span of months actually available was telescoped, with the result that little time was available within which to taper off the war production program before the fighting ceased.

Christmas, 1944, saw the Germans launch one last desperate attack against their pursuers, the so-called "Battle of the Bulge," and with such a high degree of success for a few weeks that demobilization progress was severely curtailed. Then, when the German army did capitulate, this collapse came very suddenly. To be sure, there was at this point a dramatic acceleration of reconversion activities, but before the economy could adjust itself to a one-front war, the atomic bomb had brought this dimension of the war also to an end. Thus it was that a nation devoting at V-J Day more than one-third of its productive effort to the requirements of war was confronted with the necessity of reversing its emphasis on very short notice.

Understandably, there was at first some toying with the idea of creating artificially the time interval for reconversion denied by the sudden cessation of hostilities. For three reasons, however, the decision was made not to follow that procedure. First, it was widely recognized that there were real dangers in delay; the failure to give private enterprise full leeway to make essential adjustments might actually impede the resumption of peacetime production. Second, such a procedure was soon seen to be politically dangerous; the mere rumor that the release of personnel from the armed services was to be correlated with the availability of job opportunities brought down upon the administration a disturbing flurry of angry condemnation. Third, there was no clearly equitable way of deciding which firms and individuals were to be prevented from returning to peacetime pursuits in the first instance.

The speed with which the first step calculated to get the government out of business was taken can be dramatically indicated. A rash of contract cancellations began late in July in anticipation of

TABLE 56. UNWINDING THE WAR EFFORT

Fiscal year	Receipts	Federal Government Expenditures		Deficit
		Total	War Department	
		(billions of dollars)		
1945	46.5	100.4	50.5	53.9
1946	43.0	65.0	28.0	22.0

Source: Treasury Department.

the Japanese surrender, this flow becoming a veritable torrent immediately thereafter. During the single month of August more than 70,000 government contracts were cancelled, plants in the metals and chemicals industries losing in this process more than three-fourths of all orders on their books. During the remainder of the year another 230,000 contracts were cancelled, with similar consequences for the firms so abruptly losing this vast amount of business.

On the human side, this same pell mell haste dictated government policy. During the 30 days following V-J Day more than 2,500,000 war workers lost their jobs on the basis of cuts in program, 1,000,000 of these in the first week of that period alone. And to complicate this wholesale convergence of reconverting workers on the nation's peacetime industries, the pressure to release personnel from the armed services became so intense that the rate of demobilization of these men was soon proceeding at a pace limited only by available transportation facilities. In a single 30-day period before the year was out, more than 1,500,000 service personnel were sent home.

The obvious corollary of these moves was to give business leadership maximum flexibility in filling the economic vacuum thus created. One way in which this could be achieved was for the several contracting agencies to remove promptly government-owned machinery which might now only be in the way. Another was to abolish the intricate network of controls which might also now be a liability. Here especially was a remarkable achievement recorded. On August 16, the day following the announcement of the surrender of Japan, all controls over manpower were dropped by the War Manpower Commission—while the Office of Price Administration removed ration restrictions on gasoline, fuel oil, processed foods, and heating stoves. Other ration orders were lifted in the ensuing months until by the end of the year sugar was the only commodity still subject to such restriction. During these same months, furthermore, several hundred items were removed from price control. By the end of August the War Production Board had eliminated priority controls, dropped the Controlled Materials Plan and with it all restrictions over metals except tin, lead, and antimony, eased industrial construction limitations, and revoked several hundred control orders. Similarly, the Office of Defense Transportation had lifted several thousand specific restrictions on commercial motor-vehicle traffic, and a large portion of the wartime controls over exports had likewise been abandoned.

All this was indeed, in its way, getting the government out of business—and with something of a vengeance. It must, however, have been a little ominous to conservatives that, so vital were government actions now to the functioning of the economy, the process of unwinding government controls necessitated the active use of the mechanism of government at numerous other points.[4]

For example, it was deemed essential to use the resources of the government to ease the financial burden of reconversion to the business community. One way in which this was done was to make tentative payments on claims against the government on account of war contracts (final payments to be left subject to renegotiation later when time was less vitally important), this enabling the firms involved to have at their disposal that much more liquid capital during the transition period. Another expedient adopted for the purpose of supplementing the liquid capital available to industry at this critical time was the so-called guaranteed production loan—a system of commercial bank loans for reconversion purposes conventional in every respect except that principal and interest was guaranteed by the federal government. It was at this point, too, that the "carry back" provision in the wartime excess profits tax more than proved its worth. Many a firm reimbursed itself almost entirely for reconversion losses through tax repayments. And finally, a $6 billion tax reduction, including the elimination of the excess profits tax, was of assistance in minimizing the financial problem of gearing business to production for peace.

And business firms were not the only point at which reconversion posed financial difficulties. Equally important was the need to keep purchasing power from falling and dragging the entire economy down in the familiar deflationary spiral. One safeguard here was a vast veteran education program keeping hundreds of thousands of veterans off the labor market until reconversion was well advanced. Another was the program of unemployment compensation so recently developed as one answer to the problems posed by the Great Depression. Still a third was a statutory guarantee for farmers that the prices of the major agricultural products would not be allowed to fall below 90 per cent of parity for a period of two years after the official ending of the war.

A NEW YEAR'S RESOLUTION

But government interventions such as these had from another standpoint little significance for the ideological struggle now about to be resumed. On the one hand, conservatives as well as liberals

---

[4] J. M. Clark, *Demobilization of Wartime Economic Controls* (New York: McGraw-Hill Book Co., Inc., 1944).

recognized the need for precautions of these kinds in the face of such a drastic reduction in government purchases. On the other hand, they would for the most part be short-lived, automatically ending when the reconversion need had past. Of much greater significance, therefore, would be the way the problems of peace were handled as they arose. And with respect to this question, conservatives everywhere anxiously awaited the first indication of what the orientation of the new President was to be.

They were not kept long in suspense. On September 6, 1945, less than five months after President Roosevelt's death and less than one month after the surrender of Japan, President Harry Truman sent to Congress his agenda for postwar legislation. Distinctly "New Dealish" in tenor, this document called for such things as an increase in the minimum wage to 65 cents an hour, a social security program expanded both as to coverage and benefits, a new national health insurance program ("socialized medicine," as his opponents called it), a broader national housing and slum clearance effort than had ever been undertaken in this country, and federal legislation looking toward the abolition of employment discrimination against the Negro. Immediately dubbed the "Fair Deal," this forthright statement was intended as a warning to "the Hearsts and the McCormicks" that the new administration believed its mission to be carrying on the program begun by the New Deal.

Thus early in the postwar period, in short, the gage of battle was thrown down. And when conservatives no less decisively accepted this challenge, the battle was on. From that moment, all major decisions were debated against the background of this controversy.

The way in which even reconversion decisions took reference from this issue can be illustrated by the problem of surplus property disposal. When the war ended the government had in its possession war plants and other productive facilities valued at more than $20 billion, and it was estimated that the Defense Plant Corporation alone held title to 10 per cent of the nation's entire manufacturing capacity.[5]

It was fairly generally agreed that the government should dispose of these assets as rapidly as possible, in conformity with the more basic policy of restoring the economy to a private enterprise basis. But that emphasis came into conflict with another principle important to the President and numerous other liberal leaders. These men believed that in disposing of such properties the government should

[5] Smaller War Plants Corporation, *Economic Concentration and World War II* (Washington, D.C.: Government Printing Office, 1946).

endeavor to use them to implement the antitrust laws by favoring new and small firms at the expense of large, established ones.

If this dispute can appropriately be thought of as the initial ideological skirmish of the postwar period, it must be conceded that conservatives drew first blood. Time and again it was the larger concern that was in the best position to make the government a reasonable offer or to take the property involved off the government's hands promptly. Indeed, a large part of this problem was the fact that these concerns had so typically operated the government's facilities during the war. It is safe to say, in other words, that the structure of industry was not significantly altered in the process of disposing of surplus productive facilities.[6]

While conservatives and liberals were still locked in battle on this front, a second major postwar issue came to a boil. One of the earliest questions raised by postwar planners had been the adequacy of the nation's institutional framework for dealing with the problem of unemployment and idle plant capacity. It was recalled with much uneasiness that the United States had been lifted out of a frustrating period of stagnation only by the coming of war, and a central resolve was that reconversion must not mean a return to 1937–39 conditions. Moreover, this fear was made even more pointed by the fact that every significant war in the nation's history had been followed by a sharp recession.

Although several New Deal innovations had served to provide the economy with built-in economic stabilizers of some importance (for example, unemployment insurance and agricultural price supports), it was nonetheless true that the primary orientation of the government during the 1930's had been resuscitation rather than prevention. It was only to be expected, therefore, that even during that period the question began to be seriously discussed whether there should not be created a mechanism for stopping such tragedies before they begin.

As early as 1936 the Senate Committee on Manufactures had recommended the establishment of a National Economic Council, one responsibility of which would be to keep

our economic system working as automatically and efficiently as possible. It seems entirely possible that it may require a higher order of skill and genius to keep our economic system satisfactorily working in a high degree automatically than to step in and try to operate it, as it were, by hand; just as an automatic machine represents greater skill and thought than one intended for hand operation. . . . The only primary and satisfactory way to avoid unnecessary

[6] Federal Trade Commission, *Concentration of Productive Facilities, 1947* (Washington, D.C.: Government Printing Office, 1949).

regimentation or an unnecessary amount of governmental interference in the form of planned economy is to bend our efforts to the positive and constructive task of making our economic mechanism work as smoothly and evenly and automatically as possible.

No detailed proposal was attached to this recommendation, but the idea here seems to have been the creation of an agency which would, among other things, keep itself and the ruling administration informed on all matters bearing on the problem of stabilization.

Against this background of depression and early thoughts about combating it before it has begun to do serious damage,[7] it is not surprising that side by side with discussions of the more technical aspects of reconversion there was also talk about how the predicted postwar recession might be prevented. Thus in the presidential election campaign of 1944, both of the major political parties pledged themselves to take whatever steps were necessary at this point.

Understandably also Democrats believed that more drastic steps might be necessary than Republicans were willing to see inaugurated, and it is therefore of significance with respect to the handling of this problem that the Democrats won the electoral victory. Their platform, in fact, even included the phrase "guarantee full employment," and when a bill to carry out this pledge was first presented to Congress early in 1945 the intent of this wording was reproduced intact.

The Congress hereby declares that every American able to work and willing to work has the right to a useful and remunerative job in the industries, or shops, or offices, or farms, or mines of the nation.

Popularly referred to as the Full Employment Bill, this measure at this stage in its journey through Congress provided for the appointment of economist-specialists who would draw up at intervals a national production and employment budget showing the amount of government spending required to achieve the desired goal—together with a Congressional commitment to appropriate the indicated funds.[8]

If this proposal had been voted on prior to, say, the last of September, while almost every economist in the land was anticipating a major economic downturn at any moment, it is almost certain that some such commitment would have become law. In fact the bill in essentially this form did pass the Senate during that period—and by

[7] Sir William Beveridge, *Full Employment in a Free Society* (New York: W. W. Norton & Co., Inc., 1945).

[8] Alvin H. Hansen, *Economic Policy and Full Employment* (New York: Whittlesey House, 1947).

a handsome margin. But conservatives subjected the measure to a strategy of opposition by delay, hoping that the economic situation would not compel so drastic a break with the past. This technique, moreover, was successful. When the expected recession did not develop, when the economy proved able to withstand the tremendous

TABLE 57. A PLEASANT SURPRISE

| Month and Year | Industrial Production | Prices | | Unem- ployment |
		Paid to Farmers	Cost of Living	
March, 1945	100	100	100	100
February, 1946	65	104	101	320
October, 1946	77	135	119	235

Source: Department of Commerce, *Survey of Current Business*.

shock of so abrupt a termination of intense war activity, support for the bill as written began to weaken. Fears that so sweeping a guarantee would in practice be incompatible with free enterprise became stronger than apprehensions of a swift return to chronic depression, and more moderate counsels won the day.

The act finally passed on February 20, 1946, the Full Employment Act of 1946, differed markedly from the original proposal.[9] Instead of the more operational budget, it required only that the President submit to Congress summary reports on the state of the nation's economic health together with such legislative recommendations as should seem to him to be appropriate. On the basis of its own conclusions about business conditions, drawn from the President's reports and elsewhere, Congress would then enact such legislation as it saw fit. And in making this determination, Congress was not to be bound by anything resembling a "right to work" pledge. Rather it was committed only

to coordinate and utilize all its plans, functions, and resources for the purpose of creating and maintaining, in a manner calculated to foster and promote free competitive enterprise and the general welfare, conditions under which there will be afforded useful employment, for those able, willing, and seeking to work, and to promote maximum employment, production, and purchasing power.

When this enactment is compared with the intent of its principal sponsors twelve months earlier, it is legitimately enough referred to as nothing more substantial than (as one disgruntled liberal put it)

[9] S. K. Bailey, *Congress Makes a Law* (New York: Columbia University Press, 1950).

"A New Year's Resolution." By the same token, it is easy to see in this turn of events another important conservative victory. On the other hand, however, even in 1946 this innovation could be seen without exaggeration as a step of the sort that so often marks the beginning of a new institutional development. Perhaps, furthermore, this was far enough to have gone at this time. An evolution proceeding slowly enough to permit a careful counting of its cost at each of a number of different stages is apt to be more substantial than one hastened along by crisis.

PRICE CONTROL ON THE FIRING LINE

Another problem sharing the spotlight in these early postwar months was a still different issue arising directly out of the transition from war to peace. One of the most significant residues of the war economy was a durable goods inventory in consumer hands and an inventory of plant facilities in the possession of business firms which had seriously deteriorated as a result of wartime production limitations. Another important residue, however, was an unprecedented volume of liquid assets widely distributed throughout the economy. It seemed reasonable to suppose that citizens would want to utilize their war-accumulated purchasing power to make good war-created shortages, and it was understood that an easily conceivable consequence of such a development could be a resumption of the price inflation which had been more or less halted by wartime price controls.

Although these two things were not wholly inconsistent with one another, there was nonetheless an element of paradox in a government endeavoring simultaneously to thwart recession and prevent inflation. Moreover, this paradox was accentuated by the fact that certain of the measures adopted to ward off recession were precisely the steps best calculated to bring about inflation. And when an administration thus trying to carry water on both shoulders decided to keep the Office of Price Administration in operation during the reconversion period, conservatives were given reason enough for maintaining that one of the objectives of the Fair Deal was to retain permanently as much wartime regimentation as possible.

To this point, at least, the views (and propaganda) of conservatives to the contrary notwithstanding, President Truman and those around him were not only sincere but were also standing on solid ground. In a highly fluid situation such as that which they were now confronting, it was only sensible to prepare for every reasonable contingency. But the accusations of their opponents were prophetic if not, at the moment, quite accurate. With the cessation of shooting war the powerful motivation working toward wartime unity began to fall apart, and the ruling group in Washington began taking sides. And of course, for an administration wanting nothing so much as to push forward the work of the New Deal, there was perhaps never any real doubt which way the successor Fair Deal would go.

Labor was already growing restive after several years of being shackled to a wartime no-strike pledge. In part this unrest reflected the depression-born power of organized workers, a power which had never really been tested and which had been enhanced by the accumulation of funds in union treasuries during the war. Since, however, bargaining strength cannot be effectively tested in a vacuum, even more important was the sudden appearance of a battle well worth fighting. A rapid decline in overtime hours, and hence overtime wage rates, was threatening workers with a substantial reduction in take home pay. A number of the major unions began making plans to demand increases in hourly wage rates sufficient to compensate for the decline in hours worked.

It can be persuasively argued that the United States did not in any event have the slightest chance of avoiding inflation after World War II. With the government, business firms, and consumers all vieing with one another in a mad race to put more and more purchasing power into the income stream, and without the restraining

TABLE 58. FORMULA FOR INFLATION

Year	Domestic Investment	Consumption Expenditures	Personal Saving	Consumer Credit Outstanding
		(billions of dollars)		
1945	10.7	123.1	28.0	6.6
1947	31.1	166.9	5.1	13.7

Source: Council of Economic Advisers, *Economic Report of the President, 1950.*

influence of a major struggle against a common enemy, the postwar price control struggle may indeed have been lost before it began. Suffice it to say here only that an administration torn between its concern for labor and its belief in the need to combat inflation now took a step which could not have been more ideally calculated to sabotage the price control effort.

Forgetting that one of the principal secrets of success on this front during the war had been a tolerably equitable sharing of the burdens of such a policy among all of the great interest groups, apparently oblivious of the fundamental truth that in a vigorous capitalist democracy it is only as all price lines are held that any price line can be maintained, the administration took the amazing position that business could in general afford wage increases of the order of magnitude of those being demanded without raising prices. To be sure, this position was first taken when it was as yet uncertain whether recession or inflation was the dragon most needing to be slain. To be sure also, the economic policy thus promoted would have been of much assistance if the predicted sharp recession had threatened to develop. Far more to the point than these extenuating considerations, however, is the fact that high Washington officials persisted in this stand long after the onset of a serious economic downturn became highly improbable.

Actually the administration was no doubt quite correct from the standpoint of objective fact. Most companies, perhaps, could have increased wages without raising prices. But what was less clear to them was why they should do so. America's private enterprise system had always been based upon a policy of selling for what the traffic would bear, and there seemed to be no good reason for believing that decisions of this sort were not still to be made by businessmen on the basis of profit considerations. Thus when business leaders were bluntly told that profit opportunities must be foregone in order that labor might receive a larger share of the national dividend, they were all the more convinced that the Fair Deal's major tendencies were in the direction of un-American socialist planning.

Probably angered more than frightened, the business community defiantly fought back. One of the principal devices adopted to frustrate the administration's program was refusing to grant substantial wage increases not supported by price advances approved by the Office of Price Administration, this step typically accompanied by a ceaseless propaganda campaign against the illogic and inequity of the government's position. An equally obvious technique was to convince Congressmen and Senators that the ending of price controls was essential to the prompt attainment of maximum peacetime production, an approach greatly strengthened by a tendency for businessmen to withhold goods from the market in anticipation of the abandonment of control legislation.[10]

Existing laws undergirding the price control endeavor were scheduled to expire June 30, 1946. Unless a new measure with teeth were enacted prior to that time, this battle would on that day become vir-

---

[10] L. V. Chandler and D. H. Wallace, *Economic Mobilization and Stabilization* (New York: Henry Holt & Co., Inc., 1951).

tually a thing of the past. As conservative on this issue at this point as it had been earlier on the full employment question, Congress on June 29 sent President Truman a renewal measure frankly designed to bring price controls to an end as quickly as possible. The President, however, refusing to be coerced by the calendar or publicly to concede as yet that this effort had become a hopeless cause, sent back a ringing veto in which he referred to the proposed bill as a "sure formula for inflation."

In the event, the "Man from Independence" would have done about as well to be content with what he was given first. Not until July 25 was a stronger control measure ready for White House approval, and in the interim the index of prices for 28 especially sensitive commodities at wholesale rose almost 25 per cent as compared with only 13 per cent during the preceding three years. Although a new control law was passed and a half-hearted attempt made to roll prices back to the June 30 level, and although a pretense of inflation control was kept up until about the end of the year, this episode marked the definitive end of the entire structure of price controls except for rent restrictions.

TABLE 59.   THE BREAK-THROUGH BEGINS

| Month and | Prices | |
year	Wholesale	Consumer
June, 1943	92	93
June, 1944	93	94
June, 1945	95	97
June, 1946	100	100
July, 1946	110	106
December, 1946	124	115

Source: Department of Labor.

It was, of course, a foregone conclusion that there would be a vigorous post-mortem debate. Each of the principal contestants had to be certain that the blame was put elsewhere. Thus the business community insisted that the ending of controls actually inhibited inflation by giving free enterprise a better opportunity to turn out a maximum quantity of goods and services, and that the real villain was organized labor's insistence on large increases in wages. Labor in turn insisted that the fault lay squarely with the businessman's greed for profits, that the wage increases received by labor were in fact the principal reason the economy had not suffered a serious postwar recession. As is almost always the case, too, the truth lay

somewhere in between. Business spokesmen conveniently overlooked the fact that the economy was already producing at full
capacity, while labor leaders just as conveniently ignored the fact
that the principal difficulty was actually an excess of purchasing
power. The most important point, however, is that this argument
was almost wholly academic; price control was dead and the President's opponents had won their most significant victory to date.

CONSERVATIVES TAKE THE OFFENSIVE

But if prior to the beginning of 1947 liberals had at least been
able to keep their adversaries on the defensive, that situation was
now to be drastically altered. In November, 1946, the nation's citizens went to the polls to choose whether they would prefer further
experimentation along Fair Deal lines or a still longer rest from
reform. The choice made was unequivocal; the Eightieth Congress
was to be the first Republican Congress in sixteen years.

Nor did this change in the political complexion of the nation's
capital mean only that Harry Truman would have to forget about
his own legislative program for a while. Far more fundamental was
the fact that the new Congress was pledged to reverse New Deal
policy in the labor field—among others.

Of course, this item had been high on the conservative agenda
ever since the passage of the Wagner Act. During the intervening
years, moreover, several events had occurred which brought a widening circle of popular support to this cause.[11]

One of the most important of these events took place during the
war. As inflated war demands for basic raw materials quickly transformed bituminous coal from a "sick industry" to a commodity available in adequate amounts, organized labor in this industry soon
made it clear that it did not propose to allow such a golden opportunity to slip away unused. Led by the indomitable and incom-
parable John L. Lewis, the miners in mid-1943 demanded concessions far beyond what they were legally entitled to under price
control regulations then in force—and when employers and the government refused to accede to these demands, the workers walked
out of the pits.

The nation's response was the Smith-Connally War Labor Disputes Act, a measure intended sharply to curtail labor's right to
strike in time of war. Because it was his feeling, however, that this
step would not solve the wartime strike problem (a prediction amply

[11] H. A. Millis and E. C. Brown, *From the Wagner Act to Taft-Hartley* (Chicago:
University of Chicago Press, 1950).

justified in the months to come), President Roosevelt had promptly vetoed this proposal. But so intense was antilabor sentiment throughout the country that it was decisively made into law despite the President's objections. Although, ironically, the miners already had secured most of their demands, and therefore the burden of this restriction fell primarily on other groups, this was nonetheless a most significant event in the history of organized labor. Notice was thereby dramatically served on the nation's workers that, despite all legal guarantees, the right to strike in wartime would not be tolerated without limit.

The next major episode in this evolution had taken place almost exactly three years later, this time in the midst of reconversion difficulties. Again a principal role was played by the United Mine Workers, joined this time, however, by the nation's railroad engineers and trainmen. Again, furthermore, the government had no alternative but to take drastic measures. On one side, these took the form of government seizure of both the bituminous coal mines and the railroads. Simultaneously, on the other side, Congress passed another restrictive measure, designed essentially to write Smith-Connally safeguards into permanent legislation, and sent it to the President for signature. Partly because both of these disputes were now settled (for the moment), and partly because he was actively building his administration around labor support, the President vetoed the Case Mediation bill and this time there were not enough votes to override. But the warning issued to labor was even more decisive than the earlier one; the right to strike in peacetime was also to be subjected to close scrutiny.[12]

A significance of an entirely different kind also attaches to the employer-employee difficulties that harassed the nation during the early postwar years. His patience strained to the breaking point by repeated troubles involving coal miners, the President finally was driven to take a desperate step. After seizing the nation's bituminous coal mines in the name of the government under the War Labor Disputes Act, he then secured a federal injunction against the union and its leaders. When the Supreme Court upheld this action on the ground that the Norris–La Guardia Act did not withdraw the government's right to injunctive relief against its own employees,[13] conservatives were no doubt even given a broad hint on the matter of the methods which might be used to modify the right to strike.

[12] George W. Taylor, *Government Regulation of Industrial Disputes* (Englewood Cliffs, N.J.: Prentice-Hall, Inc., 1948).
[13] *United States* v. *United Mine Workers,* 330 U.S. 258 (1947).

However, it was not merely their desire to achieve limitations along this line that had led conservatives to make labor legislation a "must" item on the agenda of the Eightieth Congress. More critically important to businessmen was the fact that the Wagner Act had been, in their opinion, one-sided. Unfair practices for employers had been enumerated—none for workers or their unions. What conservatives were now anxious to do was to redress this violation of accepted principles of fair play.

While some credit must be given to Wagner Act opponents for sincerity of purpose in launching this assault, it must nonetheless be noted that much of their argument was with tongue in cheek. What was actually desired in many cases was the outright repeal of collective bargaining guarantees. Having failed in repeated attempts to accomplish this directly, it was now proposed to take advantage of public sentiment on the strike issue to achieve as much as possible indirectly. The fair play angle simply looked like a good handlehold —even though the Wagner Act had been originally passed in order to correct a one-sidedness that already existed.

The extent to which the Labor-Management Act of 1947 (popularly referred to as the Taft-Hartley Act) did correct weaknesses

TABLE 60.   PREFACE TO TAFT-HARTLEY

Month and Year	Man-days Idle (millions)	Per Cent of Working Time
January, 1945	0.2	0.03
October, 1945	8.6	1.39
January, 1946	19.7	3.13
February, 1946	22.9	4.19
May, 1946	13.7	2.06

Source: Department of Labor.

found in the Wagner Act over a period of years, as well as the extent to which it was instead simply a part of the program of conservatives, is a matter on which scholars disagree. Suffice it here to say on this point only that the new measure amended existing law in this field in a number of significant ways.[14]

Perhaps the sharpest break with the past was a drastically altered conception of the role of government in the collective bargaining process. Whereas the Wagner Act had dealt only with prebargaining

[14] Glenn W. Miller, *American Labor and the Government* (Englewood Cliffs, N.J.: Prentice-Hall, Inc., 1948).

employer-employee relationships, seeking primarily to give labor a voice at the bargaining table, the Taft-Hartley Act undertook to write rules and regulations governing the bargaining process itself. Put differently, conservatives were so eager to protect the prerogatives of management it was felt were being encroached upon by organized labor that they were willing to accede to a basic step away from the idea of minimum government as a means to that end.

This new orientation in labor relations can be seen at a number of points. First, the closed shop was made illegal—although the union shop was still to be permitted. A more subtle way of undermining job control by unions was a provision allowing state laws on this subject to take precedence over federal legislation. (In the battle against the Wagner Act it had been discovered that in state governments the urban worker is often less adequately represented than in Washington, D.C.) Second, no union security clause could be written into a collective bargaining contract if the union was not "democratic" in the sense of charging "reasonable" fees and following nondiscriminatory admission policies. Third, the new law gave bargaining representative status to many small craft unions which had been overshadowed by their industrial union rivals under prior interpretations. Fourth, foremen's unions (as, in theory at least, spokesmen for management) were denied the protection of the Wagner Act—although these workers were not forbidden to organize. Fifth, collective bargaining in pursuit of "featherbedding" contract provisions was outlawed, and bargaining for "health and welfare" provisions was somewhat narrowed in scope.

A similarly drastic change of direction was the enunciation of several limitations on the right to strike during peacetime. Of least importance in this connection were prohibitions against sympathy strikes (and secondary boycotts), jurisdictional strikes, and strikes by federal government employees. Of somewhat greater significance were provisions denying the right to vote in National Labor Relations Board representation elections to striking workers who had been replaced, and lifting the Wagner Act ban against employers telling workers their views on the subject of labor unions. Still more important was a requirement that a 60-day notice (called a "cooling-off period") had to be given by a union of intention to terminate or modify a contract, with the proviso that a strike could not be called during that period. And most basic of all was the authority given the government to secure an 80-day injunction (another "cooling-off period") against any strike threatening the public's health or safety.

Of course Truman vetoed the Taft-Hartley Act—not because it was a "slave-labor law" as laborites insisted, but because it was a "reversal of the basic direction of our national labor policy." Of course also it was precisely this retreat from New Deal philosophies which endeared this measure to those who supported it (including southern Democrats, now more preoccupied with the problems of industrialization than they had ever been before, as well as most Republicans), and therefore there was no difficulty in securing enough votes to pass this measure over the President's veto. Thus it was that a conservative Congress, enthusiastically propounding a get-government-out-of-business philosophy, enacted a measure which did as much to put government in business at a critical point as almost any New Deal enactment which might be named.

But it exaggerates the importance of the immediate situation to discuss the Taft-Hartley Act so exclusively in terms of post-World War II conditions. Actually for a full half-century the nation's leadership had been searching for a solution to the problem posed by strikes vitally affecting the over-all community—the critical case in point in this quest being the railroad industry. Moreover, some 20 years earlier a major step toward the position now being greatly broadened (the idea of a "cooling-off" period during which the discipline of public opinion can be brought to bear) had been instituted in that industry. And while it was unquestionably a tragic blow to labor's bargaining position and prestige that the long-hated injunction was at this point added to this endeavor, it is nonetheless also clear that the public interest in an exchange economy requires drastic action in the case of strikes doing greater damage to the community at large than to the parties directly involved.

IDEOLOGICAL BATTLE IN WORDS

Certainly no imagination is required to see in post-World War II economic policy what might with a fair degree of accuracy be called a conservative reaction. This reaction, moreover, was sufficiently strong that if the United States had elected a President in 1946 Harry Truman himself would in all probability have been replaced. At the same time, however, it was by now obvious that current trends were not at all paralleling developments after World War I. Because, in other words, it was so apparent that no fundamental conservative program could be launched over White House vetoes, the existing situation might from another point of view and with equal accuracy be referred to as a "stand-off."

Perhaps it was in part because opposing forces were so nicely balanced that there arose during these years an intellectual duel over basic social-political-economic philosophy such as is rarely seen even in a high-spirited democracy. To be sure, there had always in the United States been public controversy along conservative-liberal lines. At times, moreover, such encounters had become particularly intense—as in the case of the prewar discussion of the New Deal. Indeed, the new chapter in this ever-present debate was in one sense only a continuation of the attack launched during the 1930's. On closer look, however, it is apparent that there was a difference. This post-World War II battle for the ear of the mass public was characterized by a note of urgency which can realistically be likened in this country (the slavery controversy of course excluded) only to the struggle over the ratification of the Constitution. It was as if men felt that the nation was standing at a vital crossroads, pausing to decide which route to take before commencing a journey from which there could be no turning back.

The opening thrust in this duel came from the conservative side of the ideological fence.[15] It was a book entitled *The Road to Serfdom*, a volume which in one form or another sold more than 5,000,-000 copies in this country alone. Thus hungry were American conservatives to see their views given a philosophical foundation and a persuasive form.

But even this fact does not do full justice to Mr. Hayek's book. Its achievement was far more remarkable than circulation figures suggest, for its origins and purpose were such that it would scarcely have been expected to reach any audience in the United States except the intellectually curious. The author was a native Austrian who had taken up residence in England in the backwash of Hitler expansionism in central Europe during the 1930's. Furthermore, the book he wrote was oriented to the situation he found in the country of his adoption rather than conditions in the United States—although after he had spent some time in this country he asserted that its warnings were fully as appropriate on this side of the Atlantic. It is indeed even more suggestive of the despondency of American conservatism (and perhaps its intellectual bankruptcy as well) that this book written by a "foreigner" for primary application in England became for a time virtually the standard manifesto of American conservatives.

Stripped to barest fundamentals, economist Hayek's thesis was this. Essentially because its leaders did not understand the implica-

15 F. A. Hayek, *The Road to Serfdom* (Chicago: University of Chicago Press, 1944).

tions of this decision, democratic capitalism was rapidly repudiating its heritage in favor of totalitarian planning. (Professor Hayek, by the way, felt that he was in a uniquely favorable position to discern what his contemporaries in England could not because he had witnessed at close range an essentially identical evolution in pre-Nazi Germany.) Well-intentioned leaders, he believed, had been led to move down this authoritarian road by the seductive promises of socialism's more persuasive advocates. In this way and only in this way, they had been told, can genuine freedom and true democracy be achieved. Actually, countered Hayek, the truth is exactly the reverse. Comprehensive planning by a single center of power can only result in the erosion of freedom and the ultimate overthrow of democracy, for the simple and obvious reason that placing all of society's energies and resources in the service of a single hierarchy of values is the antithesis of the freedom democracy seeks to maintain.

No doctrinaire laissez fairist, Hayek freely acknowledged the importance of sovereign government power in creating and maintaining a competitive market economy. Indeed, he on occasion even embarrassed his partisans by insisting upon an effective antitrust policy and the elimination of tariff subsidies. At the same time, however, it was one of Professor Hayek's most fundamental theses that in the "good" society market forces will be given as much room in which to operate as possible—that impersonal and hence nondiscriminatory decisions mediated by the so-called "Rule of Law" are much superior to the invariably personalized and hence often discriminatory decisions handed down by administrative officials. And although his analysis was short on specifics, offering little detail on how more appropriate relationships between government and the underlying community might be recaptured, it was also basic to this presentation that the operation required would involve in some sense a turning back of the clock of economic policy evolution.

But if conservatives evinced a little of what might appropriately be called anxiety in their acceptance of Hayek in the role of self-appointed formulator of these depressing fears, this was equally true of liberals if judgment is made on the basis of the "official" rebuttal of The Road to Serfdom.[16] Here the self-appointed spokesman was Herman Finer, an American political scientist, and the title of the volume dedicated to the task of exposing the dangerous fallacies of post-World War II conservatism was Road to Reaction.

In a number of ways Finer's work suffers by comparison with the object of its attack. One of the important reasons for this is that it

16 Herman Finer, Road to Reaction (Boston: Little, Brown & Co., 1946).

was pin-pointed to the negative purpose of annihilation rather than devoted to the more theoretical aspects of the problem at hand. As a consequence it was polemic and hot-blooded where *The Road to Serfdom* was philosophical and (relatively) detached; on occasion Professor Finer even resorted to an academic variety of name-calling—going so far in this direction as repeatedly to accuse his opponent of enmity to democracy. Moreover, in studying these two books side by side it is difficult to escape the conclusion that, quite apart from this difference in orientation, Hayek's mind has the surer grasp of fundamentals. Nor does this conclusion arise solely from the fact that the subject at hand is most effectively analyzed with the tools of the economist rather than those of the political scientist, which is probably not the case.

A still more significant reservation about Professor Finer's refutation that often made his own supporters uneasy was the ground on which he chose to make his defense. Instead of denying Hayek's thesis that reformers (whether inadvertently or with full knowledge of what they were about) were in fact promoting an economic system in which all major decisions would be made at the central government level, he seemed rather to be arguing that this responsibility in government hands would not bring the dire consequences Professor Hayek was predicting. And not only was this a much less defensible position from the standpoint of America's entire economic and political development than would have been a more moderate statement of the proper functions of government in a democracy, but it had the tactical disadvantage of pleading guilty to the very charges his opponent was making. If, in short, Professor Hayek weakened his case by adopting a semireactionary point of view, Professor Finer weakened his to an even greater extent by espousing a semiradical one.

But it is not to be concluded from these comments that *Road to Reaction* does not even so offer *The Road to Serfdom* a powerful challenge. Sweepingly but painstakingly, documenting his presentation with details from the American scene with which he was intimately familiar, Professor Finer interposed four major objections to Hayek's charges. First, the market mechanism has not historically proven itself to be nearly as effective a conservator of basic human values as it can be made to seem in discussions couched in abstract terms. Second, the political process in a vigorous democracy has not proven itself to be nearly as ineffective in conserving these same values in the face of greatly expanded government responsibilities as Hayek would have us believe. Third, although it is true that many intellectual conservatives (men like Friederick Hayek) do sincerely believe in competition, the fact is that so few practicing conservatives (businessmen) genuinely believe in it that to talk wistfully of a society built around a free market governed by competition is foolish. Fourth, the responsibilities that would have to be assumed by government if the free market were really to become the primary regulator of economic affairs might more nearly approximate the comprehensive planning which Hayek so bitterly opposes than that gentleman would be willing to concede.

During the years immediately following the publication of these works, numerous other efforts were channelled into this controversy. Two only will be specifically noted here. Another important volume on the liberal side, one to become in time even more widely quoted than *Road to Reaction*, was J. M. Clark's *Alternative to Serfdom*.[17] Written by an economist, and never intended to be more than semi-popular at most, this book is a much more balanced analysis of politico-economic realities in the modern world than either of its predecessors by a man competent to meet Professor Hayek on the latter's own ground. But if the liberal argument improved after Finer, the conservative analysis as unmistakably deteriorated after Hayek. The American version of *The Road to Serfdom* was a volume entitled *The Road Ahead: America's Creeping Revolution* by John T. Flynn, wherein the point of view there presented lost far more by being transformed from philosophy to innuendo than it gained from Americanization.[18]

In retrospect it can be seen why the postwar ideological battle took on a note of urgency—as well as why the concept of planning was given such a prominent place. When just prior to the war a decade of depression had degenerated into a painful stagnation, both conservatives and liberals had their own broad solutions to the policy impasse thus created. The former group naturally saw the country's salvation in a return to principles of economic organization which would accommodate very few of the institutional innovations inaugurated by the New Deal, while to the latter it seemed evident that the role of the government would have to become still more pervasive—and all the more so if businessmen persisted in taking fright at more or less routine government stabilization measures. Indeed, on the premises of post-New Deal liberalism, it seemed that there might well be no way of avoiding involuntary unemployment

[17] J. M. Clark, *Alternative To Serfdom* (New York: Alfred A. Knopf, Inc., 1948).
[18] John T. Flynn, *The Road Ahead* (New York: Devin-Adair Co., 1949).

short of creating what might with some accuracy be termed a "planned economy."

Moreover, the experience of the economy during the war did much to heighten this ideological tension. On the one hand, the comprehensive central planning of production necessitated by the war (or at least the injection into the economy by the government of an unprecedented amount of purchasing power) promptly restored the nation to a condition of full employment, thus adding greatly (if somewhat superficially) to the plausibility of the liberal argument. On the other hand, conservatives saw in this development all the more reason for fearing a return to policy-making by reformers in the postwar period, and when the liberal proposal for full employment legislation began to circulate, these fears could not have been more abundantly confirmed. In other words, now that the war prosperity was over and the economy was thus in danger of slipping back into prewar stagnation, those on both sides of the ideological debate understandably felt uneasy in the face of the policy drift implicit in the fact that neither group held decisive political power—and even a little desperate.

Actually, as the sequel to these events would soon demonstrate, there was no reason for panic. The United States was not about to take a crucial step, except insofar as every important decision creates unalterable history. This country had never retreated significantly after accomplishing basic reforms, nor failed to take a long look at reforms already achieved before departing further from the ways of the past. In short, the only realistic expectation was that America would continue in her historic, pragmatic way, endeavoring to resolve concrete difficulties by making as few changes in the status quo as possible.

QUESTIONS FOR DISCUSSION

1. Why were liberals and conservatives so broadly agreed on the fundamentals of reconversion?

2. What would have been the advantage of ending the war gradually rather than abruptly from the standpoint of reconversion adjustments?

3. In the circumstances, what was the advantage in making a clean break with war controls rather than adjusting to the new situation by degrees?

4. How did the government actively assist the process of reconversion?

5. What was the fundamental issue between conservatives and liberals after World War II?

6. Should the reconversion opportunity have been used to decentralize the nation's manufacturing industries? Why was this not done?

7. How feasible is an unconditional job guarantee for a free enterprise society?

8. Why was it uncertain immediately after the war whether the overriding reconversion problem would be recession or inflation?

9. Could inflation in the United States after World War II have been prevented? Explain how, or why not.

10. Was the "right" decision made on the issue of retaining price controls? What are the most important criteria to use in answering this question?

11. What problems does the right to strike pose for government in a democracy? Why must this right be limited in a modern industrial society?

12. How was the government's role in labor-management controversies altered by the Taft-Hartley Act?

13. Granting its basic premise, how sound do you think the argument presented in Hayek's book was?

14. What weaknesses in the operation of a market economy might a 1946 liberal especially appropriately have mentioned?

15. Why was the New Deal not given the same treatment in the post-World War II period as had been meted out to the New Freedom?

Chapter 27

Frictions and Frustrations

Despite the fact that Congressional committees were now stacked against him, President Truman did not resign himself to a two-year period of reform inactivity. It was simply not in this man to run away from the clang and clamor of partisan politics. Soon after the new Republican Congress began to sit he must have decided to try to pin on this group the epithet "The Worst Congress in the History of the Country." In any event he immediately set out to embarrass the opposition wherever this could be done without jeopardizing his own party's popular support.

GUERILLA WARFARE FROM THE WHITE HOUSE

It would unfairly exaggerate to say that the President's determined fight against inflation was dictated solely by a desire to gain political profit at the expense of the other end of Pennsylvania Avenue. For obvious reasons the nation was now conscious of changes in the level of economic activity as it had never been before, and for these same reasons it was understood that the federal government would henceforth assume a broader responsibility for the over-all operation of the economy than at any previous time. Here was one inheritance from the decade of the 1930's to which few seriously objected. At the same time, however, it would be almost insulting to President Truman's political acumen to suppose that he carefully counted the teeth in the mouth of this gift horse—that he scrupulously avoided using the nation's determination to maintain full employment for partisan purposes.

From both of these standpoints, furthermore, it is understandable why so much of the politico-economic discussion of inflation and related problems took reference from the brand-new Full Employment Act. On the one hand, this legislation was a prime symbol of

577

the nation's altered attitude toward economic stability, and the very process of launching a program boasting so splendid a purpose lent much prestige to activities with which it was directly associated. On the other hand, the newly created Council of Economic Advisers (the President's economic analysis arm under this legislation) rendered to Mr. Truman a report on business conditions every six months during this period, and each such report gave the President an excellent opportunity to make legislative recommendations and then to berate Congress for not taking them seriously.

In point of fact, inflation was not a continuous problem in the immediate postwar period.[1] During the last half of 1946, immediately

TABLE 61. PROGRESS OF INFLATION

Month and Year	Prices	
	Wholesale	Retail
July, 1946	100	100
October, 1946	105	106
January, 1947	116	109
April, 1947	119	112
July, 1947	120	113
October, 1947	126	118
January, 1948	132	121
April, 1948	129	122
July, 1948	135	126
October, 1948	132	126

Source: Department of Commerce, *Survey of Current Business.*

after the de facto ending of effective price controls, prices rose 15 per cent at wholesale and 10 per cent at retail. This advance continued, although at a slower pace, through the first quarter of 1947, but prices at both levels remained surprisingly stable for several months thereafter. About midyear, however, the rise was resumed. The last six months of 1947 saw the consumers' price index increase at an annual rate of 15 per cent, and an irate President began belaboring an obstreperous Congress to take decisive action on this front.

On November 17, 1947, President Truman sent a special message to Congress recommending a comprehensive ten-point inflation-control program well calculated to make conservatives wince. The response of Congress was the Anti-Inflation Act of 1947 passed in December, an enactment solemnly proclaiming its purpose to be

[1] Council of Economic Advisers, *Economic Report of The President* (Washington, D.C.: Government Printing Office, Annual).

to aid in curbing inflationary tendencies, to promote the orderly and equitable distribution of goods and facilities which basically affect the cost of living or industrial production.

Under its provisions the President was given a small fraction of the powers he had asked for. Export controls were extended and strengthened; allocation authority over transportation facilities and equipment was authorized; the Department of Agriculture was asked to encourage conservation practices in the United States and the increased production of food in foreign countries; and the President was given permission to negotiate *voluntary* allocation agreements for the distribution of goods in critically short supply. If ever a bone were disdainfully (defiantly?) thrown to a starving dog, this was that time.

The President renewed his demands in January, 1948. When still no substantial action was forthcoming he sent another special message to Congress on July 27—saying in part:

Positive action by this Government is long overdue. It must be taken now.

I therefore urge Congress to take strong, positive action to control inflation.

I have reexamined the anti-inflation program I proposed to the Congress 8 months ago. In its essentials that program is as sound now as it was then. It has been revised and strengthened in the light of changing circumstances. The program I now propose is as follows:

. . . an excess-profits tax . . . to provide a Treasury surplus and provide a brake on inflation.

. . . consumer credit controls . . . to hold down inflationary credit.

. . . Federal Reserve Board . . . authority to regulate inflationary bank credit.

. . . authority . . . to regulate speculation on the commodity exchanges.

. . . authority . . . for allocation and inventory control of scarce commodities. . . .

. . . [effective] rent controls. . . .

. . . stand-by authority . . . to ration those few products in short supply which vitally affect the health and welfare of our people.

. . . price control for scarce commodities. . . .

The White House could not of course have expected serious action on a program such as this. And if its principal occupant half hoped that Congress would ignore what he insisted was a problem fundamental to the nation's well-being, he was not disappointed. Only two matters closely related to the inflation issue were accorded the dignity of a wide public discussion, and neither of them actually grew out of the President's proposals.

From the beginning of its first session, the Eightieth Congress had been determined to make inroads on the steeply progressive income tax structure created during the war. Twice during 1947 a bill to accomplish this had passed both Houses of Congress, only to be struck down by bluntly worded presidential vetoes. Ostensibly the ground on which Truman based his resistance to this step was the impetus it would give to the upward price spiral, although it was well understood that the President would not have been nearly as negative on the subject of tax reduction if the proposed measure had dealt more generously with low-income receivers than did the revision program preferred by Republicans. In fact, President Truman did in mid-1948 sign a compromise tax reduction measure[2]—perhaps in preparation for the then pending presidential election campaign.

The second inflation-related question to be seriously discussed raised even more sharply the issues dividing conservatives and liberals. Ever since the first few weeks of reconversion progress steel had been in short supply, and therefore this was one of the most difficult trouble spots from the standpoint of price control. For many months men high in government circles, as well as others, insisted that the appropriate remedy for that situation was government-built steel capacity. From the first suggestion of this solution, businessmen in general of course opposed it—in part because the steel industry was felt to be competent to determine when more productive capacity was required, and in part because government-owned plants would then hang over the market for many years after the current crisis had passed. This matter was never openly taken up by the President, and no government building was done to supplement private enterprise in this area, but at least the nation got a hearty laugh when it developed that one of the groups most anxious to secure additional steel production by unorthodox means if necessary was the automobile industry.

Because nothing of consequence came of the President's price control program,[3] and because he nonetheless criticized Congressional-Republican inactivity at every opportunity, his efforts came eventually to be referred to contemptuously in the business press as a "jawbone attack on inflation." But Harry Truman was placing his "jawbone" to a far better use than many realized. The principal

[2] Randolph E. Paul, *Taxation in the United States* (Boston: Little, Brown & Co., 1954).

[3] L. V. Chandler, *Inflation in the United States, 1940-1948* (New York: Harper & Bros., 1951).

justification for concern about the behavior of prices, and in this approach President Truman was fully supported by the Council of Economic Advisers, was that from an inflationary boom must come a deflationary bust of approximately equal dimensions. In the words of the Council:

> But what most fully justifies every effort to halt an inflation is the certainty that, if it runs its course unimpeded, it will spread in its wake the disaster of falling markets, unemployment, and business losses.

Subsequent events have demonstrated that this causal relationship is by no means to be accepted without qualification, but at the moment it was most convincing. It gave high authority and superficial objectivity to the President's repeated announcements that wage increases were lagging dangerously behind price increases—a proposition designed to place the blame for the ensuing deflation upon the business community, even while the responsibility for the current inflation was being laid on the doorstep of the Eightieth Congress.

GHOST OF HENRY CLAY

But though the people's representatives did not choose to make a problem out of inflation, it is not to be supposed that they were in consequence unoccupied. The leaders of the Eightieth Congress had a number of ideas of their own about what would be best for the country, and after labor legislation probably the next most important item on that agenda was the inauguration of changes in America's international economic policy. Here also the nation had for all too many years been moving down a road considered by many conservatives to be most treacherous.

It was not that serious opposition was arising to the country's ebullient postwar internationalism as such—even though this development was in striking contrast to the program conservatives had successfully built after World War I. Indeed it was conceded by virtually all thinking persons that isolationism for the United States was now and would for the foreseeable future remain a relic of the nation's youth.[4] Thus American membership in the United Nations Organization, participation in such supranational cooperative endeavors as the International Monetary Fund and the International Bank for Reconstruction and Development, and foreign loans and giveaway programs such as the British Loan and the Marshall Plan averaging approximately $6 billion per year were the product of an

---

[4] Alvin H. Hansen, *America's Role in the World Economy* (New York: W. W. Norton & Co., Inc., 1945).

essentially bipartisan foreign policy by now broadly taken for granted.

The trouble, in short, was not with internationalism in principle; it was rather that the implementation of the new foreign policy required at one point in particular a repudiation of 150 years of United States history which many conservatives were not prepared to face.

TABLE 62. FRUITS OF RECIPROCITY

| | Rate of Customs Duty | |
Item	Under Smoot-Hawley Schedules	Under Effective Tariff Schedules
1934 imports	46.7	46.7
1947 imports	28.3	15.0
1949 imports	25.8	13.9
1952 imports	24.4	12.2

Source: D. D. Humphrey, *American Imports* (New York: Twentieth Century Fund, Inc., 1955), p. 129. Used by permission.

With the Fair Deal now conducting a tariff reduction program under the Reciprocal Trade Agreements Act such as had not been seen even during New Deal days, it is easily understandable why many members of the Republican Party had concluded that this concerted assault on the historic doctrine "the American market belongs to the American producer" should be brought to an end.

Nor was there even a reasonable basis for doubting that a liberal tariff policy was a necessary accompaniment of the international economic policy this nation had elected to follow. Dollars were critically short throughout the world, while in almost every country there was a powerful demand for American goods to rebuild economies ravaged by the recent war. Given these circumstances, tariff concessions were one of the most obvious tangible evidences this nation could offer of its willingness to help create a more satisfactory world order.[5]

The fact was simply that the tariff reduction shoe was beginning to pinch a good many conservative feet. Industries which had been encouraged to develop under the wide umbrella of America's traditional protective tariff would be inconvenienced by the demolition of so spacious a shelter.

This would itself have been reason enough for a Republican declaration of war on the reciprocal trade agreements program. But

[5] Howard Piquet, *Aid, Trade, and The Tariff* (New York: The Thomas Y. Crowell Co., 1953).

there was also another justification for such a stand. The price support policy devised for the farmer's benefit was based upon maintaining the domestic price of supported products above the world level. A commitment of this kind, coupled with a policy of free trade, was obviously creating an awkward situation.[6] The United States was being compelled to choose which of these two mutually exclusive policies she wished to pursue, and there was of course no question which direction the noncotton agricultural groups preferred to move.

Here was an opportunity made to order for a Republican leadership eager to restore the country to conservative principles. The political foundation on which the New and Fair Deals had been built was a coalition between labor interests and those agricultural regions which had historically been Republican, and it had long been understood that there would not again be a Republican President in the White House until the Middle West returned to its traditional political moorings. Since, therefore, one of the most basic conflicts between that area and the Democratic party was the latter's insistence upon ever lower tariffs, it can readily be seen why Republicans felt that this field needed to be cultivated with particularly great care.

The first fruit of Republican determination to breach the reciprocity stronghold was a 1947 proposal to increase the level of protection available to domestic producers of wool. Passed in both House and Senate, this sabotage of an internationalism as yet far from mature was prevented from becoming law by a presidential veto. A second dimension of this attack involved sugar, the primary instrument used here being import quotas rather than duties. Under the terms of the Sugar Act of 1948 (passed in 1947), domestic sugar producers were for the first time in the history of the industry given a share of the American market stated in absolute tons.[7] This meant that any decline in American consumption would be borne primarily by foreign producers. Because the consequences of this innovation were limited essentially to Western Hemisphere countries, the fate of the world-wide movement for trade liberalization therefore hanging less directly in the balance, the President allowed this measure to become law.

But these challenges to Democratic trade policy were only preliminary to the more fundamental contest to follow. In 1948 the

[6] C. A. Hickman, *Our Farm Program and Foreign Trade: A Conflict of National Policies* (New York: Council on Foreign Relations, 1949).

[7] Joshua Bernhardt, *The Sugar Industry and the Federal Government* (Washington, D.C.: Sugar Statistics Service, 1948).

Reciprocal Trade Agreements Act itself was coming up for renewal, and protectionists were eagerly looking forward to the opportunity of challenging this far more fundamental policy.

Two significant changes were proposed to be added to that law. First, in all future reciprocal trade agreements an "escape clause" was to be included. Such arrangements were not, in other words, to be made so rigid that the United States could not later withdraw concessions granted on the basis of changed conditions. Second, the wide open authority the President had heretofore been granted for purposes of these negotiations was to be tightened a little. The Tariff Commission would henceforth be asked to inform the President (supplying Congress also with a copy of such communications) with respect to all future proposed duty reductions the lowest tariff level that would not injure domestic industry. If, then, the President reduced any duty below this "peril-point" he would be required to send to Congress a statement of his reasons.

Obviously the enactment of these proposals would make this country a much less reliable trading partner in the family of nations. Nor was this result viewed with indifference by all conservatives, either. Important segments of the business community, particularly durable goods manufacturers, had by now developed to the point that their economic well-being was intimately related to the level of their exports. To whatever extent the American market was narrowed for foreign producers by modification of the tariff, purchasing power abroad to buy this country's exports would be correspondingly restricted. It goes without saying, therefore, that these amendments encountered stiff opposition within the Republican party before they were approved by both House and Senate.

But approved they were—and the resulting measure was then sent to President Truman in a form which made disapproval almost unthinkable. To have prevented amendment would have destroyed the entire reciprocity program, one of the key pillars of America's post-World War II foreign policy, and this Harry Truman had no intention of doing. Once again conservatives who had once made a fetish out of minimum government (when it suited their purpose to do so) literally thrust the government into a more active role in business affairs.

GHOST OF CALVIN COOLIDGE

But if the renewal of reciprocity gave the Republican party a favorable opportunity to retrieve lost fortunes in midwestern agricultural areas, other aspects of its relationship with agriculture were less fortunate. In fact it is no exaggeration to suggest that the need at this crucial time to enact basic agricultural legislation was a tragedy of the first order for Republicans anxious to extend their control over the government.

There were three major dimensions of this problem as it once again took the center of the national policy stage. First, the wartime guarantee of 90 per cent of parity during the postwar adjustment period was due to expire in 1948, and arrangements had to be made for a successor farm program. This would not in and of itself have posed particularly difficult problems. Through 1947 a tremendous volume of exports financed by this country's fabulous foreign aid program had kept the prices of agricultural products for the most part above the guarantee level, and it would have been a relatively simple matter to enact new farm legislation if this situation had continued. Unfortunately, however, in the second place, this period of grace abruptly ended early in 1948. In February the prices of a number of important farm products broke sharply; for example, the

TABLE 63. NORMALCY RETURNS TO AGRICULTURE

Period	Prices Received by Farmers (1909-1914 = 100)	Farmers Parity Ratio
1947	278	120
1948—first half	291	116
last half	283	114
1949—first half	259	105
last half	244	101

Source: Department of Agriculture.

price of grain fell 20 per cent during that single month, and continued to fall throughout the entire year.[8] As a result Congress was compelled to take action in this field under what might almost be thought of as crisis conditions. For if these prices had not yet fallen anywhere near depression levels, the fact that legislation had to be enacted against the background of a presidential election campaign—the third basic dimension of that issue—gave this price downturn a far greater significance than would otherwise have been the case.

The way in which these three factors were interconnected can be even more specifically indicated. From almost every standpoint a 90

[8] Murray R. Benedict, *Farm Policies of the United States* (New York: Twentieth Century Fund, Inc., 1953).

per cent guarantee was too high; objectively it seemed clear even in 1948 that such a policy could not stand indefinitely, and indeed even the efforts of the New Deal had not seriously endeavored to achieve so ambitious an objective. Moreover, in their more sober moments many farmers from traditionally Republican states were by no means as closely wedded to a policy of high price supports coupled with substantial government regimentation as Democratic (southern) farmers. The chances were therefore good that a downward adjustment of the guarantee level could have been achieved if prices had held fairly firm during debate on a revised law. But farmers are apt to be much less sober when their prices are falling, and a Republican Congress seeking electoral votes in the Middle West was correspondingly disturbed at the news from the "Wheat Pit" in Chicago.

It can be argued in retrospect that the Republican party in fact gave less heed to the political consequences of what was taking place than its fortunes at the polls demanded. Certainly, as events were abundantly to demonstrate, Republicans were naively overconfident as they went into the 1948 campaign. On the other hand, however, there is a special significance in politics of the saying that old dogs do not easily learn new tricks. Perhaps, indeed, it should be termed remarkable that the Eightieth Congress did not abandon the idea of agricultural prices held up by expenditures from the federal treasury. But whatever interpretation is to be placed upon what happened, the fact remains that the Agricultural Act of 1948 contained two important features which would not endear the Republican party to farmers suffering from declining incomes.

The first of these new features was a concept most popularly referred to as flexible price guarantees. Because it was by now obvious that price supports offered no *cure* for the so-called farm problem, because in other words, the only long range corrective for the current more or less chronic imbalance between the supply of and the demand for agricultural products would be a fundamental shift in demand and supply conditions,[9] it seemed reasonable to devise a payments system that would give farmers themselves a greater incentive to work toward the needed adjustment. The system now set forth as public policy on this point was one calling for relatively high guarantees (up to 90 per cent of parity) where the supply was smallest in relation to demand, and relatively low support levels (as low as 60 per cent of parity) where the supply was greatest in relation to demand.

[9] T. W. Schultz, *The Economic Organization of Agriculture* (New York: McGraw-Hill Book Co., Inc., 1953).

The second innovation in agricultural policy now introduced was closely related to the first as to underlying purpose. For a long time it had been felt by many that a too rigorous adherence to the 1910-1914 parity base period might have unfortunate consequences. Many changes had taken place during the intervening years on both the demand and supply sides of agricultural product markets, and hence free market relationships between prices of various products were now much different than at the earlier time. In order to encourage more effective private enterprise adjustments to dynamic conditions, it was considered necessary to introduce a degree of flexibility in the parity base itself. Accordingly this 1948 legislation, although retaining the 1910-1914 base as the definition of parity to be used in the farm program in general, provided that parities for individual commodities within this broader framework would be calculated on the basis of the average prices prevailing over the immediately preceding ten years. Called modernized parity, this approach was objected to in farm circles not only because any given per cent of parity as a guarantee would henceforth be a smaller dollars and cents figure for a number of products, but also because coupled with a flexible price support policy the parity position of the most seriously overproduced items would drop lower and lower.

Although with the Marshall Plan beginning now to get into full swing the farmers' plight was by no means desperate,[10] and although the innovations written into farm legislation did make provision for a gradual rather than an abrupt change to the new bases, here was unquestionably one major reason why in 1948 a sixteen-year-old voting trend away from the Democratic party west of the Mississippi River was dramatically reversed. There were also, however, other reasons for a cold shouldering of the Republicans in that year by western farmers. For one, a particularly abundant wheat crop was threatening the critical problem of inadequate storage facilities. Repeatedly Congress had been asked to vote funds for an expansion of storage capacity for Commodity Credit Corporation purchases—in the absence of which many farmers might have to sell their product for less than the loan level. But a Congress eager in any event to restrict the government's role in this industry perhaps looked upon that situation as another opportunity to confront farmers with the hard realities of the existing agricultural situation, and these pleas consistently went unheeded.

Still another way in which the Eightieth Congress was overly

[10] Seymour Harris, *The European Recovery Program* (Cambridge: Harvard University Press, 1948).

candid with the farmer from the standpoint of Republican electoral success had to do with agricultural cooperatives. Since the early 1920's these organizations had been exempt from federal income taxation, and more orthodox business interests were becoming increasingly of the opinion that the cooperative's days of infancy were sufficiently over that it could now be brought out from behind this protective shield and asked to compete for survival under the same rules which governed the rest of the economy.[11] A full dress Congressional investigation of this matter was authorized, a parade of witnesses many of whom opposed existing policy was heard and given wide publicity in the conservative press, and the decision was reached not to enact further legislation at that time. Of course, a reversal of the Capper-Volstead philosophy would have been much more injurious to Republican political prospects, but even to raise the issue in this way was most inappropriate from the standpoint of party loyalty in the Middle West—long the citadel of agricultural cooperation.

TABLE 64. FRUITS OF CAPPER-VOLSTEAD

| Type | Number of Farmer Cooperatives in 1950-51 | | |
	Local	Large-scale	Total
Marketing	5,980	527	6,507
Purchasing	3,092	116	3,208
Service	255	7	262
Grand total	9,327	650	9,977

Source: Department of Agriculture.

Is it to be wondered at, then, that western farmers did not heed the invitation offered them in November, 1948, to return to the Republican fold? Though the name on the ballot was Thomas E. Dewey, the spirit behind the platform seemed all too clearly to be that of Calvin Coolidge. The wonder, in short, is not why Dewey lost and Truman won, but why after treating the farmer the way they had the Republicans became so certain their candidate would win.

ON THE DEFENSIVE AGAIN

It would, of course, be an oversimplification to suggest that relationships between midwestern farmers and the Republican party

[11] John H. Davis, *An Economic Analysis of the Tax Status of Farmer Cooperatives* (Washington, D.C.: American Institute of Cooperation, 1950).

constitute a complete explanation of the 1948 presidential election results. No doubt another important factor was the steadfast way the President had stood by the man in the street against an insidious inflation that the Republican Congress was never quite willing to take seriously. Thus when after the nominating conventions Truman called Congress back in special session to do something constructive about this problem (as well as others), and when against the background of continued inactivity on the legislative front he waged a fighting campaign denouncing the political party responsible for the record of "The Worst Congress in the History of the Country," it was easy for millions of American voters to conclude that Harry Truman was on their side. Perhaps this is as near as an American President has ever come to making political profit out of a government so sharply divided against him.

But insofar as Truman's victory in 1948 is attributable to his unyielding stand on the inflation issue, there is here one of American history's most profound ironies. For several reasons the public's confidence at this point in a President whose intentions were unquestionably good was not well placed. First, statistics show conclusively (a fact, however, which could not have been known at that time because of the time lag in information of this kind) that when the 1948 election was held inflation had already run its course. Second, certain of the measures taken by Truman's administration in 1948—for example, a several billion dollar reduction in the national debt, and Federal Reserve actions to tighten credit—must bear a portion of the responsibility for the mild recession now setting in. Third, the tax reduction measure passed by the Republican Congress over the Democratic President's third veto was excellently timed to keep this economic downturn within narrow limits—although the kind of tax reduction Truman preferred and would perhaps have approved would have been still more useful for this purpose.

There were other reasons, too, why the recession of 1948-49 was not severe, some of which are most revealing from the standpoint of the major role in economic affairs the government had assumed since World War II (or even since the early 1930's). For one thing, the primary cause of this dip in business activity was apparently a slackening off of consumer buying now that much of the wartime demand backlog had been filled. However, since there was as yet little diminution in the rate of new house or new car buying, the resulting fall could not be severe. And at least one of the factors behind the continued strength of the demand for housing was the veterans' housing program financed directly by the government, and the fact that this was the first opportunity the nation had had to utilize depression-born innovations in home financing under prosperity conditions.

Another factor involved at this point had to do with foreign demand for American goods. A contributory cause of the recession had been a sharp fall in exports from this country as gold and dollar reserves abroad fell to dangerously low levels and as emergency-temporary foreign aid programs in this country began to taper off. But at

TABLE 65. TRIALS AND TRIBULATIONS OF WORLD LEADERSHIP

Year	Merchandise Exports	Export Surplus	American Foreign Aid	Foreign Expenditure of Dollar Reserves
		(billions of dollars)		
1946	11.9	7.8	5.0	2.0
1947	16.1	11.3	5.7	4.5
1948	13.4	6.3	4.6	0.9
1949	12.5	5.8	5.9	—0.1

Source: Department of Commerce.

just this time Marshall Plan exports were becoming a major item in United States' foreign trade, an item which could be counted on to keep exports at a relatively high level for a number of years.

Still a third benevolent force (from this standpoint) was the "Cold War" which had erupted in 1947. So difficult had relationships become between East and West that active steps were being discussed to rebuild some of the military strength which had been dissipated when the shooting war ended. Even responsible talk about spending additional billions of dollars for national defense was enough to give considerable buoyancy to the economy at this critical time.

America's first postwar recession also had a number of consequences for government-business relationships, the most important of these no doubt being the creation of a totally different environment within which to carve out policy decisions. This fact, combined with the return of the Democratic party to undisputed possession of the government in Washington, was to produce in the ensuing months several significant developments in both foreign and domestic policy.

It is not to be wondered at, to begin with, that the first decline in business activity in a dozen years would send businessmen by the score scurrying to take advantage of the modifications so recently written into the reciprocal trade agreements program. This threat to the more liberal trade policy on which America's foreign economic relationships now rested was promptly met by the retroactive repeal of the 1948 amendments to that law. Simultaneously the President launched his "bold, new program"—the so-called "Point Four" proposal—designed to make this country's industrial know-how available to underdeveloped areas so that backward peoples might more effectively raise their own standards, although this endeavor was implemented at a veritable snail's pace largely as a result of growing American fears of competition from foreign industries our efforts were helping to establish.

On the domestic front the big news was rapid progress toward several important Fair Deal objectives. The minimum wage was raised from 40 to 75 cents per hour, 10,000,000 people were added to those already covered by social security legislation,[12] and provision was made for a substantial expansion of government activity in the fields of slum clearance and low rent housing. With these developments there was confirmed a principle of American historical evolution which the Fair Deal had to date consistently ignored; reform, particularly of the sort requiring government intervention, is most apt to be popular in periods of business decline.

But it is not to be supposed that the liberal orientation swept all before it. For example, it is significant to note that even under these highly favorable circumstances no move was made to implement the President's cherished ideal of national health insurance. Similarly revealing is the fact that first a southern filibuster and then a coalition of Republicans and southern Democrats blocked an administration push for federal legislation prohibiting employment discrimination against Negroes. Even a measure designed to streamline the operation of the federal government in the interest of greater efficiency and lower cost probably resulted in a conservative victory over restrictive regulation. The Reorganization Act of 1949, by giving to the President the authority to name the chairman of each of the regulatory commissions (except the Interstate Commerce Commission) and giving the chairmen of these commissions more specific powers than they formerly possessed,[13] no doubt took away some of the political independence of those bodies.

Another major way in which conservatism raised its head during the first part of Truman's second administration had to do with

[12] Eveline M. Burns, *The American Social Security System* (Boston: Houghton Mifflin Co., 1949).

[13] Committee on Organization of the Executive Branch of the Government, *Task Force Report on Regulatory Commissions* (Washington, D.C.: Government Printing Office, 1949).

bituminous coal, labor, and the Taft-Hartley Act. Early in 1950 the miners again went out on strike, and again the administration believed that the nation's best interest demanded a quick end to this walkout. Unfortunately, however, the only action the President could reasonably take at this point was a Taft-Hartley injunction. Thus it was that the man who had initially vetoed that law, called it "bad, wrong-headed, vicious, and ineffective," and done everything in his power to get it repealed, was compelled to come to terms with this sworn enemy. Moreover, the stand the President had persistently taken to the contrary notwithstanding, the law did work. And when in March the miners went sullenly back to their jobs, the place of the Taft-Hartley Act among the economy's basic institutions was virtually assured.

And then, of course, there were those areas in which conservatism and liberalism were so intermingled that the resultant policies are difficult to classify. At the moment, the classic case in point here was agricultural legislation.

Actually the liberal instincts reflected in the policy proposal now made to Congress by the administration through Secretary of Agriculture Brannan were sound enough. This was especially true insofar as the innovations suggested would help resolve the conflict between agricultural and foreign policies, and the evident interest of the administration in channelling the lion's share of the benefits of this policy to the nation's poorer farmers was a tally on the same side of this scoreboard. It was not even specifically illiberal to seek to transfer some of the burden of payments to farmers from the urban laborer's cost of living to the general taxpayer, although there were many who felt that this indicated a somewhat too exclusive concern for the working class.

The way in which the famous "Brannan Plan" proposed simultaneously to achieve all of these objectives was as follows. Henceforth, instead of being bought by the government at an above-the-market price, farm products (particularly those which were perishable) would be sold by the farmer for whatever they would bring. The seller would then be paid a lump-sum by the government to compensate him for the difference between the free-market price and whatever percentage of parity had been agreed upon—with the proviso, however, that a fairly low limit would be set to the amount of money which could be paid to any one farmer under this program.

It would be putting it mildly indeed to say that the Brannan Plan aroused a storm of controversy. Nor is it surprising that the most bitter opposition arose within the agricultural community itself. Although the Farmer's Union, a farmer organization representing tenants, sharecroppers, and small farmers generally, warmly supported Secretary Brannan's proposal, the American Farm Bureau Federation, an agricultural group speaking frankly for the larger operators, spearheaded a powerful opposition (ostensibly based on the premise that the new program would increase the degree of farmer regimentation). So formidable in fact was resistance to policy changes in these directions that the agricultural program debate in 1949 more and more became a discussion of the pros and cons of retaining the legislation passed the year before.

The decision reached on this latter point was a compromise. Apparently feeling that it would be unwise to repeal these innovations outright, but still unwilling to see them become law at this time, the Democrats postponed the effective date of the application of flexible price supports to wheat, cotton, corn, peanuts, and rice, and the effective date for the application of modernized parity to cotton, wheat, corn, rice, and tobacco. Despite the fact that these departures promised to bring about in time a price support structure more consistent with consumer preferences, export demand, and production costs, the Democratic party was not yet ready to commit itself to the proposition that the farmers most in need of financial aid would receive the least government assistance.

There were many who mourned the demise of the Brannan Plan, maintaining that a great opportunity had thus been lost to put agricultural policy on a more defensible footing. But although the intentions of most of these mourners were sound enough, a goodly number of such tears were surely misplaced. On the one hand, even with the 1949 retreat from 1948 innovations, one major achievement had resulted from this discussion. Support levels were drastically cut back on such highly perishable items as potatoes and eggs where existing policy had become a national scandal. On the other hand, at one crucial point the Brannan Plan did fall far short of a satisfactory, long-range solution to the farm problem. While it is appropriate enough from one point of view to operate on the assumption that agricultural subsidies should not be paid to farmers because they are farmers but rather to families because they are poor (underemployed?)—to limit the benefits from this program which can be received by larger farmers while still holding them to rigorous acreage restrictions would not only raise sharply a fundamental question of equity, but would at the same time violate one of the most elementary premises of American economic life by rewarding the inefficient producer at the expense of his more efficient colleague.

"Economics in the Public Service"[14]

While Republicans and Democrats were threshing out current issues in the field of farm policy, an intra-administration row which had been seething for some time broke into the open. Less discussed at the moment by far than the Brannan Plan, it nonetheless promised to be much more significant in the long-range development of government-business relationships.

The creation of a three-man Council of Economic Advisers as a part of the implementation of the Full Employment Act inevitably raised the problem of orienting the work of this group harmoniously to other parts of the nation's elaborate governmental machinery. In a sense, of course, the widespread use by this time of such nonconstitutional bodies as the Interstate Commerce Commission and the Social Security Administration did much to minimize these difficulties. In certain respects, however, there was a vast difference in concept between the new agency and the typical quasi-legislative, quasi-judicial, administrative organization. Here was a body with no powers whatsoever, and with no responsibility save that of advising the President on stabilization policy.

To be sure, this was not the first time a President of the United States had called in specialists to advise with him on policy matters. Indeed since the early days of the New Deal this had become a common practice. But almost without exception such people had been brought in on either a temporary or an unofficial basis (or both). The Council of Economic Advisers, on the contrary, was explicitly called for in the full employment statute itself as a "permanent" addition to the government's executive branch. Here was another reason why the initial problems with which it had to cope were unique.

There was first and foremost, of course, the problem of giving the Council sufficient prestige among other government agencies that it could speak in its field with a maximum of authority. This was in part a function of the personnel chosen for these three posts—and this part was adequately although not outstandingly taken care of by President Truman. In particular was the choice of Edwin G. Nourse of the Brookings Institution as Chairman a happy one from the standpoint of professional competence and esteem in his own profession. Another part of this need, however, could only be satisfied over time in the form of (among other important items) the President's attitude toward the Council and its work. Beginning with the

[14] Title of a book by Edwin G. Nourse (New York: Harcourt, Brace & Co., Inc., 1953).

Chairman's firm insistence upon adequate office accommodations located near the White House (a matter quite trivial in substance but most vital in the symbolism of organized human society), and extending through the personal relationships established between the Council and the President, this part of the problem of becoming satisfactorily established was also successfully met in a comparatively short period of time.

But at this point a larger difficulty arose. Just what was to be the role of the Council? Was it to be a partisan advocate of its own policy recommendations? Or were these recommendations to be confidential to the President, the Council advocating rather the President's program embodying as it unavoidably would Council recommendations tempered by such political expediencies as the situation of the moment dictated? If, furthermore, this body were to become an advocate of particular policies, how should the existence of disagreement within the Council with respect to those policies be handled? Or, finally, should this group limit its policy formulation activities to advising the President, taking to the stump only for the purpose of promoting public understanding of broad economic relationships.

Almost at once the original members of the Council found themselves not only in disagreement but almost at sword's points over these issues. The Chairman, in the minority from the beginning, believed that the Council should maintain political neutrality; his colleagues felt that the President's advisers on stabilization policy should have a high place in the councils of the party in power. And to complicate matters still further, there arose also an intra-Council controversy cutting more along liberal-conservative lines, a controversy not unrelated to the question of the Council's function. For example, the Chairman opposed while his fellows approved government-built steel capacity to relieve that frustrating postwar shortage. But as the lid of this boiling pot first lifted slightly and then popped completely off, it is now evident that the central issue was more procedural than doctrinal.

For a time the newness of the Council's responsibility, the interest of President Truman in its public acceptance, and the personal prestige and force of its Chairman all contributed to a tolerable degree of harmony built around Professor Nourse's preferences. Slowly but surely, however, other considerations began to gain the upper hand. One of these, of course, was the intense sincerity with which the opposing view was held by, especially, the Council's Vice-Chairman —Leon Keyserling. Another was the President's determination to turn Congressional indifference to inflation to the advantage of himself and his party. And perhaps it is not unfair to suggest that the election upset of 1948 greatly strengthened groups supporting views sympathetic to those held by President Truman.

But whatever the factors at work, the time came when the Chairman concluded that his effectiveness on the Council was at an end. In December, 1948, Nourse sent a letter of resignation to the President. When no response was forthcoming from the White House, he reluctantly stayed at his post, and it was from this most uncomfortable vantage point that he witnessed the insistence by the administration of which he was technically a part on inflation controls long after the replacement of postwar inflation by mild recession. Finally, as of November 1, 1949, the Chairman stepped aside in favor of men more philosophically attuned to the direction President Truman's second term was so clearly taking.

Even before the Full Employment Act had been signed by the President, Senator Murray, one of its prime movers, had said:

When new legislation is enacted, it often happens that many months and sometimes many years are spent in the trial and error process in developing an administrative organization. . . . It would be a tragic commentary upon the vast efforts that have been expended in attaining a sound Full Employment Act if the passage of this legislation were to be followed by the usual period of groping and fumbling.

As of late 1949, more than three years after this had been expressed, it could not have been more obvious that this legislation was not in fact to escape "the usual period of groping and fumbling."

It was as yet too early to say for certain who was right and who wrong in the controversy which had led to this situation. Put differently, few people were willing at this stage to commit themselves on the way the Council might best ensure its survival. Events in history appear to contemporaries as events rather than as history. Two facts, however, were clear. First, the President was for a considerable time unable to secure a replacement for Nourse—the most important point here being that such a body could not long serve a useful function unless it conformed with the underlying expectations of that overwhelming majority of professional economists who essentially agreed with Mr. Nourse with respect to the issues raised in this controversy. Second, it was at this point that sentiment began to rise (in Democratic as well as Republican circles) for abolishing the Council. Was it or was it not a coincidence that this sentiment seemed to flourish broadly in proportion to the overtly political orientation of the Council's *Reports?*

A New Consensus?

Against the background of these developments, it is especially appropriate here to note with some care the content of the fourth annual report of the President's Council of Economic Advisers.[15] Submitted in December, 1949, shortly after the effective date of Nourse's resignation, this document was devoted to a philosophical discussion of the interrelationships between government and business in the United States—"because we find this subject of significance at all times and close to the forefront of general interest now." In a number of significant respects, this statement of principles marks a high point in the post-World War II battle between liberals and conservatives.

Beginning its discussion with a section entitled "Free Enterprise and Free Government," this document set the stage for the discussion to follow by saying:

The balanced emphasis which the Employment Act places upon the merits and responsibilities of free enterprise and free government is typically American and yet of universal import at this midpoint in the twentieth century. In the last century the philosophic base was laid for extremist doctrines that these two freedoms were irreconcilable. . . .

All history shows that freedom in the long run may best be safeguarded through moderation in the adjustment of seeming conflicts. And the American system is so fortunately situated that it furnishes to the world a beckoning example of this kind of moderation. . . .

The particular urgency of this subject exists because there has now grown to maturity a whole generation of Americans touched by the influence of extremists who look upon conflict between business and government as normal. Conditioned by the depression era, extremists on one side have said that our business system broke down through fatal defects and that government took the whole leadership in putting it together again; while extremists on the other side have blamed government for all the tribulations of business. The new generation of Americans should always remember that the breakdown resulted from errors on the part of both government and business; that both joined in forging some of the most practical measures for recovery; and that both must admit imperfection because the recovery was incomplete until the war restored maximum production and employment. . . .

We have now moved far enough away from the depression of the early thirties to start looking ahead, and to appraise the heartening evidence that free enterprise and free government have blended their varying strains into a rewarding effort. The conduct of the war was an example never to be forgotten. The moderate character of the 1949 recession, and the upward turn which followed, would have been impossible without business policies as well

[15] President's Council of Economic Advisers, *Business and Government* (Washington, D.C.: Government Printing Office, 1949).

as public policies based upon greatly increased understanding of economic affairs. . . .

Having thus laid the foundations for a more specific analysis, the Council next enumerated the major trends it saw in "government's attitude toward business."

1. . . . the doctrine of secular stagnation no longer finds place in any important public circle with which we are familiar.

2. . . . the realization that efforts to promote expansion of the total production and income of the economy are more significant than measures to "redistribute" the current product.

3. . . . fuller realization that the flow of income to different parts of the economy should be viewed as an economic no less than a social problem.

4. The problems of our economy appear no longer primarily of . . . preventing any one group from taking unfair advantage of another. . . . But national economic policy should center mainly upon the basic interdependence of the long-range interest of various groups.

5. No thoughtful person within government wants to abandon or vitiate the "antitrust policy." . . . Still it is important to realize that our industrial problems have changed continually and require recurrent examination.

6. . . . away from the purely negative or policing function and toward the affirmative or facilitative approach.

7. . . . in the current and foreseeable economic situation, it is far less important even to contemplate the restoration of the specific controls than it is to realize that they do not for the long pull answer the basic economic questions confronting the American system.

8. . . . "compensatory" public action can help to iron out minor fluctuations of the business cycle and must indeed be used if big ones develop, but . . . the main concentration of economic policy should be upon encouraging stability and growth within our free enterprise system itself.

And side by side with these were next laid "trends in the attitude of business toward government" as seen by this same group.

1. . . . an increased appreciation by business that business and government are not enemies but friends; and that persons permanently in the public service have the same virtues and faults as Americans elsewhere and are equally committed to free enterprise as well as free government.

2. . . . businessmen have come increasingly to realize the immense influence of public policy upon the American economy. The prevalent view that government should adopt policies which "create a favorable environment" for business is a far step from the earlier notion that government should just "let business alone."

3. Recognition by businessmen of the complexity of the modern economy has made a majority of them increasingly distrustful of mere slogans or shibboleths as a guide to the relationship between enterprise and government.

4. The informed businessman of today is acutely aware of the menacing challenge to free enterprise and free government which confronts the West. He knows that this challenge must be met by firm and comprehensive counter-measures. . . . He knows that the United States must take the leadership in these measures. . . . He knows that . . . government must help to mobilize and give leadership to the programs involved.

All of this must not, of course, be taken too literally. This description of recent evolution in the government and business field was not prepared by disinterested observers in an ivory-towered study. It was instead written by liberal partisans so immersed in the political controversies of that time as to have shortly before precipitated a minor crisis inside President Truman's official family, and is therefore properly to be considered as another key item in the ideological battle for the mind of the public then being fought out. In consequence it exaggerated the liberal-conservative harmony which had been achieved, while subtly stating objectives and responsibilities as favorably as possible to the liberal point of view.

On the other hand, however, it seems in the perspective of history legitimate to think of this document as nonetheless reporting with fair accuracy an important economic policy development. In a number of ways it was becoming evident that the tempers which had touched off and been touched off by the Hayek-Finer *et al* debate were now visibly cooling. Liberals were apparently not as anxious to stake out new reform advances as had earlier been the case, while conservatives, it seemed equally clear, were less eager to press for sweeping policy reversals than they had once been.

And what concrete evidence was available to support this dramatic and important conclusion? Two items in particular stand out in this connection. First, although too much emphasis must not be placed on the behavior of a Republican Congress working with a Democratic administration, it would seem to be highly significant that the first major piece of labor legislation since the 1930's did not seriously attack the principle of collective bargaining. Evidently organized labor was to be accepted henceforth as an ineradicable fact of modern economic life. Second, the interest currently being taken by some businessmen in the federal government's responsibility for the overall performance of the economy was another unmistakable case in point. To be sure, forward-looking business groups (the most striking instance here being the Committee for Economic Development born in 1942) were still conservative—were still eager to keep the government's activities from unnecessarily burdening traditional business relationships. The key fact here, however, was that these men were willing to follow the implications of this government responsibility wherever they might lead, and to encourage their business colleagues to do likewise.

Nor was this change in outlook any more difficult to understand than the earlier tension. Indeed, the factor which had been more responsible than any other for creating the prior climax was now contributing to the lessening of political hostility—that is, developments on the economic stabilization front. As attitudes growing out of the failure of the economy to right itself during the 1940's had set liberals and conservatives at one another's throats, just so were responses to postwar prosperity generating more moderate policy demands. As in 1946 the more radical full employment measure preferred by liberals had fallen victim to the mildness of the postwar recession, just so were the ideological extremes of 1946 falling victim to the failure of the 1948-49 recession to develop into a major economic crisis. Because liberals no longer felt compelled to think in

TABLE 66. ENCOURAGEMENT TO MODERATION

Year	Gross National Product (billions)	Industrial Production (1947-1949 = 100)	Automobile Production	Construction Expenditures (billions)	Unemployment (millions)
1948	$257.3	104	93	$21.7	2.1
1949	257.3	97	122	22.8	3.4
1950	285.1	112	159	28.4	3.1

Source: Council of Economic Advisers, *Economic Report of the President, 1955*.

terms of complete economic planning as the only way of avoiding prolonged involuntary unemployment, conservatives did not feel so pessimistic about the future of their world.

In short, and from an even more general point of view, it might appropriately be said that partisans on both sides of this controversy were losing much of their earlier panic.[16] On the one hand, conservatives could now see that their influence in policy-making was still considerable even if it was not as complete as it had once been. Liberals, for their part, were beginning to understand that a greatly lessened policy influence for them was not to mean a return to predepression laissez faire.

A term frequently used in discussing government–business relationships today is "mixed economy." Although this concept does not

[16] Samuel Lubell, *The Future of American Politics* (New York: Harper & Bros., 1952).

always carry exactly the same connotation, one of the most basic meanings ordinarily implied thereby is that a new community consensus has evolved to replace the old consensus built around 19th century institutions.[17] It was to this historic transition that a Council of Economic Advisers, itself in turmoil from the political winds without and violent dissension within, was pointing when it called attention to the new politico-economic harmony it saw developing.

What was the nature of this new consensus? Again it would be futile to attempt a complete analysis, but a few outstanding features can nonetheless be suggested.

A first point to note in this connection is that to a considerable extent the community as a whole was beginning to take for granted the simultaneous existence of two things which had historically been considered incompatible with one another—a government possessing great powers and charged with a wide variety of important responsibilities, standing side by side with an enterprise economy in which business managers continue to make policy decisions on the basis of profit considerations. In the second place, liberals were now at last conceding the desirability (inevitability?) of an economy built around a relatively small number of large concerns, whereas conservatives were (reluctantly?) conceding the need for a government powerful enough to deal with big business on even terms. Still a third key to the attitude transformation taking place was the understanding rapidly becoming current on both sides of the ideological fence that, although the economic game was henceforth to be played according to somewhat different rules, the rule book was not to be thrown away. And fourth, it was by now broadly agreed that power in the hands of private enterprise is not nearly as benevolent, and that power in the hands of government is not nearly as malevolent, as the laissez faire tradition had long insisted.[18]

When, furthermore, this new consensus is applied to the problem of economic stabilization, it can be seen how effectively it struck at the roots of the vicious circle which had paralyzed the economy in the late 1930's. The situation then existing has been described as one in which conservatives refused to permit liberals to lubricate the oil-dry gears of the economic mechanism on the grounds that the lubricant in hand contained a large admixture of sand, whereas liberals in turn refused to subject the oil they wanted to use either to

17 Frank D. Graham, *Social Goals and Economic Institutions* (Princeton: Princeton University Press, 1949).

18 Seymour Harris (ed.), *Saving American Capitalism* (New York: Alfred A. Knopf, Inc., 1948); and D. M. Keezer, *Making Capitalism Work* (New York: McGraw-Hill Book Co., Inc., 1950).

laboratory tests or further refinement. By now it was apparent to conservatives that much of what they had taken to be sand had in reality been oil, and liberals could now as clearly see that their oil had indeed contained impurities. Dropping the figure, what liberals had learned was that there are limits beyond which the government cannot go in taking over the responsibility for the economy's performance without vitally damaging the values inherent in private enterprise; by the same token the lesson being brought home to conservatives was that the American profit-and-loss system is by no means as delicate from this standpoint as they had heretofore supposed. Thus (to suggest only the classic case in point) who would have dreamed a decade earlier that this economy could generate and sustain a state of high prosperity in the face of a national debt exceeding $250 billion?

QUESTIONS FOR DISCUSSION

1. Why was Congress so reluctant to pass the inflation control legislation President Truman believed to be necessary?

2. What was the principal issue associated with taxation between Congress and the President? Which viewpoint was most nearly correct?

3. Do you approve of the use of important policy issues for political purposes? Explain.

4. Why was trade liberalism such an important factor in post-World War II foreign policy?

5. Explain the conflict between foreign trade policy and the price support program.

6. What important interest inside the Republican party no longer believed in protectionism, and why?

7. Why did agricultural policy become critical again so suddenly?

8. How were the agricultural policy innovations of 1948 to help solve the farm problem over the long pull?

9. Explain the connections between farm policy and the 1948 presidential election.

10. In what ways did the 1948-49 recession interrelate with the role of government in economic life?

11. List and explain the major strengths and weaknesses of the Brannan Plan.

12. Why did the Council of Economic Advisers have an especially difficult time establishing itself within the circle of government agencies?

13. Who was right and who wrong in the controversy over the nature of the work of this body?

14. Which of the trends enumerated by the President's Council of Economic Advisers do you consider most important, and why?

15. What is meant by the term "mixed economy"? Is such an adjustment really possible in the long run?

16. What were the most important new rules by which the economic game was to be played?

Chapter 28

Antitrust Laws Come of Age

Another important aspect of the post-World War II economy which might be attributed at least in part to the new consensus was a condition of more nearly stable equilibrium on the antitrust front than had yet been seen. Between 1890 and 1914 this effort was complicated by its own newness, and when the first experimental steps in this field met head-on a rapidly evolving economic structure the result was a very dynamic situation indeed. Before the antitrust program could settle down, furthermore, new legislation, a major war, and an uncompromising conservatism all served to keep this pot boiling for another decade and a half. At this point the Great Depression overtook normal peacetime activities, and the astonishing New Deal somersault from the National Industrial Recovery Act to the Temporary National Economic Committee claimed the center of this stage, after which an even more comprehensive war effort introduced still another major abnormality into these relationships. Now, for the first time in half a century, laws which were at this point fairly well established were to be applied in a context free of both political and economic extremes.

THE BIG STICK PADDED

One point at which this new equilibrium can be seen is in the antitrust literature of the early postwar period. One of the most widely quoted items in the liberal's library had come to be *The Decline of Competition* by Arthur Robert Burns.[1] Written in the 1930's, and making full use of the information then being developed concerning the American economy during the fabulous 'twenties, this volume painstakingly documented the thesis set forth in its title. By the early 1950's, however, this approach to that subject was on the defensive. Beginning with Professor Schumpeter's brilliant discus-

[1] (New York: McGraw-Hill Book Co., Inc., 1936).

sion of dynamic competition as a process of "creative destruction" in an industrial society in which large firms play the dominant role,[2] a formidable documentation was being prepared (in substantial part by liberals) of the proposition that effective competition can be found in the structure of consumption and the process of innovation as well as in the static rivalry of firms producing a more or less identical product.[3]

Two facts especially indicate that the focus of this debate had ceased to be the allocation of resources by way of the economists' model of pure competition. On the one hand, so deeply rooted was the new emphasis becoming that a prominent liberal of the New Deal era wrote a book in which he chastised the courts roundly for the severity with which the antitrust laws were then being applied.[4] On the other hand, the attack on big business, the plea for a more vigorous antitrust policy, was more and more taking reference from the threat of industrial concentration to political democracy rather than the historic ground of economic exploitation.[5] And in this connection it is worth noting that one of the important volumes taking that position was written by a man most of whose adult life had been devoted to a successful career inside big business.[6]

Another point at which a new emphasis in antitrust endeavors could be seen was the types of cases absorbing most of the efforts of enforcement. Thus whereas for perhaps twenty-five years after the passage of the Sherman Act the most important proceedings had been actions to break up existing combinations, suits so oriented now constituted only a minor proportion of the energies going into antitrust work.[7]

This fact can be most readily documented by reviewing the dis-

[2] *Capitalism, Socialism, and Democracy* (New York: Harper & Bros., 1942). The term "creative destruction" here refers to the way in which new products, new production processes, and new methods of business organization destroy existing business structures even while they are adding new horizons to living standards.

[3] J. K. Galbraith, *American Capitalism: The Concept of Countervailing Power* (Boston: Houghton Mifflin Co., 1952); and A. D. Kaplan, *Big Business in a Competitive System* (Washington: Brookings Institution, 1954).

[4] David Lilienthal, *Big Business: A New Era* (New York: Harper & Bros., 1953).

[5] James T. Adams, *Big Business in a Democracy* (New York: Charles Scribner's Sons, 1945); and Robert A. Brady, *Business as a System of Power* (New York: Columbia University Press, 1947).

[6] T. K. Quinn, *Giant Business: Threat To Democracy* (New York: The Exposition Press, 1953).

[7] F. W. Machlup, *The Political Economy of Monopoly* (Baltimore: The Johns Hopkins University Press, 1952); A. G. Papandreau and J. T. Wheeler, *Competition and its Regulation* (New York: Prentice-Hall, Inc., 1954); and George W. Stocking and Myron W. Watkins, *Monopoly and Free Enterprise* (New York: Twentieth Century Fund, Inc., 1951).

solution record of the post-Hoover period—that is, activity in the field of "trust-busting" in the popular sense of that term. And in all fairness it must be noted at the outset that a number of successes were achieved on this front. For example, back in the middle of the depression General Electric and Westinghouse had been compelled to make an independent firm out of their Radio Corporation of America subsidiary. A little later, during World War II, an investigation of monopoly in the broadcasting industry by the Federal Communications Commission issued in an antitrust proceeding against the National Broadcasting Company compelling that company to sell its "Blue Network" (later the American Broadcasting Company).[8]

Still more recently one of the truly classic dissolution actions of all time was brought against the Pullman Company, this case reaching its dramatic climax in 1947. The government had found that this concern had achieved its dominant position in the sleeping car business in the United States by the use of a number of questionable devices such as: (1) exclusive dealing arrangements; (2) refusal to service cars owned by others; (3) the exclusive use of cars produced by a manufacturing subsidiary; and (4) staggered expiration dates on long-term contracts making it possible for Pullman to deal with its major customers on a one-at-a-time basis. These findings seemed, in the opinion of the Department of Justice, to warrant a demand for the separation of the manufacture of these cars from their operation, and when this issue was brought before the Supreme Court the government's order was affirmed without opinion.

A similarly drastic remedy was upheld in another case involving vertical integration—this time in the motion picture industry. The most widely discussed charge against the principal integrated producers was "block-booking," a tying arrangement through which the licensing by unaffiliated theaters of second- and third-rate pictures was made the condition for the availability of first-rate films, but there were a number of other practices complained of as well. Broadly speaking, what the Antitrust Division objected to was the use of their positions as integrated producer-exhibitors by the "Big Five" to discriminate against independent exhibitors, and the Supreme Court not only accepted as proved virtually every one of the government's specific charges but in addition agreed to a divorce between production and exhibition in this industry.[9]

---

[8] T. P. Robinson, *Radio Networks and the Federal Government* (New York: Columbia University Press, 1947).

[9] *United States* v. *Paramount Pictures*, 334 U.S. 141 (1948).

Of course it is not to be supposed that the government won all of its cases of this kind in the post-depression-postwar era. Defeats were recorded as well. However, setbacks were scarcely more numerous than victories—and when it is remembered that as many antitrust actions of all sorts were launched in the decade following World War II as in the entire history of those laws prior to 1945, the only conclusion which can logically be drawn is that the responsible agencies were simply not pressing dissolution proceedings.

Nor is that surprising. From the beginning the antimonopoly "pay dirt" secured from a veritable mountain of dissolution ore had been small. And a brief glance at two epochal government defeats on this front make it clear that even jurists appointed by Democratic presidents were leaning over backwards to avoid tampering with long established property relationships.

The first of these defeats centered around the aluminum industry. Prior to the Second World War production of aluminum had for all practical purposes emanated from a single firm—the Aluminum Company of America.[10] Directly attacking this concern as a monopoly in restraint of trade under Section 2 of the Sherman Act, the Department of Justice asked the courts for a decree dissolving it in the interest of more effective competition.

Using the earlier United States Steel and International Harvester decisions as its authority, the Company invoked the rule of reason. As in these precedent-making cases, the defendant's brief maintained, whatever a study of the past might show from this standpoint, that the Aluminum Company was not now engaging in predatory practices. Because, in other words, it was the law of the land that "the existence of unexerted power" was not a violation of the antitrust laws, and because the Company had achieved its monopoly position innocently (that is without removing competitors from the field through combination), it was argued that no action could properly lie against it.

Speaking for the Court of Appeals acting here as the court of last resort, and casting grave doubts upon long-accepted Supreme Court doctrines in the process, Judge Learned Hand denied every one of the Company's major contentions.[11] He made it clear, first, that monopoly as well as price-fixing agreements as such is illegal per se. This pronouncement was then broadly supplemented by the assertion that "unexerted power" is a contradiction in terms—that the

[10] Charles C. Carr, *Alcoa: An American Enterprise* (New York: Rinehart & Co., Inc., 1952).

[11] *United States* v. *Aluminum Company of America*, 148 F. 2d 416 (1945).

power to control prices means that prices are in fact under control. And finally, Judge Hand ridiculed the idea of monopoly being achieved innocently. In the case at bar it was his belief that a monopoly position had been attained as deliberately as though based on a thousand mergers.

Here was indeed strong language, and the force of Judge Hand's opinion in this case promised at least to provide useful precedent for future antitrust opinions. As a practical matter, however, as far as the aluminum industry was concerned, its importance is easily exaggerated. An opinion in an antitrust proceeding is no better than the decree which results therefrom. In this instance, though it could hardly be said that what was done was illogical or unreasonable, the remedy actually demanded was far less thoroughgoing than the one the government had requested.

In antitrust cases the higher federal courts do not issue final decrees. Accordingly this issue was next remanded to District Court for the issuance of a decree consistent with the Court of Appeals opinion. The District Court Judge in turn decided to postpone action until after Washington had made up its mind what to do with the aluminum production facilities created for the government during the war. When a decision was made to establish two new competitors for Alcoa (Kaiser Aluminum and Reynolds Metal), Judge Knox did not feel it would be appropriate to break the defendant concern into several parts as Justice had asked. Instead Alcoa was required to sever its connection with Aluminium Ltd. of Canada, to license domestic competitors under its patents, and to refrain from using its control of the basic raw materials of this industry to "squeeze" its competitors.[12]

And one other feature of this latter decision even seemed to add insult to injury as far as the government's brief was concerned. Consistent with more than 150 years of economic theory, the government's case had been built around the idea of competition as the result of rivalry between producers of a homogeneous product. The Court, on the other hand, explicitly recognized the possibility that a whittled-down Alcoa might be less technologically progressive, and that aluminum is in active competition with producers in a variety of other industries—both of these notions coming almost bodily out of Professor Schumpeter's analysis.

The other major antitrust defeat on the dissolution front involved the United States Steel Corporation. That concern had soon after World War II acquired title to an important steel producing plant

---

[12] *Aluminum Company of America* v. *United States,* 91 F. Supp. 333 (1950).

located in the western part of the country built during the war by the government. Shortly after this deal had been consummated, the Corporation through one of its subsidiaries (Columbia Steel Company) proposed to acquire the assets of the largest independent fabricator of steel products on the west coast, the Consolidated Steel Corporation. To the businessmen who worked out the details of this transaction, it seemed only a logical integration of the Geneva, Utah production facilities with the fabrication capacity of Consolidated. To the government, however, this merger seemed to threaten exclusion of United States Steel competitors as sellers to Consolidated, and hence to be an illegal restraint of trade under the Sherman Act.

There is considerable agreement among economists that a strict extension of the reasoning developed in other postwar antitrust cases would have required Court disapproval of this combination.[13] The Court, however, felt differently. Taking note of the fact that Consolidated had over a 16-year period accounted for only 3 per cent of the demand for rolled steel products, and calling attention also to the fact that the Attorney General had approved United States Steel's acquisition of the Geneva plant, Justice Reed once again invoked the rule of reason to frustrate antitrust efforts. Specifically referring to the Paramount decision, the majority concluded that the vertical integration sought by the acquiring corporation would not "unreasonably restrict the opportunities of the competitor producers."

Four Justices objected to this reasoning, and in Justice Douglas' dissent there was set forth a ringing declaration of the liberal stand on this issue:

This is the most important antitrust case which has been before the Court in years. It is important because it reveals the way of growth of monopoly power —the precise phenomenon at which the Sherman Act was aimed. Here we have the pattern of the evolution of the great trusts. Little, independent units are gobbled up by bigger ones. At times the independent is driven to the wall and surrenders. At other times any number of "sound business reasons" appear why the sale to or merger with the trust should be made. If the acquisition were the result of predatory practices or restraints of trade, the trust could be required to disgorge. . . . But the impact on future competition and on the economy is the same though the trust was built in more gentlemanly ways. We have here the problem of bigness. Its lesson should by now have been burned into our memory by Brandeis. . . . Power that controls the economy should be in the hands of elected representatives of the people, not in the

[13] C. E. Griffin, *An Economic Approach to Antitrust Laws* (New York: American Enterprise Assoc., 1951).

hands of an industrial oligarchy. Industrial power should be decentralized. It should be scattered into many hands so that the fortunes of the people will not be dependent on the whim or caprice, the political prejudices, the emotional stability of a few self-appointed men. The fact that they are not vicious men but respectable and social minded is irrelevant. That is the philosophy and the command of the Sherman Act.[14]

There was also a sequel to the Columbia Steel decision—although one more heartening to the liberal point of view than the final episode in the postwar action against the Aluminum Company of America. Ever since the passage of the Clayton Act the prohibition against holding company mergers had been narrowly interpreted,[15] even to the point of permitting stock ownership to be used for the purpose of effecting asset merger.[16] In 1950 by means of the Celler Antimerger Act, Section 7 of the Clayton Act was amended by extending to asset consolidation the same legal restrictions long applicable to holding company type acquisitions.[17] Unfortunately, the large number of horses which had already been stolen from this barn greatly limited the value of such a step to the liberal cause—and in fact there is not even any assurance that had this law been in effect it would have prevented the Columbia-Consolidated merger.

The attitude of the courts was one reason why "trust-busting" in the original meaning of that term did not seem to be a fruitful activity during these years. Another was a dramatic new wave of consolidations making it more than doubtful if even a protracted period of successful dissolution work could keep this hole in the dike closed. In a few short years after the war more than 2,000 manufacturing and mining concerns with assets of approximately $5 billion disappeared through combination. As the Federal Trade Commission summarized this situation:[18]

The recent merger movement has extended to virtually all phases of manufacturing and mining. . . . The new wave of mergers and acquisitions which set in as the war drew to a close has, of course, been superimposed upon the plateau of economic concentration which already prevailed in this country.

Nor was any end in sight for this development.

[14] *United States* v. *Columbia Steel Company*, 334 U.S. 495 (1948).

[15] House of Representatives, *Congress and the Monopoly Problem: Fifty Years of Anti-Trust Development* (Washington, D.C.: Government Printing Office, 1950).

[16] *Arrow-Hart & Hegeman Electric Company* v. *Federal Trade Commission*, 291 U.S. 587 (1934).

[17] Commerce Clearing House, *The Federal Antitrust Laws* (New York: Commerce Clearing House, 1952).

[18] *The Merger Movement: A Summary Report* (Washington, D.C.: Government Printing Office, 1948).

CONSPIRACY IN NEW CONTEXTS

It is, however, not quite fair to draw conclusions about the status of antitrust endeavors after examining only cases involving dissolution in the technical sense. Attacks on looser combinations had also been a part of this work from the beginning, and indeed the most successful demolition activity had perhaps always been of this kind. How was the so-called double standard faring by this time—namely, the judiciary's inclination to judge "tight" corporate arrangements and "gentlemen's agreements" by a different yardstick in antitrust cases?

The short answer to this question is that it was standing approximately intact. Crude price-fixing activities were still being summarily destroyed without benefit of the rule of reason so consistently finding its way into cases involving monopolization by a single firm. But this short answer is more misleading than helpful. Of cases of simple conspiracy, there were by now very few. Thus the only postdepression decision of importance was a 1940 one reaffirming the High Court's traditional stand against direct price agreements—a stand much in need of reaffirmance after the depression-born aberration of the Appalachian Coals decision.

At issue in this proceeding was an agreement by which the major oil companies in the Middle West were controlling the price of gasoline by purchasing marginal supplies from independent producers in that area (in this way relieving pressure which would otherwise have thrown these supplies on the market regardless of the effect on price). In rejecting the contention that the price established was a fair one, Justice Douglas had this to say:[19]

Any combination which tampers with price structures is engaged in an unlawful activity. Even though the members of the price-fixing group were in no position to control the market, to the extent that they raised, lowered, or stabilized prices they would be directly interfering with the free play of market forces. . . . Whatever economic justification particular price-fixing agreements may be thought to have, the law does not permit an inquiry into their reasonableness. They are all banned because of their actual or potential threat to the central nervous system of the economy.

When the focus of attention here is broadened to include trade association cases, the horizon lifts a little. But it is worth emphasizing in this connection that the activities of these organizations did not become an important element in antitrust work until the Sherman Act had been on the statute books for two decades. Further-

---

[19] *United States* v. *Socony-Vacuum Oil Company*, 310 U.S. 150.

more, even when this extension is made little was added to the law of conspiracy in the early postwar period. At this point, too, only a single case of consequence was litigated, and, interestingly enough, it was not agreed what its outcome really was from the standpoint of the contemporary liberal-conservative tug-of-war on such questions.

In a searching opinion rendered during the Great Depression, the Supreme Court had delineated three basic principles which it felt could constructively be used to separate legal from illegal trade association price activities.[20] As long as these were confined to the collection, compilation, and dissemination of market information, if price data were made available to buyers as well as sellers, and insofar as the information disseminated were unidentified data on closed transactions—the Supreme Court had suggested that those involved in agreements of this kind might feel reasonably safe from legal attack.

Admittedly the Tag Manufacturers' Institute case (1949) was a borderline one. But of course so too are the majority of causes which get into the higher federal courts—or, indeed, almost any court for that matter. This organization had for some time been following an open-price policy in which the current price list of every member (not merely unidentified price information relating to past sales) was made available to every other member. In defending these arrangements against a Federal Trade Commission challenge, however, the Court of Appeals took specific note of several extenuating considerations—all within the framework of previous interpretations. Because the information exchanged was for all practical purposes public property, and because actual price lists in this industry were so often used only as a point of departure in negotiating with customers, it was concluded that this information service had not been used to restrain competition.[21] In the words of the Court:

Nor is there evidence of "retaliatory action" by any subscribers to coerce other subscribers into adherence to list prices. They all engaged in off-list pricing to such an extent that it would be wholly irrational to infer that the essence of their agreement was that they would adhere to their current price lists. . . .

The fact is that the conspiracy dimension of the antitrust laws was concerning itself less and less with issues of the older and simpler type, and progressively more with newer and increasingly complex varieties of that type of relationship. For example, an aspect of this problem which had only recently come into its own had to do

[20] *Sugar Institute* v. *United States*, 297 U.S. 553 (1936).
[21] *Tag Manufacturers' Institute* v. *Federal Trade Commission*, 174 F. 2d 452 (1949).

with trade association activities in the field of international trade, where the applicable legislation dated back only to 1918.[22]

For some twenty years after the Webb-Pomerene Act was passed, the Federal Trade Commission did almost nothing to supervise export trade associations claiming exemption under its terms. Then, in 1940, the Commission took its first formal action in that area, while simultaneously the Temporary National Economic Committee made public a wide variety of abuses being practiced by these groups. Beginning in 1944 the Commission launched a series of investigations, the outcome of which was a number of voluntary adjustments of cooperative activities in the international trade operations of several industries.

At this point the Department of Justice also decided to take a hand in this work. Some years prior to this the Federal Trade Commission, speaking for an isolationist America, had concluded that the Webb-Pomerene Act was no bar to an international cartel arrangement affecting only the foreign market. When, however, the Department of Justice in 1939 inaugurated its own campaign against cartel abuses, this ruling was directly challenged. And when in 1945 the Supreme Court was given an opportunity to choose between these two interpretations, it unequivocally held with Justice.[23] This decision was then supplemented by a District Court judgment against the National Lead Company[24] and a Supreme Court ruling against the Timken Roller Bearing Company[25] to the same general effect, all of these actions combined making it clear that the government was in earnest about the matter of monopoly in foreign trade.

Another new form in which the conspiracy problem was now arising was the modern railroad rate bureau. After rate regulation in that industry had been strengthened soon after the turn of the century by a series of enactments expanding Interstate Commerce Commission responsibilities and authority, it had been broadly assumed that that agency constituted the public's protection against collusive price-fixing. (Had not the Transportation Act of 1920 even gone so far as to authorize both pooling and consolidation under Commission supervision?) Furthermore, there was a special reason why rate bureaus in the railroad industry had always been considered to be in a class apart from ordinary trade association activities. Railroad

[22] G. W. Stocking and M. W. Watkins, *Cartels in Action* (New York: Twentieth Century Fund, Inc., 1946).

[23] *United States Alkali Export Association* v. *United States*, 325 U.S. 196 (1945).

[24] *United States* v. *National Lead Company*, 63 F. Supp. 513 (1945).

[25] *Timken Roller Bearing Company* v. *United States*, 341 U.S. 593 (1951).

rate-making cannot be effectively organized on a firm-by-firm basis. The entire economy is so built around the railroad price structure that a rate change of any importance must be considered in the light of its consequences for a large number of rate relationships. Thus it was that it had long been the accepted practice for groups of carriers to form rate associations as a convenient method of introducing the necessary cooperation into rate-making—even though it was admittedly a practice which, at almost any other point in the economy, would have been challenged under the antitrust laws.

Shortly before the outbreak of World War II a number of southern leaders had banded together to make a major protest against the higher rates charged southern industries on class freight by the nation's railroads than was charged in so-called "Official Territory." In preparing this case for presentation to the Interstate Commerce Commission, one of the key facts which forced itself on the attention of its sponsors was the cooperative way in which railroad rates were typically made.[26] Simultaneously, toward the end of the war, the Department of Justice brought suit against the Association of American Railroads, and the State of Georgia filed against a number of individual carriers. Both suits charged price conspiracy under the antitrust laws.

The Georgia case was concluded first. In 1945 the Supreme Court ruled that the railroads were not exempt from attack on charges of violating the Sherman Act.[27] Although the Court granted that Congress had given the Commission power "to lift the ban of the antitrust laws in favor of carriers who merge or consolidate," there did not exist similar authority "to remove rate-fixing combinations from the prohibitions contained in the antitrust laws."

For those who believed in the value of rate bureaus in the railroad industry, this decision was both a blow and a suggestion. No time was lost in giving practical effect to the suggestion. A bill was readied granting the Interstate Commerce Commission broad supervisory authority over the activities of railroad rate bureaus—thus permitting cooperative rate-making to continue. When the Reed-Bulwinkle bill finally passed both Houses of Congress in 1948 President Truman gave it a symbolic veto, but expert opinion as to the need for a mechanism allowing rate changes to be viewed in perspective was so nearly unanimous that it became law anyway.

And what of the regional freight rate discrimination issue out of

[26] Wendell Berge, *Economic Freedom For The West* (Lincoln: University of Nebraska Press, 1946).

[27] *Georgia* v. *Pennsylvania Railroad Company*, 324 U.S. 439 (1945).

which this proceeding had grown? The Interstate Commerce Commission found that such discrimination was in fact being practiced, and the federal courts refused to intervene. However, by the time this case had run a long legal gantlet it was generally recognized that this problem was by no means as important a matter from the standpoint of southern industrialization as it had been advertised as being; too small a proportion of railroad freight moved on class rates for this to have been the case. Furthermore, it was also understood that because of the intricacy of railroad regulation in general and the financial plight of so many railroads in particular, these inequities would not soon be completely removed. Nonetheless the die was cast, and a major readjustment of railroad class rates was gotten under way.

But even the matter of railway rate bureaus was not the newest type of antitrust problem tackled on the conspiracy front—nor the most important. Much more significant was an action brought against the major producers in the tobacco industry, in which two long-standing questions were given more definitive answers than had been forthcoming heretofore.

The first of these questions traced back to the United States Steel and International Harvester decisions. Ever since that time the courts had stood firm on the position then taken on price leadership. With equal persistence the government had continued its efforts to secure a modification of that interpretation. In 1946 this was accomplished through a Supreme Court opinion which, though it did not directly modify these earlier rulings, did serve to narrow considerably the behavior of this sort which would be unqualifiedly permitted.

Closely related to this question (indeed perhaps only stating it in a more technically legal way) was the matter of proof requirements where conspiracy was charged. It had of course long been accepted that unlawful cooperation may be proven, if better evidence is unavailable, by circumstantial reasoning. As the Supreme Court had expressed this point at an early date: "It is elementary that conspiracies are seldom capable of proof by direct testimony, and may be inferred from the things actually done." However, the Department of Justice had for some time been endeavoring to go beyond this. Specifically what was wanted, and what was to a considerable extent now achieved, was court approval of the following proposition: when several firms consistently follow identical policies with respect to price and related matters, each one knowing that the others are likewise following these policies, there exists prima-facie evidence of conspiracy.

A beginning had been made just prior to the war. In a case in which the government had charged unlawful conspiracy against a number of motion picture distributors, the Supreme Court first indicated a willingness to infer the existence of an agreement from the identical behavior of a group of firms.[28]

It taxes credulity to believe that the several distributors would, in the circumstances, have accepted and put into operation with substantial unanimity such far-reaching changes in their business methods without some understanding that all were to join, and we reject as beyond the range of probability that it was the result of mere chance.

This reasoning was carried further three years later in a case in which a manufacturer of hardboard had signed an identical agency agreement with each of his competitors authorizing them to distribute his product and fixing selling prices. The Court found these documents illegal on the ground that each participant must have known "that its contract was not an isolated transaction but a part of a larger arrangement."[29]

Armed with these weapons, the Department of Justice was emboldened to accuse the "Big Three" in the cigarette industry with collusion in the purchase of leaf tobacco and the sale of cigarettes. Actually had it not been for a special feature of this case it would have posed no issue at all beyond that raised by its two predecessors. In both of these other situations the parallelism complained of conformed closely with a plan the industry leader had previously proposed, whereas in the American Tobacco Company case there was not a trace of any such proposal. The basis for the new complaint, therefore, was solely a striking parallelism in behavior from firm to firm. For example, in 1931, one of the worst business years of the recent depression, these three concerns had *raised* their sale prices at precisely the same time and by exactly the same amounts.

Here also the Supreme Court was unwilling to overtax its credulity, and the doctrine of implied conspiracy became even more deeply rooted.[30] In the words of the Court:

No formal agreement is necessary to constitute an unlawful conspiracy. . . . The essential combination or conspiracy in violation of the Sherman Act may be found in a course of dealing or other circumstances as well as in an exchange of words. . . . Where the circumstances are such as to warrant a jury in finding that the conspirators had a unity of purpose or a common design and understanding, or a meeting of minds in an unlawful arrangement, the conclusion that a conspiracy is established is justified.

[28] *Interstate Circuit* v. *United States*, 306 U.S. 208 (1939).
[29] *United States* v. *Masonite Corporation*, 316 U.S. 265 (1942).
[30] *American Tobacco Company* v. *United States*, 328 U.S. 781 (1946).

It would perhaps not be argued that this decision was a major antitrust achievement[31]—even though the Supreme Court did here explicitly endorse the conclusions reached by Judge Hand in the aluminum case. On the one hand, this proceeding had been built around a criminal charge, with the result that no remedies for the future were forthcoming. On the other hand, both the courts and the Federal Trade Commission were later considerably to soften the implications of the conscious parallelism doctrine. But that a fundamentally new dimension of the conspiracy problem had been opened up there could be no doubt.

F.T.C. Versus "Pittsburgh Plus"

A third important point at which to look to get a well-rounded picture of antitrust in action under what might be termed modern conditions is the Federal Trade Commission. After the doldrums period in that agency's history, after the New Deal era had begun to restore to its work more of the dignity it had been intended to have, what kind of a contribution did this inheritance from the days of the New Freedom make?

From the outset most of the Commission's work had had to do with unfair competition as such rather than with the more basic problem of monopoly. And by the outbreak of World War II its acknowledged authority in that field was substantial—thanks to the Humphrey and Keppel decisions, and to the Wheeler-Lea Act. Moreover, the courts saw fit to expand still further their tolerance of this work. Said Justice Douglas in a trademark case in 1946:[32]

The Commission has wide discretion in its choice of a remedy deemed adequate to cope with the unlawful practices in this area of trade and commerce . . . and the courts will not interfere except where the remedy selected has no reasonable relation to the unlawful practices found to exist.

All this, of course, was to the good from the standpoint of those who believed that competition in a free enterprise society should proceed according to more or less civilized rules—that businessmen should not be permitted to profit from such practices as misrepresentation in all its many forms, false and misleading advertising, espionage, bribery, disparagement, inducing breach of contract, malicious interference, and so forth. At the same time, however, it

[31] William H. Nicholls, *Price Policies in the Cigarette Industry* (Nashville: Vanderbilt University Press, 1951).
[32] *Siegel Company* v. *Federal Trade Commission*, 327 U.S. 608 (1946).

did have its other side. The Commission had also been created to assist on the antitrust front, and it is quite obvious that policing competition in the world of little business could easily have become an all-absorbing task. It is of some significance, therefore, that although the courts were less and less preventing this body from moving ahead in the unfair competition field, they were simultaneously delimiting the range of that activity.

Two Supreme Court cases will illustrate this dimension of Federal Trade Commission evolution. In one that agency had sought to intervene in a dispute in which two small merchants in Washington, D.C., insisted on calling their store "The Shade Shop." In the other an order had been issued against an Illinois candy manufacturer selling candy in Illinois through a lottery. On both of these occasions the Supreme Court reversed the Commission—stating that the Washington case was a private matter involving no "specific and substantial" public interest,[33] and that though the behavior of the Illinois manufacturer "affected commerce" it was not "in commerce" as the law required.[34] While to be sure these were both reversals in the technical sense, it is nevertheless thought by many that they prevented the Commission from being inundated by a veritable flood of essentially trivial matters.

The larger meaning of these delimitations has been that the Federal Trade Commission has had available some resources for antitrust work—that it might make use of its concurrent powers with the Department of Justice in the antitrust field. These are of two kinds. On the one hand, the Clayton Act explicitly gave both agencies authority to act under its provisions. On the other, no less an authority than the Supreme Court of the United States had authorized the Commission to extend its responsibility for the level of competition into the realms of conspiracy and monopolization. "The Commission has jurisdiction to declare that conduct tending to restrain trade is an unfair method of competition even though the selfsame conduct may also violate the Sherman Act."

For one reason or another, the Federal Trade Commission had not gotten into the antitrust act at all seriously prior to World War II. All this time, however, that agency had been biding its time with respect to an issue first decisively raised in the 1920's. Now, with a suddenness and a ferocity quite unlike the impression of itself then existing in the public mind, the Federal Trade Commission picked up that thread once more and made itself for a time the

---

[33] Federal Trade Commission v. Klesner, 280 U.S. 19 (1929).
[34] Federal Trade Commission v. Bunte Brothers, Inc., 312 U.S. 349 (1941).

major center of interest on the antitrust front. The issue was basing-point pricing.

Americans had learned a great deal more about this business practice since the United States Steel Corporation had virtually defied the Federal Trade Commission's order with respect thereto some twenty years earlier[35]—and perhaps in part because its use had broadened considerably in the interim. In an economy of high and oftimes threatening overhead costs, the limitation of price-cutting to the amount of freight a competitor is willing to absorb had seemed to many industrialists to be an excellent solution to a troublesome problem.

The highly simplified diagram below illustrates the essential features of a basing-point system, together with the reasons why it was more or less inevitable that public policy would in time single

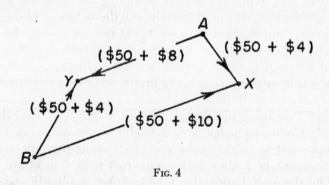

Fig. 4

out this device for special attack. To begin with, it will be noted that a producer at a basing-point B can sell at X on even terms with a producer at a non-basing-point A who is geographically much nearer. Thus although A needs to spend only $4 per ton transporting his merchandise to X, a common practice was to charge the $50 base price plus the $10 it would cost to freight the goods from the nearest basing point. The corollary of these facts is that whereas a basing-point producer is thereby enabled to compete at the very back door of any non-basing-point producer without reducing his net receipts, the non-basing-point producer is compelled to reduce his net receipts (absorb freight) when competing near a basing-point rival, say, at Y.

In like manner it can be seen from the diagram why economists and antitrust officials had long been suspicious of this pricing tech-

[35] Frank A. Fetter, *The Masquerade of Monopoly* (New York: Harcourt, Brace & Co., Inc., 1931).

nique. For one thing, it had always seemed evident that a pricing system resulting in identical quotations from widely separated firms could only result from collusion. In the second place, under a wide range of conditions price discrimination must inevitably result from this procedure; A, for example, will charge $60 per ton at X and $54 at Y even though the cost of goods laid down in X is less than the cost of those delivered at Y. Third, the practice in two ways seems to threaten a wastage of resources. On the one hand, an artificial concentration of productive resources near basing-points is encouraged.[36] On the other hand, such a system can easily result in the simultaneous sale of goods at Y by A and at X by B, thus dissipating transportation resources through cross-hauling.

Although quite naturally the industries operating with this kind of pricing arrangement have protested their innocence of wrongdoing under the antitrust laws, time and a number of administrative and court opinions have by now cut away the trimmings from most of these arguments.[37] That a basing-point system results in discrimination, even where employed by a single firm producing at several locations, was a proposition no one seriously questioned after the first court test of a Federal Trade Commission order against the practice. And that this technique, where several competing firms are involved, results *from* collusion, seemed scarcely arguable when it developed that the firms in an industry so organized habitually quoted identical prices under widely varying circumstances of production and location. On one occasion the Navy Department opened 59 bids for steel pipe, each one for $6,001.83. On another the Army Engineers opened 11 bids for cement; every one of these concerns quoted the figure $3.286854 per barrel. And if such evidence were not conclusive on this point, the following excerpt from a letter written by one executive in the cement industry to another would seem to provide the authoritative answer to the question of what is involved in this way of working out price relationships.

Do you think any of the arguments for the basing-point system which we have thus far advanced will arouse anything but derision in and out of government? I have read them all recently. Some of them are very clever and ingenious. They amount to this, however: that we price that way in order to discourage monopolistic practices and to preserve free competition, etc. This is sheer bunk and hypocrisy. The truth is . . . that ours is an industry above all others that cannot stand free competition, that must systematically restrain competition or be ruined.

[36] George W. Stocking, *Basing Point Pricing and Regional Development* (Chapel Hill: University of North Carolina Press, 1954).

[37] Fritz Machlup, *The Basing Point System* (Philadelphia: The Blakiston Co., 1949).

One of the reasons basing-point pricing had become more general throughout American industry was that (as would only have been expected) a number of National Recovery Administration codes of fair competition had incorporated this principle into their provisions.[38] However, after this interlude was summarily brought to an end by the Supreme Court, the way was again open for actively challenging the practice. In 1937 the Federal Trade Commission issued a complaint against the principal firms in the cement industry and their trade association, while the Wheeler-Lea Amendment of 1938, by making all outstanding Commission orders final unless appealed, compelled the United States Steel Corporation to file a formal protest. At the same time a number of other actions against basing-point practitioners were launched—in situations in which a single-firm system was at issue, as well as those in which collusion could also be charged.

Of course the focus of this controversy soon shifted to the courts as defendants accused the Federal Trade Commission of seeking to destroy the American free enterprise system. The first major indication of the direction the evolution of the law was about to take came in a Supreme Court decision involving a glucose manufacturer with an intrafirm basing-point system and only one basing-point. The Commission had charged discrimination against candy manufacturers located near non-base glucose plants, and the Court had no difficulty conceding that the inclusion of phantom freight was indeed a violation of the Clayton Act as amended by the Robinson-Patman Act.[39]

On the same day the Corn Products decision was handed down, the Supreme Court also decisively upheld another Commission action on this front. A competitor of Corn Products had built its own price structure around its rival's basing-point system. Against the complaint that this discriminated in favor of customers located nearest the low-price point, it maintained that, in the words of Section 2 as amended, this was only the result of a "good faith" attempt "to meet the equally low price of a competitor." When the Commission challenged this defense by asserting that the lower price had been quoted too consistently and systematically to be saved by this wording, a majority of the Justices agreed.[40]

---

[38] Temporary National Economic Committee, *The Basing Point Problem* (Washington, D.C.: Government Printing Office, 1941).

[39] *Corn Products Refining Company* v. *Federal Trade Commission*, 324 U.S. 726 (1945).

[40] *Federal Trade Commission* v. *Staley Manufacturing Company*, 324 U.S. 746 (1945).

To this point the issue of conspiracy had not been a major consideration. However, the Supreme Court's assertion in the American Tobacco Case that an agreement might be inferred from behavior without concrete proof suggested a new dimension for basing-point actions, and it was not long before the courts were incorporating such reasoning into their opinions. In a lower court opinion in 1946 the stage was set for a broad use of the implied conspiracy doctrine in cases of this kind. "On the face of the situation it taxes our credulity of belief, as argued, that petitioners employed this system without any agreement or plan among themselves."[41]

Against this background the Federal Trade Commission's challenge to the Cement Institute reached the High Court in 1948. Mincing no words, this body found basing-point pricing to be illegal on almost every conceivable ground.[42] It was first and foremost "an unfair method of competition under the Federal Trade Commission Act." In the second place, it was a violation of the Clayton Act because of the resulting discrimination, and again the "good faith" defense was rejected. And perhaps most important of all the Court had no difficulty finding in such arrangements a price-fixing conspiracy.

All this time the Commission had been moving warily against its most formidable basing-point adversary—the United States Steel Corporation and the steel industry. Apparently the Commission wanted to have both an irrefutable case and favorable legal precedents before bringing this fight into the open. But as the larger campaign swept on to victory after victory, the Corporation decided to give up without a struggle. In late 1948 it accepted the long-outstanding order against it, and in 1951 the entire industry agreed to abandon this pricing device.

It would be a mistake, however, to suppose that these administrative-judicial successes ended this matter. As in the case of railway rate bureaus, adverse court rulings only provided the incentive to take the problem to Congress.[43] Here, too, the conservative appeal for a legislative loosening of antitrust restrictions was broadly successful. Sparked by what a (liberal) Senator called "one of the best organized, one of the most heavily financed, and one of the most adroitly deceptive [lobbying efforts] that has ever been addressed to the Congress of the United States," and side by side with a

---

[41] *Milk and Ice Cream Institute v. Federal Trade Commission*, 152 F. 2d 478.

[42] *Federal Trade Commission v. Cement Institute*, 333 U.S. 683.

[43] Earl Latham, *The Group Basis of Politics—A Study in Basing-Point Legislation* (Ithaca: Cornell University Press, 1952).

wholesale abandonment of basing-point systems in which the maintenance of old base prices in the face of the elimination of freight absorption was resulting in both higher prices and higher profits, this effort secured in 1950 favorable action on a measure legalizing basing-point pricing. Then, just as he had done earlier, President Truman vetoed this antitrust retreat. But here the analogy ends. This time there were not enough votes to override, and hence recent triumphs were not repudiated.

And there was one other sequel to these developments before things became much quieter on this front. Perhaps in part because that group itself was so shaken by the power of the assault on recent achievements by basing-point proponents, but also no doubt in part to assuage the fears of those who professed to see in what was happening a condemnation of postage stamp or even zone pricing by a single firm, the Commission wrote into the 1951 steel order the following explanation of its position:

1. The Federal Trade Commission is not considering evidence of uniformity of prices or any element thereof of two or more sellers at any destination or destinations alone and without more as showing a violation of the law.

2. The Federal Trade Commission is not acting to prohibit or interfere with delivered pricing or freight absorption as such when innocently and independently pursued, regularly or otherwise, with the result of promoting competition.

Although many liberals sincerely believed in 1951 that all the ground which had been won was herein given away, the recent history of the cement and steel industries suggests that important and lasting gains had in fact been made.

Whatever had been accomplished, however, the credit lay with the Federal Trade Commission. A far cry this from the bruised and battered agency which had been so rudely rebuked in its first court test some thirty years before. But it is not to be concluded that the Commission was now fully recovered from the ineptness which had characterized its operations during its youth. Habits engendered by years of neglect were not so easily outgrown. Low morale, personnel indifference, mediocrity of staff, and a passive approach to its job still seemed to pervade this organization. As late as 1949 and 1951 first the Hoover commission on governmental reorganization and then the Small Business Committee of the House of Representatives reported at some length on the general ineffectiveness of the Commission's present work. Said a prominent civil servant (James M. Landis) as Chairman of the Twentieth Century Fund's Committee on Cartels and Monopoly:

. . . Reference must be made to what I would call the utter bankruptcy of the Federal Trade Commission. As a practical matter, the deterioration of that Commission has gone beyond redemption. If duties of this kind are to be thrust on some agency, there is really only one thing to do, and that is to wipe out the F.T.C. completely and start afresh.

PATENTS ON THE DEFENSIVE

And in one other important respect was the new equilibrium being worked out on the antitrust front particularly noteworthy. This was in the field of patent monopolies. For a number of years liberals had been groping for an effective way of challenging the excesses to which they believed this system of privileges had been carried. Now, at long last, several key pieces in this puzzle were beginning to fall into place.

The crux of the problem here as at so many other points in the world of government–business relationships was the corporation. Historically, the patent law had been intended to encourage technological progress in the public interest by giving special rewards to the individual inventor. In exchange for these rewards the inventor would be compelled both to disclose his invention to the public as a part of the foundation on which new technological advance could then be built, and to put his patent to work in the production of either more or better goods. The appearance of the large corporation, however, and especially its predominance in precisely those areas of the economy in which technology is especially important, had raised a number of questions about the applicability of the old individual-oriented patent system to the new economy.[44]

That the individual inventor was being elbowed to one side was a proposition with which few would have quarrelled. Increasingly business concerns were requiring employees to assign whatever patentable ideas they developed to their employer, usually on a royalty-free basis. Increasingly also the established concern already holding basic patents in a field constituted the only practical market for a patent resulting from the labors of an independent inventor.

But these facts in and of themselves proved little. The patent system undoubtedly still served the purposes for which it was created despite profound changes in the environment within which it operated. On the one hand, patent assignment by employees to employers is a part of the foundation upon which an expensive program of research and development in American corporations has been built. On the other hand, modern industrial technology requires that a

[44] O. R. Barnett, *Patent Property and the Anti-Monopoly Laws* (Indianapolis: Bobbs-Merrill Co., 1943).

group of patents (and sometimes a very large group) be held in the same hands. To whatever extent, in short, patent monopoly had ever been contributory to this country's productive greatness, there seemed to be reason enough for supposing that it was still playing that role reasonably well.[45]

At the same time, however, it was also evident that, from the standpoint of public interest, questionable results were creeping into patent practices—some of these largely the result of the rise of the corporation, but others rather the consequence of an admittedly lax administration of the patent law as such. With respect to this latter factor, for example, the Patent Office has for some time been unable to make more than a superficial survey of existing technology when a new application was presented, and hence the grant of a patent does not carry a particularly strong presumption of validity. Moreover, no opportunity is given other interests to be heard in connection with patent applications—not even government agencies charged with the maintenance of competition. The requirement in the law that an invention to be patentable must be useful is in turn so ambiguous that rigorous standards of selection would be difficult to arrive at even if the Patent Office were in a position to apply them. And finally, the litigation in this field, made especially crucial by administrative inadequacies elsewhere, is in the hands of men trained in the law rather than in either industrial technology or basic economics.[46]

Perhaps, when the underlying purposes of the patent system are taken into consideration, a convincing case could be made for vague criteria and loose procedures. But when these arrangements were thought of in the context of the structure of modern industry, there was much point to the growing liberal feeling that patent law was in need of tightening.[47]

An obvious difficulty here, of course, is the fact that the individual inventor is typically unable to protect his own idea, and thus tends to be drawn into the vortex of the large-overhead concern at the outset. Furthermore, a broad interpretation of the concept of "usefulness" has the result of extending monopoly rights to the outcome of routine business research and development—a consequence made all the more questionable by the fact that the advance of tech-

[45] Morris D. Forkosh, *Economics of American Patent Laws* (New York: New York University School of Law, 1940).

[46] Harold G. Fox, *Monopolies and Patents* (Toronto: University of Toronto Press, 1947).

[47] Corwin D. Edwards, *Maintaining Competition* (New York: McGraw-Hill Book Co., Inc., 1949).

nology is to a considerable extent a collective social process. A third public interest problem raised here is the duration of the patent grant itself; although nominally valid for 17 years, this protection is invariably extended several years by a period of pendency in the Patent Office, and is frequently extended much further by the patenting of improvements at strategic intervals. Still another tendency thought by many to be adverse to the larger community is the extension of a patent monopoly by tying it to unpatented goods, by using it to effect a vertical integration which would otherwise have no basis, by monopolizing the available patents within a particular technological field, by awarding highly restrictive licenses to producers of patented goods or users of patented machines or processes, and by intimidating competitors with the threat of litigation.

However, granting that improvement, substantial improvement, was at least theoretically possible, the question still remained as to how this might best be brought about. Because so much of this problem seemed to stem from the broad interpretation currently being given to the concept "patentable invention," a suggestion that had often been made was to seek a narrowing of this concept which would not at the same time destroy the fundamental economic purpose behind patent legislation—to endeavor, in other words, to separate the work of the "sole and true inventor" from the progress of technology due to sheer socio-economic evolution.

It was, of course, not certain at the time how much real progress was being made in that direction, but that some was taking place was evident. Thus in 1941 the Supreme Court held that usefulness and novelty "does not necessarily make the device patentable."[48] And Justice Douglas then proceeded to make this position even stronger by declaring:

Under the statute, the device must be not only "new and useful," it must also be an "invention" or "discovery." . . . That is to say, the new device, however useful it may be, must reveal the flash of creative genius, not merely the skill of the calling. If it fails, it has not established its right to a grant on the public domain.

Three years later this suggestion was elaborated on still further in a lower court, this time with emphasis on the contrast between the individual inventor of earlier days and the modern organization of research in the large corporation.[49]

[48] *Cuno Engineering Corporation* v. *Automatic Devices Corporation,* 314 U.S. 84 (1941).
[49] *Potts* v. *Coe,* 140 F. 2d 470 (1944).

Each man is given a section of the hay to search. The man who finds the needle shows no more "genius" and no more ability than the others who are searching different portions of the haystack. . . .

The "inventor" is paid only a salary, he gets no royalties, he has no property rights in the improvements which he helps to create. To give patents for such routine experimentation on a vast scale is to use the patent law to reward capital investment, and create monopolies for corporate organizers instead of men of inventive genius.

And again in 1950 Justice Douglas had occasion to revert to this key problem in even more caustic language in a case involving a patent for a movable rack to slide articles along the counter by the cash register clerk in a grocery store.[50]

The fact that a patent as flimsy and spurious as this one has to be brought all the way to this court to be declared invalid dramatically illustrates how far our patent system frequently departs from the constitutional standards which are supposed to govern.

Hopefully building on these foundations, liberals endeavored to broaden this achievement by embodying the "flash of genius" test in statute law. But the conservative temper in Congress quickly proved to be too much for this attempt; radical departures were not yet to be enacted into law. Although an act was passed in 1952 clarifying a number of minor aspects of existing legislation in that field, this particular innovation was decisively rejected.

A second way in which many had long thought the patent monopoly problem might be attacked was by narrowing the scope of the patent grant itself. And although it was evident that, contrary to the way patent laws typically operate in other parts of the world, the legal doctrine relieving the patent holder of the obligation to put his property to work was still the law of the land, there were nonetheless ways in which this problem could be approached.

For example, there was plainly visible during these years a tightening up of the prohibitions aimed at attempts to broaden patent monopolies by means of various kinds of tying contracts and other types of restrictive arrangements. Thus it was now being driven home that a patent monopoly could not legally be extended by tying the sale of an unpatented item to the sale of a patent-protected product.[51] Similarly unduly restrictive licenses were being repeatedly struck down by the courts, as when the Ethyl Gasoline Corporation sought to control the price of its product by confining its sale to

[50] *Great Atlantic and Pacific Tea Company* v. *Supermarket Equipment Corporation*, 340 U.S. 147 (1950).
[51] *International Salt Company* v. *United States*, 332 U.S. 392 (1947).

specifically approved dealers.[52] And in still another kind of situation the Supreme Court ruled that a patentee endeavoring to use his grant in violation of the antitrust laws cannot ask the courts to protect his claim against invasion by those he has sought illegally to coerce.[53]

But achievements along these lines, heartening though they were in many respects did not get at the most critical problem patent reform faced in this area. Some twenty years earlier the Supreme Court had sweepingly upheld the General Electric Company in a patent case by means of a line of reasoning the government had for some time now been striving to modify. General Electric had licensed Westinghouse to make certain types of electric lamps under patents it held on condition that these lamps would then be sold by Westinghouse at prices fixed by General Electric. Said Chief Justice Taft for the majority in response to the government's charge of restraint of trade:

When the patentee licenses another to make and vend and retains the right to continue to make and vend on his own account, the price at which his licensee will sell will necessarily affect the price at which he can sell his own patented goods. It would seem entirely reasonable that he should say to the licensee, "Yes, you may make and sell articles under my patent but not so as to destroy the profit that I wish to obtain by making them and selling them myself."[54]

Two cases settled in 1948 gave the Department of Justice a particularly good opportunity to see if time had mellowed the High Court's stand at this point. The principal producers of fuse cutouts on the one hand, and the major firms in the gypsum wallboard business on the other, had made cross-licensing agreements with one another which included reciprocal price-fixing. Against both of these sets of arrangement the government brought a charge of restraint of trade under the Sherman Act, and in time both suits appeared on the agenda of the Supreme Court. That body was almost unequivocal in holding against the companies.[55]

The merging of the benefits of price-fixing under the patents restrains trade in violation of the Sherman Act in the same way as would the fixing of prices between producers of non-patentable goods. . . . When patentees join in an agreement as here to maintain prices on their several products, that agree-

---

[52] *Ethyl Gasoline Corporation* v. *United States*, 309 U.S. 436 (1940).
[53] *Mercoid Corporation* v. *Mid-Continent Investment Company*, 320 U.S. 661 (1944).
[54] *United States* v. *General Electric Company*, 272 U.S. 476 (1926).
[55] *United States* v. *Line Material Company*, 333 U.S. 287 (1948); *United States* v. *United States Gypsum Company*, 333 U.S. 364 (1948).

ment, however advantageous it may be to stimulate the broader use of patents, is unlawful *per se* under the Sherman Act.

No one of course would doubt that this was a significant liberal victory. At the same time, however, it stopped well short of what the Court had been asked to do in these proceedings. The government's brief had requested that the General Electric decision be explicitly reversed. Although the effect of the Line Material and Gypsum cases was seriously to weaken the force of that decision (in the minds of many actually destroying it), the way was nevertheless left open for price control under a patent where only one patent holder is involved.

And in still a third way was the patent system being modified to make it serve the public interest in a highly developed corporate society more effectively. Slowly but surely the government seemed to be effecting a major change in the pattern of remedies applicable in patent violation cases. The Mercoid case represented one small straw in this wind—although the principle involved was there stated negatively rather than positively. Why not, the government was now insisting, make a patent available to all comers when the original holder abuses the privilege he is thereby entitled to?

The case in which this issue was first sharply raised concerned a patent pool in the glass container industry. An excellent opportunity it was, too, to test a basically new principle of law, for there was no question of the guilt or innocence of the accused. Again and again the courts had declared that if a patentee agrees to share his property with some he must do so with all, and it was precisely this that the Hartford-Empire clique was refusing to do. By following a ruthless policy of patent litigation, a policy the Supreme Court referred to as "expensive beyond the dreams of the average man," some nine concerns had secured an iron hold on this industry.

The District Court readily acceded to the government's suggested remedy. According to its decree all existing patents in this industry were to revert to the public domain, and all future patents were to be made available to all at "reasonable" royalties. The Supreme Court, however, refused to accept the reasoning behind this ruling.[56] Its conclusion was that so drastic a remedy was not necessary to end the evils complained of—that it would suffice to make existing and future patents available to all applicants on payment of a "reasonable" royalty fee. But, and this is the important point, in thus requesting the District Court to modify its ruling the Supreme Court for the first time accepted the principle of compulsory licensing as

[56] *Hartford-Empire Company v. United States*, 323 U.S. 386 (1945).

a remedy in patent cases—a principle which was to be frequently employed from that point forward.

THE OTHER SIDE OF THE COIN

If, however, all of this adds up to an antitrust endeavor both more dedicated to the achievement of positive results and more weighted in the direction of liberal ideas than ever before; it does not follow that this is all there is to be said about the new equilibrium in this field. The fact is that side by side with this unprecedented antitrust progress there was also visible a considerable amount of foot-dragging by those who had contrary views about appropriate public policy.

One dimension of this other side of the postwar antitrust picture was the fact that most of the progress being made was the consequence of court cooperation with the Department of Justice, whereas an all-out effort would have required the active assistance of Congress as well. Indeed this obstacle to more rapid evolution on this front was pointedly stated by the Supreme Court itself in its Hartford-Empire opinion.

Legislative history is also enlightening upon this point. Repeatedly since 1908 legislation has been proposed in Congress to give the courts power to cancel a patent which has been used as an instrument to violate the antitrust laws. Congress has not adopted such legislation. The Temporary National Economic Committee recommended imposition of such a penalty for violation of antitrust laws. But its recommendation was not adopted by Congress.

And there were other evidences as well. Thus numerous antitrust exemptions still held over from an earlier period—the most important of these perhaps being Webb-Pomerene Associations, farmer cooperatives, and labor union activities. Moreover, Congress was even at this moment engaged in lengthening this list, as witness the McCarran and Reed-Bulwinkle Acts exempting, respectively, insurance rate groups and railroad rate bureaus from antitrust prosecution. In this same category was Congress' refusal to write the "flash of genius" test of patentability into law. And when to all of these developments was added a revealing enactment in the trademark field, the Celler Anti-Merger Act all the more took on the appearance of a legislative reform oasis in an ocean of Congressional antitrust conservatism.

The trademark had always been a bone of contention between consumers and businessmen.[57] The former group would prefer that standard items put out by different manufacturers be subjected to

[57] Walter J. Derenberg, *Trade-Marks* (New York: American Bar Assoc., 1946).

grade labelling supervised by the federal government. Businessmen, on the other hand, have insisted on retaining the right to differentiate their products from those of competitors, and Congress had to date accepted this latter position. Now a step was taken which all the more frustrated the consumer point of view.

Ever since the passage of the nation's first trademark statute in 1905, the tendency had been to broaden rather than narrow the legal means by which producers might differentiate their products. Under the terms of the Lanham Act of 1946, something approaching the ultimate along that line was achieved by dint of much patient lobbying by a number of national advertisers. Defining a trademark as "any word, name, symbol, or device, or any combination thereof adopted and used by a manufacturer or merchant to identify his goods," this law extended legal protection to virtually any mark which has become "distinctive" in the broadest sense of that term.

The other major dimension of the nation's reluctance to push with all vigor along the antitrust road was a carryover from the reaction against competition of Great Depression days. In two important developments of the post-World War II period tracing directly to these origins was it made clear that this force in American economic life was far from dead. The first of these was an antitrust action against the Great Atlantic and Pacific Tea Company (A & P); the other was further evolution on the resale price maintenance front.

At the time suit was brought against A & P that organization was operating some 5,000 retail outlets in more than 3,000 cities in 40 of the 48 states. In addition this gigantic holding company controlled a number of manufacturing subsidiaries and several wholesaling subsidiaries. Charging violation of the antitrust laws, the government asked that this concern be broken up into seven pieces, that it be removed entirely from the manufacturing business, and that its central purchasing agencies be disposed of.

Criticism of this action as a bona fide antitrust suit has been based on several considerations. Most broadly it has been emphasized that this organization was not in any sense of the word a monopoly. Although in a number of cities A & P was doing from one third to one half of the total grocery business, it was in fact handling less than 7 per cent of all the grocery business of the country. Furthermore, this company had actively pioneered numerous aspects of distribution technology. And perhaps most important of all, it had a wide reputation as the lowest priced grocery outfit in the world.

More specifically, the Department of Justice charged that A & P engaged in local price-cutting designed to drive competitors out of particular areas. But though the tremendous financial power of the company would have enabled it to do so, there was no evidence that it had in fact increased its share of the market by means of geographic price discrimination tactics. Rather it had, as a matter of company policy, exchanged higher gross profits margins for a greater volume of sales, and it had varied its prices from market to market in response to competitive factors. Is this not, many economists wanted to know, a behavior pattern more calculated to promote competition than to weaken it?

Another charge of unfair competitive activity on the part of A & P had to do with that concern's buying policies. Here it was said to have coerced suppliers into quoting more favorable prices than competitors could obtain—by insisting on discounts on account of those services its integrated organization enabled it to perform for itself, or by threatening to begin manufacturing products its leaders considered unreasonably priced. But, came back the economist's query, if A & P were securing discriminatory price reductions, why did not the government ask for a cease-and-desist order under the Robinson-Patman Act instead of seeking dissolution under the Sherman Act? And was it not a little fanciful, they further queried, to refer to coercion where the other concerns involved were as often as not powerful, oligopolistic corporations.

The other major charge brought by the government involved A & P's vertical integration. Where that concern did do its own manufacturing, the antitrust lawyers maintained, sales to retail outlets could easily be entered on the books at unduly low prices—with the result that the manufacturing operation would subsidize the retail grocery end of the business. Similarly the so-called Atlantic Commission Company, A & P's most important purchasing subsidiary, was accused of occupying a conflict of interest position adverse to competition. This concern could not simultaneously, so this charge insisted, serve A & P suppliers as a broker and A & P as a purchasing agent without frequently resolving conflicts of loyalty in the interest of the latter concern's preferences. But even here it was not clear why it was unfair competition for a retailer to engage in manufacturing activities at a loss if it so desired, or why if ACCO was an unreliable brokerage agent A & P competitors did not turn elsewhere for that service.

In short, it seems clear in retrospect that the central issue in this contest was the protection of the independent grocer against competition from the chains[58]—or, stated in legal terms, whether the

[58] M. A. Adelman, "The Great A & P Muddle," *Fortune*, Dec., 1949.

advantages of size in this business were so great as to constitute restraint of trade. Nor was a clear answer to this question given in the settlement of the case by a consent decree in 1954. The principal outcome was dissolution of the Atlantic Commission Company, the retail concern itself remaining intact and retaining the use of its manufacturing subsidiaries. In addition A & P agreed to a number of restrictions on its operations which would not be applicable to competitors. But if the company conceded more than the strength of the government's case warranted, as perhaps a majority of students of this subject would argue, it was at least not committing economic suicide. The first year following this consent decree settlement, A & P's gross sales exceeded $4 billion for the first time in its history.

The issue of resale price maintenance had had a varied career since the passage of the Miller-Tydings Act in the late 1930's.[59] On the one hand, antitrust exemption in the interest of smaller, independent retailers had considerably broadened the use of that device. On the other hand, however, the courts had shown a disposition progressively to narrow the scope of this business practice.

The first step in the latter direction came in 1942, when the Supreme Court declared that the federal law applied only to the producers of finished goods and not to products traded at other stages of the production process.[60] A second came in 1946 in a case in which the Federal Trade Commission challenged the Eastman Kodak Company.

The Miller-Tydings Act had explicitly stated that resale price maintenance contracts would not be valid in the case of commodities not in "free and open competition" with similiar goods produced by other firms, and it was obviously of the utmost importance to the liberal position that this terminology be given a flexible interpretation. This issue was squarely raised for the first time when the Eastman concern was ordered to cease and desist from "fair-trading" Kodachrome Film and Magazine Cine-Kodak Film. The Commission's contention here was that a product's uniqueness (for example, color film as compared with black and white film) must be taken into consideration in applying the "free and open competition" clause, and with this interpretation the District Court agreed.[61]

Moreover, the courts a few years later indicated a willingness to go still farther. The 1936 decision validating state fair trade laws had

---

[59] Federal Trade Commission, *Report on Resale Price Maintenance* (Washington, D.C.: Government Printing Office, 1945).

[60] *United States* v. *Univis Lens Company*, 316 U.S. 241 (1942).

[61] *Eastman Kodak Company* v. *Federal Trade Commission*, 158 F. 2d 592 (1946).

not dealt with more fundamental constitutional issues, and thus there remained ample room for further litigation. This was all the more the case, furthermore, in view of the fact that this decision had been rendered prior to the passage of federal legislation. In short, it was almost inevitable that sooner or later a case designed specifically to test the validity of this 1937 enactment would reach the Supreme Court.

In 1951 it happened, and once again that body was asked to judge this principle in a proceeding involving the fair trading of strong drink. Directly at issue on this occasion was the nonsigner clause, still the heart and soul of effective resale price maintenance. A nonsigner in New Orleans deliberately undercut the fair trade price of Calvert Reserve whiskey, and the manufacturer brought suit to enforce compliance. When the lower courts rejected the defendant's plea that the nonsigner clause violated the Sherman Act, he appealed to the Supreme Court. Here too the deeper constitutional questions were avoided, but in a 6-3 decision the foundation on which resale price maintenance then rested was rudely chopped away.[62] The Miller-Tydings Act was construed as applying only to actual signers of fair trade agreements.

The Act sanctions only "contracts or agreements." If a distributor and one or more retailers want to agree, combine, or conspire to fix a minimum price, they can do so if state law permits. Their contract, combination, or conspiracy— hitherto illegal—is made lawful. . . . When they seek, however, to impose price fixing on persons who have not contracted or agreed to the scheme, the situation is vastly different. That is not price fixing by contract or agreement; that is price fixing by compulsion.

No doubt the enunciation of this principle would in any event have precipitated a drive for a broader legislative sanction. Such a result, however, was doubly assured when this decision touched off a price war in fair trade items which quickly spread from New York to San Francisco. A prominent item on the agenda of the next session of Congress, therefore, was a rewriting of the Miller-Tydings law to make it specifically applicable to nonsigners. This was accomplished in the so-called McGuire-Keogh Act, and although the President signed this measure with some reluctance (perhaps he was afraid to veto a measure dear to the hearts of a multitude of small retailers all over the nation on the eve of the 1952 presidential election campaign), he nevertheless did sign it. Thus the principle of resale price maintenance once again reigned supreme, and when the Supreme Court was asked the following year to consider this

[62] *Schwegmann Brothers v. Calvert Corporation,* 341 U.S. 384 (1951).

question from the standpoint of the Constitution it refused to give such a case a place on its docket.

———

It would not, of course, be argued that antitrust policy had become either noncontroversial or unimportant. Obviously the debate in this field would long go on. However, it was nonetheless possible to see in the trust-antitrust *status quo* the unmistakable replacement of policy uncertainty and drift by a fairly firm institutional framework.

This emerging pattern possessed a number of key characteristics. In the first place, it was by now broadly accepted that a high degree of concentration in American business would neither be destroyed nor even strenuously assaulted. A part of this acceptance is to be explained by the fact that much painstaking research was failing to reveal any clear tendency for monopoly to follow close behind oligopoly.[63] Another important element here was the realization at long last that where powerful motivating forces are at work the law can guarantee only the barest minimum of ethical or legitimate behavior. And perhaps both of these points can be summarized by emphasizing that a firm decision had been made to give private enterprise the benefit of this doubt as one of the prices of a belief in freedom.

In the second place, it seemed evident that the antitrust effort had made a successful adjustment to the realities of economic life in the middle of the 20th century. Ultimately rising above the oversimplified view of economic organization implicit in the Sherman Act, policy-making officials had set themselves earnestly to the task of steering a clear course between abandonment of the struggle and insistence upon a "restoration" of the pure competition ideal.

This observation in turn has two significant dimensions of its own. First, as early as 1914 it had become apparent that antitrust work would make its major contribution by concentrating primarily on business practices rather than on industrial structure as such, and it was by now little short of remarkable how accurate that foresight had been. Consistently now (if not always relentlessly) the antitrust agencies were finding their principal opportunities in attacking business activities which threatened the maintenance of competition, activities posing this problem in ever more subtle and complex ways, and almost as consistently the courts were cooperating in that en-

[63] G. Warren Nutter, *The Extent of Enterprise Monopoly in the United States* (Chicago: University of Chicago Press, 1951).

TABLE 67. TRIUMPH OF OLIGOPOLY

Industry group	Per Cent of Net Capital Assets Owned by					
	1 Company	2 Companies	3 Companies	4 Companies	8 Companies	15 Companies
Linoleum	57.9	80.8	92.1	93.6	—	—
Tin cans and other tinware	55.2	92.1	95.3	96.4	—	—
Aluminum	55.0	85.0	100.0	—	—	—
Copper smelting and refining	46.8	73.5	88.5	94.6	100.0	—
Biscuits, crackers, and pretzels	46.3	57.0	67.7	71.4	—	—
Agricultural machinery	45.3	56.8	66.6	75.4	82.1	—
Office and store machines and devices	42.0	56.3	69.5	74.3	85.3	89.6
Motor vehicles	40.9	62.8	68.7	70.7	77.3	86.1
Cigarettes	36.6	64.4	77.6	87.8	—	—
Plumbing equipment and supplies	33.2	64.9	71.3	74.3	—	—
Distilled liquors	29.0	53.3	72.4	84.6	94.3	—
Meat products	28.8	54.7	64.0	69.3	77.6	81.6
Primary steel	28.6	42.0	49.2	54.5	69.3	77.2
Rubber tires and tubes	27.8	49.9	70.3	88.3	94.8	—
Dairy products	27.5	48.9	55.8	59.6	71.3	—
Glass and glassware	24.9	49.1	57.4	62.2	73.9	—
Carpets and rugs	24.1	36.8	48.9	57.9	—	—
Footwear (except rubber)	23.6	39.6	43.4	46.8	53.1	57.5
Industrial chemicals	21.5	36.5	45.5	51.8	70.2	80.2
Woolen and worsted goods	16.7	23.5	28.1	30.3	36.4	—
Electrical machinery	15.8	28.8	41.7	47.5	55.2	60.7
Grain-mill products	15.6	23.5	30.2	36.3	48.6	56.6
Aircraft and parts	13.6	25.4	35.2	44.0	73.7	86.2
Bread and other products (excluding biscuits and crackers)	13.0	20.0	25.4	30.6	38.2	—
Canning and preserving	10.7	21.4	32.0	39.4	51.0	59.2
Drugs and medicines	8.4	16.5	23.5	30.0	47.7	—

Source: Federal Trade Commission.

deavor.[64] For the foreseeable future this would surely continue to be the central problem on this front—distinguishing between competitive and anticompetitive business behavior in a wide variety of situations in which the necessary distinctions are extremely difficult to make.

Second, the entire focus of government–business relationships was broadly complementing antitrust policy at this point. Thus, in certain areas, and especially labor and agriculture, it was now acknowledged that too much competition can pose problems fully as great as too little competition. More broadly, it was understood that serious market imperfections may often be most effectively attacked

[64] Joel B. Dirlam and Alfred E. Kahn, *Fair Competition: The Law and Economics of Antitrust Policy* (Ithaca: Cornell University Press, 1954).

by allowing a concentration of countervailing power to develop rather than by destroying institutional arrangements already in operation.[65] And if with all of this it was also true that the government was in some areas actively protecting anachronistic institutions from the "perennial gale of creative destruction" (as in the A & P case and resale price maintenance), it can at least be said that this effort to insulate small retailers from the impact of the chains was not yet particularly successful.

QUESTIONS FOR DISCUSSION

1. Why did "trust-busting" not turn out to be an effective way of dealing with business anticompetitive tendencies?

2. What feature did the successful dissolution proceedings discussed in this chapter have in common? What is the significance of this common element?

3. What do you think of what was done with respect to Alcoa's position in the aluminum industry?

4. What do you think of the quotation from Justice Douglas' dissent in the Columbia Steel case?

5. Distinguish between legal and illegal trade association price activities. Why are these particular distinctions made?

6. Justify the antitrust exemption given to railroad rate bureaus.

7. Of what value in antitrust work is the doctrine of implied conspiracy? Do you approve of its use?

8. Distinguish between the unfair competition and the antimonopoly dimensions of the work of the Federal Trade Commission.

9. Of what value to firms using basing-point pricing was this device?

10. Why was basing-point pricing so strenuously opposed by liberals? On what legal grounds was it successfully attacked?

11. How much retracting did the Federal Trade Commission do in its 1951 basing-point order to the steel industry?

12. How does today's patent problem differ from the situation for which the patent laws were originally designed?

13. What difficulties in existing patent arrangements came in for litigation during these years? How satisfactorily were they resolved?

14. Comment on the problem of remedies in patent cases, particularly with respect to the direction in which this phase of patent law was now moving.

15. What do you think of the turn trademark law took in the Lanham Act?

16. Defend the proposition that the A & P case was not really an antitrust case at all. Why would a concern sign a consent decree under these circumstances?

17. What was the significance of the Eastman Kodak case in the field of resale price maintenance?

18. Justify the nonsigner clause in fair trade legislation.

19. What was the new consensus insofar as antitrust was concerned? What do you think of it?

[65] J. K. Galbraith, *American Capitalism: The Concept of Countervailing Power* (Boston: Houghton Mifflin Co., 1952).

Chapter 29

New Fashions in Republicanism

Though Harry Truman had dramatically demonstrated that he had more than one political life, it did not follow that he was to enjoy all of the proverbial nine. Furthermore, it was not to be long before this truth would be decisively brought home. After having had the exceedingly good fortune of being visited by a mild rather than a severe depression, and after having taken advantage of the situation sufficiently to vindicate in part his earlier insistence on several items of Fair Deal legislation, Truman's new administration ran into a protracted period of stormy weather which could have had but one outcome.

THE FAIR DEAL REPLACED

The first of these squalls in point of time was the outbreak of a war in Korea for the prosecution of which the United States assumed the major responsibility. One consequence of this development was a visible deterioration in public acceptance of the foreign policy the nation had been following since the end of World War II. This policy had been broadly justified in terms of the intense interest of most Americans in building an enduring peace, and it was understandable that the appearance of new hostilities would dampen that spirit. Early in 1951 what was happening on this front was made evident when a Democratic Congress saddled the reciprocal trade agreements program with essentially the same protectionist amendments earlier enacted by the Eightieth Congress.

Another politically unprofitable aspect of a new war was its implications for domestic policy. Even a small war in modern times requires the imposition of economic controls designed to guarantee that first things come first. And while the American people have never been irretrievably stubborn about that necessity, there was nonetheless in this new demand for mobilization planning one factor which was exasperating in the extreme for the administration in charge. Partly because this was (as wars go) a minor effort, partly because it was waged over a portion of the globe in which American citizens had never before been especially interested, and partly because it was fought in the name of the United Nations—the Korean conflict did not develop the sense of imminent danger and hence the citizen acceptance of sacrifice needed to make an effective control program possible. Yet because it was not known at the outset how long or how hard this struggle was to be, a responsible leadership felt constantly under pressure to inaugurate a tighter program of controls than the people would accept.[1]

TABLE 68. CRISIS IN KOREA

		Government Purchases of Goods and Services		
Year	As Per Cent of GNP	Total	Federal (billions of dollars)	National Security
1944	45	96.5	89.0	88.6
1950	15	42.0	22.1	18.5
1951	19	62.8	41.0	37.3
1953	23	84.5	59.5	51.4

Source: Department of Commerce.

The result can only be described as an impasse. On the one hand, although a skeleton control mechanism was set up, and although war production was generally adequate to the task at hand, the restrictions imposed and attempted seemed always to generate hostility to the ruling administration. On the other hand, and here an important consideration was the fact that this military endeavor was superimposed upon an economy already characterized by full employment, the speed with which defense output was expanded coupled with the scare-buying of items thought to be in short supply produced an inflationary spiral the control program did little to mitigate and which was also held against the party in power.

But not all the public disfavor into which the Fair Deal was now falling was related to the outbreak of war. There were also troubles of a more pedestrian nature. Some of these, moreover, the President seems almost to have gone out of his way to bring on himself.

For example, 1951 was scarcely a propitious time to insert a renewed plea for national health insurance in an annual budget message. England's bold experiment with this innovation was currently

[1] A. G. Hart, *Defense Without Inflation* (New York: Twentieth Century Fund, Inc., 1951).

providing much material for election contests in that country, and the mistakes initially made there were being sensationally played up in the American press. Nor was this any more appropriate as a time to press once again for federal legislation abolishing discrimination against Negroes in employment. A series of Supreme Court decisions had recently attacked discrimination against Negro voting and segregation in interstate transportation, and many southern Democrats were hence already under more political pressure on this front than was comfortable.

In a somewhat different category are to be placed the adverse consequences flowing from the work of a Congressional investigating committee. Corruption in government is not always legitimately traced to the door of the Chief Executive, or even of the party to which he belongs, although it is quite proper in a democracy that the party in power bear political responsibility for improper use of office by public servants. On this particular occasion the instances exposed were more petty than spectacular; suspicion was cast on the loan policies of the Reconstruction Finance Corporation, and definite irregularities were uncovered in the operations of the Bureau of Internal Revenue. But the fact that Truman administration corruption was apparently retail and sporadic rather than wholesale and organized was more than compensated for by the fact that the committee bringing this information to light contained a majority of Democrats, and it is therefore no wonder that as one result of these developments the term "the mess in Washington" became an important political slogan.

It now seems likely that, everything considered, the die was already cast for a resounding Fair Deal defeat in the election of 1952 before the end of 1951. In other words, the additional adversities which befell the administration in the months leading up to the electoral contest probably only constituted gilding for that particular lily. Thus it was that the most important single event in the government and business field during Truman's second term, as well as the most serious single blow to the President's own popularity and prestige, was probably not a decisive factor in the November, 1952, voting.

For some three years prior to December 31, 1951, the nation's steelworkers had been operating under essentially the same contract. Understandably in a three-year period as dynamic as this one had been, a number of items had arisen which the workers' leaders would want arranged differently in a new contract. Accordingly, several weeks before the expiration of the old agreement the companies were presented with a list of 22 demands (including a substantial wage increase) which their employees desired to have incorporated in the revised document. When management refused to accede to as many of these as worker representatives considered adequate, and when in consequence bargaining negotiations threatened to break down, the government intervened to prevent a cessation of production in this vital war industry.

At that point the only action taken was to refer the dispute to the Wage Stabilization Board, the union voluntarily agreeing to maintain the status quo pending a report from that body. On March 30 the Board submitted recommendations as to both wages and working conditions broadly acceptable to the workers. The managements of the several steel concerns, however, refused to accede to the suggested changes unless the government in turn would agree to a substantial increase in their prices under the existing stabilization program. But this the President unequivocally refused to countenance, and indeed even answered this counterproposal with an address to the nation pointedly condemning the steel companies for the selfish, stubborn, unpatriotic stand they were taking. Once again, therefore, the nation was threatened with a shutdown of this industry.

Theoretically, the government had at least two action alternatives other than the one it chose to follow. Both the Defense Production Act and the Taft-Hartley Act contained provisions dealing with the handling of emergency labor situations. Evidently, however, neither of these possibilities appealed to those responsible for the next critical decision. Thus the President gave as his reason for not securing an 80-day injunction under the Taft-Hartley Act that the workers had already voluntarily postponed their strike for an even·longer period—99 days. Later, furthermore, it was explained that the Defense Production Act was not invoked because its procedures were considered "much too cumbersome, involved, and time-consuming for the crisis which was at hand."

But much more significant than why the President did not do some of the things he might theoretically have done is what he did decide to do. On April 8, only a few hours before the rescheduled strike was to begin, he issued an Executive Order seizing the properties of the steel companies.[2]

It goes without saying that on April 9 the companies applied in District Court for an injunction to prevent the Secretary of Commerce from carrying out this order. The primary reason given for

[2] *The Steel Seizure Case* (Washington, D.C.: Government Printing Office, 1952).

taking this drastic step (seeking an injunction in effect against the President of the United States) was the interest of owners and managers of these concerns in getting their property back intact—that is, before wages and working conditions had been altered in unacceptable ways, and before the government had illegally unearthed important trade secrets. But there was a much broader principle involved here as well. Many, and perhaps a majority, of conservatives, felt that the outcome of Franklin Roosevelt's war against the Supreme Court had been a serious weakening of the Judiciary in favor of the Presidency. Surely the handling of this action of a Fair Deal President by a New Deal-appointed Bench would furnish an excellent testing ground for that thesis. Furthermore, this case was especially well suited to such a test. The President and his lawyers cited no statutory authority for the action taken, basing it rather upon powers inherent in the Constitution. Thus the nation watched this historic battle fully conscious of its extraordinary significance.

The District Court conceded the appropriateness of injunctive relief. Upon appeal the Supreme Court granted certiorari, and on June 2 Justice Black delivered the opinion of a Court divided six to three.

In an amazingly few words, considering the importance of the case, the high Court held against the government. The creation of a legal machinery by means of which the federal government can intervene in labor disputes was said to be a legislative responsibility, and since in passing both the Defense Production Act and the Taft-Hartley Act Congress had not authorized plant seizure it could only be concluded that this technique had been implicitly legislated against.[3]

In the framework of our Constitution, the President's power to see that the laws are faithfully executed refutes the idea that he is a lawmaker. The Constitution limits his functions in the lawmaking process to the recommending of laws he thinks wise and the vetoing of laws he thinks bad. And the Constitution is neither silent nor equivocal about who shall make the laws which the President shall execute. . . .

The Founders of this Nation entrusted the law making power to the Congress alone in both good times and bad.

It is possible that at the time the steel industry was taken over by the government, a majority of the American people would have been more inclined to applaud than condemn. But as the ensuing weeks went swiftly by, as the flimsiness of the constitutional justification for this action became apparent side by side with the longest strike in the history of the steel industry (52 days), the appraisal of the

[3] *Youngstown Sheet and Tube Company* v. *Charles Sawyer*, 343 U.S. 579 (1952).

voting public began to alter. A feeling which had no doubt been strongly present for a number of months now began to crystallize into an even greater determination to substitute new leadership at

TABLE 69. A COSTLY CONTROVERSY

Month in 1952	Index of Industrial Production (1947-49 = 100)
January	121
July	115
December	133

Source: Federal Reserve Board.

the top in Washington. Prior to the Great Depression the Republican party had identified itself in the minds of citizens too exclusively with the interests of business for its own good. It now seemed evident that the Democratic party was in like manner legislating too exclusively in favor of labor. Just as in the earlier instance the party of the businessman had been compelled to pay the supreme penalty for so flagrant a bias, so now did the party of the worker have to give way to a constellation of forces promising a program resting on a somewhat broader base.

MR. EXECUTIVE GOES TO WASHINGTON

No doubt many citizens had cause to wonder during the first few months of President Eisenhower's administration if the nation had not simply traded the frying pan for the fire. For a time it appeared that, instead of merely entrusting the new consensus to a different leadership, the nation's destiny had rather been turned over to men determined to return the American economy to the point at which it had "gone astray" in the 1930's.

Nor is it to be wondered at that this issue arose in precisely this form. For just such an opportunity many conservatives had for twenty long years been waiting, and it was therefore only to be expected that steps would immediately be taken designed to resume the task of governing for the business interests where it had been involuntarily abandoned two decades before.

The clearest indication that such a movement might indeed be under way was the pattern of executive appointments which followed hard on the heels of the election. To a degree unprecedented in

American experience the top responsibilities in the new administration were to be in the hands of men called to those posts directly from key positions out in the world of industry. Conservative though the Republican party had always been, it had never before built a government so exclusively out of such materials; it was almost as if (in a violent reaction to the labor orientation in Washington in recent years) the successful meeting of a private payroll were considered the first, and virtually a sufficient, criterion of competence in government administration. Indeed, so pronounced was this tendency that when the American Federation of Labor president of the international plumbers' union was made Secretary of Labor, the quip began to go around that the Cabinet consisted of "nine millionaires and a plumber."

One incident in particular alerted the public to the possibilities inherent in the situation which seemed to be developing—and simultaneously informed the administration that the nation remembered the Republican bias of the 1920's. When Charles E. Wilson, president of the General Motors Corporation, was asked to be Secretary of Defense, he owned $2½ million worth of General Motors stock which under existing law he would be required to dispose of before being sworn into his new position. Mr. Wilson, however, was inclined to protest this requirement, insisting that no real conflict of interest was involved. He had always, he told a Congressional committee interviewing him on the subject, "operated under the assumption that what was good for the country was good for General Motors, and that what was good for General Motors was good for the country." When this statement was given wide publicity (with emphasis, of course, upon the last part rather than the first) against the background of Republican campaign inferences that 20 years of Democratic drift toward the welfare state were to be summarily reversed, sober-minded citizens had reason enough for wondering what if anything had been accomplished by the change in top management.

Against the background of these preliminaries, it came as a pleasant surprise to liberals that apparently there was not to be launched a concerted assault on New and Fair Deal social reforms—at least for the time being. Instead, getting off to a relatively slow start as a political machine somewhat the worse for lack of use began to unlimber itself for action, and concentrating at first on matters which were not even especially controversial, the nation's new leadership contented itself with a number of small steps calculated to reduce the influence of government in the world of private enterprise.

Progress on this front, although not dramatic, was immediate. With the end of active fighting in Korea now in sight it was agreed that most of the wage and price controls imposed as a result of that conflict should be allowed to expire on April 30, 1953—a decontrol measure more perfunctory than substantive in view of the fact that these restrictions had long since ceased to be a significant factor in the operation of the economy. In May the decision was made to give the states (primarily Texas, Louisiana, and California) legal title to oil lands off their coasts under waters controlled by the federal government.[4] June saw that great veteran of depression and war, the Reconstruction Finance Corporation, replaced by a Small Business Administration whose function was to make capital more readily available to smaller concerns.[5] At about this same time a commission headed by ex-President Herbert Hoover was created to (among other things) find areas of activity from which the federal government might properly withdraw. The Inland Waterways Corporation, a government barge line operating on the Mississippi and Warrior Rivers inherited from World War I days, was put up for sale and auctioned off to the highest bidder. And machinery was created whereby the government might dispose on reasonably favorable terms of the synthetic rubber plants carried over from World War II.

But of course there were limits to what could be accomplished by steps such as these, taken though they were with a distinct laissez faire flourish. To a considerable extent government had insinuated itself into business relationships through the medium of administrative activities of one sort or another rather than through simple legislative pronouncements. It was, therefore, only a logical corollary of direct moves to take the government out of business when attention began to be focused upon the agencies responsible for these more pervasive and continuous business–government contacts. Although, to be sure, such groups had become so much a part of the country's institutional framework that there could be no thought of summarily abolishing them, advantage could nevertheless be taken of many opportunities to minimize their impact on the economy.

One key battlefield of this kind was the National Labor Relations Board.[6] For some years it had been argued that Taft-Hartley achieve-

---

[4] Ernest R. Bartley, *The Tidelands Oil Controversy* (Austin: University of Texas Press, 1953).

[5] Sidney Goldberg and Harold Seidman, *The Government Corporation: Elements of a Model Charter* (Chicago: Public Administration Service, 1953).

[6] Fred Witney, *Government and Collective Bargaining* (Philadelphia: J. B. Lippincott, Co., 1951).

ments had been substantially narrowed as a result of being applied by a body reflecting the philosophy of a President bitterly opposed to it, and for an even longer time it had been felt in business circles that the National Labor Relations Act had itself been significantly broadened in scope by administrative decisions. Now it was proposed to remedy both of these defects by replacing Board members (as terms expired) with men holding views more consistent with the conservative's idea of what Congress had intended. And because President Eisenhower was required to make two appointments to this five-man agency shortly after his inauguration, a difference in labor law interpretation began to be noted very soon.

In three areas in particular was the way thus opened for a strengthening of employer advantage in collective bargaining relationships. First, using a somewhat narrowed definition of interstate commerce as the primary tool here, the new National Labor Relations Board set about pushing many local-type cases out of the jurisdiction of the federal government (and hence into the jurisdiction of less liberal local governments). Second, the securing of recognition by islands of craft workers wholly surrounded by a sea of industrial unionists was made easier—this having the effect of weakening union bargaining strength by threatening worker unity. And third, the so-called ban on employer free speech, the limitations surrounding management's freedom to propagandize against the union, was further modified.

Another major field in which Republicans moved to infiltrate a key citadel built out of a philosophy of government–business relationships alien to their own was the public generation and transmission of electric power.[7] During the preceding twenty years the government's output of this product had increased from 1 per cent of the national total to 13 per cent. Moreover, two special aspects of this fact were at this point making the federal government's power program an even livelier issue in partisan politics. In the first place, although the generation of electricity was still typically only one of the objectives served by multipurpose valley development projects, power was more and more becoming a central objective of public policy in this field. In the second place, public policy at this point was becoming less and less insistent upon a schedule of rates for government generated electricity which would return full costs, concerning itself rather with the development of a rate structure promoting a greater use of electric power. It is, in other words, small wonder that private enterprise enthusiasts were now all the more

[7] James C. Bonbright, *Public Utilities and the National Power Policies* (New York: Columbia University Press, 1940).

TABLE 70. CONSERVATIVE ARGUMENT FOR RETRENCHMENT

	Generation of Electric Energy		
Year	Total (billions of kilowatt hours)	Per Cent Private	Per Cent Nonprivate
1942	186	85.0	15.0
1947	256	81.4	18.6
1953	443	80.0	20.0

Source: Federal Power Commission.

training their sights on the $1.5 billion investment and the 20,000 miles of transmission lines represented by this government activity.

Eager though many conservatives were on this front, however, Republicans did not direct a frontal assault on the status quo. Powerful vested interests had not only formed around the principal projects already completed, but many citizens (especially in the western part of the country) were afraid that a retrenchment of government power development would mean a drastic slowing down in the construction of new plants. Accordingly the procedure followed for the most part was to "bleed" this activity rather than to pass sweeping legislation. The budgets of the Bureau of Reclamation, the Army Engineers, the Rural Electrification Administration, and the Tennessee Valley Authority were reduced; a number of new projects were cancelled; some projects already under way were abandoned; and a major effort was inaugurated designed to give private power concerns a more important role in distributing publicly generated power.

Stated in summary fashion the new policy on power development was essentially to be that of resolving whatever doubts might arise in favor of private rather than public enterprise. A case in point will illustrate the kinds of considerations involved in this approach. One of the public power projects now abandoned was the construction of a large multipurpose dam in Hell's Canyon on the Snake River as a part of the water control system for the Columbia River Valley. Instead the construction of a number of smaller dams by private companies was authorized. While the smaller dams would require a smaller total outlay and would likely be in operation sooner, they would on the other hand generate only about one half as much power as the larger dam—and might even result in the less effective accomplishment of certain of the other objectives for which multiple-purpose projects are undertaken.[8]

[8] Twentieth Century Fund, *Electric Power and Government Policy* (New York: Twentieth Century Fund, Inc., 1948).

Antitrust Under New Management

Another important agency to which new appointments were promptly made was the Federal Trade Commission. Moreover, this was a particularly significant vantage point from which to watch for clues as to the new administration's intentions, for antitrust policy had for many years been considered by liberals the key to the national government's approach to economic issues.[9] Thus it was with special interest that the nation awaited the new President's first action involving the administrative body responsible for the plane of business competition.

This step, taken three months after President Eisenhower's inauguration, seemed at first glance to confirm the worst fears of zealous "trust-busters." The new chairman of this group was to be a man who had spent most of his mature life handling antitrust cases for large corporations. Furthermore, this shift in leadership at the top began almost immediately to be reflected in changes in underlying philosophy.

One of the first shifts noted in actual policy was a cautious retreat from the doctrine of conscious parallelism. Early in 1953 a vigorous dissent by a Truman appointee recorded the following sentiment: "In my opinion, some kind of overt act which implements a meeting of the minds is a 'must' in a conspiracy." The reinforcement of this stand by two Republican appointments made it a majority position in the Commission even before 1953 was over. At the same time, too, the courts were taking a second look at the implications of this principle they had recently seemed wholeheartedly to support.

But if this trend could accurately be described as "reactionary," liberals were soon gratified to learn that it was not a representative one. Indeed, as the new administration's program on this front began to unfold, the antitrust fraternity the country over was frankly astonished at the contrast between that program and its Republican predecessor of thirty years earlier.

Still emphasizing the pattern of behavior emanating from the Federal Trade Commission, note that the same agency which was backing down on conscious parallelism was apparently endeavoring to remain as firm as possible in another important area of current controversy. In the basing-point cases the Commission had advanced the argument that a systematic price structure continued over a period of time could not be defended against a charge of discrimina-

---

[9] Clare E. Griffin, *An Economic Approach to Anti-Trust Problems* (New York: American Enterprise Assoc., 1951).

tion by use of the "good-faith" proviso of the Robinson-Patman Act—and the courts had broadly gone along with that interpretation of the law. After nailing down the basing-point issue largely in other ways, the Commission had endeavored to widen this achievement on the good faith front by utilizing it in cases involving other types of discrimination.

This effort met, initially, with a mixed success. The simplest type of issue was raised when the Minneapolis-Honeywell Company defended its regular schedule of quantity discounts, discriminations included, on the ground that the discriminatory prices were quoted in good faith to meet the equally low prices of a competitor. A Circuit Court of Appeals upheld the Commission's rejection of that defense under these circumstances,[10] and the Supreme Court refused to upset this ruling.

A more complex question was also being fought out in connection with a complaint brought some years before against the Standard Oil Company of Indiana. This concern systematically quoted jobbers a price 1½ cents per gallon less than that allowed retailers. A normal enough procedure in and of itself (the former bought in tank car lots, the latter in tank wagon quantities), this practice gave rise to difficulties because certain of these jobbers also sold at retail. A Federal Trade Commission order, based on injury to competition arising from the fact that jobber retailers were given an undue advantage over service stations, demanded that Standard cease offering its discount to jobbers on that portion of their purchases they themselves later sold at retail.

The company's contention in this proceeding was that the good faith defense should be absolute, that once good faith is in fact shown nothing more remains to be said. In the case at bar the Commission conceded that the price system in question had evolved out of a good faith meeting of competitors' prices, but insisted that the resulting injury to competition was the decisive fact. The Circuit Court supported the Commission in this contention, but the Supreme Court agreed with Standard that the good faith defense is substantive and not merely procedural in character.[11] Whereupon the Commission set about challenging Standard on the basis of the principles established in the Minneapolis-Honeywell ruling.

It was not certain what all of this meant—even apart from the fact

[10] *Minneapolis-Honeywell Company* v. *Federal Trade Commission*, 191 F. 2d 786 (1951).

[11] *Standard Oil Company* (Indiana) v. *Federal Trade Commission*, 340 U.S. 231 (1951).

that it was too early to be sure which side of this fence the "new" Federal Trade Commission would ultimately be on. To a point the limitation of the good faith defense along Minneapolis-Honeywell lines can serve useful purposes from the standpoint of maintaining competition. On the other hand, there were just as obviously elements in the Standard of Indiana case broadly reminiscent of the defense of "soft" competition (the protection of competitors rather than the maintenance of competition) first launched in New Deal days.

What could be said for certain, however, was that in a number of less dramatic but probably more important ways the Federal Trade Commission was being given the most vigorous role in the antitrust field it had ever had. Thus a campaign of systematically investigating newly announced mergers for compliance with the Celler Anti-Merger Act was inaugurated, and several significant actions were brought which still further attested to the new government's intention to enforce that law. A beginning was made at checking compliance with outstanding orders and establishing machinery to keep this information up to date—the first such program in the Commis-

TABLE 71. REGULATION IN SLOW MOTION

Age of Formal Antitrust Cases Pending July 1, 1952	
Period of Pendency	Number of Cases
Less than 1 year	2
From 1 to 2 years	6
From 2 to 3 years	13
From 3 to 5 years	21
From 5 to 10 years	12
From 10 to 15 years	25
More than 15 years	6
Total	85

Source: *Final Report of the Select Committee on Small Business*, House of Representatives, 82d Congress, 2d Session, House Report 2513, 1952.

sion's history. Plans were made to tighten up the government's handling of cases involving the cost defense under the Robinson-Patman Act, both to make the meaning of that proviso more concrete for the benefit of those business firms concerned with it and to lessen its usefulness in support of soft competition. And a stringent action was brought against the exclusive distributor contracts of Dictagraph Products, Inc.

Nor was this "new look" in Republican antitrust policy restricted to the Federal Trade Commission. Beginning almost immediately the Department of Justice also added its weight to this effort. New suits were instituted as consistently and as vigorously as under the preceding regime—some of the defendants in these actions being large and prominent firms. For example, in October, 1953, a complaint was made against American Smelting and Refining charging that certain of its long-term contracts had the effect of substantially restricting competition. A proposed merger of Bethlehem Steel and Youngstown Sheet and Tube was disapproved. And a committee was named by the Department of Justice to make a thorough investigation of policy in that field, a committee liberally sprinkled with stanch defenders of "trust-busting."

It would not be argued, of course, that there was developing anything which might legitimately be referred to as an all-out campaign to achieve a fully competitive economy (whatever that might mean). But it was nevertheless something of a paradox when the nation's courts began, ideologically, to lag behind a Republican administration in the matter of antitrust enforcement.

Note in this connection the way in which two district courts turned aside two government suits against Du Pont. In the first of these the charge was the monopolization of the production of cellophane. The court, however, refusing to define the appropriate market as consisting of cellophane alone, concluded as follows:

There has been no monopolization or conspiracy or attempt to monopolize shown. The record reflects not the dead hand of monopoly but rapidly declining prices, expanding production, intense competition stimulated by intensive research, the development of new products and uses and other benefits of a free economy. Du Pont nor any other American company similarly situated should be punished for its success.[12]

The second challenge to Du Pont reaching its climax during this period involved a charge of intra-enterprise conspiracy. The government's contention here was that the defendant had used its stock holdings in General Motors and United States Rubber to prevent these concerns from buying (for instance) paint and tire fabrics from Du Pont competitors. Holding that the charge was not supported by evidence, the court dismissed this suit.

The government was similarly reversed in an action brought against the New Orleans *Times-Picayune*, the only morning newspaper in that city. The same concern also, however, published an evening edition, and in that area it had a major competitor. Challenging

[12] *United States* v. *E. I. Du Pont de Nemours Co.*, 118 F. Supp. 41 (1953).

this company's legal right to require morning paper advertisers to buy space in its evening edition as well, the government brought suit. In one of the strangest decisions in recent years the Supreme Court rejected this complaint. The court refused to recognize the morning paper monopoly, defining this market as consisting of three daily newspapers, and consequently held the arrangement complained of to be legal.[13] And this side by side with an action being brought (later settled on the new government's terms by a consent decree) against Eastman Kodak's practice of selling color film at a price which included finishing services.

Still another adverse court decision was not a reversal for government antitrust work as such. In late 1952 the Supreme Court announced that the Food and Drug Administration could not inspect food factories without permission from the owners under existing law—a serious deprivation for an agency which had the year before condemned twenty-three tons of food every working day. On paper this damage was promptly remedied by the new Congress, but with the other hand that group virtually took away this added power by reducing the Administration's appropriation.

And even the courts were not wholly negative in the field of antitrust enforcement. With respect to patents especially the trend toward modernizing these monopoly grants was decisively carried forward. Thus the United Shoe Machinery Corporation was directed to sell its machines as well as lease them, to grant licenses to all concerns on reasonable royalties, and to revise its standard contracts in several other particulars.[14] And in a truly landmark decision the General Electric Company, as a penalty for conviction in a criminal suit charging the use of patent privileges to create a monopoly, was required to make all its patents covering the manufacture of bulbs and bulb-making machinery available to the public on a royalty-free basis—and to make all future patents available on payment of reasonable royalties.[15]

A Fresh Look at Some Old Taboos

Nor was it only in the antitrust field that the new administration began to exhibit an unfamiliar pattern of behavior for Republican governments. In the labor field, for example, although the reactionary wing of the party would have preferred legislation drawing

---

13 *Times-Picayune Publishing Company* v. *United States,* 345 U.S. 594 (1953).
14 *United Shoe Machinery Corporation* v. *United States,* 347 U.S. 241 (1953).
15 *United States* v. *General Electric Company,* 115 F. Supp. 835 (1953).

Taft-Hartley–type labor union restrictions still tighter, the President chose rather to support a measure which would have eased the legislative handicaps under which worker organizations were then functioning. To be sure, nothing came of this attempt by the administration to take seriously its campaign promises to labor. Rightist resistance to such a move was so strong that it aborted, precipitating the explosive resignation of the Secretary of Labor, but this impasse coupled with developments on the National Labor Relations Board front went a long way toward ratifying the consensus on the labor issue first proclaimed in the Taft-Hartley Act.

Another point at which the Republican party soon found itself in a strange policy environment was the field of taxation. Almost immediately after the new President took office an intense controversy over this issue arose which could hardly have developed at all in the days when Andrew W. Mellon presided over the nation's finances.

During the electoral campaign Republicans had criticized New Deal–Fair Deal budget deficits, repeatedly promising to return the Treasury to the black. By this time, too, the special taxation which had been imposed to help finance the Korean conflict was coming increasingly under fire, and Republican candidates made it clear that the need for these levies had about run its course.[16]

Under the most favorable circumstances, the conflict between these two promises would not have been complete. But circumstances were far from ideal. On the one hand, the level of expenditure associated with the war in Korea had already been drastically reduced from the rapid rate of two and a half years earlier, while in any event the nation's armament output would remain high for cold war purposes. On the other hand, there was much less fat in the Truman budget than had been assumed. It was discovered that re-

TABLE 72. EASIER SAID THAN DONE

| Calendar Year | Federal Government (billions of dollars) | | |
	Cash Receipts	Cash Payments	Excess of Payments
1950	42.4	42.0	0.4*
1952	71.3	73.0	1.6
1953	70.0	76.2	6.2
1954	68.6	69.6	1.1

* Surplus.
Source: Treasury Department and Bureau of the Budget.

[16] Roy Blough, *The Federal Taxing Process* (New York: Prentice-Hall, Inc., 1952).

ducing expenditures typically meant restricting activities—activities in the continuation of which vested interests were invariably much interested. Thus it was that Republicans were soon at odds with one another over which of two mutually exclusive goals was to be most actively pursued.

The major bone of contention here was the excess profits tax scheduled to expire June 30, 1953. While almost everyone conceded that this tax resulted in an undesirable discrimination against young concerns and industries, the fact remained that in six months it would bring into the Treasury some $800 million. Moreover, individual income tax rates were due to come down about 10 per cent on January 1, 1954, and it was thought to be politically impossible to allow the excess profits tax to expire on schedule without advancing by six months the date of relief for individual income taxpayers. Accordingly, the administration set its face resolutely—and successfully—against all midyear reductions, the sequel to this stand being the necessity for asking Congress to raise the ceiling on the national debt above $275 billion.[17]

Still another challenge to Republican preferences appeared in the area of monetary management. Beginning more or less with America's entry into World War II, a central consideration in Treasury policy had been to keep the interest rate as low as possible in order that the burden of the government debt might be minimized. Conservatives had not, to be sure, protested this objective in and of itself, but at the same time such a policy did have several overtones irritating to that group.

Stated most broadly, conservative criticism of Democratic debt management was that it was inflationary, that it created an "easy money" situation defrauding creditors for the benefit of debtors. More specifically, it was emphasized that such a policy kept the Federal Reserve System subservient to the Treasury, rather than allowing it the flexibility needed to do its part in stabilizing the economy.[18]

As is so frequently the case, the attack by the outsiders was exaggerated. The rate of interest had in fact been steadily rising since the end of World War II.[19] At the same time, however, it was possible, in the very midst of the Korean war, to mount so formidable an as-

[17] C. C. Abbott, *The Federal Debt—Structure and Impact* (New York: Twentieth Century Fund, Inc., 1953).

[18] G. L. Bach, *Federal Reserve Policy-Making* (New York: Alfred A. Knopf, Inc., 1950).

[19] J. S. Fforde, *The Federal Reserve System, 1945-1949* (Oxford: Clarendon Press, 1954).

sault against Democratic "cheap money" that an agreement was worked out whereby the Federal Reserve authorities were gradually to withdraw System support from the government bond market.

Heartened by that triumph, Republicans understandably planned to use their political victory to broaden this gain. Indeed, one of the important conservative battle crys during the campaign had been a promise to restore the nation to a "hard money" basis, and to a high post in the Treasury Department was named a man who still entertained the naive notion of putting the United States back on a gold redemption basis.

At this point, too, the results achieved left much to be desired. Although immediately after inauguration the rediscount rate was raised and the Treasury floated a long-term bond issue carrying the highest interest rate in many years, this policy soon ran into the roughest sort of weather. Partly because it coincided with and partly because it helped bring about an extremely tight money market, retrenchment began almost at once. When $1 billion worth of Treasury bonds fell to a discount before they were issued, when a $5 billion issue had to be refinanced on a short-term basis rather than the long-term basis administration policy-makers would have preferred, and especially when it began to be wondered if the Treasury would be able to carry its refinancing program through on any terms—the Federal Reserve Board was forced to lower reserve requirements and buy $1 billion worth of securities in the open market.

Once again Republicans had learned that situations often look different to those in power than to leaders of the "loyal opposition." Despite the agreement negotiated two years before which was to emancipate the Board from Treasury policy, it now seemed that little progress had been made toward accomplishing that goal—and it was even uncertain when more definitive steps in that direction could be taken. To be sure, the administration's quick reversal of policy indicated that the new government would not be stubbornly orthodox in the face of hard realities. Thus it was apparent that the Federal Reserve Board would behave responsibly, in recognition of the tremendous economic significance now of debt management. But it was nonetheless something of a shock to many conservatives to learn that the price of responsibility in monetary policy had risen so high.

But perhaps the most striking demonstration of the "new look" in the Republican party appeared in the social security field.[20] In his

[20] J. D. Hogan and F. A. J. Ianni, *American Social Legislation* (New York: Harper & Bros., 1956).

first State of the Union message, delivered in January, 1954, President Eisenhower set forth the official attitude of his administration on this issue in the following words:

This Administration recognizes a third great purpose of government: concern for the human problems of our citizens. In a modern economic society, banishment of destitution and cushioning the shock of personal disaster on the individual are proper concerns of all levels of government, including the Federal Government. This is especially true where remedy and prevention alike are beyond the individual's capacity.

Specific proposals to implement these sentiments included broadening the social security program as such, raising the minimum wage, expanding projects for rehabilitating disabled citizens, substantial expenditures in the public housing field, and a federal government program for reinsuring private health and accident insurance activities (as a device to lessen pressure for a national health insurance program).

Of course, it would not be expected that highly conservative groups within the Republican party would enthusiastically enact an agenda such as this into law. Thus the American Medical Association took almost as dim a view of the government reinsurance approach to the nation's health problem as it had earlier of Harry Truman's Fair Deal proposal. Moreover, prompted at this point by the real estate lobby, Congress appropriated funds for additional public housing grudgingly and therefore less abundantly than the President requested. However, it is nonetheless a remarkable fact that the new Republican party not only carried forward the public housing program of predecessor administrations, but also liberalized benefits and expanded coverage in both the old age and unemployment security areas and increased the minimum hourly wage from 75¢ to $1.00.

POINT OF NO RETURN

But all these developments were in a sense mere episodes by comparison with what was unquestionably the greatest challenge to the new administration. For when the time came for the nation's new leadership to stand up and be counted on the issue of economic stabilization, the conflict between the old and the new Republican parties stood out in still sharper relief.

Understandably, a Republican party taking over the responsibilities of government in America at such a time would be keenly interested in this problem. For one thing, in the preceding two decades the nation had learned that prosperity cannot be taken for granted —that the assistance of human institutions is often necessary in this area, even apart from the fact that voting citizens in a mature democracy will insist upon the acceptance of this responsibility. Even more important, the position of the United States in world affairs made a high level of economic activity the most vital component of an effective foreign policy. And finally, a serious economic downturn could easily destroy for a number of years whatever hope remained of reducing the role of government in the economy. In short, a business-dominated government had everything to gain from continued prosperity, particularly in view of the fact that the public mind still associated the Republican party with economic disaster. President Eisenhower himself had emphatically given expression to this feeling by stating during the campaign that "never again will we allow a depression in the United States."[21]

The first question to be decided in this field, of course, was what to do about the Council of Economic Advisers. Both because that agency had by this time become identified with the Fair Deal, and because it had fallen into popular disfavor in the bargain, a convincing case could be made for abolishing it and starting off on a wholly new tack. Such a procedure, moreover, was debated for a time. But when it seemed that so drastic a step would be interpreted in some quarters as indifference to the problem of unemployment, another decision was reached. The Council was retained with new personnel at the top, but on a somewhat altered basis. For purposes of internal research and discussion there were to be three Council members as required by law. When, however, it came to communicating with the administration (that is, informing those around the President about economic conditions or giving official advice), the Chairman of the Council was to speak with a single voice. And the new Chairman was a man acknowledged by his professional colleagues to be one of the world's outstanding authorities on the subject of business cycles.

All this was an excellent preparation for what was to come next. In late July, 1953, the eagerly awaited and long-expected truce in Korea became official, and an important pillar supporting American prosperity began to weaken a little. Unfortunately, furthermore, this development came close upon a general inventory adjustment which had already reduced the level of industrial production. July saw indexes of business activity begin to register declines, and this situation continued through the first quarter of 1954. By January of that

[21] Neil H. Jacoby, Can Prosperity be Sustained? (New York: Henry Holt & Co., Inc., 1956).

year it was acknowledged that the economy was in the throes of another economic recession.

There was never any question of following a "let-nature-take-her-course" policy. The President's *Economic Report* published in early 1954 made it unmistakably clear that the official policy of the government toward this situation would not be neutrality.

TABLE 73. FATE TAKES A HAND

Month and Year	Industrial Production*	Unemployment†	Corporate Profits†
July, 1953	100	100	100
March, 1954	90	300	84

* Federal Reserve Board.
† Department of Commerce.

The decisions currently made by government, whether in the sphere of taxes or housing or defense or agriculture or bank credit or any other major area, inevitably have implications for economic growth and stability. . . . The new concept that is emerging in the practical art of government . . . is to subject every act of proposed legislation or administrative decision, as far as that is humanly possible, to review from the standpoint of the contribution it is likely to make . . . to the attainment of an expanding economy with maximum employment and without price inflation. That was the basic intent of the Employment Act of 1946, and it is a guiding principle of this administration. If our economy is to have a good chance of staying firmly on the road that separates inflation from recession the Government must be alert and sensitive to every economic development, including its own myriad activities; it must be prepared to take preventive as well as remedial action; and it must put itself in a state of readiness to cope with new situations that may arise.

There was, on the other hand, much debate over whether the action now to be taken by the government was to be drastic or mild. The decision here, of course, revolved around the view taken as to the seriousness of the situation confronting the economy, and on this the Republican administration remained optimistic throughout. (Was not General Motors currently announcing a $1 billion expansion program to be financed out of earnings?)[22] That attitude perhaps in part reflected conservative hopes coupled with preferences as to the relationship between government and business, but it must not be forgotten that the President was also constantly receiving interpretations of business conditions from specialists in that field.

Largely because the government's decisions were based on opti-

---

[22] National Bureau of Economic Research, *Regularization of Business Investment* (Princeton: Princeton University Press, 1954).

mistic expectations, there were no dramatic developments in stabilization policy. As administration spokesmen pointed out, the care which had been taken the year before not to let the money market get too tight had after all been an important protective measure. Similarly, it was emphasized that the reduction in individual income taxes and the demise of the excess profits tax scheduled for January 1, and reductions in corporation income and excise taxes scheduled for April 1, were also fundamental antideflationary steps. Apart from these more or less routine actions, no specific stabilization measures were inaugurated except a liberalization of credit terms on government housing loans, a further reduction in reserve requirements, and perhaps the acceptance of a larger budget deficit than would have been tolerated under more propitious circumstances.[23] It was at one time understood that if the business slide-off continued beyond the first quarter more stringent measures would be readied, but when the decline began to level off in April, these further actions were not taken.

Because the 1953-54 recession was as mild as it was, and because in consequence little of importance happened on the antidepression front, the significance of this period for the evolution of government–business relationships lies primarily in a policy development having no direct connection with recession as such but which was no doubt conditioned by the fact that it coincided with a period of economic discomfort and uncertainty. The subject here was another aspect of tax policy. Years ago Republicans had pledged themselves to overhaul the tax structure which had grown up during successive Democratic administrations and under emergency conditions. It was therefore nothing more than a political accident that the first opportunity for fulfilling this pledge was rendered much less favorable than would otherwise have been the case by a wholly extraneous factor.

There was of course an element of pure class bias underlying conservative hopes in this field. One of the most basic aspects of New Deal–Fair Deal tax policy had been an emphasis upon the progressive feature of the individual income tax, and it is understandable that those in the higher income brackets would want to shift some of this tax burden to other shoulders. At the same time, however, the principal proposals now put forward by the administration could also be convincingly defended on the basis of fundamental economic

---

[23] Kenyon E. Poole (ed.), *Fiscal Policies And The American Economy* (New York: Prentice-Hall, Inc., 1951).

policy. And of course it was along these lines that Republican orators elected to present their case.

The primary argument advanced was that the existing tax structure had developed while the nation was too preoccupied first with depression and then with defense to give serious thought to the impact of fiscal policy on economic progress.[24] Now, however, this matter could no longer be treated as secondary. Only an economy in which business was not fettered by antibusiness policies could produce the goods needed for defense in addition to providing a rising standard of living for a rapidly growing population.

Two changes in tax policy were especially emphasized in this connection.[25] First, it was urged that business managers should be allowed more flexibility in determining their own depreciation rates. In order to encourage expansion of private enterprise production of war goods during World War II, plants had been granted the privilege of accelerating their depreciation write-off, and this expedient had worked so well as to suggest a similar technique for speeding up peacetime innovation. Second, pressure was exerted to secure at least significant modifications in the policy of taxing corporate dividends twice—once in the hands of the corporation and again in the hands of dividend receivers. Here the argument was that present policy discouraged equity investment and hence was also a drag on innovation.

It goes without saying, that the Democrats stood on ideological grounds poles apart from considerations such as these. Their preference would have been a reduction in taxation for lower income bracket taxpayers rather than concessions to big business and clippers of coupons.[26] But this preference too was clothed in the raiment of public interest. Over and over again it was emphasized that in a period of business recession taxes should be reduced for income spenders rather than income savers. Accordingly what the Democrats wanted was an increase in the personal exemption allowed in the individual income tax from $600 to $700.

There was merit on both sides of this controversy—enough, in fact, to justify building policy in either of these directions, depending upon the nature of the economic crisis then at its crest. For weeks

[24] Lewis H. Kimmel, *Taxes and Economic Incentives* (Washington, D.C.: Brookings Institution, 1950).

[25] D. T. Smith, *The Effects of Taxation on Corporate Financial Policy* (Cambridge: Harvard Graduate School of Business Administration, 1952).

[26] Simon Kuznets, *Shares of Upper Income Groups in Income and Savings* (New York: National Bureau of Economic Research, 1953).

the issue was genuinely in doubt, as spokesmen for both sides closely watched developments on the business activity front. But when in early April it became evident that the worst was over, at least for the time being, the administration's approach clearly had the advantage. To be sure, the changes written into the ensuing legislation were not as substantial as conservatives had hoped. Thus depreciation liberalization fell far short of the five-year amortization privilege allowed during the war, and only the first $50 of dividends received were excluded from double taxation. But a beginning had been made, and, what was perhaps of even greater importance, the Eisenhower administration had won a resounding victory for the principle that economic progress is not to be taken for granted—that the use of fiscal policy for stabilization purposes carries with it an equal responsibility to keep constantly under review the consequences of stabilization policy for underlying growth and development.

It was frankly a little confusing. The first Republican administration in almost a quarter of a century was turning out to be conservative by the smallest possible margin. The very men who had claimed that sweeping changes would be made as soon as they were in power seemed after the fact to be quite tame.

QUESTIONS FOR DISCUSSION

1. Why was the government's attempt to control the economy during the Korean war much less successful than during World War II?
2. What was the significance for government–business relationships of the steel seizure controversy in 1952?
3. Why was the Fair Deal replaced?
4. Describe the most important steps taken in 1953 to reduce the influence of government in the private enterprise economy.
5. What did the new administration primarily expect to accomplish in the labor field, and how?
6. Explain the major aspects of the public versus private power controversy at this time.
7. How would you characterize the new administration's antitrust policy as it began to unfold?
8. How should the good faith doctrine be used in implementing an effective antitrust policy?
9. Why was a return to the business economy of the 1920's more easily talked about than accomplished?
10. What was the essence of the 1953 controversy over taxation within the Republican party?
11. Explain the major factors involved in the dispute over monetary policy.

12. Why was the maintenance of prosperity so important to the Republican party at this time? How adequate were the government's measures to assure this result?

13. From the standpoint of the public interest was the right decision made on the tax question in 1954?

14. Why did the new Republican administration ratify the public policy consensus at so many points?

15. Describe the "New Republicanism" in terms of the concept "mixed economy."

Chapter 30

Lances and Windmills

REVOLT OF THE MODERATES

Of course this mystery could in a superficial way be clarified by making reference to the new consensus. But the most important question would remain. What forces were at work keeping public policy so nicely balanced?

One explanation here might approach this question from the standpoint of the ideology current within the two major parties. On the Democratic side a key fact was the achievement under the New and Fair Deals of the basic objectives sought. Thus it was suggested by some that prosperity and social legislation to date had made conservatives out of so many Democrats that a comprehensive reform program could no longer secure party endorsement.

Republican ideology, moreover, had over the years been placed under even greater stress by a drastic alteration in the popular conception of government responsibilities. Whether this was because changed conditions demanded that the federal government assume additional functions, or whether the people had simply become accustomed to the assumption by government of new tasks would long be debated by both conservatives and liberals. But that no political party could again interpret the functions of the federal government as narrowly as had been done under Harding, Coolidge, and Hoover, and survive at the polls, was a proposition no one seriously disputed.

Again, however, it may be profitable to probe deeper. Not only is it true that the major parties had moved closer together, but the balance betwen them on the public policy stage was at the moment remarkably even. In 1952, although Mr. Eisenhower won a veritable landslide victory in his own contest (a fact apparently attributable to personal popularity rather than ideological considerations), the

Republican majority in the Congress then elected was exceedingly narrow. Two years later this experience was repeated—in reverse. Without Eisenhower coattails to cling to Republican candidates fared less well, and in consequence the Democrats were enabled to organize both Houses of Congress. But the Senate in the Eighty-fourth Congress was Democratic by the paper thin margin of a single vote, while the parliamentary advantage in the House was almost equally slight. Why was it that neither party seemed able to achieve a decisive majority?

Perhaps the most plausible explanation of the phenomenon is that the parties had drifted into a period of ideological confusion. As a consequence, so this contention ran, their propaganda efforts were ritualistically rather than realistically oriented—by which was meant that prewar issues built around prewar alignments continued to dominate national campaigns even though these issues themselves had already been resolved or had ceased to divide the parties in the same old way. As Professor Galbraith put it:

The noise and the violence and imaginativeness of the invective are no measure whatever of the importance of the issue. (Later I shall show in fact that the correlation is more likely inverse.) . . .

Much of our debate is loud and violent, not because the issues are close but because they are not. There is anger not because issues are being settled but because they are settled. The noise nonetheless leaves the impression that the matter is still in doubt.[1]

Using a somewhat different terminology, Samuel Lubell advanced the thesis that the mid-century stalemate in American politics stemmed from a revolt against extreme proposals by moderates of all types. Two reasons were given for this rebellion:

In part this persistent uncertainty reflects the harsh choices posed by the cold war, choices which have often made inaction seem more desirable than action. But it also reflects the fact that these choices have had to be registered through political parties which still are wedded to perpetuating prewar hatreds and ideologies.

The whole of Western civilization is caught up in this same struggle between the past and future which is the essence of the American political trial.

. . . It is the drama, in miniature, of a world in transition, with every nation being forced to break free of the past so it can find a new internal balance that can be fitted into a new world equilibrium. Human thought seems fated to follow a cycle of imprisonment and liberation. When first set forth, intellectual concepts free our imaginations. But as what was once new hardens into dogma, these same concepts become like so many prison walls that shut in

[1] J. K. Galbraith, *Economics and the Art of Controversy* (New Brunswick: Rutgers University Press, 1955), pp. 16 and 103.

our minds. In no field is the need for a mental prison break more urgent than in what we call "politics."[2]

And even the President of the United States made a significant contribution to this analysis. In late January, following the Budget and State of the Union messages, Mr. Eisenhower was asked in a press conference if the views he had just expressed to Congress were not New and Fair Dealish in tenor. The President's answer, a response he so firmly believed reflected his feelings on this subject that he permitted himself to be quoted directly, will long remain a classic in the literature on the government's role in the American economy:

When it comes down to dealing with the relationships between the human in this country and his Government, the people in this Administration believe in being what I think we would normally call liberal, and when we deal with the economic affairs of this country we believe in being conservative.

While it is true that from the standpoint of strict logic this statement was little more than the jumble of words it was promptly accused of being by liberals (but let it be remembered that it had been the architect of the New Deal himself who said in the middle of the 1930's: "I am that kind of a liberal because I am that kind of a conservative"), it perhaps nevertheless explained much about the prevailing politico-economic environment. Furthermore, if this quotation can appropriately be thought of as a declaration of confusion, it would be difficult to find a more fitting platform on which moderates might stand than the following taken from the *Economic Report of the President* transmitted to Congress January 20, 1955:

The economic actions of this Administration and its program for the future rest upon certain basic propositions. *First*, competitive markets, rather than governmental directives, are as a rule the most efficient instruments for organizing production and consumption. *Second*, a free economy has great capacity to generate jobs and incomes if a feeling of confidence in the economic future is widely shared by investors, workers, businessmen, farmers, and consumers. *Third*, the Federal Government creates an atmosphere favorable to economic activity when it encourages private initiative, curbs monopolistic tendencies, whether of business or labor, avoids encroachment on the private sector of the economy, and carries out as much of its own work as is practicable through private enterprise. *Fourth*, the Federal Government generates confidence when it restrains tendencies toward recession or inflation, and does this by relying largely on indirect means of influencing private behavior rather than by direct controls over people, industries, and markets. *Fifth*, the Federal Government contributes to economic growth when it takes

[2] Samuel Lubell, *Revolt of the Moderates* (New York: Harper & Bros., 1956), pp. 12-13.

its part, at the side of the States, in promoting scientific research and in providing public facilities, such as highways, hospitals, harbors, and educational institutions, on which the expansion of the private economy heavily rests. *Sixth,* the Federal Government strengthens the foundations of the economy when it widens opportunity for its less fortunate citizens and, working in cooperation with the States and localities, helps individuals to cope with the hazards of unemployment, illness, old age, and blighted neighborhoods.

These economic tenets are basic and inseparable. They constitute guides to policies which, if pursued persistently, will advance us toward the goal of an increasing national income, shared equitably among those who contribute to its growth, and realized in dollars of stable buying power. In broadest outline they constitute the framework of an economic system that is at once strong and humane, a system that can provide both greater material abundance and a better quality of living.

POLITICS OF CONFUSION

And in the final analysis it matters little whether the accent was placed on party confusion or citizen moderation. An abundance of both are to be found in this four years of Republican rule, and indeed policy items of these two kinds constitute a fairly full account of the achievements of this administration.

On the confusion side of the ledger, to begin with, what terminology could more accurately describe the phenomenon of a Republican President preparing for submission to Congress a bill amending the Taft-Hartley Act in labor's favor—even though conservative Senators and Congressmen did succeed in blocking this move? Similarly, how better describe the repudiation by a Republican administration (although here again over the opposition of a sizable group of its own stalwarts) of the Mellon philosophy that the lower the rate of taxation assessed against business enterprise the greater the tax revenues received by the government? And is it not traditional American politics turned upside down when a Republican leadership calmly accepts a federal government deficit in the face of economic recession, while highly placed Democrats threaten refusal to raise the debt limit as a weapon to compel fiscal economies?

A somewhat more complex confusion arose in connection with the minimum wage increase. This proposal was officially made and actively promoted by the administration, a striking enough fact in and of itself in view of the stand Republicans had customarily taken where security guarantees by the federal government were involved. When Congressional lines began to form around a measure implementing this recommendation, moreover, it developed that both support and resistance were bipartisan. Because the largest group of workers which would be affected were southern factory laborers, northeasterners discomfited by the drift of industry toward the South enthusiastically supported the higher minimum. Thus the controversy was essentially between North and South, and it is worth noting in this connection that the President's proposal of a 90 cents per hour minimum became in the Senate a bill suggesting $1.00 per hour as the minimum—and it was this version of what the nation needed which became law.

Still more confusing were the political dimension of developments on the money front.[3] Of course Democrats promptly assumed an "I-told-you-so" attitude when their opponents found it impossible to make the Federal Reserve System "independent" in a few short weeks. But even Democrats were hardly prepared for what happened next in this area. As soon as the 1953-54 recession was safely past, the Federal Reserve Board thought it detected signs of inflation on the horizon. Acting accordingly that body continued to tighten the supply of credit, until the Treasury Department openly and repeatedly asserted that these officials were courting economic disaster.

Imagine! A Republican Secretary of the Treasury declaring that the central banking authorities were becoming *too* independent! And the sequel to this state of affairs was even more entertaining to Democrats and uncomfortable for Republicans. Although risks had been run in endeavoring to combat inflation, and a rift thereby created in Republican ranks, inflation came nevertheless. After re-

TABLE 74. THE UNKINDEST CUT OF ALL

Period	Index of Consumer Prices (1947-49 = 100)
1954	114.8
1955: June	114.4
1956: January	114.6
March	114.7
May	115.4
July	117.0

Source: Department of Labor.

maining roughly constant for some 3 years, the index of consumer prices began to rise in the second quarter of 1956—with the result that the man who promised to bring to an end the long period of erosion in the value of the dollar was forced to seek a vote of con-

[3] National Planning Association, *The Employment Act—Past and Future* (Washington, D.C.: National Planning Assoc., 1956).

fidence against the backdrop of the highest price level in the history of the country.

Yet another confusing development in the business–government realm had to do with the tariff. Historically Republicans had stood for a high tariff, and without a single exception the replacement of a Democratic administration by a Republican one had resulted in a significant increase in customs levies. Securing power at a time when the level of import duties had been pushed by a succession of Democratic regimes lower than it had been in more than a century, many conservatives naturally supposed that advantage would also be taken of this opportunity.

But here as at so many other points Republican cohesion was, for the time being at least, a thing of the past. For one reason, the cold war and the foreign exchange dollar shortage still persisted, and hence it continued to be of the utmost importance that America's allies be assured of this country's interest in their well-being.[4] Moreover, at this historical juncture there were a number of key American industries (automobile production being the classic case in point) so certain of their ability to compete with all comers as to have a pronounced preference for lower rather than higher tariff barriers. Thus it was that Democrats enjoyed ring-side seats as isolationist and internationalist Republicans stood toe to toe in a grim contest to decide on next steps in this crucial area.

However, the role of the Democratic party was not on this occasion limited to that of objective bystander. The Reciprocal Trade Agreements Program, after all, was a Democratic policy, and it was therefore important to that group as well that this law be extended without serious change. And unfortunately for the peace of mind of Democratic leaders a traditionally agricultural South was rapidly industrializing, with the result that southern support for reciprocity could no longer be taken for granted. And to make this intraparty conflict even more acute than would otherwise have been the case, post-World War II recovery in Japan was just then reaching the point where Japanese exports to the United States of cotton textile goods was placing southern Congressmen and Senators under severe pressure.

The situation in Georgia will illustrate. Over a quarter of a century prior to 1955, in nine key votes on tariff measures, Georgia representatives in the House had cast a total of eleven protectionist votes—as against seventy-seven nonprotectionist ones. In a single

---

[4] D. D. Humphrey, *American Imports* (New York: Twentieth Century Fund, Inc., 1955).

key vote in 1955 Georgia representatives cast nine votes on the protectionist side by comparison with one vote opposed to protectionism. So critical was this repudiation of the traditional Democratic position by southerners that the Democratic Speaker of the House was compelled to descend from the rostrum to make a special plea for passage of a strong low-tariff pledge to the rest of the world.

The result was a draw. Speaker Rayburn secured passage of a strong reciprocity renewal bill, only to have this victory seriously diluted in the Senate as permissible reductions in tariff rates were greatly narrowed—especially on Japanese imports. Put differently, President Eisenhower's wing of the Republican party (to be thought of in this connection as broadly synonymous with the Committee for Economic Development) did not win the kind of victory for internationalism which would have been required at this point to reassure foreign friends, but it did demonstrate to the world that it could not be pushed around on this issue. The line had been held against a full-scale retreat away from a freer trade policy, but no more than this could be claimed.

But perhaps the most confusing situation of all, especially within the administration, was the handling of the so-called farm problem.[5] Ever since the early months of the Korean conflict the government's investment in agricultural commodities under the price-support program had been increasing, until by the beginning of 1954 it had reached the staggering total of $7 billion. Thus it was not merely nostalgic memories of the "good old days" of laissez faire on the part of Republicans which gave rise to strong feelings that current policy in this field needed rethinking. In the absence of new wars to absorb Treasury holdings, the federal government would clearly have to come to terms with the tremendous productive power of American agriculture more decisively than had yet been done.

A strong Republican inclination, inherited from the past and now powerfully advanced by right-wingers, would have been to do away with government supports entirely. More than a hint of this attitude was expressed during the 1952 campaign, when no less a person than candidate Eisenhower himself promised farmers "100 per cent of parity in the market place." And in his first press conference after taking office, the new Secretary of Agriculture emphasized that the price-support program would henceforth be used only to provide insurance against "undue disaster." However, as actual prices of

[5] Murray R. Benedict, *Can We Solve the Farm Problem* (New York: Twentieth Century Fund, Inc., 1955).

TABLE 75. FEAST AND FAMINE

Year	Farmers' Parity Ratio (1910-14 = 100)
1932	58
1943	113
1949	100
1951	107
1954	89

Source: Department of Agriculture.

farm products fell lower and lower, and especially as it became evident that most farmer-voters had in fact only heard the President's reference to 100 per cent of parity without catching the significance of the words "in the market place" (and possibly this result had even been intended), the new administration was shortly called upon to indicate how seriously it wanted its protestations of economic orthodoxy in this area to be taken.

As it turned out the party was not willing to run the political risks implied in its bold pre-election talk. Confronted with the necessity of taking a stand on this issue which party members were willing to have associated with their organization in future campaigns, few Republicans spoke openly of removing the government from that segment of private enterprise. Instead official talk shifted to the necessity of working toward a program more compatible with the intra-industry adjustments essential to remedying the fundamental supply-demand imbalance from which this industry was suffering.

Committed, then, to an aid program of some kind, and stressing the need for a policy attacking this problem at its source, Republicans were soon turning their thoughts toward the flexible parity mechanism their party had legislated some six years before but the full operation of which had been repeatedly postponed. After all the central difficulty at the moment, judging by the content of the government's inventory of surplus farm commodities, was precisely the five basic items on which that innovation was not yet operative —wheat, cotton, corn, peanuts, and rice. Accordingly, one of the administration's most determined purposes became to breach this stronghold.

As this controversy settled down to open warfare, it did not resolve itself into a battle between farmers on one side and the rest of the country on the other. On the one hand, many larger operators, speaking through the Farm Bureau, were now solidly in favor of flexibility as a device by means of which the economic superiority of large- as compared with small-scale agriculture would over the longer pull be allowed to assert itself. On the other hand, wool growers were brought to the support of flexibility for other farmers by a 90 per cent guarantee for their own product. With these resources at the administration's disposal the new program was at long last made effective for the overwhelming majority of the country's farmers, although even then the range of flexibility in the new law was substantially less than its proponents had hoped.

But this was in 1954—when Congress as well as the presidency was in Republican hands. And though they had in this rather backhanded way ratified the new consensus at still another point, it was not surprising that when Republicans lost control of Congress their version of the appropriate compromise at this point would at once be put on the defensive.

Actually, had misfortune bordering on catastrophe not befallen the administration a decisive test on this issue could have been avoided. Unfortunately, however, each year of the Republicans' term of office saw the farmer's parity ratio fall lower until by the end of 1955 it stood barely above the 1939 level. Thus it was that

TABLE 76. EROSION ON THE FARM

Period	Farm Operators' Net Income (billions of dollars)
1952	15.1
1953	13.3
1954	12.5
1955	11.7
1956	11.4

Source: Department of Agriculture.

with one eye on the next presidential election campaign now less than a year away, the President felt compelled to recommend further agricultural legislation.

The most revolutionary and hence most discussed item on the new agenda was a so-called "soil-bank" program. The idea here was to pay farmers for taking out of production entirely land which would otherwise be devoted to producing crops already in surplus. This approach would break with the past in that heretofore acreage not planted to products in surplus could be cultivated otherwise—tending thereby to create still other surpluses. And the name given to this innovation suggested another important selling-point. The land not used would provide a sort of a "storehouse of fertility" which could be drawn upon in time of need.

When this proposal was submitted to Congress, the last phase of this particular confusion reached a dramatic climax. It proceeded in two stages. First, the Democrats were unable to hold the line in favor of rigid, 90 per cent of parity supports as their time-honored alternative remedy—even though the parliamentary machinery was now in their hands. Second, after achieving a decisive victory against this attempt to breach the flexible price-support principle, the President by administrative action raised substantially the support level for farmers under the heaviest economic pressure.

POLITICS OF MODERATION

However, though it is often difficult to draw a convincing line between these two things in practice, the concept of moderation comes nearer the spirit of some aspects of the new government's program than the term "confusion." And perhaps this characteristic of Republican policy-making was nowhere more evident than in a field which was still almost virgin territory as far as relationships between government and business were concerned. Surely if it had been deemed desirable to introduce drastic changes in existing arrangements at any point, the atomic energy industry would have afforded an excellent opportunity.

To be sure, that area of the economy had already been the subject of legislation.[6] But in 1946 this activity had been only one year old from the standpoint of public knowledge of its existence, and at that time almost no thought had been given to the peacetime possibilities of the atom. Between 1946 and 1954, however, the war importance of this fearful yet wonderful achievement had given way somewhat to its nondestructive uses, and policy directions had to be set governing that development.[7]

In a sense the most remarkable fact about the 1954 Atomic Energy Act was the limited extent to which it altered the control pattern established eight years before—and such changes as were made reflect the altered status of this industry in the economy much more than the change in political complexion of the government in Washington. Under the new law, as under the old, comprehensive responsibilities for promoting the technology and output of this in-

---

6 J. R. Newman and S. Miller, *The Control of Atomic Energy* (New York: McGraw-Hill Book Co., Inc., 1949).

7 R. Dahl and R. Brown, *Domestic Control of Atomic Energy* (New York: Social Science Research Council, 1951).

dustry and regulating all important phases of its operation were lodged with the Atomic Energy Commission—and these responsibilities were to be met while still maintaining the degree of secrecy required for national security. In short, Republicans as well as Democrats felt committed to the proposition that the atomic energy industry was to be government controlled in every essential respect.

But this way of putting the matter may exaggerate. Perhaps an even more remarkable fact about control of the atom is the way a liberal, Democratic government had elected to regulate this industry in the first place. To the greatest possible extent President Truman's appointees had chosen to operate on the basis of contracts negotiated with private enterprise concerns, the Commission reserving to itself the right of almost unlimited supervision to make sure that contract terms were met. On this foundation the Atomic Energy Commission had by 1954 built a $6 billion industry, an industry expected moreover to double this investment in a few more years to become one of the biggest enterprises on the face of the globe.

In taking this step, the United States government had unquestionably embarked on a fundamentally new departure in government activity to safeguard the public interest. Not public enterprise (even in the government corporation sense), not private enterprise (at least in the historically accepted sense), nor yet government regulation of enterprise (in the public utility commission sense), this new approach actually contains elements of all of these. Most of the facilities used in this work are neither owned by the government nor manned by government employees, although the government never-

TABLE 77. A PUBLIC INTEREST EXPERIMENT

Fiscal Year	Atomic Energy Commission	
	Expenditures (millions of dollars)	Employees
1948	466	5,018
1951	897	5,709
1954	1,895	6,195

Source: Bureau of the Budget.

theless makes the basic management decisions with respect thereto. While such capitalistic procedures as competitive bidding and profits are practically eliminated as policy guides, fullest advantage is still taken of private organizations with their technical competence and framework for cooperation. And though the central feature of utility control—rate regulation—is here absent, the results achieved are analogous to those attained by, say, the New York Public Service Commission.

It would, however, be misleading to leave the impression that no difficulties arose here. In the process of passing the Atomic Energy Act of 1954 a spirited debate arose over the private possession of fissionable materials, atomic facilities, and patents relating to atomic technology. A Republican administration naturally leaned toward maximizing private possession as the best way of stimulating the generation of electricity from atomic fuel, while opponents argued that private ownership of patents—especially in view of the extent to which the government had financed the basic research in this industry—would unfairly advantage first comers. Moreover, the appearance of atomic power on the horizon immediately raised the question of public versus private power in a new and potentially quite volatile form.

But even on points such as these satisfactory compromises were worked out. Private ownership of patents was permitted—although with the proviso that all such patents were to be open to the public for five years at royalty rates approved by the Atomic Energy Commission. And as would only have been expected in the circumstances the Commission was forbidden to go into the commercial power business. Indeed, about all that had really taken place was the transition of that body from nonpolitical to political status, with the result that as 1954 drew to a close it seemed likely that the details of business–government relationships on this front would be in flux for some time.

Moderation was likewise the keynote in connection with another issue which came to a dramatic climax at this time. Involved was a long-standing controversy over the jurisdiction of the Federal Power Commission under the Natural Gas Act of 1938.[8]

This legislation stated specifically that it was to apply to the transportation of natural gas in interstate commerce for public consumption. And just as specifically it stated that the production and gathering of natural gas were not included within its purview. Prompted largely by this statement of Congressional intent, the Commission from the outset ruled that it had no authority over gas sales by independent producers. Only the transportation of gas by the big, integrated producers was to be regulated.

Admittedly there was an ambiguity here in the law itself, and from time to time attempts were made to clear it up. In 1950, for

[8] F. F. Blachley and M. E. Oatman, *Natural Gas and the Public Interest* (Washington, D.C.: Government Printing Office, 1947).

example, both Houses of Congress approved a measure to exempt producers from control—only to have this step frustrated by a Truman veto. Four years later, furthermore, this ambiguity was resolved in the opposite direction when the Supreme Court ruled that the Federal Power Commission possessed regulatory jurisdiction over *all* sales of natural gas for resale in interstate commerce.[9] When that agency moved to bring its activities into conformity with this ruling, efforts to secure exemption were zealously renewed.

Proponents of this change in the status quo presented several convincing arguments in support of their position. Thus they pointed out that natural gas was the only fuel subject to federal point-of-production regulation, and that this fact complicated the competitive battle between gas and oil and coal. Stated more broadly, they contended that the independents were caught in a network of restrictions working against maximum output by inhibiting exploration and discovery of new sources of supply—a very high-risk activity. And in any event, they maintained, this control was not essential for the protection of consumers because the Federal Power Commission would continue to regulate the price received by producers through the supervision of rates paid by interstate pipelines.

But opponents also had several strong points in their favor, the most important contention here being the great difference in the conditions under which natural gas is distributed by comparison with competing fuels. If a consumer desires (or has need) to do so he can play one distributor of oil or coal against another for his own protection, but he is not similarly flexible when hooked onto

TABLE 78. THE CRUX OF THE MATTER

Year	Natural Gas Consumption (trillions of British thermal units)
1905	383
1915	658
1925	1,332
1935	2,116
1945	4,392
1954	9,720

Source: Bureau of Mines.

the only gas line in town. And as to indirect protection through Commission supervision of interstate rates, this was branded as grossly inadequate. The new law would establish "reasonable mar-

[9] *Phillips Petroleum Company* v. *Wisconsin*, 347 U.S. 672 (1954).

ket price" as the test of fairness in this regulation, which would be
no safeguard at all if that concept became identified with the prevailing market price in the field.

No partisan controversy, this; the lineup was essentially producing
versus consuming areas, with high-ranking members of both parties
on each side. Relatively little difficulty was encountered in securing
House approval in 1955 for the exemption sought, although in the
Senate in 1956 opposing forces were so evenly matched and so determined that a major contest ensued. Slowly but surely, however,
sponsors ultimately garnered enough votes to have their way. And
though the President had not taken a position on this issue while it
was in Congress, it was known that he stood ready to approve a
revision of existing law whenever a measure so providing came to
him for signature.

Then it was that the cyclone struck. A Senator accused producer
interests of paying him (more or less directly) $2,500 for his vote, a
Congressional investigation of "improper influence" in the bill's passage was launched, charges of subservience to big business lobbyists
were directed at the White House, and President Eisenhower vetoed the measure—giving as his reason the questionable activities
of some of its promoters.

Still another field of endeavor for the new administration in which
the concept moderation (in 1955-56 as well as 1953-54) is perhaps
most descriptive was antitrust. And here more than at any other
point so many things were happening that there was no problem
of classifying the ideological foundations on which action rested.

One item on this agenda was a study by the Federal Trade Commission of a new wave of business combinations. Ironically, whereas
the year before the Celler Anti-Merger Act was passed less than 150
such unions were recorded, by 1952 this figure had risen to more
than 800—a consolidation movement surpassing anything seen to
date with the possible exception of the 1920's. What the Commission was now endeavoring to do was determine how much of this
development reflected a desire to eliminate competition and how
much was resulting from other causes.

No important recommendations were forthcoming from this investigation, its principal conclusion being that the causal factors
at work had little to do with anticompetitive attitudes.[10] Nor could
this outcome be reasonably referred to as a "whitewash," for it appeared almost simultaneously with the *Report of the Attorney Gen-*

[10] Federal Trade Commission, *Report on Corporate Mergers and Acquisitions*
(Washington, D.C.: Government Printing Office, 1955).

eral's Committee to Study the Antitrust Laws—a document highly disappointing to men who had supposed that a Republican administration in Washington would bring about a marked relaxation of antitrust enforcement.[11] Although this committee concluded that the good faith defense ought to be broadened in its application, that the retreat from the conscious parallelism doctrine could appropriately be carried further, and that the narrow line separating legal patent monopoly from patent abuse should be accented in antitrust work —it also registered itself as opposed to fair trade legislation, in agreement with existing antitrust exemptions, anxious to see the ban on mergers strengthened, and generally in favor of stiffer enforcement procedures all along the line.

Interestingly enough, however, Democrats were still unwilling to accept the new government's record in this area at face value. Obviously endeavoring to develop campaign material by charging Republican favoritism for big business in this work, an investigating committee (headed by none other than the principal author of the Celler Act—Representative Celler of New York) was created to "bring the facts to light."

Unfortunately for the objective in view, the facts as they came to light were not reassuring. On the quantitative side the key refutation item was a record of more antitrust suits launched per year under President Eisenhower than during President Truman's last four years in the White House. And this record held up extremely well when viewed qualitatively, too. The concerns selected as defendants in these proceedings were by no means inconspicuous members of the business community.

Note, for example, that stringent efforts were being made to clarify the ambiguity inherent in the Celler Amendment to the Clayton Act—to determine when mergers do and do not "substantially lessen competition or tend to create a monopoly." One step along this road was Justice disapproval of the Bethlehem-Youngstown merger. Another was a Federal Trade Commission action against Pillsbury Mills, one of the largest food processors in the country. And in quick succession similar proceedings brought the government into conflict with the Crown Zellerbach Corporation, Schenley Distilleries, and General Shoe—all of these concerns being leaders in their respective fields.

Moreover, even apart from the problem of mergers as such, events were demonstrating that a revitalized Republican antitrust

[11] (Washington, D.C.: Government Printing Office, 1955).

policy offered no immunity for big business. Early in 1956 the Justice Department concluded by consent decree two cases which had been commenced under the predecessor administration. In one International Business Machines was summarily required to inaugurate major policy changes directed toward helping lesser concerns share IBM's hitherto dominant market position—including making all present and future patents available to all comers on payment of a reasonable royalty. In the other, the consenting party was American Telephone and Telegraph Company. Here too the purpose was to help other concerns break into an otherwise tightly held preserve. And here the new required behavior included making all patents currently held available to all comers without charge, and giving rivals technical assistance in putting Bell patents to work most effectively.

There were other areas, too, in which decisions were made illustrating this same tendency toward middle-of-the-road positions. Thus a special committee appointed by the President to recommend policy changes in the transportation field made no important suggestions which were not already common coin among students of American transportation[12]—and such recommendations as were made did not seem likely soon to become the law of the land. Also in the realm of transportation was a mammoth highway policy measure which did pass Congress. Included were a thirteen-year program greatly increasing the federal government's share of the nation's road-building burden, and tax increases on motor fuel, rubber, and commercial motor vehicles. But here again the net result

TABLE 79. THE GASOLINE ENGINE GROWN UP

| Year | Motor Vehicle Registrations | |
| | Cars and Taxis | Trucks and Busses |
	(thousands)	
1900	8	—
1915	2,332	159
1930	22,973	3,559
1940	27,372	4,663
1945	25,691	4,947
1950	40,185	8,382
1955	51,989	10,031

Source: Bureau of Public Roads.

[12] Committee on Transport Policy and Organization, *Revision of Federal Transportation Policy* (Washington, D.C.: Government Printing Office, 1955); and C. L. Dearing and W. Owen, *National Transportation Policy* (Washington, D.C.: Brookings Institution, 1949).

was essentially the writing into law of a consensus already reached by those most actively concerned with the problems created by the rapid expansion in the car, truck, and bus population.

And finally, a particularly striking instance of moderation was the new administration's power policy. Although its leaders had initially denounced Democratic trends in this field as "creeping socialism," and indeed kept up a running fire of criticisms relating thereto, no fundamental changes in the organization of this industry were in evidence. Not only did the installed capacity of publicly owned electricity-generating plants increase in absolute terms, but the percentage of total capacity accounted for by government-operated facilities continued to inch upward.

"You Never Had It So Good"

It was against this background of confusion and moderation that the nation went to the polls in November, 1956, to pass judgment on the policies promulgated during the preceding four years. And on the character of that judgment depended much of the future of American business–government relationships. Republicans quite naturally pressed for a continuation of the middle-of-the-road equilibrium they had arrived at by a painful trial and error process. Democrats just as understandably were inclined to argue that the social justice promised by the "American Creed" could only be achieved by further drastic measures along New Deal–Fair Deal lines.

Of course in such a contest the party of the "ins" adopted as its theme song the refrain "You never had it so good," a propaganda standby of incumbent administrations in this country in times of prosperity. Moreover, this slogan could be convincingly defended. During four years of Republican rule gross national product had risen $65 billion to well over $400 billion, and the index of industrial production had climbed one-sixth to a level significantly above that achieved during World War II. And even on a smaller canvass this picture was much the same. In four years per capita disposable personal income in current prices had increased almost 45 per cent ($200) on an annual basis, while factory weekly earnings had gone up more than 20 per cent ($15).

Even Democrats privately conceded that these were formidable odds. The fact of the matter was that only twice in the twentieth century had an administration been turned out of office when economic skies were bright—and on each of these occasions certain noneconomic factors were particularly decisive. Thus in 1912 the

Republicans had been unseated in good times against the background of a deep split within that party's own rank, while in 1952 the Democrats were unhorsed in the midst of high prosperity in a context of popular dissatisfaction over the Korean War.

But a major political party dares not succumb to defeatism. The world must see only the face of optimism, and Democratic leaders accordingly set about exploiting such soft spots in the Republican's armor as could be found. And what more likely handlehold could be secured for this purpose than the standby propaganda item of Democrats to the effect that their opponents were probusiness—that prosperity for the business community was being promoted at the expense of other large groups of citizens.

For example, a favorite focus of attention in this connection was corporate profits and net farm income. Comparing 1955 and 1956 with the first two years of President Eisenhower's administration, corporate profits after taxes had risen 30 per cent although national income as a whole had increased only 15 per cent. Furthermore, not only were corporate profits greater in 1955-56 than in any other two-year period in the nation's history, but dividend payments had set a new record in every one of those four years.

By contrast the agricultural side of the economic ledger had steadily worsened in over-all results. On the one hand, the parity

TABLE 80. A REVEALING COMPARISON

Year	Corporate Profits after Taxes (billions of dollars)	Dividend Payments	National Income	Net Farm Income per Farm
1952	16.1	9.0	290.2	$2,821
1953	16.7	9.3	302.1	2,531
1954	16.4	10.0	298.3	2,449
1955	21.1	11.2	324.0	2,336
1956	21.1	12.0	335.0	2,340

Source: Department of Commerce and Department of Agriculture.

ratio had fallen 15 per cent, and with it net income per farm by an even greater proportion. On the other hand, farm mortgage indebtedness had risen more than 10 per cent at the same time that the farmer's share of the consumer's food dollar was falling from 47 cents to 41.

Placing this same charge in a somewhat broader context, organized labor emphasized that from the standpoint of basic social justice relatively little had yet been done to bring about a more equitable distribution of income in the United States. Thus it was pointed out that in 1954 the 10,000,000 lowest income families received an average of only $1,300 per family as compared with the almost $12,000 per family received by the 10,000,000 highest income families, and that this lowest one-fifth received less than $14 billion in income while the highest one-fifth received $56 billion. Further, it was concluded from Department of Commerce figures that although income distribution improved significantly during New Deal

TABLE 81. A PROBLEM IN SOCIAL JUSTICE

Families by Fifths	Share of Total Family Income by Fifths		
	1935-36	1944 (per cent of total)	1954
Lowest	4.1	4.9	4.9
Second	9.2	10.9	11.4
Third	14.1	16.2	16.6
Fourth	20.9	22.2	22.4
Fifth	51.7	45.8	44.7
Total	100.0	100.0	100.0

Source: Department of Commerce.

days, this trend had come to an untimely end in recent years.

Of course, too, this accusation meshed especially well with what Democrats had all along been saying about the 1954 tax legislation —particularly the tax credit on dividends included therein. The Republican party had been making much campaign material out of what they called our "peoples' capitalism," the wide distribution of corporate securities in this country. Moreover, the 1956 Republican platform contained this sentence: "Good times in America have reached a breadth and a depth never known by any nation." Against the background, however, of labor's stress on income distribution, the 1954 revenue law, and the fact that a large majority of American income receivers received no dividends at all, the Democrats' campaign could at least raise some significant questions about their opponents' record on this front.

Still another challenge by the "out" group took the form of an outright denial of the prosperity thesis. Here analysis centered on a theoretically attainable "full prosperity," and actual accomplishments were compared with this hypothetical ideal. To be specific it was maintained by the full prosperity advocates that during President Eisenhower's term of office the nation's production deficit had amounted to $57 billion, and that this huge deficit had resulted in serious income "shortfalls" for many citizens.

Our national economic policies and programs are caught in the vise of The Great Complacency. For three years at least, we have been coasting along on the economic reforms and social gains built into the structure during the two decades after the Great Depression. Thus far, the momentum has been sufficient to avoid depressions, and to maintain a high and somewhat advancing level of general prosperity.

But this great Nation cannot coast forever. New motive power is needed. During the most recent years, the momentum of our economic growth has seriously slackened, and some new national policies have contributed to the slowdown. In consequence, total production and employment have been far too low for full prosperity. And while the whole economy has moved forward too slowly, millions have been forced tragically backward by the inequities in the general prosperity, and by national policies which have aggravated this decline. Our traditional concepts of economic and social justice have faded into the background.

. . . Most serious of all, we are preening ourselves with false pride because we are in some respects "higher" than last year or years ago. We are setting low goals, based on the dead statistics of the past, instead of high goals for the ever-increasing abundance and security which our technology and skills promise if only we show the creative intelligence to move forward.

It is easy to talk about a better future for all. But in what direction are we actually moving—and at what pace?[13]

Other illustrations of the character of the 1956 political debate could be presented. Enough has been said, however, to make clear the central problem posed for the American people in the government–business field by that campaign. Farmers were in economic difficulty largely as a result of economic adjustments which had been a part of the American scene since the beginnings of industrialization; to what extent were citizens willing to see the government interjected even further into this evolution? Income redistribution as a policy objective had risen to the forefront in the midst of deep depression, and certain of the principles developed at that time had continued to govern policy; but how important did voters want this objective to become during prosperity? Poverty was currently arising in large part from the low economic status of farmers and Negroes, and from the economic tragedies following in the wake of old age and the break-up of families by death or otherwise; how far did Americans want their government to go in guaranteeing living standards in situations such as these? An economy perhaps never operates at full capacity; do we, in time of high prosperity, want to place our economic mechanism under the forced draft of

13 Conference on Economic Progress, *The Gaps in our Prosperity* (Washington, D.C.: Conference on Economic Progress, 1956), p. 1.

an accentuated government responsibility in order to expand output by 3 or 4 per cent?

Actually, of course, it is difficult to see an electoral contest in perspective except against the background of the votes which are in fact cast. On the other hand, as the campaign itself was drawing to a close one conclusion at least seemed almost inescapable. The Republican party (for purposes of argument, at any rate) had successfully pre-empted the vast middle-of-the-road area in American economic ideology—forcing the Democrats to press their cause in terms of fringe issues of a mildly radical variety. Put differently, the Republicans had succeeded in identifying President Eisenhower's administration with a moderate, "you-never-had-it-so-good" status quo, and their opponents with the urge to unsettle a comfortable equilibrium.

Be all of this as it may, however, the outcome of the balloting provided much additional food for speculation. As an indication that an end to moderation was not in sight, the presidency was to continue in Republican hands, while both House and Senate would remain under Democratic control. And perhaps as an indication of how comprehensive political confusion still was, this came about despite the fact that the President's victory was even more decisive than four years earlier—457 electoral and 36,000,000 popular votes, as compared with only 74 electoral and 26,000,000 popular votes for his Democratic rival. Not since the Civil War had a newly elected President taken up his duties with both House and Senate on the other side of the political fence.

To be sure, it was conceded that "Ike" was still an exceedingly popular figure—and that serious flare-ups in the Middle East and in Central Europe just prior to the election had worked to the President's advantage. But these considerations would scarcely account for the much wider gap now between the success of the leader of the Republican party and that of his political colleagues than had appeared in 1952. It was as if the people believed that the party had campaigned on the President's principles but could not be depended upon to carry out the indicated policies. Or was it that, after all, a Republican president in cooperation with a Democratic Congress had brought about the "you-never-had-it-so-good" situation in the first place?

Although most people who lived through these years would perhaps not have argued that this was an especially dynamic period, it was evident in retrospect that much had happened. And the most significant single development was undoubtedly a rapid progress in the direction of outlining in more concrete terms the nature of America's new mixed economy. Prior to this, before the new consensus had been made official through the medium of this country's two-party democracy, the outline of this ideological adjustment was of necessity essentially abstract and hence somewhat vague. But by the time the people went to the polls in 1956 to pass judgment on the first Republican administration since 1928, a number of major details of the new center of gravity in political debate had been spelled out quite fully.

It was clear, for example, that big labor's right to coexistence with big business had been definitely established, although just as clearly both businessmen and workers would continue to fight for more elbow room within that adjustment. By the same token, it was plain that conservatives now recognized the necessity for matching their efforts to achieve additional flexibility for themselves on the labor side of the economy with a sincere endeavor to keep big business operations within some bounds.[14] And just as the worker's bargaining power weaknesses were now accepted, so too were the farmer's; henceforth this battle would be fought out in terms of the problem of flexibility versus rigidity within a control and support framework. At a more fundamental level it was evident that no important group would again insist upon treating the economy as a self-equilibrating, automatic mechanism, although conservatives would no doubt continue to bring to the stabilization issue their accustomed interest both in economic growth and in minimizing the impact of government activities on the enterprise sector of the economy. Even in the welfare field, the new adjustment stood out in bold relief. While conceding the need to expand government's security activities as new ways to do so become feasible, the better-off segments of the community would at the same time endeavor to chip away at their own tax burden.

All this can be summarized with profit, too, in lighter vein. It has been said that the difference between an optimist and a pessimist is that the former says his glass is half full while the latter refers to his as half empty. Applying this figure to America's politico-economic ideology, much campaign oratory would surely henceforth revolve around Republican emphasis upon the extent to which government decisions have displaced private ones countered by Democrats re-

[14] Marshall E. Dimock, *Free Enterprise and the Administrative State* (Tuscaloosa: University of Alabama Press, 1951).

minding us how much of our economic life is still the responsibility of men operating within the price-profit nexus.

QUESTIONS FOR DISCUSSION

1. Why was the Republican party becoming more liberal? Why was the Democratic party becoming more conservative?

2. Explain and evaluate Mr. Galbraith's thesis. Mr. Lubell's.

3. Discuss the quotation from President Eisenhower's January, 1954, press conference from the standpoint of the new consensus.

4. Discuss the excerpt from the 1955 *Economic Report of the President* in terms of the new consensus.

5. Relate the concepts "new consensus," "mixed economy," and "moderation."

6. In what respects do the terms "the politics of confusion" and "the politics of moderation" really refer to the same phenomenon?

7. What is the farm problem today? What is the solution?

8. What is the Federal Reserve–Treasury problem today? What is the solution?

9. What is the public-versus-private power problem today? What is the solution?

10. What do you think of the control pattern developed in the atomic energy field, and why?

11. Evaluate the merits of the two sides of the controversy over natural gas regulations.

12. Why in a mixed economy are indirect controls (such as fiscal and monetary policies) so important?

13. Summarize the 1956 electoral campaign from the standpoint of the business–government issue.

14. Could it be concluded from the results of this election that attacks on big business are not to be politically profitable in the future? Explain.

15. Is government in the United States now assuming too many responsibilities for the good of the country? Why or why not?

16. At what points in the government–business field do you think the most changes will be forthcoming in the foreseeable future?

Part VII
AN OVERVIEW

Chapter 31

Beyond Politics

This, then, is the record—an account of the step-by-step process through which government acquired the multitudinous responsibilities it now performs in connection with economic activities in the United States. So full an account is useful for some purposes, indeed illuminating aspects of an historical topic which can be seen clearly in no other way. At the same time, however, a detailed exposition of a complex evolutionary development has limitations. Of these the major one is surely that the reader's attention is thereby directed so exclusively to pedestrian concerns that the more dramatic sweep of events, the deeper significance of what has taken place, may escape notice.

But it does not follow, happily, that this particular scene can be surveyed from a single vantage point, that having once been viewed at close range it cannot later profitably be seen from afar. Thus in the hope of achieving this further objective, the observation center will now be shifted to some of the highest points in the terrain being surveyed. From these elevations it may be possible more fully to appreciate the broader panorama.

A THESIS PROPOUNDED

Of first importance here is perhaps an examination of government-business relationships from the standpoint of partisan politics. Thinking and writing about American institutions attach great importance to our system of party government, and rightly so, for the healthy competition of political parties for popular support is fundamental to the maintenance of a vigorous democracy. Unfortunately, however, that discussion is all too prone to accept at face value what the parties themselves say about this competition. Unless the student of business-government relationships can develop a capacity for distinguishing between realities and superficialities at this point he is apt to be bewildered by the further evolution which will take place in these areas during the remainder of his lifetime. The fact is that a careful review of almost two centuries of American history makes it clear that the matter of which political party secures the most votes at this or that time is not *in and of itself* a significant causal factor in determining next steps in the economic policy realm. Put differently, *the actions which have been taken on this front were dictated by underlying forces that partisan politics was competent to reflect but was not powerful enough to shape.*

The Thesis Defended

This observation, of course, is not put forward as either a profound or a novel truth. It is rather only the application to the subject at hand of principles long understood by social scientists—principles worth elaborating here only because the typical discussion of business-government relationships rests on different presuppositions. From that standpoint, however, this truth is so fundamental to a mature perspective on one of today's central problems that a brief survey of its foundations would seem to be in order.

A preliminary point is that the situation could really not be otherwise in a satisfactorily functioning democracy. It is essential that democratic processes embody in concrete institutions the policy preferences of the community at large, and to the degree that they fail to achieve this ideal they are not democratic. Politician-statesmen in a democracy are to give effect to rather than create the "general will."[1]

Building further on this premise, certain aspects of decision-making in a democracy as presented earlier may appropriately be reiterated. It will be recalled, to begin with, that one of the indispensable characteristics of a democratic society is a core of agreement among all classes of citizens solid enough to withstand a constant and often exaggerated conflict between differences. It will also be remembered, moreover, that several key characteristics of party politics operate to hold both major parties in a two-party system to a middle-of-the-road position, to compel them to lay greatest stress upon the values and attitudes citizens hold in common. For one thing, each party is made up of a heterogeneous and unstable aggregation of interests, and hence concessions to a fringe group are apt to alienate more support than is thereby won. For another, interest groups

[1] A. V. Dicey, *Law and Public Opinion in England During the Nineteenth Century* (New York: The Macmillan Co., 1930).

themselves are so heterogeneous that almost never does a party succeed in mobilizing to its support 100 per cent of any such grouping. The result is that most elements within either party are intimately associated with an element within the other, and the party in power cannot therefore oppress any major segment of the opposition without at the same time oppressing some of its own members.[2]

But though the differences between the parties in a two-party democracy are moderate, they are nonetheless both real and significant. To the extent of these differences is it not correct to think of the parties as independent causal forces in the forging of economic policy? No, even this does not follow. In the rough and tumble of real-life politics there is yet a third reason why the creative as distinct from the reflective role of the parties must be minimized.

A case in point will illustrate what is here involved. In 1932 the American people, ravaged by a tragic depression, the end of which could not as yet be seen, went to the polls to choose between a leadership which had exhibited every reluctance to use the powers of the federal government to destroy the scourge of unemployment and one promising to use those powers with great vigor to restore prosperity to a tortured economy. When the Democrats were on that occasion overwhelmingly elected, they set to work at once replacing an historic laissez faire policy toward economic downturns with an insistence upon the government's positive responsibility toward those able and eager to work—a conception which was never thereafter to be relinquished.

It is immediately apparent from this brief review of a few familiar facts why it is misleading to assert that politico-economic policy took a decisive turn at this point because Democrats were in power rather than Republicans. On the contrary, Democrats were swept into office because the voting public was anxious to abandon an economic policy which had obviously gone bankrupt. And to put this matter in a still more specific perspective, it can be pointedly inquired if America's response to the depression would have been significantly different if a Democratic administration had been inaugurated on March 4, 1929, or if the Republicans had put up and elected a progressive group of leaders in 1932. Although questions such as these are speculative, it is hard to believe either that Democrats would have been much more enlightened than Republicans

[2] E. E. Schattschneider, *Party Government* (New York: Rhinehart & Co., Inc., 1942).

before 1932 or that Republicans would have continued to be so inflexible for very long thereafter.

To generalize the principles at issue here, each party endeavors to read the "signs of the times" as accurately as it can, which in essence means determining how far the people will permit policy to be turned in the direction of that party's own predilections.[3] However, partly because gauging the temper of a large and heterogeneous body of citizens poses great difficulties at best, and partly because the assessment faculties are prone to be somewhat warped by wishful thinking, the two parties will typically arrive at a somewhat different set of conclusions. The one which in the voting is adjudged most nearly correct is then given an opportunity, not as such to create policy conforming to its preferences, but to translate into policy the ideals and attitudes the people took to the polls. And perhaps the most important point to emphasize here is that carte blanche authority is not given. Frequently the party in power finds that its interpretation of underlying sentiment is in error and is compelled in consequence to beat a hasty retreat, just as the party losing out in the election is forced to reassess the interpretations that brought it into disfavor.

And finally, these relationships can constructively be put into a somewhat more fundamental context. An evolution toward a basically different pattern of government responsibilities in the economy such as this country has experienced (and is, indeed, still experiencing) is after all a part of a process of social change which could only take place in a disturbed society. A brief account of the most important factors underlying institutional change in a more or less integrated community will make it even clearer why partisan politics in and of itself explains very little in the government and business field.

One of the primary ways in which societies differ from one another is in the structure of beliefs common to their citizens. Man as the rationalizing animal has always labored at developing explanations of various aspects of the world about him capable of making him more comfortable in his sojourn through life. These beliefs extend all the way from the most obvious certainties to the speculations advanced to round out man's understanding of his environment beyond the point of certain knowledge—all the way from the simplest of facts to the most profound of values.

Such a structure of beliefs is also often referred to in terms of

[3] Bertrand M. Gross, *The Legislative Struggle* (New York: McGraw-Hill Book Co., Inc., 1953).

the concept *myth*, a concept that has been explained by an eminent social scientist[4] as follows:

By *myths* we mean the value-impregnated beliefs and notions that men hold, that they live by and for. Every society is held together by a myth-system, a complex of dominating thought-forms that determines and sustains all its activities. All social relations, the very texture of human society, are myth-born and myth-sustained. . . . Every civilization, every period, every nation, has its characteristic myth-complex. In it lies the secret of social unities and social continuities, and its changes compose the inner history of every society.

Wherever he goes, whatever he encounters, man spins about him his web of myth, as the caterpillar spins its cocoon. Every individual spins his own variant within the greater web of the whole group. The myth mediates between man and nature. From the shelter of his myth he perceives and experiences the world. Inside his myth he is at home in the world.

When we speak here of myth we imply nothing concerning the grounds of belief, so far as belief claims to interpret reality. We use the word in an entirely neutral sense. . . . Whatever valuational responses men give to the circumstances and trials of their lot, whatever conceptions guide their behavior, spur their ambitions, or render existence tolerable—all alike fall within our ample category of myth.

A second major way in which societies differ is in the institutions devised to transform their values into reality. In placing these into a social change context, Professor MacIver says:

By *techniques* we mean the devices and skills of every kind that enable men to dispose of things—and of persons—more to their liking, so as to ease their toil, to increase the return to their labor, to enlarge their satisfactions, to organize and preserve their advantages, to subdue their enemies, to harness the forces of nature, to extend their knowledge, and so forth. A technique is a way of knowing that is primarily a way of control. It is not the instrument man fashions, not the tool or the machine as such, but the craft he employs in making the machine and in putting it into service. A technique is a way of manipulating objects, including persons as objects. It is knowledge compactly applied to the world of objects, changing the relation of the subject and the object in a direction desired by the subject.

Beliefs and institutions, furthermore, are very closely related to one another.

To achieve anything man resorts to his techniques, develops his techniques; but what he seeks to achieve, how far he cultivates or inhibits one set of potential aptitudes or another, how he chooses between the various paths always opening up before him, what play he gives his sheer organic drives as he imposes upon their exuberance proportion and limit—that depends upon his myths. His myths and his techniques are interdependent. As his myths change he turns his techniques to different uses. . . .

[4] R. M. MacIver, *The Web of Government* (New York: The Macmillan Co., 1947). All references taken from chap. i.

On the other hand, as his techniques advance, his myths responsively take a new range. . . . In all human activity myth and technique are for ever interacting. One man may take the myth cherished by other men and make it an instrument to control them, embodying their myth within his own system of techniques, but he still is moved to do so by his own compelling myth. The technique can never become a substitute for the myth. Only when the myth points out the goal does the technique build the road to it.

With the aid of these two concepts the process of social change can be succinctly summarized. To begin with, that process can be defined as a significant alteration in the pattern of beliefs and institutions which interact to make society what it is. Although this interaction is so intricate that it is rarely possible to say with assurance whether a given change has its origin at the myth or the technique level, for present purposes it will be useful simply to think of the first link in this chain as being either an altered formulation of man-nature relationships or a different way of managing society's affairs. But whatever the impetus, it is essential to visualize a change at any point in the system as setting off a series of mutually interacting consequences. New techniques tend to cut new channels in human thought processes, new presuppositions suggest different ways of getting the work of the world done, and all the while the entire framework must be readjusted to keep its several parts tolerably congruent one with another.

Here also illustration will perhaps be helpful. When the American Constitution was written, political democracy as we understand that term had not yet taken deep root. Stated from the standpoint of the language of social change, the prevailing structure of beliefs in this country (the American myth) was distinctly aristocratic in temper. This fact was reflected (among other ways) in the technique devised for selecting a president. Thus care was taken not to accomplish this by direct vote of the people. On the one hand, the laws of most states denied the franchise to large segments of the adult population (nonproperty-holders); and on the other, even voting citizens were allowed only to vote for electors who would perform the function of designating a chief executive for the ensuing four years in an atmosphere far removed from the passions and biases of the "lower classes."

As long as the American myth remained aristocratic in emphasis, this technique for electing presidents was reasonably satisfactory. But as the years went by this structure of beliefs began significantly to alter. The attitudes appropriate to aristocracy were placed more and more on the defensive, with sentiments congenial to democracy crowding in to take their place. Closely paralleling this evolution came a broadening of the base of political privilege and responsibility. One by one, laws limiting suffrage were revised until almost all adult, white males possessed the vote. And when the so-called lower classes had succeeded in annihilating this barrier to gain a share in decision-making, they made short work of the elector device in presidential elections. The convention system of making party nominations for this office was substituted, and nominees thus chosen were subject to an elimination contest by direct, popular vote.

A second illustration of this process takes reference more immediately from government-business relationships. During the early days of industrialization in the United States, a key element in the American myth was belief in the efficacy of competition for protecting the public interest. Focusing attention on the atomistic competition contemplated by classical economics, this way of thinking insisted that free enterprise alone would prevent consumer exploitation. But that approach to economic organization reckoned without a technique devised by businessmen under severe competitive pressure, and when the top officials of great railroads began to use free enterprise prerogatives to combine rather than compete, modifications were promptly introduced into American thinking concerning private enterprise.

In this pattern of change the sequence of events was approximately as follows. The myth structure, insisting upon the adequacy of competition in holding the forces of industrialization in check, placed primary reliance at the technique level upon private decision-making. When, however, this technique developed into something which had not been anticipated and which at the same time could not be condoned, the belief system had to be altered to accommodate important new facts. And of course with changes in myth there came also corresponding alterations in technique; the almost unconditional acceptance of the results of nongovernmental decisions which had heretofore been the rule gave way before a reluctant but nonetheless decisive imposition of governmental restraints.

Although these accounts of key changes in this country's institutional structure are greatly oversimplified, they at least make clear what is meant when it is said that significant social change takes place only in a disturbed society. To be sure, evolution of this kind does not imply that the society involved is diseased; indeed the capacity to introduce change slowly and peacefully is, if anything, conclusive evidence of health and vigor. But a society that is changing is seeking a new internal equilibrium, struggling to bring its myths and its techniques into congruency on a different basis. Disequilibria of this sort are never superficial, never surface phenomena alone. It is precisely because they are not that it is misleading to suppose that such adjustments are either initiated in party platforms or pushed through to completion by political propaganda or even electoral competition between the parties—however far they may go toward explaining political results. Who can doubt that the idea of universal suffrage had long been nourished in the breasts of frontiersmen before a political party risked espousing the cause of direct election of presidents, or that the possibility of regulating railroads existed in the thinking of midwestern farmers long before it became an institutional reality? In short, the party system in a democracy can effectively perform the midwife function at the birth of new institutions, but the basic forces at work lie much deeper.[5]

POLITICAL PARTIES AND GOVERNMENT CENTRALIZATION

It is not enough, however, to explain in theoretical terms that partisan politics has been only a secondary phenomenon in the evolution of business-government relationships in the United States. In order that the student may more fully appreciate the implications of this proposition, and more surely distinguish realities from superficialities in this field in the years to come, it will also be helpful to examine several dimensions of the historical material from this standpoint.

No better starting point could be found for this purpose, perhaps, than the struggle over the issue of government centralization in the midst of which our nation came into existence and which was a key item in the competition between the parties for some two decades thereafter. The essential facts of this controversy were as follows. Agrarians, identifying centralized government with those aspects of British rule which had borne most heavily upon them, were strongly opposed to the concentration of power in the hands of a national government. America's embryonic but nonetheless burgeoning business community, on the other hand, associated centralized government with the protection it had received under British rule from the anticapitalist inclinations of fellow-citizens, and therefore the merchant group stood stanchly for the superiority of the new national government over the states.

At first the victory went to the states'-righters—an appropriate enough outcome in view of the fact that at this point in time agrarians greatly outnumbered merchants. As a document the Ar-

[5] Charles A. Beard, *The Economic Basis of Politics* (New York: Alfred A. Knopf, Inc., 1945).

ticles of Confederation accorded little more than a polite nod in the direction of a central government and surrounded the obligations of the sovereign state governments to the "league of friendship" with all manner of frustrating impediments. A little later, however, against the background of the trials and tribulations of war, independence, and postwar depression, businessmen were able to mount an attack on this government effective enough to replace it with that of the American Constitution—a government allowing much more scope for the work of a coordinating central power, and one administered for a little more than a decade by those groups most interested in its success.[6]

To this point it would almost seem as if government centralization had been primarily a function of the party in power. However, with the election of Thomas Jefferson as President in 1800 such a relationship was rebutted in a way which could hardly have been more striking.

It is to be noted at the outset in this connection that from a number of standpoints no administration ever had a more favorable opportunity to give effect to the policy preferences of its following. Thus states' rights had continued to be a live issue throughout the period of Federalist rule; virtually every major item in the ruling administration's program added fuel to the fire of anti-Federalist antagonism to centralization, and the election campaign of 1800 was fought out against the background of that issue. Indeed, agrarian resistance to the concentration of government power had only recently reached a particularly high point in the form of the reaction to the Alien and Sedition Acts; and candidate Jefferson had himself authored one of the famous Resolutions of this controversy, setting forth the right of the several states to nullify acts of Congress violating the original pact of union.

But with the accession of the Jeffersonians to power, what happened? With almost monotonous regularity steps were taken which, far from reducing the role of the central government, actually enhanced its position. Among the more important developments in this category were the Tripolitan War which went far toward nullifying the determination to eliminate the national debt, the liberal construction of the Constitution implicit in the Louisiana Purchase, Albert Gallatin's strenuous efforts on behalf of internal improvements financed by the federal government, and the gallant fight made by the ruling administration to renew the charter of the First

[6] W. W. Crosskey, *Politics and the Constitution in the History of the United States* (Chicago: University of Chicago Press, 1953).

Bank of the United States which agrarians had fought against so
bitterly twenty years before. And as the more radical of the agrarians
of that day deliberately pushed the United States into a major war
with England in 1812, it was all the more certain that eighteenth-
century government particularism was dead.

Of course, it can be argued from a certain superficial point of view
that had circumstances been more accommodating the anti-Federalists would have stuck by their principles and carried the new
nation along with them. But this is precisely the point. It is to the
circumstances of real life that political parties in a vigorous democracy respond. Where a set of principles can be formulated accurately
reflecting underlying popular sentiment, well and good. But when
a party's symbolism runs counter to deep-rooted community prejudices or preferences, that party must either abandon this appeal or
step aside. In the case at hand the American people were oriented
toward a position of power and prestige among the nations of the
world that was simply not compatible with the interpretation of the
role of the central government agrarians had heretofore found
reasonably satisfactory.

And there is also an interesting and instructive sequel to this early
struggle over the concentration of governmental power. During those
years the strongest supporter of centralization had been the business
community. On the one hand, that group saw in the concept of a
United States of America the answer to the colonial-type policy
particularism which stood in the way of the most rapid development of an industrial economy. On the other hand, agricultural
leaders (especially in the South) did not immediately and completely
give up the notion that the farmer's interest required the states to
retain considerable authority. Furthermore, the major parties faithfully mirrored this cleavage. The Democratic party stood consistently
on a program of resistance to the expansion of federal power at a
number of key points, while the party of the business interests, the
Whigs, sought to break down this resistance.

With the victory of industrialism over agrarianism, with the development of a sufficient amount of centralization to permit the
forces of specialization and exchange freedom to create a fundamentally different kind of society, this pattern of attitudes changed
significantly. Farmers as a politico-economic force growing weaker
decade by decade, together with workers as a power in government
steadily gaining in strength, began to see in the federal government
the only force powerful enough to hold a dynamic industrialism in
check. By the same token businessmen were now compelled in their

own self-defense to resist the further expansion of central government power—to defend with greatest vigor the sovereignty of state governments now clearly unable to cope with the power the corporate world had attained.

Nor were the parties unequal to the requirements imposed upon them by these policy-preference gyrations. When the Republican party emerged from the Civil War as the champion of industrialism and its needs, it stood solidly for the minimization of federal authority in favor of allowing state governments maximum freedom to exercise their constitutional responsibilities. By contrast the new Democratic party, through which the rising labor group and frustrated farmers were able from time to time to join forces, just as consistently championed the cause of centralization against the claims of state governments unable to protect nonindustrial interests from the most threatening features of the new economy.

POLITICAL PARTIES AND THE EVOLUTION OF BANKING

A second vantage point from which this phenomenon can constructively be viewed is the development of banking institutions. Here, furthermore, the lack of party influence as such was less a result of the abandonment of principles by partisan groups committed to particular policies than the consequence of a failure of the parties to develop unequivocal positions on this question.

To be sure, this was less true when banking was young in America than it came to be later. Federalists, it will be recalled, went into office in 1789 sworn enemies of state autonomy in money and banking matters, while their agrarian opponents were as determined to keep the federal government from elbowing the states out of this field. The merchant group, in other words, was seeking relief from the business uncertainties and occasional outright confiscations attributable to paper money issued by state governments and state-chartered banks, whereas farmers wanted to see to it that the money mechanism did not become so "sound" that they could not pay their debts.[7]

In quick succession the business interests won two sweeping victories on this front—at least on paper. A Constitution was written forbidding the states to issue paper money, and the First Bank of the United States was created. For a number of reasons, however, these decisions did not significantly alter monetary policy. In the first place, the institution of paper money was undergoing a marked

[7] Harry E. Miller, *Theories of Banking in the United States Before 1860* (Cambridge: Harvard University Press, 1927).

change which did much to nullify the intent of the Constitution at that point—and no doubt one effect of the constitutional prohibition was to accelerate these trends. In the second place, this shift from paper money as such to bank notes could not have been kept within the intent of the Constitution's framers except by outlawing all state-chartered banking institutions; and so agrarian was the United States at the time (that is, the business interests were so politically helpless without farmer allies) that this alternative was never seriously discussed. And finally, the party of the businessman did not as consistently make war on state banks as might have been expected, in large part because state banking became such a profitable business.

This Federalist fiasco was promptly followed up by a series of equally revealing developments on the Anti-Federalist side of the fence. First, an agrarian administration in 1811 fought for the renewal of the charter of the First United States Bank, an institution agrarian leaders had bitterly opposed 20 years earlier. Second, when the zeal for nationalism growing out of the War of 1812 reached its crest, and motivated in addition by the confusion of the currency occasioned by the war and the demise of the First Bank, another agrarian administration secured a charter for a Second Bank of the United States. Third, when economic and political life had settled down to a more nearly normal pace, still another agrarian administration declared war to the death against that organization. And when after 1840 the party of the businessman held control over the government for a brief period on two occasions, central banking proponents were chagrined to discover that Whig ranks had become so heterogeneous in the process of making a successful bid for power that it was impossible to overhaul the banking system.

After the Civil War much of this history was broadly repeated. The war crisis plus the accession to power on a more decisive basis than ever before of the business interests made possible the passage of the National Banking Act, in effect outlawing state bank notes. Interestingly enough, however, this step also coincided with a technical evolution in the money field which again largely nullified the progress toward the more centralized system which had been intended—and the question is legitimately raised if the emergence of checkbook money at this time was not itself one of the major factors making politically feasible the proscription of state bank notes. Moreover, primarily because businessmen were still politically dependent upon farmer support, coupled with the fact that the sound money controversy was especially heated between 1865 and 1900, it was all the Republican party could do to maintain the status quo, to say nothing of achieving fundamental banking reforms. Thus it was that for more than fifty years, through three major panics and a number of smaller ones, the nation limped along with a banking system suffering from essentially the same lack of unified control which had made the Panic of 1857 so severe.

Against this background of economic difficulties at all too frequent intervals it is understandable why sentiment favoring greater centralization of money and banking policy eventually crystallized to the point that such an innovation could be enacted into law, and by 1912 the business community was looking forward to the prospect of reformulating banking policy along lines more congenial to its interests. Unfortunately for these expectations, however, at this critical moment the Republicans lost their hold on the federal government, with the result that the party of monetary radicalism took over the responsibility of creating new financial institutions.

Of three things in particular were businessmen afraid. First, the Democratic party had always had a strong inflationist bent, and it was feared that use would be made of the need to reshape banking policy to give effect to those proclivities. Second, although there was a fairly general agreement on the desirability of greater centralization, it was nonetheless a well-known fact that farm spokesmen were pressing for a substantially lesser degree of concentration than the business interests. Third, farmers were especially opposed to centralization in the hands of private bankers; they preferred instead control by government. In short, conservative Republicans were concerned lest the farmer element in their own ranks join with the ruling administration in enacting an unacceptable measure.

From one standpoint these fears were well grounded, for Republican lines did not hold firm against all proposals opposed by party leaders. But on the other hand they did not take into account a powerful conservative group within the Democratic party. In the event, the conservative elements in both parties were able to compel their opponents to concede enough points to add up to a tolerable compromise. No inflationist provisions as such were included. A genuinely central bank was created, even though this institution was loosely organized into 13 separate centers of power. And in 12 of these centers private enterprise was given a dominant position; only in the coordinating, supervisory agency, a body possessing at first little real authority, was the government given a decisive responsibility.

That the Federal Reserve Act accurately reflected underlying sentiments toward banking institutions is abundantly illustrated by developments in this field since its passage. The only change of consequence in the adjustment arrived at some fifty years ago has been a continuation of the trend toward greater monetary policy concentration which has itself been a fixed feature of American economic evolution for nearly two centuries. This has, to be sure, meant a progressively greater control over financial institutions by the federal government (because it was the central Federal Reserve agency which in 1913 was made most responsive to the will of government), but here again money and banking centralization has always tended to move toward federal supervision.

Nor have the parties been any more influential in the making of recent banking history than they were in its earlier phases. It is of course quite true that the major steps toward unification of monetary policy in the last third of a century were taken during Democratic administrations, and that it was a Republican government which more recently led a minor retreat on this front. But the facts seem to warrant the conclusion that the primary forces bringing about more centralization were first the Great Depression and then World War II, and that the reaction from these developments was essentially the result of the passing of emergency conditions. Indeed, in this latter connection, the Republican retreat from centralization in the hands of the federal government unquestionably owed its beginnings to steps taken while the government was still in the hands of the Democrats.

POLITICAL PARTIES AND THE ATTACK ON LAISSEZ FAIRE

But it may be thought at this point that the issues selected for discussion here are those pointing most obviously in the direction of the thesis with which this chapter began. And perhaps there is no way of dispelling that suspicion other than by discussing from this same standpoint those policies which would seem at first glance most likely to contradict the thesis. Of such issues surely the general question of modifying laissez faire as it arose and became ever more troublesome after the Civil War is the most promising candidate. Is it not a fact well understood by everyone that the Republican party has always been the party of laissez faire, and that the Democratic party has been the group insistent upon major modifications of that philosophy?

This inquiry can at the outset be put into its proper perspective by a few brief comments concerning the span of time here involved. In the first place, the period itself can reasonably be bounded by the years 1866 and 1929. The former was the first full year after the close of the Civil War, before which time the matter of laissez faire was of very little significance. By 1929, on the other hand, it would be generally agreed that the attack on laissez faire had already been carried quite far, and that immediately thereafter this effort was dwarfed by something which might more appropriately be referred to as the attack on the Great Depression. Stated in terms of the language used in this volume, before 1929 laissez faire was under attack whereas after that date it was being replaced. Indeed, one outstanding American historian identifies the first two decades of the twentieth century with what he calls "the decline of laissez faire,"[8] while an eminent European commentator was discussing "the end of laissez faire" in the middle of the 1920's.[9]

In the second place, it can readily be seen that the idea that laissez faire was only seriously challenged when the Democrats were in power is up against several formidable historical facts. During the 64-year period under review the Democratic party held the presidency only 16 years, and during only 8 of these 16 did it control both Houses of Congress as well. Only, in other words, during the years 1885–1888, 1893–1896, and 1913–1920 did the country have a Democratic President, and only during the years 1893–1894, and 1913–1918 were both the legislative and executive branches of the federal government also in Democratic hands. Is it, now, to be contended that laissez faire came under threatening attack only during those years?

This proposition needs only to be stated to be dismissed as absurd. Even if the 16 years of Democratic presidents is taken as the test period (and a strong case could be made for using the 8 years of full Democratic control instead), it can readily be demonstrated that assaults on the laissez-faire stronghold did not at all discriminate between administrations.

Consider railroad regulation, for example. The Granger movement, the authentic origin of the decisive control over railroads to be established later by the federal government, was a product of the deeply Republican Middle West—the Grangers at one point in this development even prevailing upon Congress to bring an abrupt end to railroad land grants. In 1887 the beginning of common carrier control over the railroads on a nationwide basis was launched by a Democratic House, a Republican Senate, and a Democratic

[8] H. U. Faulkner, *The Decline of Laissez Faire* (New York: Rinehart & Co., Inc., 1951).

[9] J. M. Keynes, *The End of Laissez Faire* (London: Leonard & Virginia Woolf, 1927).

President. But when a few years later it was discovered that this first step had not been effective and that better teeth were required for the Interstate Commerce Act, the Hepburn and Mann-Elkins Acts were enacted by governments strongly Republican in all branches. By contrast with these Republican achievements in railroad regulation the New Freedom did little of consequence in this area, and even the Transportation Act of 1920 making railroad regulation in a number of respects still more comprehensive was passed by a Republican Congress.

Or take labor policy during these years. Surely the beginning of the breakdown of the rigid "the-employer-is-always-right" philosophy held by government officials, a beginning clearly visible in the period under discussion, must be classified as a part of the attack on laissez faire. Yet it was a Democratic President who used federal troops to break the Pullman strike in Chicago over the protest of the Governor of Illinois, and it was the Attorney General in a Democratic administration who did so much to make the injunction a major antistrike weapon. On the other hand, it was a Republican President who first put the power and prestige of the federal government on the worker side of a major strike controversy. To be sure, it was during Woodrow Wilson's administration that labor received its greatest boost during the years under review here, but it is nonetheless important to remember that it is to Theodore Roosevelt that Wilson would be most naturally compared in this respect rather than Grover Cleveland.

How about antitrust policy? Could it be that in this field also the party of big business does not stand out in sharp contrast with its rival? Broadly reviewed, these facts are as follows. To begin with, the Sherman Anti-Trust Act was enacted by an administration which was Republican throughout, and neither the Clayton Act nor the Federal Trade Commission Act—both of New Freedom origin—were as fundamental in this field as the 1890 law. Furthermore, Democrat Grover Cleveland is not to be distinguished from Republicans Benjamin Harrison before him and William McKinley after him in the matter of rigorous antitrust enforcement, while Republicans Theodore Roosevelt and William Howard Taft compare quite favorably with Democrat Woodrow Wilson as trust-busters. And finally, even Republicans Harding, Coolidge, and Hoover do not suffer in this respect when their antitrust records are compared with Grover Cleveland's and the first few years of the New Deal, while recent Republican endeavors in this field have been as vigorous as any in the entire history of this legislation.

And in conclusion the considerable evidence bearing on the point at issue here may perhaps be summarized by comparing 1902-1910 with 1911-1917 from this perspective. The first of this group of years starts with the beginning of Theodore Roosevelt's term as President and ends with the frustration of William Howard Taft's administration by the election of a Democratic House; the second begins at that point and ends with the entry of the United States into World War I. It is submitted that when the Republican achievements during the former span of years is held alongside the Democratic accomplishments of the second from the standpoint of what has here been termed the attack on laissez faire, it is not easy to say which party was responsible for the most profound changes in American business-government relationships.

POLITICAL PARTIES AND THE TARIFF

Another issue on which it would seem that the popular association of particular policy positions with particular parties could not be in error is the tariff. If ever there was a party issue par excellence, surely the tariff is that issue. From the beginning of their existence as a major American party Republicans stood for a highly protective tariff, while their Democratic opponents almost as consistently pressed for a tariff for revenue only. Furthermore, for a period of three-quarters of a century and with not a single exception, every time Republicans succeeded Democrats to full control over the government in Washington the tariff was markedly increased; and every time Democrats replaced Republicans it was significantly lowered. Can such facts be interpreted in any way other than that American tariff policy has been largely a function of which major party was in power?

As a matter of fact they can. On closer examination it turns out that this view of what has taken place in that area of public policy is essentially superficial. A few observations will make clear why this conclusion seems to be warranted.

The first point to be made in this connection is that the results of the tariff controversy visible on the surface were in large part the consequence of a process of selectivity between the parties on that question. Thus after southerners in the early 1820's turned bitterly against the protectionism they had tolerated and even half-heartedly supported during the nation's formative years, it became a foregone conclusion that the Democratic party would be aggressively anti-protectionist. At the same time first the Whigs and then the Republicans enthusiastically grasped the opportunity thus thrown into their lap to espouse what was undoubtedly the most popular side of that issue. With major party positions on the tariff thus determined in advance, and with these positions remaining stable for a long period of time what could be more logical than for those interests favoring protection to throw in their lot with the Republican party and for those interests opposed to protection to join forces in the Democratic party. In other words, the situation was not so much that tariff policy was altered because the parties changed places in Washington as that with virtually all interests committed to protectionism included within Republican ranks, and vice versa for the Democratic party, a change in administration would almost inevitably result in a change in tariff legislation.

Nor is this mere quibbling. As long as the emphasis is on the parties as such, the way is of course left open for the conclusion that had the Democratic party been more successful at the polls in the seventy-five years following the Civil War, American tariff history would have been very different. But such an interpretation begs almost the entire question—as can be seen when a second important consideration is made the focus of attention.

A strong case can be made for the proposition that a major reason for the poor showing of the Democrats during this period was the unequivocal way in which it repulsed protectionist groups. This is not, of course, the place to defend such a proposition at length, but a few of the principal points which would enter into its defense will suffice as an indication of its force. First, in order to elect a President it was vital that a political party secure support in the nonsouthern regions west of the Mississippi River. This area, however, was the heart and center of the beet sugar, wool-raising, and dairy industries—all strongly protectionist interests—and was eager to minimize competition from Canadian wheat and pork in the bargain. Second, it was also essential for a political party to win electoral votes in the industrial East in order to secure control over the federal government. Here the key interest to be wooed was labor, another political force primarily protectionist in its orientation. In summary, it seems reasonable to doubt that there was ever a time during the entire period of intense protectionism in the United States when a dogmatic stand against high duties would not have alienated more votes than it attracted.

And finally, these conclusions can be still further documented by noting two important features of recent tariff history. On the one hand, the Democrats secured office in 1933, and hence the power necessary to inaugurate the most comprehensive tariff reduction program ever witnessed in this country, against the background of two presidential campaigns in which they pointedly promised not to do what they immediately set about doing—that is, to lower duties. On the other hand, the Republican party more recently altered traditional behavior in this field in a similarly striking way. For the first time in its history it did not raise the tariff immediately after taking over the government. In the last quarter of a century international affairs have so altered in importance and character that the tariff can no longer be treated as a domestic issue, while at the same time American industry has so grown in stature and confidence that many businessmen are now more concerned about the capacity of foreigners to buy American exports than about their ability to undersell American producers in the American market. The result is that strong anti-high tariff interests now reside within the Republican party, and that this traditionally protectionist organization is going through the painful process of altering its orientation accordingly.

PARTY POLITICS AND THE WELFARE STATE

And one last topic might constructively be discussed from this standpoint. For some years now much has been heard about the welfare state. Some there are who are delighted to see government in the United States move in this direction; others are repelled by the very thought of such a trend. But there is little doubt in anyone's mind that there is in evidence today a marked evolution toward the assumption by government of more and more functions belonging in the welfare-state category. Furthermore, it is generally assumed that the Democratic party is actively hastening this development, while the Republicans are just as vigorously applying the brakes. How true is this popular impression?

Unfortunately, this is an area in which a meeting of minds in debate is made especially difficult by the problem of definition. Not only are numerous definitions (for the most part implicit rather than explicit) of the welfare state in current use, but even when a particular definition is explicitly put forward for analytical purposes most disputants at once have major reservations about its suitability. Given this situation, it will not be supposed here that all such reservations can be summarily disposed of. But because serious discussion of this subject is impossible in the absence of a fairly concrete definition, one must in any event be advanced.

Historically, and this seems to be a proper approach since the phenomenon at issue is an historical evolution, the concept of the welfare state arises in opposition to the concept laissez faire. In other words, the definition sought must offer something of a contrast with the rugged individualism of the nineteenth century. Moreover, a central facet of the first attack on laissez faire was based on the proposition that the injustices growing out of historic individualism arose because the so-called "night-watchman government" was not really neutral as it claimed to be—that it surreptitiously, although nonetheless decisively, granted special privileges to the few at the expense of the many. It follows that a definition designed merely to do away with government favoritism (e.g., by doing away with tariff protectionism) and calculated to implement the laissez faire philosophy even more rigorously would not fill the bill here. Only when an ideology developed supporting government intervention in economic affairs to achieve positive purposes as distinguished from the policeman function of enforcing a "law of nature" could it be said that a welfare-state concept had come into being.

On the basis of this definition, how have the parties stood on the welfare-state issue? To begin with, the thesis has been ably presented that such a concept of government was first expounded by a major political figure in America in connection with the presidential election campaign of 1912—and not by Woodrow Wilson, as would at first be supposed, but by Theodore Roosevelt.[10] According to this view the New Freedom of 1912 was essentially superficial from the standpoint of aggressively using the government for broad, socioeconomic purposes by comparison with the platform of the "Bull-Moosers," and that as the victorious party set to work translating its campaign promises into a legislative program it found itself drifting steadily toward the T. R. philosophy. The technical point can, of course, be raised that Roosevelt was not a Republican in 1912, but this scarcely affects the argument here. Speaking generally, the membership of this maverick organization came from Republican ranks (note Roosevelt's 88 electoral votes by contrast with the 8 garnered by Taft), and it is therefore not stretching a point to suggest that it was the Republican party which first gave way before welfare-state pressures.

Now it is true that if there was a lesson to be learned by the Republican party in the events of 1912 and after, it was not heeded. The reaction which set in after World War I against Woodrow Wilson and all that he stood for, coupled with the high prosperity that characterized most of the 1920's, made it possible to eradicate

[10] Arthur S. Link, *Woodrow Wilson and the Progressive Era* (New York: Harper & Bros., 1954).

all traces of the welfare-state heresy. In the event this was accomplished so successfully that even in the face of the most devastating depression in the history of the country there was surprisingly little resurgence of such views.

Because the Republicans did not read aright the handwriting on the wall shortly after the turn of the century, because the Democrats were quick to capitalize on their rivals' failure to respond effectively to the human tragedy of the early 1930's, and because it was twenty years before Republicans were again entrusted with full control over the nation's government, the notion has understandably arisen that welfare state doctrines are a monopoly of the Democratic party. But even when the historical period under review is thus shortened to the interval from 1929 to the present, this case is by no means as clear-cut as it seems at first glance to be.

For example, as has already been emphasized in connection with the tariff, it was not so much Democratic espousal of a new philosophy of government responsibilities which brought a government broadly reflecting that philosophy into being. It was rather a deep-rooted public insistence upon such a government which led Democratic leaders to put their party behind the associated philosophy. Moreover, only a casual examination of public policy evolution between 1929 and 1933 is required to demonstrate that even Republican orthodoxy was unmistakably giving ground before the upsurge of this sentiment. Let it not be forgotten either that Herbert Hoover's last full year in the White House saw the national debt rise by $3 billion, and that Franklin Roosevelt in 1932 received considerable conservative support on the basis of his promise to put an end to Republican deficit-financing.

But these facts, revealing though they are, are only shadow-boxing with this issue by comparison with what has happened in the "welfare politics" area since World War II. The tip-off here came in 1949 in the form of a special senatorial race in New York between Mr. John Foster Dulles, the incumbent Republican, and Mr. Herbert Lehman, an aspiring Democrat. Mr. Dulles campaigned vigorously in opposition to the welfare state, while his opponent pleaded guilty to the charge of believing in the welfare of democracy's citizens. Mr. Lehman won a decisive victory. A few weeks later in an address at Princeton University Thomas E. Dewey, the leader at that time of the Republican party, publicly drew the obvious conclusion. "It must," he said, "have been a very clumsy Republican" who sought to make a party asset out of the term "Welfare State." To this caustic comment he then added, "Anyone who thinks an attack on the fundamental idea of security and welfare is appealing to the people is living in the Middle Ages."

That the Republicans took this lesson to heart can be seen by post-1949 events on the national policy stage. Who would have thought a quarter of a century ago that a Republican administration would aggressively take the initiative in expanding the social security program, raising the minimum wage, accepting in practice if not in principle the idea of price supports for farmers, and appropriating funds for public housing. Thus does a major political party in a two-party democracy become chastened as a result of twenty years on the outside looking in. To be sure, it may be both correct and meaningful to say that the Democrats espoused the welfare-state cause enthusiastically while the Republicans did so reluctantly, but that fact rather proves than challenges the basic proposition at issue here.

In conclusion, and at the risk of being accused of taking back with the left hand everything that has been given with the right, it is essential to make one last observation tempering these conclusions a little. It is, of course, recognized that there are from time to time historical accidents altering temporarily the pace of economic policy development. Thus it could be called an accident that, in part because of the post-World War I reaction to Woodrow Wilson's administration, evolution in the government and business field almost ceased for a dozen years. In the same sense it was an accident that public revulsion against the Republican party was so great after 1932 that evolution in this policy area was much accelerated—although a substantial part of this acceleration was no doubt due to the virtual cessation of evolution in this field during the 1920's.

The course of history, working in a democracy through the medium of competition between political parties, generates lags and leads in policy formulation which are of some importance on a short time scale but which have a way of averaging out over the longer pull. With this qualification included, the significant points in this chapter can be broadly summarized as follows. First, the shorter the period of time and the less important the issues under consideration, the greater is the significance of party fortunes as such for economic policy; conversely, *the longer the period of time and the more important the issues under consideration, the smaller is the significance of ebbs and flows in party politics.* Second, any *fundamental discussion of public policy evolution must revolve primarily around the temper of the times, the sentiment of various major citizen groups, the pres-*

sures under which the population is laboring, and the available alternatives for relieving those pressures.

QUESTIONS FOR DISCUSSION

1. What is the relationship between partisan politics and the evolution of economic policy?

2. Explain the interrelationships between beliefs and institutions. How do these interrelationships contribute to social change?

3. What is social change? Why is the evolution of different relationships between government and business properly thought of in these terms?

4. Explain the rise of the public utility concept from the standpoint of the process of social change as here described.

5. Why were the Anti-Federalists unable to make good on their pledge to save the nation from Federalist concentration of power in the hands of the federal government?

6. Why did the major parties reverse their respective stands on the issue of government centralization?

7. Analyze the major features of American banking history from the standpoint of public interest.

8. What are the main lines of evidence supporting the proposition that money and banking evolution has not been primarily a product of American political history?

9. Where did the major parties stand on the issue of laissez faire early in the twentieth century? Compare these positions with the situation today.

10. Defend the thesis that the Democratic party was no more responsible for either regulation of railroads or the recognition by government of the right of workers to organize and bargain collectively than the Republican party.

11. How might the Democratic party's stand on the tariff have contributed to its poor showing after the Civil War? Why was protectionism the popular side of this controversy?

12. Why have both major parties changed their basic approach to the tariff in recent years? Are they now closer together on this issue?

13. What is meant by the concept "the welfare state"?

14. To what extent is it correct to refer to the Democratic party as the welfare-state party?

15. On the basis of the discussion in this chapter, explain the dominance of businessmen in policy-making after the Civil War.

16. How accurate is it to refer to the Republican party as the party of the businessman? Is this any more or any less accurate today than formerly?

17. Can you think of any policy in the government and business field in which party positions as such have played a major role?

18. If party politics is not a major causal factor in public policy development, what is?

Chapter 32

Looking Backward—Ideological Foundations

If partisan politics as such has not been a primary cause of the institutional changes under review here, what has? If more fundamental forces have been at work, what has been their nature? As we look back at the road we have traveled in the government and business field over a period of two centuries, what common denominators for the complex evolution which has taken place can be isolated?

SOCIAL CHANGE AND HISTORICAL DETERMINISM

It does not go far toward the development of specific answers to questions such as these, and indeed it is almost a truism, to assert that the key to an investigation of this kind is the process of social change. At the same time, however, that thread can appropriately be picked up here by stressing an important feature of the particular changes which emanate from a given set of underlying social conditions. Thus because myths and techniques are intricately interrelated, because significant alterations at one point in a society's make-up invariably set in motion other transformations, and especially because the myth-structure must not only be congruent with the existing state of technology but must also be internally consistent, social scientists are coming more and more to believe that institutional evolution is to a considerable extent deterministic. That is, at any given point in time most avenues of change are closed to a particular society by the very nature of the disequilibrium it is experiencing.

710

This point of view has been particularly well expressed by J. A. Schumpeter in a classic piece of writing built almost wholly on this theoretical foundation.[1]

For mankind is not free to choose. This is not only because the mass of people are not in a position to compare alternatives rationally and always accept what they are being told. There is a much deeper reason for it. Things economic and social move by their own momentum and the ensuing situations compel individuals and groups to behave in certain ways whatever they may wish to do—not indeed by destroying their freedom of choice but by shaping the choosing mentalities and by narrowing the list of possibilities from which to choose.

By bringing Schumpeter's formulation into the realm of the workaday world, this premise can also be stated in the language of a brilliant American statesman—a man whose greatness rests in large part upon a capacity for reducing abstract ideas to more common-sense terms. Shortly before the Civil War Abraham Lincoln said of slavery (in paraphrase): "This institution is doomed. Whoever shall assist in its destruction can ride out the tides of history. But whoever endeavors to stand in their way will be crushed." It was, in other words, Lincoln's view that the disequilibrium the United States was then experiencing could be remedied only by the elimination of slavery. When this prediction is viewed today against the background of the more recent controversy over segregation, it can be appreciated both how keen was Lincoln's foresight and how long-range are the forces under consideration here.

PRIVATE PROPERTY BEGINNINGS

In order to comprehend social change, then, it is necessary for analysis to work its way from a set of basic belief-institution interrelationships, through whatever disequilibria develop out of these relationships, to a resultant set of beliefs and institutions—or in the reverse direction. It follows, of course, that every process of dynamic evolution has remote beginnings, and that any starting point for either analysis or presentation must be in high degree arbitrary. To select just such an arbitrary point of departure, discussion of the broad development of present-day business-government interaction in the United States will be based chronologically on the replacement of feudal institutions by more modern ones in the sixteenth and seventeenth centuries. Attention will be focused first on the

---

[1] J. A. Schumpeter, *Capitalism, Socialism, and Democracy* (3d ed.; New York: Harper & Bros., 1950), pp. 129-30.

major features of the myth-development which has taken place, after which the more important institutional changes will be related to these several ideological stages.

Surely no extensive justification is necessary for beginning an overview of such a key aspect of American history in the British Isles. This country was for a long time only a tributary of the great stream of western civilization, fed largely from the springs of socio-economic development in England. More specifically, it was in England that the industrialization the New World inherited from the Old first took root, and hence it was in England that a myth-technique appropriate to an industrialized society first appeared.

Nor is any more justification required for beginning such a discussion with a review of some of the essential features of John Locke's classic treatise *Of Civil Government*. Before the modern-type economy could develop it was essential that the complex and overlapping person-property relationships found reasonably satisfactory in feudal society be replaced. The new structure of relationships devised for this purpose has for more than two centuries been referred to by the name "private property," and it was John Locke who more than any other single individual brought together the various strands out of which an effective rationalization of this alternative in social organization could be woven. In the terminology of social change, this achievement was the development of a set of beliefs (myths) highly congruent with the most basic institutions of an embryo industrial society.

The fundamental interconnection between past, present, and future in any significant myth-development can be clearly seen in Locke's starting point. For centuries men had been accustomed to a situation in which more than one person or family shared rights to the same piece of real estate, the most extreme case of this being the vast acreages held in common by the entire community. Furthermore, a major pillar of feudal society had always been the Church, and it is, therefore, readily understandable why the central task Locke set for himself in his justly famous chapter "On Property"[2] was to explain that the resources "which God gave to mankind in common" may nonetheless be appropriated for the sole use of a particular individual.

This explanation took first the ground that the new arrangement was the only reasonable one—despite the fact that for many generations a much different alternative had served quite well.

[2] Book II, chap. v.

God who hath given the world to men in common, hath also given them reason to make use of it to the best advantage of life and convenience. . . . And though all the fruits it naturally produces . . . belong to mankind in common . . . yet being given for the use of men, there must of necessity be a means to appropriate them some way or another before they can be of any use . . . to any particular man. The fruit or venison which nourishes the wild Indian . . . must be his, and so his—*i.e.*, a part of him, that another can no longer have any right to it before it can do him any good for the support of his life.

But Locke could scarcely have rested his case on the fact that only one person can secure bodily nourishment from the same bit of food. After all, the more or less forcible conversion of feudal types of land tenure to private property had long been a burning issue in Locke's England. A myriad of socio-economic relationships which had existed for many generations were thereby abruptly severed, a process occasioning a great deal of bitterness. Clearly nothing less than a particularly strong moral foundation for private property could give the new orientation deep roots in Britain's institutional soil.

Locke's position on this issue was that all production is the outcome of human labor, and that an individual has an unequivocal right to the fruit of his own efforts.

Though the earth and all inferior creatures be common to all men, yet every man has a "property" in his own "person." This nobody has any right to but himself. The "labour" of his body and the "work" of his hands, we may say, are properly his. Whatsoever, then, he removes out of the state that Nature hath provided and left it in, he hath mixed his labor with it, and joined to it something that is his own, and thereby makes it his property. It being by him removed from the common state Nature placed it in, it hath by this labour something annexed to it that excludes the common right of other men.

And because it seemed so important that at this crucial point nothing be left to chance, Locke developed this thesis still further by considering private property from the standpoint of social justice— the problem of the fairness of the distribution of resources. The conclusions reached here were twofold. On the one hand, Locke repeatedly assumed that there was enough property for everyone.

For this "labour" being the unquestionable property of the labourer, no man but he can have a right to what that is once joined to, at least where there is enough, and as good left in common for others. . . .

Nor was this appropriation of any parcel of land, by improving it, any prejudice to any other man, for there was still enough and as good left, and more than the yet unprovided could use. . . .

. . . ground which God had given him, in common with others, to labour on, and whereof there was as good left as that already possessed, and more than he knew what to do with, or his industry could reach to. . . .

. . . So that it was impossible for any man, this way, to entrench upon the right of another or acquire to himself a property to the prejudice of his neighbor, who would still have room for as good and as large a possession. . . .

On the other hand, a definite and readily defensible limit was set to the right of accumulation.

It will, perhaps, be objected to this that if gathering the acorns or other fruits of the earth, etc., makes a right to them, then any one may engross as much as he will. To which I answer, Not so. The same law of Nature that does by this means give us property, does also bound that property, too.

"God has given us all things richly." Is the voice of reason confirmed by inspiration? But how far has He given it to us—"to enjoy"? As much as any one can make use of to any advantage of life before it spoils, so much he may by his labor fix a property in. Whatever is beyond this is more than his share, and belongs to others. . . .

As much land as a man tills, plants, improves, cultivates, and can use the product of, so much is his property. . . .

The measure of property Nature well set, by the extent of men's labor and the conveniency of life . . .

Whatsoever he tilled and reaped, laid up and made use of before it spoiled, that was his peculiar right. . . .

. . . everyone hath a right . . . to as much as he could use, and had a property in all he could effect with his labor; all that his industry could extend to, to alter from the state Nature had put it in, was his.

This, then, is the substance of the most influential defense of private property ever penned. Its importance for present purposes, however, does not lie with the defense as such, but with the conclusion drawn therefrom as regards the role of government in a private property society. Because this institution was thought to embrace an incentive system adequate to get society's chores done, and because it could at the same time be counted upon to resolve the principal questions of social justice which are constantly arising, it seemed to follow that the "true end of government" (the abbreviated title for the entirety of Book II of Locke's work) is to protect property rights.

The great and chief end, therefore, of men uniting into commonwealths, and putting themselves under government, is the preservation of their property.[3]

Here, in short, was a pioneer statement of the plea for a government limited to a very restricted range of responsibilities.

From Private Property to Free Enterprise

But myth-building is a never-ceasing human activity, and hence these intellectual achievements must submit to modification as soon

[3] Book II, chap. ix.

as they begin to circulate. This is not, it must be emphatically stated at the outset, because they are logically defective in the sense that they will not bear close scrutiny by minds shaped through different traditions, ideas, and institutions. A social myth does not owe its vitality to its ability to withstand critical examination from every conceivable frame of reference; its function is only to relate existing realities to human values and aspirations, and therefore its strength rests upon how securely it is rooted in its own times. Thus, in the case of John Locke's justification of private property inadequacy had little to do with the dependence upon the labor theory of value latter-day analysts have made such sport of—even the unequivocal denial of the existence of economic scarcity. For many years after 1690 the labor theory of value, in the form of the proposition that personal income is a reward for individual productive efforts, remained an article of faith with many citizens, while the assumption of abundance likewise was given by the wide-open frontiers outside Europe (and particularly in North America) enough plausibility to have a long and eventful career.

The shortcoming of Locke's analysis was that, although it performed the highly useful task of rationalizing the first great step away from a feudal organization of society, it did not by itself complete that transition. Western civilization was on the march, and no sooner had Europeans begun to incorporate Lockeian principles into their thinking than institutional change advanced decisively beyond the range of the rationalization thus achieved. Although Oswald Spengler would have his readers believe that comprehensive myth-structures never appear until the related institutional evolution has already reached an advanced stage,[4] it is true that John Locke's approach to economic organization was very nearly anachronistic on the day it was first published.

This fact can be demonstrated in two ways. In the first place, it is evident that Locke's thought processes did not take into account specialization and exchange. The concept of property around which his thinking revolved was the direct use of physical assets for the benefit of the user. By contrast England was already a great mercantile power, and hence ownership was becoming more and more bound up with exchange values and the intangibles so important in a specialized society. Whereas, in other words, Locke's illustrative material was taken almost entirely from the field of agriculture, the area within which exclusive possession most needed to be justified was coming to be trade and manufacturing activities.

[4] *The Decline of the West* (New York: Alfred A. Knopf, Inc., 1926).

It is equally obvious, in the second place, that Locke's discussion of social justice could be no more realistic than the conception of property from which it was derived—entirely apart from the fact that even in the field of agriculture social philosophy would soon be compelled to come to terms with the unpleasant truth that there was not "enough and as good" for everyone. In a specialized society the institution of money inevitably becomes an intermediary between production and consumption, with the result that the simple principle that a family is entitled to receive only so much of its own output as can be consumed before it spoils becomes hopelessly inadequate. One of the essentials of a good money system is that it be capable of serving effectively as a store of value, that, in other words, it will not spoil no matter how long it is kept. Inexorably, therefore, whatever progress was made toward developing a more satisfactory monetary system—and progress on this front was extremely rapid—could only undermine the conception of social justice enunciated by Locke.

In all fairness it must be recorded that Locke himself saw the difficulties of his position, and that he made an attempt to adapt his conclusions to the commercial world growing up about him.

But since gold and silver, being little useful to the life of man, in proportion to food, raiment, and carriage, has its value only from the consent of man—whereof labour yet makes in great part the measure—it is plain that the consent of men have agreed to a disproportionate and unequal possession of the earth—I mean out of the bounds of society and compact; for in government the laws regulate it; they having, by consent, found out and agreed in a way how a man may, rightfully and without injury, possess more than he himself can make use of by receiving gold and silver, which may continue in a man's possession without decaying on the overplus, and agreeing those metals should have a value.[5]

However, whether it is a kindness to Locke to complete this record is another question. Surely no approach to the problem of justice in a money economy could be more naive. From a justification of exclusive possession of however much an individual and his family can produce and consume, discussion has arbitrarily shifted to a situation in which anyone is entitled to whatever he has enough purchasing power to buy. In the absence of a careful investigation of the source of the purchasing power commanded by a particular person, here was no social justice proposition at all.

Because of these limitations of Locke's analysis it is not surprising that his view of "the great and chief end" of government went unheeded for many years. Indeed, not only was this evolution not pro-

[5] Book II, chap. v.

ceeding along Lockeian lines, but it was instead moving in an exactly opposite direction. Feudal society had been organized around the virtually self-sufficient manor as the most effective unit of social, political, and economic life, the consequence being a fragmentation of sovereignty inappropriate to the growth of business enterprise. Exchange activities require considerable elbow room for best development; where a trading area is subject to numerous legal jurisdictions and hence conflicting patterns of regulation, modern-type business operations are impossible. The second great step away from feudalism, therefore, was to solidify sovereignty in the hands of *national* governments. Side by side with the rise of private property this institutional change had also long been underway, reaching something of a climax at approximately the time Locke was writing.

This process was also accompanied by active myth-construction. The resultant body of doctrine has been popularly dubbed "mercantilism," so-called because its most prominent concern was the proper ordering of merchant affairs. By the same token mercantilism is most often discussed in terms of international economic relationships, but when its numerous threads of philosophy and policy are viewed as a whole it can be seen that underlying this structure was an interest in elevating the nation-state from the position of secondary social institution it had held for so long to one of first importance.[6] And in the process of furthering that interest mercantilism contributed a great deal to the rise of commercial enterprise to an activity of major significance in western nations.[7]

But this assistance was not all net gain. For as the central government more and more brought the life of the nation under its control, business operations were more and more closely supervised by the new power. Rarely has the adage "from the frying pan into the fire" so aptly described a predicament. Rarely has a group of social innovators been caught in such a difficult dilemma. They could not see clearly how to do without their central government ally; no more could they tolerate the central government paternalism they saw stretching out endlessly before them.

This dilemma, plus the inadequacy of John Locke's justification of private property, set the stage for the next great development on the ideological front. What was needed was a defense of the new order resting squarely on the assumption of specialization and exchange, but which would at the same time relieve business enterprise of the

---

[6] E. F. Heckscher, *Mercantilism* (London: George Allen & Unwin, Ltd., 1935).

[7] F. L. Nussbaum, *A History of The Economic Institutions of Modern Europe* (New York: Appleton-Century-Crofts, Inc., 1933).

incubus of comprehensive government regulation. And precisely this was soon forthcoming. In his classic *An Inquiry Into the Nature and Causes of the Wealth of Nations,* first published in 1776, Adam Smith utterly demolished the doctrine of mercantilism, at the same time converting Locke's reasoning into a rationalization of private enterprise in the nineteenth century meaning of that concept.

That the edifice Smith erected was built on Lockeian foundations can be readily demonstrated.

The property which every man has in his own labor, as it is the original foundation of all other property so it is the most sacred and inviolable. The patrimony of a poor man lies in the strength and dexterity of his hands; and to hinder him from employing this strength and dexterity in what manner he thinks proper without injury to his neighbor, is a plain violation of this most sacred property.[8]

The value of any commodity, therefore, to the person who possesses it . . . is equal to the quantity of labour which it enables him to purchase or command. Labour, therefore, is the real measure of the exchangeable value of all commodities.[9]

But that these principles were for Smith only a point of departure is equally evident. Chapter I of Book I of this work announces quite matter-of-factly that the division of labor is responsible for "the greatest improvement in the productive powers of labor, and the greater part of the skill, dexterity, and judgment with which it is anywhere directed," thus serving notice at the outset that specialization and exchange are to be central to this system of thought, rather than peripheral as with Locke. Furthermore, Smith goes even farther along this road by asserting in Chapter II that the division of labor so important to his thinking is rooted deep in human nature.

This division of labor, from which so many advantages are derived, is not originally the effect of any human wisdom, which foresees and intends that general opulence to which it gives occasion. It is the necessary, though very slow and gradual, consequence of a certain propensity in human nature which has in view no such extensive utility; the propensity to truck, barter, and to exchange one thing with another.

And not only does Smith stress the exchange aspect of economic life, but he explicitly distinguishes between an earlier state of affairs in which Lockeian principles could be directly applicable without serious modification and a later stage of development in which more advanced concepts were required.[10]

[8] Book I, chap. v
[9] Book I, chap. x, pt. ii.
[10] Book I, chap. viii.

In that original state of things which precedes both the appropriation of land and the accumulation of stock, the whole produce of labour belongs to the labourer. . . .

But this original state of things, in which the labourer enjoyed the whole produce of his own labour, could not last beyond the first introduction of the appropriation of land and the accumulation of stock . . .

. . . rent makes the first deduction from the produce of the labour which is employed upon land. . . .

. . . profit makes a second deduction from the produce of the labour which is employed upon land.

To this point Smith has done little more than state the problem. The issue remained. What justification is there for a system of social relationships based on private property?

To begin with, here also an appeal is made to universal principles which men cannot alter and in consequence have no alternative but to accept. Thus it is effectively argued that a system of exchange relationships based on personal gain succeeds admirably in getting the world's work done—a crucial test for any economic system.[11]

In civilized society he [an individual] stands at all times in need of the co-operation and assistance of great multitudes, . . . and it is vain for him to expect it from their benevolence only. He will be more likely to prevail if he can interest their self-love in his favour, and shew them that it is for their own advantage to do for him what he requires of them. . . . It is not from the benevolence of the butcher, the brewer, or the baker, that we expect our dinner, but from their regard to their own interest. We address ourselves not to their humanity but to their self-love, and never talk to them of our own necessities but of their advantages. . . .

Among men . . . the most dissimilar geniuses are of use to one another; the different produces of their respective talents, by the general disposition to truck, barter, and exchange, being brought, as it were, into a common stock, where every man may purchase whatever part of the produce of other men's talents as he has occasion for.

And in the second place, this way of thinking goes to some lengths to demonstrate that a self-interest orientation does not, as might at first be supposed, create individual well-being at the expense of the well-being of the community as a whole, but is in fact the orientation most consistent with this larger objective.[12]

Every individual is continually exerting himself to find out the most advantageous employment for whatever capital he can command. It is to his own advantage, indeed, and not that of society, which he has in view. But the study of his own advantage naturally, or rather necessarily leads him to prefer that employment which is most advantageous to the society. . . .

11 Book I, chap. ii.
12 Book IV, chap. ii.

By preferring the support of domestic to that of foreign industry, he intends only his own security; and by directing that industry in such a manner as its produce may be of greatest value, he intends only his own gain, and he is in this, as in many other cases, led by an invisible hand to promote an end which was no part of his intention. . . . I have never known much good done by those who affected to trade for the public good.

But neither of these points attacks directly the critical issue of social justice as such. What of conflicts between one social group and another? Between rich and poor? Between employer and employee? Between producer and consumer? Note that questions of this order become both more important and more difficult in an exchange society when employer and employee, producer and consumer, are not one and the same person.

Our author, actually, had little to say about the problem of poverty in and of itself. For one thing, it seemed to him a sufficient guarantee at this point that every individual would have the opportunity to employ whatever resources he possessed most advantageously to himself. For the rest, he was apparently content to let his resolution of the other two social justice issues stand for this one also.

With respect to employer-employee conflict Smith pointed to two major reasons why no real issue was involved. On the one hand, he relied on the so-called "Iron Law of Wages" to keep wages from falling below a certain irreducible minimum.[13]

But though in disputes with their workmen, masters must generally have the advantage, there is however a certain rate below which it is impossible to reduce . . . the ordinary wages even of the lowest species of labor.

A man must always live by his work, and his wages must at least be sufficient to maintain him. They must even upon most occasions be somewhat more; otherwise it would be impossible for him to bring up a family, and the race of such workmen could not last beyond the first generation.

On the other hand, the wealthier members of society could be counted on to use whatever capital they accumulate for additional wage payments.[14]

When an independent workman . . . has got more stock than what is sufficient to purchase the materials of his own work, and to maintain himself till he can dispose of it, he naturally employs one or more journeymen with the surplus, in order to make a profit by their work. Increase this surplus, and he will naturally increase the number of his journeymen.

The demand of those who live by wages, therefore, necessarily increases with the increase of the revenue and stock of every country, and cannot possibly increase without it.

[13] Book I, chap. viii.
[14] *Ibid.*

Even for Adam Smith, however, the matter of consumer-producer conflict could not be shrugged aside. Quite candidly he observed that:

Merchants and master manufacturers are . . . an order of men whose interest is never exactly the same with that of the public, who have generally an interest to deceive and even to oppress the public, and who accordingly have, upon many occasions, both deceived and oppressed it.[15]

And proceeding still further along this same general line Smith even went so far as to say:

People of the same trade seldom meet together, even for merriment and diversion, but the conversation ends in a conspiracy against the public, or in some contrivance to raise prices.[16]

But though an exchange society does have this problem to contend with, it was not thought to be particularly serious. Again natural law was relied upon to assure the desired results. The "invisible hand" operating through a price-profit nexus—in short, the competition of the market place—will see to it that the public is supplied with as much and only as much of every product as is demanded.[17]

The quantity of every commodity brought to market naturally suits itself to the effectual demand. It is the interest of all those who employ their land, labour, or stock, in bringing any commodity to market, that the quantity never should exceed the effectual demand; and it is the interest of all other people that it never should fall short of that demand.

This, then, is the way Adam Smith, writing almost one hundred years after John Locke, converted the latter's defense of private property for use into a justification of private property for profit. But that necessity, it will be recalled, was only one of the ideological problems confronting the evolution of capitalist institutions in 1776. The other was to challenge the concept of a strong central government with comprehensive economic responsibilities. Nor did Smith's elaborate consideration of the first of these problems cause him to neglect the second. Indeed, it might almost be said that his analysis of the virtues of a private enterprise society was but the essential background for the bitter attack he launched against mercantilism.

Three major points were made in this connection. First, to a considerable extent a vigorous private enterprise economy will so frustrate a government having mercantilist preconceptions as to make it little more than a nuisance.

15 Book I, chap. xi, pt. iii.
16 Book I, chap. x, pt. ii.
17 Book I, chap. vii.

The natural effort of every individual to better his own condition, when suffered to exert itself with freedom and security, is so powerful a principle, that it is alone, without any assistance, not only capable of carrying on the society to wealth and prosperity, but of surmounting a hundred impertinent obstructions with which the folly of human laws too often incumbers its operations; though the effect of these obstructions is always more or less either to encroach upon its freedom, or to diminish its security.[18]

Second, there is little if anything that government can do to assist the operation of such an economy.

What is the species of domestic industry which his capital can employ, and of which the produce is likely to be of the greatest value, every individual, it is evident, can, in his local situation, judge much better than any statesman or lawgiver can do for him. The statesman, who should attempt to direct private people in what manner they ought to employ their capitals, would not only load himself with a most unnecessary attention, but assume an authority which could safely be trusted, not only to no single person, but to no council or senate whatever, and which would nowhere be so dangerous as in the hands of a man who had folly and presumption enough to fancy himself fit to exercise it.[19]

And finally, it was thought to be of the utmost importance that the government keep its activities within the bounds dictated by natural law in order to hold in check the conflict between producers and consumers in an exchange society.

Consumption is the sole end and purpose of all production; and the interest of the producer ought to be attended to, only so far as it may be necessary for promoting that of the consumer. The maxim is so perfectly self-evident, that it would be absurd to attempt to prove it. But in the mercantile system, the interest of the consumer is almost constantly sacrificed to that of the producer; and it seems to consider production, and not consumption as the ultimate end of all industry and commerce.[20]

Then, having thus carefully explained what government in the new society was *not* to be, Smith states fairly specifically the responsibilities a private enterprise society government might properly perform.

All systems either of preference or of restraint, therefore, being thus completely taken away, the obvious and simple system of natural liberty establishes itself of its own accord. . . . According to the system of natural liberty, the sovereign has only three duties to attend to; three duties of great importance, indeed, but plain and intelligible to common understandings: first, the duty of protecting the society from the violence and invasion of other independent societies; secondly, the duty of protecting, as far as possible,

[18] Book IV, chap. v.
[19] Book IV, chap. ii.
[20] Book IV, chap. viii.

every member of the society from the injustice or oppression of every other member of it, or the duty of establishing an exact administration of justice; and thirdly, the duty of erecting and maintaining certain public works and certain public institutions, which it can never be for the interest of any individual, or small number of individuals to erect or maintain; because the profit could never repay the expense to any individual or small number of individuals, though it may frequently do much more than repay it to a great society.[21]

Clearly the concept Locke had earlier advanced of the "great and chief end of government" had undergone substantial change in the course of the eighteenth century. But there remained a strong family resemblance.

FROM FREE ENTERPRISE TO MATURE CAPITALISM

There is an interesting element of paradox in this ideology custom-built, so to speak, for an industrial society. On the one hand, it breathes a spirit of high optimism: no particular thought need be given to the matter of how the economy can be made to function more effectively, for it will perform best when allowed to operate by itself. On the other hand, it also exudes the chill air of pessimism: even when the economy is functioning at its best there is no prospect of a significant improvement in living standards for rank-and-file citizens, because the "Iron Law of Wages" stubbornly intervenes. Indeed so pronounced was this strain of pessimism that classical economics came to be known as "the dismal science."

And a second paradox also marked this system of thought. While in one sense it rested on the use of reason in human affairs, this rationalism was essentially negative. As a consequence of their strong belief in natural law, the classicists could not give intelligence a continuing, guidance role in socio-economic relationships. Its task instead consisted of two other responsibilities: first to discover the natural laws governing human existence, and second to destroy man-made obstacles to their operation. To undertake more would not only fail to improve the mechanism but might seriously damage it in the bargain.

So uneasy was this equilibrium of concepts that it is no wonder dissenting voices were soon raised. In the same way that John Locke's formulation began to be outdated almost before it was penned, so too did Adam Smith's. Once again the ideological framework constructed soon ceased to correspond at all closely with the realities of a dynamic industrial society.

[21] Book IV, chap. ix.

The promptness with which the classicists were first challenged can be illustrated by the fact that in 1804, only a few years after Smith's death, the optimism of *The Wealth of Nations* was called into question by a man who fully shared Smith's own distrust of the mercantile system. In a volume entitled *An Inquiry Into The Nature And Origin Of Public Wealth And Into The Means And Causes Of Its Increase,* the Earl of Lauderdale emphatically denied that the "simple and obvious system of natural liberty" can be as completely trusted to achieve public well-being as so many of his contemporaries seemed to be assuming.

The most basic ground for this denial lay in the definition of public wealth. To Lauderdale it seemed evident that an individualistic, self-interest definition of that term could only result in serious conceptual error.[22] Thus, whereas in Smith's analysis the "wealth of the nation" was determined by simply totaling the private wealths of individual citizens, this critic maintained that a more macroeconomic interpretation would have to be substituted. Specifically, although individual riches must be thought of as "all that man desires as useful or delightful to him which exists in a degree of scarcity," national wealth may properly be thought of as "all that man desires as useful and delightful to him"—and in an exchange society there are all too many ways in which national wealth can be destroyed in the process of creating individual riches. In fact Lauderdale went so far as to summarize his analysis of various possible situations as follows:

The conclusion is therefore inevitable that there exists only one case, and that a very improbable one, —. . . in which an increase in the mass of individual riches produces a similar effect on the wealth of the nation.

Furthermore, where his adversaries would have preferred to insist that inequities in distribution would more or less automatically work themselves out because those who received "excessive" incomes would invest the "excess" by adding to the nation's total employment, Lauderdale advanced a second reason for challenging classical optimism. In his opinion the useful employment of such incomes could no more be taken for granted than can the identity of public wealth and individual riches.[23]

Thus the distribution of wealth not only regulates and decides the channels in which the industry of every country is embarked, and of course the articles in the production of which it excels; but a proper distribution insures the increase of opulence, by sustaining a regular progressive demand in the

[22] Chap. ii.
[23] Chap. v.

home market, and still more effectually, by affording to those whose habits are likely to create a desire of supplanting labour, the power of executing it.

In other words, too exclusive a preoccupation with individual riches may result in the failure of mass purchasing power, and thereby in a falling-off in the rate of capital accumulation, in this way striking at one of the key avenues for increasing national wealth.

And not only did Lauderdale question laissez faire's optimism, but he even suggested that laissez faire pessimism could appropriately be discounted as well. Here the target of his attack was the Iron Law of Wages. Perhaps, he ventured, there is no such relationship; perhaps natural law does not set an upper limit to the incomes of members of the working class. However, Lauderdale did not pursue this point at length. The western world was just beginning to fall under the spell of the Malthusian "Law of Population Growth" (the idea that human beings tend to reproduce to the limit of subsistence), and against this handicap questions about the validity of the Iron Law of Wages could obviously make little headway.

It is of particular interest that Lord Lauderdale, having presented in embryo the principal ideas which were one day to transform America's politico-economic ideology, drew no specific policy conclusions. That is, he offered no amendments to laissez faire thinking on the role of intelligence in human affairs. At one point it had been his intention to issue simultaneously a companion volume setting forth the implications of his analysis from the standpoint of the functions of government. This project, however, he tells us in his Preface, was put aside because he "thought it more prudent to pause, and delay the execution of the remaining part of his plan, until he discovers how far the opinions he has advanced in the present publication shall stand the test of public criticism."

Evidently our author did not conclude that his work had successfully stood the test of time for the projected volume on "legislation" was never prepared. Moreover Lauderdale himself in later years grew increasingly conservative in his views, until by the time of England's great reform movement of the early 1830's he was to be found in the forefront of the defenders of the status quo. Thus easily did a hardening orthodoxy deflect one of the most powerful challenges it was ever to encounter. Thus decisively did one of the most brilliant minds of the early nineteenth century give way before the onward march of a business civilization.

Although Lauderdale's wholesale revision of Adam Smith bore no fruit directly, lesser modifications of laissez faire began to make their way immediately. Boring from within, a small but influential group of thinkers known as utilitarians were soon stretching Smithianism slightly out of shape, while at the same time giving a strong impetus to some of the ideas which had figured prominently in Lauderdale's challenge.

The chief concern of utilitarianism was the function of reason in working out a society's institutional arrangements. And here too the tone was open criticism. Whereas, according to one of the leading proponents of utilitarian philosophy, Jeremy Bentham, social and political thinkers customarily dealt in unmanageable generalities, the primary objective of the new approach was to reduce this branch of thought to the concrete objectivity of mathematics. The great concept which was to make this possible was the principle of utility.[24]

Every man, so this thinking went, is guided by two masters—pleasure and pain. Seeking always to maximize the one and minimize the other, men order their lives insofar as they are able in such a way as to achieve the largest net balance of "pleasure-minus-pain." From the standpoint of society as a whole, it was then asserted that total social well-being would be maximized when and only when this favorable state had been attained by as many individuals as possible. A maximum number of men enjoying a maximum number of pleasures minus a minimum number of men suffering a minimum number of pains—the greatest good of the greatest number—was set as the highest goal toward which a society might strive.

To a point no controversy need have developed between this way of thinking and laissez faire philosophy. Indeed, as long as utilitarianism confined itself essentially to the repeal of the Corn Laws and the eradication of numerous other feudal remnants, as long, in short, as it was preoccupied with problems relating to production, it was no less than the principal cutting edge of classical economics. But the time was to come when utilitarian thinking began to merge with Lord Lauderdale's concern with problems of distribution, and from that point onward tension mounted rapidly.

This tendency for utilitarianism to outgrow its origins can be seen especially clearly in the writings of John Stuart Mill, the systematizer of that philosophy and perhaps its greatest proponent. Viewing industrial society some fifty years after Adam Smith, and bringing to his works a greatly altered perspective on the limits of reason in social innovation, Mill's conclusions on the functions of government were quite different from those reached by the "father of modern economics."

24 Crane Brinton, *English Political Thought in the Nineteenth Century* (Cambridge: Harvard University Press, 1949).

The entirety of the fifth and last book of Mill's *Principles of Political Economy* (1848) is given over to what he calls "The Influence of Government." In the first chapter of this book, entitled "Of the Functions of Government in General," he makes explicit the fact that the theoretical limitations here had in the preceding half-century become much broader.

In attempting to enumerate the necessary functions of government, we find them to be considerably more multifarious than most people are at first aware of, and not capable of being circumscribed by those very definite lines of demarcation, which, in the inconsiderateness of popular discussion, it is often attempted to draw round them . . .

. . . the admitted functions of government embrace a much wider field than can easily be included within the ring-fence of any definition, and . . . it is hardly possible to find any ground of justification common to them all, except the comprehensive one of general expediency. . . .

These introductory observations are followed by nine chapters in which various aspects of the subject at hand, especially taxation, are discussed. Then comes Chapter XI, "Of the Grounds and Limits of the Laissez-Faire or Non-Interference Principle," in which Mill becomes quite explicit about the consequences of applying pleasure–pain analysis to social organization in an exchange community.

First the principle itself is summarized, together with the major grounds for adhering to it as closely as possible. These comments are concluded with the following statement:

The preceding are the principal reasons . . . in favour of restricting to the narrowest compass the intervention of a public authority in the business of the community: and few will dispute the more than sufficiency of these reasons, to throw, in every instance, the burthen of making out a strong case, not on those who resist, but on those who recommend, government interference. *Laissez-faire*, in short, should be the general practice: every departure from it, unless required by some great good, is a certain evil.

There are, however, exceptions to this general rule that "the business of life is better performed when those who have an immediate interest in it are left to take their own course," and to these Mill devoted some thirty pages. The character of the situations placed in this category of exceptions are a far cry from the premises of *The Wealth of Nations*.

Thus intervention can be justified in the public interest where the consumer is not competent to judge the commodity he is buying; where some persons are in a position to exercise an excessive power over other persons; where in any event not individuals themselves but a delegated agency (e.g., a corporation) is the responsible entity;

where unduly long contract periods are involved; where the desires of those most interested could not otherwise be protected (e.g., regulating the hours of labor); where the business at hand is done for the benefit of others than the persons concerned (charity); and where private enterprise defaults on its responsibilities even though it could perform the task required more effectively than government.

To such a state had classical optimism concerning "the obvious and simple system of natural liberty" been reduced. Surely there can be no mistaking the import of these words on the next to the last page of Mill's treatise:

In the particular circumstances of a given age or nation, there is scarcely anything really important to the general interest, which it may not be desirable, or even necessary, that the government should take upon itself. . . .

However, Mill's concessions to economic liberalism were scarcely more influential in his times than Lauderdale's analysis had been in his. On the one hand, Mill himself repudiated the most extreme policy implications of his philosophy. On the other hand, such sentiments were still so counter to prevailing views that they could hardly have had widespread consequences in any event. And thus it was that laissez faire ideas continued to hold the field without effective opposition from within.

Perhaps in large part because orthodoxy could not bring itself to attack its own problems in a really fundamental way, the next significant development in this ideological evolution was to shake that doctrine to its deepest foundations. That was the appearance, also in 1848, of *The Communist Manifesto*. And what made this assault especially damaging was its use for diametrically opposite purposes of some of the basic elements in classical political economy.

The first of these was the doctrine that labor creates all value and the Iron Law of Wages. Actually the first of these ideas was no longer a cornerstone of orthodox belief. Adam Smith had carefully distinguished between natural value and market value; Lauderdale had gone to some pains to deny that labor is the only factor of production; and a long line of classical thinkers had been working toward a theory of value having a much broader foundation. In like manner the Iron Law of Wages was being subjected to increasing pressure. But neither of these propositions had been explicitly repudiated in the sense that a formulation wholly free of them could convincingly be advanced, and therefore when revolutionary socialism seized upon them as weapons with which to attack capitalism no adequate defense was immediately available. The fact is that classical economics *was* pessimistic in tenor.

Observe how neatly the tables were turned here. What the Marxists succeeded in doing was to tie the labor theory of value and the Iron Law of Wages together by insisting that the "value" of labor is the cost of subsistence for the working class. Very well, they said, let us agree that the source of all value is labor. What follows? Wherever we look we see the creator of value, the workingman, receiving only a part of what he has created while a handful of capitalists are growing wealthy at his expense. Paying labor only its "value," but forcing workers to produce many more goods each day than the value equivalent of worker subsistence, the entrepreneur creates a "surplus value" which roughly measures the extent of labor exploitation.

A second way in which revolutionary socialism used orthodox concepts as a basis for condemning capitalism was the twist thereby given natural law. In the hands of this group that idea became an historical determinism in which laissez faire arrangements are inevitably undermined and replaced by institutions of a drastically different character. Thus workers are the victims of natural law when they reproduce to the limits of subsistence; capitalists are compelled by market forces to get as much output out of every worker as possible; the bourgeoisie naturally acts to protect itself from labor-class unrest by creating government as an instrument of oppression; and capitalist evolution must inevitably proceed to a point at which there are so few plutocrats as compared with the size of the exploited group that the latter will rise up and destroy the former.

Note again how deftly classical pessimism was turned completely around. Because the majority of citizens had no prospect of improving their lot in the existing order, they obviously had no reason to defend that order.[25]

You are horrified at our intending to do away with private property. But in your existing society, private property is already done away with for nine-tenths of the population; its existence for the few is solely due to its non-existence in the hands of those nine-tenths. You reproach us therefore with intending to do away with a form of property, the necessary condition for whose existence is the non-existence of any property for the immense majority of society. . . .

The Communists are further reproached with a desire to abolish countries and nationality.

The working men have no country. We cannot take from them what they have not got. Since the proletariat must first of all . . . constitute itself *the* nation, it is, so far, itself national, though not in the bourgeois sense of the word.

[25] Karl Marx and Frederick Engels, *The Communist Manifesto*.

AN OVERVIEW

And in the third place, it is worth noting in passing that the socialists were even able to make skillful use of the movement toward democracy in the Western world during the nineteenth century.[26]

We have seen . . . that the first step in the revolution by the working class is to raise the proletariat to the position of ruling class, to win the battle of democracy. . . .

When, in the course of development, class distinctions have disappeared, and all production has been concentrated in the hands of a vast association of the whole nation, the public power will lose its political character. . . . If the proletariat . . . sweeps away by force the old conditions of production, then it will, along with these conditions, have swept away the conditions for class antagonisms and of classes generally, and will thereby have abolished its own supremacy as a class.

In place of the old bourgeois society with its classes and class antagonisms, we shall have a condition in which the free development of each is the condition for the free development of all.

The degree of influence quickly achieved by Marxism posed a challenge for orthodoxy which could not be ignored. Clearly, ideological pessimism and first thoughts about natural law would have to be revised—to say nothing of the modifications in classical optimism already under way.[27] On the defensive and under heavy ideological pressure, orthodoxy set itself to the task of completing the work so ably begun by the utilitarians.

The first need here—counteracting the "dismal" elements in economic science—was met by abandoning the Iron Law of Wages, introducing in its place the so-called marginal productivity approach to wage theory.[28] According to this analysis an increase in the quantity of nonlabor factors of production (say, capital) relative to the quantity of labor employed will result in an increase in the quantity of output attributable and hence payable to each unit of the labor factor. This notion conceded a wage basis for the participation of the "proletariat" in the fruits of an industrial civilization—and when over the years it developed that mankind did not necessarily reproduce to the limit set by bare subsistence, the working man was restored to full citizenship in his country.

And not only was the individual worker given a secure position in capitalist society, but organizations of workers were also. Here it was

---

[26] *Ibid.* But see also G. B. Shaw, *et al., Fabian Essays* (Boston: Ball Publishing Co., 1908).

[27] Lionel Robbins, *The Theory of Economic Policy in English Classical Political Economy* (London: Macmillan & Co., Ltd., 1952).

[28] The more comprehensive idea here was the view that the history of civilization is the story of mankind improving its lot here on earth. See J. B. Bury, *The Idea of Progress* (New York: The Macmillan Co., 1932).

emphasized that the demands made on corporate managements are such that workers can never quite feel that the employer is vitally concerned about the employee's welfare. In consequence the worker turns to his own "legitimate government," the union.[29] And because these organizations have made a place for themselves in the organizational framework of modern life on this premise, it is even argued by some that collective bargaining agencies have been capitalism's first line of defense against socialism.[30]

This obstacle surmounted, the way was opened for further modifications of mid-nineteenth-century ideology. It will be recalled that Mill's conclusion at this point had been that though numerous exceptions can be found, laissez faire ought nonetheless to be the general rule. Toward the latter part of the last century and especially during the present century, this approach has been essentially supplanted with the idea that no particular presumption should govern here, but that human intelligence must examine alternatives as problems arise and decide on the basis of the evidence what institutional arrangements should govern.

The result of this reorientation is an approach to political economy which now goes by the generic name of "welfare economics." Analyses of this kind may be said to have originated in 1912 with the publication of Pigou's *Wealth and Welfare*,[31] and since that time this endeavor has become an important branch of economic science.

There are a number of dimensions of this development important to an understanding of recent ideological change. Pigou's own emphasis, and what might be termed the main stem of welfare economics, was a focus of attention on distribution: the general problem of income inequality and, more specifically, questions involving the circumstances under which a gain in income for some at the expense of others may be classified as an over-all social gain. In a sense approaching these same issues from the opposite direction, other studies inquire into the wastes of laissez faire—"the manner in which private enterprise under conditions of unregulated competition tends to give rise to social costs which are not accounted for in entrepreneurial outlays but instead are shifted to or borne by third persons and the community as a whole."[32]

[29] Peter Drucker, *The New Society* (New York: Harper & Bros., 1950).

[30] Frank Tannenbaum, *A Philosophy of Labor* (New York: Alfred A. Knopf, Inc., 1951).

[31] (London: Macmillan & Co., Ltd.).

[32] K. W. Kapp, *The Social Costs of Private Enterprise* (Cambridge: Harvard University Press, 1950), Preface.

Somewhat more comprehensive in orientation is the modern-day, so-called Keynesian attack on the widespread unemployment which often appeared in laissez faire society. Two emphases have predominated in this approach. One is an advance in economic theory along lines first laid down by Lord Lauderdale; that is, recognition of the possibility of a failure of aggregate purchasing power in an exchange economy.[33] Second, one of the key lessons learned during the Great Depression was that the benefits of an individualistic economic organization can most effectively be realized in an environment conducive to a high level of business activity. And finally, there is the still more comprehensive analytical procedure now quite common of listing over-all social goals and determining what control mechanisms are best calculated to achieve these particular objectives.[34]

IDEOLOGY FOR AN INDUSTRIAL SOCIETY

Though it is not easy to summarize ideological developments in the government-business field over the past two centuries, a few generalizations can nevertheless be made. Thus it is worth noting that the extreme individualism of the eighteenth and nineteenth centuries had itself been a reaction against the collectivism of the Middle Ages. For centuries the human spirit had been entrapped within a paternalistic social system, and it is therefore not surprising that the breakaway when it came was a radical one. The Reformation, the Renaissance, the disintegration of feudal institutions were all a part of this beating of newly found wings against decaying bars. Obviously the spirit thus freed would not soon consent to reimprisonment by the rising nation-state, and an effective defense seemed to be the separation of politics from economics contemplated by the laissez faire position.[35]

Unfortunately for this position, however, a reaction of such intensity is in turn vulnerable to counter-reaction, and the case at hand was no exception to this historic truth. As a social system which had submerged the individual was replaced by one in which society was almost equally ignored, it was almost inevitable that in time this missing element too would be rediscovered. When this did indeed happen one consequence was a general realization of the artificiality

[33] J. M. Keynes, *The General Theory of Employment, Interest and Money* (New York: Harcourt, Brace & Co., Inc., 1935).

[34] R. A. Dahl and C. E. Lindblom, *Politics, Economics, and Welfare* (New York: Harper & Bros, 1953); and A. D. Ward (ed.), *Goals of Economic Life* (New York: Harper & Bros., 1953).

[35] H. J. Laski, *The Rise of European Liberalism* (London: George Allen & Unwin, Ltd., 1936).

of the structure which had been created, and a new recognition of the positive role government must play in a society of any complexity. But in this reaction against extreme individualism more is involved than the swinging of a pendulum. Another key aspect of this development can be brought into focus by referring to what one student has termed the inherent conflict within a so-called market society.[36] Markets, so this argument runs, are organized on the basis of self-interest. Buyers and sellers confront one another, men having no mutual obligations and interested only in calculating on a coldly rational basis where the greatest net advantage in a particular series of bargains lies. However, this analysis continues, societies cannot in fact be constructed out of self-interest materials alone. There must also exist obligations, behavior which does not limit itself to close calculations of personal advantage—relationships, in short, which are freely spontaneous, and which are at the same time powerful enough in many types of situations to override considerations of self-oriented gain which might arise but which in actuality do not.[37]

It does not follow of course from the fact that the concept "market society" is a contradiction in terms, from the rediscovery of society, that the existence of a market mechanism precludes the existence of a genuine community. What is involved is rather the proposition that the market must operate within a framework dictated by society's needs rather than being encouraged to destroy its legitimate master. And while even acceptance of this proposition does not make either economics or political science exact disciplines in the mathematical-scientific sense, it is clear that capitalist society has always harbored something of a revulsion against a too exclusive preoccupation with values readily reducible to monetary terms.[38]

Nor does the addition of this consideration completely round out an explanation of why government activity has come to be much less narrowly restricted. Still a third way of viewing this phenomenon takes as its point of departure a principle developed by both John Locke and Adam Smith. Locke had concluded, and gone to some lengths to demonstrate, that the resources of the earth originally belonged to mankind in common, but that when human intelligence was applied to the task of determining how this common possession might best be utilized, the decision had been made to divide it out into private property units. Smith's version of this same

[36] Karl Polanyi, The Great Transformation (New York: Rinehart & Co., Inc., 1944).

[37] F. Tonnies, Community and Association (London: Routledge & Kegan Paul, Ltd., 1955).

[38] John D. Glover, The Attack on Big Business (Boston: Graduate School of Business Administration, 1954).

process was that although in the ideal organization of society's affairs men will be left to pursue their own advantage, the superiority of this procedure is that it best contributes to the interests of the community as a whole.

A. TOWARD A SOCIAL THEORY OF PROPERTY

From this small seed a mighty tree was one day to grow, the so-called social theory of property.[39] According to this interpretation, the extent and nature of the private property rights existing at any one time are the result of deliberate community decisions, that with regard to either property or enterprise society reserves the right to impose limitations whenever and wherever it appears that the public interest will thereby be served.

But while this way of thinking was closely related to the ideological foundations of capitalism in one respect, it was just as certainly a fundamental departure in another. Both Locke and Smith had leaned heavily on the concept of natural rights and had rested their most basic conclusions on this cornerstone. Thus, although on the one hand private property and free enterprise were presented as a rational way of organizing social relationships, they were on the other hand thought to be so firmly fixed as a part of the natural order that no useful purpose could be served by wishing for different arrangements. Obviously until this conviction had been dispelled, the idea of human decisions in the realm of institutions could not take root.

Five factors, all interrelated, contributed particularly to modifications in the concept of natural law, permitting a less limited view of the functions of government to develop. First and foremost there was the change in the conditions under which economic life came to be lived. In a world in which it is realistic to think of every citizen as a property-owner using these resources to produce directly for his own needs, a certain plausibility attaches to the concept of absolute individual sovereignty over land advanced by John Locke. When, however, a majority of citizens become urban residents owning virtually no *productive* property, when the essence of property became an exchange relationship in which every individual's standard of living becomes a function of the operation of an intricate, scarcity-oriented market mechanism, it was only to be expected that the absoluteness of property rights would be hedged about by restrictions.

---

[39] Richard T. Ely, *Property and Contract* (New York: The Macmillan Co., 1914), Vol. I.

In the second place, as industrialization mediated by a laissez faire philosophy proceeded apace, it became increasingly apparent to less favored groups that this ideology was being exploited by merchants and manufacturers for class purposes. It could not of course have escaped notice indefinitely that the government did not merely protect property rights, that it first created those kinds of property rights which it then chose to protect—and it is understandable that the classical view of natural rights could not long survive that discovery. And stating this matter in a slightly different way, once it became evident that laissez faire institutions were after all man-made, the way was open for the abandonment of the idea of automaticity in socio-economic relationships in favor of the use of human rationality in constructing a more suitable institutional framework.

A third factor here was the impact of scientific advance on social thought. Consistently during these years men were uncovering important new truths about the natural world around them, penetrating farther and farther into the unknown and demolishing in the process understandings which had theretofore been taken for granted. Gradually, out of this experience, the conviction became widespread that more and more of nature's secrets would be wrested from her. Inevitably, still broader implications appeared. If human intelligence could thus devise increasingly complex experiments and equipment by means of which human understanding of natural relationships could be increased, and especially if this new knowledge could be used to produce a much higher standard of living for a greatly increased population, it seemed reasonable to suppose that that same intelligence could also be used to improve the institutions through which social affairs are ordered. Here, too, was an idea against which the historical concept of natural rights could not long stand.

As still another important consideration, there developed a fundamental antipathy between natural rights in the concrete Lockeian sense and belief in a government responsive to the will of the people. Indeed, the very essence of democracy is the proposition that government is a means to an end, the end being the creation of institutions which will contribute to the good life desired by citizens; and therefore the underlying theory of democratic government must fall to the ground if institutional arrangements are accepted as irrevocably given. Stated differently, the natural right of private property and free enterprise becomes in the philosophy of democracy the "natural right" of citizens to create their own institutions.

It follows that as democracy flourished during the nineteenth century, becoming toward its close one of the dominant features of western civilization, the significance of the concept of natural law was much altered.

Lastly, it is of importance to note that in the years after Adam Smith so enthusiastically echoed Locke's objections to major economic responsibilities for government, this institution did a considerable amount of growing up. In point of fact, the governments Smith and Locke knew were no doubt incompetent to manage the various and intricate affairs which must today be conducted by every modern state. But as the industrial evolution advanced, as for example improved transportation and communication greatly extended the reach and power of a bureaucratic organization (governmental as well as corporate),[40] the capacity of governments correspondingly expanded. Because nothing succeeds like success, the more effectively the responsibilities given the governments of commercial societies were handled the less reason did there seem to be for not utilizing this resource even more fully.

And perhaps all of these considerations can constructively be summarized by referring once again to Professor Schumpeter's approach to history. In a society in which change is limited and gradual, a doctrine of inherited and virtually unchanging law will carry conviction. Citizens in such a society do not "choose" to think in terms of deliberate institutional innovations because their mentalities are shaped in an environment which does not list social invention as a realistic alternative. On the other hand, in a society in which change is both profound and rapid the idea that law and tradition are close companions cannot be similarly persuasive. Here the "choosing mentality" is shaped by a situation demanding a high degree of institutional nimbleness as the price of maintaining a reasonably harmonious (and hence tolerably stable) social system.

These, then, were the more important factors behind the appearance of the social theory of property as a major challenge to the doctrine of laissez faire. Can the theory itself now be succinctly stated? This is difficult, of course, both because it is so general in its implications and because it is still locked in ideological combat with residual laissez faire concepts and is hence still in the process of being formulated. But with these qualifications in mind it will perhaps be helpful to append a fairly concise statement of what is here involved. As Benjamin Franklin expressed it:

[40] Kenneth E. Boulding, *The Organizational Revolution* (New York: Harper & Bros., 1953).

Private Property therefore is a Creature of Society, and is subject to the Calls of that Society, whenever its Necessities shall require it, even to its last Farthing.

And T. H. Huxley put the matter if anything still more bluntly.

At present the state protects men in the possession and enjoyment of their property, and defines what that property is. The justification for its so doing is that its action promotes the good of the people. If it can be clearly proved that the abolition of property would tend still more to promote the good of the people, the state will have the same justification for abolishing property that it now has for maintaining it.

B. Toward a More Democratic Individualism

But viewing recent ideological evolution in terms of a social theory of property does not, after all is said and done, explain much about government-business relationships in the United States. For one thing, this approach is fundamentally a negative rather than a positive orientation to the subject at hand. Furthermore, it is by the same token abstract rather than concrete.

What is needed is a concrete, positive analysis calculated to bring this idea to life. Precisely because there is today a greater willingness than formerly to use governmental powers to limit and define property and enterprise for the benefit of the community as a whole, it is essential to understand what sorts of things are considered to be in the public interest. If a desirable social order is thought of as one in which citizens create their own institutions, it becomes important to know what kinds of institutions citizens wish to create. In short, having observed the social theory of property coin on one side, it is now necessary to examine it on the other.

This dimension of ideological evolution has its deepest roots in the fact that laissez faire thinking focused its attention mainly on problems of production; personal distribution was for the most part left to its own devices.[41] With full employment taken for granted, and on the assumption that wages would be held within a narrow range bounded on one side by Malthusianism and on the other by competition between employers, it seemed reasonable to suppose that the achievement of maximum aggregate output was *the* economic problem.

Although the economic system which grew up under that emphasis was outstandingly successful from the standpoint of increasing output, the experience of Western civilization with laissez faire

[41] Gunnar Myrdal, *The Political Element in the Development of Economic Theory* (London: Routledge & Kegan Paul, Ltd., 1953).

capitalism gave rise to two kinds of pressures on prevailing thought-patterns. On the one hand, dissatisfaction arose from the resultant concentration of wealth and income. On the other hand, discontent developed because of various other kinds of inequities which seemed to thrive in such an environment.

The macroeconomic assault appeared as an essential part of the attack on capitalism by socialism. Basing their argument on a principle popularly known as the diminishing marginal utility of money, for long an important item in the neoclassical economist's kit of concepts, socialists insisted that a nation's aggregate real output would create a greater "value in use" if distributed more nearly equally. Not only, in other words, would a given aggregate of goods and services provide more "utility" if the purchasing power with which it was to be bought were more evenly distributed, but a more "useful" aggregate of goods and services would be produced if much of the income of the rich were transferred to the poor. Indeed, some socialists even carried this conclusion to the extreme of demanding that every individual receive the same income.[42]

A revised capitalist ideology obviously could not go so far; it was too important to take every precaution not to interfere with the forces making the free enterprise economy so productive. At the same time, however, here was a challenge to be met. The distribution of income resulting from the institution of private property had to be either justified or altered.

A reasonably satisfactory compromise was ultimately arrived at, one involving both justification and alteration. In justification *differential rewards were defended on the ground that leveling down the more fortunate and leveling up the less fortunate would threaten output* in two ways. First, it was feared that this might interfere with the incentive system. Second, it seemed that it might divert production from capital formation into consumption to such an extent that economic progress would virtually cease. By way of alteration, plausible principles were developed on the basis of which the differential could be reduced without serious consequences. For the benefit of the destitute the concept of the social minimum was devised; *in a democratic society the community as a whole must see to it that every individual receives the minimum standard of living consistent with the inherent dignity of the human personality.* At the other end of the income scale, the corresponding principle was the idea that *because social organization as such contributes greatly to the wealth-getting process, those receiving the largest incomes have*

[42] Edward Bellamy, *Looking Backward* and *Equality*.

a proportionately greater responsibility for supporting the community's basic functions—for example, government activities.

The other major challenge directed against "rugged individualism" looked less at the over-all results of the operation of a capitalist economy than at a number of more specific aspects of that process in and of themselves. Whereas Adam Smith's "obvious and simple system of natural liberty" did indeed within the pages of the *Wealth of Nations* appear to be both obvious and simple, the more mature industrialism and democracy became the less did that system seem either obvious or simple.

The essence of Smithianism at this point had been the sharp distinction drawn between those economic activities suitable for private enterprise and those for which the government would have to assume the principal responsibility. Of secondary though substantial importance was the assumption that the fields of endeavor properly belonging in the latter category (namely "public works" and "public institutions") were relatively few—and easily recognized in the bargain, for they could not be erected or maintained at a profit. Of far greater importance was the fact that these two types of economic organization, private and public, could be kept almost completely separate. Where private enterprise was an effective approach, the operation of the invisible hand would make it unnecessary for the hand of government to appear at all.

With respect to the first of these propositions, American capitalism has not seen fit to formulate a sweeping restatement. Doubts still tend to be resolved in favor of the private sector of the economy; the contribution of the profit motive to total production is thus safeguarded. The modern version of the second, however, differs strikingly from its predecessor. Nor was this wholly because the hand of government was seen to be already so important in holding the field for the so-called invisible hand. The decisive point was rather that profit-seeking for personal gain was found to generate such a marked bias in favor of property owners and the unscrupulous that a society more and more professing the ideals of democracy was compelled to devise a different principle of interventionism.[43]

Three major requirements had to be simultaneously fulfilled by the new formulation. First, the prejudice against government participation in the economic process had to be softened. Second, the all-important emphasis of democracy upon the inherent worth of the individual personality had to be recognized. Third, account had to be taken of the great and growing complexity of modern indus-

[43] J. A. Hobson, *Work and Wealth* (New York: The Macmillan Co., 1926).

trial society—the fact that the achievement of basic goals increasingly demands a pattern of intervention varying from situation to situation over a wide range of circumstances.

Of course an ideological position fully meeting these specifications did not arise at once. Step by step, however, a head-on collision between industrialization and democratization was prevented by appropriate modifications of Adam Smith's "obvious and simple system." Today the content of the prevailing myth explaining the relationship between public and private spheres of economic activity can be broadly summarized as follows. *Although the market mechanism performs indispensable functions, imperfections in its operation are apt to arise at any point and are certain to arise at many. Wherever such a condition does develop, it is the responsibility of a democratic community to see to it that its values are protected.*

And perhaps the ideological evolution described here can be still more succinctly summarized by reproducing a modern scholar's distinction between what he calls constructive liberalism and laissez faire liberalism.[44]

Freedom of action cannot be reduced realistically to an absolute datum; it is inseparable from the behavior of the group. The group necessarily prescribes the conditions of freedom enjoyed by the individual, and the growth of personal liberty depends fundamentally upon the progress of the group. There-fore liberal policy rests necessarily upon complementary postulates of individual freedom and group action. It demands both freedom of action for the individual and a constructive public program designed to release the productive energies of all individuals and to curb those proclivities of some who would obstruct the freedom of the many. Practically speaking, the state is able to provide the only instrument of total group action and, hence, the widest possibility of representation and enforcement of the collective will. In itself government is only a means of group action just as the business unit, or any other form of organization, may serve a group purpose. Both are designed, in liberal theory, to advance the welfare of the individual—the term welfare being used in the broadest possible sense to include the creative, enterprising, and contemplative, as well as the consumptive capacities of the individual. Therefore, liberal policy can never have as its aim the aggrandizement of the state, but solely the elevation of the individual. *This positive conception of liberal policy, which contemplates individual freedom and group action as complementary, and the former as the object of the latter, will be termed constructive liberalism . . . in order to distinguish it from laissez-faire liberalism which has advocated as the guiding hand of public policy almost exclusively the constructive role of individual initiative.* The latter is not in essence antithetical to constructive liberalism but rather is only a constituent part of it.

[44] Milton S. Heath, *Constructive Liberalism* (Cambridge: Harvard University Press, 1954), pp. 4 and 5. Italics added.

It cannot, however, be overemphasized that to study social change from the standpoint of ideological evolution is to look at only one dimension of that process. Or, more accurately, from this point of view only a bare skeleton can be seen. The other dimension, the flesh and blood with which the skeletal framework of society's institutions is covered, can be appreciated only when attention is focused upon the interaction between the way men think about social relationships and the actual problems they encounter in trying to maintain satisfactory relationship patterns—particularly in the face of comprehensive environmental change. And so the developments portrayed here will next be discussed in terms of the institutional aspects of the evolution of business-government relationships in the United States.

QUESTIONS FOR DISCUSSION

1. Explain the meaning of the concept historical determinism as applied to social change. How plausible do you think this concept is?

2. What was the significance of John Locke's discussion of private property in the context of his own times?

3. How did Locke solve the problem of social justice? How reasonable do you think his analysis was as of 1690?

4. At what point did Locke's defense of private property break down most seriously?

5. How did mercantilism fit into the picture of ideological evolution?

6. In what ways did Adam Smith improve upon Locke's thought system from the standpoint of developing capitalism?

7. How did Smith solve the problem of social justice? How reasonable do you think his analysis was in 1776?

8. What was "the obvious and simple system of natural liberty" on which Smith was willing to rely so heavily?

9. Evaluate Lord Lauderdale's critique of the laissez faire ideal.

10. Enumerate some specific ways in which utilitarianism would threaten Adam Smith's system.

11. Translate John Stuart Mill's exceptions to the "non-interference principle" into government policies now taken for granted.

12. To what extent did the Marxists distort orthodox thinking, and to what extent did they only draw obvious conclusions from classical premises?

13. Describe the major features of "welfare economics" from the standpoint of government-business relationships.

14. Explain the major factors which undermined the eighteenth-century belief in natural law?

15. State the social theory of property. How convincing do you think this proposition is?

16. How has the rise of democracy altered men's belief about the functions of government?

17. What is the meaning of the distinction sometimes made between property rights and human rights? Is such a distinction useful in understanding the ideological evolution under review here?

18. How has the issue of concentration of wealth and income been resolved in the ideology of mature capitalism?

19. List a number of specific ways in which the laissez faire conception of separating politics from economics has been violated in recent years.

Chapter 33

Looking Backward—Institutional Responses

Although private property is still often defined as the right of an individual to do whatever he wants with that which is his, it is nonetheless almost universally understood that such a definition is highly unrealistic. However, when one pushes behind this common assertion, its significance apparently lies less in a belief that property relationships can today be so described than in the widespread idea that at some point in American economic evolution property was appropriately thought of in those terms.

A Point of Departure

Nor is this interpretation particularly fanciful. While a situation in which property is held by citizens without obligation to the larger community (or, what amounts to the same thing, without supervision by government) is quite inconceivable, the fact remains that an institution which can be described without undue exaggeration as individual sovereignty over property did at one time exist in the western world. Indeed this condition can serve as an excellent point of departure in recounting the evolution of government-business relationships in the United States.

Let us first, in this connection, apply our imaginations briefly to the task of determining the circumstances under which the highest degree of property sovereignty can be permitted in a civilized community. Obviously, there would be little basis for objection from neighbors as long as A's use of his property does not make more difficult B's enjoyment of his. And this happy situation will prevail where A's noise, odors, garbage, and economic activity do not make significant contact with B's sphere of operations.

743

It is at once apparent that this is exactly the state of affairs with which John Locke was preoccupied. A society composed of self-sufficient family farms would meet the postulated requirement almost to perfection. Here sheer distance would protect each family from its neighbors' noises, odors, and garbage, while the very fact of self-sufficiency would guarantee the absence of those types of economic relationship out of which economic injury or exploitation can so easily arise. Nor is it to be doubted that Locke was himself keenly aware of these advantages of his favorite mode of social organization. Note how insistent he was that a family is justified in possessing only as much land as its members can till without hired help.

Equally significant is it that the emphasis upon self-sufficient households was also especially meaningful in the context of economic organization in colonial America. Here was an overwhelmingly agrarian society, and one in which an unusually large proportion of land operators was made up of either actual or prospective land owners. Again, moreover, Locke's penetrating understanding sheds much light on the key relationships involved; in early America, if anywhere, the free land condition on which he premised his main argument was abundantly fulfilled. To be sure, from the beginning some men did make payments to other men for the privilege of using land belonging to the latter, but this suggests no more than that many families were willing to pay rent in settled areas to avoid the necessity of braving the interior wilderness. The essential fact remains. Given an economic environment all but ideally suited to that institution, individual sovereignty over property understandably became a vital tradition.

THE GENIE FREED

The fable about the genie imprisoned in a bottle is familiar to most Americans. A passer-by, it will be recalled, innocently picked up the bottle and removed the stopper. Whereupon what appeared to be a black gas poured out of the opening, transforming itself almost immediately, however, into a giant eager to repay an unsuspecting world in kind for the indignities he had suffered as a result of his imprisonment.

Perhaps it does not unduly tax credulity to suggest in the association of the institution of private property, thought of as individual sovereignty over assets, with a self-sufficient agriculture type of economic organization an analogy with a giant compelled to occupy uncomfortably small quarters. A man with property could indeed do virtually anything he desired with it. But this legal freedom to act was sharply restricted by the narrow choice available as to what an owner might *realistically* desire to do with his property. Because property by definition consisted of a land area, and because the character of such property is what it is, it could not readily be hoarded, disposed of in small quantities, or converted into a more liquid form. For all practical purposes it could either be used or sold as a unit—with the added qualification that the man who sold his livelihood would have to use the proceeds to secure another. Property, in short, consisted of tangible assets held for the use of their owner.

Naturally a giant thus restrained began to press against his prison walls. As an agrarian society evolved into a commercial one, as various kinds of business property became an important element in the economy's operation, as the types of property in common use became more flexible from the standpoint of the uses to which they could be put, it was only to be expected that businessmen would want to exercise the same sovereignty over their assets that farmers were given over theirs. And as businessmen squared away to do battle on that front, the struggle of new property forms to achieve social and legal acceptance on a basis of equality with agricultural real estate made up the largest proportion of the early development of American business-government relationships.

No doubt the key to the rapid progress made in this contest in the early years of capitalist evolution was the gross economic inefficiency of post-medieval production methods. Where very small groups produce only for their own needs, per capita real income is typically small and the goods so produced are apt to be very poor quality in the bargain. It was therefore found that when the manufacture of goods for a much larger group was concentrated in one place, per worker productivity rose immensely.

From this discovery a widening circle of significant consequences promptly appeared. Potential customers could profitably drop this or that item from their own production programs, buying what they needed from a central supplier. But in order to take advantage of this opportunity, it was necessary for them first to do a certain amount of specializing of their own to secure the funds required for the desired purchases. With these things taking place among consumers, ambitious entrepreneurs could find any number of points in the economy at which production could be economically concentrated. As these interacting factors began to gain a powerful

momentum, a cumulative process of comprehensive social change
was set in motion which has not yet come to an end.

Clearly such an evolution could not have prospered had not the
state been brought to its assistance. By the same token, herein lies
the significance of the mercantilism which guided the destinies of
young America until the new nation was well started on the road
to becoming a great power. A commercial society requires very different institutions from an agricultural one, and these can only develop insofar as they are at least tolerated by the sovereign power.
Enterprises expressly designed to perform specialized production
services must have permission to do so. A medium of exchange must
be provided under government auspices. Bankruptcy legislation
more specifically fitted to a world mediated by businessmen has to
be enacted. Improved transportation facilities must be made available, and experience has demonstrated that private enterprise activities often need government supplementation at this point. Uniformity in standards of weight and measure takes on an entirely
new and much heightened importance. A commercial society that
rates continued economic progress as an important value must make
arrangements to treat generously the possessors of new inventions.
And while few economists today would insist that tariff protection
played a fundamental role in United States' industrialization, this
was nevertheless a central mercantilist preoccupation in the early
years of that development.

But these general observations do justice neither to the position of
property nor to that of government in the evolving socio-economic
order. To appreciate more fully these aspects of what was happening
it is necessary to focus attention upon several more specific relationships.

Note for example the special problem created by the need for
permission to operate a commercial enterprise, and the way that
problem was handled. Obviously every system of land tenure, including one built around private property, must rest upon a foundation of government sanctions. The point at which this fact is most
clearly visible in a private property society is the deed book in the
county court house; literally every square inch of the earth's surface
within the jurisdiction of the particular county has its place in
these voluminous records setting forth in full the historical account
of changes in ownership from the time of use by the Indians. But as
soon as business firms appeared on the scene the traditional network
of sanctions became inadequate; in addition to approving the ownership of real estate, it was now necessary to approve the specific uses

to be made of business property. Here, in other words, was an excellent opportunity for the law to discriminate against enterprise as compared with agriculture. But the law did not choose this way out. Instead it elected to clothe the permit for businesses to operate in the most charismatic concept in the vocabulary of private property. Mercantilist John Marshall, ever watchful for ways in which capitalist activities could be enhanced in public esteem, elevated the permit to do business to the status of a contract.

As a second case in point here, note the legal acceptance of various kinds of nontangible assets as property—the most basic single step away from the inflexibility of medieval property forms. While no question would be raised in a private property society about the purchase and sale of the physical assets of a shoe manufacturing concern, it is important to bear in mind the vast difference between these kinds of transfers and the purchase and sale of the business of manufacturing shoes. Here the intangible asset goodwill enters the picture, an asset often made more valuable because it includes a contract with the state granting the firm the right to exist. Not only goodwill, moreover, but other intangibles as well were similarly accepted as valid property forms. And perhaps the most significant item on this list is the negotiable instrument—the many varieties of written contracts which are legally binding, regardless of the identity of their possessors at the stated time of performance.

Both of these innovations were next made even more sweeping in their consequences through the development of the corporation. By means of this device, as opportunities for enterprise profits became increasingly available, permits to do business became both more numerous and more valuable. Here, moreover, the negotiable instruments par excellence were developed. By creating a bewildering array of corporate security types, the new middle class was able to distribute property rights and obligations in almost any conceivable way. And as if this were not achievement enough for a single new institution, the limitation of liability therein and its endowment with permanent existence made this departure still more fundamental.

Actually it can be argued that in the appearance of the corporation business property more than achieved institutional equality with preindustrial ownership forms. Implicit in the concept of limited liability is the idea of the corporation as a person, and it was not long before the courts were explicitly recognizing this implication. An individual must pay his debts or go into bankruptcy. So too must a corporation, of course, but there is this vital difference between the two situations. Where natural individuals are the contracting parties the law insists that bankruptcy proceedings leave them much worse off than it found them. By contrast the principal individuals involved in a corporation bankruptcy action might very well be millionaires after all outstanding liabilities have been settled on some fractional basis.

But even emphasis upon the value to a corporation of limited liability does not adequately portray the privileged position accorded those organizations in the American scheme of things. Not only is individual property outside a corporation protected by the state in the event of bankruptcy, but property held for individuals inside a corporation secured a special protection from the state under the Fifth and Fourteenth Amendments. Time and again these guarantees of individual rights were invoked to prevent government from imposing one or another kind of sanction upon the corporate world. In precisely the same way the vast aggregation of various kinds of assets which is the corporation was frequently treated as the legal equal of the individual employee—as, for example, when state laws specifying the number of hours workers might be kept at their jobs in a single day were declared to be violations of employees' freedom of contract. It was not quite a situation of "Heads I win, tails you lose," but the property owner was to a degree enabled either to magnify his legal stature through the corporation or to withdraw from easy visibility as circumstances dictated.

And finally, mention must be made of the element with which these various institutional innovations were welded together into a more or less consistent whole. This was the idea of natural law, and especially the private property dimension of that concept. Of course, in a sense all of the more concrete ways in which property sovereignty was applied to new property types were manifestations of the continuing strength of this myth-element. But if a single phenomenon were to be designated as an especially clear indication of its power, that phenomenon would be judicial review. In that doctrine, securely imbedded in American legal practice after 1803, the philosophy inherited from England that law is found not made and that only lawyers are competent to find it became one of the most important protections private property was to have in this country.

As all these interpretations were one by one grafted onto the institutional framework of the country, those seeking to establish business property upon a legal par with prebusiness property could properly have considered their mission complete. Figure 5 roughly shows

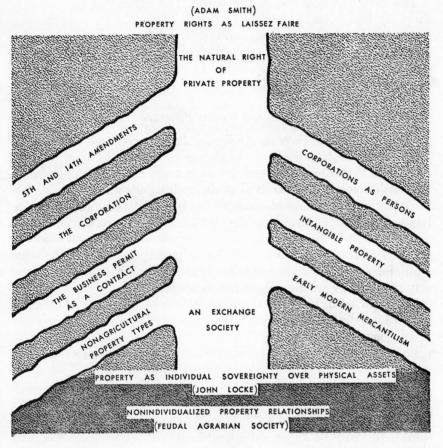

(ADAM SMITH)
PROPERTY RIGHTS AS LAISSEZ FAIRE

THE NATURAL RIGHT
OF
PRIVATE PROPERTY

5TH AND 14TH AMENDMENTS

THE CORPORATION

THE BUSINESS PERMIT AS A CONTRACT

NONAGRICULTURAL PROPERTY TYPES

CORPORATIONS AS PERSONS

INTANGIBLE PROPERTY

EARLY MODERN MERCANTILISM

AN EXCHANGE
SOCIETY

PROPERTY AS INDIVIDUAL SOVEREIGNTY OVER PHYSICAL ASSETS
(JOHN LOCKE)

NONINDIVIDUALIZED PROPERTY RELATIONSHIPS
(FEUDAL AGRARIAN SOCIETY)

Fig. 5

the transformation which was taking place. Out of the crumbling subsoil of feudalism the roots of modern industrialism were visibly forming. A taproot representing the economic superiority of an exchange society over a self-sufficient one emerged first. This vigorous growth was then rapidly extended by a number of subsidiary roots, the entire network leading to the base of the trunk of the tree of modern property concepts in the support given the industrialization process by the emphasis on natural law. With this development, aided as it was by direct government action, John Locke's emphasis upon property as individual sovereignty over physical assets was converted in almost imperceptible stages into Adam Smith's definition of property as laissez faire.

The cork was now out of the bottle. The genie was free at last. Property had been made flexible beyond even the most optimistic expectations of the earliest capitalists, while simultaneously the sovereignty over property once associated primarily with the family farm was made broadly applicable to commercial firms producing for the market.

A Giant on the Prowl

But if property owners, and especially prosperous ones, had reason to feel satisfied about the course events were taking, it does not follow that all segments of the community were able to share in this enthusiasm. The fact is that the industrialization process was bringing with it profound changes in the entire network of under-lying social relationships, making these at once more complex and more delicate. A brief review of some of the most pervasive conse-quences of specialized production will make eminently clear why a number of groups soon began doubting the compatibility of prop-erty sovereignty with an exchange economy.

To begin with, production specialization means production con-centration: the development of economic activities much less scat-tered geographically than self-sufficient farming. Large numbers of people are now brought together to work in huge factories—people who, because their livelihood is no longer directly dependent upon the extensive use of land, find it convenient to live relatively near their workplace. Other things being equal, the conditions which en-courage one factory to locate at a particular point will also draw others, and with them the workers required for their operation. And the concentration of several factories in a single small area will in turn bring in those industries needed to supply factory workers with such other goods as they can afford to buy. In short, the specializa-tion of production leads inevitably to urbanization, perhaps the most fundamental change in the circumstances under which the or-dinary citizen lives his life that industrialization brings in its wake.

On the one hand, as population density increases the earlier indif-ference to a neighbor's noises, odors, and garbage quickly disappears. Excessive noises now become a public nuisance. Odors originated by one citizen make up a part of the external environment of a dozen families. Garbage improperly disposed of may menace the health of thousands. Even the indispensable rural watchdog comes now to be judged more by the way he responds to passers-by and children than by his reaction to prowlers. In literally hundreds of ways behavior which was essentially private prior to urbanization takes on a community-wide significance where many people must live in close proximity to one another; and the phenomenon of property sovereignty in the new urban world was understandably judged accordingly.

On the other hand, putting this phenomenon in a somewhat broader perspective, it soon developed also that an urban society required for its survival the provision of a number of services which could either be ignored or taken for granted in a simpler economic context. For example, the residents of a great city cannot produce their own food and many of the other necessities of life. Indeed their very congregation in the vicinity of their specialized workplaces is predicated upon the assumption that these goods and services will in fact be provided by others. Thus, a complex network of external transportation and communication facilities must be at the disposal of these concentrations of people. A similarly complex network of such facilities must exist within the city, both to give citizens ready access to essential goods and services and to facilitate movement between home and workplace. Obviously, here too was a point at which the right of an individual to do whatever he desired with his own property was soon being scrutinized very carefully.

In a frame of reference less arbitrarily restricted than urbanization as such, these relationships can even be seen in a still more vital setting. A high degree of specialization means that any given individual produces only a tiny fraction of the goods and services he himself consumes. Instead he sells the fruits of his productive efforts, and then purchases such other items as he wants and can afford. This means, however, that a citizen's standard of living is determined not only by how much (in the purely quantitative sense) he produces, but in addition upon the prices of the goods he sells and buys. Economic well-being for perhaps a majority in the community is made dependent upon the operation of a market mechanism over which most have no direct control, a fact giving citizens in an industrial society a still stronger reason to keep in close touch with the more subtle ramifications of the prevailing property ownership system.

But these general observations put this matter much too mildly. Nonbusiness groups were not merely inclined to be suspicious—and hence watchful—as the implications of laissez faire abruptly transformed the entire fabric of social life. Indeed a majority of citizens gradually reached the conclusion that both the undoubted benefits and the very real burdens attributable to the industrial revolution were being most inequitably distributed.

Note for example some of the concrete problems faced by the residents of the new urban areas. A concern is organized to engage in the slaughtering business—in the middle of a residential district. It is conducted on a competent, businesslike basis, paying its bills promptly and yielding a net profit to its owners. Unfortunately for those who live nearby, however, all the costs associated with this enterprise could not in an immature free enterprise society be presented to it in the form of bills to be paid, and had therefore to be borne in the community rather than being charged against profits. Or consider the difficulties inherent in making the necessary arrangements for intracity transportation. The most feasible solution here, let us suppose, was a traction company, which of course had to be granted the privilege of using the city streets. But since it was not ordinarily practicable to give this privilege to more than one such concern, the price and profit system often resulted in gross customer exploitation.

And note, in the second place, the impact of commercialization upon the farmer. As the new exchange economy became more elaborately organized, this group found itself increasingly separated from the ultimate consumer by various groups of middlemen. Whereas farmers were many and widely scattered, the handlers of their products were relatively few and correspondingly better organized. Thus when the farmer came to market with his produce, usually in dire need of the proceeds from their sale, he was more often than not confronted with a buyer enjoying a decisive bargaining advantage. Small wonder farmers also decided at an early date that the "natural" operation of the market mechanism should not be allowed complete freedom.

Again, consider the situation of the consumer as a consumer. Obviously in a self-sufficient household no conflict of interest can arise between producer and consumer. Even in the early phases of commercialization when goods are few and simple and buyer-seller relationships are still close, no serious interest divergence is likely to appear at this point. When, however, the variety of goods on the market becomes bewilderingly complex, when the goods themselves are typically much more complicated from the standpoint of content and uses, and when producers normally do not know and are not known by consumers, a wide range of opportunities appears for adding to profits at the expense of consumer well-being. Here also the unassisted market mechanism produced results many citizens were soon challenging.

The worker constituted still another group which came in time to conclusions boding no good for property sovereignty in the form of unrestricted enterprise. As the farmer found himself bargaining with business concerns under highly disadvantageous circumstances, so too did the laborer. Possibly, indeed, the threat to the urban worker was even greater than that to his rural counterpart. For one thing, the farmer at least had at his disposal resources by means of which he could keep body and soul together; his city compatriot, in other words, was more critically dependent upon the market than he. For another, the labor force included several important elements (such as women and children) especially easy to exploit to the detriment of a large circle of fellow workers. Given this situation, who could doubt that it would be only a matter of time before workers would also conclude that individual bargaining with an aggregation of acres, buildings, and tools was an activity offering no bright prospects for the future.

Mention can also appropriately be made here of the investor in a corporate world. The essence of modern industrial society is capital and its productivity, and hence one of its basic institutions is a market mechanism funneling liquid capital from many different individuals into productive economic endeavors. However, investors are often no more competent than most consumers to evaluate the market situation correctly, with the result that this market lends itself almost as readily to obtaining money under false pretenses as to assisting in the capital-formation process. And though perhaps a case can be made for the proposition that abuse in this market is of little moment as long as those who lose can afford their losses, the appearance therein of a multitude of small investors committing much of their life savings to the economy's growth created yet another ally for those looking askance at the unrestrained pursuit of profits.

Finally, the incidence of a mushrooming industrialization can be concretely seen by focusing attention upon the individual as such. In medieval times, although the general standard of living was extremely low by modern standards, most individuals were prevented from falling below a certain level of well-being by the very fact of having been born to a particular status. By contrast, if in an infant capitalist society there were no discernible limits to how high ability, determination, and circumstances might elevate one in the reward scale, there were likewise no dependable limits to how far one might be plunged by adversity in a system in which status had been replaced by contract. A key dimension of the change in the position of the individual generated by the industrial revolution was job in security. Whatever the shortcomings of a less advanced social order, stable precapitalist societies could at least offer their citizens a useful labor to perform—a guarantee which ups and downs of the business cycle made very difficult in a commercial context. Another important dimension of the security issue raised by recent economic evolution was the problem of the aged. A rural, relatively immobile people somehow seem to have little difficulty caring for those who have made their primary contribution to the community's on-going life. On the other hand, modern urban societies characterized by a high degree of family mobility found here a problem which did not readily take care of itself.

Now it might be supposed that all these factors in and of themselves would have been sufficient to generate a vigorous struggle between frustrated citizens and the giant now on the loose in the western world. And perhaps it would have been. In the event, however, the more important point to note is that each and every one of these problems was accentuated by the dramatic growth of the spirit of democracy taking place at the same time.

Because of the power of this spirit, for example, it became a far more vital matter to society at large whether citizens were threatened or injured by the new institutions. Thus the implications of the market mechanism for farmers, workers, consumers, and small investors were placed significantly higher on the public policy agenda. The uncompensated costs attributable to property sovereignty in an exchange society were correspondingly more certain to be given a share of policy attention. Individuals and their needs moved much closer to the top of the community's hierarchy of values, especially where "invisible" compulsions such as poverty, unemployment, or old age were contributing to a wholesale degradation of the human personality. A more sympathetic understanding was given to the pressure in an urban, industrialized, democratic society to have made available at government expense more services of various kinds than would otherwise have been the case.

But there is no need to elaborate further. The consequences of allowing the laissez faire giant to roam across the land unfettered were excellently summarized years ago in an address made all the more remarkable by the fact that it was delivered by a Republican at a time when it would not have been commonly supposed that a prominent conservative would possess so keen an insight. The speaker was Elihu Root—the year, 1916.

The real difficulty appears to be that the new conditions incident to the extraordinary industrial development of the last half-century are continuously and progressively demanding the readjustment of the relations between great bodies of men and the establishment of new legal rights and obligations not contemplated when existing laws were passed or existing limitations upon the powers of government were prescribed in our Constitution. In place of the old individual independence of life in which every intelligent and healthy citizen was competent to take care of himself and his family we have come to a high degree of interdependence in which the greater part of our people have to rely for all the necessities of life upon the systematized cooperation of a vast number of other men working through complicated industrial and commercial machinery. Instead of the completeness of individual effort working out its own results in obtaining food and clothing and shelter we have specialization and division of labor which leaves each individual unable to apply his industry and intelligence except in cooperation with a great number of others whose activity conjoined to his is necessary to produce any useful result. Instead of the give and take of free individual contract, the tremendous power of organization has combined great aggregations of capital in enormous industrial establishments working through vast agencies of commerce and employing great masses of men in movements of production and transportation and trade, so great in the mass that each individual in them is quite helpless by himself. The relations between the employer and the employed, between the owners of aggregated capital and the units of organized labor, between the small producer, the small trader, the consumer, and the great transporting and manufacturing and distributing agencies, all present new questions for the solution of which the old reliance upon the free action of individual wills appears quite inadequate. And in many directions the intervention of that organized control which we call government seems necessary to produce the same result of justice and right conduct which obtained through the attrition of individuals before the new conditions arose.

GROPING FOR A HARNESS

What was to be done? What steps should be taken to protect society from the giant now stalking up and down the land?

One alternative here of course was to try to induce the genie to go back into the bottle. This, it will be recalled, was the happy outcome of the tale as told in the celebrated fable. But this was hardly a realistic alternative in the history of Western civilization; fundamental historical development is essentially irreversible. To be sure, there were sporadic attempts to destroy wholesale commercialization in its infancy. Indeed, the entire way of life of precapitalist society cried out against the transformation of social relationships implicit in the laissez faire spirit. Unfortunately for these vested interests, however, the attraction of a materially higher standard of living was too great; and the institutional evolution taking place was a prerequisite to rapid economic progress.

Almost at the opposite pole from a return to the precapitalist status quo was another way in which many people thought the giant might be made to disappear. In one sense the crucial institutional difference between early modern and medieval times was the ambiguous intermingling of private and public property rights characteristic of the earlier period. Why not, inquired socialists in Europe and innumerable varieties of utopians in the United States, maintain the new distinction but, rather than emphasizing the private property dimension, accentuate instead the control of property in the name of the larger community? In this way, it was argued, full advantage could be taken of the new kinds of property while still guaranteeing their use for the common welfare.

Three closely related factors especially operated against acceptance of this solution to the problem at issue. In the first place, the pendulum swing against feudal and mercantilist collectivism was too powerful to be thus abruptly reversed. Second, the new middle class, the group enjoying the greatest opportunities for personal achievements in an exchange economy, was a decisive force at precisely the point at which such policy determinations would have had to be made; that is, in government circles. And third, there was reason to have grave doubts whether per capita output could be expanded as rapidly under public as under private enterprise.

But if the giant would not go away, clearly he had to be brought under some kind of control, at which point the question posed became this: Could he be encouraged to continue making economic abundance more readily available, and at the same time be prevented from trampling innocent bystanders under foot? Could he, in short, be domesticated? Against the background of this vital problem, an intensive search for compromise institutional arrangements got under way.

The answer ultimately hit upon was to introduce sharp modifications of individual sovereignty over property into prevailing practice in key areas, taking care to interfere as little as possible with the essence of that relationship in the process. However, before noting the points at which this dilution was primarily aimed, it is appropriate to take special note of a fact all too seldom emphasized in this connection. Thus it is commonly thought that the separation of individuals from full control over their property has been essentially a function of the broadening of government responsibilities. Actually this is misleading. Side by side with the dilution of property rights for which governments were responsible, there developed an equally profound dilution worked out by resource owners among themselves.

This dimension of capitalist evolution can readily be illustrated. Property sovereignty, in Lockeian analysis, carries the implication that every economic good, every unit of any of the factors of production, could be assigned to some individual in the sense of saying, "that is his." (Nor did Adam Smith's distinction between private and public works significantly alter this implication; all that was changed thereby was the addition of the collective entity called government as *the* controller of some resources.) But note how radically that situation changed when the simple agricultural society gave way to a corporate type of economic organization. Who owns the poles, wires, and other equipment by means of which Western Union delivers messages from one part of the country to another? Who owns the tracks on which Pennsylvania Railroad trains run?

To be sure, the superficial answer can be given that ownership resides in the corporate entity in whose name such assets are held, and the legal fiction of the corporation as a person lends special plausibility to that conclusion. But when ownership is conceived in

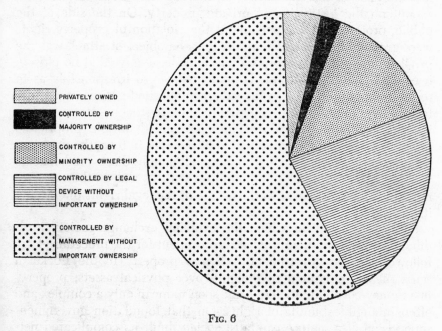

FIG. 6

FIG. 6. Type of control of the two hundred largest nonbanking corporations in the United States—1929. Source: A. A. Berle and G. C. Means, *The Modern Corporation and Private Property* (New York: The Macmillan Co., 1932). Used by permission.

terms of Locke's identification of property as physical assets over which flesh-and-blood individuals have sovereign disposition rights, it is at once evident how far that concept had already evolved before governments began seriously encroaching upon laissez faire arrangements. No corporation stockholder, as a stockholder, has *any* disposition rights over corporate property. And perhaps still more important, the small group of men which customarily makes the decisions that constitute the on-going life of the corporation (they do, in a manner of speaking, have disposition rights over corporate property) often hold only a minor fraction of the outstanding ownership rights.

Too much could perhaps be made of this phenomenon. Certainly the fact that men have agreed to a system of reciprocal limitations on their own rights does not in itself justify or make citizens any more receptive to the imposition of such limitations by government. However, from the standpoint of the evolution of government-business relationships two implications of this process were particularly important.

First, as a result of this development government regulation when it came took on the appearance of an oblique rather than a frontal assault on the institution of private property. On the side of the public, protests from owners about the violation of property rights were greatly blunted by the retort that the object of attack was the privileges of "soul-less" corporations and these only—that no *citizen*, it could be taken for granted, would behave so irresponsibly as to require such sanctions. On the side of propertied groups, two other factors were at work. For their part, corporate stockholders were less inclined to resist government interventions than sole proprietors or partners similarly situated would have been. In turn, the decision-making group within the corporation ultimately discovered that its well-being was more closely bound up with its skill in the management of resources than with the nature of the legal rights underlying its decisions.

Second, the way in which the evolving exchange society itself diluted property rights furnished a precedent for the procedure later followed by the government. Whereas property in the Lockeian sense meant individual sovereignty over physical assets, property in a money-corporate society came soon to mean only a complex and often intangible bundle of rights. On that foundation government supervision of a mature capitalist society built its complicated network of interrelationships with business. Here too the fact of private property was not basically disturbed; the emphasis was rather on altering the make-up of the rights bundle. And if those among us who are more pessimistic than the rest insist that in reality the substance of private property has been largely dissipated in this process, it can at least be said that this erosion has its deepest roots in the institutional arrangements devised to implement a laissez faire philosophy.

THE GENIE TAMED

In the same way that the early development of business-government relationships in this country can meaningfully be thought of as the root system of a great tree, so can the later stages of that growth be visualized in terms of the tree itself. As the huge trunk grew taller and taller one after another mighty branches pushed outward from it, each delimiting some basic area (or areas) of free enterprise operation.

It is not, of course, to be supposed that the roots of this particular tree grew to maturity before the branch system began to form. Following closely the pattern of its natural counterparts, root and branch grew together. Perhaps the reason was the same in both cases; it is after all a tree's under-the-ground stability which makes possible its above-the-ground display. At any rate, although the root system continued to grow vigorously under the impetus of the rise of the corporation beginning early in the nineteenth century, the appearance of the New Jersey holding company toward the end of that century, and the perfection of the Delaware corporation during the 1920's, the emergence of the first main branch can be dated as accurately from 1837 as from any other time. And it is worth more than passing notice that this was the same year which saw enacted the nation's first general incorporation statute, that of Connecticut.

Actually it is not wholly realistic to date precisely the beginning of a development such as this. Because, however, the Supreme Court's decision in *Charles River Bridge* v. *Warren Bridge* was handed down in 1837, a case can be made for placing particular emphasis upon that year. In that opinion the High Court unequivocally established the principle that there continued to exist, even in a regime built so fundamentally around private property, a public interest which could not be overridden at will by the operation of a free enterprise society.

Figure 7 broadly charts the major ramifications of this first stage in fashioning an effective harness for laissez faire capitalism—the first great branch on the tree of government-business relationships

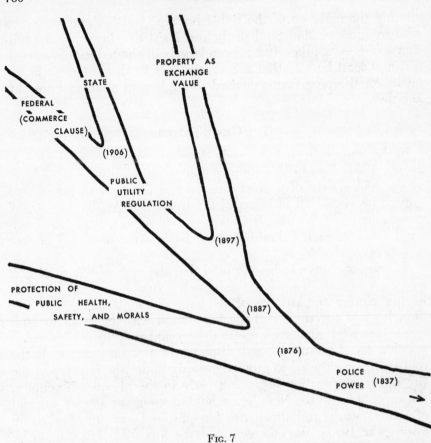

FIG. 7

in a modern exchange society. At first police power restrictions were narrowly construed to permit intervention only where the community's most basic needs were obviously at stake, especially citizen health and safety. However, although that emphasis remained important, in time it proved to be inadequate. During the last three decades of the nineteenth century the dependence of the average man, and particularly urban residents, upon certain key services led to another major departure from property sovereignty. This was the public utility concept; first the federal government in the field of railroad transportation, and then state governments with respect to urban utilities, undertook a program of comprehensive price control designed to limit consumer exploitation in situations in which effective competition was clearly impossible. Furthermore, out of this innovation there was to develop before the end of the century the legal concept of property as exchange value which was later to make contact with another dimension of the regulation network in a vitally important way.

But even a steady strengthening of public utility regulation was found to be an incomplete harness for a giant beginning to flex his muscles in ever more threatening ways. The assumption behind this step had been that if a very few industries which do not lend themselves to restraint through competition were rigorously supervised, the preponderance of the economy would respond sufficiently well to the operation of competitive forces as to pose no special public interest problem. Almost before the implications of the decision to make a special category out of these few industries had become apparent to more than a handful of people, however, it was beginning to be understood that this fundamental assumption was seriously in error.

The difficulty here was that in a number of areas in which the public utility category could obviously not be applied, the industrial revolution was rapidly destroying the vision of a capitalism consisting of firms small enough and hence numerous enough to make consumer exploitation impossible. Phase two, therefore, in the campaign to keep the institution of private property congruent with other important values was a program in which the community through its government set out to impose competition on the new industrial economy by force.

Figure 8 depicts the principal dimensions of this policy as it matured. At first the central concern was to protect the citizen from monopoly, or the perversion of the possibilities inherent in specialization by means of engrossing the available supply of an important economic good. In consequence the primary emphasis of this program was the breaking-up of aggressive concentrations of economic power.

After a quarter of a century of experience with this approach, however, it seemed apparent that much more would be necessary. On the one hand, the most critical problem on this front turned out to be, not monopoly, but oligopoly, or the concentration of control over an industry in a small number of firms. On the other hand, it developed that even where competition was adequate from the standpoint of consumer protection, there seemed a need to insist that the war of competitors on one another follow civilized rules. The first of these discoveries resulted in almost a right angle turn in antitrust work, from "trustbusting" to the channelling of business practices in directions more favorable to the long-range health of vigor-

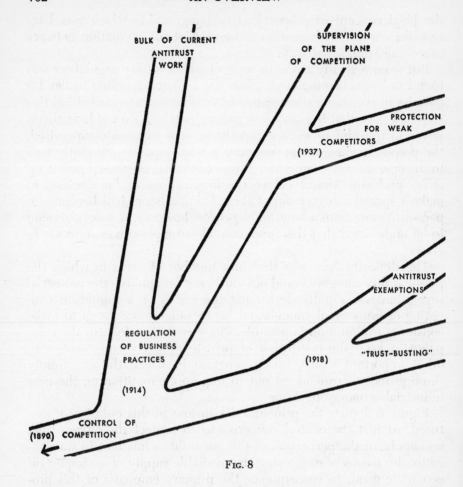

BULK OF CURRENT
ANTITRUST
WORK

SUPERVISION
OF THE PLANE
OF COMPETITION

PROTECTION
FOR WEAK
COMPETITORS
(1937)

ANTITRUST
EXEMPTIONS

REGULATION
OF BUSINESS
PRACTICES

(1914)

(1918)   "TRUST-BUSTING"

CONTROL OF
(1890) COMPETITION

FIG. 8

ous competition. The second brought about an interest in the plane
of competition which had not theretofore prevailed. And to complicate this picture still further a number of exemptions to the antitrust laws were authorized for a variety of reasons, while simultaneously there grew up a pattern of regulations manifestly designed to
protect weak competitors from some of the more painful consequences of economic evolution.

Once again, however, breaches already made in laissez faire principles were soon thought to be inadequate. And once again America's reform conservatism—this country's preference for minimum
changes in the status quo—was frustrated. Scarcely had the decision
to regulate competition been made than the need was felt to challenge free enterprise in still another way.

In public utility regulation the conclusion had been reached that certain types of markets in a market economy require detailed supervision. Similarly antitrust legislation was based on the proposition that all important markets must be given a particular type of supervision. Now it was discovered that in a society in which the well-being of every person is vitally bound up with the operation of an incredibly complex market mechanism remediable defects may appear at almost any point, and that when this happens it is the responsibility of a democratic government to devise the appropriate remedies.

Figure 9 outlines the most important consequences of this determination, a decision intermingling government and business activities at a greater number of points than either of the preceding steps.

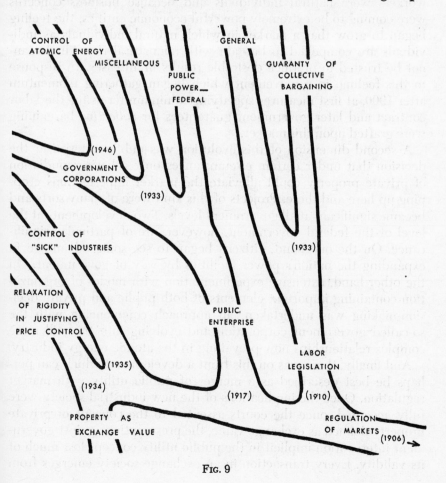

CONTROL OF ATOMIC ENERGY

MISCELLANEOUS

GENERAL

PUBLIC POWER— FEDERAL

GUARANTY OF COLLECTIVE BARGAINING

(1946)

GOVERNMENT CORPORATIONS

(1933)

CONTROL OF "SICK" INDUSTRIES

(1933)

RELAXATION OF RIGIDITY IN JUSTIFYING PRICE CONTROL

PUBLIC ENTERPRISE

(1935)

LABOR LEGISLATION

(1934)

(1917)

(1910)

PROPERTY AS EXCHANGE VALUE

REGULATION OF MARKETS (1906) →

Fig. 9

It is especially arbitrary to attempt to date with any precision the start of this development—both because here as in so many other areas the dramatic landmarks were preceded by a steady evolution of legal theory and practice going back a great many years, and because the legal foundations undergirding this departure was the police power. However, a landmark which can lay much claim to denoting the historical line of demarcation between public utility regulation and less comprehensive market supervision was the federal government's taking over from the states a large share of the task of protecting consumers in the food (including meat) and drug industries.

Three major stems were soon cropping out of this huge branch. One of these was legislation aimed at the labor market. Because workers were natural individuals and because business concerns were coming to be extremely powerful economic entities, the feeling began to grow that a market in which natural individuals as individuals are compelled to bargain with nonnatural individuals cannot be trusted to produce desirable results in all cases. In response to this feeling, in a movement which began gathering momentum after 1900, at first measures specifying minimum terms for the labor contract and later government guarantees for *collective* bargaining were grafted upon this market.

A second dimension of this evolution was public enterprise: the decision that under certain circumstances only a basic repudiation of private property could alleviate the market imperfections cropping up here and there. Projects of this kind were of many sorts and became significant at all government levels. Two developments at the level of the federal government, however, are of particular significance. On the one hand, citizens began to see some advantage in expanding the nation's power facilities by way of government. On the other hand, extensive experimentation with modes of organization containing important elements of both public and private decision-making was undertaken, an approach commencing with the so-called government corporation and evolving into the still more complex relationships now prevailing in the atomic energy industry.

And finally, there was on this front a development which can perhaps be best described as a merger of public utility with market regulation. Once the implications of the new industrial society were fully accepted, once the courts assented to the concept of private property defined as exchange value, the presumption against government intervention implicit in the public utility concept lost much of its validity. Every transaction in an exchange society emerges from a bargaining relationship, and the question of the public interest involved therein accordingly becomes a matter of degree. With only a little oversimplification, the government can appropriately be thought of here as a countervailing power endeavoring to make its weight felt for the benefit of economically disadvantaged groups.

After thus breaking through the rigid limits initially placed on market intervention, government regulation rested on a foundation which could be used as the basis for extending the *microeconomic* control pattern in any direction deemed desirable by a democratic legislative body. From this point forward, therefore, the principal economic policy innovations took the form of developing a comparable set of *macroeconomic* interventions.

The first major development of this kind is summarized in Figure 10. Partly because it was decided that income distribution in a

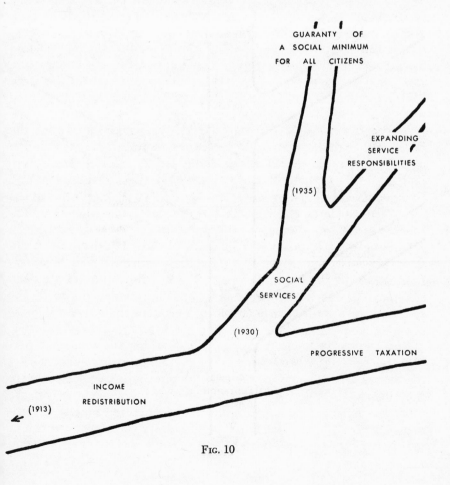

Fig. 10

laissez faire society is highly arbitrary, partly because it seemed that urbanization was progressively multiplying situations in which services could be furnished more economically by governments than otherwise, and partly because the nation's rising per capita real income was bringing to the foreground a public demand for facilities most appropriately provided by government, expenditures for so-called social services of all kinds began to increase. With the coming of the Great Depression, furthermore, an important aspect of this departure became an aggressive expansion of government guarantees for human rights as distinguished from bare property rights—this approach turning soon in the direction of government acceptance of a responsibility to see that each person receives the minimum real income necessary to maintain the human dignity and self-re-

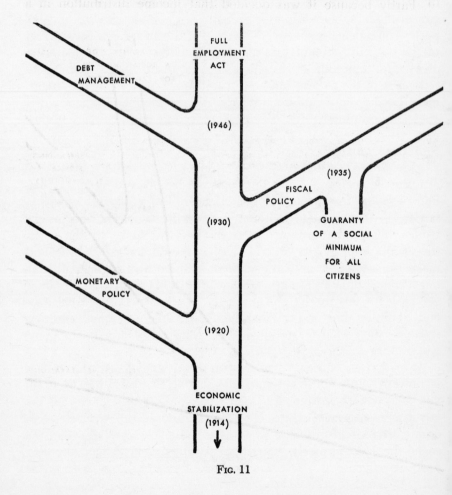

FIG. 11

spect every individual is entitled to. Of course, it goes without saying that this entire development was undergirded by a policy of progressive income taxation.

Figure 11 portrays a second great area of macroeconomic interventionism, together with the final major development in the difficult task of domesticating the private property giant. Aggravated by a series of frustrating business downturns, citizens early in this century began devoting much attention to the problem of economic stabilization, control of the tendency for a regime of decision-making by private capitalists periodically to bring economic ruin to large numbers of people who are in no way responsible for the tragedy befalling them. This interest culminated in the passage of the Federal Reserve Act, and during the 1920's the tools forged by that legislation began unmistakeably to evolve into a deliberate and constant concern about the medium of exchange by money and banking experts. The especially severe contraction of the 1930's saw fiscal policy merge with this stream, and also make contact with the guarantee of a social minimum for all citizens. As a result of the tremendous federal debt the nation inherited from World War II, debt management became an important element of this larger effort, while in 1946 the complexity of stabilization as well as its status as a permanent government policy were made official by the passage of the Full Employment Act.

After thus depicting each major branch of the great tree of modern property concepts, it will perhaps not be amiss to picture in outline form the tree itself. Rooted in the soil of property defined as laissez faire in the Adam Smith sense, towering skyward by means of a trunk which can most meaningfully be thought of as the social theory of property, its several branches with their own offshoots make up a complex network of members constituting a greatly altered conception of property—a bundle of rights relative to economic goods. With this reaching of maturity (not to be confused with the end of either life or growth), the American government-business scene became what it has since been: a *mixed economy*. The genie was no longer a threat to organized society.

At least this is the way one version of this analogy would read. It is, however, only fair to emphasize in passing that this history has not yet been wholly written. And many there are who believe that the government controls which have been imposed on American economic life present problems as great as those they resolved—that the social theory of property growth may well turn out to be malignant. More specifically, it is felt that the mixed economy tree may in the

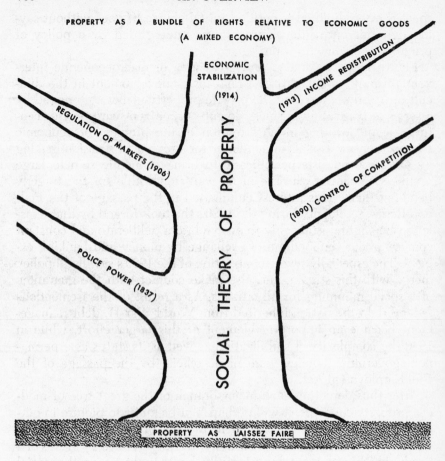

PROPERTY AS A BUNDLE OF RIGHTS RELATIVE TO ECONOMIC GOODS
(A MIXED ECONOMY)

ECONOMIC
STABILIZATION
(1914)

(1913) INCOME REDISTRIBUTION

REGULATION OF MARKETS (1906)

SOCIAL THEORY OF PROPERTY

(1890) CONTROL OF COMPETITION

POLICE POWER (1837)

PROPERTY AS LAISSEZ FAIRE

Fig. 12

end drain our people and their institutions of the flexibility, the creativity, and the prodigious productivity which have made the United States' economic organization the envy of much of the rest of the world. Just as a real tree may on occasion so sap the fertility and moisture around it that other vegetation cannot exist in competition, so it is thought that the expansion of government responsibilities may undermine individual initiative and ingenuity.

Most would probably agree that, should this happen, the price of surcease from the depredations of the giant will prove to be too great. But only time can tell whether the social theory of property tree, so carefully nurtured over so long a period of time, once it becomes strong and vigorous, can be prevented from destroying the other institutional vegetation which once thrived in its vicinity. Here is the dimension of this history yet to be written.

———

The outline below brings together in another way the principal threads of the interrelationships between government and business as they exist today. Here each major development as set forth earlier is accompanied by several concrete illustrations of the kinds of government activities comprehended therein.

I. Police power intervention:
    A. Protection of public health, safety, and morals
      (City zoning, license regulations)
    B. Public utility regulation—federal
      (Transportation, telephone and telegraph, electric light and power)
    C. Public utility regulation—state
      (Transportation, telephone, electric and gas utilities)

II. Control of competition:
    A. "Trustbusting":
      (American Tobacco, Standard Oil, Pullman)
      1. Antitrust exemptions
        (Regulated industries, labor unions, farmer cooperatives)
    B. Regulation of business practices—antitrust dimension
      (Collusion, coercion, exclusion)
    C. Supervision of the plane of competition:
      (Simulating a competitor's product, false and misleading advertising)
      1. Protection for weak competitors
        (Robinson-Patman prohibitions, fair trade)

III. Market regulation:
    A. Government as countervailing power:
      (Food and drug regulation, supervision of markets for farm products, security market regulation)
      1. Control for "sick" industries
        (Bituminous coal during the 1930's, agricultural price supports)
      2. Relaxation of rigidity in justifying price control
        (Milk industry regulation, commodity exchange controls)
    B. Labor legislation—general:
      (Maximum hours, minimum wages, employers' liability)
      1. Guarantee of collective bargaining
        (Restrictions on use of injunction, unfair labor practices)
    C. Public enterprise—miscellaneous:
      (Urban utilities, employment exchanges, special temporary projects)
      1. Public power—federal
        (Tennessee River, Colorado River, Missouri River)
      2. Government corporations:
        (Reconstruction Finance Corporation, Tennessee Valley Authority)
        (a) Control of atomic energy
          (Supervision of contractees by Atomic Energy Commission)

IV. Income redistribution:
  A. Progressive taxation
     (Federal and state individual income, federal corporation income)
  B. Expanding government service responsibilities:
     (Recreation, health, education, rehabilitation)
     1. Guaranteeing a social minimum for all citizens
        (Housing, social security, income tax exemptions)

V. Economic stabilization:
  A. Monetary policy
     (Rediscount rate, reserve requirements, open market operations, qualitative controls)
  B. Fiscal policy
     (Tax structure, expenditure timing)
  C. Debt management
     (Structure of maturities, integrating refinancing with money market conditions)
  D. Full Employment Act
     (Council of Economic Advisers, coordinating government activities relative to stabilization)

This classification does not, to be sure, pretend to be complete. Not only could the breakdown easily be made finer, but it cannot even be said that all of government's far-flung activities relative to business fit in one and only one of the categories listed. However, this summary does have the virtue of being manageable without being seriously misleading, and perhaps this is all that can really be helpful in an introduction to an exceedingly complex subject.

QUESTIONS FOR DISCUSSION

1. Under what circumstances can property sovereignty be permitted in a civilized community?

2. Why did production for use give way to production for sale? How important was the institution of private property to this process?

3. Enumerate the major steps in the evolution of a laissez faire society from the standpoint of property relationships.

4. What was the role of the state in bringing an industrial society into being?

5. Distinguish between property as physical assets and property as laissez faire.

6. Explain the major consequences of urbanization for business-government relationships.

7. What groups in particular were disadvantaged by laissez faire industrialization, and how?

8. In what major ways could the giant have been made to disappear? What was wrong with these alternatives?

9. How did property-owners, quite apart from the expansion of government's economic responsibilities as such, modify property relationships in a capitalist society? Of what significance was this development?

10. From the standpoint of private property relationships how meaningful is the common distinction between corporate bondholders as creditors and stockholders as owners?

11. Trace the major steps in the abandonment of laissez faire in favor of a mixed economy.

12. Define private property and explain your definition.

13. State briefly the special significance of each date shown in Figures 7 through 11.

14. Classify each of the major items of New Deal legislation from the standpoint of the outline suggested in Figure 12.

15. What government activities in the business and government field can you think of that cannot be fitted into the summary on pages 669-70 without strain?

16. What are the major factors which have brought about a steadily increasing intervention by government in economic affairs?

17. Has the power of government expanded more rapidly than the size and influence of the forces it must mediate?

18. To what extent are security and freedom mutually exclusive? Is the level of security now guaranteed to Americans a threat to freedom?

19. What problems relating to government-business relationships would you say are now most in need of solution?

20. It is often maintained that once a trend toward government intervention in the economy sets in, it cannot be reversed. From your study of this subject would you be more inclined to agree or to disagree with this conclusion? Why?

Case Index

773

Name Index

Abbott, C. C., 95n, 653n
Abrams, E. R., 392n
Adams, James T., 604n
Adams, John, 68
Adams, Samuel Hopkins, 219
Adams, Walter, 351n
Adelman, M. A., 631n
Albion, R. G., 76n
Aldrich, N. W., 224, 259
Aldrich, Winthrop W., 420–21
Allen, F. L., 208n, 231n, 369n
Almond, Gabriel, 27n
Ames, Oakes, 112–13
Anderson, Don S., 444n
Anshen, M., 533n
Arnold, Thurman, 529n
Atkins, W. E., 433n

Bach, G. L., 653n
Bacon, Nathaniel, 50
Baer, George F., 212
Bailey, S. K., 561n
Baker, George F., 232
Baker, R. H., 502n
Bakke, E. W., 405n
Baldwin, L. P., 66n
Barnett, O. R., 623n
Bartlett, R. W., 442n
Bartley, Ernest R., 644n
Baruch, Bernard, 270n, 275, 554
Bassett, J. S., 63n
Bauer, John, 190n, 245n
Baum, Robert D., 361n, 543n
Beale, H. K., 106n
Bean, L. H., 409n
Beard, Charles A., 58n, 65n, 694n
Beard, Mary R., 139n
Beard, William, 357n
Beer, G. L., 48n
Bellamy, Edward, 151n, 154, 197, 738n
Belmont, August, 206
Benedict, Murray R., 585n, 668n

Benns, F. Lee, 80n
Benson, Lee, 161n
Bentham, Jeremy, 726
Berge, Wendell, 613n
Berle, A. A., 342
Berman, Edward, 235n, 326n
Bernhardt, Joshua, 583n
Bernstein, M. H., 336n
Beveridge, W. H., 517n, 560n
Biddle, Nicholas, 87
Billington, Ray A., 173n
Blachley, F. F., 673n
Black, Hugo L., 414, 641
Black, John D., 366n, 412n
Blaisdell, Donald C., 220n, 334n, 359n, 504n
Blakely, M. Murphy, 322n
Bland, R. F.,135
Blough, Roy, 652n
Bobbe, Dorothie, 76n
Bogart, E. L., 282n
Bonbright, James C., 190n, 503n, 645n
Boulding, Kenneth E., 736n
Bowden, Witt, 44n
Bradford, F. A., 418n
Brady, Robert A., 604n
Brandeis, E., 248n
Brandeis, Louis D., 256n, 330, 397
Brinton, Crane, 726n
Brown, E. C., 566n
Brown, R., 671n
Bryan, William Jennings, 220
Buck, S. J., 167n
Bunyan, John, 202
Burns, A. R., 342n, 603
Burns, Eveline M., 591n
Burton, T. E., 168n
Bury, J. B., 730n
Butler, Smedley D., 444

Caldwell, S. A., 88n
Calhoun, John C., 39, 72, 74

777

Subject Index